BUSINESS LAW

BUSINESS LAW

Principles and Practices

Fourth Edition

Arnold J. Goldman
Law Firm of Goldman & Goldman

William D. Sigismond
Monroe Community College

HOUGHTON MIFFLIN COMPANY   BOSTON   TORONTO
Geneva, Illinois   Palo Alto   Princeton, New Jersey

Editor-in-Chief: Bonnie Binkert
Senior Project Editor: Paula Kmetz
Associate Production/Design Coordinator: Jennifer Meyer
Senior Manufacturing Coordinator: Marie Barnes
Marketing Manager: Michael Mercier

Arnold J. Goldman is an attorney with the firm of Goldman & Goldman in Rochester, New York. In addition to practicing law, he has taught courses in constitutional law at the University of Rochester and has been a guest lecturer in several schools in the Rochester area.

William D. Sigismond is Director of Cooperative and Experiential Learning and Adjunct Professor in the Department of Business Administration at Monroe Community College, Rochester, New York. He has taught business law at both the high school and college levels for over twenty-five years and is a member and past president of the New York State Business Teachers Association, as well as a member of many other professional organizations. He is a certified arbitrator for the American Arbitration Association.

Cover design: Len Massiglia, LMA Communications
Cover image: Created by Len Massiglia, LMA Communications

Printed in the U.S.A.

Library of Congress Catalog Card Number: 95-76944

ISBN: 0-395-74660-4

789-DH-99

Contents

Preface

The fourth edition of *Business Law: Principles and Practices*, retains the overall organization and chapter format of the third edition. Each chapter contains a topical outline; a brief introduction to alert students to what will be covered in the chapter; narrative text; a summary, which aids in a general review of the chapter; key legal terms found in the chapter; and questions, problems, and cases. In many instances, material in the chapters has been rewritten or reorganized to improve clarity. Some chapters have been expanded to cover timely new topics, while others have been thoroughly updated to reflect changes in the law. As in previous editions, the material is presented in a nontechnical, succinct manner, yet in depth sufficient enough to provide comprehensive, authoritative coverage of the basic rules and principles. It is written in a clear, conversational style that avoids confusing courtroom language in both the text narrative and the case examples at the end of the chapters. Legal terms are clearly defined and highlighted, and there is an abundance of real-world examples.

This text is designed for use in business law courses offered at postsecondary schools. It begins with an introduction to the study of law through a brief look at these topics: how law developed; the legal system in the United States; the function, organization, and work of the federal and state court systems; criminal and civil law; and the steps in a civil law suit. The text then presents all of the important areas of business law students need to know, such as contracts, sales, commercial paper, agency and employment law, business organizations, property, and bailments. Other important and timely topics are also covered, including insurance, wills and estate planning, and consumer and creditor protection.

COURSE OBJECTIVES

Before beginning the study of the various chapters in *Business Law: Principles and Practices*, Fourth Edition, students should review the broad course objectives listed below. These broad objectives describe the desired outcomes of the course—that is, what students should get out of the entire course. After completing the business law course using this text, students will:

- Become legally literate—more informed about what laws are "on the books," how these laws affect their lives, what their legal rights and responsibilities are, and how legal disputes in which they become involved can be resolved.

- Recognize when it is important to seek professional advice from an attorney as common legal problems arise in their personal lives or work sites.

- Develop a basic understanding of legal terms used in personal, consumer, and business situations.

- Grasp the legal implications of various business transactions.

- Gain familiarity with a variety of legal documents common to personal and business transactions.

- Develop analytical skills and reasoning power.

In addition to the broad course objectives, there are specific objectives at the beginning of each part of the text to help students focus on the key points to be learned.

A SPECIAL NOTE TO STUDENTS

Business law affects everyone—it is the one aspect of law that people deal with on a daily basis. Therefore, we have written this text to provide you with a readily understandable explanation of business and general law topics that are of practical use as you live each day "on the street," so to speak. As you read the text narrative, you will honestly be able to say that you understand the material. The material covered in the text will also serve as background for advanced law courses you may elect to take in the future. To help reinforce your learning of the legal principles presented in the text narrative, to motivate you to do your best, and to facilitate instruction, we've presented study materials at the end of each of the chapters, at the end of each unit, and in a separate study guide. Some of the distinctive features of this text's coverage are listed below.

1. Chapter summaries. At the end of each chapter is a summary of the narrative information presented in the chapter. You should read this summary before proceeding to the questions and case problems.

2. Questions and case problems. At the end of each chapter there is a series of questions and problems designed to help you review the basic concepts discussed in the chapter and to apply the basic rules of law to factual situations.

3. Key legal terms. Within the chapters, key terms are boldfaced where defined. They are also compiled in a list at the end of each chapter. In addition, key terms (many more than are in the chapters) are defined in the glossary, which contains over 900 entries.

4. "You Be the Judge." At the end of each unit is an expanded case problem that requires you to apply legal principles you learned in the unit. These cases will challenge you since there are no easy answers.

5. Appendixes. The text contains three appendixes. Appendix A will guide you when "briefing" cases; Appendix B will help you make the transition from the study of contracts under the common law to the study of contracts under the Uniform Commercial Code; and Appendix C, the Constitution of the United States, will be a point of reference throughout the text but especially as your instructor covers Part I of the text.

6. Study Guide. The study guide, which includes several types of questions based on material presented in the text, can be used for individualized study and self-testing.

We hope that the good instruction you will receive, your continued effort to attend class regularly, and the material presented in this text along with the study materials provided, will motivate you to do your best in the course. Good luck.

ACKNOWLEDGMENTS

We would like to express thanks to the many instructors who have used previous editions of the text in their classes and to those reviewers who provided us with comments regarding earlier editions. We also express our gratitude to the following reviewers who offered suggestions for preparing the fourth edition:

Hakim Ben Adjoua
Columbus State Community College

Vince DiMaria
Bryant & Stratton Business Institute

Janine S. Hiller
Virginia Polytechnic Institute and State University

Jeff Holt
Tulsa Junior College

Sam Markovits
Orange County Community College

Louie J. Michelli
Belmont Technical College

Mary Michels
Anoka-Hennepin Technical College

Stephen Warner, J.D.
Keystone Junior College

Sara E. Zurenda, Esq.
Elmira College

We are grateful to the Houghton Mifflin staff members who worked with us for their loyal support, their understanding at times when things didn't always go right, and their patience in dealing with us while we worked on this fourth edition.

This text is dedicated to our wives Lynn Goldman, Mary Beth Sigismond (in her memory), and to our children Jonathan Goldman, Lisa Goldman Pelta, Ruth Goldman Heller, Jacquelyn Sigismond Mery, and Todd Sigismond.

A.J.G.   W.D.S.

PART I

UNDERSTANDING THE LAW

*After studying Part I,
you should be able to*

1 Define law.

2 Demonstrate a knowledge for the need of a legal system.

3 Trace the development of our own law from Roman law and the English common law.

4 Demonstrate a knowledge of the four primary sources of law for the American legal system.

5 Discuss the differences between civil law and criminal law.

6 Outline the structure of the federal and state court systems in the United States.

7 Distinguish between a private wrong and a public wrong.

8 Demonstrate a knowledge of legal wrongs, both criminal and civil.

9 Compare the procedures in a civil action and a criminal action.

10 Evaluate alternative ways to settle disputes between two or more parties other than by litigation (a lawsuit).

Chapter 1

Foundations of Law

CHAPTER PREVIEW

This opening chapter focuses on law and ethics, what law is, why it is needed, where it came from, what functions it serves, and how it is affected by ethical concepts. The chapter points out that, although the modern emphasis in the United States is on statutory law, Americans also rely heavily on case law and rules of administrative agencies to protect a right or to correct a wrong. Civil law, which protects individuals from harm by other individuals, is discussed in contrast to criminal law, which protects society (a neighborhood, a town, a city, a state, a nation, or the entire world), from harmful acts of individuals. The chapter ends by pointing out that our laws will be changed over time in response to the changes and needs of our society.

WHY LAWS ARE NEEDED

Suppose someone broke into your house, did extensive damage, and, in addition, stole many of your valuables. And suppose you found out the thief's identity. Isn't it reasonable to believe that you might seek revenge on the thief and on his or her family? Isn't it also reasonable to believe that the thief and his or her family might in turn seek revenge on you? Can you imagine what it would be like to live in a society in which these situations would occur but there would be no laws? Maybe your first reaction is that you'd like that because no one could stop you from taking revenge. But remember, no one could stop the thief from taking revenge, either. You can be sure that if you and the thief and your families decided to take revenge, injury or death would result. If we are to avoid chaos and live together in peace, we must have laws.

Since the earliest times in history, and as society developed, it has become obvious that the only alternative to chaos is some system of rules of order for society's members. At first, these rules were customs or practices, but they had the same effect as laws. Through a gradual process, law has become more formalized, and today it governs almost everything we do. It is therefore important for all of us to understand our legal duties to other people and to society as a whole.

THE NATURE OF LAW

Law can be defined as an enforceable set of rules established by a government—federal, state, or local—to regulate the conduct of individuals and groups in a society. Just as there are rules for playing a game, so there are rules for living with other people in society—whether that society is a neighborhood, a town, a city, a state, a nation, or the entire world. The rules that make up law are actually legal duties that are imposed on people and that require them to act in a certain way. When people do not follow these rules, they violate the law. Through the courts, individuals injured by those who violate the law are provided with legal remedies, such as requiring the wrongdoer either to pay money damages, go to prison, or in some cases both.

THE RELATIONSHIP BETWEEN LAW AND ETHICS

Ethics is the study of what is right or good for human beings as they live each day. People are moved to deal with others because of their own ideas of what is right and wrong. Often their conscience is their guide, and they do what they think they ought to do based on religious upbringing and family customs and traditions. Legal action is not generally taken against a person who does something that is only ethically wrong.

> While driving home from a shopping center one evening, you saw a car strike a pedestrian crossing the street at a designated intersection. Without stopping, the driver of the car drove away. The following day, the newspaper reported the hit-and-run accident and stated that the victim was in critical condition. Since you did not want to get involved, you did not tell the police what you had seen. ■

In this example, failing to report the incident might be considered ethically wrong on your part; however, it was not legally wrong, since you have broken no law.

The distinction between law and business ethics is especially important. Business ethics is the branch of ethics that relates to what is right or good in business settings. In the past, businesses felt only an obligation to act legally in determining a course of action. Today, while some businesspeople still feel this way, others have acknowledged that businesses have an obligation to consider their ethical as well as legal responsibilities—especially in sensitive areas such as the marketing of dangerous products, fairness in hiring and firing practices, and controlling pollution in the communities in which they operate.

> The Myers Company legally continued to promote, advertise, and sell its brand of cigarettes after learning through research that cigarette smoking causes or predisposes people to lung cancer, contributes to heart disease, and might cause emphysema. ■

In the above example, some would assert that the Myers Company, although operating within the law, has an ethical responsibility to discontinue the manufacture of cigarettes based on its research findings, whereas others would contend that the only responsibility of the Myers Company is to make a profit (while obviously staying within the law) and that this obligation overrides any ethical responsibility.

Thus, while it is tempting to say that what is legal is also ethical, such a proposition is not necessarily true. But it could be said that law is strongly affected by ethical concepts. For example, laws that people feel are unethical are often successfully challenged through intensive lobbying and court challenges. These tactics positively influence government bodies as they consider future changes to present laws or as they enact new laws.

FUNCTIONS OF LAW

Early in the chapter, it was pointed out that if people are to live together peacefully, law must be an important part of their lives. This need for law presents a dilemma: Every time a law is created, a person's freedom to act is in some way restricted; at the same time, trying to settle disputes without resorting to law will produce chaos. Given this dilemma, what functions can law legitimately serve without unduly restricting a person's freedom? These are four functions of law (see Figure 1.1):

- Protection of the individual
- Protection of society
- Protection of property
- Promotion of worthwhile social objectives

Protection of the Individual

One of the major reasons for the development of law was to protect the individual. People in a society do not all behave in the same manner, and sometimes it's hard to tell where one person's rights end and another's begin. The rules of law guide people in a society in deciding what an individual's rights are. For example, the U.S. Constitution guarantees the right of free speech. But local laws may say that if you exercise that right at 3 A.M. in your front yard, your neighbor can call the police and have you arrested for disturbing the peace. You have violated your neighbor's right to peace and quiet.

Law thus serves to protect the rights of each individual and to regulate conduct between persons in a society. Law provides stability, allowing people to develop their own interests without infringing on the rights of others.

Figure 1.1
The Four Functions of Law

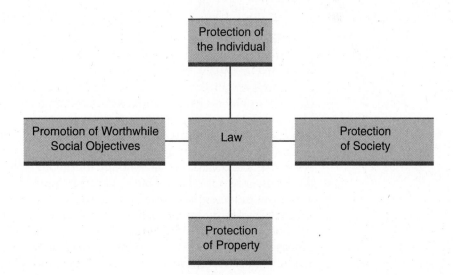

Protection of Society

Protecting society is an equally important task of the law. All people are members of one group or another. Just as individuals need protection and stability, so does the group as a whole. For example, a person who refuses to hire a qualified job applicant just because she or he is of Asian parentage harms not only the individual but also society as a whole.

Many laws that are designed to protect society help to make our cities and towns safe places in which to live and work. For example, society needs protection from thieves, muggers, murderers, vandals, and others who violate all individuals' rights when they commit harmful acts.

Protection of Property

Law protects property as well as people. Our society places much value on the importance of property and the need to protect it. Our laws protect property in many ways. Those who destroy or damage property may be punished or may have to compensate the injured party. The government may not take private property for public use without just compensation. Governments may tax property, but only if the tax is fair and reasonable. Those who own property may, upon dying, pass it on to other persons, subject only to reasonable rules.

Promotion of Worthwhile Social Objectives

Law is not limited to regulating conduct between individuals or between individuals and their society. Law may also be used as a positive force to promote worthwhile social goals. The Social Security system is a good example. The system was established by Congress to aid the aged, the poor, and the disabled. Through a system of contributions and salary deductions required by law, our government helps those who need some form of public assistance.

Promoting good health and educational opportunities is another example of the use of law to promote worthwhile objectives. Congress has enacted many laws establishing and financing medical centers and research facilities. Grants are given each year for extensive medical research, treatment programs, and immunization. Both federal and state governments assist education through legislation. Tax dollars help support many colleges, and many students receive government scholarships to study in this country and in other countries. Many states help pay for the high cost of education by giving tax deductions for educational expenses.

Promoting commerce is also an important goal. Our society believes that law should not be limited to regulating competition in promoting trade. It should also be used to assist in other ways. One example is the use of tax dollars for research to improve trade and develop new products. Another example is the use of public funds to finance businesses and business expansion. By providing direct loans or insuring private loans, government enables many small businesses to get started and to expand as the need arises.

DEVELOPMENT OF LAW

Although many societies and nations have contributed to the development of law, Roman law and English common law were the most important influences on law as we know it today.

Roman Law

Prior to the Romans, most law was oral. Decisions were made by judges or juries, but a written record of those decisions was not kept. Instead, the decisions were passed on by word of mouth from generation to generation. The Romans developed the concept of written codes that everyone could know and understand. These codes, or laws, were to be so complete that they would guide almost every aspect of life. During the reign of the Emperor Justinian (527–565 A.D.), a great body of law was developed and written. It eventually became known as the Justinian Code. When this code was revised by Napoleon I of France in 1804, it became known as the Napoleonic Code. The Napoleonic Code is the basis of much of the law of Europe today, as well as the law of Louisiana. Louisiana state law is based upon the Roman law because the state was settled primarily by people of French descent.

Common Law

The second great influence on the development of law was the English system of law. Developed in England following the Norman conquest of 1066 A.D., the English system of law is called common law. **Common law** refers to the body of legal decisions made by English court judges over a period of many years. Unlike the written Roman law, the common law in its early stages was oral. Judges traveled to various communities to hold court and try cases. They made legally binding decisions based on local customs but did not write those decisions down. As a result, common law is often referred to as the "unwritten law." Each case produced a new oral law that served as a **precedent,** an example or standard for deciding later, similar cases. This practice of judges following the precedents established by previously decided cases is called *stare decisis,* which means "to stand by a decision."

After many years, these oral laws became so numerous that they were put in writing so that anyone could become familiar with them. One of the first printed books containing important decisions of English court judges was *Blackstone's Commentaries,* published in several volumes from 1765 to 1769. The English common law system became the model for the legal system of the United States.

SOURCES OF LAW

Although much of our law originated in English common law, we also rely on other sources of law to meet the changing needs of our society. Our primary sources of law are constitutions, statutes, court decisions, and administrative regulations (see Figure 1.2).

Constitutions

A **constitution** is the fundamental written law of a state or nation. It defines the individual's rights and duties and describes the government's power and limitations.

There are fifty-one constitutions in the United States—the federal or U.S. Constitution and one for each of the fifty states. Most state constitutions are modeled after the U.S. Constitution. The U.S. Constitution, the supreme law of the land, takes precedence over all state constitutions. No law, whether enacted by Congress or by a state legislature, may conflict with the basic principles of the U.S. Constitution. If it does, a court may declare the law invalid or "unconstitutional" and, thus, unenforceable. Each state has its own constitution, which is the supreme law within its boundaries. If a state or local government passes a law that conflicts with the state constitution, that law may also be declared invalid by a court of law.

Figure 1.2 **Sources of Law in the United States**

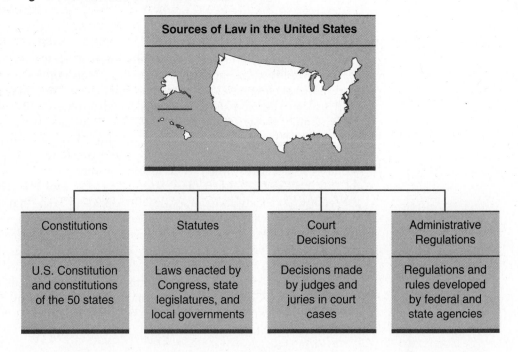

Constitutions	Statutes	Court Decisions	Administrative Regulations
U.S. Constitution and constitutions of the 50 states	Laws enacted by Congress, state legislatures, and local governments	Decisions made by judges and juries in court cases	Regulations and rules developed by federal and state agencies

Constitutional law evolves primarily from judicial interpretation of the meaning of the Constitution as issues arise. Because the Constitution is written in broad general terms, interpretations are necessary to allow for unanticipated circumstances. For example, the Fourth Amendment to the Constitution protects people from unreasonable searches; however, the term *reasonable search* is not spelled out. In a landmark case, the Supreme Court interpreted this amendment. The interpretation stated that if a lawful custodial arrest has taken place, a full search of the person is permitted and is considered a "reasonable" search under the amendment (*United States v. Robinson,* 414 U.S. 218).

Statutes

Statutes, also called legislation, are laws that have already been formally passed by legislative bodies, rather than by the courts. Legislative bodies exist at all levels of government. At the federal level, legislation passed by Congress is called "**acts.**" At the state level, this same legislation is referred to as "**statutes.**" Legislation passed by local governments (cities, towns, and villages) is called "**ordinances.**" In contrast to common-law court cases, which are written as opinions of judges explaining court decisions and are called "holdings," statutes are written in textbook form. Statute law is frequently referred to as the "written law."

The modern emphasis is upon statutory law and especially on its more specialized subfields, such as bankruptcy law, workmen's compensation laws, consumer protection laws, marriage and divorce laws, and laws dealing with the sale of goods. One reason that statutory law is emphasized is that legislatures usually take the initiative in identifying and acting on issues that result from the numerous technological, social, and economic changes in our society. The laws legislatures make can be sweeping and comprehensive and, if necessary, can be enacted rapidly. In contrast, the courts deal only with issues that arise in actual cases brought before them by individuals and businesses. The journey of a case through the courts is often slow, and the issues the case focuses on are generally narrow in scope. Changes in the law that result from such cases are usually small and are limited to a specific situation.

Congress has the power to pass laws that have national importance. Such areas as national defense, commerce between the states, and postal regulations are all within the power of Congress to regulate. As stated earlier, these federal laws take precedence over any state laws. State and local governments may pass laws involving matters over which Congress does not exercise control. For example, state and local governments have enacted laws and regulations covering such matters as marriage and divorce, zoning, vehicle and traffic control, and taxation for local purposes. Just as state laws may not conflict with federal law, local laws may not conflict with state or federal law.

Court Decisions

Although the modern emphasis is on statutory law, a substantial portion of United States law is created through decisions that judges and juries hand down in court cases. This law is known as **case law,** a modern version of the common law of England. In some court cases, no statute may exist governing the dispute. Or, if a statute does exist, it could be interpreted in different ways. In such cases, federal and state courts must decide what the law is. The court will decide the matter and set forth in a written opinion the rule or principle on which its decision was based.

These court decisions produce precedents that have the force of law. Other courts will follow these precedents when they decide similar cases in the future. The advantage of the *stare decisis* concept (the practice of following previous decisions) is predictability; it enables people to act in a certain way, knowing that they can rely on established law.

You can see that, although legislatures are primarily responsible for passing laws, courts in effect pass laws by interpreting or modifying existing laws or by making decisions that create new precedents. These precedents are as effective as laws passed by the U.S. Congress or by state legislatures.

A classic example of case law is *Robinson* v. *California,* decided by the Supreme Court in 1962 (370 U.S. 660). Robinson's conviction by the Municipal Court of Los Angeles as a narcotic addict was based upon a California statute making it a criminal offense (punishable by a jail sentence) for a person to "use, or be under the influence, or be addicted to the use of narcotics. . . ." A higher state court affirmed the lower court's decision. Upon appeal to the United States Supreme Court, the decision was reversed, on the theory that being "addicted to the use of narcotics" was an illness. The court reasoned that a statute (law) that made a criminal offense (punishable by a jail sentence) of that or any other illness—such as insanity, leprosy, or veneral disease—is unconstitutional, because it would be an infliction of cruel and unusual punishment and would thus violate the Eighth and Fourteenth Amendments to the Constitution. The significance of *Robinson* v. *California* is that it is now a precedent case: the high court's decision, namely, that narcotics addiction is no longer punishable as a crime, represents case law in the United States.

Administrative Regulations

A great deal of the regulation of individuals and businesses in this country is done by administrative agencies at the federal, state, and local levels. These agencies have been delegated the power to make rules called **administrative regulations,** which have the same force and effect as statutes and court decisions. In addition to making laws, these agencies can also take legal action against violators of their rules, in much the same way that courts do.

The federal agencies are created by Congress. The Federal Trade Commission is an agency created by Congress to regulate commercial activities and prevent unfair trade practices. The Federal Communications Commission regulates various forms of communication, including radio and television.

Protecting the environment from abuse is the task assigned to the Environmental Protection Agency.

State administrative agencies are created by state legislatures. The Bureau of Motor Vehicles, one such agency, develops rules and regulations for the operation of motor vehicles within each state.

Local administrative agencies are created by city councils or by town or village boards. A zoning board, one example of a local agency, regulates the height, size, uses, and suitability for particular purposes of residential and commercial land and buildings.

Although administrative regulations have the same force and effect as statutes and court decisions, these rules can be challenged in the courts. A business or an individual may challenge them on the basis that they are unconstitutional, vague, or beyond the power granted to the agency.

Over the last several years, administrative agencies have grown rapidly. A major reason for this growth is that many laws needed to deal with social and economic issues in the United States today—such issues as unsafe automobiles, pollution of the environment, unfair competition, and employee discrimination—cannot be addressed by legislatures in the traditional manner of passing laws. Legislatures have neither the expertise possessed by the staff of a particular administrative agency nor the necessary time to devote to the specialized problems that continually emerge and often require new or changed legislation. Furthermore, the courts are already overburdened. Given these conditions, an administrative agency's ability to make rules and regulations that have the same force and effect as statutes and court decisions offers a viable alternative for individuals and businesses that wish to recover a right or correct a wrong.

CIVIL LAW VERSUS CRIMINAL LAW

In the United States, law can be divided into two broad categories: civil law and criminal law. All law other than criminal law is known as civil law. The differences between these two categories of law are significant because in our legal system, civil actions are completely separate from criminal proceedings.

Civil law establishes rules that protect the rights and property of individuals from harmful acts by other individuals. The person who is harmed because another person violated civil law may initiate a civil action (lawsuit) against that person seeking compensation (money damages) for the harm caused. An example of a case title indicating a civil action is *Temple v. Mann*. Civil actions may be brought, for example, for child support, contract violations, injuries or damage caused by automobile accidents, divorce, libel, invasion of privacy, and violations of property rights.

> While crossing at an intersection marked as a pedestrian walk, Temple was struck by a speeding car driven by Mann. Since Mann violated her duty to Temple to drive safely, she is subject to a lawsuit for Temple's injuries (*Temple v. Mann*). ∎

Civil lawsuits are discussed in detail in Chapter 5.

Criminal law establishes rules to protect society from acts of individuals that are considered so dangerous, or potentially so, that they threaten peace and order within a society. A person accused of committing a crime is subject to arrest and, if convicted, punishment. It is for this reason that in criminal cases the government (state or federal) brings the proceeding against the accused individual. An example of a case title indicating a criminal action by the state is *State of Ohio* v. *Darling;* an example of a case indicating a crime against the federal government is *United States* v. *Darling.* Crimes include such acts as stealing, murder, breaking into a house, forging a person's signature on a check, and violating some traffic laws.

> Darling, a resident of Ohio, was arrested for stealing a car in Cleveland, Ohio. The state of Ohio brought action against him. (*State of Ohio* v. *Darling*). ■

Violations of criminal law are discussed in detail in Chapter 3. See Table 1.1 for a comparison of civil law and criminal law.

In a civil lawsuit, courts generally are confined to just awarding money damages as relief to the injured party. But money damages are not always suitable or adequate for certain violations of rights. In such cases our legal

TABLE 1.1 A Comparison of Civil and Criminal Law

	Civil Law	Criminal Law
Protects:	An individual's rights and property from the harmful acts of other individuals, such as slander or trespass, or from a person's breach of contract.	Society from the harmful acts of individuals, such as theft, murder, or driving while intoxicated.
Provides:	Money damages (compensation) or equitable relief to a person who is harmed by the wrongful conduct or breach of contract of another person. Equitable relief consists of ordering a person to perform a certain act (specific performance) or to cease carrying on certain conduct (injunction).	Punishment in the form of capital punishment, imprisonment, or fines imposed on a person who is found guilty of violating the law.
Requires:	A civil lawsuit by the person harmed (plaintiff) in order to recover.	Prosecution (criminal action) by government (federal or state) acting for society (plaintiff) against the accused person.
Type of wrong addressed:	Private (individual versus individual). An example of a case title indicating a civil action is *Ramirez* v. *Ames.*	Public (society versus individual). Examples of case titles indicating a criminal action are *United States* v. *Moll* (federal) and *State of Nevada* v. *Martin* (state).
Required in order to win:	Preponderance of the evidence (one party presenting more convincing evidence to the jury than the other party).	Determination of guilt beyond a reasonable doubt (jury entirely convinced of guilt).

system recognizes the principle of **equity,** or nonmonetary relief. Equity grants relief in accordance with principles considered fair and just. For example, if a lawsuit arises and money damages are an unsuitable remedy, a court of equity may allow the injured party to seek specific performance (order the other party to perform a certain act) or an injunction (order the other party to refrain from certain conduct).

> ■ The Dyer Company, a company that makes copiers, hired O'Leary, an executive recently fired from the rival Riverton Corporation. O'Leary had some notes and papers on Riverton's new copier, which was a cleaner and faster machine than Dyer's copier. When she was hired, O'Leary gave this information to the Dyer Company. A court can prevent the Dyer Company from using O'Leary's notes and papers on Riverton's copier to its advantage. ■

Although judges hear equity cases today, virtually no states have special equity courts (often called *chancery courts*). A judge hears the case of a person seeking a remedy in equity in the same court where other cases are also tried. (For centuries, common law and equity were administered in England by two separate sets of courts.) Some basic distinctions between law and equity are described in Table 1.2.

THE ROLE OF BUSINESS LAW

Business law is not a separate branch of law. Business law is the part of the law that deals with business or commercial transactions. To protect their commercial rights, early merchants and traders established their own laws (or customs), which became known as the *law merchant*. The law merchant

TABLE 1.2 Differences Between Law and Equity

	Law	Equity
Remedy sought by the injured party	Sum of money for damages to compensate for the loss sustained	Enforcement of a right (specific performance) or the prevention of further violation of a right (injunction)
Reason remedy is sought	Money adequately repays the injured party for a loss.	Damages are difficult to measure in money terms; therefore, an award of money to an injured party would be unfair.
Decision on the remedy is made	By a judge or jury	Solely by a judge, (with an advisory jury in some states)
Legal name for the decision	Judgment/Order	Decree/Order

became a part of English common law and, in the same way that much of our law developed from English common law, much of our business law developed from the law merchant.

In the past, each state passed its own statutes to govern most commercial transactions. Now, however, states have adopted the Uniform Commercial Code (UCC), enabling a businessperson to know that the rules governing certain transactions will be the same throughout the country. The UCC has been adopted in all fifty states, although Louisiana has adopted only portions of it. The District of Columbia and most U.S. territories, such as the Virgin Islands, have also adopted the UCC. The UCC will be discussed in some detail in Parts III and IV of the text.

Business law is only a small part of the total body of rules and regulations known as law. To understand business law and its significance, you will have to understand law in general. The chapters in Part 1 are designed to give you this general introduction to law.

THE CHANGING NATURE OF LAW

Law is constantly changing to reflect the changes that take place in society. Through our governing bodies, such as Congress and state legislatures as well as the courts, we as a society reexamine and reinterpret our existing laws and pass new laws that reflect social and economic changes. When new products or machines are developed, for example, new laws are often needed to govern their use. New laws are also needed as people change their opinions about social issues. The civil rights laws are one example of such a change. Another is the age at which a person is considered to be an adult, which almost all states have lowered in recent years. Still another example is the change in the status of capital punishment over the years.

We live in an era when technology brings many new developments to our lives. As our society—and societies in other parts of the world—change in the years to come, law will also change, to reflect the needs and concerns of the people who are governed by that law.

Summary of Important Legal Concepts

Law, a legally enforceable set of rules to regulate the conduct of individuals and groups in society, developed out of a need to keep order. Individuals injured by those who violate the law have legal remedies through the courts.

Ethics is the study of what is right or good for individuals in personal life and in business settings.

What is legal is not necessarily ethical, but law is strongly affected by ethical concepts.

Law has many important functions. Four of them are protecting the individual, protecting society, protecting property, and promoting worthwhile social objectives.

The most important influences on our legal system were Roman law and English common law. Roman law is the basis of much of the law of Europe today, while English common law and equity became the model for the legal system of the United States.

The primary sources of law in the United States are constitutions, statutes, court decisions, and administrative regulations. Although the modern emphasis is upon statutory law, including the regulations of administrative agencies, a substantial portion of our law in the United States is created through court decisions.

One way to classify law is as civil law and criminal law. Civil law protects the rights and property of individuals from harm by other individuals. Criminal law protects society from the harmful acts of individuals.

Business law is not a separate branch of law. Business law is the part of the law that deals with business or commercial transactions. The Uniform Commercial Code (UCC), which has now been adopted in all fifty states, assures businesspeople that the rules governing certain commercial transactions will be the same throughout the country.

As society changes, law will also change, to reflect the needs and concerns of people who are governed by that law.

Key Legal Terms to Know

Match the terms with the definitions that follow.

acts
administrative regulations
business law
case law
civil law
common law
constitution
criminal law
equity
ethics
law
ordinances
precedent
stare decisis
statutes

1. Laws that deal with the relationships between individuals and society and that maintain peace and order
2. Law arrived at through court decisions
3. Unwritten law based on local English customs
4. Law dealing with the relationships between individuals
5. Nonmonetary relief granted by courts when money damages are inadequate
6. An enforceable set of rules of conduct
7. An example or standard to be followed
8. The study of what is right or good for human beings
9. Laws passed by legislative bodies rather than by the courts
10. The fundamental written law by which a government derives its power and authority
11. The practice by which judges follow precedents in previously decided cases
12. Laws passed by Congress
13. Laws passed by local governments, such as cities, towns, and villages
14. Law that deals with business or commercial transactions
15. Rules that are made by administrative agencies and that have the same force and effect as statutes and court decisions

Questions and Problems to Discuss

1. What does *stare decisis* mean? Why is this concept important in American law?
2. List and describe four important functions of law.
3. In the presence of several of your friends, you remarked that "my attorney knows about as much law as can be placed in a small prescription bottle." The attorney learned of your remark and brought an action in court against you for injury to her reputation. Is this a civil matter or a criminal matter? Explain.
4. Clay stole a car from Mooney's driveway. While driving the car down the main street of town at an excessive rate of speed, Clay ran into Page's store window, causing extensive damage. Can Mooney and Page bring a civil action against Clay? Can the state take action against Clay? Explain. What functions does law serve in this case?
5. A state legislature passed a law making fourteen the minimum age for working in a dangerous occupation. Congress then passed a law making eighteen the minimum age for such employment. Which law prevails?

6. If you lived in a society with no rules, how do you think people would determine their relationships with each other?

7. What is the difference between statute law and case law? Is one more important than the other in the American legal system?

8. Do you think that law is just? Explain.

9. Why should a person have a knowledge of law? Can you give reasons for not having a knowledge of law?

10. Discuss the role that administrative agencies play in the regulation of individuals and businesses in the United States.

Chapter 2

The U.S. Court System and Its Constitutional Foundation

CHAPTER PREVIEW

This chapter presents an overview of the state and federal court systems in the United States, names the personnel who play a primary role in helping the courts to function smoothly, points out the different names given to the courts in each system, and describes the types of cases that these courts have the authority to decide. (It may come as a surprise to you that the U.S. Supreme Court will not hear every case that is presented for consideration.) Finally, the chapter outlines briefly the constitutional principles that have a significant impact on the U.S. legal system and that set it apart from legal systems in other countries.

THE COURT SYSTEM IN THE UNITED STATES

People's rights are meaningless unless the rules protecting these rights can be enforced. Chapter 1 pointed out that nonpeaceful means of settling disputes not only are unlawful but could create more trouble. Of course, two people engaged in a dispute could simply forget what happened and get on with their lives, and sometimes this is what happens. In other cases, however, the issues involved are simply too important to allow the dispute to die. In such cases, what does a person do? The answer, of course, is take the case to court.

Under our system of government, the courts have been assigned the responsibilities of interpreting and enforcing law. The courts carry out these responsibilities by deciding cases that are brought before them. To decide a case means to listen to a dispute and then render a decision. Whatever the issue—civil or criminal liability of a wrongdoer, enforceability of a contract, or the resolution of a constitutional question—when the case is decided, the court will enforce the law by imposing punishment for a criminal violation, or, in the case of a civil violation, by awarding damages to the injured party or granting relief in equity as illustrated in Chapter 1.

The United States has two separate and distinct court systems: the federal court system and the state and local court system. With courts located throughout the country, principally in the larger cities, the federal court system uniformly follows the same rules and procedures. In contrast, each state has its own court system, with courts located in virtually every town and county; these are the courts with which citizens most often have contact. Although rules and procedures vary somewhat among the states, there are similarities between the two systems. Both systems have various levels of courts with different types of jurisdiction. **Jurisdiction** is the authority to hear and decide a case. Both systems have lower level courts, called **trial courts,** where cases are first tried. Because these courts try cases for the first time, they are said to have *original jurisdiction.*

Above the trial courts are higher-level courts called **appellate courts.** These courts have *appellate jurisdiction,* that is, the authority to review cases that have already been tried in the lower courts and to make decisions about these cases without holding a new trial. Appellate judges determine only whether errors of law were made during a trial. They reach decisions by listening to the oral arguments presented by the attorneys for the parties to the appeal, reading the written information (briefs) presented by these attorneys, and reviewing the record of the trial court proceedings. No new information such as additional facts or proof is permitted. Appellate court judges may affirm the trial court decision, reverse it, or order a new trial. Both federal and state systems have a *highest* court, which has the last say in a case.

At both the federal and state levels there are civil and criminal courts. Civil courts handle cases involving disputes between individuals, between a person and a business, or between businesses. Disputes are usually settled by an award of money damages or a relief in equity to the "winning party." Criminal courts hear cases between a governmental unit—such as the state or federal government (acting for society)—and a person or business accused of a crime. Criminal courts determine whether a crime has been committed and also set punishment for those who are found guilty of committing a crime. Finally, a few special courts at both the federal and state levels deal only with certain types of cases.

No court can decide every kind of case. A case can be properly brought in a certain court only if the court has jurisdiction over the person and over the subject matter of the dispute. "Jurisdiction over the subject matter" means that the court can hear and decide the *kind* of case (for example, civil or criminal) being brought before it. Some courts have *general jurisdiction,* the power to hear and decide almost any type of case brought before them; other courts have *limited jurisdiction,* the power to hear only certain cases limited by type (such as civil *or* criminal), by the amount of money involved, and by the geographic area. Some courts, for example, can handle cases involving civil money damage claims, but only up to a certain amount and only within city or county limits. Other courts can handle cases involving civil money damage claims of any amount within a wide geographic area. Still others deal only with specific disputes, such as those relating to juveniles.

> ■ Otero wished to sue Clawson for $100,000, claiming that a permanent injury resulted from a car accident due to Clawson's carelessness. Both parties reside in New York State, County of Monroe, Rochester, NY. This case lies within the jurisdiction of the New York Supreme Court Monroe County, which is a trial court in that state. ■

In the above example, if Otero goes to the wrong court, proper jurisdiction will not exist, and she will not be able to obtain a valid hearing.

"Jurisdiction over the person" means that a court can hear and decide a case because it has authority over the *parties* in the case. The party who brings the case into court automatically comes under the court's jurisdiction. The defending party is brought under the court's jurisdiction through a legal process that describes the nature of the complaint and names the person or legal authority requesting that the case be brought to court. For example, the issuance of a summons (described in Chapter 5) in a civil lawsuit brings the defending party under the jurisdiction of the court.

> Lloyd sued Schnell to recover a sum of money for a financial loss he suffered when Schnell backed out of a legal contract. Both parties live in the state of Nevada. Lloyd should file a lawsuit in the appropriate Nevada court and then issue a summons to Schnell in order to bring him (Schnell) within the jurisdiction of that court. ■

In a criminal case, an arrest (described in Chapter 3) made by means of an arrest warrant issued by a judge brings a person accused of a crime (the defending party) into court.

THE STATE COURT SYSTEM

As noted above, each state has its own court system established by state law. Nevertheless, it is possible to make some general observations about the organization of state courts. Each state court system includes lower-level trial courts, which have various degrees of original jurisdiction, and an appellate court of final resort, which is the highest court in the state. In addition, about half of the fifty states have an intermediate appellate court system. It is important to recognize that the names of the individual courts handling the same types of cases vary from state to state. Figure 2.1 shows a typical state court system. State courts have authority to decide nearly every type of case, subject only to the limitations of the U.S. Constitution, their own state constitutions, and state law. A state court decision is not binding on the courts of other states.

Trial Courts of Limited Jurisdiction

The lower-level trial courts may be courts with both limited and general jurisdiction. Trial courts of general jurisdiction are discussed in the next section. Trial courts of limited jurisdiction generally try traffic cases and minor civil and criminal cases. These courts have such names as justice court, magistrate's court, and municipal (city) court.

A court of special interest is the **small claims court,** a local court established to provide a fast and inexpensive hearing on a claim (the average case takes about five minutes). Small claims courts exist in practically all states. Although their jurisdiction is limited, both in subject matter and dollar amount, there are three distinct advantages to taking a case to small claims courts. First, technical rules of evidence and procedure normally followed in a court trial are not strictly applicable. Second, the parties may proceed without attorneys, although most states do not bar attorneys from small claims court. Both of these advantages allow disputes to be settled without long delays. The third advantage is that a dispute that can be resolved only by court action remains economically feasible because such action does not involve attorneys' fees. The maximum amount for which a person may sue in small claims court varies by state. The amount may be as much as $15,000 (in one state, although the usual top amount is $5,000) or as little as $1,000.

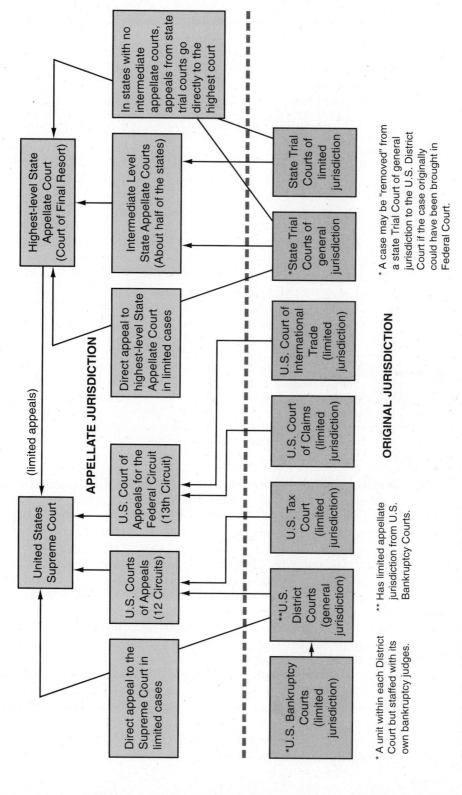

Figure 2.1 The Federal and State Court Systems

The upper limit for which suits can be brought in a small claims court is continually on the rise.

A small claims action is fairly easy to file. The injured party simply goes to the small claims court clerk's office, fills out a statement of his or her claim, and pays a modest filing fee. After the claim is filed, the court notifies the defendant (the person against whom the action is being brought), usually by certified mail. The claim notice tells the defendant when the case will be tried. The notice also gives a brief statement of the claim of the plaintiff (person bringing the action) and the amount of money he or she is seeking. A trial date is usually set within four to six weeks of filing. At the trial, the plaintiff and defendant each have a chance to tell their story to the judge and to present evidence and/or witnesses. After hearing both sides of the argument, which in some cases may take no more than twenty minutes, the judge considers the evidence and renders a decision. A typical small claims court case might be a suit by a tenant against a landlord who for no good reason refuses to return the tenant's security deposit. Other typical cases include a suit by one person against another who breaks a contract and refuses to return the cash deposit; a suit against a person who damages another's car but refuses to pay for repairs; a suit against another who passed a bad check; and a suit for a personal injury, such as assault, committed by one person against another.

> Levin, a tenant, rented an apartment from Hale, the landlord, for one year. Levin gave Hale a security deposit amounting to one month's rent. At the end of the one-year lease, Levin moved out, but Hale refused to return the security deposit, claiming tenant damage beyond normal wear and tear. Although Levin proved she had not caused the damage to the apartment, Hale still refused to return the security deposit. Levin sued Hale in small claims court to secure the return of the security deposit. ■

Although the tenant in this example had a valid claim, she might have been discouraged from pursuing it in another court, where legal fees and court costs might have exceeded the amount of the security deposit. Small claims court was a convenient, inexpensive way to recover her legitimate claim.

In a few states, for example New York, where corporations or partnerships are not allowed to sue in small claims court, there is a **commercial claims court,** allowing businesses to sue debtors up to a certain limit (in New York the amount is presently $3,000). This court is especially convenient for small businesses, which can take customers, subcontractors, and other businesses to court, typically to receive payment for their bills. Commercial claims courts offer businesses the same low-cost, represent-yourself alternative that small claims court offers to individuals. For example, a veterinarian who runs an animal hospital under the corporate name of "Caring for Animals" may take the owner of a dog treated at the hospital to court for not paying the bill.

There are other trial courts that have a greater amount of limited jurisdiction to try cases. These courts have the authority to hear civil matters involving large sums of money (for example, $25,000) and/or major criminal cases involving felonies. These courts may also have appellate jurisdiction to hear cases from the lowest courts of limited jurisdiction. There are also specialized courts with limited jurisdiction. Examples of these courts include the probate (or surrogate's) court, which handles wills, the administration of estates, and the guardianship of minors and incompetents; and domestic relations (or family or juvenile) court, which deals with family difficulties and juvenile delinquency cases.

Trial Courts of General Jurisdiction

Trial courts of general jurisdiction may hear cases involving any question (civil or criminal), any amount of money, or any degree of crime. They generally handle all serious disputes. A civil injury case involving a large sum of money or a major crime could be handled by such a court. Pursuing petty claims in this court is discouraged if the case can be settled in one of the local courts of limited jurisdiction, as for example city or justice court. In some states, a trial court of general jurisdiction is called the superior court; in others, it is called the court of common pleas, the circuit court, or the district court. In at least one state, New York, it is called the supreme court.

Intermediate Appellate Courts and the Court of Final Resort

At a higher level of the state court system are the appellate courts. As mentioned previously, these courts review cases decided in the trial courts of both general and limited jurisdiction and determine whether a mistake of law was made during the trial. A mistake of law may consist, for example, of a trial judge allowing attorneys to ask witnesses improper questions. In about half of the states (the more populous ones), intermediate courts of appeal exist to review these cases. In the remaining states, the court of final resort is the only appellate court. Where intermediate courts do exist, they usually decide a majority of cases, which relieves the burden of cases on the court of final resort.

The state's court of final resort may be called by various names—the court of appeals, the supreme court of appeals, the supreme court, or the supreme judicial court. This court will hear a case that has come from a lower court through an intermediate appellate court only when permission is given to the appealing party by the intermediate appellate court. If an appeal is denied, the intermediate appellate court's ruling stands. In limited cases, appeals may be taken directly to the state's court of final resort from the trial court, for example, when the question involves the constitutionality of a state or federal statute or the death penalty. There is no appeal from the decisions of this court to a federal court unless a federal law or question of constitutionality is involved.

There is a common misconception that anyone can appeal a case. Actually, the opportunities for successful appeal are limited. The appealing party must show that he or she would have won the case if the error of law had not been made during the trial. Another factor that limits the appeals process is its cost. One major expense is attorney's fees. Another major expense is the cost of reducing to writing the entire record of the court trial (word for word). A copy of this record of the trial must be presented to each appellate court judge so that he or she can study it in great detail.

THE FEDERAL COURT SYSTEM

The federal court system was established under Article III, Section 1, of the U.S. Constitution. Article III provides for the U.S. Supreme Court and any other lower courts that Congress may wish to establish. Under this authority, Congress has established U.S. district courts, U.S. courts of appeals, and special federal courts. The specialized federal courts with limited jurisdiction include the U.S. Bankruptcy Court, which handles the process by which financially troubled debtors are relieved from paying some of their debts; the U.S. Court of International Trade, which settles controversies over matters involving import transactions; the U.S. Tax Court, which has jurisdiction over matters involving collection of federal taxes; and the U.S. Claims Court, which deals with money claims against the U.S. government (except personal injury). Judges within the federal court system receive lifetime appointments from the president, subject to confirmation by the Senate. Figure 2.1 illustrates the organization of the federal court system.

Federal Trial Courts

The federal district courts (referred to as United States district courts) are the trial courts of the federal court system for both civil and criminal cases. (They are the equivalent of state trial courts of general jurisdiction.) The United States is divided into judicial districts. The number of districts is determined by Congress and varies over time, primarily because of population changes. Each state has at least one district court, and the more populous states—such as California, New York, and Texas—have several. Federal district courts are also located in the District of Columbia, Puerto Rico, and the territories of Guam, the Virgin Islands, and the Northern Mariana Islands.

Cases heard in the federal system originate in the district courts, with one exception: those cases for which the U.S. Congress has established special trial courts. Federal district courts have general jurisdiction, but as noted earlier, these special trial courts have only limited jurisdiction. District courts hear cases that fall into two categories: federal issues and diversity of citizenship.

Federal issues are those that pertain to federal statutes (federal law) passed by Congress. They include crimes such as narcotics sales, bank robbery, and treason committed against the federal government; injury cases in which citizens suffer damages caused by federal employees; environmental pollution cases; and problems with copyrights and patents. Also included under the umbrella of federal issues are those that pertain to the federal constitution—such as a violation of a person's rights under the federal consti-tution—and problems concerning treaties of the United States.

Diversity-of-citizenship cases apply to citizens of different states who are involved in a lawsuit based on state laws. Such cases can be tried in a federal district court. The amount of the claim, however, must be at least $50,000. A major reason for allowing this type of suit is to prevent the court of one state from showing partiality for its citizen over the citizen of the other state during any court procedure stemming from the lawsuit.

■ Marta Rollands, a citizen of Ohio, was walking along a sidewalk on a busy street in Athens, Ohio, one day when a large drum containing cleaning fluid rolled off a passing truck traveling at high speed. She suffered severe injuries and incurred a great deal of pain and suffering. As a result, she could not work for one year. Rollands now wishes to sue the trucking company for $200,000 to cover her injuries, pain and suffering, and loss of work over and above what her insurance will cover. The trucking company does business in Ohio but has its headquarters in Indiana. Because the amount of the claim exceeds $50,000, Rollands could bring her lawsuit in federal court on the basis of diversity of citizenship. ■

In the above example, Rollands could, if she wished, sue not in federal court but instead bring the lawsuit either in Ohio (because the trucking company did business there) or in Indiana (because the trucking company was head-quartered in that state). For the reasons stated above, however, it would be wiser for Rollands to bring the lawsuit in federal court.

Intermediate Courts of Appeal

Circuit courts of appeal hear appeals from federal district courts. The United States, including the District of Columbia, is divided into twelve circuits (regions), each with a court of appeals. Each circuit court hears appeals from all of the district courts located within its region. A region includes three or more states. The District of Columbia, however, is a separate region and has its own Court of Appeals. A thirteenth federal circuit court of appeals is authorized to hear appeals from federal courts of any district if the case relates to certain copyright, trademark, and patent issues. It may also hear appeals from the U.S. Court of Claims and the U.S. Court of International Trade. Decisions of this court are binding throughout the country. The thirteen federal circuits, including the D.C. Circuit and Federal Circuit are shown in Figure 2.2.

Neither the U.S. Courts of Appeal nor the U.S. District Courts have jurisdiction to review decisions of the highest state courts.

The U.S. Supreme Court

The Supreme Court of the United States, located in Washington, D.C., is the highest court in the federal court system and the highest court in the land, (see Figure 2.1). The vast majority of the Court's work is appellate. The

Figure 2.2 The Thirteen Federal Judicial Circuits

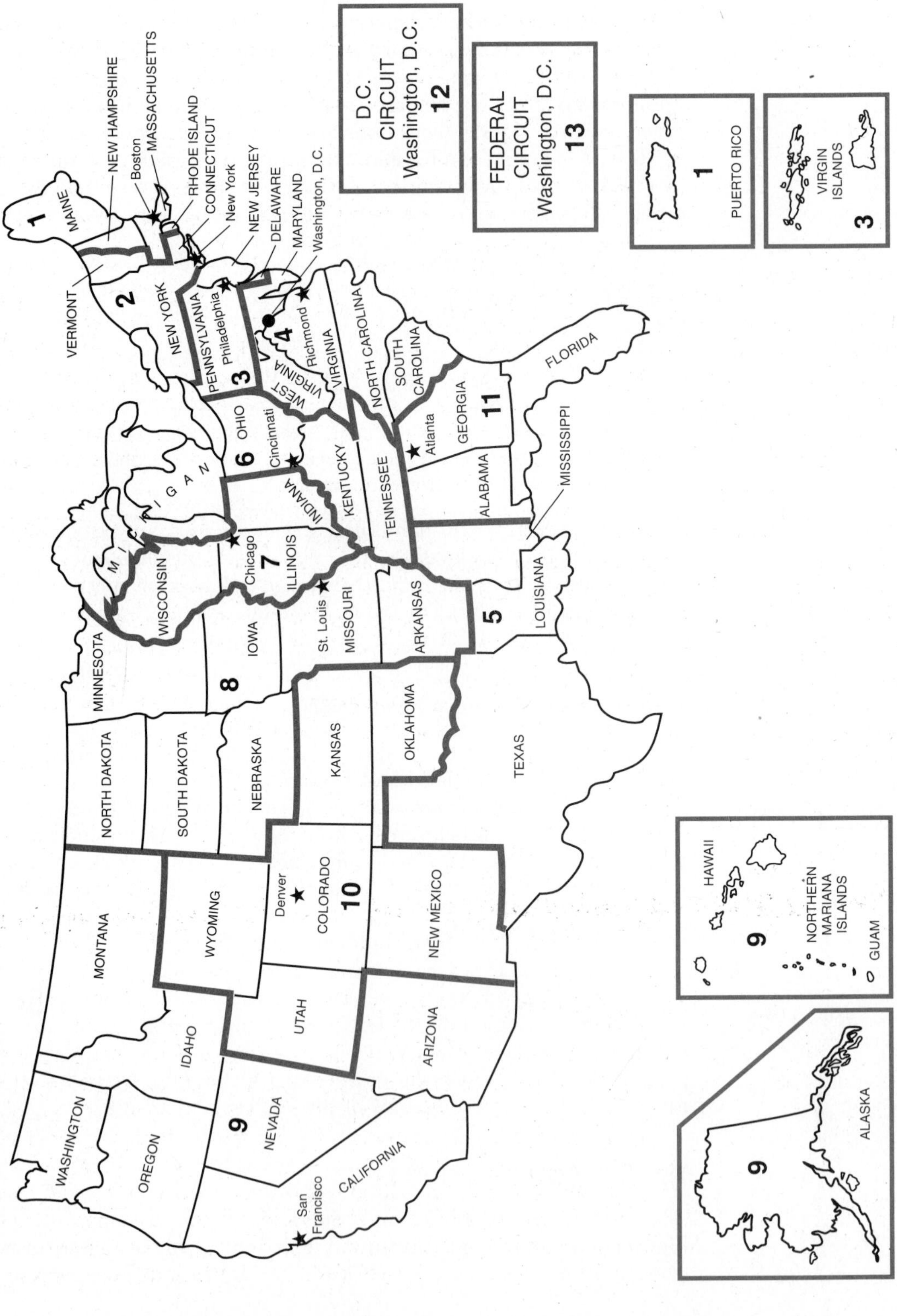

Supreme Court does have original jurisdiction in some instances, for example, in cases involving foreign ambassadors or those involving two or more states, but the Court rarely exercises this power.

The Supreme Court hears appeals from the thirteen U.S. Courts of Appeal and from the highest state courts when a question about a constitutional issue or some other federal question is involved. Ordinarily, a case must first be tried in one or more of the state or lower federal courts before it will be heard in the Supreme Court. Sometimes, decisions rendered in the U.S. District Courts may be appealed directly to the Supreme Court.

The statement, "I'll take my case all the way to the Supreme Court" is more an expression of a person's frustration or dissatisfaction with a lower court ruling than a reality. Those who direct an appeal to the Supreme Court cannot demand, as a matter of right, that the Court hear their case, even if a federal question is involved. In other words, there is no absolute right of appeal to the United States Supreme Court. Actually, very few cases go all the way to the Supreme Court; only the nine justices who comprise the Court (eight associate justices and the chief justice) and hear the cases decide which ones they will take. There is good reason for this. Each year, thousands of civil and criminal cases are tried in state and federal courts. Consequently, only the toughest cases containing the most important legal questions in the nation are heard (about 150 cases). The most common means of bringing a case before the Supreme Court is known as *certiorari*, a writ in which the Court grants permission for the case to be brought before it.

The justices of the Supreme Court meet to decide which appeals they will hear. By tradition, an appeal will be heard only with the consent of at least four justices. Although the justices are mandated by law to review some cases, most cases are subject to this "rule of four."

PARTICIPANTS IN THE LEGAL SYSTEM

The federal and state courts require the assistance of many people. Some of the personnel who play a primary role in helping the courts to function smoothly are the attorney, the paralegal, the judge, and the jury.

The Role of the Attorney

An attorney is a person professionally trained and licensed to practice law, that is, to assist individuals (clients) on legal matters. Attorneys may be consulted by individual clients on such matters as making out a will or settling a marital dispute, or they may act as legal representatives for individual or business clients who decide to bring a lawsuit in court against others. Large corporations have full-time attorneys who advise them in the management of potential legal problems resulting from, for example, labor-management disputes, securities violations, and antitrust issues. In serving clients, the attorney must provide the best advice possible and must represent them with skill and integrity. It is important to know when to consult an attorney; often, legal help is not required or other consultants may be used instead.

Sometimes it is absolutely essential to consult an attorney. An arrest or an indictment for a crime (discussed in Chapter 3) is an example of a situation in which legal counsel is essential. The risks of being treated unfairly or improperly, of being held without bail, or of being found guilty and being sentenced improperly are too great to bypass legal advice. If you have been accused of a crime and you cannot afford an attorney, the court will appoint an attorney to represent you.

You should also consult an attorney before executing any legal document. For example, contracts are binding legal documents that may have serious, long-term effects. An attorney may be helpful in negotiating the terms of a contract.

There are other times when the services of an attorney are advisable but not essential. Planning for the development of real estate or for the start of a business is often helped by the advice of a knowledgeable attorney. Seeking and obtaining financing for the purchase of a home or the expansion of a business are also occasions when the assistance of an attorney is helpful.

There are many ways to find a reliable attorney. The bar association in your community is a good source of information. Other sources are friends, relatives, employers, accountants, bankers, and other professionals. In addition, many attorneys now advertise and provide information about their areas of specialization.

The Role of the Paralegal

A paralegal is a person who, although not an attorney, possesses the legal knowledge, skills, and training to assist lawyers in many aspects of legal work. The importance of paralegals cannot be overemphasized, especially in the area of litigation. They help attorneys prepare for trial by interviewing potential witnesses, investigating facts, doing legal research, and preparing court documents. Paralegals also have other responsibilities. They often draft legal documents such as contracts, wills, mortgage agreements, and separation agreements.

The Role of the Judge and the Jury

A trial judge is the person who presides over a trial, listens to attorneys argue their clients' cases to ensure that the evidence presented during the trial on behalf of the parties is relevant, and determines that the rules of trial procedure are not violated. The judge rules on points of law that arise during the trial, and at the conclusion of the trial instructs jurors regarding the law of the case before they retire to the jury room. If there is no jury, the judge alone decides the outcome of the case. In criminal cases it is the judge who sentences those who are found guilty.

The jury is a body of citizens randomly chosen from within a community to listen to the facts presented during a civil or criminal trial and to reach a conclusion (money damages, equitable relief, or punishment) about that case.

The number of jurors will vary depending upon whether the trial is civil or criminal and according to the particular state where the jurors reside.

More information about the roles of the attorney, the judge, and the jury is given in Chapters 3 and 5.

THE CONSTITUTIONAL FRAMEWORK OF THE UNITED STATES LEGAL SYSTEM

Our legal system is unique. Although other countries have legal systems that resemble ours, the U.S. system combines elements almost unknown in other countries. The following sections discuss briefly the constitutional principles on which this system is based.

Separation of Powers

The U.S. system of government and law is based on a concept known as **separation of powers,** which is set out in the U.S. Constitution. This concept establishes the three branches of the federal government—the legislative branch, Congress, which makes laws; the executive branch, the President, which enforces laws; and the judicial branch, the Supreme Court and lower courts, which interprets the laws. Each branch is independent of the others, and each has its own predominant power. This organization of the federal government was established when the Constitution was originally drafted. It was meant to prevent any one branch from obtaining more power than another branch and from gaining absolute control of the government.

As a practical matter, the concept of separation of powers is not always followed. Courts often "make law" by interpreting existing law. That interpretation may change a law in the same manner that a legislature might change it. Courts also make decisions that are often political in nature, such as deciding whether a certain political party may appear on an election ballot. These acts are incidental, however; for the most part, our judicial system concentrates on interpreting laws.

A distinctive characteristic of our legal system is that it combines statute laws (laws enacted by legislatures) and decisions made by courts. In contrast, most other civil law systems rely almost completely on statutes.

Another important principle of our legal system is that of "constitutionality." The U.S. Constitution is the supreme law of the land. Each state also has a constitution that is the supreme law in that state. Statutes, governmental actions, and court decisions may be declared invalid if they violate the principles of either the state or the federal constitution.

Judicial Review

The concept of **judicial review,** an important part of our legal system, gives higher courts the power to review decisions of a lower court. Federal courts review acts of the U.S. Congress and state legislatures, and the U.S. Supreme Court reviews decisions of the highest state courts. This review process allows decisions and laws to be reversed or changed if they are not in harmony with existing laws and constitutions. The Supreme Court case of *Marbury* v. *Madison*, 5 U.S. 137; 2L. Ed. 60, established the basis for the concept of judicial review by declaring an act of Congress unconstitutional. In a more recent decision, *Roe* v. *Wade*, 410 U.S. 113; 93 S. Ct. 705; 35 L. Ed. 2d 147, the Court struck down a Texas statute that made performing an abortion a crime.

Judicial review is a cornerstone of our Constitution. In the United States, our courts serve as the supreme protector of the rights of the individual. In no other country do so many citizens look to the courts to advance the interests of both individual citizens and society in general. In other countries, those who feel that their rights are being violated seek help from the legislature or from the administration. In this country, it is more likely that these matters will be brought to the courts.

Accommodation of Interests

Another principle of our legal system is that of **accommodation of interests.** As it is practiced in the United States, law is not simply a matter of right versus wrong. Law is more a matter of acknowledging the equitable considerations of the parties involved in a dispute. A tenant, for example, may be evicted for nonpayment of rent. A court, however, will often give the tenant time to raise the money needed to pay the rent, even though the law doesn't provide for this. This action helps the tenant and may prevent the tenant from becoming a burden on society.

Litigation

Our legal system operates almost exclusively within the framework of **litigation**—that is, a lawsuit or legal action. The Constitution does not give the courts the power to offer advisory opinions or to answer hypothetical questions. Courts may provide answers only to the questions brought before them in the form of lawsuits. This framework ensures that the courts will not interfere with the rights and duties of the legislative and executive branches of government.

Judicial decisions that are based on litigation depend upon an *adversary system.* Opposing parties enter our courts represented by attorneys who are adversaries (opponents) of each other. Each attorney attempts to ensure that her or his point of view should prevail and that the opposing attorney's point of view should lose. They do this by producing evidence in the client's favor and by attempting to disprove the evidence presented by the opposing party. The underlying thought is that this process will bring out all important evidence and that the result will be the truth.

The Bill of Rights

The first ten amendments to the United States Constitution, known as the *Bill of Rights,* have a substantial impact on the rights and liberties of the individual within the framework of the legal system in the United States. The U.S. Constitution and the state constitutions guarantee U.S. citizens individual personal rights against infringement from government, called **civil rights.** The First Amendment guarantees religious freedom. Government must be neutral concerning religious organizations, neither approving nor disapproving of them. The First Amendment also guarantees freedom of speech, freedom of the press, and the right to peaceful assembly. Because determining the boundaries of individual rights is sometimes difficult, many First Amendment cases have been decided by the courts.

The Fourth Amendment protects the individual's right to privacy by prohibiting unreasonable search and seizure by government. If an unreasonable search and seizure should occur, the evidence obtained cannot be used in a trial. The Fifth and Sixth Amendments guarantee a number of rights that fall under the heading of "due process of law." One such right is the right against self-incrimination. To guard against the use of torture to extract confessions, the founders of our nation declared that individuals could not be compelled to be witnesses against themselves. It is up to government to prove guilt, not up to the individual to prove innocence. In addition, a person may not be tried twice for the same offense, and private property may not be seized for public use without just compensation for the property owner.

With a few exceptions, the Fourteenth Amendment applies the Bill of Rights to the states. In addition, it guarantees the equal protection of the law to all persons. Equal protection means that the state and federal governments cannot treat one person differently from another unless there is a legitimate reason for doing so.

Summary of Important Legal Concepts

Sometimes, people involved in disputes with others have issues serious enough to bring to a court of law. This alternative may be the only way to protect each party's legal rights. Under our system of government, the courts have been assigned the responsibilities of protecting our legal rights by interpreting and enforcing law. (In Chapter 1 we learned that law consists of rules of conduct that require people to act in a certain way.) The courts carry out their responsibility by deciding cases that are brought before them.

The court system of the United States is made up of state and federal courts. Both court systems have various levels of courts with different types of jurisdiction—general, limited, original, and appellate. Jurisdiction covers both civil and criminal cases. In both systems, there are lower-level courts called trial courts, where cases are first tried. These courts have original jurisdiction. Higher-level courts have appellate jurisdiction, the authority to review lower court cases. In both systems, a highest court has the last say in a case. A state's highest court may be called by various names; in the federal system, the highest court is called the Supreme Court. The Supreme Court is the highest court in the land. Very few cases reach this Court because it hears only the toughest cases involving the most important legal questions. The Supreme Court, which has mainly appellate jurisdiction, will hear a case only if it was first tried in a lower court and only if a federal question, such as a constitutional issue, is involved (see Figure 2.3).

The attorney, the paralegal, the judge, and the jury all play a key role in helping the courts to function smoothly.

U.S. SUPREME COURT

U.S. Supreme Court may hear appeal if a constitutional issue is involved.

Appeals court ruling is submitted to U.S. Supreme Court.

State court of final resort rules on case.

Loser takes case to a U.S. circuit court of appeals.

Loser takes case to state appeals court.

Case is tried in a U.S. district court.

Plaintiff or defendant loses in state trial court.

Figure 2.3
The Road to the Supreme Court

State Route

Federal Route

Several constitutional principles significantly influence the U.S. legal system. One important principle is separation of powers—the independence of the legislative, executive, and judicial branches of government. A second important principle is judicial review, the power of higher-level courts—especially the U.S. Supreme Court—to review decisions of lower courts and to reverse or change laws that are not in harmony with existing laws, state constitutions, and the U.S. Constitution. A third important principle that makes our legal system unique is accommodation of interests, where equitable considerations of the parties involved in a dispute are acknowledged. A fourth principle, litigation, gives courts the power to provide answers to questions brought before them in the form of lawsuits. Finally, the underlying principles of the Bill of Rights (the first ten amendments to the U.S. Constitution) have a substantial impact on court decisions when it comes time to determine the boundaries of individual rights of citizens.

Key Legal Terms to Know

Match the terms with the definitions that follow.

accommodation of interests
appellate courts
civil rights
commercial claims court
judicial review
jurisdiction
litigation
separation of powers
small claims court
trial court

1. The concept of independent branches of government
2. A lawsuit or legal action
3. Freedoms and rights guaranteed by the federal and state constitutions
4. The power of a court to review decisions of a lower court
5. The power of a court to hear and decide a case
6. A court of original jurisdiction
7. Courts that hear appeals of decisions of lower courts
8. A local court established to provide a fast and inexpensive hearing on a claim
9. A special local court similar to a small claims court that allows businesses to sue debtors up to a certain limit
10. Equitable considerations of the parties involved in a dispute are acknowledged

Questions and Problems to Discuss

1. Explain the concept of judicial review.
2. Discuss the advantages of taking a case to small claims court.
3. Villar, who lives in San Bernardino, California, was seriously injured near his home when an out-of-state car driven by Ames, from Seattle, Washington, negligently struck him. Villar wished to sue Ames to $200,000, the amount of his (Villar's) injuries. In what court should he file his case?
4. Would the U.S. Supreme Court hear the following cases? Explain why or why not.
   a. A Fourth Amendment search and seizure case is appealed from the highest state court of Pennsylvania. Three justices of the U.S. Supreme Court vote to hear the case. The remaining six justices believe the issue has already been decided in a similar case heard by the Court a year prior to the case currently being considered. The six vote not to hear the Pennsylvania court appeal.
   b. A female college student is fined $150 for speeding on a major street in a large city. She claims she wasn't speeding and vows to take her case directly to the Supreme Court.
   c. A state has made it a crime to criticize state government. Nichols, the publisher of a small-town newspaper, sued in the appropriate state courts to declare this law unconstitutional (in violation of the First Amendment right of free speech), but lost.

5. What is the function of an appellate court in the federal and state court systems?
6. The state of Ohio has a state statute that prohibits the manufacture and sale of fireworks. The Rainbow Corporation of Ohio was charged with violating this statute, and the state brought a civil action in state court to recover profits the corporation made from illegal sales. Rainbow, believing that federal rules of procedure were more favorable to its case, asked to have the case transferred to a federal district court in Ohio. Will Rainbow's request be granted?
7. In what ways are the state and federal courts similar?
8. Vira was owed $60,000 by Caldwell and sued in a state court to collect the amount due. Vira won. Caldwell was unhappy with the decision and appealed to the highest state court, where she also lost the case. Caldwell then thought about appealing to a federal court, hoping for better treatment. Does a federal court have jurisdiction to hear her case?
9. Kline was tried and convicted in a county court for killing her husband during a family argument. She claimed that she was innocent. Can Kline appeal the decision of the county court?
10. Sullivan owned land and a cottage bordering a lake. The Town Board passed a resolution taking ownership of the beach in front of Sullivan's home for a public bathing area. The resolution did not provide for any compensation to Sullivan. What can Sullivan do to prevent this action?

Chapter 3

Public Wrongs/Crimes

CHAPTER PREVIEW

This chapter deals with crimes called public wrongs, which are wrongs against society. Initially, the chapter describes the two major classifications of crimes. It then goes on to list and describe the crimes most often handled by criminal justice agencies at the state and local levels. Another part of the chapter deals with some common defenses, or excuses offered by accused persons for committing a crime, and the primary steps in the criminal justice system that are followed when a person actually commits a crime or is suspected of committing a crime. The remainder of the chapter is devoted to a discussion of the handling of juvenile delinquents when they commit unlawful acts equivalent to adult crimes.

NATURE OF PUBLIC WRONGS

Public wrongs, called **crimes,** violate criminal laws. Those who commit such acts can be punished by the courts upon conviction. Depending on the seriousness of the crime, punishment may consist of a prison or jail sentence, a fine, or even death. Persons found guilty of criminal acts have permanent criminal records.

Crimes are classified according to their degree of seriousness (see Figure 3.1). A **felony** is a crime of a serious nature for which the punishment may be death or imprisonment for more than one year, usually in a state or federal prison. A **misdemeanor** is a crime that is less serious than a felony and is punishable by imprisonment for no more than one year, usually in a local institution such as a county jail.

A few states have another classification of wrongs, less serious than misdemeanors; these wrongs are variously termed *violations, infractions,* or *petty offenses.* Although the punishment for these wrongs may be confinement in a local jail, the acts are not considered to be criminal acts. The offender therefore has no permanent criminal record. Violations of town, city, or county ordinances, public disturbances, and minor traffic violations are included in this category of wrongs.

STATE AND FEDERAL CRIMINAL LAWS

The U.S. Congress has passed federal criminal laws (statutes) making certain crimes federal offenses. State legislatures in each of the fifty states have also passed laws (statutes) making certain offenses crimes against the state.

Criminal statutes vary from one state to another. Consequently, an act that is a crime in one state may not be a crime in another. Similarly, a violation of a criminal statute may be a felony in one state but a misdemeanor in another.

Some crimes, such as bank robbery and the possession and sale of narcotics, violate both federal and state criminal laws. Offenders can therefore be tried in either state or federal court.

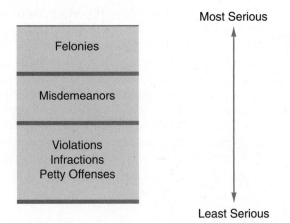

Most Serious

Felonies

Misdemeanors

Violations
Infractions
Petty Offenses

Least Serious

Figure 3.1
**Classification of
Crimes According to
Degree of Seriousness**

COMMON CRIMES

Many acts are prohibited by federal and state laws. The acts discussed here represent crimes most often handled by criminal justice agencies at the state and local levels; they include assault, robbery, arson, burglary, theft, driving while intoxicated, drug law violations, and computer crimes.

Assault

The crime of **assault** occurs when one person unlawfully causes physical injury or substantial pain to another. A person commits an assault by striking, beating, kicking, choking, or wounding another person. Assault can be either a felony or a misdemeanor depending on the severity. In the past, the crime of assault referred only to the *threat* of physical injury; the crime of "battery" referred to the actual physical contact. Modern criminal statutes have abolished assault and battery as separate crimes and use the term "assault" to cover both acts.

■ Gitano, a reputed mobster charged with racketeering, struck Russ, a cameraman for WRXZ-TV, Channel 17, in the face as Russ was shooting films of Gitano leaving a federal court building. For striking Russ, Gitano could be charged with the crime of assault. ■

Robbery

Robbery is the act of unlawfully taking another person's money or personal (movable) property against his or her will, by means of force or the threatened use of force. The money or property may be on the victim's person or simply in the victim's presence. (If the use or threat of force is absent, no robbery has taken place, but rather another crime, such as larceny, which is discussed below.) Pushing, jostling, or striking with a fist are sufficient to substantiate the force element in robbery. Robbery is generally regarded as a felony.

A salesperson at a downtown department store was approached by a man who pointed a gun at her and demanded all the money in her cash drawer. Upon receiving the money, he fled. The man has committed a robbery. ■

Arson

The intentional, illegal burning of any dwelling house, other building (such as a warehouse), or motor vehicle, by fire or by means of explosives is called **arson** and is a felony. In some states arson includes the property of the arsonist if there is an attempt to defraud the insurance company. Two frequent motives for arson are revenge and a desire to collect on fire insurance policies.

Manny set fire to and destroyed a federal court building because one of his children had been arrested by federal authorities for the sale of dangerous drugs. Manny was guilty of arson. ■

Burglary

In most states **burglary** is the crime of unlawfully entering another person's dwelling house (home), building, or boat used for regular residence at any time of the day or night, without permission and with the intent to commit a felony. An offender who successfully carries out a burglary may be charged with both burglary and the other crime. Burglary is a felony. Even if the person does not commit a crime inside the building, the *intent* to commit the crime is enough to classify the act of entering as burglary.

Thinking no one was home, Carroll entered Petrie's house through an unlocked door. Carroll's intent was to steal what he could, especially cash and jewelry. As he entered the den, much to his surprise he spotted Petrie sitting in a chair. Petrie screamed and Carroll ran from the house without taking anything. Carroll could be charged with burglary even though he did not steal anything. ■

Theft

Recall that robbery is the act of taking another person's property through force or the threat of force. *Theft* is a broader term, and it describes offenses relating to the unlawful taking of another person's property *without the use of force* and with the intent to deprive the person of the property permanently. The most common forms of theft are listed here.

Larceny Intentionally stealing (taking and carrying away) money or the personal (movable) property of another person is known as **larceny.** The law classifies larceny as either *grand larceny* (generally a felony) or *petit larceny* (generally a misdemeanor). The classification depends on the value of the property stolen and the state in which the crime was committed. For example, stealing an item worth $1,000 or less in New York state would be petit larceny.

> Glassjean parked her van in a mall parking lot while she shopped at various stores throughout the mall. When she returned to the van, she discovered that several musical instruments that had been stored there, worth a total of $5,298, had been stolen. In most states, if the person responsible for stealing these instruments were caught, he or she would be tried in criminal court for grand larceny, a felony. ∎

Shoplifting is a form of larceny. **Shoplifting** is the crime of taking merchandise from a store without paying for it. Merchants' rights in shoplifting incidents are mentioned in Chapter 4 in the discussion of the tort of false arrest.

Embezzlement The crime of **embezzlement** is the unlawful taking of money or other personal property by an employee to whom the money or property has been legally entrusted by his or her employer.

> Butler was the accountant for a construction company. She set up a false account and regularly took money from the company, hiding her act by recording payments to a company that did not exist. Butler was guilty of embezzlement. ∎

Forgery The making or altering of any document with the intent to deceive is called **forgery.** Documents that are commonly forged are checks, credit card invoices, driver's licenses, and identification cards.

> Quatro found on the street a blank personalized check on Speedy's account at Chase First Bank. She filled in the blanks on the check, making it payable to cash for $200, and she signed Speedy's name. Quatro then took the filled-in check to a local grocery store where she was known, and she cashed it. Quatro committed the crime of forgery. ∎

Fraud When one or more individuals obtain money or personal property under false pretenses—for example, by misrepresenting or by creating a false impression—they have committed **fraud.** In the case of some frauds, the victims are consumers; in other frauds, the primary targets are businesses and businessmen.

> Jardine needed money to pay some heavy debts that he had run up through gambling. To raise funds to pay these debts, he induced some of his friends to invest in a telecommunications company he claimed he was starting. He gave his friends a brochure that contained pertinent information about his company and assured investors that it had good earning potential. Leslie, one friend who had already invested several thousand dollars, discovered through an investigation that the brochure produced by Jardine was false and that no such company existed. Leslie attempted to recover her money, but it was too late. Jardine used the funds to pay his debts and then disappeared. If found, Jardine could be charged with fraud. ∎

Blackmail The crime committed by a person who illegally obtains money or other property by making threats is called **blackmail,** or extortion. The threats may be to do physical harm; to destroy property; or to harm another's reputation, career, or business.

> ■ The leader of a street gang in a large city threatened to burn several small businesses in a certain section of the city unless the owners paid a weekly "protection fee." The gang leader is guilty of blackmail. ■

Receiving Stolen Property   It is generally a felony to take **possession of property known to be stolen** with the intent of depriving the true owner of the property. It is no defense to say that you did not know that the property was stolen. Courts hold that you are guilty of the crime if you accepted the property having some knowledge leading you to believe that it may have been stolen.

> ■ Wilkins is offered a telephone answering machine for $15 from a person who says he got it and several others from the phone company during a special inventory sale. The fact that these machines are usually rather expensive should prompt Wilkins to contact the phone company and ask about that special sale. Otherwise, Wilkins may be prosecuted for possession of stolen property. ■

Driving While Intoxicated

If you operate a motor vehicle while intoxicated, you are subject to criminal penalties. The courts have defined **driving while intoxicated** (DWI) to mean that a person has knowingly and voluntarily consumed alcohol to such an extent as to substantially affect his or her ability to properly operate a motor vehicle. Without guidelines, this definition would be difficult for a court to apply to a DWI case. Accordingly, states have set a standard to determine legal intoxication, and they use chemical tests to measure the standard. Several states say that a motorist is legally intoxicated and can be arrested for driving while intoxicated when his or her blood-alcohol content is .10 percent or higher. A reading of .10 percent means that .10 percent of one's blood consists of alcohol. As the blood-alcohol content rises, a person becomes increasingly intoxicated. Some states—California, Utah, Oregon, Maine, and Virginia for example—use .08 percent as the standard for determining legal intoxication, and others are studying reduction. Generally, a first-time DWI conviction is a misdemeanor, whereas second and third charges within some limited period of time are treated as felonies. Over forty states now have laws that mandate prison time for any driver twice convicted of driving while drunk.

A police officer has the right to run a preliminary test on a suspected offender's breath for the presence of alcohol. One device commonly used in this test is the Alcolyzer. This portable device measures both the presence of consumable alcohol in a driver's breath and the *approximate* quantity of the alcohol. The results obtained from the Alcolyzer can provide legal grounds for an arrest and for conducting a full-scale blood-alcohol content test at the police station. A full-scale test determines the presence and quantity of consumable alcohol in a person's blood. One test analyzes body fluids such as blood, urine, or saliva. Another measures the quantity of alcohol by taking samples of deep lung air produced by the driver rather than of body fluids. A machine often used for this purpose is the Breathalyzer. An arrested person who refuses to take a full-scale test risks the loss of driving privileges. Courts usually take a tough stand on people who drive while intoxicated because drunk drivers are a major cause of vehicle-related fatalities in our country. According to statistics, they are twenty-five times more likely to have accidents than are drivers who are not intoxicated.

In some states, public awareness of the drunk-driver problem revived a century-old law called the "dram shop act." The dram shop act imposes liability on bars or taverns selling alcoholic beverages to an intoxicated person or to any person under the influence of an alcoholic beverage. Two Rochester, New York, restaurants together paid $2 million to a person injured in a DWI-related crash. The injured person was struck by an intoxicated driver who earlier had been drinking at the two restaurants. Some state courts have extended civil liability under the dram shop laws to include liquor stores and grocery stores that sell to intoxicated persons and minors and have also extended liability to persons who host private parties.

Drug Law Violations

State and federal laws make the sale and possession of illegal drugs a felony and, therefore, a serious crime. The Federal Controlled Substances Act, passed by Congress in 1970, has served as a model for state laws. As a result, there is much uniformity between the federal and state drug laws and among the various state laws. The federal act classifies drugs into five groups, ranging from the most to the least dangerous, and defines the penalties associated with the manufacture, distribution, and dispensing of any drug in each group. Drugs are rated on such factors as their actual abuse or potential for abuse, medical usage, risk to the public health, capability to create physical or psychological dependence, and the scientific knowledge of the drug.

In some states the trend has been to "decriminalize" possession of small quantities of marijuana by removing the offense to the lowest level of seriousness. First-time offenders are summoned to court and pay fines, in much the same way traffic violators do. Under federal law, simple possession (with no prior conviction) has not been decriminalized and continues to be a misdemeanor.

Computer Crimes

As computers have grown more important in our society, the ways in which they are used have also increased. It is very common for various family members to use computers in private homes to track personal finances, to play entertaining games, to prepare income tax returns, and for other utilitarian reasons. Computers have become such an integral part of the business environment that companies have made substantial changes in the way they do business because of them. Unfortunately, with the growth of computers and computer applications, a negative effect has emerged: computer crime. Computer crimes have become one of the fastest-growing categories of crime in America.

The variety of computer crime is almost infinite, and therefore trying to define it concisely is difficult. Computer crimes include unauthorized access to data (called *snooping*), stealing information from a computer (called *raiding*), fraudulently manipulating computer information, deliberately destroying computer information (e.g. out of revenge), and the outright theft of computer hardware (which includes the actual computer and its attachments such as tape drives, monitors, and printers) and computer software (programs). A computer criminal may range from a highly experienced technician to a minimally experienced professional with little or no technical experience. Here are a few examples of typical computer crimes:

- A bank employee obtained a computer printout of the names and addresses of current bank customers and the maturity dates of their investments. He thereafter resigned from the bank and used this printout to make sales in his own investment business. ■

- A disgruntled computer programmer at a nuclear weapons plant created a destructive computer program (a virus) that, when used, made copies of itself and multiplied so rapidly that it clogged computers in the plant's computer room and effectively shut these computers down. ■

- A disloyal department head carried a totally fictitious person on a computerized payroll, paid this person a weekly salary, and then used the money for his own personal benefit. ■

- A college student infiltrated the computerized files of her college and made unauthorized grade changes. ■

- A computer operator used his employer's computer installation to run his own private computer business. ■

- A college student who received a $10,000 auto loan purposely sent in the last payment stub with her first payment. A week later she received a computer-generated letter from the bank congratulating her on the quick retirement of her loan. ■

- A government employee altered a computer program and wrote herself $150,000 in government checks from taxpayers' money. ■

- A college student wrote a program and placed it on the college's computer system. The program caused computers in the system to "choke to death" and generate vast amounts of nonsensical data. ■

Most states and the federal government have now enacted legislation to prosecute those who commit computer-related crimes. Many state laws specify stiff fines and prison terms for those who tamper with or illegally gain access to data in computers. At the federal level, the Computer Fraud and Abuse Act of 1986 covers situations that involve federal government computers or an interstate crime. An example of an interstate crime that would be covered by the 1986 act is that of a disgruntled employee who leaves his job, moves to another state, gains access to his former employer's computer system by phone transmissions, and triggers a destructive program. Many companies are reluctant to prosecute such cases because they do not wish to publicize their vulnerability to computer crimes.

In many investigations of computer-related crimes, federal agencies assist local investigators. (One of the duties assigned to the Secret Service is the investigation of computer fraud.) Even if the case results in a local prosecution, federal agencies may assist, as long as the crime violates federal law.

DEFENSES TO CRIMES

Sometimes individuals are not criminally responsible for their acts due to certain defenses. Figure 3.2 depicts these defenses. A **defense** is a reason that a defendant (the accused) offers to excuse his or her guilt in a criminal action. Defenses that have been raised include infancy, insanity, involuntary intoxication, duress, justification, and entrapment.

Infancy

Under modern law today, all states provide that a boy or girl who is less than a certain age (eighteen in most states) and who commits an unlawful act will not be charged with the commission of a crime but only with being a juvenile delinquent. The decision of how to handle a juvenile is based on the seriousness of the crime; the manner in which the offense was committed;

Figure 3.2
Defenses to Crimes

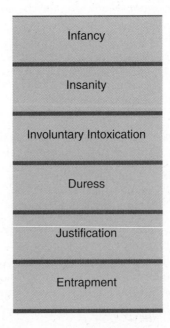

Infancy

Insanity

Involuntary Intoxication

Duress

Justification

Entrapment

the juvenile's prior record; and the cooperation, attitude, and behavior of the juvenile and parents involved. The juvenile may be placed on probation and under the supervision of a probation officer or in a rehabilitation facility, such as a group home. Juveniles who commit serious offenses and whose behavior poses a threat to society are placed in a secured juvenile detention facility.

When juveniles above a certain age commit serious crimes, they may be tried as adults. In most states children below the age of seven cannot be charged even with juvenile offenses, no matter how serious their actions may appear to others.

Insanity

Whether an accused was insane (of unsound mind) at the time he or she committed a criminal act is generally decided by a court, after hearing all the evidence in the case. Psychiatrists for the defense usually produce evidence that the accused had a mental disease or defect and, consequently, did not know right from wrong. Psychiatrists for the prosecution often testify in court that the accused did indeed know what he or she was doing. The court weighs the conflicting testimony before rendering its decision. A few jurisdictions recognize that an accused can be partially insane in respect to the circumstances surrounding the commission of a crime, but sane as to other matters.

Involuntary Intoxication

Like insanity, involuntary intoxication resulting from alcohol or other drugs is a defense to a criminal act because the intent (the desire) to commit a crime is lacking. A person with a drugged mind cannot distinguish right from wrong. Intoxication is involuntary when the accused can show that he or she was forced to take the intoxicating substance or to consume the alcohol without knowing what it was.

Duress

An accused who has committed a crime under duress—forced to act against his or her own free will—may have no criminal liability for the unlawful act. A typical example of duress is that inflicted by bank robbers who hold up a bank and force a customer doing business in the bank to drive them to a certain destination. There is no criminal intent on the part of the customer, and therefore the customer has committed no crime. The customer must, however, show that there was a threat of death or serious bodily harm, either to the customer or to another person, such as a family member. The customer must also show that there was fear that the threat would be carried out and that there was no reasonable opportunity to escape the threatened harm. Duress will excuse a person from liability from any crime except one in which the accused is compelled to take someone else's life.

Justification

This defense excuses a person for the commission of an act that otherwise constitutes a crime. The act is generally committed to protect one's person or property. Justification might be used as a defense in a case in which a burglar entered a house to commit a robbery and was killed by the victim, who shot in self-defense. In this case, if reasonable cause existed to take another's life, the victim may have no criminal liability.

Entrapment

Entrapment applies when a law enforcement officer persuades a person to commit a crime. The key to the entrapment defense is that the accused had no intention of committing the crime and in fact would not have committed it until persuaded to do so by the officer. Why would a law enforcement officer "set up" a person to commit a crime and then make an arrest? An officer might use this strategy to trap a known criminal who has committed crimes and has been arrested but, for lack of evidence or through legal technicalities, has not been convicted. Entrapment is not a defense if a person has already made up his or her mind to commit a crime and then does so with assistance from a law enforcement officer.

> Johnson, a known drug dealer, offered to sell cocaine, an illegal drug, to Evans, a police undercover officer who was posing as a drug addict. Evans bought the drug and then she arrested Johnson. Johnson cannot plead entrapment as a defense. ■

In the above case, the police officer did not *cause* the crime to happen; she simply provided the opportunity for Johnson to make the sale.

THE CRIMINAL JUSTICE SYSTEM

The United States has two distinct criminal justice systems, federal and state. Each system is composed of three elements: the police, courts, and corrections. A person who has committed a crime or is suspected of having committed a crime is handled through one of these two systems. Figure 3.3, which displays the primary steps in the criminal justice system at the state and local levels, outlines the process that takes place when a felony is committed. The steps broadly parallel the federal system. A person accused of a crime is protected by many guarantees found in the Constitution, particularly the Fourth, Fifth, Sixth, and Eighth Amendments in the Bill of Rights. These guarantees apply to federal crimes and, through the Fourteenth Amendment, to crimes covered by state laws.

Police

The first step in the criminal justice process is the arrest by a police officer of a person who has actually committed a crime or is suspected of committing

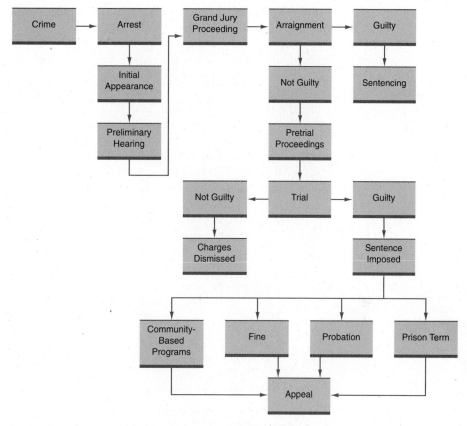

Figure 3.3 **Primary Steps in a Felony Criminal Case**

a crime. The term **arrest** means that a person is taken into custody for the purpose of charging him or her with a crime. An arrest occurs whether a person submits to authority or is seized by force. If the criminal act was not committed in the police officer's presence, the arrest must be made on **probable cause,** a reasonable belief that a crime has been committed and that this person is probably the one who committed it.

> Pulvino, a police officer, received a report that a burglary was in progress at the Trio Jewelry Store and a description of the suspect. As she neared the store, Pulvino saw a person who matched the suspect's description running away from the store. The officer can stop and arrest that person based on probable cause. ■

After a police officer arrests a person, the Fourth Amendment gives the police officer the legal right to conduct a reasonable search of that person and the area immediately around him or her for evidence and for hidden weapons. If the arrested person is driving a car, it may also be searched. As the result of expanded U.S. Supreme Court rulings (*United States* v. *Ross,* 456 U.S. 798; *New York* v. *Belton,* 453 U.S. 454) the police, with probable cause, may search the entire passenger compartment and trunk of the car, as well as any sealed containers and packages found in these places.

Following an arrest, the suspect is usually taken to a police station and "booked." Booking is a procedure by which a record is made of the arrest. It consists of entering in the police log the suspect's name, the time of arrest, and the offense. The suspect is then fingerprinted and photographed and may be required to participate in a lineup. A lineup is a procedure in which a suspect is placed in a group for the purpose of being viewed by a witness. All suspects who are interrogated (questioned) must, according to the Fifth and Sixth Amendments, first be warned that they have the right to remain silent, that anything they say may be used against them in a court of law, and that they have the right to an attorney. These rights, which are read to a suspect, are commonly called the **Miranda warnings,** based on the famous *Miranda* v. *Arizona* case. Figure 3.4 shows an official document listing these rights. An accused who decides to answer any questions may also stop and

Figure 3.4
Rights Read to a Suspect Who Is Interrogated After Arrest

MIAMI POLICE DEPARTMENT
NOTIFICATION AND WAIVER

Mr.
Mrs. . . . ., I am now advising you that you have
Miss

a right to remain silent and that you do not have to answer any questions if you do not wish to; also, that anything you do say to me can be used against you in a court of law; also, that you have a right to consult with an attorney before answering any questions and to have the attorney present with you during the questioning by me if you so desire; also, that if you cannot afford an attorney, then one will be provided for you. If you do consent and agree to discuss this matter with me without an attorney present, you can terminate the discussion at any time.

Do you understand what I have just told you?   RESPONSE: . . . .

Do you agree to waive these rights and do
you consent to discuss this matter with me?   RESPONSE: . . . .

Officer: Complete reverse side of this card.

THE UNDERSIGNED POLICE OFFICER READ THE NOTIFICATION ON THE REVERSE OF THIS CARD TO THE INDIVIDUAL NAMED AND RECEIVED THE RESPONSES INDICATED AT THE TIME AND DATE NOTED BELOW.

DATE . . . . TIME . . . . .M.

PLACE. . . . .

PERSON INTERVIEWED . . . .

OFFICER(S) INTERVIEWING . . . .

. . . .

. . . .

. . . .

This Waiver/Notification, properly completed, will become a part of the Case File.

refuse to answer further questions at any time. Generally speaking, police officers do not elicit any statements unless a defense attorney is present.

In most cases, an arrested person can be released on bail at any stage in a criminal proceeding. **Bail** is the security given to the court to release a person from jail and to ensure the person's appearance at a hearing or trial. Bail usually consists of cash or other property. The amount of bail depends upon the seriousness of the crime and the probability that the accused may flee. If the accused shows up in court when required, the bail is returned; if not, the bail is forfeited. A defendant who fails to make bail is confined in jail until the required court appearance. Instead of bail, the court may release the person "on recognizance"—a promise to appear in court when required—when the accused has strong community and family ties and steady employment.

Courts

Within a reasonable time (usually forty-eight hours) after arrest, the accused must be brought before a judge for a procedure called the **initial appearance.** At this appearance, the suspect will be informed of the charge for which he or she is being held, given the Miranda Warnings, and told of the right to post bail (if this was not determined at the arrest phase). It is quite possible that at this point the judge may determine that there is not sufficient evidence to hold the suspect for further criminal proceedings and will dismiss the case.

After the accused has been arrested and booked and has made an initial appearance before a judge, the next step in some states is a rather formal hearing called a **preliminary hearing,** held to further evaluate whether sufficient evidence exists to proceed to trial with the accused's case. Both the prosecutor and the defense counsel are usually present at this hearing. If a judge believes that the chance of a conviction is slight, the charge against the accused is dismissed.

Whether a preliminary hearing takes place, the next step in the criminal justice process is to formally accuse the arrested person. One method for accomplishing this is the indictment by a grand jury. An **indictment** (sometimes called a *presentment*) is a formal, written accusation of a crime by a grand jury against an individual. (See Figure 3.5) A grand jury consists of a group of people (generally about twenty-three) from the community. It does not try cases—that is, it does not determine guilt or innocence—but formally (by majority vote) determines whether the accused should go to trial for a crime, or have the charges against him or her dismissed for lack of evidence. Generally, the grand jury hears only the prosecutor's side of the case. The prosecutor—usually the district attorney (D.A.)—represents "the people." The prosecutor often presents witnesses to testify against the accused (the defendant). Instead of an indictment by a grand jury, some states bring formal charges by means of an *information*. This document serves the same purpose as an indictment. However, the information is filed by the prosecutor based on the evidence obtained from the preliminary hearing.

```
STATE OF NEW YORK
COUNTY COURT
COUNTY OF MONROE


_____

                  THE PEOPLE OF THE STATE OF NEW YORK

                                VS.

                    LINDA SUZANNE GORDON

_____



        THE GRAND JURY OF THE COUNTY OF MONROE, by this indictment,
    accuse the defendant, LINDA SUZANNE GORDON, of the crime of Burglary
    in the First Degree, in violation of Section 140.30, subdivision 2,
    of the Penal Law of the State of New York, committed as follows:

        The defendant, on or about August 11, 1996, in the County of
    Monroe, State of New York, did enter the dwelling house of another,
    to wit, James Mason, with the intent to commit a crime therein, and
    while in the dwelling, caused physical injury to James Mason by
    shooting him in the neck.

                                        Ronald A Vats
                                  RONALD A. VATS
                                  DISTRICT ATTORNEY
                                  OF MONROE COUNTY
```

Figure 3.5
**A Grand Jury
Indictment**

A person who has been formally accused of a crime, by either an indictment or an information, must then be arraigned. An **arraignment** occurs when the accused (the defendant) is brought before a judge, formally notified of the charges in the indictment, and asked for a plea to the charges—either guilty or not guilty to all elements of the crime. If a guilty plea is entered, the judge must determine if the defendant understands the consequences of such a plea. If the judge is satisfied, the defendant is scheduled for sentencing. Prior to the sentencing, the court orders a presentence report. This report gives detailed background information about the defendant's education, family, employment, and previous criminal record, as well as personal, social, and emotional histories.

If the defendant pleads not guilty, the next stage will be the *pretrial proceedings.* These proceedings consist of hearings on behalf of the accused (by his or her attorney) asking that the charges be dismissed because of lack of evidence or because of other defenses, such as insanity. At this time, plea negotiations may also take place—the accused may enter a guilty plea in return for the prosecutor's assurance that he or she will ask the judge to reduce the charge or sentence. If the pretrial proceedings do not bring results, the case will be scheduled for trial. During the trial both the prosecutor and the defendant's lawyer may present evidence. Acting for the state, the prosecutor must present evidence to substantiate the charge against the defendant. The defense attorney may challenge the validity of the prosecutor's evidence and may also present additional evidence.

Though in many respects the trial itself resembles a civil trial (discussed in Chapter 5), several significant points apply only to a criminal trial:

■ The defendant is presumed innocent until proven guilty.

■ The defendant must be proven guilty beyond a reasonable doubt (i.e., the proof must be so conclusive and complete that all reasonable doubts no longer exist in the mind of the ordinary person).

■ Evidence obtained in an illegal manner must be excluded from the trial.

■ The defendant does not have to testify, and no unfavorable conclusions may be drawn from this failure to testify.

■ The defendant has the right to be present to hear all the evidence presented.

■ The defendant has a constitutional guarantee of a speedy trial.

If the verdict is not guilty, the charges are dismissed, and the defendant is released from the criminal process. After either a conviction or a plea of guilty, the defendant is brought before the judge for sentencing. The judge, who has studied the presentence report, tries to make the sentence appropriate for the defendant and yet remain within the guidelines set down by the law. Options open to judges include prison with the possibility of parole, fine, probation, community-based programs, or a combination of these. In states that allow it, the death penalty is also an option in some murder cases.

After conviction, however, the defendant can appeal to the next higher court asking for a review of the case. In most jurisdictions, this right of appeal is automatic. The appeals court, based upon its review, may uphold the conviction reached in the lower (trial) court. If the appeals court decides to reverse the conviction, the defendant is discharged. Also, if an error of law—such as improper introduction of evidence—is found in the procedures used in the case, the appeals court may reverse the decision of the lower court and order a new trial. It should be noted that there is no absolute right on the part of a criminal defendant to appeal a criminal conviction to the

United States Supreme Court. (Chapter 2 discussed ways in which cases reach the U.S. Supreme Court.)

Although the defendant can appeal a conviction to the next higher court, a prosecutor normally cannot appeal the case if the defendant is found not guilty.

Corrections

After a convicted offender is sentenced, the responsibility of carrying out the sentence moves to the state, or to the federal government if the conviction is for a federal crime. Offenders sentenced to prison serve their time as inmates in a maximum-, medium-, or minimum-security institution. If prison personnel believe the inmate is ready to live in the community, the inmate may be paroled from prison after serving only part of the sentence. **Parole** is a reward allowing early release for felons who have done well in prison and seem to be a good risk for successful return to the community. The inmate is then required to participate in a community-based correction program under the supervision of a parole officer. Community-based correction programs include a variety of activities and programs within the community; for example, the paroled inmate may be required to attend personal- and job-counseling seminars and behavior modification sessions, or to live in a nonsecured halfway house, departing daily to attend work or school and returning after work to participate in group therapy sessions. Parolees are subject to strict rules that guide their behavior and limit their activities. Any parolee who violates these rules can be returned to the institution to serve the remainder of the sentence.

Instead of receiving a prison sentence, an offender may have the sentence suspended and instead be given probation. **Probation** allows a person convicted of an offense to avoid prison and remain free in the community subject to certain rules and conditions, usually under the supervision of a probation officer. If the rules are violated, probation may be revoked and the offender sent to prison under the terms of the original sentence. Rules imposed upon a probationer will depend upon the offense committed. For example, a child molester can be forbidden to associate with young children, and a tax violator can be required to submit his or her tax return to the probation officer periodically for review. In many cases, the probationer is required to pay restitution to the victim of his or her crime.

THE JUVENILE JUSTICE SYSTEM

A young person who commits an unlawful act (an intentional violation of the criminal law) but who has not yet reached the age at which he or she can be treated as an adult criminal offender is called a **juvenile delinquent.** This young person would be charged with "juvenile delinquency," whereas an adult who commits the same unlawful act would be charged with a crime.

> Kemp, a troubled fifteen-year-old, deliberately shot and injured his father with a hunting rifle while the father was sleeping on the couch. Rogers, age twenty-five, shot a neighbor during an argument. Kemp would be charged with juvenile delinquency, whereas Rogers would be charged with a crime. ∎

The age at which an individual is considered a juvenile delinquent varies among states, but in most states young people are considered juveniles until age eighteen. However, some states set the limit at sixteen or seventeen.

A juvenile who commits an unlawful act is handled through the juvenile justice system. Like the adult criminal justice system, the juvenile justice system consists of the police, courts, and corrections. A 1967 Supreme Court decision (In re Gault 387 US 1) guarantees juveniles, like adults, such constitutional rights as the right to remain silent, the right to an attorney, the right to be free from unreasonable searches and seizures, the privilege against self-incrimination, and the right to due process at the pretrial, trial, and posttrial stages of the juvenile process. (Table 3.1 describes some basic similarities and differences between the juvenile and adult justice systems.) All states now waive jurisdiction over serious cases such as murder, allowing juveniles to be tried in adult courts. Nevertheless, in many states juveniles convicted in an adult court are sentenced to a juvenile institution rather than to an

TABLE 3.1 Comparison of Adult Criminal Justice and Juvenile Justice Systems

Adult	Juvenile
1. Three basic subsystems: police, courts, corrections.	1. Same.
2. The primary purpose of the system is punishment.	2. The primary purpose of the system is protection and treatment.
3. Police may use discretion in deciding whether to take a person into custody.	3. Same.
4. Charged with a crime if arrested.	4. Charged with juvenile delinquency if taken into custody.
5. Proceedings held at the pretrial, trial, and posttrial stages are considered criminal.	5. Proceedings held at the pretrial, trial, and posttrial stages are not considered criminal.
6. Guaranteed constitutional rights and due process at pretrial, trial, and posttrial proceedings.	6. Same.
7. Arrest is based on probable cause.	7. Many states allow a juvenile to be taken into custody on less than probable cause.
8. Right to trial and appeal.	8. Same.
9. Standard of evidence in criminal trials is proof beyond a reasonable doubt.	9. Standard of evidence in juvenile delinquency adjudication hearings is proof beyond a reasonable doubt.
10. Can receive the death penalty.	10. If tried as an adult, can receive the death penalty.

adult prison and may be transferred to an adult prison when they have reached a certain age.

The steps in the juvenile justice system vary from state to state, but the process in general is shown in Figure 3.6.

The Role of the Police

The police may take a juvenile into custody (the equivalent of an adult arrest) for an act that is a crime. Generally, probable cause must exist that a crime has been committed and that the juvenile committed it. Many states, however, give the police broad authority in juvenile cases by authorizing the police officer to take a child into custody with less than probable cause if it is determined that the child's welfare requires it. Once in custody, the constitutional guarantees mentioned earlier apply. Any questioning of the juvenile must be done in the presence of parents, unless the parents cannot be located or refuse to appear.

Figure 3.6 **Steps in the Juvenile Justice System**

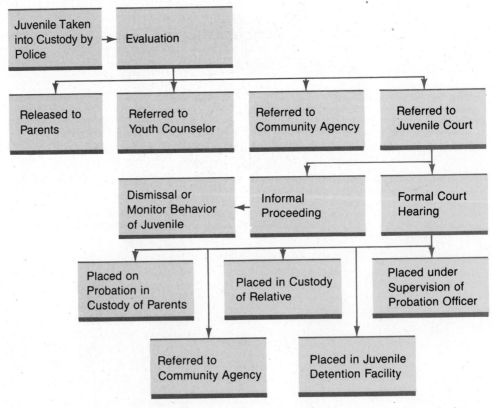

The police may handle a juvenile offender in one of the following ways:

1. Release the juvenile to the parents with a warning.
2. Refer the juvenile to a youth counselor.
3. Refer the juvenile to a community agency that rehabilitates young people.
4. Refer the juvenile to juvenile court.

Cases involving violence, serious property offenses, or victim-related crimes are generally referred to court.

The decision of how to handle a juvenile is based on the seriousness of the crime; the manner in which the offense was committed; the juvenile's prior record of contact with police; the cooperation, attitude, and behavior of the juvenile and parents; and the ability of the parents to effectively manage the child.

■ Osgood, age fourteen, was detained at Beir's Department Store for shoplifting. The police were notified, and Osgood was taken into custody. Further action by the police will depend on the circumstances of the case. ■

Juvenile Court

Juvenile courts are special courts that handle referrals of juvenile delinquents. While most of these referrals to juvenile court come directly from the police, some may come via a **juvenile petition** by teachers, school administrators, store managers, or others who have frequent contact with juveniles, or by parents unable to control the behavior of their teenager. A juvenile petition is like a criminal complaint in that it alleges illegal behavior.

When a case has been referred to juvenile court, the first step is generally **intake,** a screening process to determine whether the case can be handled in some way other than a formal hearing. Intake officers have substantial discretion. Most cases are in fact handled informally, and the juvenile does not appear before a judge. In such cases the juvenile may be released into parental custody for many different reasons, one being the ability to afford private counseling or therapy. A release of the juvenile to the parents amounts to an outright dismissal of the case. The juvenile may instead be required to participate in either informal meetings with a probation officer or some other program that can monitor and control her or his behavior. Such a program may involve a mental health facility, a drug treatment center, or perhaps job training. The juvenile's attitude, the family situation, any previous offenses, and the seriousness of the present accusation greatly influence the intake officer's decision.

If a formal hearing—called an **adjudication hearing**—is scheduled, it will be conducted like an adult trial but without a jury. Pending this hearing, a decision is usually made whether to release the child to the parent or guardian or to detain the child in a shelter. Most states require that a hearing be held on the appropriateness of placing the child in a shelter if the initial decision is to keep the child in custody. At this hearing, the juvenile may exercise his or her constitutional safeguards, such as the privilege against self-incrimination and the right to question and cross-examine witnesses. When the adjudication hearing is under way, a judge hears evidence and then decides whether the young person committed the alleged act (crime). Later, at a **disposition hearing**—the final stage in the juvenile court process—the judge decides the sentence for a guilty juvenile offender.

When a serious offense, such as a homicide or rape, is involved, many states have mandated the transfer of serious juvenile offenders to adult courts. The impact of this legislation has been to send juveniles to adult prisons rather than to provide treatment through the resources available under the juvenile justice system.

Corrections

A judge who finds a minor guilty of being a juvenile delinquent (which is similar to an adult conviction) has several options to help the youth. As with adults, the seriousness of the crime and the offender's past record determine the actions the judge will take. One of the most commonly used options is to place the juvenile on probation, thus allowing the young person to remain at home. The juvenile is under the supervision of a probation officer and must meet with this officer regularly for counseling and supervision. The judge often sets certain guidelines for the juvenile to follow while on probation. Juveniles placed on probation may be ordered to pay fines or make restitution. Because juveniles rarely have financial resources, most economic sanctions take the form of court-ordered work programs, for example cleaning buildings or refurbishing schools.

Summary of Important Legal Concepts

Crimes are public wrongs, and those who commit such acts can be punished by the courts upon conviction. The punishment may be a prison or jail sentence, a fine, or, in certain cases, death. Serious crimes called felonies are punishable by death or by imprisonment for more than one year. Misdemeanors, less serious than felonies, are punishable by confinement for up to one year. Wrongs less serious than misdemeanors—variously termed violations, infractions, or petty offenses—are not crimes but could bring a short jail sentence in a local jail.

There is no uniform law of crimes. The federal government and each state define and punish crimes according to their own guidelines. Even among states, criminal statutes vary. An act that is a crime in one state may not be a crime in another state.

The selected crimes discussed in this chapter are assault, robbery, arson, burglary, theft, driving while intoxicated, drug law violations, and computer crimes. The defenses—reasons that defendants offer to excuse guilt for criminal acts—raised in the chapter are infancy, insanity, involuntary intoxication, duress, justification, and entrapment.

People who commit crimes are handled through either the federal or state criminal justice system, which consists of the police, the courts, and corrections. The first step is the arrest of the individual suspected of committing a crime. This arrest is usually based upon probable cause, a reasonable belief that a crime has been committed and that the arrested person is probably the one who committed it. When arrested for a felony, the accused is "booked," interrogated, and, at an initial appearance before a judge, formally notified of the crime he or she is suspected of committing. A preliminary hearing may then be held to further evaluate whether sufficient evidence exists to proceed to trial. If the charge is not dismissed at this point, a grand jury is convened. This body is generally composed of twenty-three people who examine evidence presented by the prosecutor; they may issue an indictment, formally accusing the defendant of the crime. (Sometimes the formal accusation is made by means of an information filed by the prosecutor.)

At the arraignment, the next step, the accused is formally notified of the charges in the indictment and asked to plead guilty or not guilty. If the defendant pleads not guilty, the next stage will usually be pretrial proceedings. If these proceedings produce no results, a trial will be scheduled. At the trial, the prosecutor, acting for the state, must prove beyond a reasonable doubt that the accused has committed the crime of which he or she is accused. Only upon conviction can the defendant be sentenced. If there is no appeal or if the appeals court upholds the conviction rendered in the lower court, the sentence will be carried out.

From arrest to conviction, the defendant is entitled to numerous constitutional guarantees, including the right to Miranda Warnings and the right to bail.

A juvenile—in most states, a person up to the age of eighteen—who commits an unlawful act that is the equivalent of an adult crime is charged with juvenile delinquency and is handled through the juvenile justice system. Like the adult criminal justice system, the juvenile justice system consists of the police, courts, and corrections. As the juvenile proceeds through the juvenile justice system, he or she has the same constitutional rights and the same right to due process that an adult has as he or she proceeds through the criminal justice system.

When a serious offense such as a homicide or rape is involved, many states have mandated the transfer of serious juvenile offenders to adult courts.

Key Legal Terms to Know

Match the terms with the definitions that follow.

adjudication hearing
arraignment
arrest
arson
assault

bail
blackmail (extortion)
burglary
crimes
defense
disposition hearing
driving while intoxicated
embezzlement
entrapment
felony
forgery
fraud
indictment
initial appearance
intake
juvenile delinquent
juvenile petition
larceny
Miranda warnings
misdemeanor
parole
possession of property known to be stolen
preliminary hearing
probable cause
probation
robbery
shoplifting

1. The unlawful use or stealing of money or other property by a person who has been legally entrusted with the property
2. The intentional, illegal burning of a home or building
3. Public wrongs that violate criminal laws and are punishable by the courts upon conviction
4. Intentionally stealing money or personal property of another person
5. Taking merchandise from a store without paying for it
6. Obtaining money or personal property under false pretenses
7. Unlawfully entering another person's home or building with the intent to commit a crime
8. A serious crime punishable by death or imprisonment for more than one year
9. Forcibly taking money or personal property from another person
10. Making or altering a document with the intent to deceive

11. A less serious crime punishable by a jail sentence of one year or less
12. Possession of property acquired as the result of some wrongful or dishonest act of taking
13. The formal, written accusation by a grand jury that a certain person has committed a crime
14. Driving after having knowingly or voluntarily consumed alcohol to the point that it substantially affects one's ability to properly operate a motor vehicle
15. The act of taking a person into police custody for the purpose of charging him or her with a crime
16. The unlawful physical injury of another person
17. The security given to the court to obtain the release of a person from jail and to ensure that person's appearance at a hearing or trial
18. Use of threats to obtain money or property
19. A reason that an accused person offers to excuse his or her guilt in a criminal action
20. The reasonable belief that a crime has been committed
21. The rights read to a suspect upon arrest
22. A strategy used by a law officer to persuade a person to commit a crime
23. The first appearance before a judge by a suspect to a crime following arrest in which he or she is formally notified of the reason for the arrest
24. A hearing by a judge to determine whether a person charged with a crime should be held for trial
25. Bringing the accused before a judge to secure a plea to a charge in an indictment or an information
26. A young person who has committed an unlawful act but who has not yet reached the age at which he or she can be treated as an adult criminal offender
27. Screening of cases by the juvenile court system
28. A formal hearing for a juvenile accused of committing a crime
29. An arrangement by which, instead of a prison sentence, a convicted person remains free in the community subject to certain conditions
30. The final stage in the juvenile court process, in which the judge decides the sentence for a juvenile offender
31. A procedure used to refer a juvenile delinquent to family court
32. An early release from prison based on a prisoner's good behavior

Questions and Problems to Discuss

1. Walkman, a student at Banes College, stole several new football helmets from the college sports locker room. He sold the helmets for a very low price to Favor, the owner of a local sporting goods store. After reading an article in the newspaper about the theft, the owner of the store was quite sure the helmets he purchased from Walkman were the ones that had been stolen. Nevertheless, he did not notify either the police or the appropriate college personnel that he had bought the helmets. Instead, he marked them for sale at a special price and placed them on a shelf with other football gear. Although he paid Walkman for the football helmets, is Favor liable for the commission of any crime? Is Walkman? Explain.
2. Distinguish between misdemeanors and felonies.
3. Lynn entered the lobby of the Royal York Hotel about 1 A.M., jumped over the counter and hit Gigliotti, the night clerk, over the head with a small iron chain. Gigliotti fell to the floor unconscious. Lynn then removed $1,000 in cash from an open safe and also took a safe deposit box containing guests' jewelry. What crime (or crimes) has Lynn committed?
4. Furenya was employed as the manager of a state-controlled betting parlor, the Off Track Betting Corporation. One of her responsibilities was to deposit the daily receipts of money in a local bank. Since she was heavily in debt, Furenya devised a way to take $300 from each deposit to pay her personal creditors. She continued this practice for over a year until the state auditors made a surprise check of the betting parlor's accounting records. When a shortage was discovered and traced to Furenya, she was arrested. With what crime could she be charged?
5. Pogus was one of several people invited to a New Year's Eve party at Nennp's house. During the evening, Pogus made several trips to the kitchen for refreshments. On one of these trips, he spotted a coin collection in another room, consisting of gold coins valued at over $3,000. He placed several of the coins in his pocket and, when the party was over, left with them. Has Pogus committed the crime of robbery or larceny?
6. On the way home from the bank, Lasham lost her checkbook containing her personalized checks. Ramos found the checkbook, wrote out a $500

check payable to himself, signed Lasham's name to the check, and cashed it at his bank. Ramos was later arrested and accused of committing a criminal act. What was it?

7. How can a computer be used to commit a crime?

8. What defenses can be raised that may excuse individuals from guilt in a criminal action?

9. A police officer on routine patrol in her police car at about 3 A.M. received a call over the police radio describing a burglary in progress at a pizza parlor in her patrol zone. When she arrived at the pizza parlor, a short distance from where she received the call, she spotted a person who was getting into a car parked next to the pizza parlor. If the police officer wished to make an arrest in the belief that this person had committed the robbery, what would be the basis for the arrest?

10. If a person is arrested for committing a felony crime, what steps must be taken before he or she can be tried for this crime?

11. Using a homemade bomb, a group of picketers on strike at the C & R Printing Company destroyed part of the building that housed the company's printing presses. What crime have the picketers committed?

12. Sagan, a police officer on patrol near a bank, heard the bank alarm go off and saw a man running out the front door carrying a paper bag. As Sagan approached the bank, the man jumped into a waiting vehicle and fled. Sagan radioed a description of the car and the driver to back-up units that were in the vicinity of the bank. The man was taken into custody and informed of his rights. During a lawful search at the police station, $25,000 was discovered in the paper bag. What crimes should the man be charged with? Why?

13. Arden, who was intoxicated, broke into an apartment near and similar to his own, believing that his spouse had locked him out. Has Arden committed a burglary?

Cases to Decide

1. Danny Escobedo was arrested for fatally shooting his brother-in-law in Chicago. He was taken to the police station for questioning but was repeatedly denied the right to consult with his attorney. He was specifically told that he could not talk with his attorney until the police had finished their questioning. During the course of the questioning, Escobedo was not advised of his constitutional right to remain silent. Consequently, he made incriminating statements that led to his conviction of murder, and he was sentenced to prison. When the police refused to honor Escobedo's request to consult with his attorney, did they violate his constitutional rights under the Sixth Amendment? (*Escobedo* v. *Illinois*, 378 U.S. 478)

2. Swanson obtained a $3,000 loan from the Lincoln Bank by using his cattle as security for the loan. However, the bank did not know that Swanson had only 80 head of cattle, not the 629 head he stated on his application. Soon after the bank credited the money to Swanson's account, an agent for the bank discovered the falsity of Swanson's statement about the cattle. Swanson immediately drew the $3,000 from his account. The bank prosecuted him for obtaining property by fraud. Swanson defended on the ground that he had not actually drawn the money from the bank until after the bank discovered the fraud and that he was therefore not guilty of any crime. In fact, he claimed that it was the bank's own negligence that created the loss. Do you agree? (*Nebraska* v. *Swanson*, 179 Neb 693, 140 NW 2d 618)

3. Davis snatched a purse and a shopping bag from a pedestrian. The pedestrian did not see Davis approach her, did not resist, and was not in danger. Can Davis be convicted of robbery? (*People* v. *Davis*, New York 71 App Div 2d 607)

4. Bowman was a foreman for an engineering company. He was given three signed blank checks with which to pay his crew and was authorized to fill in the names of the employees and the amounts they were owed. Bowman filled in his own name on one check, entered the amount of $3,900, cashed the check, and used the proceeds. Charged with forgery, Bowman claimed that it is not forgery to complete, even though in an unauthorized manner, an otherwise genuine instrument. Is Bowman's defense a good one? (*Bowman* v. *State*, Ind 398 NE 2d 1306)

5. Davis and another person were seen inside the office of a manufacturing company by police late one evening. The office was supposedly locked, and the desk drawers and file cabinets had been closed for the evening. Davis and the other person were unlawfully on the premises and, although some cabinet and desk drawers were

found open, nothing was reported to be missing. Davis was charged with burglary but claimed he could not be convicted of burglary because nothing was taken. Was Davis correct? (*Davis v. State,* Ind 398 NE 2d 704)

6. Bower was encouraged by an acquaintance, who was actually an informer, to sell cocaine to a government undercover agent. The agent then arrested Bower for the possession and sale of a drug. Bower claimed entrapment as a defense. During the trial, evidence was introduced to show conclusively that Bower was in the business of selling cocaine and that the sale to the undercover agent was not really induced by the agent but was actually just another opportunity that presented itself to Bower. Is the defense of entrapment valid in this case? (*United States v. Bower,* 575 F2d 499 U.S. Court of Appeals)

7. Ward, a former employee of ISD, a computer company, was employed by UCC, a competing computer service company. Ward was charged with obtaining trade secrets illegally through the use of a computer terminal. Using a UCC data telephone, Ward dialed a secret number and gained access on his terminal to an ISD program without authority to do so. He then got a printout of the ISD program. The ISD program gave ISD an advantage over its competitors, including UCC. When charged with theft, Ward claimed he stole nothing tangible and therefore that no crime had been committed. He contended that he only caused impulses to be transmitted over the phone and onto a screen and that, once he did that, getting a printout was not theft. Does making a printout of secret information taken from another's computer constitute computer theft? (*Ward v. Superior Court, Alameda County Cal* 3 Computer Law Service Reptr, 206 Super Ct Cal 1971)

8. Gault, a fifteen-year-old boy, was accused by a female neighbor of making indecent phone calls to her. A probation officer filed a juvenile delinquency petition, reciting no facts but stating that Gault was a delinquent and in need of the protection of the juvenile court. Gault's parents never saw the petition. No witnesses appeared at the hearing. Gault was never advised of his right to be represented by an attorney, and he was never told about his right against self-incrimination. He was committed as a juvenile delinquent to the State Industrial School for six years. Gault claimed that his constitutional rights had been violated. Is Gault correct? (*In re: Gault,* 387 US 1)

9. Schlicht opened a checking account at the Bank of Winter Park and deposited $1,900. In entering the deposit to the checking account the bank made a computer error, so that the amount credited was $10,900. Shortly thereafter, Schlicht withdrew the entire amount and closed the account. When the bank learned of its mistake, it requested Schlicht to return the money, but he refused, claiming that he now owned the money since the bank had made an error. The bank then prosecuted Schlicht for theft. Should Schlicht be found guilty? (*Colorado v. Schlicht* [Colo App] 709 P 2d 94)

Chapter 4

Private Wrongs/Torts

CHAPTER PREVIEW

This chapter deals with the wrongful acts, called *torts,* that harm others, and with the legal rights that victims have. Intentional (deliberate) torts are discussed first. Negligence, an unintentional tort, is discussed next. The third and final category of torts discussed in this chapter is strict liability, or "liability without fault." A person being sued for a tort may offer certain defenses, or reasons to either reduce or eliminate his or her liability for a tort. The chapter discusses these defenses. Early in the chapter the point is made that tort law is changing to meet both the social changes in this country and the changing relationships between and among individuals.

AN OVERVIEW OF TORT LAW

People have a duty not to cause harm to others. If they violate that duty and someone suffers a loss, the victim may sue the wrongdoer in tort. A **tort** occurs when a person sustains either physical or mental injury to his or her person or property damage as the result of some other person's wrongful act or failure to act.

Tort law developed to protect people from the wrongful conduct of others in areas that are not covered by criminal law. As you will see in the next chapter, *criminal law* is concerned with "public wrongs"—wrongs such as murder that affect society as a whole. *Tort law* deals with a body of "private wrongs"—wrongs, such as slander and trespass, against an individual's personal and property rights. For a wrong to be considered a public wrong, it must go beyond harm to the individual and be so inherently undesirable as to be flatly prohibited by a state or federal statute.

A violator of a public wrong has committed a crime and will be prosecuted and punished by the state. The violator of a private wrong has committed a tort, is subject to a civil lawsuit, and will be required to pay the victim money damages. Many wrongful acts are both torts and crimes because they harm both society and the individual. In such cases, the wrongdoer could be brought to court as the defendant (person against whom an action is brought) in separate civil and criminal trials.

> During a bank holdup, Martell intentionally shot and killed Dorais, a bank teller. Martell was tried and convicted for the crime in criminal court. Dorais's family could also sue Martell for money damages in a tort action in civil court for wrongful death as a result of Martell's intentional killing of Dorais. ■

It is interesting to note that criminal law is primarily statutory, but, even in this age of legislation, tort law still has strong ties to the common law and has evolved primarily from particular cases. As social conditions change, relationships between individuals also change. New technologies, different moral values, and different fundamental beliefs have led to new torts being recognized, others being abolished, and present torts being applied to new situations. In recent years, for example, there has been increased recognition of a person's right to be protected against intrusions on peace of mind. This increased recognition has given rise to a tort called *mental distress* (discussed later in the chapter). This tort has been used successfully against those who harass others—for example, against collection agents who use unorthodox tactics to secure payment of a debt and in the process cause the victim to suffer severe mental stress. Another response to social change has occurred in the area of the tort of defamation (libel and slander). The case of *New York Times Co.* v. *Sullivan* (376 U.S. 254), decided by the Supreme Court in 1964, laid the groundwork for the rejection of the concept that all defamatory speech is subject to a lawsuit. More will be said about this case and its impact on the law of defamation later in the chapter.

Under the law, torts are classified as intentional torts, torts resulting from negligence, and torts based on the concept of strict liability. In intentional and negligent torts the law imposes liability because of one person's "fault" in causing another person's harm. On the other hand, in strict liability torts a person is held liable in the absence of either intent or negligence, that is, the person is liable without fault.

All persons, including minors (those who have not yet reached adulthood), are legally responsible for their torts.

INTENTIONAL TORTS

An **intentional tort** occurs when one person deliberately inflicts injury on another or deliberately does damage to his or her property. There may be no intent on the part of the wrongdoer to harm, but there is an intent to interfere.

> As a practical joke, Callens threw a small stone at the window of a parked car, intending to scare his friend who was sitting in the car. The window shattered and seriously cut the friend's face. Although Callens did not intend to cause harm to his friend, he nevertheless committed an intentional tort because he intentionally threw the stone. ■

Intentional torts include (1) assault and battery, (2) false imprisonment, (3) infliction of mental distress, (4) defamation, (5) invasion of privacy, (6) wrongful death, (7) malicious prosecution, (8) fraud, (9) interference with contractual relations, (10) trespass, (11) conversion, and (12) nuisance.

Assault and Battery

Under civil law, an **assault** is a threatening act by one person that leads another person to believe that he or she is about to suffer bodily harm. The victim, as a reasonable person, must believe that the threat is real—that something is going to happen here and now, although the person making the threat may not actually intend to carry it out. Pointing an unloaded gun at someone and threatening to shoot, for example, is an assault as long as the person being threatened believes that the gun is loaded. However, a person who threatens to shoot but has no gun will generally not be considered to have committed a tort.

Additionally, a threat to carry out an unlawful act cannot be considered an assault if it does not seem reasonable that the threat can be carried out.

> ■ Clawson was a member of a citizen's group being given a tour of a medium-security prison by several armed guards. During the tour, one of the inmates who was securely locked in his cell put his face up against the bars of his cell. He doubled his fist and, as he waved it between the bars, yelled in an angry voice at Clawson, "If you don't get out of this cell block now, I'll push your face in." Since it is unlikely that the prisoner could carry out his threat, the prisoner's conduct generally will not be considered an assault. ■

The tort of **battery** consists of the intentional and wrongful physical contact with a person without consent. The physical contact may be harmful and cause injury, as in kicking, shoving, throwing an object that strikes a person, or disfiguring a person, but merely touching a person offensively, for example by displaying affection without permission, also constitutes battery. Battery very often also includes an assault, because the wrongdoer will generally threaten to commit the battery (assault) before actually doing it; and when the threat is carried out, a battery occurs.

> ■ Cambisi, a waitress in a coffee shop, got angry with a customer and threatened to throw a cup of coffee in the customer's face unless he left the restaurant. The customer refused to leave, so the waitress carried out her threat and threw coffee in his face. Cambisi committed both assault (the customer saw the coffee coming at him) and battery (the customer got the coffee in his face). ■

The courts have held that a battery occurs even if there is no physical contact, as, for example, when a prankster pulls a chair out from under a person who then sits down and is injured when he or she "hits" the floor. Although there is no physical contact between the prankster and the person sitting down, the prankster has committed a battery, since the injured person's contact with the floor is the intended result of the prank. Thus, the injured person's contact with the floor is considered equivalent to an injury directly inflicted by the prankster.

Injuries inflicted during contact sports such as boxing, football, and wrestling are generally not considered the result of a battery as long as the contact is within the rules of the game.

False Imprisonment

False imprisonment occurs when a person is unlawfully and intentionally forced by another person to remain in a certain place—a room, an automobile, a boat, a building, or some spot on the open street—so that his or her freedom of movement is restricted, and no reasonable escape route is available.

> ■ At the beginning of his psychology class, Professor Hicks asked Mary Sullivan to remain after class to discuss her poor attendance record. At the end of

the class, Sullivan refused to stay because of another commitment. Professor Hicks then blocked the entrance to the door so that she was not able to leave as she wished to do. Sullivan may claim false imprisonment. ■

In the above case, if the classroom had another exit (that would not lead to injury) and Sullivan could easily have left through that exit, she would have no claim for false imprisonment. To be falsely imprisoned, the confinement must be total.

When a person is unlawfully detained by an authorized official, such as a police officer, a security guard, or a loss prevention officer in a store, the term **false arrest** is used.

■ Kessler, a taxi driver parked at a cab stand, was suddenly approached by several police officers. They ordered him out of his cab at gunpoint, frisked and handcuffed him, and put him in the back seat of a squad car. He was driven to the police precinct station and charged with breaking into a house, assaulting the homeowner, and stealing her money and jewelry. Kessler's arrest was based on the victim's identification of him from a photo that had been "doctored" by the police investigators to resemble the description of the man believed to have attacked her. Police suspected a cab driver was involved, but at first the victim could not identify Kessler from the group of photographs presented to her. When the real assailant was arrested a few hours later, Kessler was officially freed from all blame. Police action in this case constituted false arrest. ■

One of the most common and most litigated false arrest situations is that of the retail merchant who detains a customer suspected of shoplifting (the crime of theft). In most states a merchant has no legal liability for the detention if he or she can prove that reasonable grounds existed to believe the customer had shoplifted. In a lawsuit, the test of reasonableness will be left to the jury. The jury will weigh this question after taking into consideration what the average, cautious, intelligent person would have done in similar circumstances, given the facts in the case. However, even if the test of reasonableness is met, the merchant could still be liable if the customer is detained for an unreasonable length of time or in an unreasonable manner.

One way for the retailer to avoid liability in a false arrest suit is to prove that the customer consented to being detained—perhaps by freely accompanying a security guard to the detention area after being stopped as a suspected shoplifter. Whether the customer went freely may again be a question decided by a jury.

■ While vacationing, Phoenix, a seventy-year-old man, went shopping in the men's department of a large clothing store. While trying on a suit, he changed his clothes in the dressing room and placed his expensive belt in his overcoat pocket, with the gold buckle hanging out. Phoenix purchased the suit but left it for alterations. As he stepped out of the door to leave the store (forgetting to place the belt back on his pants), a security guard standing at the door spotted the belt. He firmly grasped Phoenix's arm and told him that he had better come to the security office and explain to the manager where he got the belt. In the meantime, another security guard stepped in front of Phoenix to prevent him from leaving. Under these circumstances, Phoenix agreed to return to the store. As he returned, he suffered a heart attack and subsequently was hospitalized for several weeks. A jury in this case would probably determine that Phoenix was illegally detained and would award him damages. ■

In the above case, the jury would reason that the conduct of the security guards was not reasonable under the circumstances and that Phoenix, with one security guard firmly grasping his arm and the other standing in front of him, had no choice but to return to the store.

Some courts have dismissed shoplifting cases because a customer was stopped inside the store and had not passed the checkout counter. Customers accused of shoplifting defended on the grounds that, although it may have appeared to the security guard that the items in question were being concealed, they intended to pay for the items when they reached the checkout counter. In these cases, a reasonable doubt as to the intention of the customers existed in the minds of the jurors.

Infliction of Mental Distress

The tort of **infliction of mental distress** occurs when one person's extreme and outrageous conduct causes severe mental suffering in another as a result of public humiliation, shame, anxiety, fright, or grief. Courts today allow a person to recover damages for the infliction of mental distress, regardless of whether this distress is associated with physical injury.

To prevent people from flooding the courts with lawsuits for the normal mental stresses of day-to-day living—such as insults, obscene or abusive language, discourtesies and profanity—the person suing must prove that his or her emotional stress was beyond the bounds of decency and was severe. The stress must be more than a reasonable person would expect to endure.

■ Pogue, a practical joker, amused himself late one evening by phoning his friend's wife and telling her an untrue story. He said that her husband, while on the way home from the business meeting he was attending, had been in a serious accident and had been taken to a local hospital, where he was listed as being in critical condition. Pogue's friend's wife became hysterical, requiring sedation and weeks of hospitalization. The shock produced serious and permanent physical consequences. As a result, the wife could legally sue Pogue for intentionally inflicting mental distress on her. ■

Today, lawsuits for the infliction of mental distress are often brought against collection agencies for the unreasonably humiliating tactics they use to force debtors to pay bills. A review of court cases indicates that representatives of collection agencies have harassed debtors by making threatening remarks ("you will lose your job if you don't pay") and calling them names ("deadbeat"). The conduct of these representatives in some cases caused their victims to require hospitalization for severe emotional stress, and the victims brought lawsuits against them.

Defamation

Oral or written false statements that injure a person's reputation are called *defamation.* A person's reputation is injured when she or he is held up to hatred, contempt, or ridicule, causing others to lose respect for or avoid that person as a result. Oral defamation is called **slander,** whereas written defamation is called **libel.**

To sue for either slander or libel under the states' laws, a private citizen must prove that the false (untrue) statements were "published," that is, communicated to at least one other person.

> ■ Eagan, the pastor of a church in Detroit, Michigan, formally applied to be pastor of a church in Largo, Florida. Jobes, a member of the Detroit congregation, sent a letter to a friend who was a member of the Largo church congregation stating that Eagan would not make a good pastor because he was a "heavy user of drugs and very often abused his family physically." These statements about Eagan were not true. Jobes made them in anger because he did not want Eagan to leave the Detroit congregation. Jobes's friend shared this letter with many others in the congregation. As a result, the board of directors of the Largo congregation decided not to hire Eagan. Jobes's statements constituted libel because they were written in a letter shared with others (published) and because they were false. ■

Sometimes, determining whether an oral or written statement is defamatory becomes a question of law for a court to decide. In such cases, the court must review the phraseology used and decide whether it is reasonable to assume that the offending words are defamatory in the context in which they were said or written. Courts may be guided by the First Amendment's guarantee of free speech. This amendment protects a person's right to state an opinion (make a personal comment) about someone else. For example, ridiculing (making fun of) a person, calling him or her names, or making an insulting remark about the person's ancestry generally cannot become the basis of an action for defamation, no matter how offensive the remarks might be.

The defamatory statement communicated to a third person may be made either intentionally (deliberately) or negligently (carelessly).

> ■ Judge Crance was at a party when she told another judge that he was incompetent and should not run in the next election. Others at the party overheard Crance's statements. Her remark amounts to slander. ■

In the above case, the publication element would be satisfied even though Crance intended her remark only for the judge. She was negligent in her communication. However, Crance would have had no liability if only the judge had heard her remark. Derogatory remarks made directly to a person in a face-to-face conversation that others do not hear do not constitute publication, even though these remarks are false. Similarly, sending a letter containing derogatory remarks directly to the victim, with the intention that no one else read it, does not amount to publication.

True statements are not defamatory, no matter how much hurt a person suffers. For example, if you tell people that your family attorney has a long history of mental instability and the attorney does have this history, you cannot be sued for defamation.

Only a living person may be defamed. Legally, defamation of a deceased person is not possible, no matter how embarrassing the remarks may be to the deceased person's family and relatives.

In 1964, the United States Supreme Court swept aside states' laws on defamation as they applied to certain people who were involved in matters of public concern. Until the 1964 ruling, state law allowed any person to succeed in a lawsuit for defamation simply by proving that statements made about him or her were false and defamatory. The Supreme Court's 1964 decision in *New York Times Co.* v. *Sullivan* changed this. Balancing the right of states to protect the good names of their citizens against the right of free expression, the Court stated that from now on, a public official must prove that published statements about his or her public—not private—life were not only false and defamatory but that the person or persons who published them did so with actual malice. Without proof of actual malice, the public official would most likely lose the case. Actual malice is defined as either a deliberate lie or reckless indifference to truth (the person publishing the statements doesn't care whether they are true or false). In this *New York Times* decision, the Court held that people in public life must both expect and accept a harsher degree of criticism about their conduct and motives than must private citizens. The Court reasoned that public persons have access to the media and thus can rebut criticisms about their life; also, public persons place themselves in the limelight and therefore leave themselves open to discussion by the public. Public officials have been broadly defined as holders of major offices (having substantial administrative or policy-making responsibilities) in the executive, legislative, and judicial branches of the government; also included in this definition are low- and middle-level public employees, such as police officers, public school teachers and college professors, incumbents in public office, and candidates running for public office.

> In a newspaper editorial, Alent, the governor of a large midwestern state, was called "corrupt and a graft collector and not worthy of being elected to another term." Alent, claiming that these statements were untrue, initiated a lawsuit against the newspaper for libel. Because Alent can be considered a public figure, she would have a more difficult time proving her case. ∎

In other leading cases since 1964, the Supreme Court extended the actual malice requirement to public figures, further reasoning that information about their public life also deserves constitutional protection. As defined by the court, public figures fall into two categories: those who are famous or widely known, giving the public a legitimate interest in all phases of their lives, and those private citizens who voluntarily attract public attention to promote a cause. Famous and widely known public figures include sports figures, movie stars, well-known entertainers, inventors, and former presidents. An example of a private citizen who voluntarily attracted public attention would be a college football coach who came into public prominence by being accused of fixing a college football game. Also, a retired general (no longer a public official) who made a speech on a college campus to influence public opinion and caused students to protest is another example of those who become public figures by thrusting themselves into public controversy.

In view of the above discussion, it can be said that the law of defamation has been significantly affected by the *New York Times* rule. Whereas suits against private citizens are governed by state laws, suits against public officials and public figures are now governed by the stricter federal constitutional standard (requiring proof of actual malice) as set down in *New York Times Co. v. Sullivan*. Comparing the state standard with the federal constitutional standard, you will discover that it is easier for a private person to recover for defamation.

Invasion of Privacy

A person has the right to be left alone, to be free from unauthorized publicity and from wrongful intrusion into his or her private life by another person or the government. A violation of these rights is called **invasion of privacy.** Invasions of privacy generally occur in one of the following forms:

1. Using a person's name or picture for an advertisement or other commercial purpose without consent.

■ Downey, a leading sports figure in the football world, discovered that his picture was appearing on billboards throughout the country endorsing a large food company's new oatbran cereal product. The food company had not obtained Downey's express or implied permission for use of either his picture or his endorsement. Downey could sue the food company for damages for invasion of privacy. Downey could also sue to force the food company to stop using his picture. ■

A statement called a *release* (generally in writing), giving another permission to use a picture for the purpose covered in the release, waives any right of privacy that might be infringed upon as a result of the publication of the photograph.

2. Intruding upon a person's right to be left alone. Examples include peeping in windows or entering, without permission or legal authority, into a person's house or office or tapping a person's telephone and then listening to the person's private conversations when such tapping is prohibited by federal and/or state law. In this context, there is increasing concern about the amount of information on individuals that is stored in databases (computer data files). Computers have made it possible to collect and store a vast amount of private information concerning people's income, phone calls, credit purchases, and other personal data. Many people fear that these data files threaten our right to privacy. Since the early 1970s, the federal government has passed several laws to limit the use of and access to computer data banks.

3. Wrongfully disclosing true but offensive and embarrassing information about another person's private life that the public does not have the right to know.

> Aman was attacked and beaten by an assailant as she attempted to enter her car in a parking garage. A reporter who wrote the news story about her attack delved into her past and discovered embarrassing, offensive, and unflattering facts about her life, and he incorporated these facts in the story. ∎

In the above case, although the reporter made true statements about Aman's past, he (and perhaps the newspaper for whom he works) nevertheless could be found liable for invasion of privacy, because the remarks wrongfully invaded Aman's privacy and were not of legitimate concern to the public, that is, not newsworthy. The remarks did not relate to the parking garage incident. On the other hand, if Aman was a member of the U.S. Congress (a public official) and one of the discoveries was that she had a criminal record, she most likely would have no cause of action against the reporter or the reporter's newspaper. The right to privacy of a public official or a public figure is given less protection than that of private citizens who become involved in matters of public interest and whose personal and/or family background is then exposed to public view (as in the above case). The courts permit an invasion of a person's privacy in these cases because there is a legitimate public interest in newsworthy events.

4. Publicizing information that creates a false picture of a person. The information must be untrue, highly offensive, and place the other person in a false light. An example of such information would be an article written in a law journal implying that a certain attorney was unethical and dishonest, when in fact she or he was not. Publishing such a story would also involve the tort of defamation. However, a person might be more inclined to bring suit for being placed in a false light, because the law allows more time to bring that type of suit than it does for defamation.

Wrongful Death

A person who commits a wrongful act that intentionally causes the death of another can be sued for damages for **wrongful death.** Intentionally killing a bank teller during the course of a bank robbery is an example of a situation in which the family of the deceased person (usually the spouse, children, or parents) could sue.

A wrongful death action can also be pursued if the victim was killed accidentally (for example, by a person driving in an intoxicated condition) or died as a result of the negligent (careless) act of another, as in the following example.

> At eighty-one years of age, Cardinalli entered the hospital for routine cataract surgery. She died the next day, after drinking a glass of juice that had been mixed with liquid air freshener. The mixture had been given to Cardinalli in error by the nurse on duty the day of Cardinalli's surgery. Cardinalli's surviving relatives can sue the hospital and the nurse for wrongful death. ∎

The measure of damages is the loss of income (for example, as a wage earner), companionship (enjoyment of a close relationship), and services (as a mother, wife, husband, and so on) that the surviving relatives would have received from the deceased had she or he not been killed. Damages are sometimes hard to determine, especially when juries must measure such intangibles as the value of companionship. Courts nevertheless instruct juries in these cases to "fix" an award based on what they think is appropriate, keeping in mind that every life has some pecuniary value.

Malicious Prosecution

The tort of **malicious prosecution** arises when one individual, without a legitimate reason and solely to harass another individual, initiates either a criminal or a civil action against that other individual. To sue for this tort, a person must show among other things that (1) there were no real grounds for the criminal or civil action (that is, the instigator of the action did not honestly believe that the accused did anything wrong), (2) there was an intent to injure, and (3) the action was not successful.

> Wentis gave Bright, his fiancée, a diamond bracelet as an engagement gift. When Bright broke off the engagement, Wentis became very angry and promised to "get even with her." He then sued Bright for conversion, claiming that he had lent her the bracelet to wear to a formal party and that she had then refused to return it to him. During the trial Bright introduced testimony from the jeweler to prove that she was with Wentis when he purchased the bracelet and that Wentis had told the jeweler that it was an engagement present. Wentis lost the case. Bright could then sue Wentis for malicious prosecution. ■

Fraud

The tort of **fraud** occurs when false statements of fact are deliberately made to deceive, resulting in injury or loss to another. Facts that are deliberately hidden may also constitute fraud. Fraud is discussed in greater detail in connection with the law of contracts in Chapter 14.

> Randy, owner of Rolf Tire Company, told Conrad, a customer, that "all the tires on sale in this store are new." Conrad, relying on Randy's statement, bought five tires for $90 each. Later, Conrad discovered that the tires were retreads. Randy committed fraud. ■

Interference with Contractual Relations

A person who intentionally and without proper justification persuades one party to breach his or her contract with another party has committed the tort known as **interference with contractual relations.** The rationale for such a tort is that to allow a third person to interfere with a contract to the point where one of the parties breaches it would weaken the value of contracts.

■ Petrosino, a well-known computer consultant, was in the second year of a three-year contract with the Rex Corporation. Convinced that Petrosino was the only person who could solve their computer problems, the chief executive officer of Computer International lured Petrosino into breaking his contract with Rex and coming to work for Computer International at a substantially higher salary. Petrosino did break his contract, and as a result, Rex suffered a huge monetary loss on a new project that Petrosino was working on. Rex has a cause of action against Computer International for intentional interference with a contract. ■

Trespass

Trespass is an unlawful interference with someone else's possession of his or her real or personal property. Real property is land and anything permanently attached to the land, for example, a building, whereas personal property consists of something tangible and movable. Walking on or driving over another person's land without permission or refusing to leave a building after the owner has withdrawn permission to remain are examples of a trespass to real property. Vandalizing a car by breaking a window and destroying a person's car phone is an example of a trespass to personal property.

■ A group of college students held a picnic on McDowell's beach-front property without permission while McDowell was on vacation. These students committed a trespass. ■

A person who owns real property generally owns a reasonable amount of the air space above the land. Therefore, a person may be liable as a trespasser by allowing the branches of a tree growing on his or her property to hang over onto a neighbor's property, thus violating this neighbor's air space.

A person also commits a trespass by wrongfully throwing or placing an object on another's property, as for example by dumping garbage on another person's land.

Conversion

The tort of **conversion** occurs when one person wrongfully takes control of the personal property (a car, an item of clothing or jewelry, and so on) of another and exercises the right of ownership, thus depriving the owner of the use of the property.

■ One evening, in front of a neighborhood grocery store, Cooper spotted a car with its motor running. He drove away in the car and left the state for several weeks to visit a friend. On the way back to his home state, he was stopped for speeding. When he could not produce evidence to show that the car was registered in his name, he was taken into custody. Cooper admitted the car was stolen. The owner of the car could bring an action against Cooper for conversion. ■

Conversion also occurs when someone purchases stolen property and then, after a proper demand is made, refuses to return it to its rightful owner. Still another example of conversion is taking building materials from a neighbor's garage for personal use and with no intent of returning them.

A person who commits the tort of conversion may also be found guilty of the crime of theft (stealing).

Nuisance

A **nuisance** arises when a person uses her or his property unreasonably or unlawfully or when her or his conduct is unreasonable, causing discomfort or inconvenience to others. There are two types of nuisances: public and private. A public nuisance is an act that affects the general public, for example, the foul odor in a neighborhood caused by burning flesh and decaying matter from a plant that processes animal parts into commercial byproducts. A private nuisance is an act affecting a limited number of individuals—often just one person—for example, excessive noise, smoke, pollution, or fire hazard.

Schultz operated a small music shop in his garage that was open in the evening between the hours of 7:00 P.M. and 11:00 P.M. The loud noises from people trying out various musical instruments disturbed the next-door neighbors. This may be a nuisance, and the next-door neighbors may be able to stop Schultz from running his shop out of his garage. Also, there may be a zoning ordinance prohibiting a for-profit business in a residential area. ■

There are no hard-and-fast rules to determine when a certain act is considered a private nuisance. The courts tend to consider the effect of the act on the average person and the commonsense realities of the situation. For example, a college student races the motor on his or her cycle several nights a week at midnight, causing a neighbor to lose sleep from the loud noise. This act may be considered a nuisance. However, if done during the day, this same act would probably not be considered a nuisance.

It is often more important to end a nuisance than to sue and recover money. To end a nuisance, the injured party would ask the court to issue an **injunction,** a court order restraining a person from doing or continuing some act.

DEFENSES TO INTENTIONAL TORTS

Earlier in this chapter, some defenses were discussed under the various categories of torts—such as truth as a defense to the tort of defamation. The following defenses can also reduce or eliminate liability for the tort:

1. Consent. A person may consent to a tort by words or may imply consent by conduct. For example, a professional football player implicitly consents to the physical contact associated with that sport by agreeing to participate. Therefore, an injured player usually cannot sue for battery.

2. *Privilege.* The privilege to say or do something, even if another is injured, is allowed by law under certain circumstances. For example, a witness at a criminal trial is allowed to make statements that might constitute slander outside the courtroom. The statements are privileged as long as they relate to the issues in the trial. Self-defense is a privileged action available to a person who is in danger of being physically harmed and who cannot seek police protection in time to prevent bodily injury.

3. *Necessity.* In an emergency, a person may need to act to protect himself or herself from harm or the threat of imminent harm but in the process may commit an intentional tort. If the emergency is sufficiently great and the person acts reasonably, the law may excuse the tort, recognizing that what the person did constituted a necessity. Many of the decided cases involve threats of harm from forces of nature, such as fires, floods, and storms. Consider the case of a person who docks his or her small boat on private property during a severe storm and then finds shelter on the property. This person is not a trespasser in the sense that he or she can be expelled from the land. Nevertheless, this person may be required to compensate the owner of the land for any damages done to the property by the boat.

TORTS RESULTING FROM NEGLIGENCE

In addition to the intentional torts, there is the tort of negligence. Negligence is an unintentional tort. In negligence cases the defendant (person being sued) is not intentionally motivated to commit the act he or she is accused of committing. Rather, the act of **negligence** occurs because the defendant became careless. The result of this carelessness proximately (directly) causes injuries to another person or damages to another person's property. Torts are one of the largest areas of litigation, and the charge of negligence is the source of a large percentage of these lawsuits.

A person bringing a lawsuit for negligence must prove certain elements. Generally, the courts decide whether the proof is adequate or not. The elements are the same whether the plaintiff was injured by a careless driver, exposure to asbestos, or a surgeon who performed an incorrect operation. Each of these elements is now discussed.

1. *The defendant had a legal duty to act carefully.* A duty of care arises whenever a person should reasonably anticipate (foresee) that harm or injury is likely to result if he or she acts or fails to act in a certain way. This "foreseeability" test implies that the defendant should have known better and, consequently, should have behaved differently.

> Anglin was late for work. As he approached a busy intersection in his car, he began to speed up because the caution light was showing and was about to change to red. The light changed before he got to the intersection but, because of his lateness, Anglin decided to "chance it" and go through the red light. As he did, he injured a pedestrian who had the right of way and was crossing the street at the crosswalk. ■

A court in the above case would probably decide in favor of the pedestrian, reasoning that Anglin had a legal duty to stop at the red light (motor vehicle laws require this) and that he should have "foreseen" that "chancing it" by going through a red light created the risk of injury, property damage, or both as a result. In contrast, take the case of a patient's death after a successful operation because careless orderlies dropped the patient down a flight of stairs. In this case, a court would probably rule that the doctor who performed the operation is not liable for negligence, because the patient's death was not "foreseeable" by the doctor.

2. *The defendant breached the duty to act carefully.* Once it is determined that a duty exists, the person suing for negligence must show the court that the defendant breached that duty by failing to act carefully. In making its decision, the court will apply the hypothetical "reasonable person" standard, which constitutes society's judgment on how a person should behave in certain circumstances. The court will compare the conduct of the defendant with the conduct of the "reasonable person," defined as a normal, average individual. In deciding what is normal, the court will consider the person's age, intelligence, experience, and physical condition—for example, is he or she blind or deaf? It is not enough that the defendant believed in good faith that he or she was being careful. The real issue is how the "reasonable person" would have acted. Because of this issue, a minor child, for example, may not be held to the same standard for a negligent act as an adult.

3. *The defendant's failure to act carefully proximately caused the plaintiff's (person suing) injury.* After proving that the defendant had a legal duty and that there was a breach of that duty (that is, the defendant failed to act carefully), the plaintiff in a negligence action must demonstrate that the breach proximately caused the plaintiff's injuries. In the example of the patient who died because of being dropped down a flight of stairs after a successful operation, the doctor's operation was not the proximate cause of the patient's death. The direct cause of the patient's death was the carelessness of the orderlies.

4. *The defendant's negligence caused the plaintiff to suffer physical injury or damage.* As the final element of a negligence action, the plaintiff must prove that he or she suffered a physical injury or damage. In most states a defendant may also be liable if, in addition to physical injury (such as the loss of an arm or leg) the defendant caused emotional distress (for example, mental harm such as shock or fright).

A number of lawsuits for negligence center on malpractice. **Malpractice** occurs when a professional's improper, immoral, or illegal conduct in rendering services causes the recipient of these services to suffer an injury, loss, or damage.

The term "professional" is usually applied to a doctor, dentist, attorney, accountant, public official, or any person who is considered to be a member of a profession.

Dr. Peters, a well-known surgeon, improperly sewed the veins of a patient during a heart bypass operation. While in the recovery room, the patient suffered severe chest pains and massive bleeding. The doctor's error was corrected, but it left the patient in a coma for several weeks. When he recovered, he was in a weakened condition for several months. Peters is liable to the patient for malpractice. ■

DEFENSES TO NEGLIGENCE

People who are sued for negligence may present defenses for their actions that can reduce or even eliminate their liability for this tort. One such defense is contributory negligence. **Contributory negligence** refers to any negligence on the part of the injured person that led (contributed) to the injury. If contributory negligence can be proved, the injured party may be denied damages, even if the negligence was slight.

■ You were hit by Arnold, who was speeding at the time of the accident. You sued Arnold for negligence. At the trial, Arnold's attorney proved that you did not cross the street at the crosswalk, nor did you look to the right and left before stepping off the sidewalk into the street. Because your own negligence contributed to the accident, you could lose your case. ■

In most states, the harsh rules of contributory negligence have been replaced by the doctrine of comparative negligence, which is considered to be more fair. With **comparative negligence,** the negligence of the injured party who is suing and that of the person being sued are compared. An injured party who contributed to the accident but was not primarily responsible may still collect. However, the amount collected would be in proportion to the injured party's share of negligence. For example, if the wrongdoer is found to be 80 percent to blame (perhaps due to having been drunk and speeding), then this person would pay only 80 percent of the damages the injured party is asking for. The injured person would be responsible for the remaining 20 percent of the damages for being slightly negligent. If the wrongdoer and the injured party are equally at fault, according to the statutes of most states, no damages would be awarded.

Another defense is assumption of risk. People who voluntarily expose themselves to a risk of harm, suffer an injury, and then sue may be met in court with the defense known as **assumption of risk.** This defense can be raised by defendants (the persons being sued) who present evidence that they have been freed of responsibility for any wrong. A prime example involving assumption of risk is the fan who buys a ticket to attend a baseball game and then, while sitting in the spectator section in the ball park, is injured by a stray baseball hit by a player. In this case, the fan may not have grounds to sue. Spectators who purchase a ticket assume the risk and accept the harm that may result (that is, when they enter a ballpark to watch a game, a stray ball hit by a player may end up in the spectator section, hit someone, and cause an injury).

STRICT LIABILITY IN TORT

The third and final category of torts is **strict liability.** Under this concept of tort law, people who are not at fault may be held liable for injuries they cause others. The law imposes liability on them even though they have committed no intentional wrongdoing or negligent act. For this reason, strict liability is referred to as "liability without fault." The courts and legislatures responding to society have concluded that, regardless of how careful a person is, certain activities and certain products on the market present high risks of harm. Those who carry on these activities or sell these products should therefore be liable for any harm caused to innocent victims. For example, people who keep on their property trained or domesticated animals (such as wolves and lions) considered to be naturally dangerous to humans are strictly liable for harm caused by the animals if they escape. Strict liability is also imposed on merchants, such as manufacturers of consumer products, who sell these products in an unreasonably dangerous and defective condition. More will be said about the sale of defective products to the public in Chapter 18 under the topic of "Product Liability."

REMEDIES FOR TORTS

The usual remedy available to the injured party for a tort is to sue in a court of law and recover money damages from the person who committed the wrong. Contrary to what many people think, however, damages are not automatically awarded every time a tort is committed and a lawsuit filed in court. Nor will the fact that the person being sued in tort is insured through an insurance company result in automatic damages. An important requirement must be met before a person injured by a tort has a cause of action: he or she must prove damages. Generally, the purpose of damages is to restore the injured party to the position he or she was in before the tort was committed (status quo).

The amount of damages a person can recover depends on the harm caused and the kind of tort committed. Million-dollar awards are not uncommon in the areas of medical malpractice and product liability, especially if the victims have suffered a seriously disabling injury. In the case of a deliberate tort, both compensatory damages and punitive damages may be awarded. **Compensatory damages** are actual, measurable damages suffered, such as hospital bills, doctor's bills, pharmacy bills, and wages lost while a person's injuries prevent him or her from working—as well as those damages not so easy to measure, which courts call "pain and suffering." Pain and suffering refer to both the actual physical pain and the mental anguish that result from the tort. Examples of pain and suffering include the pain suffered from a back injury or the loss of an arm or leg and the emotional trauma of a permanent disfigurement caused by an automobile accident. Since there is no fixed rule by which to calculate pain and suffering, there is wide latitude for the amount that can be awarded. **Punitive damages** (also called *exemplary damages*), often referred to as "vindictive damages" or "smart money," are imposed upon the wrongdoer by the court as punishment for an intentional tort. In some personal injury cases, the award for punitive damages exceeds the award for compensatory damages. The case of *Pacific Mutual Life Insurance Co.* v. *Haslip* (499 U.S. 1) involved an award of $19,000 in compensatory damages and $10 million in punitive damages—a ratio of over 500 to 1. While juries have broad discretion to award punitive damages in personal injury cases, in recent years the U.S. Supreme Court has expressed its unease with the size of punitive damages. (See *Browning-Ferris Indus., Inc.* v. *Kelco Disposal, Inc.*, 492 U.S. 257; *Pacific Mut. Life Ins. Co.* v. *Haslip*, 499 U.S. 1; and *TXO Prod. Corp.* v. *Alliance Resources Corp.*, 113 S.Ct. 2711.)

> Clar was attacked in the parking lot of a shopping mall one evening by two strangers attempting to steal her purse. She suffered a broken arm and the loss of her front teeth. Clar could sue for assault and battery. ∎

Clar's award for compensatory damages would depend on the actual amount spent for medical and dental bills. In addition, the court could direct the wrongdoers to pay additional money as punitive damages.

When a tort is caused by negligence, compensatory damages will be awarded for any resulting physical injury or damage to a person or the person's property.

Sometimes money damages will not provide the kind of relief needed. Remedies in equity (as discussed on page 13) protect parties when monetary damages are not adequate. If, for example, someone is disturbing you by creating a nuisance, what you may really want the court to do is to stop the nuisance rather than award you money damages. You can do this by seeking an injunction, which is a remedy in equity (see nuisance, page 71).

TORT REFORM

It appears that litigation has now become embedded in this country's legal culture. Americans used to think that by just behaving themselves they could stay out of legal trouble. This is no longer true. Honest, careful, competent people, businesses, and public agencies are now sued in large numbers. Doctors are a good example. Statistics show that 80 percent of the the physicians in this country have been sued, many losing their cases. Some physicians have left their profession because they are unable to afford the large malpractice premiums charged by insurance companies. One reason for the "heavy" litigation is that legislators, judges, and juries have been pushing out the frontiers of responsibility, so that individuals, businesses, and public agencies are required to compensate injured people more readily, and more generously, than ever before. Million-dollar verdicts are not uncommon.

Several possible reforms have been discussed in state legislatures and in the U.S. Congress in the past few years—from alternate dispute resolution (discussed in Chapter 5) to fee shifting (shifting attorney's and court fees to the loser) to placing a cap on the amount of money that judges and juries can award in certain tort cases. Reform, however, will not come easily unless the prolitigation advocates can be convinced that change is in the best interests of everyone involved in the litigation process.

Summary of Important Legal Concepts

A tort, known as a private wrong, is a harmful act or simply a failure to act. In either case, physical or mental injury to a person or damage to a person's property results. The violator of a private wrong is subject to a civil lawsuit and will be required to pay money damages. Generally, all persons, including minors, are legally responsible for their torts. Torts are classified as either intentional, negligent, or strict liability.

Intentional torts, those deliberately committed, include assault and battery, false imprisonment, mental distress, defamation, invasion of privacy, wrongful death, malicious prosecution, fraud, interference with contractual relations, trespass, conversion, and nuisance. A defendant (person being sued) in a civil lawsuit, may avoid liability for these torts by proving defenses such as consent, privilege, and necessity.

Negligent torts arise because someone was careless. Negligence may be defined as the failure to act carefully when there is a foreseeable risk of harm to others. When a lawsuit is based on negligence, the courts will apply the hypothetical "reasonable person" standard. A "reasonable person" is a normal, average individual. Three defenses are available to a defendant in a lawsuit for negligence: contributory negligence, comparative negligence, and assumption of risk. Comparative negligence is the rule in most states, because it is considered to be fairer than the other two defenses.

The third and final category of torts is strict liability, often referred to as "liability without fault." In strict liability lawsuits, defendants may be held liable even though they acted carefully (without negligence) and had no intention of harming others or their property. Society, however, acting through the courts, requires those who carry on high-risk activities or who sell products that could be unreasonably dangerous to the public to assume responsibility for their actions.

The usual remedy available to an injured party for a tort is to sue in court and to recover money damages. The amount of damages that can be recovered depends on the harm caused and the kind of tort committed. Sometimes, millions of dollars are awarded. Damages generally are classified as compensatory or punitive (also called *exemplary damages*). In the case of an intentional tort, the injured party is entitled to both categories of damages. Compensatory damages refer to an award of money that repays the injured party for losses actually suffered, such as hospital and doctor's bills, and for "pain and suffering" resulting from any physical injury. Punitive damages are above and beyond compensatory damages and are imposed by a court as punishment on the wrongdoer.

Equitable remedies, e.g. an injunction, protect parties when monetary damages are not adequate.

Tort reform has been discussed at the state and federal levels. Reform, however will not come until prolitigation advocates are convinced that change is in the best interests of everyone involved in the litigation process.

Key Legal Terms to Know

Match the terms with the definitions that follow.

assault
assumption of risk
battery
comparative negligence
compensatory damages
contributory negligence
conversion
false arrest
false imprisonment
fraud
infliction of mental distress

injunction
intentional tort
interference with contractual relations
invasion of privacy
libel
malicious prosecution
malpractice
negligence
nuisance
punitive damages
slander
strict liability
tort
trespass
wrongful death

1. Illegally entering or remaining on the property of another
2. A court order restraining a person from doing or continuing some act
3. Actual measurable damages suffered by an individual as a result of a wrongful act
4. The wrongful exercise of control or ownership over the personal property of another
5. An unauthorized detainment by an officer of the law
6. A professional's improper, immoral, or illegal conduct in the performance of his or her duties either intentionally or through carelessness
7. Injury to another person through intentional and wrongful physical contact, such as the unlawful stroking of one person by another
8. The failure to act carefully, resulting in injury to another person or in damages to another person's property
9. Wrongfully initiating a lawsuit against a person who has done no wrong
10. Written false statements that injure a person's reputation
11. Use of one's own property to annoy or disturb others
12. Damages imposed as punishment for intentionally committing a wrongful act
13. Oral false statements that injure a person's reputation
14. A wrongful act that causes injury to another person or to his or her property
15. Unlawful and intentional restriction of a person's freedom of movement

16. The wrongful intrusion into a person's private activities
17. Mental suffering caused by another person's extreme and outrageous behavior
18. The defense that the negligence of the injured party led to the injury
19. The defense of comparing the negligence of the injured party and the negligence of the person being sued
20. A threatening act by one person that places another person in fear of bodily harm
21. A deliberate harmful act done to a person
22. A wrongful act that causes the death of another
23. False statements of fact that are deliberately made to deceive
24. Persuading one party to breach a contract with another party
25. Results when a person either expressly or implicitly assumes responsibility by exposing himself or herself to risk
26. A concept of tort law in which people not at fault may be held liable for injuries they have caused others

Questions and Problems to Discuss

1. Explain the meaning of the following statement: "Many wrongful acts are both torts and crimes because they harm society as well as the individual."
2. When his wife died of Alzheimer's disease in an Ohio hospital, Gomez instructed the attending physician to have her brain preserved for research purposes to help determine causes of the disease. The brain was placed in chemicals and sent to the National Research Lab for study. However, the package containing the brain was lost when it arrived at the lab; it was never found. The husband, who said he would "never be able to totally bury" his wife because of the loss, suffered severe mental shock and was treated for several years by a well-known psychiatrist. For which tort or torts, if any, can the husband sue the National Research Lab?
3. Davidson was walking into Midtown Mall when he was attacked by two men. They hit Davidson with brass knuckles, knocked him down, took his wallet containing $200, and seriously injured him. The two men were apprehended about

twenty minutes later and taken into custody by the police. They were charged with the crimes of assault and robbery. Since they were charged with crimes, is Davidson prevented from bringing a civil action against these two men for money damages?

4. Christian, a certified public accountant, carelessly maintained the financial records for several clients, which caused the financial statements of each client's business to show a large profit over one year. Actually, however, each of the businesses had instead suffered a heavy loss and, as a consequence, was forced out of business. For what tort can these clients sue Christian?

5. Madama was taking the bus home from work. At the stop where she was to get off, the driver opened the door, but a very rude individual in a hurry to board the bus positioned himself directly in front of the bus entrance. The individual refused to let Madama leave the bus even after she asked him several times. Now hysterical, Madama screamed and ran back into the bus and out the rear door. Once off the bus, she engaged a nearby police officer, asking the officer to get the details of what had happened. Madama then sued the man for false imprisonment, claiming that, on her doctor's recommendation, she remained out of work for several weeks as a result of severe emotional strain. Is Madama entitled to a claim of false imprisonment?

6. What impact did the Supreme Court decision in *New York Times Co.* v. *Sullivan* have on the laws of defamation as they existed in the various states?

7. Russ, aged sixty, was struck by a snowplow in the parking lot of the Manor Hotel as she was walking toward her car. Russ suffered multiple fractures and internal injuries. As a result, she had to walk with a cane. Russ sued the driver and owner of the snowplow and was awarded $500,000 in damages to pay for hospital and doctor's bills, as well as to compensate her for the fact that she will be required to walk with a cane indefinitely. The $500,000 would be classified as what type of damages? Explain.

8. Frank Blaine, aged fifty-five, a famous singer-actor, announced his retirement from show business. The headline of a story in the *Red Glow Express* the day after Blaine announced his retirement was "FRANK BLAINE HAS CANCER." The article said that the singer-actor had been forced to retire because "he was suffering from cancer of the throat and that within a period of one year he would be forced to be confined to a hospital to await his death." Blaine filed a $3 million lawsuit against the newspaper, claiming that he never had and does not now have cancer and that no diagnosis had been made by any doctor that he has cancer. Blaine sued to recover damages from the *Red Glow Express*. Should he succeed? Explain.

9. Coleman, a salesperson for a security company, wanted to get even with Cloos, the superintendent of the West Ridge School District, for not purchasing burglar alarms for the school district from Coleman's company. She (Coleman) wrote a letter to the board of education falsely accusing Cloos of having been arrested in a neighboring community for possession of drugs. She also wrote that Cloos paid the local politicians to keep the incident off the police records. On what grounds could Cloos sue Coleman?

10. Discuss the relationship of "foreseeability" and "proximate cause" to a victim's claim during a civil lawsuit that she or he has suffered from another person's negligence.

11. Hazardous wastes from the Hooker Chemical Company were being dumped at a local dump site and, through seepage, contaminated the groundwater supply of a nearby residential neighborhood. Neighbors living near this site filed suit against Hooker Chemical. What will be the basis of their lawsuit? Instead of suing, what other action might the neighbors wish to take?

12. One spring evening, around 6:30 P.M., Baranek was driving her car down a two-lane highway, heading back to her college dorm. The weather was cool, clear, and dry and, though it was nearly dark, the visibility was good. Baranek proceeded down the road going about 40 mph, but slowed to 20 mph in anticipation of making a left turn at an intersection. She turned on her left directional signal and looked in the rear-view mirror. She saw a set of headlights behind her and began to turn left when her car was struck by the vehicle whose headlights she had seen in her mirror. The vehicle turned out to be a tractor-trailer, which, in the process of passing Baranek's vehicle, struck it and caused Baranek to be ejected from her car. She then rolled under her car, which landed on her legs and caused her to suffer serious injuries.

Although Baranek's car had seat belts, she was not using them at the time of the accident. Baranek sued the driver of the tractor-trailer for his negligence in striking her car and injuring her. The driver of the tractor-trailer maintained, however, that he should not have to pay for Baranek's injuries because she had contributed to the accident by not wearing her seat belt. Is Baranek prevented from receiving any money for her injuries caused by the tractor-trailer driver because she failed to wear her seat belt? Discuss the possibilities.

13. Marks was meeting her sister and a friend for dinner at a swanky restaurant. It was a warm summer evening, and because she was early, Marks decided to wait outside. She stood in front of the restaurant until her sister and friend arrived. Within a few minutes, a police car drove up and a police officer got out and forced Marks into the car, accusing her of being a prostitute. She was taken to the police precinct station, where she was questioned and released without being charged. She had no previous convictions and was employed as a full-time account executive at a local securities investment firm. Can Marks sue the police department for false arrest?

14. Popovici, an untenured college English teacher, was being considered for a permanent appointment. When the president of the college discovered that she was separated from her husband and seeking a divorce, he brought this information to a Board of Trustees meeting and recommended that she not be rehired at the end of the current school term. The Board of Trustees agreed, and Popovici was not granted tenure. She was then requested to leave her current position as soon as the current school year ended. The president's request to the Board that Popovici not be rehired was based strictly on his fear that her divorce would harm the college's "image." Popovici was otherwise considered an "excellent teacher" and had been recommended for tenure by her department chairperson. Did the president's recommendation to deny Popovici's tenure appointment, based on her marital situation, constitute a wrongful intrusion into her private life?

15. Without permission, Pasto took her good friend's car keys and drove the friend's car to a mall to shop. On the way home later the same day, Pasto had an accident that caused minor damage to the front of the car. What torts has Pasto committed?

Cases to Decide

1. Mary Jane LaBrier, the wife of car salesman James LaBrier, sued Anheuser Ford (her husband's employer) and two of its employees for emotional distress. Her cause of action was based upon the extreme and outrageous conduct of two Anheuser Ford employees. The two employees appeared at the LaBrier residence and questioned Mrs. LaBrier as to the whereabouts of her husband and the company car that he had borrowed for a short trip. In loud, threatening voices and in the presence of neighbors and house guests, they harassed and humiliated her by repeatedly asking where her husband and the automobile were. The two employees accused Mr. LaBrier of stealing the car and threatened to have the police issue an "all-points bulletin" and arrest him. Mrs. LaBrier, a highly emotional individual who had previously suffered severe emotional problems, became very upset. She had to start her medication again and be hospitalized. At the time of the incident, the employees knew of Mrs. LaBrier's prior emotional problems. The house guests and neighbors who heard the conversation between Mrs. LaBrier and the employees testified in court that the employees were harsh and cruel and made Mrs. LaBrier tremble. Should Mrs. LaBrier be successful in her lawsuit? (*LaBrier* v. *Anheuser Ford*, 612 SW 2d 790)

2. Gonzalez was injured while a passenger in Garcia's car. Garcia, who had been drinking heavily, lost control of the car and caused it to roll over, landing on its side. Gonzalez sued for damages for negligence. Garcia claimed comparative negligence as a defense. Testimony in court revealed that Gonzalez knew Garcia was intoxicated. The court concluded that Gonzalez could have taken a cab or called his wife for a ride. Instead, he took a dangerous route and rode with Garcia. Does Gonzalez's decision to ride with Garcia amount to negligence that makes him partially liable for the accident? (*Gonzalez* v. *Garcia*, 142 Cal Reptr 503)

3. Russo charged in a lawsuit that Iacono pointed a gun at her and shouted, "I got to kill you," and

that she, Russo, became frightened. She further charged that Iacono had used objectionable and violent language toward her before. If Russo can prove the facts alleged, would this be sufficient to show assault? (*Russo v. Iacono*, 423 NYS 2.53)

4. Gielskie was left totally paralyzed from the chest down as a result of an injection of tetanus antitoxin serum. The serum was provided by the New York State Department of Health, which included instructions on how to give the injections. The instructions stated that there were a number of methods of giving injections of this serum. Evidence indicated that doctors differed on which method to use. Gielskie sued the state of New York, claiming malpractice. Should Gielskie succeed? (*Gielskie v. State*, 9 NY 2d 834)

5. Berger, a firefighter, responded to a chemical boilover at Lipson's chemical manufacturing plant, the boilover having been caused by Lipson's negligence. When Berger arrived on the scene, he asked whether any toxic chemicals were involved and was told there were none. Actually, toxic chemicals were involved, and Berger was injured when he attempted to control the boilover. In response to Berger's suit for damages, Lipson argued that a person, such as a firefighter, who engages in a hazardous activity in the normal course of duty assumes the risk of danger and should be barred from recovery for injuries. Should the court accept this line of reasoning? (*Lipson v. Superior Court*, 644 P. 2d 822)

6. Gibson was a salesclerk at a 7–11 store of which Hummel was the supervisor. After a shortage of inventory was noted, Gibson was asked to take a polygraph test against her will. All signs of guilt pointed to Gibson, and she was given the choice of resigning or being fired. She quit and then sued Hummel and the store owner for intentional infliction of emotional distress, claiming that being forced to take a polygraph test against her will was improper and that she suffered a major mental disorder as a result. Should her claim succeed? (*Gibson v. Hummel*, 688 S.W. 2d 4)

7. Dun & Bradstreet, a credit reporting agency, sent a report on Greenmoss Builders to several subscribers interested in dealing with Greenmoss. Through the error of a D&B employee who prepared it, the report erroneously reported that Greenmoss was bankrupt. Although D&B make it a routine practice to verify the accuracy of their reports with the businesses themselves, no such check was made in this case. Greenmoss Builders sued for libel. Would Greenmoss be entitled to damages, even though there was no actual malice on the part of Dun & Bradstreet? (*Dun & Bradstreet, Inc. v. Greenmoss Builders, Inc.*, 472 U.S. 749)

8. Hairston purchased and took delivery of a new car from Haygood Lincoln-Mercury. As he drove home from the Lincoln-Mercury dealership, the left rear wheel came off the car. Because there was no shoulder on the road, he stopped the car in the far right lane. A passing motorist who stopped to help parked his van 20 feet behind Hairston's car. A flatbed truck, driven by Alexander and owned by the Alexander Tank and Equipment Co., came along and struck the van, knocking it into the rear of Hairston's automobile. Hairston, who had been standing between his car and the van, was killed. There was conclusive evidence that Alexander was negligent in failing to keep his truck under proper control. Hairston's wife Bettye sued both Haygood and the Alexander Tank and Equipment Co. for damages, alleging that their negligence had caused her husband's death. Should Hairston's wife succeed in her lawsuits? (*Hairston v. Alexander Tank and Equipment Co.*, 311 S.E. 2d 559)

Chapter 5

Litigation and Alternatives for Settling Disputes

CHAPTER PREVIEW

The first part of this chapter outlines the general procedures that one may go through when a decision is made to bring a civil lawsuit. The remainder of the chapter explores several alternatives for settling legal disputes outside the courtroom.

PROLOGUE

The governor of a midwestern state once told the *Washington Post*, "Filing lawsuits has replaced baseball as our national pastime. . . . 'See you in court' used to be a real threat. Now it's as common as 'Have a nice day.' " Many Americans are now demanding their day in court. Thousands of civil cases are filed in federal and state courts every year (19 million new cases a year, an increase of 40 percent since 1984). Juries in these cases often award large sums of money to victims of torts and to those suffering losses from breach of contract, inappropriate real estate transactions, matrimonial problems, illegal or unconscionable consumer transactions, antitrust violations, patent infringements, and other causes. Each of us is now a perennial candidate for a part in a civil damage lawsuit.

As you will see later in this chapter, there are ways to settle a disagreement between two or more parties other than by **litigation** (a lawsuit). It goes without saying that if you become involved in a legal controversy, you should try to settle out of court. There are advantages to an out-of-court settlement. A major reason for finding alternatives to a lawsuit is that the person you are thinking of suing may be *judgment proof*—that is, unable to pay even if you win the case. Also, because of the backlog of court cases, delays of up to three years (and sometimes even longer) before a case can be heard are not unusual. During such delays, witnesses may die or move away, and evidence may be lost or forgotten. Furthermore, if the losing party appeals the trial court's decision to a higher court, settlement could be delayed as much as ten years. Also, consider the fact that lengthy legal proceedings can be an emotionally draining experience. The prospects of a prolonged courtroom battle may require you, and possibly other members of your family, to face hostile attorneys involved in the trial as well as in pretrial hearings. And, although all the signs of winning may be in your favor, you still run the risk of losing. Finally, you must ask yourself whether a successful court battle is worth its cost to you in court and attorneys' fees.

The first step in deciding whether to sue is to discuss your legal problem with an attorney. After you have this discussion and fully understand your options, you may discover that the case cannot be settled in any way other than by litigation.

To help you better understand what litigation is all about, the next several pages of this chapter discuss the steps in a lawsuit from beginning to end. (Remember, however, that each court has its own rules and regulations governing the procedures for bringing a lawsuit.) Although procedures vary from court to court and from state to state, certain procedures or stages are basic to all suits. Figure 5.1 illustrates these steps. The following scenario traces one person's experiences in the litigation process.

SCENARIO

Bill Allen (age thirty-five), an executive for a large advertising firm, had a wife, Martha (age thirty), and a daughter, Karen (age five). His job was secure and paid him a salary of $100,000 a year; he had a good future with the firm. He and his wife shared an excellent relationship—they enjoyed doing things together, such as playing tennis; going to concerts, plays, and movies; and gardening and landscaping around their new house. Above all, they were both devoted parents who took an active interest in bringing up their young daughter.

One evening, Bill Allen was driving home from work and, as he traveled (within the speed limit) on an open stretch of road, his car was struck by a tractor-trailer belonging to the Laiden Trucking Company. The driver of the truck, who was traveling in the opposite direction at a high rate of speed and in an intoxicated condition, had crossed the white line, driving head on into the Allen car. Allen, trapped inside the car, had to be removed by a special crew called to the accident scene. Witnesses verified Allen's version of the accident, and police called to the scene verified that the driver of the truck had been drinking.

After several months in the hospital, where he was recovering from serious internal injuries and undergoing painful therapy, Allen's doctors determined that he would be paralyzed from the waist down and would have to spend the rest of his life in a wheelchair. He also would face many years of pain and the possibility of additional medical treatment. It was also determined that he was suffering emotionally. He was upset that he could no longer work to support his family or do the things his wife and he had done together and with their daughter. Allen had some savings but, because his wife was not working, the money would not be enough for the family to maintain the same standard of living they were used to before the accident occurred. The Allens also would have to pay thousands of dollars in medical bills not covered by his health insurance. Allen decided to seek the advice of an attorney but, not having had any legal problems, he had no idea which attorney could best handle his case. His friends recommended attorneys whom they had retained in the past. One friend also suggested that he contact the local bar association for the names of attorneys.

Allen contacted Jan Heisman, an attorney for a large law firm with a good reputation for settling negligence cases similar to his. At their meeting, Allen described in detail all the facts relating to the accident and provided the names of the witnesses. Heisman indicated to Allen that before she took the case, she would first conduct a preliminary investigation. Heisman obtained a medical release from Allen so that she could examine the hospital and medical records relating to his case. She also interviewed the witnesses

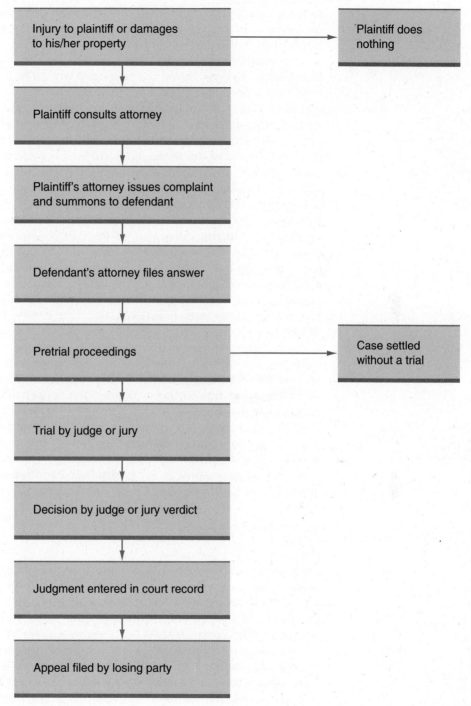

Figure 5.1
The Primary Steps in a Civil Lawsuit

to the accident. The preliminary investigation completed, Heisman then requested another meeting with Allen to present her evaluation of his case in terms of the course of action she would recommend.

Heisman concluded that Allen indeed had a case (or cause of action) based on negligence, that if the case came to trial he stood a good chance of achieving a favorable verdict, and that the amount of the award would be considerable because of his high medical bills and because his earning capacity had been destroyed by his inability to return to work as a result of the "pain and suffering" (physical pain and emotional stress) inflicted in the accident. Heisman discussed with Allen the possibility of settling out of court, noting, however, that the amount of the settlement would be considerably less. Heisman made the point that the trucking company's attorney, knowing that Allen would probably receive a large award of money, might use shrewd legal tactics to delay the start of the lawsuit. This delay would be aimed at inducing Allen, out of desperation and frustration, to settle out of court for less money. Heisman also pointed out that even if Allen won his case in the lower court, the trucking company might appeal the case to a higher court. This appeal would delay even further any decision on an award because of the appeal court's crowded schedule.

Given all these facts, Allen evaluated them carefully, including Heisman's advice to go to trial. He decided to proceed to trial and to retain Heisman as his attorney. Heisman discussed with Allen the expenses of litigation, including the matter of attorneys' fees. Heisman explained that there were at least three bases for attorneys' fees: an hourly rate, a flat rate, and a contingency fee. She further explained that in personal injury lawsuits, the attorneys were often paid a *contingency fee*—in Allen's case a percentage (at least 33.33 percent) of the money damages collected from the trucking company if the case was decided in Allen's favor but, if Allen lost the case, no fee. Heisman then drew up a client-attorney contract and indicated in the contract that payment was to be based on a contingency fee. Heisman was officially retained to represent Allen, and preparation for the trial began.

HOW A LAWSUIT BEGINS

Bill Allen's lawsuit begins when Heisman, as an officer of the court, prepares and delivers a complaint and summons to the appropriate representative of the Laiden Trucking Company. A **complaint** (Figure 5.2) states the names of the parties to the lawsuit, in this case, Bill Allen and the Laiden Trucking Company. The complaint also sets out the *cause of action*—the facts and circumstances that Bill Allen, on whose behalf the suit is brought, believes are the basis for the legal action and states the remedy being sought. In this case, Allen is seeking $3,000,000 for medical expenses, "pain and suffering," and court costs. A **summons** (Figure 5.3) is a written notice to the party being sued (in this case, the Laiden Trucking Company), indicating that a lawsuit has been filed and ordering an authorized representative of the

STATE OF NEW YORK
SUPREME COURT
COUNTY OF MONROE

BILL ALLEN

                              Plaintiff,   COMPLAINT

                         VS.

LAIDEN TRUCKING COMPANY

                         Defendant
_____

     The Plaintiff, BILL ALLEN, complaining of the Defendant, LAIDEN
TRUCKING COMPANY, and through his attorney, Jan Heisman, Esq.,
alleges and respectfully shows the Court as follows:

  1. That at all of the times hereinafter mentioned, the Plaintiff,
BILL ALLEN was a resident of the City of Rochester, County of
Monroe, State of New York.
  2. That at all of the times hereinafter mentioned, the Plaintiff,
BILL ALLEN was the owner and operator of a 1988 Chevrolet automobile
bearing New York State license plate number: NY 689-42.
  3. Upon information and belief, and at all of the times hereinafter mentioned, the Defendant, LAIDEN TRUCKING COMPANY, was a domestic corporation organized and existing under and by virtue of the
laws of the State of New York, and had its principal place of
business located in the City of Rochester, County of Monroe, and
State of New York.
  4. Upon information and belief, and at all of the times hereinafter mentioned, the Defendant, LAIDEN TRUCKING COMPANY, owned a 1989
International Tractor-Trailer bearing New York State license plate
number: NY 138JJ.
  5. Upon information and belief, and at all of the times hereinafter mentioned, and more particularly, on the *3rd day of July, 1995,*
employee of the Defendant, LAIDEN TRUCKING COMPANY, was operating
the tractor-trailer owned by the Defendant with its permission,
knowledge and consent, and within the scope of its business
interests.
  6. That Route 390 is a public road running in a general northerly
and southerly direction in and through the City of Rochester, County
of Monroe and State of New York.
  7. That on or about the *3rd day of July, 1995,* between the hours
of 6 and 7 o'clock in the evening of said day, the Plaintiff, BILL

Figure 5.2
Complaint

company to appear in court or to answer in writing within a designated
period of time (such as twenty days).

   Now that the lawsuit is officially under way, Bill Allen legally becomes
known as the **plaintiff** because he is bringing the lawsuit. The Laiden Trucking Company becomes known as the **defendant** because it is the party against
whom the lawsuit is brought. (It should be noted at this point that in a
criminal action, the plaintiff is the state or federal government acting for the

ALLEN was operating his motor vehicle in a general northerly direction on Route 390 at a point approximately one-quarter of a mile south of Exit 29.

8. That at the same time and place, the tractor-trailer owned by the Defendant, LAIDEN TRUCKING COMPANY, was traveling in a general southerly direction on Route 390 and crossed into the northbound lanes of traffic striking the automobile of the Plaintiff, BILL ALLEN, causing the Plaintiff BILL ALLEN to sustain serious permanent personal injuries as will be hereinafter more particularly set forth.

9. That the Defendant, LAIDEN TRUCKING COMPANY, was careless and negligent, in that its employee was operating Defendant's tractor-trailer at a high and excessive rate of speed in view of the conditions then and there prevailing; that he failed to sound, signal, or give any notice or warning of his approach; that he failed to keep the tractor-trailer in the southbound lanes of traffic, and crossed into the northbound lanes of traffic; that said employee was further careless and negligent, in that he was operating said tractor-trailer when his ability to do so was impaired by alcohol, or additionally, when he was driving while intoxicated.

10. That as a result of the carelessness and negligence of the Defendant, LAIDEN TRUCKING COMPANY, as has hereinbefore been set forth, the Plaintiff, BILL ALLEN was made sick, sore, lame, and disabled; that he suffered and will in the future continue to suffer great pain and physical as well as mental anguish; and that the Plaintiff, BILL ALLEN is informed and believes that he has sustained permanent injuries, and that he will never fully recover from the effects of same.

11. Due to the carelessness and negligence of the Defendant, LAIDEN TRUCKING COMPANY, as aforesaid and the injuries resulting therefrom, the Plaintiff, BILL ALLEN has been, and will in the future be, incapacitated and prevented from performing the duties incident to his usual occupation in life, and that he lost, and will in the future lose, the wages therefrom.

12. That no fault or negligence on the part of the Plaintiff, BILL ALLEN herein contributed to or caused said accident herein and the injuries resulting therefrom, but that the same were caused wholly and solely by reason of the carelessness and negligence of the Defendant, LAIDEN TRUCKING COMPANY herein.

Figure 5.2
**Complaint
(continued)**

people—society—and the defendant is the person accused of committing a crime.) A person called a *process server* usually delivers a copy of the summons and complaint to the defendant, wherever that person can be found. In some cases, the "papers" may be left with a responsible individual at the home of the defendant or may be sent by certified mail.

After the representative of the Laiden Trucking Company has been served with the complaint and summons, he or she should contact the company's

```
BILL ALLEN    Plaintiff,                    Complaint        page 3
              VS.
LAIDEN TRUCKING COMPANY    Defendant
```

13. Due to the carelessness and negligence of the Defendant, LAIDEN TRUCKING COMPANY herein, the Plaintiff, BILL ALLEN, sustained among other things, serious internal injuries and paralysis from the waist down, which will be permanent in nature, and he has been out of work for a year, all in compliance with Section 5102 of the New York State Insurance Law.

14. That as a result of the carelessness and negligence of the Defendant, LAIDEN TRUCKING COMPANY herein and the injuries sustained by the Plaintiff, BILL ALLEN, the Plaintiff, BILL ALLEN has been damaged in the sum of $3,000,000.00.

WHEREFORE, the Plaintiff, BILL ALLEN, demands judgment against the Defendant, LAIDEN TRUCKING COMPANY, in the sum of $3,000,000.00, together with the costs and disbursements of this action.

Dated: August 15, 1996

```
                                        Jan Heisman, Esq.
                                        Attorney for Plaintiff
                                        350 Main Street
                                        Rochester, NY 14606
                                        (716) 555-9201
```

```
TO: HILL AND DALE
    Attorneys for Defendant
    2700 Bleek Tower
    Rochester, NY 14732
    (716) 555-9348
```

Figure 5.2
**Complaint
(continued)**

lawyer, who will then draw up an **answer** (see Figure 5.4) to the complaint. The answer is a written response to the *allegations* (claims) made by the plaintiff. The answer may deny all charges and give legally sound reasons in defense of these charges, or it may deny some charges while admitting others. An actual appearance in court by the defendant to deliver the answer is not necessary. In this case, the Laiden Trucking Company's attorney would simply deliver a *notice of appearance* to Bill Allen's attorney. This notice

```
STATE OF NEW YORK
SUPREME COURT
COUNTY OF MONROE


BILL ALLEN
301 Blaine Street
Rochester, New York 14839
                              Plaintiff              SUMMONS
                          VS.

LAIDEN TRUCKING COMPANY
383 Ipswich Avenue
Rochester, New York 14631
                          Defendant
_____


To the above named Defendant
     YOU ARE HEREBY SUMMONED to answer the complaint in this action
and to serve a copy of your answer, or, if the complaint is not
served with this summons, to serve a notice of appearance, on the
Plaintiff's Attorney(s) within 20 days after the service of this
summons, exclusive of the day of service (or within 30 days after
the service is complete if this summons is not personally delivered
to you within the State of New York); and in case of your failure to
appear or answer, judgment will be taken against you by default for
the relief demanded in the complaint.
     Upon your failure to appear or answer, judgment will be taken
against you by default for the sum of $3,000,000.00 together with
the costs and disbursements of this action.

Dated: August 15, 1996

Notice: The object of this action is to recover for injuries sus-
tained in a motor vehicle accident caused by defendant's negligence.
The relief sought is monetary damages in the sum of $3,000,000.00
for medical expenses, pain and suffering, and court costs.


                              Jan Heisman, Esq.
                              Attorney for Plaintiff
                              350 Main Street
                              Rochester, NY 14606
                              (716) 555-9201
```

Figure 5.3
Summons

acknowledges that the defendant has received the summons. A failure to acknowledge gives the plaintiff the right to a *judgment by default*, which means that Bill Allen could then proceed to prove his case in the court having jurisdiction and, if successful, could receive money damages. The judge of the court would make a decision based only on the evidence presented by Allen's attorney. In a judgment by default, the attorney for the Laiden Trucking Company would not be permitted to present evidence on behalf of the company.

```
                 STATE OF NEW YORK
                 SUPREME COURT
                 COUNTY OF MONROE

                 BILL ALLEN
                 301 Blaine Street
                 Rochester, New York 14839

                                          Plaintiff                    ANSWER
                                       VS.

                 LAIDEN TRUCKING COMPANY
                 383 Ipswich Avenue
                 Rochester, New York 14631

                                          Defendant
                 _____

                    1. Defendant, LAIDEN TRUCKING COMPANY, admits the allegations in
                 paragraphs 3, 4, and 6 of the complaint.
                    2. Defendant, LAIDEN TRUCKING COMPANY, states that it lacks know-
                 ledge or information sufficient to form a belief as to the truth of
                 the allegations in paragraphs 1 and 2 of the complaint.
                    3. Defendant, LAIDEN TRUCKING COMPANY, denies each and every other
                 allegation of the complaint.

                                        AFFIRMATIVE DEFENSE
                        That any injuries or damages which the plaintiff may have
                 sustained, if any, at the time and place mentioned in the complaint
                 herein were caused for the most part by the carelessness and
                 negligence of the plaintiff himself and that if any carelessness,
                 negligence, or want of care upon the part of defendant caused or
                 contributed to such injuries and damages of the plaintiff it bore
                 only a slight proportion to the entire negligence attributable to
                 both plaintiff and defendant in causing such injuries and damages.
                        WHEREFORE, defendant LAIDEN TRUCKING COMPANY, demands judg-
                 ment against plaintiff dismissing the complaint, plus costs and dis-
                 bursements.

                 Dated: August 30, 1996

                                                     HILL AND DALE
                                                     Attorneys for Defendant
                                                     2700 Bleek Tower
                                                     Rochester, NY 14732

                 Jan Heisman, Esq.
                 Attorney for Plaintiff
                 350 Main Street
                 Rochester, NY 14606
```

Figure 5.4
Answer

PRETRIAL PROCEEDINGS

Before a lawsuit is brought to trial, both parties to the suit have a chance to develop their cases and prepare for trial. Pretrial proceedings usually consist of *motions, discovery,* and a *pretrial conference.*

A **motion,** which may be filed by either party, is an application to a judge for a ruling on a point of law. For example, after studying the complaint, the attorney for the Laiden Trucking Company may choose to file a motion to dismiss the lawsuit, claiming that the facts stated in the complaint are not adequate and do not entitle Bill Allen the relief he is seeking ($3,000,000). If the judge grants a motion to dismiss, the case is dismissed, effectively ending the lawsuit. Or, if Heisman, Bill Allen's attorney, thinks the Laiden Trucking Company lacks a sufficient defense to win the suit, she may, for example make a motion for immediate judgment (called a *summary judgment*). By this motion, Heisman asks the court to decide the issue based on the statements in the complaint and in the answer.

In either case, if the judge grants the motion, further proceedings, including a trial, are avoided.

Discovery refers to the pretrial steps taken by the plaintiff and the defendant to learn in detail the nature of the other's claim or defense. In today's court systems, every effort is made to encourage discovery so that both parties will be fully prepared for trial and surprises will be avoided. The process ensures that all potential testimony and other evidence is made available to both sides. Discovery techniques include a series of written questions that are sent to the opposing party, who must truthfully answer them under oath; **depositions**—sworn statements from witnesses who, for good cause, may not be able to be present at the trial; compulsory physical and mental examinations by doctors chosen by the other party in personal injury cases where a person's condition is a matter of controversy; and the request for production of documents or other things in the possession of the other party for inspection. At this time, Heisman will introduce the records of the hospital, statements from the doctors who examined Bill Allen, and the statements of the witnesses to the accident. The attorney for the Laiden Trucking Company may even require Allen to submit to a physical examination by an independent doctor. Discovery techniques, which generally take place after the motions have been filed and dealt with, sometimes result in the compromise and settlement of a claim at this stage.

After a lawsuit is placed on the court's trial calendar, awaiting its turn to be heard, a **pretrial conference** may be held to see whether the suit can be settled without a trial. The pretrial conference includes a judge, the opposing attorneys, and, often, the parties to the suit. At this conference the judge and the two opposing attorneys discuss, evaluate, and narrow down the issues in the case (taken from the complaint and the answer), and they review the results of the discovery process with a view to working out a settlement if possible. A *settlement* is an agreement between the parties to resolve the lawsuit without a trial. Many suits are settled at the pretrial conference stage after the judge has made recommendations for settlement. When a settlement is reached, the parties agree to dismiss the lawsuit. If no settlement can be reached, the judge and the attorneys then discuss the details of the trial.

THE TRIAL

Unless Bill Allen reaches a satisfactory settlement agreement with the Laiden Trucking Company during the pretrial proceedings, the case will be placed on the calendar (sometimes called the docket), which lists the cases to be heard over a certain period of time. Bill Allen's case will come to trial as *Bill Allen* v. (versus) *The Laiden Trucking Company*. If Allen and the Laiden Trucking Company do not demand a jury trial (both must agree), the case will come to trial before a judge. If either party demands a jury trial, the case will be set for trial and a jury will be selected (impaneled). (*Assume for the remainder of this discussion that the parties have requested a jury trial.*)

The first step of the trial is to select jurors—called **petit jurors**—from a panel of prospective jurors summoned to the courthouse for jury duty. They are chosen at random from voter registration lists, driver license lists, and income tax lists. (Traditionally, the number of jurors has been twelve, but many states have reduced that number to eight or even fewer in civil actions.) Those selected must be citizens of the United States and within a certain age group. Some states, like New York State, are loosening the age requirement and now allow citizens of any age beyond adulthood to serve as jurors if they wish to do so. Some other states have eliminated all exemptions from jury duty.

Jurors are subject to examination before serving. This examination to determine potential jurors' qualifications and suitability to serve is called the *voir dire* examination. In the typical procedure, jurors take their seats in the jury box in the courtroom where the case will be heard. The judge and the attorneys then question potential jurors to determine whether they are impartial and will decide the case fairly. A prospective juror who is biased, is related to someone involved in the case, or has an interest in the outcome of the case will be dismissed. This is called **removal for cause.** Each attorney may also question jurors to determine which ones will be most favorable to his or her client's case. Each attorney has a limited number of **peremptory challenges.** This means they can dismiss a limited number of potential jurors arbitrarily without giving any reason.

When the jury has been selected or impaneled, the opposing attorneys make *opening statements*. These statements give the judge and jury an overall picture of the facts and issues in the case and an idea of what each attorney intends to prove.

After the opening statements, the plaintiff presents his or her case. In our case, Heisman will therefore be first to present **evidence**—legal proof—to support Bill Allen's claims. She will do this by questioning witnesses for Allen through **direct examination.** (If witnesses do not voluntarily appear to testify, they can be ordered to do so by means of a court order called a **subpoena.**) Heisman may also present further evidence in the form of documents or charts, such as Allen's hospital record and other medical records attesting to his serious internal injuries, the painful therapy, and the fact that he will be paralyzed for the rest of his life. The attorney for Laiden Trucking

Company as the opposing attorney may then cross-examine Allen's witnesses. The purpose of **cross-examination** is to enable the opposing attorney to discover and bring to the attention of the jury any false or inconsistent statements that Allen's witnesses have made in their direct testimony. When all of Allen's witnesses have been questioned, the trucking company's attorney calls his or her witnesses for direct examination. Allen's attorney will then have a chance to cross-examine these witnesses.

After all the evidence has been presented, the attorneys make their *closing arguments,* summarizing for the jury the testimony supporting their clients and arguing that they should win the case because they have proved their cases by a *preponderance of evidence*—their evidence is more convincing than that presented by the opposing side. The judge then instructs or *charges the jury,* which means that he or she advises the jurors of the rules of law that must be applied to the facts presented during the trial. In this case, because Allen is suing for negligence, part of the judge's instructions to the jury will state the elements that must exist to constitute negligence. Following the instructions, the jurors retire to the jury room to discuss the facts in the case. When they reach a **verdict**—a decision—the jurors return to the courtroom. (In some states, the verdict does not have to be unanimous in a civil case.) After the verdict is announced in open court, a judgment is entered. A **judgment** is the official decision of the jury entered into the court record. If a jury verdict awards Allen $3,000,000, for example, the court clerk at the request of the judge will enter the amount in the court records as a judgment against Laiden Trucking Company. After the judgment is entered in the records, the case is then said to be decided or **adjudicated.**

POSTTRIAL PROCEEDINGS

The party who loses the lawsuit has options. One option is to appeal the decision of the trial court to a higher court. (The appeals procedure was discussed in Chapter 2.) If the Laiden Trucking Company loses to Bill Allen and has to pay him $3,000,000, the company, through its attorney, may request a higher court to review the case. The attorney may ask that the trial court's decision be reversed or at least modified—reducing the amount of damages—or may request a new trial. Such a request is unlikely to happen, however, unless the trial court judge made a critical legal error during the trial. For example, in this case, the attorney for Laiden Trucking may show that the judge disallowed certain evidence that the attorney wanted to introduce and that was favorable to the company, which may have changed the outcome of the jury's decision.

As noted in Chapter 2, the appeals procedure is not simple. It requires a lot of preparation on the part of the attorneys and consequently is quite expensive. (In an appeal, attorney's fees could run as high as 45 percent of the amount collected as money damages, instead of the usual 33.33 percent.)

Not all legal disputes end up in a courtroom. Increasing numbers of individuals and businesses in the United States who are frustrated about the expensive, stressful, and time-consuming nature of the judicial process are voluntarily giving up their day in court and agreeing to participate in other, faster, and less expensive ways of settling their disputes. Some of these alternative programs are arbitration, mediation, minitrials, the summary jury trial, a private trial, and informal settlement between the parties. These programs, especially arbitration and mediation, are becoming the trend in resolving disputes that arise in business and industry. For example, the number of disputes between corporate employers and their employees involving termination or forced retirement has increased, and the expense of litigating these disputes has escalated in recent years. Businesses have responded by including in their labor contracts with employees a clause that requires the parties to submit their disputes to arbitration or mediation and, in some cases, minitrials. One big advantage of this method is that disputes can be dealt with while they are "live," rather than having the parties reconstruct facts at great cost years later before judges or juries.

Arbitration

In **arbitration,** a dispute is brought before one arbitrator or a panel of arbitrators—a neutral third party or parties who listen(s) to both sides of the story and then decide(s) what the settlement should be. The decision of the arbitrator(s) called an **award,** is binding on both parties. This means that the parties must comply with the award.

The arbitrator may be an attorney or a person who is not an attorney but who is skilled in an area that is the subject of the dispute. A list of arbitrators is available through such organizations as the American Arbitration Association. Arbitration cases are scheduled for hearings quite rapidly, and the normal rules of evidence are often waived. It is usually not necessary for a party to be represented by an attorney at an arbitration hearing. The parties agree in advance to be bound by the decision of the arbitrator or arbitrators and not to appeal the case to a formal court unless either party can show that a gross error or fraud took place in the proceedings or that the award was illegal. Unless specifically required to by the agreement, the arbitrator may not provide the reasons for rendering the decision.

Better Business Bureaus provide arbitration services to consumers who have complaints against merchants. Individuals selected to arbitrate for the Better Business Bureaus are generally volunteers, such as high school teachers, college professors, businesspeople, and other professionals, who are given training in arbitration procedures.

Business owners who don't want the delays, legal fees, and public exposure that accompany lawsuits have turned to arbitration. Binding arbitration clauses are often added to business contracts. In some communities, referral to arbitration is mandatory for civil cases involving a certain sum of money.

Mediation

Another method of resolving disputes outside of court is **mediation.** Mediation is similar to arbitration except that a decision reached through mediation is only advisory, not binding. The mediator, generally a person with expertise in the disputed area, helps the parties reach agreement and offers recommendations for settlement. Mediation is particularly useful in settling labor disputes to achieve better working conditions and wages, in resolving insurance claim disputes, and in family conflicts. In such cases, advice from a third party may be invaluable.

Minitrials

The minitrial has also been used successfully by large corporations in cases involving complex litigation. Lawyers for both sides present their case to a neutral adviser, and the plaintiff and defendant (generally officers of the corporation with decision-making powers) are both present. These presentations may last a few days and will include an exchange of information; opposing lawyers will point out the strengths and weaknesses of their respective positions. To support their positions, the attorneys may produce witnesses and documents.

At the end of the presentations, with some questioning in both directions, the plaintiff and defendant will retire, without their lawyers, to consider what they've heard. If this first stage of the minitrial does not produce a settlement, the minitrial adviser lets the parties know how he or she thinks the case would be decided in court. The plaintiff and defendant take this additional information and try to work out a solution. This process, which requires intensive, direct communication between plaintiff and defendant, helps each side reach a better understanding of the other's position and thus enhances the chance for a settlement that will be less costly than going to court.

The Summary Jury Trial

The summary jury trial is used for cases that would normally be heard by a jury. The opposing lawyers present a summary of their cases to a "sample" jury of five or six people. The lawyers then converse with jury members and ask such questions as "Why did you reach that decision?" The jury's decision, although it has no binding effect, gives the lawyers some idea of how a jury might decide in an actual trial. When the lawyers see the reaction of the sample jury, they may temper their positions and negotiate a settlement.

Private Trial

The private trial is an approach based on the "rent-a-judge" concept. The disputing parties hire a retired judge with the power to enter a legally binding judgment. A number of states have passed legislation giving these judges the power to try cases and to make decisions relative to these cases. The judges are paid by the hour (the current rate is about $125) plus administrative costs. This approach to settling disputes has led to the creation of firms that employ retired judges of many ranks for hire to those in need of their services.

Informal Settlement Between Parties

Many disputes are settled informally by the parties themselves, without resort to third parties, litigation, or any of the alternatives described above. Many people decide to settle informally after talking with an attorney and discovering the merits of settling a dispute in this fashion. The attorney may view the client's case as weak and suggest that more could be gained by simply sitting down and talking with the other party to the dispute. Most people dislike trouble, and many fear engaging in any kind of legal "warfare." Sometimes our values encourage compromise and settlement, but our stubborn side tells us to push on and cling to the "I'll show him (or her)" attitude. A compromise and settlement may lay the legal matter to rest quickly, make you feel better personally, and allow you to divert the funds that you would otherwise spend to more worthwhile endeavors. Of course, if informal compromise and settlement doesn't work, don't leap to litigation. Try the alternatives to litigation discussed in this chapter. Remember, litigation should be your last resort!

Summary of Important Legal Concepts

If legal disputes cannot be resolved informally by the parties themselves through agreement and compromise, they may end up in court. Settlement by litigation—a lawsuit—is expensive, time-consuming, and emotionally draining, and the outcome of the court trial is uncertain. Besides, the person being sued may be judgment proof.

People who, after discussing their options with an attorney, decide that their case cannot be settled in any other way generally end up in court. Before a court trial takes place, however, the plaintiff's attorney prepares and delivers to the defendant a complaint (the basis for the legal action) and a summons (a written notice to appear in court). Through an attorney, the defendant then issues a response called an answer. Once the issues in the case are known (taken from the complaint and the answer), pretrial proceedings follow. Pretrial proceedings usually consist of motions, discovery, and a pretrial conference.

If no settlement is reached at these proceedings, the case will come to trial.

If the plaintiff and defendant do not demand a jury trial, the evidence in the case will be presented to a judge alone. If either party demands a jury trial, the first step before the trial begins is to select, or impanel, a jury. Once the jury is impaneled, each attorney—the attorney for the plaintiff and the attorney for the defendant—presents evidence to this jury to support his or her client's case. After all the evidence has been presented, the judge instructs the jury as to the law that must be applied in the case. The jury then deliberates and reaches a verdict. After the verdict is announced in the courtroom, it is officially recorded in the record as a judgment against the losing party. The party who loses the lawsuit may appeal the case to a higher court.

Increasing numbers of people are turning to quicker, less expensive ways to settle their legal problems—for example arbitration, mediation, minitrials, the summary jury trial, and private trials.

The general steps followed in criminal and civil cases are compared in Table 5.1.

Key Legal Terms to Know

Match the terms with the definitions that follow.

adjudicated
answer
arbitration
award
complaint

cross-examination
defendant
deposition
direct examination
discovery
evidence
judgment
litigation
mediation
motion
peremptory challenges
petit jurors
plaintiff
pretrial conference

TABLE 5.1 Comparison of Civil and Criminal* Procedures

Civil	Criminal*
1. *Complaint.* Paper prepared by injured party's (plaintiff's) attorney informing defendant of the reasons for legal action. Complaint accompanied by a summons officially announcing to the defendant the commencement of a lawsuit based on the allegations (claims) made in the complaint.	1. *Arrest.* Accused person taken into custody, "booked" (record of arrest entered in police records), fingerprinted and photographed, interrogated, released on bail, or confined.
2. *Answer.* Defendant forwards to plaintiff's attorney a response to the charges made in the complaint. Defendant will be in default for failure to respond to complaint.	2. *Initial appearance.* Accused informed of the charges and advised of his or her legal rights. Judge reviews case and possibly dismisses charges; or, accused is released on bail (if not already released) or confined.
3. *Pretrial proceedings.* Consists of filing motions, discovery, and pretrial conference.	3. *Preliminary Hearing.* (Some states) Formal hearing with attorneys present to evaluate evidence against accused. Judge reviews evidence and possibly dismisses charges.
4. *Trial.* Selection of jury. Presentation of evidence by attorneys to the jury (or a judge if a nonjury trial). To win a successful verdict, an attorney must prove his or her case by a preponderance of evidence (evidence more convincing than that of opposing counsel). In some states, verdict of jury need not be unanimous.	4. *Grand jury proceeding.* Prosecutor (D.A.) presents evidence to the grand jury, which then brings formal charges against the accused (an indictment) or dismisses the charges for lack of evidence. (Formal charges in some states are made by the D.A. through issuance of a document called an information, the contents of which are based on evidence obtained from the preliminary hearing.)
5. *Judgment.* The official decision of the jury is entered in the court record. Case is now said to be adjudicated.	5. *Arraignment.* Formal notification to accused of charges against him or her made in the indictment or information. Accused is then asked for a plea of guilty or not guilty. If accused pleads guilty, date for sentencing is set. (There is no trial.) If accused pleads not guilty, pretrial hearings are scheduled. Bail may be reexamined.
6. *Appeal.* The party who loses the lawsuit has the option to appeal the decision of the trial court to a higher court.	

TABLE 5.1 Comparison of Civil and Criminal* Procedures (cont.)

Civil	Criminal*
	6. *Pretrial proceedings.* Hearings on behalf of accused asking that charges be dismissed for various reasons. Plea negotiations may also take place. If these hearings do not bring results, the case is scheduled for trial.
	7. *Trial.* Selection of jury. Presentation of evidence by the prosecutor (D.A.) for the state and by the accused (generally by accused's attorney) to the jury (or to a judge alone if a nonjury trial). Guilty verdict by jury must be unanimous (in most states), and must be proven beyond a reasonable doubt. If convicted, date is set for sentencing.
	8. *Sentence.* Presentence report made detailing defendant's previous criminal record and his or her personal, social, and emotional background. Sentence may be prison, fine, probation, community-based programs, or a combination of these.
	9. *Appeal.* Defendant may request review of case by higher court if found guilty in lower court. If defendant is found not guilty, the prosecutor cannot appeal the case.

*Based on the proceedings in a felony case.

removal for cause

subpoena

summons

verdict

voir dire

1. Questioning a witness by the attorney who called the witness
2. A written statement detailing a defendant's response to a plaintiff's complaint
3. Jurors selected for a civil or criminal trial
4. The term given to a dispute that has legally been decided
5. A written notice informing a party that a lawsuit has been initiated against him or her
6. Any type of proof presented at trial to support a fact
7. Pretrial steps taken by the plaintiff and the defendant to learn the details of a case
8. The decision of a jury
9. A lawsuit

10. A court order requiring a person to give testimony in a case
11. A document that sets out the facts and circumstances that form the basis for a lawsuit
12. Hearing that is held before a trial in which parties discuss the facts and that may lead to a settlement of a case
13. Questioning of a witness by the attorney who did not produce the witness
14. The submission of a dispute to a neutral third party for settlement
15. The person who sues in a civil action
16. The binding decision of an arbitrator
17. Request to a judge for a ruling on a point of law
18. The party against whom criminal charges or a lawsuit is brought
19. The official decision of a jury entered into the court record
20. Dismissal of a prospective juror during jury selection based upon the juror's inability to render an impartial decision

21. The process of questioning potential jurors by the judge and opposing attorneys to determine their fitness to serve as jurors
22. The right of each attorney to dismiss prospective jurors arbitrarily without having to state a reason
23. Nonbinding, advisory intervention by a third person to settle a dispute between two parties
24. Testimony of a witness under oath, taken outside the court and put in writing for use as evidence during a court proceeding

Questions and Problems to Discuss

1. Rose Gallup purchased a new automobile from a car dealer in her home town. After Gallup drove the car 20,000 miles, problems occurred with the engine, air conditioner, radiator, and power steering gear rack. The dealer refused to do anything about these problems, claiming that the warranty period on the car had expired and claiming further that the problems were the result of normal wear and tear on the car. Gallup decided to bring legal action against the dealer for $1,500, the amount it would cost to repair the car. Is a lawsuit Gallup's best course of action? Explain.
2. What effect do motions made by either the plaintiff or the defendant, and granted by the judge, have on the course of the litigation?
3. What is the purpose of discovery as a pretrial procedure?
4. Outline and briefly describe the steps in a civil trial; begin with the opening statements by the attorneys.
5. Compare petit jury with grand jury as mentioned in Chapter 3. How are they similar? How do they differ?
6. Describe three alternatives to litigation for settling legal disputes.
7. In your opinion, what could be done to encourage parties to settle out of court instead of pursuing litigation?
8. Gruhn was fraudulently induced to make a large stock purchase from a broker who was a member of the New York Stock Exchange. The stock was actually of little value. Claiming damages of $75,000, Gruhn agreed to arbitrate her case under the New York Stock Exchange rules. Without explanation, the arbitrator awarded her $500. Can Gruhn appeal her case to a court of law?
9. Compare the burden of proof required in a civil case mentioned in this chapter with the burden of proof required in a criminal case as mentioned in Chapter 3. Why do you think a higher burden of proof is required in a criminal case?
10. This chapter described a lawsuit involving Bill Allen, a thirty-five-year-old advertising executive and the Laiden Trucking Company. Allen sued Laiden for $3,000,000. Based on the facts in this case, do you think a jury would consider this amount excessive? Why or why not?
11. Why do you think a court is reluctant to impose a default judgment?
12. In conducting the *voir dire* examination for the trial of *Bill Allen* v. *The Laiden Trucking Company*, Allen's attorney Jan Heisman got the following response from a prospective juror:
   Heisman: "Have you been reading the newspaper accounts or listened to any news reports about the accident in question?"
   Juror: "Yes. After reading and listening to the reports, I felt that Allen should assume much of the responsibility for the accident."
   What step should Heisman take at this time to protect Allen from this prospective juror?
13. Can Heisman, as attorney for Bill Allen, request that a juror be dismissed simply because Heisman has the feeling that this juror will be detrimental to Allen's case?
14. Bill Allen retained (hired) Heisman, his attorney, on a contingency-fee basis. Explain how Heisman will be paid under this type of fee arrangement. (Mention a major argument in favor of a contingency-fee basis for retaining an attorney.)
15. What are some of the advantages to settling disputes informally without resort to litigation or other third-party alternatives?
16. Why has the United States become a litigious society (a society prone to lawsuits)?

Blake Johnson, an intern at a local hospital, was driving on the road that bordered a lake when he noticed that a swimmer was having trouble in the middle of the lake and appeared in danger of drowning. Johnson parked his car and, at great risk to himself, dove into the water—not knowing how deep the water was or how cold it might be. He reached the swimmer, who was thrashing in the water and, fearing that the swimmer might pull him under, grabbed the swimmer around the neck and towed him to shore. Because of the way that Johnson struggled with the swimmer and swam with him to safety, the swimmer suffered a broken neck, resulting in paralysis.

The swimmer brought an action against Johnson for negligence as the cause of the injuries that he sustained.

The Trial

During the trial, the intern testified that he was an excellent swimmer and had taken courses in lifesaving and water safety. A medical expert testified that the neck injuries sustained by the swimmer could only have been caused by the manner in which Johnson towed the swimmer to shore. Johnson testified that he had used his best efforts to save the swimmer's life but that he might have used other means of towing the swimmer to shore had the swimmer not been thrashing around so much.

The Arguments at Trial

During the trial, the attorney for the swimmer argued that negligence could exist in this type of case regardless of Johnson's motive and that Johnson should be judged by the standard of reasonable care. The attorney further argued that there was no proof that the swimmer would have drowned had Johnson not come to his rescue and that both as a physician and as an excellent swimmer with lifesaving experience, Johnson should have taken greater reasonable care in attempting to save the swimmer's life.

Johnson's attorney argued that in almost all states in the United States, Johnson had no legal or moral obligation to attempt to save the swimmer's life. However, in attempting to save the swimmer's life at great risk to his own, Johnson should not be held liable for negligence even if his lifesaving activities produced the injuries that actually occurred. Johnson's attorney further argued that if good samaritans are held liable for negligence, there will ultimately be no good samaritans—and people who might otherwise be saved will die.

Questions to Discuss

1. Who has the stronger arguments, the swimmer or Johnson? Why?
2. Do you need any additional information to determine the facts?
3. If you were the judge or jury hearing this case, for whom would you decide? Why?
4. What type of legislation, if any, do you think should be enacted to protect good samaritans against whom actions are brought for negligence?

PART II

CONTRACTS

1 Recognize the requirements of a valid contract.

2 Classify contracts as being either valid, void, voidable, or unenforceable.

3 Explain the requirements of a valid offer and acceptance, the first important elements in a binding contract.

4 Summarize the various forms of consideration, when consideration is necessary to form a binding contract, and the exceptions to the rule requiring the presence of consideration in a contract.

5 Determine what makes parties competent to contract and the effects of various incapacities.

6 Distinguish between a legal and an illegal agreement and the consequences of entering into an illegal agreement.

7 Demonstrate a knowledge of the six types of contracts that are frequently required to be in writing to be enforceable and point out the effects of failure to comply with the writing requirement.

8 Point out the circumstances in which parties to a contract may transfer their rights and obligations after the contract has been made.

9 Summarize ways in which contracts may be ended and the various remedies available to the parties for breach of the contract.

Chapter 6

The Basics of Contract Law

CHAPTER PREVIEW

This chapter is the first of nine chapters dealing with contracts. It defines what a contract is and in what circumstances a contract is not formed, identifies the essential elements necessary to form a contract, and then briefly discusses each element. The remainder of this chapter is devoted to the terminology associated with contract law. An example is also included of a special type of contract that the law creates to prevent a person from unjustly receiving a benefit at the expense of another person. A sample contract is presented in the chapter to show what a typical written contract looks like.

WHAT A CONTRACT IS

A **contract** is any agreement between two or more parties that a court will enforce because the agreement creates legally binding obligations between or among the parties. No aspect of modern life is free from contractual relationships. You make a contract when you take your car to a garage for repairs, enroll in a college, rent an apartment, purchase a stereo, sell your bicycle, buy something at a garage sale, take clothes to the cleaners, use your credit card, or have a plumber install a garbage disposal in your house. Each person, or "party," obtains certain rights and assumes certain obligations that will be enforced in a court of law.

■ Hunt promised in writing to resurface Inya's driveway for $700. Under the terms of the contract, Inya has a right to have the driveway resurfaced and an obligation to pay Hunt when the job is completed. Hunt has a right to collect $700 when the job is completed and an obligation to resurface the driveway. ■

Contracts are often simple and easy to understand, as, for example, when you buy clothing in a store or order food in a restaurant. Other contracts, such as buying a car or a house, are more complicated. In some cases, you do not sign your name to a formal document, but that does not make the contract any less significant, since an informal written contract—or even an oral contract—may be binding. Often people fail to realize that a contract has been made and, therefore, also fail to live up to the agreement. If the contract is trivial, no one really suffers if it is broken. But if the contract is important, it causes a hardship if the parties fail to live up to its terms.

People form many agreements that at first glance appear to be contracts but are not real contracts because no legally binding obligations between the parties are created. Such agreements will not be enforced by the courts. A strictly social agreement—generally considered to be one that does not create legally binding economic obligations for the parties or one in which the failure by one party to carry out his or her part of the agreement would not cause the other party to suffer damage recognizable by courts—is an example of an agreement that a court will not enforce.

■ Marlo, president of a small-town bank, agreed to drive you, a large depositor at the bank, to the golf course. Marlo forgets and you have to take a taxi. ■

■ Cohen, a close friend, agreed to sell her 1980 car for $1,000, and you agreed to buy it. ■

The courts would hold that the first example, the invitation to drive you to the golf course, is admittedly an agreement but it is a social agreement and, therefore, legally unenforceable. Marlo will not be required to pay your taxi fare. The second example, the sale of the used car, created binding economic obligations on both sides and is enforceable in court. Cohen, therefore, must sell you the car and you must buy it.

THE ELEMENTS OF A VALID CONTRACT

Four essential elements must be present for an agreement to have the status of a contract: agreement, consideration, competent parties, and legal purpose (see Figure 6.1). These elements are introduced briefly below, but each element will be covered in detail in Chapters 7–10.

Agreement is the initial step toward forming a contract. It is accomplished by a process called *offer* and *acceptance*. The person who makes the offer is called the *offeror*. The person to whom the offer is made is called the *offeree*. When the offeree accepts an offer, the first requirement of a valid contract has been satisfied.

■ Hudek (the offeror) offered to sell Hopkins (the offeree) some camera equipment for $300. Hopkins accepted the offer. This was offer and acceptance, one of the elements of a binding contract. ■

Figure 6.1
The Elements of a Valid Contract

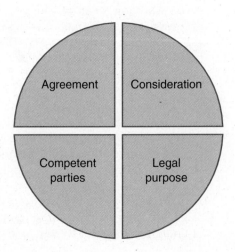

Agreement

Consideration

Competent parties

Legal purpose

Consideration is something of value exchanged by each party to bind the agreement. Consideration may be money or it may be property, such as a watch or a car.

Consideration may also consist of doing something you are not legally bound to do, refraining from doing something you have a legal right to do, or promising to do or not to do something.

- At a garage sale O'Grady agreed to buy a set of used encyclopedias from Moran for $100. The $100 and the set of encyclopedias are the consideration for this contract. ■

- A seriously ill uncle offered Ling, a pharmacy student at a local college, $10,000 to leave school and run the uncle's business. Ling agreed. Because Ling had a legal right to continue in pharmacy school, this act of refraining (not continuing in pharmacy school) was consideration for the uncle's promise to pay Ling the $10,000. ■

Competent parties are those people who have the legal and mental ability to enter into binding contracts. In the eyes of the law, however, some parties lack the ability to enter into contracts freely. These people may legally avoid (cancel) contracts made with others and demand the return of the consideration paid. Among those not considered competent are minors (in most states, persons under the age of eighteen), persons under the influence of alcohol and other drugs, and mentally ill persons.

- Harris, age sixteen, lives in a state where the legal age for making contracts is eighteen. She entered into a contract with Michaels, an adult, to buy computer software for her computer but then changed her mind. Since Harris is a minor, she can legally avoid the contract. ■

Legal purpose means that the contract must not be against the law. The courts will not enforce a contract if the parties knowingly enter into an illegal agreement and then demand performance. This is true even if all the other elements of a contract are present. A contract that interferes with the proper administration of justice is one example of an illegal contract.

- You were an eyewitness to an automobile accident caused by a negligent driver. The driver who caused the accident promised you $1,000 if you would not testify at the upcoming trial. You agreed not to testify. Since this contract interferes with the proper administration of justice, it is illegal and would not be enforced by a court. ■

If offer and acceptance, considerations, competent parties, and legal purpose are present, a contract has been created. If any one element is missing, a contract does not exist and the agreement will not be enforced against either party by a court of law. If one of the parties does not carry out her or his part of the contract, that person may be sued for breach of contract. *Breach of contract* is the failure to carry out one's part of the agreement. Breach of contract is discussed in detail in Chapter 14.

It should be noted at this time that for certain types of contracts, there is another requirement: the agreement must be in writing. This requirement will be discussed in Chapter 11.

CONTRACT TERMINOLOGY

All contracts may be classified in the following ways: (1) bilateral or unilateral; (2) valid, void, voidable, or unenforceable; (3) formal or informal; (4) express or implied; and (5) executory or executed. These classifications are not mutually exclusive and may apply to the same contract. Consequently, a contract could be express, valid, bilateral, and informal.

Bilateral and Unilateral Contracts

A contract is either bilateral or unilateral (see Figure 6.2). An offer for a **bilateral contract** is one in which a promise (offer) is made by one party in return for a promise made by another party. In other words, both the offeror and the offeree make promises.

> Oliver promised to pay Douglas $500 if Douglas promised to drive Oliver's car from Los Angeles to Boston. As soon as Douglas promises to perform the act required, a bilateral contract will be formed (a promise for a promise). ■

An offer for a **unilateral contract** is one in which a promise (offer) is made by one party in return for the performance of a specific act by the other party.

> Noble promised to pay Duffy $35 if he washed and waxed Noble's car. The contract is not effective until Duffy actually performs the act of washing and waxing Noble's car (a promise for an act). ■

Figure 6.2
Ways in Which Parties Reach Agreement

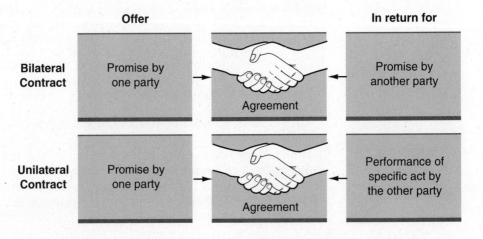

	Offer		In return for
Bilateral Contract	Promise by one party	Agreement	Promise by another party
Unilateral Contract	Promise by one party	Agreement	Performance of specific act by the other party

Valid, Void, Voidable, and Unenforceable Contracts

Contracts may be classified in terms of their enforceability. A **valid contract** is one that contains all the essential elements of a contract: offer and acceptance, consideration, competent parties, and legal purpose. It is legally binding on all parties to the agreement.

> Colt, a competent party, offered to sell some fence posts to Craft, also a competent party, for $100. Craft accepted. This is a valid contract because it has all the essential elements of a contract. ■

Technically, a void contract is not a contract at all. A **void contract** has no legal effect and neither party can enforce the contract against the other in a court of law. A void contract usually is an agreement that lacks any one of the essential elements of a contract or that has a subject matter which, unknown to the parties, does not exist at the time the agreement is made, thus making performance impossible.

> You purchased a CD player that you knew was stolen. Since selling stolen property is illegal, the essential element of legal purpose is missing. The contract is void and therefore unenforceable by either party to the agreement. ■

A **voidable contract** is a contract that is completely enforceable against all parties unless and until a party legally entitled to avoid the contract decides to do so. A minor, for example, may avoid some contracts.

> Miller, a minor, purchased some sports equipment for $200 from Darby, an adult who owned Darby Sporting Goods. Two days later, Miller returned the merchandise and asked for a refund, claiming the equipment was no longer needed. Because he is a minor, Miller has the right to avoid the contract and get his money back. Until it is canceled, however, the contract is enforceable against both parties. ■

An **unenforceable contract** is one that is legal in all respects but fails to meet some requirement of the law. As a result, a court will not enforce the contract against either party. For example, the law requires that some contracts, such as contracts for the sale of land, be in writing. If they are not, the contracts are unenforceable, even though they are legal in all other respects.

Formal and Informal Contracts

A **formal contract** is a written contract prepared with certain formalities. A check is one example of a formal contract because it must use a particular form or style of language.

An **informal contract** does not require any particular formalities. The parties are free to use any style of language they wish. Informal contracts may be oral or implied; they do not have to be written unless required by statute. Although the language used in an informal written contract may be as elaborate or as sketchy as the parties desire, it should include the date, the name and address of each party, the consideration of one party, the consideration of the other party, and the signature of each party to the agreement. These elements are shown in the example of an informal, written contract in Figure 6.3.

Express and Implied Contracts

An **express contract** is one in which the agreement is specifically stated. An example of an express contract is an insurance policy, in which all the terms of the contract are written as part of the policy. Express contracts may be either oral or written.

Many contracts are made orally. When you buy gasoline for your car, groceries for your dinner, or film for your camera, you make an oral contract. As simple as these transactions seem, all the necessary elements of a contract are present. Oral contracts should be limited to simple transactions that can be carried out quickly.

Written contracts should be used whenever important matters are involved or the agreement is complicated. Written terms cannot be easily changed. If a misunderstanding arises later, it is easy to establish the terms actually agreed upon. For example, you orally agree with Innes, a friend, to buy her used bicycle for $300. If Innes changes her mind, you could sue her for breach of contract, but you might lose the suit because you lack proof. A written contract of Innes's original intention to sell you the bicycle would make it easier for you to win in court.

It may be harder to prove the existence of oral contracts but, from a practical standpoint, if all contracts had to be in writing, our daily lives would be very complicated.

An **implied contract** (a contract implied in fact) is one in which the parties form a contract from their actions rather than from a specific oral or written agreement.

> You wanted to visit a friend who lives across town. The bus fare was $1.25. You got on the bus and dropped $1.25 into the coin box. The resulting contract is implied, since neither you nor the bus driver agreed either orally or in writing to form a contract. Rather, your actions and those of the bus driver created the contract. ■

In some instances a contract may be partially express and partially implied.

> Johnson was enrolled in the auto technology program at a local college. A classmate asked her to make some repairs to his car but did not mention paying Johnson for the work. Johnson agreed to do the work, expecting to be paid. When the job is completed, the classmate has a legal obligation to pay the "going price" (the price generally charged by mechanics in business for doing the same work). Although the agreement between Johnson and her classmate to make the repairs was express, the agreement by the classmate to pay the going price was implied. ■

CONTRACT

THE COLONIAL HOME IMPROVEMENT COMPANY
18 Brickstone Drive
Washington, D.C. 22182

April 22, 1997

The Colonial Home Improvement Company agrees for the sum of eight thousand dollars ($8,000) to construct a deck at the rear of the premises at 12 Harris Street, Washington, D.C. owned by Ruth Boyd. Said porch shall be constructed of redwood and shall be seven (7) feet in width and ten (10) feet in length, and shall stand five (5) feet off the ground. The expected date of completion is May 13, 1997.

TERMS:

Consideration from Ruth Boyd shall be the sum of one thousand dollars ($1,000) as down payment immediately upon signing the contract. The balance of seven thousand dollars ($7,000) shall be paid as follows:

One thousand dollars ($1,000) upon commencement of construction

Six thousand dollars ($6,000) upon completion of construction

Upon commencement of construction, any payment two days in default shall render the entire balance due and owing.

The Colonial Home Improvement Company agrees to furnish quality building materials; experienced workers; and top quality service. Any dispute arising from the terms of this contract including an interpretation of the term ''quality'' and ''experienced'' shall be settled by arbitration consisting of two (2) arbitrators, one of whom must be a member of the Building Trades Association.

This writing constitutes the full agreement and understanding of the parties signed herein.

Mark Peterson

The Colonial Home
Improvement Company

Ruth Boyd

Customer/Homeowner

**Figure 6.3
Informal Written
Contract**

In certain cases the courts create a fictional contract, called a *quasi contract,* in order to promote justice. A **quasi contract** (a contract implied in law) means "as if there were a contract." Actually, no real promises have been made by the parties and none of the other elements of a true contract are present. The courts create the quasi contract so that one party will not be *unjustly enriched* (that is, receive a benefit) at the expense of the other party. For example, Dr. Restov comes upon the scene of an accident and renders the necessary medical aid to Claire, who is injured and unconscious. Restov has a claim in quasi contract against Claire for the reasonable value of services rendered. The explanation for allowing Restov to collect is that Claire, if able, would have promised to pay for the services rendered and, therefore, the court will impose that promise on Claire.

Executory and Executed Contracts

In regard to performance, a contract is either executory or executed. An **executory contract** is one that has not been fully performed by one or all of the parties. An **executed contract** refers to a contract in which all parties have completely carried out their parts of the contract.

■ You hire a friend to install a stereo system in your new car. At this time, the contract is executory because neither party has performed. When your friend completes the job satisfactorily and presents the bill to you, the contract is still executory because you have not yet paid for the work. When you pay your friend, the contract will be executed because it has been completely performed by both parties. ■

Summary of Important Legal Concepts

A contract is any agreement between individuals that a court will enforce because it creates legally binding rights and obligations. Some agreements appear to be contracts but are only social in nature and are therefore legally unenforceable in the courts.

A valid contract must fulfill the following four requirements: (1) agreement, reached through a process called offer and acceptance; (2) consideration, something of value given up by each party; (3) competent parties, those having the legal and mental ability to enter into binding contracts; and (4) legal purpose, an agreement not against the law.

Contracts may be classified as bilateral and unilateral; valid, void, voidable, and unenforceable; formal and informal; express and implied; and executory and executed. These classifications are not mutually exclusive and in fact may apply to the same contract.

In certain cases, the law considers it unjust that a person should receive a benefit (called unjust enrichment) at the expense of another person. Under these circumstances, a court-created contract (called a quasi contract) allows the person who conferred the benefit to recover its value from the benefited

person, even though there is no contract between the two parties requiring any payment.

Key Legal Terms to Know

Match the terms with the definitions that follow.

contract
bilateral contract
executed contract
executory contract
express contract
formal contract
implied contract
informal contract
quasi contract
unenforceable contract
unilateral contract
valid contract
void contract
voidable contract

1. A contract that contains all the essential elements and is legally binding on all parties
2. A contract in which an agreement is specifically stated in spoken or written words
3. A contract that is completely enforceable against all parties unless and until a party legally entitled to avoid the contract does so
4. A written contract prepared with certain formalities
5. A contract in which a promise is made by one party in return for a promise by another party
6. A contract that is legal in all respects but fails to meet some requirement of the law
7. A contract that has no legal effect and cannot be enforced against either party
8. A contract formed by the actions of the parties rather than by their spoken or written words
9. A legally binding agreement between two or more parties enforceable in a court of law
10. A contract implied in law
11. A contract in which a promise is made by one party in return for the performance of a specific act by another party
12. A contract fully performed by all parties
13. An oral, written, or implied contract that is not prepared with certain formalities
14. A contract that has not been fully performed

Questions and Problems to Discuss

1. The Radiant Heating and Air Conditioning Company installed a central air-conditioning unit in Randy's house. At the time of signing the contract with Radiant Heating, Randy made a down payment. However, she has not as yet paid the balance due. Is her contract with Radiant Heating executory or executed?
2. Stacy agreed to sell Haag a set of used encyclopedias if she paid him $150. Haag paid Stacy the $150. Is this contract
   a. valid, voidable, or void?
   b. express or implied?
   c. unilateral or bilateral?
3. Flynn, a popular college athlete, agreed to take Alison, one of his many friends, to the college sports banquet. A few days prior to the banquet, Flynn changed his mind and decided to take another friend. Although Alison had not yet spent the money to purchase a new dress, she felt humiliated and embarrassed. Does Alison have a claim against Flynn for breach of contract?
4. Stacey, out of a job and on welfare, was arrested on suspicion of burglary. Following his arrest, the city's legal aid bureau provided free legal services for his defense. After he was acquitted of the crime, however, the legal aid bureau discovered that Stacey had hidden assets and actually did not qualify for the free legal services he received. The city sued Stacey for the value of the services provided. Must Stacey now pay for them?
5. By telephone, McKay agreed to buy Dodd's CB radio for $75. When Dodd attempted to deliver the radio, McKay refused to accept it, claiming the contract was not enforceable because it was not in writing. Is McKay correct?
6. While shopping at a grocery store, Garr took a carton of soft drinks from a shelf, placed it in her shopping cart with other food products, and paid her bill to the cashier at the check-out counter. Because of a defect in one of the soft drink cans, Garr cut her mouth while drinking the beverage. She sued the grocery store for her injuries. As a defense, the store claimed it could not be sued because it never made a contract with Garr for the sale of the soft drinks. Was the grocery store correct?
7. Ross, who was being sued, offered to pay Cone $500 if Cone would appear as a witness and give false testimony that would be favorable to Ross. Cone agreed. Was Cone legally entitled to the $500? Why or why not?
8. Hart agreed in writing to hire Page as a salesperson in Hart's appliance store for $1,200 a month. When Page received his first month's pay, the check was written for only $1,100, $100 less than the contract amount. Page insisted on the full $1,200. Hart refused, claiming that business was not good and the extra $100 was needed to pay bills. Is Page entitled to the full $1,200 for the month's work?
9. Compare and contrast an implied contract and a quasi contract.
10. Griffin went away for the weekend to a resort area. While he was gone, a lawn service seeded his lawn and landscaped his backyard by mistake. The lawn service had actually contracted with Griffin's neighbor. Nevertheless, the lawn service billed Griffin for $750. Griffin refused to

pay, claiming he had not contracted with them to have lawn work done. Is Griffin liable for the payment?

Cases to Decide

1. Michelle and Lee Marvin, who lived together from October 1964 through May 1970 without marrying, entered into an oral agreement stating that while they lived together they would share their earnings and all property acquired, and they would hold themselves out to the general public as husband and wife. Michelle even took Lee's name. She agreed to give up her career as an entertainer and singer to devote herself full time to Lee as a companion, homemaker, housekeeper, and cook. In return, Lee agreed to provide her with financial support for the rest of her life. In May 1970, Lee asked Michelle to leave and refused to provide further support for her. She then sued him for one-half of the money and property acquired during the time they lived together. Lee defended on the grounds that Michelle was not entitled to anything. He claimed that their agreement was illegal, having been based on an immoral and illicit relationship in which Michelle was to perform sexual favors for him. Michelle claimed that, although part of their relationship was sexual, the agreement to live together with Lee was not tied to their engaging in sexual relations but rather to sharing their earnings and property rights. Is Michelle entitled to her claim? (*Marvin* v. *Marvin*, 557, P.2d 106 Cal.)

2. Dobos was admitted to a hospital with a serious condition that required around-the-clock nursing care. The hospital, on orders from Dobos's doctor, requested Nursing Care Services, Inc. to care for Dobos while she was in the hospital and for a two-week period while she was at home. When Nursing Care Services sent a bill, Dobos claimed she was not liable because she had not signed a written contract or personally made an oral agreement for their services, although she was well aware of what her doctor had requested and readily accepted the care provided. Under what theory can Nursing Care Services collect? (*Nursing Care Services, Inc.* v. *Dobos*, 380 So.2d 516)

3. Schor, a dentist, became ill and asked Radnay, a dental assistant, to handle his patients. He orally agreed to pay Radnay a salary plus a bonus. Radnay was not in fact a dentist and Schor, therefore, refused to pay the salary and the bonus agreed upon. Radnay sued Schor for the amount owed. Was Radnay legally entitled to collect the salary and bonus even though she was not a licensed dentist as required by law? (*Radnay* v. *Schor*, New York 41 Misc 2d 789)

4. Antonucci went to the Stevens auto showroom to discuss the purchase of a pickup truck. After looking over a catalog and discussing the terms, Antonucci signed a purchase order prepared by the dealer and left a $500 deposit. The dealer never signed the form, which stated: "This order will not become binding until accepted by the dealer or his authorized representative." Six weeks later, the truck came in. It was not exactly what Antonucci had ordered and he refused to take it. Did a contract exist between Antonucci and the dealer? (*Antonucci* v. *Stevens Dodge*, New York 73 Misc 2d 173)

5. Swetman and others were college teachers whose contracts expired at the end of the school year. They had been teaching for a number of years and all had tenure (permanent status). However, they had no specific contract for the coming year and applied for unemployment compensation for the summer months. Compensation was denied because the teachers had tenure and both the teachers and the college expected that the teachers would be teaching next year. Was it implied that the teachers would have a teaching job for another year? (*Swetman* v. *Gerace*, Fla 349 So 2d 977)

Chapter 7

Agreement: Offer and Acceptance

This chapter discusses the first and foremost element of any contract—agreement, reached through a process called offer and acceptance. Offer and acceptance are first defined. Then there is a discussion of the offer: what is required to make it valid and how it ends. The chapter concludes with a discussion of the acceptance: who can accept, what makes an acceptance legally binding, and whether a person who has been made an offer assents to it by remaining silent.

HOW AGREEMENT IS REACHED

The first and most important requirement of a legally enforceable contract is that the parties must agree on what the contract is all about. **Offer and acceptance,** often called mutual assent or a "meeting of the minds," is the process by which the parties to a contract agree to its terms. An **offer** is a *promise* by one person to do something if the other person either *performs* an act or *promises* to do or not to do something. An **acceptance** takes place when the person to whom the offer was made agrees to do what was requested in the offer. The **offeror** (promisor) is the person making the offer (promise) and the **offeree** (promisee) is the person to whom the offer (promise) is made.

> You (the offeror) say to Malloy, "I'll sell [meaning I promise to sell] you my golf clubs for $200." If Malloy (the offeree) says, "I'll buy them at that price," she has accepted your offer (promise). If the other elements are present, a contract is formed. ■

THE OFFER

The first step toward making a contract is for the offeror to make an offer (a promise) to the offeree. It is essential that the offer be seriously intended, definite, and communicated to the offeree by the offeror.

Offer Must Be Seriously Intended

The offerer must clearly and seriously intend to make an offer to the offeree. If no offer is intended, acceptance by the offeree cannot result in a legally binding agreement. An offer obviously made in jest, anger, or under great excitement is not binding on the offerer.

> Your expensive new lawnmower has been giving you a lot of trouble. After it stopped running several times while you were mowing the lawn, you yelled to your neighbor, "For five bucks, I'll sell you this lemon!" Your neighbor said, "You've got a deal." Your neighbor then came over to you and held out $5. Since you were obviously angry at the time you made the statement, you did not make a valid offer and do not have to sell the lawnmower. ■

If the offeree as a reasonable person (average individual) believes an offer was made seriously, the offer may be accepted. For example, as a joke, you offer to sell a friend an expensive painting worth $1,000 for $100. Your friend, who knows nothing about paintings, accepts the offer. If your friend is honestly unaware of your joke, a binding agreement will result.

Offer Must Be Definite

An offer that is indefinite—not clearly stated, vague, or ambiguous—cannot be accepted. A court will not enforce contracts with unclear terms because the court will be unable to determine whether both parties intended to contract.

> ■ Hayness said to Lee, "I'd like to sell my mobile home if I could get a good price for it." Lee promptly replied, "I'll pay you a good price for it."
> Because Hayness's statement was simply one of intention to sell the mobile home at some time in the future and was too indefinite to be taken as an offer, no legal acceptance by Lee was possible. ■

Actually the type of statement that Hayness made to Lee in the above problem may be the start of what is called **preliminary negotiations,** whereby the potential offeror "sounds out" the potential offeree's intention to enter into a contract. The parties will talk back and forth until one party eventually makes a genuine offer that can be accepted.

An offer may be considered definite even though an important detail does not appear in the offer, as long as the parties intended to make a contract. For example, you asked a plumber to come to your house immediately to repair a broken pipe that was flooding your cellar. Although you did not discuss the cost of the repairs ahead of time, a court would decide that a reasonable fee had been implied because of your request (offer) to enter into a contract for the plumber's services. A reasonable fee would be determined by what other plumbers in the area receive for performing the same service.

Offer Must Be Communicated

The offeree must know that an offer has been made and must know the terms of the offer. If not, there can be no legal acceptance by the offeree. The offer may be communicated orally, as by telephone or face to face, or in written form, as by letter or telegram. In either case, the offer must be communicated directly from the offeror or the offer is not valid.

> ■ You mailed a letter to Hughes offering to sell Hughes a used cellular phone for $100. The letter was lost in the mail. Since the letter was never delivered, no offer was communicated to Hughes. ■

An offer may also be implied from the conduct of the offeror. An implied offer results, for example, when you deposit the proper coins in the fare box on a bus. Although you do not state your offer in words, the driver understands that when you deposit the coins you are making an offer.

Invitations to Make Offers

Some things are not considered offers. Advertisements—whether placed in newspapers, magazines, mail order catalogs, and circulars or on radio and television—displays in store windows, price tags on merchandise, and even price quotations that companies send out to customers are ordinarily in this category. The wording used in these examples is too general to form an offer. Most courts consider these advertisements, displays, price tags, and price quotations to be preliminary negotiations, which only invite a potential customer to make an offer to the advertiser to purchase. Because of this interpretation, an advertiser may reject offers, but only for legitimate reasons. Most states have advertising statutes that impose civil or criminal liability upon unethical businesspersons who refuse to sell goods or services in conformity with the terms of their advertisements.

> An advertisement for the Hartman Floor Company appeared in the local newspaper offering floor tiles at 5¢ per tile. The correct price was actually 50¢ per tile. Barnhart entered the store and ordered 200 tiles at 5¢ each. The salesperson refused to sell the tiles at that price, claiming there was an error in the advertisement. Since the newspaper advertisement was only an invitation to make an offer, the store was not obligated to sell the tiles to Barnhart at 5¢ each. ■

If the language used is specific, an advertisement can constitute an offer. The following advertisement is worded in a way that creates an offer: "On Friday, December 6, we will sell one brand-new Arco stereo with component parts for $75 to the first customer who buys $75 worth of cash merchandise."

At auction sales an auctioneer invites members of the audience to make offers. At an ordinary auction, called an auction "with reserve," the bidder makes the offer in the form of a **bid.** Acceptance of a bid takes place when the auctioneer either says "Sold" or lets the gavel fall. The auctioneer does not have to accept a bid, even from the highest bidder. Until acceptance takes place, an article may be withdrawn from the sale by the auctioneer. Likewise, a bidder may withdraw a bid before it is accepted by the auctioneer. All auctions are held "with reserve" unless otherwise announced.

If an auction is announced or advertised to be "without reserve," the auctioneer may not withdraw the article from sale once a bid has been made and must sell it to the highest bidder. The bidder, however, may withdraw a bid at any time before the auctioneer accepts it. Withdrawal of the bid does not automatically restore a prior bid.

How an Offer Ends

An offer ends when it is accepted by the offeree. An offer may also end by lapse of time, rejection, counteroffer, revocation, death or insanity of the offeror or offeree, illegality, and impossibility.

Lapse of Time   If the offer contains a fixed time limit, the offer ends at that time. When no fixed time is stated, the offer ends at the end of a reasonable time. What is a "reasonable" time depends upon the circumstances in each case. Among the factors considered in determining reasonable time are whether the price of the article (such as shares of stock) changes rapidly, whether the article is perishable, or whether the offeror has a chance to sell the article to a third party.

> On April 2 Isaac wrote to Leary and offered to sell several household items for $400. Isaac did not state how long the offer would remain open. On November 10 Leary contacted Isaac and accepted the offer. Isaac, however, refused to sell the items to Leary, claiming that a reasonable time had passed and the offer had ended. ■

Rejection An offer is ended by **rejection** when the offeree refused the offer made by the offeror. The offeree cannot later decide to accept the offer. The offer does not end, however, until the offeror receives notice of the rejection directly from the offeree.

> Macey sent a letter to Stevens offering to sell a fur coat for $750. Stevens sent a return letter to Macey rejecting the offer. A week later Stevens decided to accept the offer. Since the rejection terminated the offer, Stevens could no longer accept it. ■

Counteroffer A **counteroffer** is an offer made by the offeree to the offeror changing the terms of the original offer. The counteroffer ends the original offer and replaces it with a new offer. The two parties now switch roles, and the offeree becomes the offeror. If the original offeror (now the offeree) accepts the counteroffer, a legally binding agreement results.

> Forster, owner of a used car lot, offered to sell you a used car for $1,000. You said, "I'll pay you $900." If Forster accepts your counteroffer, agreement has been reached. ■

A counteroffer may be worded by the offeree in a way that clearly indicates the original offer has not yet been rejected and is still being considered. The offeree may simply wish to find out whether other terms would be acceptable. Under modern law, this inquiry will not prevent the formation of a contract.

> Bean offered to sell Rand six prerecorded cassette tapes for $8 each. Rand replied, "I'm considering your offer, but I think the price is high. Would you take $6 a tape?" ■

In this example, Rand's response to Bean's offer does not end the original offer. Rand was simply asking about the possibility of getting the tapes at a lesser price. He was not indicating an unwillingness to accept the original offer. If Bean states that she will not take anything less than $8 a tape and Rand agrees to pay this amount, a legally binding contract will result.

Revocation The offeror has the legal right to withdraw an offer at any time before it is accepted. Withdrawing an offer is known as **revocation.**

Revocation is possible even though the offeror has promised to hold the offer open for a stated period. The offeror may not be able to revoke the offer, however, if an option exists.

An **option** is actually a contract in which the offeror agrees to hold an offer open and irrevocable for a certain time or until a certain date. In return, the offeree gives the offeror consideration (generally money) to keep the offer open.

> A friend offered to sell you a used amplifier for $100. You gave your friend $20 to hold the offer open for five days. You have five days in which to decide whether or not to buy the amplifier. If you decide to buy the amplifier, your friend must sell it to you for $100 (the $20 is ordinarily applied to the purchase price). If you let the five days pass without making a decision or if you reject the offer, you lose the consideration (the $20) and your friend may sell the amplifier to someone else. ■

The offeror may not revoke the offer during the time the option is in effect if the offeree has paid consideration to the offeror to hold the offer open. If the offeree has not paid any consideration, the offeror may revoke the offer at any time before acceptance, even though promising to hold the offer open for a stated period.

In some states a written promise by the offeror to hold an offer open for an agreed time cannot be revoked even though no consideration is paid by the offeree.

Usually the offeror must notify the offeree directly about the revocation. But the offer also ends if the offeree indirectly hears about the revocation from another person or if the offeror does something that indicates revocation, such as selling the subject of the offer to another person.

> Croft, by telegram, offered to sell Finch a complete set of plans for an apartment complex for $500. Two days later Croft notified Finch that the plans were no longer for sale. Since Finch had not accepted the offer, the revocation was legal and ended the offer. ■

If an offeree has begun to perform the act requested in an offer, and the offeror knows that performance has begun, modern law holds that the offeror generally cannot revoke the offer until the offeree has had a reasonable time to perform. For example, you offer your neighbor $150 to repair the damage to your storage shed, and he begins the work. You can revoke your offer only after your neighbor has had a reasonable time to complete the repairs but has not done so.

An offer that has been properly accepted can no longer be revoked.

> On November 25 Crombach sent a telegram to Mayer offering to sell a camper for $1,500. Mayer sent a telegram to Crombach at 11 A.M. on November 26 accepting the offer. Late in the afternoon of November 26, Crombach telephoned Mayer and indicated that he (Crombach) was withdrawing the offer. The withdrawal of the offer was ineffective because Mayer had already properly accepted the offer. ■

An offer made to the general public may be revoked in the same manner that was used to tell people of the offer. If the announcement of a reward, for example, is placed in a local newspaper, it may be revoked by running another notice in the same paper. A member of the general public who performs the act requested without knowing that the offer has been revoked cannot ask to have the offer enforced. It is impossible to give personal notice to all the people who had learned of the offer.

Death or Insanity   If the offeror dies or becomes insane before the offer is accepted by the offeree, the offer ends even though the offeree does not know of the offeror's death or insanity. An offeror declared insane by the courts is incompetent and, therefore, not able to understand the offer made or the consequences of making the offer.

> ■ Chan offered to sell you a set of golf clubs for $175. You accepted the offer a week later, unaware that Chan had just died in a hunting accident. Your acceptance was not effective because Chan's death ended the offer. ■

The death or insanity of the offeree also terminates an offer. Agreement cannot be reached if the offeree is not alive to accept the offer. Although death ends an offer, it does not terminate a contract already formed before the death of one of the parties (except one for personal services). In the previous example, if you had accepted Chan's offer before he died, a legally binding contract would have been made. The person in charge of Chan's estate would be obligated to sell you the golf clubs.

Illegality   An offer ends if the offer itself becomes illegal before it is accepted by the offeree.

> ■ Kelvin offered Spicer, a contractor, $25,000 to build an addition on her house, which she planned to use as a dental office. Before Spicer accepted the offer, the city passed an ordinance making it illegal to operate such a business in Kelvin's neighborhood. Because the city made it illegal for Kelvin to operate the dental office, the offer ended. ■

Impossibility   An offer ends if the offer becomes impossible to carry out before the offeree accepts it.

> ■ You offered to sell a motorboat to a friend for $900. Before your friend could accept the offer, the boat was destroyed in a fire at the marina where it was docked. Since the boat was destroyed, the offer ended. ■

THE ACCEPTANCE

A legally binding agreement is reached when the offeree accepts the offer made by the offeror. For the acceptance to be valid, it must meet certain requirements. The acceptance must be accepted only by the offeree, agree with the offer, and be communicated to the offeror by the offeree.

Acceptance Only by Offeree

Since the offer is directed only to the offeree, only the offeree can accept it. If a person other than the offeree accepts the offer, the acceptance does not result in a legally binding agreement.

■ You offered to sell Hickman a camera for $75. Hickman refused, but told Agnew, a friend, about the offer. Agnew then accepted your offer. Since the offer was intended only for Hickman, Agnew could not legally accept it. ■

An offer of a reward made to the general public may be accepted by any person who knows of it. This offer is accepted by performing the act requested.

■ The Tri-State Transit Company placed an ad in a local newspaper offering a $1,000 reward to anyone who furnished information leading to the arrest and conviction of the person or persons who had damaged several Tri-State buses. Holmes, who knew Watson was responsible for the damage, learned of the reward and notified the police. Based on Holmes's information, Watson was arrested and convicted. Holmes acted in response to the reward offer and the information given to the police led to Watson's arrest and conviction, and Tri-State was therefore legally obligated to pay Holmes the $1,000. ■

Most states have concluded that the offeree is not entitled to the reward without prior knowledge of the offer. Some states, however, have ruled that a person may collect a reward with or without prior knowledge of the offer. If there has been partial performance before learning of the offer or reward, modern law generally permits the offeree to accept by completing the requested act.

Acceptance Must Agree with the Offer

Under common-law rules, the acceptance must be a "mirror image" of the offer. In other words, the acceptance must match, term by term, what was requested in the offer. Any material change in, or addition to, the terms of the original offer automatically terminates that offer. The acceptance then becomes a counteroffer that need not be accepted. The original offeror can, however, accept the terms of the counteroffer and create a valid contract. Counteroffers were discussed on page 119.

In a *unilateral contract* (a promise for an act), acceptance is the doing of the act requested. For example, you say to Fields, "I promise to give you $20 if you rake my yard and trim the bushes." Acceptance of your offer takes place when Fields completes the yard work. This is a unilateral contract because Fields accepted by performance (completing the yard work), not by a promise (that he would complete the yard work).

In a *bilateral contract* (a promise for a promise), the offeree's promise is the acceptance. For example, you say to Fields, "I promise to give you $20 if you promise to take my yard and trim the bushes." Acceptance of your offer takes place when Fields promises to do the work requested. This is a bilateral contract because Fields accepted by a promise (to complete the yard work), not by performance (completing the yard work).

Often the offeror does not care how the offeree accepts, or it may not be clear from the offer whether acceptance is to be by a promise or by the performance of an act. In either case, modern law permits the offeree to accept the offer either by promising to perform the act requested (creating a bilateral contract) or by actually performing the act (creating a unilateral contract).

In very important transactions, it is common for both parties to sign a written document. If the offeree is required to accept by signing the written document, which has already been signed by the offeror, agreement is reached when the document has been signed by the offeree and delivered to the offeror.

Acceptance Must Be Communicated to the Offeror

An acceptance is not effective until it has been communicated to the offeror. Furthermore, the offeror is in control of the offer. As such, the offeror has the power to determine both the manner (performance or promise) and medium (mail, telegram, etc.) of acceptance. If the offeror asks for performance (a unilateral contract) then the offeree can accept only by doing the act requested. If the offeror specifically seeks a promise (a bilateral contract), then the offeree can accept only by making a promise. In a unilateral contract, once the offeree completes the act requested in the offer, no further communication to the offeror is required. However, as a practical matter, the offeror must know about the completed act before the promise made to the offeree can be carried out.

> You stored your motorcycle at a local motorcycle center for the winter. You agreed to pay a mechanic $100 to make necessary repairs to it. Acceptance took place when the repairs were completed. If, however, the mechanic wants the $100 before the winter is over, you must be notified that the repairs have been completed. ■

In a bilateral contract, the offeree's acceptance must be properly communicated directly to the offeror. If the offeror specifies that a certain means of communication be used—for example, face-to-face meeting, telephone message, mail, telegram, fax machine, or some other means—acceptance takes effect (even though the offeror has not yet received the communication) as soon as it is properly communicated by the offeree using the method specified by the offeror (e.g. properly depositing a letter of acceptance in the mailbox).

When the parties are negotiating orally—face to face or by telephone— acceptance is properly communicated when the offeror clearly hears and understands the offeree's acceptance. A letter properly communicates acceptance when it is dropped—stamped and addressed—into a mailbox. A telegram properly communicates acceptance at the time it is given to the telegraph company to be sent.

If the offeree uses a method other than that requested by the offeror, acceptance is not effective until the offeror actually receives the communication (assuming that the offer is still open).

Ordinarily the offeror will not insist on a specific means of communicating the acceptance. In this case, the trend of modern court decisions is to allow acceptance of an offer by the same method the offeror used to send the offer or by any other reasonable method of communication. The definition of "reasonable" may be a question for a court to decide. Generally, however, the method of communication chosen by the offeree is considered reasonable if it falls into one of the following categories:

- It was the same one used by the offeror.
- It was one that the parties customarily used in prior dealings with each other.
- It was customarily used within the trade or business in which the parties are engaged.
- It appeared to be appropriate as determined by the language of the offer. (For example, the offeror sends an offer by fax but indicates that the offeree need not respond immediately; an acceptance by letter would probably be considered reasonable under these circumstances.)

The various means of communication that the offeree may use to accept a written offer are letter, telex, telegram, fax machine, telephone, or in person. A written acceptance takes effect at the time the acceptance is properly given to the sending agency. The offeror is bound at this time, even if the acceptance is not received. If, however, a method of acceptance is not considered to be reasonable, acceptance is not effective until the offeror actually receives the communication.

> ■ Tay, a resident of New York City, wrote to Morasse, of Buffalo, offering to sell computer software at a reduced price. Morasse, realizing that the offer was a "good deal," immediately sent a telegram agreeing to buy the software at the stated price. Morasse's telegram was lost and never reached Tay. An agreement resulted, however, because Morasse's acceptance was valid as soon as he gave the telegram to the telegraph company to send. ■

The offeror may place other conditions on the acceptance. The offeror may, for example, state that the acceptance must be received by a certain date. If the offeror's conditions are not met, the acceptance is not legally binding.

> ■ Sanford sent a letter to Zebart offering to sell a personal computer for $3,500. In his letter Sanford stated that "Acceptance of this offer is not binding unless it is received by me in my office by 5 P.M. on May 1." Zebart's acceptance would take place only if Sanford receives the acceptance by 5 P.M. on May 1. ■

Silence as Acceptance

As a general rule, the offeree's silence is not regarded as acceptance. An offeree has no legal obligation to reply even if an offer says, "Failure to reply will amount to acceptance."

Huff wrote to Walden offering her $300 for her pedigree show dog. In the offer Huff stated, "If I do not hear from you within ten days, I shall consider my offer accepted." Walden, the offeree, has no legal obligation to reply to the offer and her silence cannot be regarded as acceptance. She does not have to sell the dog to Huff. ■

In some cases acceptance may be implied by an act of the offeree. For example, when the offeree silently accepts benefits, knowing that they are not made as a gift, an implied acceptance arises. In such a case, the offeree is equally bound unless he or she speaks out and rejects the offer.

Martin, the owner of a fruit and vegetable stand at the farmer's market, buys regularly from Bart, a local farmer. Bart arrived at the farmer's market early one morning and left a load of assorted fruits and vegetables at Martin's stand. Since Martin had not yet arrived, Bart left a note that included the price. Bart had left fruits and vegetables at Martin's stand in this manner on four other occasions; each time, Martin accepted and paid for the items. Arriving at the stand, Martin read the note and tore it up. He left the fruits and vegetables to spoil without notifying Bart that he did not want them. Martin is liable for the price of the fruits and vegetables. ■

In the example, Martin's silence amounted to an implied acceptance. Because he had accepted fruits and vegetables in this manner on four previous occasions, Martin led Bart to believe that Martin would continue to accept fruits and vegetables unless notification to the contrary was sent to Bart.

If both the offeror and offeree agree, silence may be considered to be acceptance. For example, you say to a friend who has offered to sell you a set of law books for $250, "If you don't hear from me by Friday, you may assume that I accept your offer."

Summary of Important Legal Concepts

Agreement, the first and most important requirement of a legally enforceable contract, is reached through offer and acceptance. An offer made by one person, the offeror, is a promise to do something if the other person performs an act or promises to do or not to do something. An acceptance is an agreement by that other person, the offeree, to do what was requested in the offer.

To be legally effective, the offer must be made with serious intent, be definite (clearly stated), and be communicated to the offeree. Advertisements are too indefinite to be offers. Rather, the law interprets them as invitations for potential customers to make offers to the advertisers. If the language used in an advertisement is specific enough, the advertisement can constitute an offer. At an ordinary auction, the offer made by the bidder is accepted when the auctioneer (the offeree) says "Sold" or lets the gavel fall.

Some offers are not accepted. An offer can be ended in seven ways: lapse of time, rejection, counteroffer, revocation, death or insanity of the offeror, illegality, and impossibility. Neither a rejection nor a revocation is effective until it is communicated to the other party. A counteroffer terminates the original offer and, in effect, is a rejection of that offer unless the wording clearly indicates that the original offer is still also being considered. Unless an option exists, the offeror can revoke an offer even though he or she has promised to hold it open for a stated period. An option is a contract in which the offerer agrees not to revoke the offer for a certain period of time in return for some consideration, usually money, from the offeree.

Only the offeree can accept the offer. Offers of reward made to the general public are legal. Most states, however, require that offers of reward must be communicated to the offeree in order for a valid acceptance to occur. Under common-law rules, the acceptance must be a "mirror image" of the offer, which means that the acceptance must match, term by term, what was requested in the offer. Any changes or additions to the terms of the original offer would amount to a counteroffer. In bilateral contracts, communication of the acceptance usually is necessary, but this is not true for unilateral contracts. In unilateral contracts, the offeree accepts simply by completing the act requested in the offer. As a practical matter, however, the offeror must know about the

completed act before the promise made to the offeree can be carried out.

A rejection and a revocation must be received by the other party to be effective. In contrast, an acceptance to an offer may be effective when properly sent if an offeree uses a means of communication requested by the offeror or uses any reasonable means when none is specified. But, if an unauthorized means is used (one other than that requested by the offeror or one not considered to be reasonable), acceptance is not effective until the offeror actually receives the communication (assuming the offer is still open). (The rules relating to the communication and acceptance of an offer are summarized in Table 7.1.)

Key Legal Terms to Know

Match the terms with the definitions that follow.

acceptance
bid
counteroffer
offer
offer and acceptance
offeree
offeror

TABLE 7.1 Communication of Offer and Acceptance

Situation	Made by	Communicated	Effective
Offer	Offeror	Directly	When received by offeree
Revocation	Offeror	Directly or indirectly	When received by offeree
Rejection	Offeree	Directly	When received by offeror
Acceptance	Offeree	Directly (bilateral agreement)	When sent, if the means of communication requested by offeror is used or any reasonable means is used (when none is specified by the offeror)
			When received, if the offeree uses a means other than that requested by the offerer
			When received, if the offeror specifies that acceptance will not be effective until actually received
Acceptance	Offeree	By beginning to perform act requested (unilateral agreement)	When act requested is completely performed

option
preliminary negotiations
rejection
revocation

1. One to whom an offer is made
2. An offer made at an auction
3. The offeror's withdrawal of an offer
4. Offer made by the offeree, changing the terms of the original offer
5. One who makes an offer
6. An offeree's refusal of an offer
7. An agreement to keep an offer open for a stated time in return for the payment of consideration (money) by the offeree
8. A promise by one person to do something if the other person either performs an act or promises to do or not to do something.
9. An agreement by the offeree to do what the offeror requests in the offer
10. The process by which the parties to a contract agree to its terms
11. An invitation to a party to make an offer

Questions and Problems to Discuss

1. How can a person be bound on a contract and not be immediately aware of it?
2. Under what circumstances will a counteroffer by the offeree terminate an offer?
3. The following advertisement appeared in your local newspaper: "1 12-HP Lawn Tractor, 4-speed transaxle, large 38-in. mowing deck, with electric starter, regular price $999. $100 to the first person to appear at the store and present this ad to the salesperson in the hardware department." You were the first person to arrive at the hardware department of the store and to present the required ad. Has a contract been formed? Explain.
4. West Star Bank offered a $5,000 reward for information leading to the arrest and conviction of whoever set off explosives at two of its automatic teller machines. Noonan provided information that led to the arrest of two individuals suspected of the crime. At their trial, however, these two individuals were acquitted. Is Noonan entitled to the reward?
5. Julian asked his neighbor Gibbons, a carpenter, to build a storage shed in Julian's backyard. Gibbons agreed. They discussed the layout of the shed and its exact location but did not discuss a price. After completing the shed, Gibbons submitted a bill to Julian for a sum that, compared with the going rate for other carpenters in their county, was unreasonable. Julian refused to pay that sum but offered Gibbons the going rate. If this case went to court, do you think a judge would be likely to rule in favor of Julian?
6. Byers, who lived in Albany, New York, received a letter from the Sweeta Corporation, also located in Albany. The letter stated that the company would send her a year's supply of low-calorie sweetener in individually wrapped packets at an introductory price of $100. In the letter the company stated that if it did not hear from Byers within seven days it would ship the sweetener to her. Byers made no reply. The sweetener arrived in the mail COD; Byers refused to sign for and accept the sweetener. The company filed a suit in small claims court. Would Byers be legally obligated to pay?
7. Hykes wrote to Gross, "I'm thinking of selling my sports car, and I'd like to get at least $3,500 for it." Gross promptly replied by mail, "I'll buy your sports car at the price mentioned in your letter to me." Is Hykes legally bound to sell the sports car to Gross?
8. On June 1 Essler mailed an offer to Weinberg to sell some household furniture at a special price of $375, stating, "Your acceptance must be received by me no later than June 12." Weinberg then mailed an acceptance on June 7 but, due to a postal strike, the acceptance did not reach Essler until June 15. Was Weinberg's acceptance binding on Essler?
9. Braun read an advertisement in the local newspaper stating that automobile tires, regularly $90, were on sale for $10. Braun went to the store and ordered four tires at the special sale price. The salesperson informed her that the advertisement was in error and that the actual sale price of the tires was $60. Could Braun hold the store to the advertised price?
10. At an auction, O'Connell bid $50 for some jewelry. Her bid was the only one made. Before the auctioneer declared the item sold, O'Connell withdrew the bid. The auctioneer maintained that once a bid was made it could not be withdrawn. Is the auctioneer correct?
11. Ballister offered in writing to sell her summer home to Washington for $40,000. In response to

this offer, Washington offered Ballister $38,900, which was refused. Washington later notified Ballister that she would give her the $40,000 for the property. Would Washington's acceptance of Ballister's original offer of $40,000 create a binding agreement?

12. On February 8 Leggett sent a telegram offering to sell Picarro a personal computer. Picarro received the telegram the same day (February 8). Picarro mailed a letter of acceptance on February 9 at 11 A.M., which reached Leggett on the afternoon of February 12. At 1:30 P.M. on February 9, Picarro received a telegram from Leggett revoking the offer. Was the revocation effective?

13. On April 13 Afton offered by mail to sell his lawn care business to Baird for $35,000. On April 19 Baird telegrammed his acceptance, which was delayed and did not reach Afton's office until April 21. On April 20, Afton died. Was there a legally binding agreement?

Cases to Decide

1. Robinson, a college football player, signed a contract on December 2 with the Detroit Lions, a professional football club. The contract was a standard form that contained a clause stating, "This agreement shall become valid and binding upon each party only when and if it shall be approved by the League Commissioner." In late December, Robinson informed the Detroit Lions that he would not be playing for them because he had signed on with the Dallas Football Club. On January 12, the Commissioner approved the contract. Detroit then sued Robinson for breach of contract. Was there ever a contract between Robinson and the Detroit Lions? (*Detroit Football Company* v. *Robinson*, 188 F. Supp. 933)

2. Steinberg applied to the Chicago Medical School, paying the required $15 application fee. He was later notified that his application was rejected. He sued the school for breach of contract, claiming that the school did not evaluate his application according to the academic entrance criteria printed in the college's informational brochure. He claimed that the medical school instead made its decisions on criteria that were not listed in the brochure, such as the ability to pledge large sums of money to the school. Was there a contract formed between the college and Steinberg to re-

view his application based on the criteria in the informational brochure? (*Steinberg* v. *Chicago Medical School*, 41 Ill. App. 2d 804, 354 N.E. 2d 58)

3. Zehmer and his wife owned a 471-acre farm. In a restaurant one night, Lucy said to Zehmer that he bet Zehmer wouldn't take $50,000 cash for the farm. When Zehmer replied he didn't think Lucy had the cash, Lucy said he would get it if Zehmer would put it in writing that he would sell him the farm. Zehmer then wrote on a piece of paper, "I agree to sell the . . . farm to W. O. Lucy for $50,000 cash." Zehmer said in an undertone at the time that he thought it was a joke. When Zehmer later refused to sell the farm to Lucy, Lucy brought an action to enforce the contract. Is Lucy entitled to purchase the farm? (*Lucy* v. *Zehmer*, 196 Va 493, 84 SE 2d 516)

4. Leavey owned a ranch in Wyoming. He entered into negotiations to sell it to Trautwein. Leavey finally made an oral offer to sell, which was then incorporated into a written contract. Trautwein signed the document but added a sheet with three changes. Could Leavey refuse to go through with the deal? (*Trautwein* v. *Leavey*, Wyo 472 P2d 776)

5. Ledbetter, sheriff of Dallas County, posted a reward of $500 for the capture of an escaped murderer. Broadnax, not knowing of the reward, captured and returned the prisoner to the sheriff. After he returned the prisoner, Broadnax learned of the reward and claimed it. The sheriff would not pay. Was Broadnax legally entitled to the reward? (*Broadnax* v. *Ledbetter*, Tex 99 SW 1111)

6. Morrison prepared a contract in Florida to purchase some Florida land owned by Thoelke. Morrison then mailed the contract to Thoelke, who was in Texas. Immediately after receiving the contract, Thoelke signed it and placed it in the mail, addressed to Morrison's attorney in Florida. Before the contract was received by Morrison's attorney, Thoelke called the attorney and canceled the contract. Morrison, however, recorded the contract. Thoelke filed a lawsuit to have the contract declared void, claiming that canceling the contract prior to its receipt by Morrison was a valid cancellation. Is Thoelke correct? (*Morrison* v. *Thoelke*, Fla 155 So 2d 889)

7. Hunkin-Corkey, a construction company, entered into a contract to build an apartment building for Brook Towers. The contract called for comple-

tion by a certain date. Because of problems that arose, Hunkin-Corkey asked for an extension of time. Requests for the extensions were contained in a printed form that was sent to Brook Towers's architect. The architect agreed to certain extensions and ignored the requests for others. Brook Towers then sued for damages because the building was not completed on schedule. Was there a valid agreement that permitted the extensions requested? (*Brook Towers Corp.* v. *Hunkin-Corkey Co.*, 454 F2d 1203)

8. Cushing sent a written request to the adjutant general's office of the state of New Hampshire to rent the Portsmouth Armory for a dance to be held on the evening of April 29, 1978. The request was received by the adjutant general's office on March 30, 1978. The adjutant general mailed a signed contract on March 31 agreeing to rent the armory on the requested date and requiring Cushing to sign and return it within five days after receipt. Cushing received the contract offer on April 3, signed it, and mailed it back to the adjutant general's office that same day. When Cushing received a telephone call from the adjutant general at 6:30 P.M. on April 4 revoking the offer to rent the armory, he told the adjutant general that he had already signed and mailed the contract. The adjutant general sent a written confirmation of the withdrawal on April 5. On April 6 the adjutant general's office received the signed contract, dated April 3 and postmarked April 5 in the mail. Did a binding contract exist between Cushing and the adjutant general's office of the state of New Hampshire? (118 N.H. 292, 386 A.2d 805)

Chapter 8

Consideration

CHAPTER PREVIEW

This chapter deals with consideration, the second element required in a contract. It opens with a discussion, supported by illustrations, pointing out that if an agreement lacks consideration, neither party can enforce the agreement unless it has already been carried out. The chapter then goes on to describe what consideration consists of and how much consideration is necessary to make a "deal." There is a brief discussion of the terms *moral consideration* and *past consideration*. The remainder of the chapter is devoted to special problems relating to consideration and some exceptional situations in which agreements without consideration can be enforced.

THE REQUIREMENT OF CONSIDERATION

Chapter 7 discussed agreement, the first element of a contract. Another requirement of a legally enforceable contract is consideration. **Consideration** is something of legal value that each party gives to the contract to bind the agreement. Suppose, for example, that your friend (the offeror) promised to give you (the offeree) $200 if you rebuilt the motor in her car. You rebuilt the motor, and your friend paid you $200. The consideration your friend gave to the contract was $200. The consideration you gave to the contract was the rebuilding of the motor.

Since the parties to a contract are not bound unless both give consideration, a promise to make a gift is unenforceable. A **gift** is a voluntary transfer of property without consideration. If you promise to give a friend an electric razor as a birthday gift, your promise is not legally binding even if your friend accepts. You, the offeror, have received nothing of value (consideration) in return from your friend, the offeree.

The presence or absence of consideration is unimportant when an agreement has been executed (carried out). For example, you and a friend agree to exchange graduation gifts. You give your friend an FM radio as a graduation gift, but she does not give you anything. A court will not cancel the agreement and return the radio to you because your friend gave no consideration.

Generally, both written and oral promises require consideration. Some states have laws providing that certain written contracts are valid without consideration.

THE NATURE OF CONSIDERATION

The consideration demanded by the offeror and given by the offeree may be a benefit to the offeror, such as money, a computer, jewelry, or a tape recorder. Often, however, the consideration does not have a monetary value and does not benefit the offeror. Instead, the consideration may consist of a sacrifice by the offeree. This sacrifice is called **legal detriment.** Legal detriment is consideration when the offeree, at the request of the offeror:

1. Does something (an act) or promises to do something he or she is not legally bound to do.

▪ Meredith promised her daughter $5,000 if she completed law school. The daughter, relying on her mother's promise, accepted the challenge and completed law school. Her completion of law school (an act she was not legally bound to do) was consideration for Meredith's promise to pay her $5,000. ▪

2. Refrains (from an act) or promises to refrain from doing something she or he has a legal right to do. This refraining is called **forbearance.**

▪ Carr promised his twenty-year-old nephew $2,000 if he would refrain (forbear) from smoking until the age of twenty-one. The nephew, relying on the uncle's promise, did refrain from smoking until age twenty-one. The nephew had a legal right to smoke, and therefore refraining from this act was consideration for Carr's promise to pay him $2,000. ▪

ADEQUACY OF CONSIDERATION

As stated earlier in the chapter, the presence of consideration in an agreement is essential. In the past, however, courts have not questioned whether the consideration received by each party was sufficient or fair in light of the consideration the other party gave. The parties have been free to enter into an agreement on terms they can agree upon, even though one party may obtain a "better deal."

▪ Because you needed money urgently, you offered to sell a friend your $600 stereo for $200. Your friend accepted the offer and you delivered the stereo. A short time later you demanded that the stereo be returned because the consideration was too small. Because your friend legally accepted your offer and gave the consideration you requested, you are bound by the agreement even though the stereo is worth $600. ▪

Modern courts and legislative bodies have changed the historical view of consideration. They now protect individuals from contracts that are so one-sided as to be unconscionable (unfair). Unconscionable contracts are discussed in Chapter 10.

The courts will question the adequacy of the consideration if the contract calls for the exchange of different quantities of things that are identical in nature or have a fixed value, such as money. A promise to pay a friend $200 in return for the friend's promise to immediately pay you $20 (money promised for money) is not enforceable. Yet, a promise to pay $200 in return for a promise to deliver a book worth $20 is binding. Since the items exchanged are not identical in nature, the adequacy of the consideration is unimportant to the validity of the contract. It is difficult to compare the worth of different items, so adequacy of consideration must be judged by the parties to the contract.

In extreme cases, the courts will also question the adequacy of the consideration. In such cases, inadequate consideration can indicate fraud, duress, or undue influence (discussed in Chapter 14). For example, at the time Fleming purchased a used motorcycle, the salesperson deliberately misrepresented the condition of the motorcycle and charged him more money than it was worth. Under these circumstances, the courts will permit Fleming to avoid the agreement because he relied on the salesperson's statements.

Often, a written contract states that the consideration given for a promise is $1 or some other small amount. This small sum of money is called **nominal consideration.** Courts will enforce contracts with such small consideration if the amount was actually paid and if the offeror intended that amount to be the price for the promise. If, however, the $1 amount was stated in the contract only to make it appear that the contract contained consideration but the $1 was not actually paid, the courts will not enforce the contract.

MORAL CONSIDERATION

Sometimes, an offeror makes a promise because he or she feels it is the right thing to do. In other words, this person (the offeror) feels a moral commitment to make such a promise. In most states, however, a moral promise is no more enforceable than any other promise unsupported by consideration. At best, a court would conclude that the offeror intends to make a gift. Take the following example:

■ Speedy, who had a great deal of affection for her aunt, promised to pay the rent on her apartment while the aunt was in the hospital and unable to work. Since Speedy received no consideration from her aunt for Speedy's moral promise to pay, the promise Speedy made is not legally binding. ■

A minority of courts would take a different position and hold that a moral obligation is sufficient to enforce a promise even without return consideration, especially if the promise of the offeror involved a humanitarian gesture. In these few states a promise such as the one Speedy made in the above example might very well be enforceable.

PAST CONSIDERATION

Past consideration is a promise made for an act that has already taken place. Since consideration is something of value given by the offeree at the time of the promise made by the offeror, past consideration is legally no consideration at all in most states. In other words, for the consideration to be valid, the offeror's promise must induce the offeree to act.

■ A friend helped you study for a final exam in your business law course. After the exam you promised to give your friend $25 for the help. Since this was a promise to pay for help that had already been given, you are not obligated to pay the $25. ■

The offeree must give the consideration *after* the offeror makes the request. If before the exam you had promised your friend $25 to help you study for the final exam and your friend had agreed, the promise would be binding. In that case, your promise induced or motivated your friend to help you.

In some states, a written promise to pay for an act already performed (past consideration) is binding.

SPECIAL PROBLEMS RELATING TO CONSIDERATION

Many problems involving consideration (or the lack of it) arise during the performance of a contract. Courts often deal with these problems on an individual basis. Although many such problems occur, one common one involves the pre-existing legal obligation.

Pre-existing Contractual Agreement

Sometimes the offeree, after beginning performance under the terms of an already existing agreement, will not continue to perform unless the offeror makes a new promise to pay more money. A new promise by the offeror to pay more money is not legally binding. The offeree has furnished no additional consideration for the new promise.

> ■ Pierre-Philippe, a building contractor, prepared a bid in writing to build a small shed behind Medford's house for $475. After beginning work, Pierre-Philippe discovered that he required more materials than originally planned. Pierre-Philippe informed Medford that he would not continue the job until Medford agreed to pay an additional $200 for the extra necessary materials. Medford orally promised to pay. Pierre-Philippe was already legally obligated to complete the work for $475. He furnished no additional consideration for Medford's promise to pay him $200 more. Medford is therefore not legally required to pay the additional $200. ■

By doing or agreeing to do something extra—something not covered by the existing agreement—the offeree *would* be providing the additional consideration required in return for the offeror's promise to pay more money. If, in the example, Pierre-Philippe had agreed to make the shed larger than originally agreed, he would have provided consideration in return for Medford's new promise to pay an additional $200 and Medford would be required to pay the additional money.

The courts in some states (and this appears to be a modern trend) would allow Pierre-Philippe to collect the extra compensation agreed upon ($200) if he had honestly run into some unforeseeable circumstance causing him to lose money. A hurricane (considered an act of God) that destroys part of the shed during the construction period is one example of an unforeseen circumstance. These states believe that as long as a person in Pierre-Philippe's position is not in any way negligent or dishonest, he should be entitled to collect.

In some states, a written agreement that changes an existing agreement and that is signed by the promisor needs no additional consideration.

Pre-existing Duty to Pay a Debt

Some promises are not legally enforceable because one of the parties (the debtor) has a pre-existing duty to pay a debt to the other party (the creditor). For example, the creditor may agree (promise) to accept part payment (a smaller sum of money) from the debtor in full payment of the debt. Nevertheless, if there is no dispute about the existence of the debt or its amount, the debt is called a **liquidated claim** and the promise is not legally enforceable. The debtor has given no consideration for the creditor's promise to accept less money; the debtor is already legally obligated to pay the full amount. Even if the creditor accepts the smaller amount, the creditor may still collect the remainder of the debt.

> ■ Sellers owed you $500. On the due date, Sellers told you that she could not pay the full $500. You orally agreed to accept $400 in full settlement of the debt. Sellers agreed and paid you the $400. Since Sellers gave you no consideration for your promise to accept less than the full amount owed ($500), you may recover the balance due of $100. ■

If a creditor accepts less money plus additional consideration from the debtor, the debt will be canceled. If, in the above example, you agreed to accept $400 plus three record albums worth $25, the entire $500 debt would be canceled because you have agreed to the additional consideration. The additional consideration may take any form, since the value of the consideration is unimportant as long as it is an *additional* consideration.

In some states, if a creditor accepts part payment of a debt and gives the debtor a written release from the remainder of the debt, the release cancels the entire debt without additional consideration.

Part payment of a debt can cancel a debt if there is an honest dispute over the correct amount of the debt—called an **unliquidated claim**—and the parties agree to a compromise. Instead of going to court to settle the dispute, the debtor and creditor each give up this legal right. They agree instead to settle out of court on an amount somewhere between the amount the debtor claims is owed and the amount the creditor claims is correct. This compromise is legally binding and represents full settlement of the entire debt. The consideration in the compromise agreement is each party's refraining, or promising to refrain, from contesting the amount in court.

> ■ Rice retained an attorney to prepare her will but did not discuss the cost of the attorney's services. The attorney sent her a bill for $500. Rice, feeling that this amount was unreasonable compared with the fees other attorneys charged, offered $300 in full settlement of the bill. Although the attorney claimed that the will was complicated and required many hours of legal research, he nevertheless was willing to settle the dispute for $350. Rice agreed and paid the attorney in cash. The $350 paid by Rice cancels the $500 debt. ■

Part payment of a disputed debt may also cancel that debt if the creditor accepts and cashes a check marked on its face "payment in full." Courts in most states reason that if any part of the debt is in dispute, the entire debt is unliquidated. A payment that is made by the debtor and accepted by the creditor as payment in full is binding.

> Crandall, who owned a landscaping service, orally gave Drake an estimate of $475 for cutting down two trees on Drake's property. Crandall then cut down the trees, claiming that Drake orally agreed to the work. Drake insisted, however, that she had authorized only an estimate. In an effort to settle the dispute, Drake mailed Crandall a check for $325 with the notation on the check "paid in full." Crandall cashed the check and then sued Drake for the additional $150. ■

In this example, Crandall could not collect the $150 ($475 − $325). Drake's check for $325 was an offer to settle the dispute. When Crandall cashed the check, he accepted this offer to settle. The result would be the same even if, before cashing the check, Crandall had crossed out the "paid in full" notation.

Not all states would consider that part payment of a disputed debt by a check marked "paid in full" would cancel the debt. Some, like New York State, hold that a creditor may collect the balance of the debt if he or she indorses the check with the statement, "This check is cashed under protest." Courts in these states argue that the amount of money a debtor claims he or she owes is liquidated and that there is a pre-existing duty to pay it. Actually paying this debt, therefore, cannot be consideration for the creditor's implied promise (cashing of the check) to release the debtor from the unpaid balance.

If a person owes money to several people, part payment of the debt owed to each of the creditors may cancel the entire debt if all the creditors agree. A **composition of creditors** is an arrangement in which all creditors agree to accept a certain percentage of the total amount owed by the debtor in full settlement of a debt. Creditors who agree to the composition actually receive no additional consideration from the debtor in return for their promise to accept less money. Courts, nevertheless, will enforce such an agreement since no one creditor receives the full amount of the debt owed. Creditors generally agree to this type of arrangement only when they believe they will never be able to collect the full amount owed to them by the debtor.

> Werner owed $4,000 to Vienna and $2,000 to Hobbs, for a total of $6,000. The two creditors agreed to accept 50 percent of their claims in full settlement of the debt. Under this arrangement, Vienna received $2,000 (50 percent of $4,000) and Hobbs received $1,000 (50 percent of $2,000). Since Vienna and Hobbs agreed to take less money in full payment of the total debt owed by Werner, the remainder of the debt is canceled. ■

A creditor's promise to extend the due date of a debt is not enforceable unless the debtor gives additional consideration. If no additional consideration is given by the debtor for the creditor's promise to extend the time for payment, the creditor may legally demand repayment before the end of the extension.

> Graves owed McHale $400. When the debt was due, Graves did not have the money and asked McHale for a three-month extension. McHale orally agreed. Before the three months were up, McHale changed his mind and sued Graves for the money. Since Graves gave no consideration for McHale's promise to extend the time of payment by three months, McHale's promise is not legally enforceable. ■

A debtor may legally obtain an extension of the due date if the creditor agrees to the extension and receives additional consideration. Suppose, in the example, McHale agreed to extend the due date and accepted a part payment of the debt from Graves before the original due date. The part payment by Graves would be the additional consideration needed in return for McHale's promise to extend the due date by three months.

In some states, a creditor's written promise to extend the due date of a debt is enforceable without additional consideration.

Pre-existing Duty to Perform a Legal Obligation

A person who performs or promises to perform his or her legal obligation gives no consideration for an offeror's promise to pay money. Into this category would fall police officers, judges, legislators, and other public officials. A promise, for example, to pay a police officer a reward for the arrest of a criminal is not legally enforceable. The arrest of criminals is part of a police officer's legal obligations. He or she cannot gain privately from this obligation.

AGREEMENTS ENFORCEABLE WITHOUT CONSIDERATION

Up to this point, the chapter has emphasized situations in which consideration was required for promises to be enforceable. There are exceptional situations, however, in which promises can be enforced without consideration. Courts base their decisions to enforce such promises on principles of equity, in an effort to avoid injustice. If ordinary contract law instead of equity were the basis, these same promises would not need to be enforced because consideration is lacking.

Promises to Charitable Organizations

A promise to make a gift to a charitable, religious, educational, or scientific organization or to some other institution such as a library, museum, or hospital that depends upon voluntary contributions is usually enforceable without consideration. This promise is called a **pledge** or subscription. The pledge can be oral (such as a donation called in to a TV station during a charity telethon), but it is usually in writing. Before your pledge is binding, you must acknowledge it. In states where a pledge is required to be in writing, the donor is often asked to sign a pledge card (see Figure 8.1). There are different theories for enforcing such a promise.

One theory is that the organization, even before payment of the pledges, will rely on the total amount of pledged money and enter into various contracts or make other expenditures. Under the circumstances, it would be unfair to the organization to permit any person to withdraw a pledge.

> The Thompson Memorial Hospital conducted a fund-raising campaign to raise money to add a new intensive-care wing to the present building. Fries, along with other citizens, pledged in writing to contribute $5,000 to the building fund. Based on these pledges, construction of the hospital wing was started. Fries later refused to pay her pledge. Because the hospital had started construction, Fries is legally obligated to pay the pledged amount. ∎

Another theory is that the promise to pay is made in consideration of the promises of others to give too. The promise of each promisor is supported by the promises of others.

Figure 8.1 **Pledge Card**

Yes, my gift to the Highland Hospital Foundation will help provide new and expanded services for Highland's patients and will directly support the high quality of personalized patient care to which Highland is committed. My tax deductible check is enclosed for $_____.

Through this gift, I/we will be considered a:

☐ *Contributor* ($5–24)

*☐ *Member* ($25–99)
Receives "Highland Highlites" four times a year. Recognition in hospital publication.

*☐ *Fellow* ($100–499)
Receives all of the above plus free personalized Emergency Medical Card. Invitation to annual reception.

*Second Century Associate

*☐ *Patron* ($500–999)
Receives all of the above plus invitation to annual recognition dinner.

*☐ *Founder* ($1000 or more)
Receives all of the above plus recognition in hospital lobby as leading contributor. Invitation to special Founder's event. Free tickets to hospital functions.

Please make check payable to:
Highland Hospital Foundation, Inc.

Every gift large or small is important to Highland.

Thank You

PLEASE PRINT
Miss Ms.
Name (circle) Dr. Mr. Mrs. _____
Please specify the way you wish your name to appear in the annual report of gifts. *

Address _____

City _____ State _____ Zip _____

Telephone ( ) _____

Please designate my (our) gift:
☐ A regular donation; †☐ In honor of; †☐ In memory of; †☐ In appreciation of:

Name _____ Occasion _____
*Donors' names are acknowledged in our hospital publication unless you instruct us otherwise.
†Acknowledgement of gift is sent immediately and no amount is mentioned

Send acknowledgement of gift to:

Name _____

Address _____

_____ Zip _____

Relationship to person honored _____

☐ This gift will be matched by my (spouse's) employer. Enclosed is the Matching Gift Form supplied by my (spouse's) employer.

☐ Please send me more information in regard to estate tax and income tax savings from a charitable gift to Highland.

Generally, a pledge may be withdrawn at any time before the institution takes steps to begin construction. However, some courts hold that, once made, a pledge may not be withdrawn.

Promissory Estoppel

Courts occasionally apply the equity doctrine of **promissory estoppel** to enforce a promise unsupported by consideration on the part of the offeree if it would be grossly unfair not to enforce the promise. In short, the offeror is prevented by law (stopped) from claiming a defense (no consideration for his or her promise) that would normally be available.

> Martin was an employee of Case for twenty-five years but had not received any benefits. Nevertheless, Case promised to pay Martin a pension of $1,300 a month for life whenever Martin decided to take retirement. Case made it quite clear to Martin, however, that he was not asking her to retire, nor did he wish her to retire. Martin retired two years later, making no plans to work anywhere else. Instead she simply relied on the monthly income Case agreed to provide; in fact, she would not have retired without it. After a few years, Case discontinued the pension. Martin was then too advanced in age to begin looking for another job and sued Case to continue payment of the pension. Case claimed that his promise to pay the pension in the first place was never supported by consideration on Martin's part. ∎

The court in this example would probably rule in Martin's favor based upon the equity doctrine of promissory estoppel because the purpose of this doctrine is to enforce a promise even though consideration is lacking. Case made a promise of a monthly income for life, and Martin relied on this promise. It would obviously be grossly unfair if she were not able to continue to collect the pension. An injustice could be avoided only by enforcing Case's promise.

Summary of Important Legal Concepts

As a general rule, the parties to a contract are not bound unless consideration is given by both of them. Consideration consists of a promise on the part of the offeror in return for some tangible benefit such as money or a computer, given by the offeree. Or, as is often the case, consideration on the part of the offeree may consist of legal detriment. Legal detriment is a sacrifice by the offeree—the doing of an act or refraining (forbearance) from doing an act or merely a promise to do or to refrain. An example of legal detriment would be that, in exchange for a

promise of $5,000 by the offeror, the offeree agrees (promises) to stop smoking.

Although the presence of consideration in an agreement is essential, courts do not usually question whether the consideration received by each party is sufficient or even fair. The courts may raise this question if there is evidence of fraud, duress, or undue influence or if the contract is unconscionable (grossly unfair), because the parties who entered into the contract had unequal bargaining powers.

In most states, a moral promise is no more enforceable than any other promise unsupported by consideration. A minority of courts, however, hold that, if the promise of the offeror involved a humanitarian gesture, a moral obligation is sufficient to enforce a promise even without return consideration. Past consideration is also not consideration because the offeror's promise did not induce the offeree to act. Instead, the offeree acted first and then was promised something by the offeror.

The performance of a pre-existing contractual obligation by the offeree (other than the payment of debts) is not consideration for an offeror's promise because the offeree is not required to do more than was originally agreed to. But by doing or agreeing to do something not covered by the existing agreement, the offeree would be providing the additional consideration required in return for the offeror's promise to pay more money. Some states, however, have modified these rules when unforeseeable circumstances are involved.

Applying the pre-existing rule to the payment of debts, a distinction is made between liquidated and unliquidated debts. If a creditor agrees (promises) to accept part payment from a debtor in full payment of a liquidated claim (no dispute exists about the existence or amount of the debt), the promise is not enforceable. The debtor is already legally obligated to pay the full amount. But if a debt is unliquidated (an honest dispute does exist over the amount of the debt), the acceptance by the creditor of a part payment of that debt cancels the remainder. The debtor and creditor each gave up the legal right to go to court to settle the dispute. Part payment of a disputed claim also cancels the remainder of the debt if the creditor accepts and cashes a check marked "paid in full." Regardless of this majority view, some states still hold that a creditor may collect the balance of the claim. A person such as a public official who is already legally obligated to perform a duty under the law gives no consideration for his or her promise to pay money. This public official cannot gain privately from the duty to perform a legal obligation.

In exceptional situations, courts will enforce promises made without consideration. The most common of these situations involve pledges, promises to make gifts to charitable, religious, educational, or scientific organizations or under the doctrine of promissory estoppel, cases in which it would be grossly unfair not to enforce the offeror's promise because the offeree has justifiably relied on that promise.

Key Legal Terms to Know

Match the terms with the definitions that follow.

composition of creditors
consideration
forbearance
gift
legal detriment
liquidated claim
nominal consideration
past consideration
pledge
promissory estoppel
unliquidated claim

1. An agreement among creditors to accept a certain percentage of the total amount owed by a debtor in full settlement of the debt
2. Consideration that is a sacrifice by the offeree
3. A dollar or other small sum of money used to bind a contract
4. A promise to make a gift to a charitable, religious, educational, or scientific organization
5. Refraining from doing something one has a legal right to do
6. A promise made for an act that has already taken place
7. Something of value given by each party to bind an agreement
8. A voluntary transfer of property without consideration
9. A debt, the amount of which is subject to an honest dispute
10. An equitable doctrine applied by the courts to enforce a promise unsupported by consideration
11. A debt, the amount of which is not in dispute

Questions and Problems to Discuss

1. A boss says to her faithful, loyal employee who is about to retire, "In consideration of your thirty-five years of faithful service, I will give you a check for $5,000." The employee never receives the check and sues the employer. Is the employer legally obligated to pay the money?
2. When Glocker received her bill from Lawnmark, a lawn-care company, she became very angry about the amount that the company claimed she

owed. She immediately wrote a letter to the company's general manager, giving her version of the amount owed and including a check for that amount. She marked on the face of the check "paid in full settlement of the claim by the Lawnmark Company." The general manager cashed the check and immediately sued Glocker to recover the remaining balance. Can the general manager legally collect?

3. Baker had a one-year contract with the printers at his print shop. Just before printing the yearbooks for several local schools, the printers walked off the job, claiming that they had been given additional duties not included in their present contract. Baker, not wishing to lose any more business, called a meeting and promised to give the printers more money for their new duties. After the yearbooks were printed, Martin paid the printers at the old rate. They brought suit for breach of his agreement to pay them additional money. Are the printers legally entitled to the additional pay?

4. Brindle was under contract to work for Lange for one year at a salary of $3,000 per month. After working six months, Brindle threatened to quit unless Lange raised his salary. Lange orally promised Brindle a $1,000 bonus at the end of the year if Brindle stayed on the job according to the original agreement. Brindle agreed. At the end of the year Lange refused to pay the bonus. Is Lange legally bound to pay the bonus?

5. Kirk was a guest at a hotel. She tripped on a torn carpet while walking down a flight of stairs and severely injured her leg. The hotel owner orally promised to pay Kirk $1,000 for her injury if she promised not to sue. Kirk agreed. Several months later, the hotel owner refused to pay Kirk the $1,000, stating that the injury wasn't as bad as originally thought. Was the hotel owner legally bound on his promise to pay Kirk $1,000?

6. Sill borrowed $500 from Huber. When the debt became due, Sill, who was unemployed, had only $250 in cash. Sill asked Huber to accept this $250 and a dinner ring worth $150 as full payment. Huber agreed. Is the entire debt now canceled?

7. The board of directors of Hill Haven, a home for the elderly, was accepting donations to build an additional dormitory at the home. Hogan promised in writing to donate $3,000 for the proposed addition. Relying on this and other pledges, the directors contracted for the construction of the dormitory. Is Hogan bound by the promise to donate $3,000?

8. Davies was employed in the data processing division of a bank. Desmond and Zwick, owners of a firm that manufactured athletic equipment, orally promised Davies a position as office manager if she would quit the bank job and work for them. Davies quit her job at the bank, but Desmond and Zwick did not keep their promise to hire her. Can Davies legally enforce the promise made by Desmond and Zwick to hire her?

9. Scholler, a dentist, performed a root canal on Mays. Scholler billed Mays for $600. Mays refused to pay this bill, claiming that other local dentists charge $400 for the same service. After much discussion, they agreed to settle for $450, which Mays paid. Scholler then sued Mays for the additional $150. Is Mays legally obligated to pay the additional amount?

10. Zwart sold a chair to Polizzi for $50 cash. The chair, which Zwart had inherited from a relative, turned out to be a valuable antique worth at least $1,000. Zwart demanded that Polizzi return the chair, claiming $50 wasn't a fair price. Is Zwart entitled to the return of the chair?

Cases to Decide

1. Ralston was injured when she fell down a church stairway. Matthew, agent for the company that insured the church, promised Ralston that the insurance company would pay her hospital and medical expenses if she did not sue the church. Ralston agreed, but the insurance company refused to pay her expenses, claiming that charitable and religious organizations in the state of Kansas were not liable for negligence. The company stated that Ralston had no valid claim and her promise not to sue was not consideration. Did Ralston have a valid claim? (*Ralston* v. *Matthew*, 173 Kansas 550)

2. Hoffman wished to establish a franchised grocery store as part of the Red Owl chain. The district manager of Red Owl informed Hoffman and his wife that they would be given a franchise if they would sell their bakery in Wautoma, Wisconsin; acquire a lot in Chilton, Wisconsin; and put up a certain amount of money. Hoffman did sell his business and acquire the lot, but he was

A minor cannot ratify part of an agreement and disaffirm another part. The *entire* agreement must be either ratified or disaffirmed.

> ■ The week before Apter reached majority, he purchased a tuxedo and its accessories from Varden's Tuxedo Shop. A few days after reaching majority, Apter returned the accessories and demanded the return of the purchase price for these items. Since he purchased the items together, Apter must either keep the tuxedo *and* accessories or return the whole outfit for a refund of the entire purchase price. ■

Minors' Liability for Necessaries

Minors are generally responsible for payment for necessaries purchased from adults. If this were not the case, adults would be unwilling to supply minors with those things necessary for their existence. This rule, therefore, is for the protection of the adult.

Necessaries are those things a person actually needs to live. Traditionally, necessaries are food, clothing, and shelter. The concept of necessaries, however, has been expanded by court decisions to include medicine and medical services, the services of an attorney in tort and criminal cases, a basic public school education, an education to learn a trade, the tools necessary for that trade, and services reasonably necessary to enable the minor to earn money required to provide the necessities of life (such as paying an employment agency for securing a job). Luxury items (items used for pleasure) such as tape recorders, boats, television sets, jewelry, cameras, and sporting goods are generally not considered necessaries.

Courts usually consider changing community standards and hold that the decision about whether an item is a necessary actually depends upon the minor's station in life. A minor's **station in life** refers to the minor's social and economic status in the community. It takes into consideration such things as the minor's financial condition, marital status, whether the minor already has a supply of necessaries, whether the parents or guardians are presently furnishing the necessaries, and whether the minor is emancipated. An **emancipated minor** is one who is self-supporting and is no longer subject to parental control and authority. The usual ways in which a minor becomes emancipated are by marriage, by court order, by consent of the parent, and by living apart from parents. The emancipated minor is self-supporting and exercises general control over his or her life. Some courts even consider minors who live at home emancipated if they pay living expenses to parents and use the remainder of their earnings as they see fit. Emancipation, however, must be proved, and the burden of proof is on the person claiming emancipation.

> ■ Scott, an emancipated minor living away from home, was injured in a skiing accident. A physician called to the scene of the accident set Scott's broken leg. Later the physician sent a bill for her services. Scott refused to pay, claiming that as a minor she was not responsible for the bill. Since Scott was a self-supporting minor, she was responsible for paying the physician's services, a necessary. ■

Applying the station-in-life rule sometimes makes it difficult to determine whether an item is or is not a necessary. When a minor and an adult disagree about whether an item is a necessary, the outcome may have to be decided in a court of law.

A minor must pay only for necessaries actually furnished, not for necessaries to be furnished in the future.

> To learn a trade, Goodman, an emancipated minor, contracted with a correspondence school to take a twenty-week course in computer programming. After five weeks Goodman lost interest and dropped out of the course. He did, however, pay the school for five weeks of instruction. The correspondence school claimed that Goodman was liable for the remaining fifteen weeks of instruction according to the agreement. Goodman may avoid the original contract made with the school and pay only for the five weeks of instruction he actually received. ■

The minor's obligation to pay for necessaries is based on a quasi contract (a contract implied in law). The minor is required to pay only the reasonable value of the item or service received, not the price stated in the agreement. Thus, while an adult is protected when selling necessaries to a minor, there may be a disagreement about the price, which may have to be settled in a court of law.

> Kelly, an emancipated minor, obtained a job as a mechanic with a large car agency. Under the terms of the employment agreement, she was to complete a three-month training program with the company at her own expense. At the end of the training period she would purchase from the company the tools she needed for the job. Kelly discovered that whereas she paid $900, several of her friends taking the same training program paid only $600. Kelly is entitled to a return of $300. ■

Parents' Liability for Minors' Contracts

Unless parents agree to become liable, they generally have no legal liability for contracts made by their minor children. For this reason, businesspeople often require parents to sign any contract made with a minor. The parents then become personally liable even if the minor backs out of the contract. Parents do, however, have the legal duty to support their minor children. So, whether they have signed a contract or not, parents who neglect a minor child are liable for the reasonable value of any necessaries furnished to him or her. Consequently, if a minor child needs clothing that isn't being provided by the parents, the child may purchase the needed items and the parents can be held liable for payment. This obligation to support generally continues until minors are emancipated.

Minors' Liability for Torts

Minors can disaffirm most contracts they make, but they are generally liable for their torts. (Refer to Chapter 4 for a discussion of torts.) A minor's age is important in determining the minor's tort liability. In the case of deliberate torts, a minor is generally liable regardless of age. For torts of negligence, the age varies from state to state. In many states, minors under the age of fourteen are considered incapable of committing an act of negligence. In those states, minors over the age of fourteen who commit negligent acts are treated as adults.

> While driving through town, Marks, age seventeen and a minor, threw an empty soft drink can from a car window. Rossini was crossing the street and the can hit her in the eye, causing injury. Although Marks is a minor, she is liable for her tort of negligence. ■

Parents are not usually responsible for the torts of their children. However, they may be held responsible if they tell a child to commit a tort or if they fail to take action to prevent a tort from being committed—for example, if they fail to take action to stop a child from repeating acts that they have been warned about in the past. Parents are also liable if they place a dangerous instrument in the hands of a child, as would be the case if they gave their child a pellet gun and the child injured someone. The parents are held liable because, in the case of a lawsuit, the victim has a better chance of recovering damages from the parents than from the child.

> Neighbors warned the Bakers that their son Todd had thrown rocks at other children on several occasions. The Bakers could be held liable for injuries caused by Todd to other children. ■

In many states, parents are automatically liable for the intentional damage caused by children under a certain age. These state laws were passed with the idea that parents who knew they were liable for their children's intentional acts would exercise more control over their children's behavior. State statutes vary in strictness and in the maximum parental liability.

PERSONS UNDER THE INFLUENCE OF ALCOHOL OR OTHER DRUGS

Another category of incompetency applies to persons who are so intoxicated by alcohol or other drugs that they do not realize what they are doing when they enter into agreements. Slight intoxication is not enough to destroy a person's ability to make contracts. Nevertheless, it is not necessary that a person be so intoxicated that she or he is completely helpless. The person must be so affected that she or he does not understand the seriousness or the consequences of the agreement.

Courts have little sympathy for individuals who want to disaffirm their contracts because of intoxication; therefore, avoidance due to intoxication is rather uncommon. As a result, a person who enters into a contract while intoxicated may avoid it on becoming sober only if the other party purposely caused the person to become drunk or had reason to know that the person was drunk and unable to understand the consequences of the transaction.

If the intoxicated person has the legal right to disaffirm, she or he must do so within a reasonable time after becoming sober. Otherwise, the person loses that right to disaffirm and the agreement is considered ratified. Most courts will not permit disaffirmance unless the intoxicated person returns any consideration received from the other party.

> ■ While intoxicated, Babitz sold a valuable coin collection worth several hundred dollars to Lyness for $5. Lyness knew that Babitz was intoxicated and unable to understand the consequences of the deal. When Babitz became sober and discovered her mistake, she immediately offered to return the $5 to Lyness in exchange for the coin collection. Lyness refused, claiming that an agreement had been formed. ■

In this example, a court would probably determine that, because Lyness knew that Babitz was intoxicated and unable to understand what she was doing, Babitz would be allowed to disaffirm the agreement.

Like minors, intoxicated persons are liable in quasi contract for the reasonable value of necessaries actually furnished to them.

MENTALLY ILL PERSONS

Mentally ill persons are considered incompetent because, unlike normal persons, they are unable to comprehend either that they are making a contract or the effect of the contract on them. A distinction must be made, however, between a mentally ill person who has been judged incompetent by a court and one who has not been so judged.

If a mentally ill person has been determined incompetent by a court, the person is considered to be legally insane. Such a determination is usually made only after legal hearings and examinations by psychologists or psychiatrists. After the formal declaration of insanity, any agreement made by the insane person is void even though the other party to the contract was unaware of the court order. The court will usually appoint a guardian to take care of the business affairs of the insane person and, if necessary, to enter into agreements on her or his behalf. The appointment of a guardian serves as public notice that the insane person (called a *ward*) cannot make contracts. If the insane person does make a contract, the guardian may disaffirm it. The guardian must first return any consideration that the ward received, unless it has been damaged or destroyed or has deteriorated. A party dealing with an individual under guardianship may recover the fair value of any necessaries provided to the insane person. The money for these necessaries usually comes from the insane person's savings or other property. When guardianship ends, the insane person regains the capacity to make a contract.

The contracts of mentally ill persons not judged incompetent by a court are voidable. These persons may be suffering from an illness, such as serious depression, split personality, or loss of a sense of reality brought on by a traumatic experience (such as a war experience) or by brain damage. During these periods, they may be incompetent to enter into any contract. There may be other times, however, when they can enter into contracts just as any other person could. The burden of proof is on the person claiming the incompetency. A mentally ill person who can prove mental illness at the time of the contract may, during a period of normalcy, disaffirm or ratify the contract. Once the contract is ratified, it can no longer be disaffirmed. Innocent parties who are unaware of the other person's mental illness and who could not reasonably be expected to know about it are protected when they deal with these individuals. To disaffirm a contract under these circumstances, the mentally ill person must be able to return the consideration (or its equivalent in money) received under the contract to the innocent party.

> Garrison suffered brain damage in an automobile accident and had periods of confusion. During one of his confused periods, he sold a used VCR to Atkinson for $200. Atkinson was unaware of Garrison's mental illness. Garrison then wished to get his VCR back but was unable to return the $200 because he had spent the money foolishly. Because Garrison could not return the money and Atkinson was unaware of Garrison's condition, the courts generally would not permit Garrison to disaffirm the contract. ■

Like minors, this class of mentally ill persons is liable in quasi contract for the fair value of necessaries actually furnished to them.

It should be pointed out that in cases involving intoxication and mental illness (except those cases involving people judged incompetent by a court), incapacity of the individual is not the only basis used by the courts to make a decision. The fairness of the agreement to the parties involved is very important. Thus, if the contract seems fair and reasonable, the court most likely will declare that the party is competent and not allow a disaffirmance.

Summary of Important Legal Concepts

Competent parties are those persons legally and mentally capable of entering into agreements that are enforceable by law. Some persons, such as minors, persons under the influence of alcohol and other drugs, and mentally ill persons not declared insane have only a limited capacity to contract. Incompetent persons with a limited capacity to contract may back out of their contracts. This legal right to back out is called disaffirmance. Others are so completely incompetent that they have no legal capacity at all to contract. Mentally ill persons declared insane by a court are in this category. Competent parties generally deal with incompetent parties, especially minors, at their own risk.

Minors may usually disaffirm (avoid) ordinary

contracts they make any time before reaching majority and for a reasonable time thereafter. Adults who make contracts with minors, however, do not have this right to disaffirm and are bound by agreements they make. A minor cannot disaffirm an agreement for the sale of real estate (real property) to an adult until the minor reaches his or her majority. Moreover, statutes in many states prevent minors at varying ages from disaffirming certain agreements such as those relating to life insurance, a loan of money, a sale of stock, and a contract involving the minor's business. In most states, minors who deliberately lie and claim to have reached the age of majority may still disaffirm an agreement and recover any consideration paid. Minors may ratify (approve) agreements they make with adults only after reaching the age of majority. Once ratified, these agreements become legally binding and the privilege to disaffirm ends. However, minors cannot ratify only a part of an agreement and disaffirm another part. The entire agreement must be either ratified or disaffirmed. Minors have a quasi-contractual liability for the reasonable value of necessaries (items a person needs to live) actually received. A minor's station in life determines whether an item is a necessary. Parents generally have no legal liability for contracts made by their minor children unless they agree to become liable. Parents do, however, have the legal duty to support their minor children until the minors are emancipated.

Some agreements made by persons under the influence of alcohol or other drugs are voidable. Upon becoming sober, these persons may disaffirm an agreement made while intoxicated only if the other party purposely caused the person to become drunk or knew that the person was drunk and did not understand the consequences of the transaction. An intoxicated person who has the right to disaffirm must do so within a reasonable time after becoming sober or lose that right. He or she is, however, liable for the reasonable value of necessaries actually furnished to him or her.

Agreements made by mentally ill persons who have been declared legally insane by a court are void. Agreements made by mentally ill persons not declared insane by a court are voidable if these persons can prove their disability. When they understand what they did, they may disaffirm or ratify the contract, provided they return the consideration received under the contract to the innocent party. All mentally ill persons (whether legally declared insane or not) are liable for the reasonable value of necessaries furnished to them.

Key Legal Terms to Know

Match the terms with the definitions that follow.

competent parties
disaffirmance
emancipated minor
guardian
necessaries
ratify
station in life

1. Things that a person needs to live, such as food, clothing, shelter, and medical services
2. An adult appointed by the court to have custody and care of an incompetent person
3. A person's status in the community
4. The right of an incompetent party to refuse to carry out the terms of an agreement
5. Those persons legally and mentally capable of entering into agreements that are enforceable by law
6. To approve something, such as a previously voidable agreement
7. A self-supporting minor who is no longer subject to parental control and authority

Questions and Problems to Discuss

1. A minor has a quasi-contractual liability for necessaries. How does this differ from contractual liability?
2. Name some contracts that a minor may not disaffirm. For what reasons do you think minors may not disaffirm them?

Unless otherwise stated, assume that the age of majority is eighteen in all of the following problems.

3. Why does the law make minors liable for necessaries? How does a court determine what is a necessary if the parties cannot agree?
4. What is meant by the term *emancipation?* What is the significance of this term as it relates to a minor's liability for contracts?
5. Schaber, a minor, paid $950 for a used motorcycle. Two months later, while driving around town, she ran into a fire hydrant and wrecked the motorcycle. Schaber, still a minor, returned the wrecked motorcycle to the dealer and demanded the return of her $950. Is she entitled to recover the entire $950?
6. Luna, a minor, took out a low-interest college loan for one year to help pay her first year's tuition at a major university. Luna did use the money for her tuition. When payment was requested by the bank, she refused, claiming that she had the legal right to disaffirm the contract. Will Luna be allowed to disaffirm?
7. Martinson, who was legally insane and under guardianship, purchased a TV set for $750 from Mart's Department Store and charged it on his credit card. The store was unaware of Mar-

tinson's disability. Would Martinson be liable for payment?

8. Jefferson, a minor, contracted with the Keyes Employment Agency to find him employment as a chef. The agency found him a chef's job with a local hotel and he immediately started work. Jefferson refused to pay the $350 fee to the agency, claiming he was a minor and therefore not liable for his contracts. Can the employment agency legally collect its fee?

9. Week, a band leader, hired Taylor on a one-year contract to work as a soloist, not knowing that she was only seventeen years old. Taylor had said nothing about her age. When Week discovered Taylor was only seventeen, he discharged her. Did Week have a legal right to break the contract?

10. Moses, a self-supporting minor, purchased a van to carry on his business activities and to commute from his home to the college he attended part time. Before reaching majority, he tried to disaffirm the purchase of the van, but the dealer refused to accept return of the van or to refund the purchase price. Can Moses require the dealer to take back the van and return the purchase price?

11. Three months before his eighteenth birthday, Klick purchased a used pick-up truck for $2,500 from Page. He agreed in writing to pay $500 down and the balance in monthly payments of $50. After making ten payments, Klick tried to return the truck to Page and get his money back. Was Klick within his legal limits in returning the truck and asking for a refund of his money?

12. While intoxicated, Newton sold an antique pocket watch to Frank, an antique collector, for $20. Frank was unaware that Newton was intoxicated. The watch had actually been valued at $500. The next day when he was sober and learned what he had done, Newton returned the $20 to Frank and demanded his watch. Is Newton entitled to have the watch returned to him?

13. Connor, age seventeen, moved away from home. She rented a room in a nearby town and orally agreed to pay the landlady $160 a month for six months. Connor paid rent for three months and then moved out without paying the remaining three months' rent. The landlady claims that Connor is liable on her agreement to pay rent for the remaining three months even though she moved out. Is the landlady correct?

14. Mauro, a minor, traded his ten-speed bike to Grossman, an adult, for a used minibike. He later asked Grossman to return the ten-speed bike but was told that it had been sold to Seeley. Seeley did not know that the bike originally belonged to Mauro. Can Mauro recover the bike from Seeley?

15. Phillips, who was well known in his home town and whose actions generally appeared normal, charged $150 worth of candy in a department store. Phillips later returned the merchandise and asked the store to give him credit for $150. The store refused, stating that the sale was final. Phillips then returned to the store with a letter from his doctor stating that at times, he (Phillips) suffered periods of temporary insanity and was not totally capable of managing his affairs. In these circumstances, is Phillips entitled to a return of his money?

Cases to Decide

1. Husband, who was suffering from schizophrenia and manic depression, had been in and out of a mental hospital, but at no time had he been declared insane by a court. In fact, he continued to work at his job as a design engineer during the day, returning to the hospital at night. His wife initiated a separation agreement because of the husband's mental condition, although her husband did not really want a separation. At a time when he was depressed and did not fully understand the impact of the agreement, he did sign it. The agreement was signed by both parties in the presence of the wife's attorney, although the husband did not receive any legal advice from an attorney and did not really know the exact contents of the agreement. Later, when the husband realized what he had done, he requested that the separation agreement be canceled. The wife refused. Is the husband entitled to have this agreement canceled? (*G.A.S.* v. *S.I.S.*, 407 A2d 253, Family Court of Delaware)

2. Robertson, a minor, purchased a pick-up truck from King. For certain reasons, Robertson decided after he reached majority to disaffirm the contract, return the truck, and get back the purchase price he had paid. There was no evidence that he needed the truck in connection with his work. Is Robertson entitled to disaffirm the contract? (*Robertson* v. *King*, 225 Ark 276)

3. Goldberg, a minor, hired an attorney to sue Perlmuter for personal injuries. When the case was

settled, the attorney asked for his fee. Goldberg, however, asked the court to hold that the contract with the lawyer was void because Goldberg was a minor when the contract was made. Is this request valid? (*Goldberg* v. *Perlmuter*, 308 Ill App 84)

4. Bethea, a minor who needed a car for her work, purchased one and financed it through Bancredit. Bethea could not make the payments and Bancredit sued for the balance due on the car. Bethea claimed she was not liable because she was a minor when she signed the contract. Is Bethea liable for the balance due? (*Bancredit, Inc.* v. *Bethea*, 65 NJ Super 538, 168 A2d 250)

5. Watters was nineteen when he entered into a contract to buy a car. He stated that he was twenty-one (the age of majority in his state) and that he was in business. A short time later the car was destroyed in an accident. Watters then sued the seller to recover his payments on the grounds that he was a minor. Will he succeed? (*Watters* v. *Arrington*, 39 Ga App 275)

6. Vichnes, age fifteen, paid $160 to Transcontinental for an airline ticket from New York City to Los Angeles. She used the ticket but then tried to get her money back on the grounds that she was a minor. Could Vichnes legally avoid this agreement? (*Vichnes* v. *Transcontinental and Western Air*, 18 NY 2d 603)

7. Lange, a minor, borrowed $3,000 with interest from her guardian but didn't repay the loan. After the guardian's death, Ruehle, the person in charge of the guardian's estate, attempted to collect from Lange the amount due. Lange, who was no longer a minor, never formally ratified the contract but said, in the presence of witnesses, that she knew she would have to pay the interest on the loan. Is Lange bound to pay? (*Ruehle* v. *Lange*, Mich 194 NW 492)

8. Rogers, a minor, quit college when his wife became pregnant. Rogers signed a contract with Gastonia Personnel Agency and agreed to pay a fee if they found him a job. He had been a civil engineering major at college, and the agency secured him a job as a draftsman. Rogers, however, refused to pay the agency's fee, claiming that, as a minor, he was not legally bound on his contract with the agency. Was Rogers liable for payment of the fee? (*Gastonia Personnel Corporation* v. *Rogers*, 172 S.E. 2d 19)

9. Farrar, age seventeen and a minor, used her father's Master Charge to pay for membership in a Health Spa. When the father received the bill, he paid the amount due, including his daughter's charge for the spa membership. However, before her membership elapsed, Farrar attempted to disaffirm the contract on the grounds of infancy. Should Farrar be released from her contract because she is a minor? (*Farrar* v. *Swedish Health Spa*, 337 So. 2d 911)

Chapter 10

Legal Purpose

CHAPTER PREVIEW

This chapter examines the last requirement of a valid contract: legal purpose. Initially the chapter discusses the nature and general effect of illegal agreements, the circumstances under which agreements are deemed to be illegal, and the exceptions to the rule that courts will not enforce illegal agreements.

The remainder of the chapter lists and describes the agreements that are generally recognized as being illegal in most states. The final paragraph of the chapter points out the effect of an agreement that is partially legal and partially illegal.

THE NATURE AND GENERAL EFFECT OF ILLEGAL AGREEMENTS

The fourth and last requirement of a valid contract is that it must be made for a legal purpose. As discussed in Chapters 7–9, an agreement must contain an offer and an acceptance, both parties must receive consideration, and both parties must be competent. Even if these requirements are fulfilled, however, the agreement will be void and not enforceable in a court of law if the purpose of the agreement is illegal.

Some agreements, such as agreements to commit crimes, are entirely illegal; others contain only clauses that are illegal. In the event of a lawsuit, a court will simply refuse to hear a case involving an illegal agreement if both parties know the agreement is illegal—in such a case, both parties are *in pari delicto.* Neither party can successfully sue the other to seek enforcement of the agreement, to recover for breach of contract, to regain any consideration given, or for unjust enrichment. The court will sometimes hear a case involving an agreement that contains one or more illegal clauses if the agreement is legal in every other respect. If the court hears the case, it will simply not enforce the illegal clauses.

An agreement (or a clause in an agreement) is illegal if its purpose, or the manner in which it is carried out, is forbidden by state statute or opposed to a state's public policy. Courts in each state have their own interpretation of the term *public policy*—what is right and wrong. Generally, however, agreements opposed to public policy contain terms that are immoral or unethical or that interfere with the health, safety, or general welfare of the public. Courts often refuse to enforce such agreements even though they have not been expressly declared illegal.

There are exceptions to the rule that courts will not enforce illegal agreements. These exceptions are intended to prevent the injustice that can result from a rigid application of the general rule. One exception occurs when the two parties are not equally at fault. A court may rule in favor of the more innocent party. For example, when one individual unknowingly deals with a person who is not licensed as required by state law, a court will permit the innocent party to recover any money paid to the unlicensed person for services performed. Generally, ignorance of the law is no excuse, but in exceptional cases—as when it is necessary to protect the public from untrained people—a court will come to the aid of the party who was unaware of the facts that made the agreement illegal. Another exception relates to gambling. Statutes in some states permit a person who suffers gambling losses over a certain amount at such forms of gambling as cards and dice to recover these losses from the winner. These statutes apply only to gambling that is held at places other than legalized gambling casinos. Under such a statute, for example, a person may recover losses over a certain amount that occurred at a "friendly" poker game at a house party. The purpose of these statutes is not to protect those who lose money. Their purpose is to discourage gambling by putting people on notice that they may have to return their winnings to the loser.

One final aspect of illegal agreements is that one or both parties to an illegal agreement can be subject to criminal penalties if the act to be performed according to the agreement is a crime. The illegal agreements discussed in this chapter are generally recognized as illegal in most states.

AGREEMENTS FORBIDDEN BY STATE STATUTES

State legislatures have passed laws declaring certain types of agreements illegal and void because they cannot be performed without violating the state's civil and criminal statutes, licensing statutes, gambling statutes, usury statutes, or Sunday statutes.

Agreements That Violate Civil and Criminal Statutes

Agreements are illegal if they require one party to commit a tort or a crime. Examples of common torts are assault and battery, slander, libel, and fraud, and the infliction of mental distress on another. Arson, murder, burglary, larceny, robbery, selling illegal drugs, and buying stolen property are examples of acts that are considered crimes. Agreements to commit any one of these torts or crimes could not be enforced by either party. They would be absolutely void. To allow people to go to court to obtain enforcement of these types of agreements, which are so obviously contrary to law, would be ridiculous.

■ Lark, a candidate for mayor, agreed to pay Gordon, a newspaper reporter, $500 to write an article containing false statements that would damage the reputation of Barron, Lark's opponent. This agreement required Gordon to commit libel, and it was therefore illegal. A court would not enforce the agreement if Lark refused to pay Gordon. ■

Agreements to protect one party from the consequences of his or her tort or crime are also illegal.

■ The mayor induced one of her campaign workers to break into the home of an opponent in the upcoming election and to remove papers that would be helpful in the mayor's re-election campaign. The mayor agreed to pay the worker a large sum of money and to protect the campaign worker from criminal charges if caught. The agreement was illegal. The mayor and the campaign worker were both criminally liable for their illegal acts. ■

Agreements That Violate Licensing Statutes

All states have **licensing statutes,** laws that require individuals to have a license or permit to practice their occupations. These laws are designed to protect people from dealing with unqualified individuals. In most states, doctors, dentists, nurses, lawyers, pharmacists, public accountants, surveyors, architects, real estate brokers, insurance agents, funeral directors, barbers, beauticians, electricians, plumbers, and contractors must be licensed. When state statutes require a person to have a license to perform services for the general public, an agreement made with an unlicensed person is illegal.

Since the agreement is illegal, an unlicensed person cannot legally collect for the services performed. In some states, a person who performs services without the required license is guilty of a crime punishable by a fine, imprisonment, or both.

■ Lucas had graduated from law school but was not yet licensed to practice law. She spent several hours giving you legal advice and then sent a bill, which you refused to pay. Since Lucas was practicing law illegally (without a license), she cannot collect a fee for her services. Lucas may also be criminally liable for practicing law without a license. ■

If a person *unknowingly* deals with an unlicensed individual, the courts will allow that person to recover any money paid.

Some licensing statutes are merely intended to obtain revenue for the state or local government. Any person paying the fee can obtain a license without showing competence in a particular trade or profession. Since the purpose of such revenue-raising licensing statutes is not the protection of the public, agreements made with unlicensed persons are legally binding. The unlicensed person, however, is still subject to a criminal penalty for violating the licensing statute.

■ For $250 Arden hired Gammons, an auctioneer, to sell Arden's household goods at a public auction. The state's only requirement for an auctioneer's license, which Gammons did not obtain, was the payment of a $100 fee. After the auction, Arden learned that Gammons was not licensed and, as a result, refused to pay Gammons the $250. Since the statute was for revenue purposes only, Arden must pay Gammons the $250. Gammons, however, is guilty of violating the licensing law and may face action from the state. ■

Agreements That Violate Gambling Statutes

Gambling agreements are those in which one party wins and another party loses purely by chance, even though some skill is involved. In most states, gambling agreements are illegal. Agreements of this nature may include card playing for money, money wagers or bets on elections or such sports events as races and prize fights, or buying tickets for a football pool (called a lottery). Giveaway games, such as those used by stores for promotional purposes, are legal as long as they do not require participants to buy some article or ticket.

At one time, most states prohibited gambling. In recent years, however, many states have changed their laws to allow some kind of regulating gambling. State-run public lotteries, parimutuel betting at racetracks, off-track betting, and licensed bingo games conducted by churches and volunteer groups are examples of gambling permitted by statute. Other states have gone even further and permit casinos to operate various games of chance. For example, through a constitutional amendment, Atlantic City, New Jersey, has been authorized to carry on casino gambling. In return for permission to operate, the state collects a percentage of the gambling profits.

Those who gamble may be classified as casual gamblers or professional gamblers. **Casual gamblers** are those who participate in a gambling event socially and for pleasure. Casual gamblers are not ordinarily subject to a criminal penalty, but they may not enforce their gambling agreements in court; as gamblers, they are performing an illegal act.

■ Vaughn and Wren lived in a state where gambling agreements were illegal. They made a $200 bet on the World Series. When Vaughn won the bet, Wren refused to pay the $200. Vaughn then threatened to sue Wren in small claims court. Since the bet was illegal, Vaughn could not collect from Wren. Because they were casual gamblers, neither party was criminally liable. ■

A casual gambler in some states who loses a "friendly bet" (a small amount of money) in a gambling transaction may recover that money from the winner, even though the gambling agreement is illegal. In other states the "friendly" bettor cannot collect at all.

Professional gamblers are those who gamble as a business or profession, hoping to make a profit. In some states professional gamblers who operate gambling establishments are guilty of a crime.

Agreements That Violate Usury Statutes

Each state by statute sets a maximum interest rate that lenders can charge for loans of money. Although rates vary from state to state, the interest ceilings currently range from 10 to 16 percent per year. **Interest** is the compensation, or fee, that a borrower pays to a lender for the use of money. The interest rate the lender and borrower agree upon when the agreement is made cannot be more than the maximum rate allowed by state law.

■ You loaned $1,000 to a friend for one year and agreed on an interest rate of 20 percent. If you live in a state in which 12 percent is the maximum allowed by statute, the agreement with your friend is illegal. ■

Charging a higher rate of interest than that allowed by law is called **usury.** Usurious agreements are illegal. The civil penalty for usury varies among states. In most states the lender will be denied the right to collect any interest. In a few states, the lender forfeits both the principal and interest. In some states, the lender forfeits the excess interest received over the rate allowed. And in still other states, the injured party (the borrower) may recover damages equal to double or triple the usurious interest amount.

Usury laws were passed to protect borrowers from paying excessively high interest rates. By creating many exceptions to the usury laws, however (and this seems to be the trend), states have lessened the impact of these statutes. For example, special lenders such as small-loan companies, credit unions, and pawn shops may charge interest rates above the maximum rate allowed by state law. Borrowers also pay more than the state's maximum interest rate on consumer loans (such as car loans) and on real estate mortgage loans. Loans to corporations are also exempt from usury statutes in many states.

Usury statutes apply only to loans of money, not to sales of merchandise on credit. Although credit sales are not governed by state usury laws, they are regulated by other state statutes and by the federal Truth in Lending Law. Usury laws and the Truth in Lending Law are discussed in greater detail in Chapter 41.

Agreements That Violate Sunday Statutes

Sunday laws, or blue laws as they are sometimes called, govern the types of transactions that can be performed on Sundays. People's attitudes have changed since Sunday laws were first passed. As a result, laws restricting business and other activities on Sundays have been changed by modifying state statutes, by passing local ordinances, or by court decisions. Most states have either repealed or modified their Sunday statutes. In the few remaining states that have such statutes, the types of contracts that are illegal vary from state to state. The most common statute declares an agreement illegal and void if it is made on a Sunday or is to be performed on a Sunday. A court will not aid either party if there is a violation of a Sunday law.

Some courts hold that parties to an agreement made on a Sunday may ratify it on a regular business day. Complete performance by both parties or partial performance by one party also acts as a ratification of the agreement. After ratification, the courts consider the agreement remade on the weekday and enforce it as such.

In most states, repayment of money due on a Sunday or legal holiday can be postponed until the first business day after the Sunday or holiday.

> Murphy, who borrowed $250 from McGrath, agreed to repay the loan in sixty days. The due date of the loan fell on a Sunday. Murphy would not be obligated to repay the loan until Monday, the next business day. ∎

Sunday laws do not apply to agreements made to protect life, health, or property or made on behalf of religious or charitable organizations. In some states, Sunday laws do not apply to persons who observe the Sabbath on some other day.

AGREEMENTS OPPOSED TO PUBLIC POLICY

Agreements that are considered illegal and void in most states because they are opposed to public policy include agreements that disclaim liability for negligence, interfere with the administration of justice, interfere with the performance of a public duty, harm marriage, unreasonably restrain competition and trade, or are unconscionable.

Agreements That Disclaim Liability for Negligence

Businesspeople and others often place **exculpatory clauses** in agreements, excusing themselves in advance (or at least limiting their liability) from any payment for injury or damages caused by their acts. Courts tend to judge the legality of such clauses on a case-by-case basis. An exculpatory clause is generally held to be contrary to public policy and therefore void and unenforceable against an injured party. While recognizing the importance of freedom of contract, the courts also wish to protect members of the general public who are not always alert to the consequences of signing a contract containing a clause that relieves businesspeople from liability. Such clauses are especially likely to be held to be unenforceable if one party is required to sign the agreement on a take-it-or-leave-it basis because the other party is in a superior bargaining position. Examples of those in superior bargaining positions include businesses that perform services for the general public, such as common carriers, public utilities, hospitals, apartment owners, banks, car repair shops, and public garages.

> ■ McGinnis parked his car in a public parking lot and received a claim check. His attention was called to the back of the claim check, which stated that the owner of the lot was not liable for the loss of cars through fire or theft. When McGinnis's car was stolen from the lot because of the lot owner's negligence, the lot owner was liable in spite of the exemption provision on the claim check. ■

Not all exculpatory clauses are against public policy and void. In cases where such a clause is worded so that the exemption from liability is narrow in scope and the wording in the exemption is conspicuous (that is, not in fine print), the clause may be upheld in court as valid and binding on the parties.

> ■ When Benz became a member of the Supercare Health Spa, he was required to complete and sign an application that included a release, on which was written in bold print, "relieving the spa owners and operators from all risks of injury that a member suffers while participating in club activities." One evening as Benz was leaving the shower at the spa, he slipped on the wet tile floor, fell, and was injured. It was determined that the injury resulted from the spa's negligence in maintaining the shower room. The spa claimed that regardless of this fact, the release form that Benz signed relieved the owners from liability. The spa would probably lose this case. ■

In the above example, a court would probably rule that the exculpatory clause contained in the application was against public policy and void. The clause as written was too broad—it relieved the club of liability *for all injuries* sustained by a member while participating in club activities (that is, regardless of how the injury occurred). If the spa wished to include in its application a clause that could be upheld in court (and that would therefore be binding on those who signed), the clause should have been worded so that the spa was relieved of liability *for negligence only* (negligence of spa employees or negligence in maintaining spa equipment). Wording that narrowed the grounds for relieving the spa of liability would have increased the chances of the court's ruling in favor of the spa if a lawsuit arose.

Exculpatory clauses that relieve a party from liability for injury or damage beyond its control will usually be upheld in court.

In most cases, courts will not enforce exculpatory clauses that attempt to relieve a contracting party from his or her own criminal conduct, from intentional injury or damages, or gross negligence. To uphold such clauses would place the rights and safety of the party or parties signing such agreements in jeopardy.

In some states, exculpatory clauses in certain types of contracts, such as leases, have been declared illegal by statute.

Agreements That Interfere with the Administration of Justice

Agreements that tend to interfere with the proper administration of justice— that prevent the law from being applied fairly—are illegal. Examples of agreements that tend to obstruct justice include an agreement to pay a witness to give false testimony or to conceal evidence during a court trial, an agreement to pay a juror to vote a certain way in a trial, and an agreement not to prosecute a person who has committed a crime in return for a sum of money.

> Kern, an employee at Van's Automobile Agency, stole $5,000 from the company safe. Kern returned the stolen money, and Van promised not to prosecute if Kern agreed to pay him $1,000. Kern agreed but then refused to pay Van the money. Van could not enforce this illegal agreement in a court of law. ■

Furthermore, since these agreements may also require the commission of a crime, the parties may be subject to criminal penalties.

Agreements That Interfere with the Performance of a Public Duty

People have the right to expect that elected and appointed officials will perform their duties properly and honestly. Agreements that tend to prevent the proper performance of duties by public officials are opposed to public policy and therefore illegal. An agreement to bribe a judge, a police officer, or the district attorney in return for a favor is illegal. Likewise, an agreement is illegal if a public official agrees to accept money for performing a legal duty, for promising *not* to perform a legal duty, or for promising to use personal influence to affect the passage of a law.

Lobbying is the practice of trying to influence the members of a legislative body to pass or defeat certain bills. As a rule, lobbying is not illegal. You can make an agreement to pay an attorney or an expert in a particular field to present your case to the lawmaker, leaving it up to the lawmaker to decide on the issue. However, an agreement to influence a legislator's decision by using bribery, threats, or other improper means is illegal.

> An influential state senator agreed to accept $100,000 from Taber in return for influencing other legislators to pass a law permitting casino gambling. The senator succeeded in getting the law passed, but Taber refused to pay. Since this agreement was illegal, the senator could not seek payment from Taber in a court of law. ■

Because these agreements, like many other agreements mentioned in this chapter, often involve the commission of a crime, the parties to an agreement that interferes with the performance of a public duty may be subject to criminal penalties.

Agreements That Harm Marriage

Our society favors and encourages marriage and family life. Therefore, agreements that place unreasonable restraints or tend to discourage marriage completely are generally illegal. For example, agreements are illegal if one party promises never to marry, promises not to marry for an unreasonable amount of time, or promises not to marry a certain person.

> Siegel, fearing his only daughter would leave him, promised to give her $15,000 if she would never marry. The daughter agreed and accepted the $15,000. Two years later she married. Siegel sued to recover the $15,000. The agreement is illegal, and he is not entitled to recover the money. ■

On the other hand, an agreement that places a reasonable restriction on marriage is legally binding. For example, the courts have held that an agreement to postpone marriage until reaching the age of majority is legal. This postponement is considered to be legal detriment.

Since the law seeks to preserve marriage, an agreement between a husband and wife to obtain a divorce for consideration is illegal and will not be enforced.

> Jason promised to give his wife $10,000 and a trip around the world if she would divorce him. His wife obtained a divorce, but Jason refused to carry out his part of the agreement. Because this agreement was illegal, Jason was not legally bound. ■

Agreements That Unreasonably Restrain Competition and Trade

Agreements or clauses that unreasonably restrain or restrict competition and trade are illegal. These agreements take many forms; two such agreements are an agreement not to compete and an agreement to create a monopoly or limit competition.

An Agreement Not to Compete   When a person buys a business, such as a pizza parlor, printing business, or a stereo center, that person is also buying the seller's goodwill—the continued patronage of old and loyal customers. No one would want a business if the seller could open a similar business nearby and draw away the old customers. The purchaser needs some assurance that customers will continue to trade at the old store. Consequently, it is customary to include in the purchase agreement a clause that prevents the seller from competing in the same business within a certain territory for a certain period of time. These clauses are legal and enforceable if the territory and time restrictions are reasonable enough to protect the purchaser. If the restrictions are unreasonable, the clause is illegal and void.

A territory restriction should not go beyond the trade area of the business. The trade area for a small card and gift business might be a mile or two. If a business is citywide, such as a laundromat with stores in various neighborhoods, a clause restricting competition anywhere in the city might be reasonable. Similarly, if the business is statewide or national, such as a well-known chain of motels, a restriction not to compete anywhere in the state or nation may be upheld as reasonable.

A time restriction should not be longer than is reasonably necessary for the purchaser to obtain the goodwill of previous customers and attract new customers. In the sale of a popular local restaurant, twenty-five years would be unreasonable, but two or three years probably would not be.

> Skerritt operated a bakery in a village of approximately 5,000 people. She sold her bakery to Van Gelder. The written sales agreement included a clause preventing her (Skerritt) from opening another bakery in the village for a period of six months. Since both the time and territory restrictions were reasonable for a shop located in a small village, the clause in the sales agreement was legally enforceable. ■

Territory and time restrictions imposed by the purchaser of a business may also be imposed by an employer upon an employee. As loyalty between businesses (especially corporations) and their workers hits an all-time low, employers claim that more people are defecting to competitors and divulging company secrets. Many companies, therefore, are increasingly asking employees—especially middle- or top-management personnel—to sign "noncompete" agreements preventing these workers from either setting up a similar business or working for a competitor. Noncompete agreements generally are upheld even when someone is forced out of a job. To be legally enforceable, the territory and time restrictions must be reasonable and necessary to protect the employer's interests. Today's noncompete clauses generally bar someone from working for a rival for six months to five years.

> ■ Crowley was hired as a consultant by Jensen, the owner of several weight loss clinics throughout Ohio. When she took the job, Crowley signed an employment agreement containing a clause stating that upon termination of her employment she would not start a similar business for three years in the state of Ohio. Since the weight loss clinics were statewide and the time limit was only three years, the territory and time restrictions were reasonable. ■

Frequently, a partnership agreement between professional people contains a clause stating that upon retiring or leaving the partnership, the partner will not start a competing business. These clauses are also enforceable if the restrictions on territory and time are reasonably necessary to protect the remaining partners.

When clauses are found to be unreasonable and therefore illegal and void, the modern view is for courts to throw out the clause, leaving the remainder of the agreement to be enforceable. (The traditional view still followed in some states is for the courts to throw out the entire agreement.) However, in some instances some courts have enforced the clause to a reasonable extent to prevent undue hardships to the parties. For example, if a clause states that a person will not open another business in the entire state of Ohio for fifty years, the court may change its terms to cover only the city of Cleveland for a period of three years.

An Agreement to Create a Monopoly or Limit Competition A monopoly occurs when one person or business controls all or nearly all of the trade or supply of a particular item within an area to the exclusion of all competition. An agreement to create or maintain a monopoly is not only opposed to public policy but also a violation of federal and state laws. These laws, called *antitrust laws,* are discussed in more detail in Chapter 28.

> ■ Bonney, who owned an established sporting goods store, learned that Sibinski planned to open a sporting goods store less than a block away. Bonney agreed to pay Sibinski $25,000 if Sibinski would not open the sporting goods store as planned. Since this agreement tended to create a monopoly and was illegal, a court would not enforce the agreement if Sibinski opened up the sporting goods store as originally planned. ■

Not all monopolies are illegal, however. Some occur because the person or business has a superior product or service that consumers are willing to buy. The efficiency, skill, and innovative practices of a person or business may also enable that business to develop naturally into a monopoly. Still other companies, such as utilities companies, are given the exclusive right to provide a product or service within a certain area by government. It is only when a business deliberately and unreasonably seeks to eliminate competition that it is illegal.

An agreement that limits competition by controlling or fixing prices, dividing up trade territory, or limiting production is also considered illegal and violates both federal and state antitrust laws.

■ Flanigan and Rinhart both sold class rings to students in schools within a ten-county area. After raising the price of the rings, they agreed that Flanigan would sell only to schools in five counties and Rinhart only to schools in the other five counties. This agreement tended to control prices and trade territory, and it was therefore illegal. ■

Agreements That Are Unconscionable

An **unconscionable agreement** is one that is too grossly unfair or harsh to be upheld in court. Unconscionable agreements violate public policy. Since public policy is a concept reflecting a court's idea of what is right and wrong, there are no limits to the types of contracts a court will find unfair or harsh. Among modern court decisions, including decisions governing the sale of goods under the UCC, unconscionability has been applied to contracts involving questionable sales tactics, unequal bargaining power of the parties, the basic illiteracy of one party, grossly excessive price terms, terms written in small print limiting the liability of one of the parties, or hidden clauses in fine print. Unconscionability has been applied to standard contracts that favor one party over another, such as a lease that favors the landlord or an insurance policy that favors the company and must be accepted on a take-it-or-leave-it basis; contracts with clauses disclaiming liability; and contracts with provisions requiring a buyer to waive certain legal rights.

■ Smith purchased a stereo system for $700 (which included the total finance charge) by making a down payment of $100 and agreeing to make twelve equal monthly payments of $50 each. A clause in the fine print of the contract stated that the buyer would also have to pay an additional charge of $75 with the final payment to cover additional costs identified by the seller as reasonable and necessary to make the sale. Smith refused to pay the $75 and the seller sued. Since this contract seemed unfair under the circumstances, a court may refuse to enforce it. ■

Recently decided cases show that most unconscionable contracts involve poor and otherwise disadvantaged consumers.

PARTIALLY ILLEGAL AGREEMENTS

An agreement may be partially legal and partially illegal. The legal part of the agreement may be enforced if it can be separated from the illegal part. If the agreement is so complicated that it is not possible to separate the illegal part, the entire agreement is void and unenforceable.

■ McGrail was studying to become a licensed electrician. It was illegal in his state to perform services for the public without a license. Nevertheless, he purchased and then installed some light fixtures for a neighbor. Even though McGrail could not collect for the cost of his labor in installing the light fixtures because he was not properly licensed, he could collect for the cost of the light fixtures. ■

Summary of Important Legal Concepts

In addition to offer and acceptance, consideration, and competent parties, the law imposes a requirement that the purpose of the agreement be legal. Agreements that are completely illegal are usually void and unenforceable. Some agreements are entirely illegal; others may only contain illegal clauses. There are exceptions to the rule that courts will not enforce illegal agreements. One exception occurs when both parties are not equally at fault. A court may in this case come to the aid of the party who was unaware of the facts that made the agreement illegal. For example, an individual who unknowingly deals with an unlicensed person may be permitted to recover any money paid to this person for services performed. Another exception relates to statutes that in some states permit gamblers who lose a "friendly bet" (a small amount of money) in a gambling transaction to recover the money from the winner.

An agreement may be illegal either because it is forbidden by state statute or because it is opposed to a state's public policy. Agreements that have been made illegal by most state legislatures are those that violate civil and criminal statutes, licensing statutes, gambling statutes, usury statutes (those in which a lender charges a higher rate of interest than that allowed by law), or Sunday statutes. Agreements that are illegal in most states because they are opposed to public policy (as decided by the courts in each state) include agreements that disclaim liability for negligence (exculpatory clauses), interfere with the administration of justice, interfere with the performance of a public duty, are harmful to marriage, unreasonably restrain competition and trade, or are unconscionable (grossly unfair).

An agreement may be partially legal and partially illegal. If it can be separated from the part that is illegal, the legal part of the agreement may be enforced.

Key Legal Terms to Know

Match the terms with the definitions that follow.

casual gambler
exculpatory clause
gambling agreement
in pari delicto
interest
licensing statutes
lobbying
professional gambler
Sunday laws
unconscionable agreement
usury

1. The fee paid for the use of money
2. A person who gambles for pleasure
3. A person who gambles as a profession
4. An agreement in which one party wins and another loses purely by chance
5. Trying to influence lawmakers to vote for or against certain legislation
6. Laws requiring individuals to have a license or a permit to practice their occupation
7. Laws that govern the types of transactions that can be performed on Sundays
8. A clause in a contract that excuses a party in advance from liability for negligence
9. Charging a higher rate of interest than allowed
10. An agreement considered too grossly unfair to be upheld in court
11. A term indicating that both parties know an agreement is illegal

Questions and Problems to Discuss

1. What is an exculpatory clause? When is it legal to include such a clause in a contract? When is it illegal?
2. Courts generally do not enforce illegal agreements. What are the exceptions to this rule?
3. What effect does an illegal contract have on the parties?
4. Marta's parents promised to give her $25,000 if she promised not to marry until she reached the age of majority. She agreed. Just before reaching majority, she married. Her parents requested the return of their $25,000. Are Marta's parents legally entitled to the money?

5. Stanford, president of a local labor union, wanted to open a restaurant and bar. Because of a criminal record, however, he could not obtain a liquor license. Stanford agreed to secure the votes of the members of his labor union for a local judge running for re-election. He also agreed to keep the voters who disliked the judge away from the polls in a certain ward on election day. In return, the judge was to use her influence with the state liquor commission to obtain the necessary liquor license for Stanford. Was this agreement legal?

6. Argo, a crane operator, was hired by a local hospital to excavate an area for a new surgical wing to be added to the hospital's existing structure. A series of accidents occurred on the job as a result of the crane operator's poor judgment, which caused problems for the hospital. When the hospital discovered that Argo was an unlicensed operator, it fired him and refused to pay any more money due under the terms of the contract. Argo sued for breach of contract. Will he succeed?

7. Nichols paid Rivera, her state senator, $1,000 in exchange for the senator's promise to vote for the passage of a malpractice bill when it came up for a vote in the legislature. Rivera failed to vote yes; Nichols then demanded the return of her $1,000. Is Nichols entitled to a return of her money?

8. While visiting a friend at Solar Prison, Kelly was offered $10,000 by Martinez if Kelly promised to help him (Martinez) plan and carry out an escape from prison. Kelly agreed and received $10,000 through a friend of Martinez. Kelly then decided not to carry out his promise and Martinez demanded the return of his money. Is Martinez legally entitled to this money?

9. A Vietnamese family was relocated in New York City by the U.S. government. Because Troung, the father, was unable to find work, the family was temporarily provided housing and a small monthly allowance by the New York City Welfare Department. In need of a stove, Troung purchased one at the S & M Appliance Center. Knowing that Troung had a very limited knowledge of the English language, the salesperson sold him a stove for $1,100 on an installment basis, although the same stove was selling to the general public for $900. During a routine interview with the family, an interpreter from the welfare department discovered the circumstances in which Troung had purchased the stove. She returned to the S & M Appliance Center with Troung and asked the owner to refund the $200 to Troung. The owner refused. Troung took the case to court, claiming that the agreement was unfair. In the circumstances, could the court require the owner of the S & M Appliance Center to refund the $200?

10. Banner, a dentist in Boston, Massachusetts, retired and sold his practice to a younger person. The sales agreement included a provision preventing Banner from re-entering the practice of dentistry for ten years within the state of Massachusetts. Was this agreement enforceable by the purchaser?

11. Peacock, a student in her last year of medical school, treated Reston at the scene of an accident and billed her for $50. Reston claimed that since Peacock did not have a license to practice medicine, Reston did not have to pay the $50. Is Reston correct?

12. You and Higgins made a $50 bet on the outcome of the Super Bowl. After your team won, Higgins refused to pay you the $50. Could you legally sue Higgins for the $50?

13. Kilmer, a prison guard, promised McKay, another prison guard, $300 to assault a prisoner who had given Kilmer trouble. McKay agreed and Kilmer paid him the $300. McKay then changed his mind and refused to carry out the agreement. Kilmer demanded the return of his $300, but McKay refused. Is Kilmer legally entitled to recover the $300 in a lawsuit?

14. Lando, chairwoman of an environmental group, was interested in the passage of a bill that banned smoking in all public places. For $2,000 she hired an attorney to draft the bill and argue for its passage before a senator interested in environmental matters. This senator was convinced of the value of the bill and urged other senators to vote in favor of its passage. The bill was passed by the legislature and became law. The attorney then demanded payment. Can Lando refuse payment on the grounds that what the attorney did was illegal?

15. Ryan purchased a rifle and other hunting equipment in a local department store on credit. Ryan made a down payment and agreed to pay the balance due with interest in six monthly installments. The interest Ryan was charged exceeded the maximum amount allowed under the usury

statutes of the state. The penalty for usury in this state allowed the borrower to withhold payment of both the principal and interest due. Ryan learned of the usury statute and stopped making payments to the department store. The department store sued, claiming that the usury statutes did not apply in this case. Is the department store correct?

Cases to Decide

1. Berner and a number of other investors purchased stock from a San Francisco–based stock brokerage firm known as Bateman Eichler by getting an inside tip from one of the brokers employed by the firm (an illegal practice called *trading on insider information*). Based on the tip, the stock would rise in value and the investors would make a large profit. When the tip turned out to be false, Berner and the other investors sued the stock brokerage firm for its losses because the market price of the stock fell far below the prices they paid for it. The trial court dismissed the complaint, concluding that the agreement to purchase the stock was illegal because the parties to the lawsuit were *in pari delicto*. Consequently, the plaintiffs were absolutely barred from recovery. An appeals court reversed the lower court's ruling and claimed that, regardless of the *in pari delicto* ruling by the lower court, Berner and the investors could still collect. Bateman Eichler appealed this decision to the U.S. Supreme Court. Should the Supreme Court decide in favor of Bateman Eichler, the stock brokerage firm? (U.S. Supreme Court, 472 U.S. 299)

2. The University of California Medical Center admitted Tunkl as a patient. While under sedation and unable to read, Tunkl was required, as a condition for admission, to sign a document containing a clause releasing the hospital from any and all liability for the negligent or wrongful acts of its employees. Alleging personal injuries from the negligence of two physicians at the Medical Center, Tunkl sued the hospital for damages. Can the hospital excuse itself from any and all liability from the wrongful acts? (*Tunkl* v. *Regents of University of California*, 383 P.2d 441)

3. Water Services, Inc., developed a secret process to purify water for industrial use. All employees of Water Services, as part of the contract of em-

ployment, promised that for two years after leaving the company they would not engage in any business that could be considered competitive to Water Services in any territory in which they had performed services under their contract. Glad, an employee of Water Services, had worked on the secret process and was familiar with it. Glad resigned from Water Services and immediately got a job with Tesco, the competitor of Water Services. Tesco had been trying to develop a water purification system of its own. Using the confidential information he had acquired from Water Services, Glad helped Tesco develop a competitive system. When Water Services sued to enforce its employment agreement with Glad, Tesco claimed that Glad's contract with Water Services was illegal because it was in restraint of trade. Do you agree? (*Water Services* v. *Tesco Chemical, Inc.*, 410 F2d 163)

4. Tovar was hired as a full-time resident physician at Paxton Hospital. He was not licensed to practice medicine in Illinois as required by Illinois state law. Upon discovering that he had no Illinois license, the hospital fired Tovar. He sued for breach of contract. Did the hospital have the right to fire Tovar? (*Tovar* v. *Paxton Community Memorial Hospital*, 29 Ill App 2d 218, 330 NE 2d 247)

5. EPI and Basler entered into an employment contract providing that if Basler's employment was terminated, Basler couldn't compete with EPI for one year within a 200-mile radius of Cleveland, EPI's home base. When his employment terminated, Basler went into business selling some of the same items. EPI sought to stop Basler from continuing in business. Basler offered evidence to show that EPI did little business beyond a 60-mile radius. Should EPI be successful in preventing Basler from continuing in business? (*EPI of Cleveland, Inc.* v. *Basler*, 12 Ohio App 2d 16)

6. Womack, a gambler, paid Maner, a judge, $1,675 to prevent him from being prosecuted and sentenced in the judge's court for illegal gambling. Womack later sued to recover the $1,675, claiming that the agreement was illegal and void. Is Womack entitled to recover the money? (*Womack* v. *Maner*, 227 Ark 786)

7. Eden and Berle entered into a contract whereby Eden, an author, would write a novel to be published with Berle's name as sole author. They also agreed to divide equally all the profits from the work. Eden wrote the book, but Berle

wouldn't permit the book to be published. Eden then sued Berle for damages for breach of contract. Should Eden be successful in the lawsuit? (*Roddy-Eden* v. *Berle,* 108 NYS 2d 597)

8. Haynes, of Austin, Minnesota, sold his business, the Haynes Bookkeeping and Tax Service, to Monson. In the sales contract, Haynes agreed that for a period of five years he would not engage in the business of bookkeeping, accounting, or tax practice within a 50-mile radius. Haynes then moved 100 miles away to Red Wing, Minnesota, and opened a new office. Haynes kept his home in Austin and continued to furnish bookkeeping and tax services for his old customers. Contacts with old customers were maintained by a telephone answering service at Haynes's Austin home. Haynes returned to his Austin home every week or two to obtain the information he needed to do the work. Information was also left with relatives who mailed it to his Red Wing office. When sued by Monson for breach of contract, Haynes claimed that he did not actively solicit the business from the people of Austin and, therefore, did not breach the clause not to compete. Would you agree? (*Haynes* v. *Monson,* 301 Minn 327)

Chapter 11

Contracts That Must Be in Writing

CHAPTER PREVIEW

This chapter identifies the relatively few contracts that are required by law to be in writing to be enforceable in court. The chapter also summarizes the essential information that the writing must contain in order to satisfy the law. A brief opening discussion points out the advantages that written contracts have over those that are made orally. The concluding pages of the chapter explain a rule that protects the terms of a contract from changes by one of the parties after the contract has been reduced to writing and is the final expression of their intentions.

THE STATUS OF ORAL AND WRITTEN CONTRACTS

Few people realize that oral contracts are just as enforceable as written contracts if they contain all the elements necessary to make a contract legally binding (those discussed in Chapters 7–10) and if the terms of the oral contracts can be proved in a court of law. In fact, most contracts are *not* in writing. Nevertheless, many lawsuits based on breach of valid oral contracts have been dismissed by courts because the parties who brought them could not sufficiently establish their terms.

Unless an agreement falls into one of the categories that is required by law to be in writing, a contract may be either oral or written. But written contracts have advantages over oral contracts. A written contract needs no witnesses to establish its existence and its terms. If there are no witnesses to an oral contract, one of the parties might deny that the contract ever existed or might disagree on the exact terms of the contract. Even if there are witnesses to an oral contract, they may disagree about the contract's exact terms. To avoid misunderstandings and disagreements, you should ensure that all important contracts are in writing.

Relatively few contracts are required by law to be in writing; they are discussed in the pages that follow.

CONTRACTS REQUIRED TO BE IN WRITING

Every state has a law requiring that, to be enforceable, certain kinds of contracts must be in writing. This law, called the **statute of frauds** (based on the English Statute of Frauds passed in 1677), does not pertain to all contracts but only to six specific types. The statute of frauds does not eliminate the other essential elements of a valid contract (offer and acceptance, consideration, competent parties, and legal purpose). It simply adds the requirement of written evidence that a contract existed. The types of contracts that are frequently required to be in writing in the various states are the following:

1. A contract to pay the debt of another person.
2. A contract by an executor or administrator to pay the debts of a deceased person from his or her own pocket.

3. A contract for the sale of real property or an interest in real property.

4. A contract in consideration of marriage.

5. A contract that cannot be performed within one year.

6. A contract for the sale of goods or merchandise for the price of $500 or more. This particular type of contract is governed by the Uniform Commercial Code and is discussed in Chapter 15.

In addition to these contracts, some states require other types of contracts to be in writing. These contracts include a contract appointing an agent to sell real estate, a promise to pay a debt discharged in bankruptcy, a promise to be released from an ordinary debt, as well as various types of consumer transactions such as a loan of money. If a state statute does not require that a contract be in writing, an oral contract is enforceable.

The statute of frauds applies only to executory contracts; that is, contracts that have not been fully performed. As a result, if two parties fully perform an oral contract that should have been in writing, it would be unenforceable for either party to try to have the contract set aside because it was not in writing.

■ Carpenter sold Black, her neighbor, a half acre of land that bordered on Black's property. The contract was an oral one. A short time later, Carpenter changed her mind, returned the purchase price to Black, and asked for the document of ownership for the land. Black refused. Carpenter then asked the court to void the contract because it was not in writing. Since the agreement had been fully performed, the statute of frauds does not apply. Carpenter is bound by the contract terms. ■

A Contract to Pay the Debt of Another Person

A contract one person (the guarantor) makes with a creditor to pay a third person's debt must be in writing to be enforceable. Under this type of agreement, called a *guaranty*, the guarantor's promise to pay is secondary to the promise of the person who owes the money (the debtor). That is, the debtor is still responsible for paying the debt; the guarantor is responsible *only* if the debtor fails to pay. If necessary, the creditor would first be required to sue the debtor and obtain a judgment. A judgment, in this case, is a court order directing the debtor to pay the debt owed to the creditor. If the debtor refuses, the creditor could then proceed against the guarantor.

■ Marks, a dentist, agreed to perform a root canal for Derringer. Derringer was short of cash and would not have the money to pay for the dental work until several months after it was scheduled to be completed. Simons, Derringer's brother-in-law, telephoned the dentist and said, "Go ahead and do the root canal. If she doesn't pay for it, I will." When Derringer failed to pay, Marks billed Simons. Simons would not be liable for payment, however, since his guaranty was not in writing. ■

An agreement does not come within the statute of frauds if you make yourself primarily responsible for the payment of a debt. An oral agreement in this case would be enforceable.

> Brandon said to the owner of Allston Video Sales, "Sell my daughter (an adult) a stereo and send the bill to me." ■

In the above example, Brandon did not promise to pay if the daughter did not pay. Instead Brandon assumed primary responsibility for the amount of the daughter's purchase. Since the debt became Brandon's and Brandon's alone, the owner of Allston Video Sales would look only to Brandon for payment.

A Contract to Pay the Debt of a Deceased Person

An *executor* or *administrator* is one who handles the property (or estate) of a deceased person. An executor gathers the assets of the deceased, pays all debts, and distributes the remaining property according to the terms of a will or state law. The executor is not personally responsible for the debts of the deceased; the debts are paid out of the deceased person's estate. If, however, there is not enough money to pay all the debts, an executor may promise to pay the debts from her or his own personal funds. Such an agreement, which is actually an agreement to become responsible for the debts of another, must be in writing to be enforceable.

> When he died, Morten had an estate worth $10,000 but owed creditors $12,000. Morten's daughter, the executor of the estate, wanted to clear her father's name. She made an oral agreement with the creditors to pay the additional $2,000 owed by her father out of her own pocket. This oral agreement by Morten's daughter was not legally enforceable by the creditors. ■

A Contract for the Sale of Real Property

A contract for the sale of real property must be in writing to be enforceable. **Real property** is land or anything permanently attached to the land such as a building. The contract of sale, sometimes called a purchase offer, consists of an offer by the buyer and an acceptance by the seller. The purchase offer must also contain the other essential elements of a contract.

> Newman placed a sign on her front lawn advertising her house for sale. Julian saw the sign, stopped, inspected the house, and orally offered Newman the $40,000 asking price. Newman accepted. After Newman had taken down the sign and worked out the details of the sale, Julian refused to go through with the purchase of the property. Since the statute of frauds requires that all contracts for the sale of real property be in writing, Julian was not bound by the oral contract. ■

It is not uncommon for people to enter into oral contracts involving real property. If, in the above problem, Julian made a deposit on the house, the oral contract for the sale of the house would still not be enforceable. In the eyes of the law, the deposit could be returned without injury to Julian. On the other hand, Newman may have immediately transferred possession of the house to Julian, with the deed of ownership to be given later. In this case, if Julian made improvements to the house, such as painting and making certain repairs, the law most likely would not permit Newman to cancel the sale and retake possession of the house because the agreement was not in writing.

A contract for a temporary transfer of an interest in real property must also be in writing. An *interest* in this sense is a legal right to the use of or a claim on real property. Examples of interests include mortgages, easements, and leases. A *lease* is an agreement by which an owner of real property rents that property to another party. In most states an oral lease for a term of one year or less is valid.

■ Clinton orally agreed to rent a house from Jeffers for one year. This oral agreement does not have to be in writing to be enforceable because it is only for one year. ■

A Contract in Consideration of Marriage

Two people who plan to marry for the first time may agree to give up rights or take on obligations that are not an implied obligation of the marriage itself. They may do so through a **prenuptial agreement.** Prenuptial (also called *antenuptial*) agreements, however, are not enforceable, unless they are in writing.

■ Harmon a wealthy, middle-aged man, orally promised Shanna that he would give her a $500 weekly allowance if she would marry him. After they were married, Harmon refused to pay his wife the weekly allowance. Harmon was not bound by his promise because it was not in writing. ■

Prenuptial agreements are especially useful for couples who, having been married before and having accumulated property, plan to marry a second time but wish to regulate inheritance rights.

■ Whitney and Banks decide to marry. It is a second marriage for both. They sign a prenuptial agreement whereby each promises to waive any inheritance rights to the other's money and/or property accumulated up to the point of their second marriage. Each wishes the children of his or her prior marriage to be the sole heirs (those entitled to inherit) of the money or property. ■

In the above example, a court will hold the agreement enforceable as long as Whitney and Banks understood the legal consequences of what they agreed to do and knew the full extent of each other's property. Courts are increasingly upholding prenuptial agreements, provided they are fair and reasonable, and were entered into freely (that is, made without threats).

A Contract That Cannot Be Performed Within One Year

A contract must be in writing if its terms cannot be carried out within one year of the date of the agreement. The year legally begins when the contract is made, not when performance is to start.

■ Carson, who owned a bakery, planned a trip to Arizona for health reasons. On March 13 she orally agreed to hire Warren for one year to manage her business while she was away. Warren was to manage the bakery from May 1 of that year to April 30 of the next year. Since this contract cannot be completed within one year of the date of the agreement (March 13), it must be in writing to be enforceable. ■

The statute of frauds does not apply if it is possible to carry out the terms of the contract within one year. The key is the *possibility* of performance, not the actual performance. Therefore, a contract to care for someone for the rest of her or his life need not be in writing. Even though such a "lifetime" agreement may not be completed for several years, it is possible that the person being cared for may die within one year. (Some states require lifetime agreements to be in writing to be enforceable.) A contract to perform lawn work for as long as the lawn service company "is in business" need not be in writing. The company could be in business for many years, but it could also go bankrupt next month.

■ Darwood orally agreed to support his elderly aunt until she died rather than have her placed in a nursing home. In return, his aunt promised to turn over to him the stock she owned and the money in her bank account. Since it was possible for Darwood's aunt to die within one year of the date of the contract, this oral contract is enforceable. ■

THE MEMORANDUM

In most states the written evidence of an agreement required by the statute of frauds is an informal **memorandum.** A formal, written contract signed by both parties is not necessary. However, the memorandum must contain the essential information about the agreement—enough to let a court know, in case of a lawsuit, what the contract was about.

Generally the memorandum should contain at least the following information:

■ The names of the parties

■ The subject matter of the agreement (real property, a debt, employment, and so forth)

■ The consideration

■ Any important terms

■ The signature of the party against whom enforcement is sought, that is, the party being sued, normally the buyer. (The party seeking enforcement need not have signed the memorandum.)

The signature of the party being held responsible may be handwritten, printed, typed, or even stamped. An example of an informal memorandum is shown in Figure 11.1.

■ While visiting Stein at her cottage on the lake, Wayne convinced Stein to sell the cottage to him. Wayne wrote out a memorandum of the agreement, signed it, and sent it to Stein. Stein did not sign the memorandum. When Stein changed her mind about selling the cottage, Wayne brought an action in court to force her to sell. Since Stein, the party being sued, had not signed the memorandum, there was no valid evidence of an agreement. The court would not require her to sell the cottage to Wayne. ■

Figure 11.1
Informal
Memorandum

Phoenix, Arizona
January 18, 1997

AYERS MANUFACTURING COMPANY AND DONOVAN JENKINS JR. hereby
agree as follows:

    AYERS MANUFACTURING COMPANY agrees to hire DONOVAN JENKINS JR.
as sales manager at a guaranteed salary of $5,000. per month
for the duration of the contract. The employment period to
begin February 1, 1997, is to continue for five (5) years,
until February 1, 2002.

AYERS MANUFACTURING COMPANY

By *Roy Ayers*
President

Donovan Jenkins Jr.

The memorandum may consist of a single document or a series of documents (letters, telegrams, or receipts) that refer to the same transaction. A sales slip or an invoice may also be attached to the memorandum. If the memorandum consists of several documents, at least one of them must contain the signature of the party who will be held responsible. The other, unsigned documents in the series must show that their content is related to the signed document.

PAROL EVIDENCE RULE

It is useless to require certain contracts to be in writing if either party can go to court and claim that the contract isn't really correct or doesn't show the real intentions of the parties. For this reason, the courts have adopted the parol evidence rule. The **parol evidence rule** states that when a contract has been put in writing as the final expression of agreement between the parties, parol evidence—evidence of an oral agreement made prior to or at the time of signing the written agreement—cannot be presented in court to change or add to the terms of the written contract. In other words, neither party can say that he or she agreed to do something other than what was included in the written contract. A court will not allow parol evidence because the court presumes that the written contract contained all the terms and provisions intended by the parties. Any term not included is, by law, considered intentionally omitted by the parties. In short, "What you see is what you get."

"Now and Then," a band, entered into a written contract with Tiffany Community College to play at the spring fling for $1,200. Shortly before the contract was signed, the band leader asked the student activities director to reimburse the band for hiring four persons to help set up and tear down the band's equipment. The student activities director orally agreed to pay this expense. After the spring fling, the student activities director paid the band leader $1,200, but refused to pay the additional $150 for the extra workers. The band sued the college to recover the $150. Since the written contract did not contain a provision to pay for the set-up people, a court will not permit the band leader to introduce evidence that the student activities director orally agreed to pay this additional sum. The band is bound by the terms of the signed, written contract. ■

Parol evidence may be introduced, however, when the evidence does not change the terms of the written contract. For instance, parol evidence may be introduced to explain certain terms or words that are vague or confusing. Parol evidence may also be introduced to prove that the written contract lacked certain terms originally agreed upon but accidentally left out of or typed incorrectly in the written contract. Parol evidence may also be presented to show that the written contract was illegal, that one party was persuaded to make the contract by the fraud (deceit) of the other party, or that one person was mentally incompetent.

■ Campo, on an application for a job as manager of a large store, lied when he said that he had never been arrested and convicted of a major crime. He had actually been arrested, convicted, and sentenced to prison for robbery. Campo was hired and signed a three-year contract. Six months later the store owner discovered the lie and fired Campo, who sued for breach of contract. The owner could introduce parol evidence to show that, since he relied on Campo's statement of having no arrest record, he was persuaded through fraud to make the contract with Campo. ■

The parol evidence rule applies only to agreements made prior to or at the time of signing the written agreement. As a result, oral proof of any changes to the writing after the written contract was made can be presented in court. The party presenting the proof, however, must show that the later agreement contained consideration.

■ Carlson, a person knowledgeable in electronics, agreed in writing to repair your stereo system for $200. After beginning work she discovered that more things were wrong than she had previously thought. Carlson informed you that she would not continue the work until you agreed to pay her an additional $50. You orally promised to pay and Carlson agreed to continue. When the work was completed, you refused to pay the additional $50. Carlson sued in small claims court and offered as proof your oral agreement to pay her the $50. This oral agreement could legally be introduced in court, but Carlson would still lose the case. Carlson, already legally obligated to complete the repairs for $200, furnished no consideration for your promise to pay the additional $50. ■

A written contract may be changed by a subsequent oral agreement if the written contract was not required to be in writing under the statute of frauds. If the contract being modified must be in writing, the modification must also be in writing.

Summary of Important Legal Concepts

Although a written contract has an advantage over an oral contract in that it needs no witness to establish its existence or its terms, most contracts are made orally. Oral contracts are just as legal as written contracts if they contain offer and acceptance, consideration, competent parties, and legal purpose—and if the terms of these oral contracts can be proven in a court of law. Every state, however, has a law called the statute of frauds, which requires certain contracts to be in writing in order to be enforceable. The most common of these are (a) a contract to pay the debt of another person, (b) a contract to pay the debt of a deceased person out of personal funds, (c) a contract for the sale of real property or an interest in real property, (d) a contract in consideration of marriage, (e) a contract that cannot be performed within one year, and (f) a contract for the sale of goods or merchandise worth $500 or more.

The written evidence required by the statute of frauds may be an informal memorandum. It must, however, contain all the essential terms of the agreement—including the names of the parties, the subject matter of the agreement, the consideration, and any important terms. It must be signed at least by the party who will be held responsible.

The courts assume that a written contract contains all the agreed-upon terms of an agreement. Therefore, in the event of a lawsuit, the courts will not allow the introduction of parol evidence to change or add to the terms of a written contract. Parol evidence, however, may be admitted in court to explain vague or confusing terms in a written contract; to show that agreed-upon terms were accidentally omitted or incorrectly typed; or to prove that the written contract was unenforceable because of illegality, fraud, or mental incompetence. A written contract may be changed by a subsequent oral agreement if the written contract was not required to be in writing under the statute of frauds. If the contract being modified must be in writing, the modification must also be in writing.

Key Legal Terms to Know

Match the terms with the definitions that follow.

memorandum
parol evidence rule
prenuptial agreement
real property
statute of frauds

1. A rule stating that the terms of a written contract cannot be changed by prior agreements, oral or written.
2. A law requiring that certain kinds of contracts be in writing to be enforceable
3. Land or anything permanently attached to the land
4. The informal written evidence of an agreement required by the statute of frauds
5. An agreement entered into by two people who plan to marry each other, agreeing to give up rights or take on obligations that are not an implied obligation of the marriage itself

Questions and Problems to Discuss

1. The written evidence of an agreement required by a states' statute of frauds is an informal memorandum. What information should this memorandum contain?
2. Under a state's statute of frauds, what types of contracts relating to marriage must be in writing to be enforceable? Explain.
3. Why is the parol evidence rule important?
4. Explain when the payment of a debt does not have to be in writing to be enforceable.
5. Lopez orally leased Payne's house for one year at $450 a month. After moving in and paying the rent for one month, Lopez moved out. When Payne sued to recover the rent for the eleven months remaining on the lease, Lopez claimed that since the lease was not in writing she was not liable. Is Lopez correct?
6. Lisi, vice president of the National Football Association, made arrangements to hold the association's annual convention at the Marvel Hotel and Convention Center. He met with Brock, the hotel manager, one year before the scheduled event. They orally came to terms on several important points—including room rates, meal prices, and exhibit space charges. Brock was then replaced by a new manager, Talbot. Lisi met with Talbot to review the oral agreement he had made with Brock, intending to draw up a written contract to cover these points. Talbot had no record of this agreement and refused to honor any prior arrangements claiming that, because of inflation, prices should be raised 20 percent. Can Lisi legally require Talbot to abide by the original oral agreement he had with Brock?
7. Hoover was hired as superintendent of schools by the Mayville School District in 1985 and signed a written contract that expired at the end of the 1987–1988 school year. In January 1987, the school board voted unanimously to extend Hoover's contract through the 1988–1989 school year. Hoover immediately prepared and signed a contract for 1988–1989 but never got the signatures of board officers. Six months later, the school board changed its mind and voted not to extend Hoover's contract. Will Hoover succeed in a suit against the board of education for breach of contract?
8. D'Angelo wanted to buy a used car from Prestige Auto Sales on thirty days' credit. Prestige would not sell D'Angelo the car unless someone else guaranteed payment. D'Angelo's father telephoned Prestige and said that he would pay for the car if his son did not pay at the end of the thirty-day period. If the son fails to make payment, will his father be held legally liable for payment?

9. McLean orally agreed to manage several of Orcini's aerobic studios in Los Angeles for three years at a salary of $35,000 a year. After six months, McLean decided to quit her job and move to the East Coast. Orcini had to hire a new manager at a salary of $38,000 a year. Orcini claimed that McLean was liable for damages of $3,000 a year for breach of contract until McLean's original contract expired. Is Orcini correct in its claim?

10. Eckert orally agreed to sell a section of land to Levinson for $2,000 and accepted a deposit of $500 to bind the agreement. Later, after she learned that another purchaser would pay a higher price, Eckert refused to honor the contract with Levinson. Levinson sued to have the contract carried out. Would Levinson succeed in this action?

11. Germano died owing the Empire Bank and Trust Company $5,000. When she died, she had assets totaling $4,500. Germano's brother, who had been named administrator of her estate, phoned the bank and promised to pay the additional $500 his sister owed. Two months after the telephone conversation, the bank made a formal demand on the brother for the $500, but he refused. The bank then sued him for the money. Can the bank collect from the brother?

12. Tonny and Kerr were married on July 1, the second marriage for both. Their state's law for the distribution of property after the death of one spouse specified that the surviving spouse automatically inherited one half of the deceased spouse's property. Tonny did not want his children by a previous marriage excluded from receiving his money or property when he died. Tonny had, therefore, promised to marry Kerr if she agreed in writing to give up any rights as the surviving spouse to the money or property Tonny had prior to July 1. Was this written agreement legally enforceable?

13. While driving her van, Siebert slightly injured Meyer, a hitchhiker. She immediately drove Meyer to the emergency ward at the nearest hospital for treatment. Siebert told the doctor that she (Siebert) would pay for Meyer's treatment. Siebert received the bill but refused to pay. Siebert claimed that the agreement to pay was not legally binding since it was made orally. Is Siebert correct?

14. Eisenhower entered into a written contract to sell Lang a used moped for $300. Two weeks after the sale, the moped developed mechanical problems. Lang asked Eisenhower to provide the labor and the parts to correct the problems, as agreed to in the contract of sale. Eisenhower felt that the wording of the contract required him to furnish only the parts. Lang reminded Eisenhower, however, that Eisenhower had orally agreed, before the written contract was prepared, to furnish both the labor and the parts in case of mechanical problems. If he sued Eisenhower for breach of contract, could Lang introduce this oral agreement as evidence to clear up the wording in the written contract?

15. Bain lived in Bristol Harbor, a resort area along the Atlantic coast. She entered into a written agreement to sell her daily catch of fresh lobster at an agreed price to a local restaurant owner during the tourist season. At the end of the tourist season, Bain sued the restaurant owner for an additional $2,000. At the trial she claimed that shortly before signing the contract, the restaurant owner orally agreed to pay her a $2,000 bonus. Can Bain introduce the oral agreement as evidence and collect the $2,000 bonus?

Cases to Decide

1. A landlord entered into a lease (contract) with a tenant. A clause in the lease stated that the tenant would use the premises only for a gasoline station, car wash, and related activities. The landlord sued to terminate the lease, claiming that the tenant had violated an oral agreement, which was made at the time the lease was drawn up, not to add a convenience store to the gas station. Was this oral agreement binding on the tenant? (*Snow v. Winn* 607 P. 2d 678)

2. D & N Boening, Inc. was franchised by the American Beverage Corporation to sell a certain beverage in a certain part of New York State. An oral agreement between the parties stated that the franchise would continue indefinitely into the future as long as the franchisee (Boening) performed satisfactorily. Kirsch Beverage bought out American Beverage and terminated Boening's franchise agreement. No cause was given for the termination, so Boening sued Kirsch and American for breach of the franchise agreement. Kirsch and American defended on the grounds that the contract was for more than one year and therefore

had to be in writing to be enforceable. Were Kirsch and American correct? (472 NE 2d 992)

3. Windberg made an agreement in writing to pay Rincones a specified sum of money to write some educational materials. Nothing was stated in the written contract to indicate that payment was conditional on state funding. Windberg refused to pay Rincones for the materials, claiming that the duty to pay was conditional upon receiving funding from the state of California and that, since such funding was not received, there was no obligation to pay. Is parol evidence by Windberg stating how payment was to be made admissible in court? (*Rincones* v. *Windberg* 705 SW 2d 846)

4. Bratman, an attorney, had a client who was injured in an automobile accident and was being treated by Dr. Healy. Bratman orally promised to pay Healy his medical fees out of the proceeds of any award made to his client as the result of a lawsuit based on the accident if the client did not pay the fees. When the client was awarded $15,000 for his injuries, Bratman refused to pay Healy, invoking the statute of frauds. Can Healy legally hold Bratman liable for his oral promise to pay? (*Healy* v. *Bratman*, 409 NYS 2d 72)

5. Mr. and Mrs. Brett owned a farm that had a mortgage on it. When they failed to make the mortgage payments, the bank foreclosed. Allen orally agreed to buy the farm at the foreclosure sale and to sell it back to the Bretts. He failed to buy it and the farm was sold to someone else. The Bretts sued Allen for breach of contract. Is Allen legally liable for breach of contract? (*Brett* v. *Allen*, NC 247 SE 2d 17)

6. Selame Associates owned a ferry boat, which it tied to a dock owned by the Holiday Inn motel. The motel's general manager orally agreed to let Selame moor the boat at the dock for a monthly fee; the motel was obligated to take care of the boat. Nothing was said about how long the agreement would last. During a storm the boat sank due to the negligence of motel personnel. Selame sued for the value of the boat. The Holiday Inn claimed there was no contract because it was not in writing. Is the Holiday Inn correct? (*Selame Associates, Inc.* v. *Holiday Inn, Inc.*, Mass 451 F Supp 412)

7. Malo, an architect, signed a contract with Gilman to design an office building. Nothing was said in the contract about the size, style, or maximum cost of the building—only an estimated cost. When the bids for the building came in, they were so much more than the estimated cost that Gilman decided not to build the building. He also refused to pay Malo for his services. In court, Gilman tried to introduce evidence that there had been conversations about maximum costs. Malo claimed that this was not possible under the parol evidence rule. Is Malo correct? (*Malo* v. *Gilman*, Ind 379 NE 2d 554)

Chapter 12

Transfer of Contract Rights and Obligations

CHAPTER PREVIEW

CHAPTER HIGHLIGHTS

This chapter focuses on a discussion of the transfer of contract rights and obligations, at some point in time after the contract has been drawn up, to people not originally connected to the contract. You will discover that certain rights and obligations can be transferred freely from one person to another, whereas others can be transferred only with the permission of all parties involved. The chapter points out the responsibilities of those individuals to whom rights and obligations have been transferred. The chapter also points out that some rights may not be transferred if prohibited either by statute or public policy or by the contract itself. You will also learn that in some cases, the transfer is accomplished automatically by law.

TRANSFER OF RIGHTS AND OBLIGATIONS

In Chapter 6 you learned that when parties enter into a contract they acquire rights and assume obligations (duties). For instance, take the following example: Heil promises to sell to Viera a used computer, for which Viera promises to pay $2,000 in monthly installments over the next year. Heil's right under this contract is to receive the payment from Viera; Heil's duty is to deliver the computer to Viera. Viera's right under the contract is to receive the computer, and his duty is to pay for it.

From your reading in earlier chapters, you should know that the parties to a contract (Heil and Viera in the above example) may, if they wish, transfer their rights and obligations to other people through an assignment or a delegation. The sections that follow discuss how this transfer is accomplished and the rights and duties the parties have after the transfer.

Transfer of Rights

A party to a contract may legally transfer her or his rights under the contract by an **assignment.** The person transferring the rights is called the **assignor.** The person to whom the rights are transferred is called the **assignee.** The assignee is a third person who is not a party to the original contract. In the above example, suppose that Heil owed Mack $2,000 and that Heil transferred to Mack the right to receive the monthly payments from Viera. After receiving notice of the assignment, Viera would be required to make the monthly payments directly to Mack, as noted in Figure 12.1. In this agreement, Viera's status is that of obligor, whereas Heil would be the assignor and Mack the assignee. An **obligor** is a party to a contract who is required to perform for another by paying money or by completing an act.

As a general rule, rights may be freely transferred without the permission of the other party to the contract. Therefore, in the above example, Heil does not need Viera's permission to transfer to Mack the right to receive Viera's monthly payments. Rights to the payment of money (such as wages, accounts receivable, or royalties on books) and rights to the delivery of goods are the most common types of rights that may be assigned without permission of

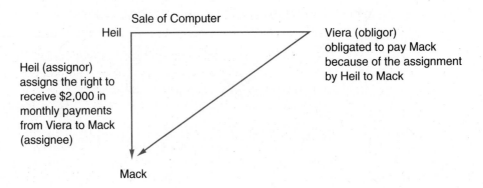

Figure 12.1
An Assignment of
Rights

the other party to the contract. After the assignment, the assignor (in this case, Heil) no longer has an interest in the right that was assigned ($2,000 in monthly payments). This right now belongs exclusively to the assignee (Mack).

Transfer of Obligations

Although rights under a contract can be assigned, obligations cannot. Obligations under a contract are legally transferred by **delegation.** Unless a clause in the contract prohibits delegation, a party to a contract may ordinarily delegate, or appoint, another person to perform the obligation in her or his place even over the objections of the other party to the contract. The person appointed to perform this obligation is, like an assignee, a third person who was not a party to the original contract. Even though the performance of an obligation may be delegated, the *responsibility* for making sure that the obligation is carried out *cannot* be delegated. The delegating party continues to be liable for breach of contract if the terms of the contract are not properly carried out or not carried out at all.

▌ ■ As owner of a lawn-care business, you agreed to mow, rake, and trim several lawns in different neighborhoods for various prices, depending upon the size of the lawns. A short time later you decided to take a two-week cruise, and you delegated the care of your lawns to another lawn-care business owner while you were gone. However, as the original obligor, you are not relieved of your responsibility. You are liable to your customers if the other lawn-care business owner does not maintain the lawns properly. ■

Only obligations that are nonpersonal may be delegated. An obligation is nonpersonal if its performance is standardized and does not depend upon a unique skill, knowledge, or talent. For example, a building contractor often hires plumbers, electricians, and carpenters and delegates to them the duties of completing certain portions of a building. In these cases, the law presumes that the jobs these people perform are mechanical in nature and can be performed by any qualified person.

Rights and Obligations That Cannot Be Transferred

Not all contract rights and obligations may be legally transferred. The right to receive a person's services cannot be assigned without the consent of that person. Since a personal relationship may have led to a contract in the first place, it would be unfair to force one party to perform personal services for someone who may be a stranger or may not be agreeable to the obligor. The right to work for someone, for example, is so personal that it cannot be assigned without permission.

> You were hired as a swimming instructor at a private club for one year. Six months after you started work, Jason, the owner of the club and your employer, sold the club to Culkins. Jason assigned the remaining six months of your contract to Culkins. Since you signed a contract to work for Jason, Culkins could not require you to work for her without your permission. ■

In this example, the personal relationship you enjoyed with Jason was affected by the change of employers from Jason (the assignor) to Culkins (the assignee). You are free to choose whether to work for Culkins or to seek employment elsewhere.

Contract obligations that require a special skill or knowledge or that involve personal trust and confidence may not be delegated without permission. The special qualities of a person are often the reason a contract is made. If you make a contract with another person based upon your trust and confidence in that person's ability, you are entitled to receive performance from that person and no one else, unless you agree to a substitution.

Members of a profession, such as doctors and lawyers, as well as such other individuals as musicians, artists, athletes, singers, and public speakers, are recognized as having special skills and talents. Individuals in trades, such as plumbers, bricklayers, and carpenters, are not included because the law recognizes that their work can be performed by any other person having the same skills. The skilled person who delegates an obligation under a contract to another person without permission is subject to a lawsuit for breach of contract.

> As student senate president at Benton Community College, you signed a contract with "The Leftovers," a band, to play for a fund-raising concert at the college. The band was chosen because of its national fame and its ability to draw large audiences. One week before the concert, the band leader called and said that, because the band was going on a European tour, another well-known group would play at the college. You not only could refuse to accept the services of this other band but could also sue the original band for breach of contract for not performing according to the contract. ■

Another situation in which rights may not be transferred is if the parties include a provision in their contract prohibiting an assignment without consent, or if the assignment is against public policy (such as assigning to someone else your right to sue) or otherwise illegal. A clause in a contract making it clear that a right is not assignable is usually honored, but some exceptions do occur. For example, a contract cannot prevent an assignment of the right to receive money. The purpose of this exception is to encourage the free flow of money as part of today's modern business practices. State statutes also place some restrictions on assignments. Most states, for example, have laws controlling the assignment of wages to creditors, in an effort to protect the wage earner. Two such states are Missouri, where an assignment of future wages is permitted only for child support, and New Mexico, where an assignment of wages is permitted for any reason but only up to 25 percent of each wage payment.

FORM OF ASSIGNMENT

An assignment usually requires no special form. Any oral or written words that clearly indicate a person's intent to make an assignment are sufficient. It is always best, however, to put an assignment in writing. This writing may be made on a separate paper or on the back of a written contract containing the rights to be assigned. An example of an informal, written assignment is shown in Figure 12.2.

Sometimes a written assignment is required by the terms of the contract or by a state statute (as is the case with wage assignments). If the *original contract* was required to be in writing under a state's statute of frauds, the assignment must also be in writing. An example of a formal, written assignment is shown in Figure 12.3.

NOTICE OF ASSIGNMENT

The assignee must notify the obligor about the assignment as soon as possible. Unless and until the obligor receives a notice, the assignment has no legal effect. If no notice is sent, the obligor would not know that an assignment had been made and would perform the obligation for the assignor.

Full performance before being notified of an assignment releases the obligor from any legal obligation to the assignee.

Rowley owed $300 to a dermatologist for treatment of a skin problem. The dermatologist, who owed $300 to a local bank, assigned to the bank his right to collect the money from Rowley. Before receiving a notice from the bank, however, Rowley paid the dermatologist in full. The bank cannot legally collect the $300 from Rowley. It must collect from the dermatologist. ■

Part performance before receiving notice of an assignment reduces the obligor's responsibility to the assignee. If, in the example, Rowley had paid the dermatologist $100 before receiving a notice from the bank, the bank could collect only $200 from Rowley. It would have to collect the other $100 from the dermatologist.

FDIC
Federal Deposit Insurance Corporation   New York Region

January 29, 1997

Dear Mortgage Holder:

On January 26, 1997, the rights of your mortgage loan were transferred from Monroe Savings Bank, Buffalo, New York to Manufacturers and Traders Trust Company (M & T Bank), Buffalo, New York. This transfer does not affect or alter the original terms of your mortgage loan in any way.

All future mortgage payments should be made payable to M & T Bank and mailed to the following address:

M & T Bank
PO Box 92814
Buffalo, NY 14692-8914

If you should have any questions about this transfer, please call M & T Bank, Loan Operations, at (315) 555-3250.

Sincerely,

R Peter Morrow

R. Peter Morrow
Manager
M & T Branch Bank

Figure 12.2
Informal Assignment of a Contract Right

After a notice of assignment is received, the obligor must pay or perform for the assignee. Payment or performance to the assignor would not relieve the obligor of the obligation to the assignee. Of course, acceptance of pay or performance by the assignor under these circumstances is a wrongful act. The assignor would be bound to return any benefits received under the assignment to the obligor.

A notice of assignment may be oral or written. If, however, the original contract was in writing as required under a state's statute of frauds, the notice of the assignment must also be in writing. After receiving a notice of

Know all Men by these Presents:

That, *on this* Tenth *day of* May ,19—

I, JANET JONES of 1419 Scott Street, Tempe, Arizona,

party of the first part;

for and in consideration of the sum of - - - ONE ($1.00) - - - - - - - - - - *Dollar*

and other good and valuable considerations, the receipt whereof is hereby acknowledged, ha ve *sold, and by these presents* do *sell, grant, assign, convey, transfer, set over and deliver unto*

JASON HUNTER of 3640 Grandin Road, Tempe, Arizona, party of the second part, all my right, title, and interest to moneys due me from Roger Sing of 125 Mt. Vernon Street, Tempe, Arizona, for his purchase of my camping and hiking equipment on April 12, 19--, and for which he agreed to pay two hundred dollars ($200.00) on or before June 1, 19--.

In Witness Whereof, the said party of the first part has hereunto set her *hand and seal the day and year first above written.*

Signed, Sealed and Delivered
in presence of

Janet Jones .... (L.S.)

Eve Mason .... (L.S.)

John H. Hunter .... (L.S.)

Figure 12.3
Formal Notice of Assignment

assignment, the obligor should contact the assignor to make sure that the assignment was actually made. This is especially true if the obligor does not know the assignee.

ASSIGNMENT BY LAW

Most assignments are made voluntarily. However, when a person dies, her or his nonpersonal rights and obligations are transferred automatically by law to an executor or administrator (an individual who handles a deceased person's property).

> Marlowe owed Jordan $250. Jordan died before Marlowe could repay the loan. The right to collect the $250 from Marlowe was assigned by law to Jordan's executor or administrator. ■

If a person owes money when he or she dies, the responsibility for paying that debt is also assigned to the person's executor or administrator.

Nonpersonal rights and obligations are assigned or delegated automatically by law to a trustee when a person becomes bankrupt. Bankruptcy (discussed in Chapter 41) legally excuses the borrower from paying certain debts. However, rights the borrower has against others are first collected by the trustee to help pay off the outstanding debts.

RIGHTS OF THE ASSIGNEE

When rights under a contract are assigned, the assignee receives exactly the same rights that the assignor had before the assignment took place. It is said that the assignee "steps into the shoes of the assignor." This means that if the obligor has a valid excuse for not performing for the assignor under the original contract, the same excuse is also good against the assignee.

> You purchased your college ring for $250 on thirty days' credit from a local jewelry store selected to sell the rings for your college. The jeweler persuaded you to buy a particular ring because she said that it was 18-karat gold. Actually, the jeweler knew the ring was only 10-karat gold. A few days after the sale, the jeweler assigned her claim against you for the $250 to a creditor. You discovered that the jeweler had lied about the quality of the ring and refused to pay. Because you refused to pay the jeweler because of her deliberate misstatement (fraud), you can also legally refuse to pay the assignee. ■

The assignor does not guarantee that the obligor will perform after the assignment is made. But the assignor does guarantee that the right exists and that it is a legally enforceable claim against the obligor. If the obligor has a valid legal excuse for not performing, the assignee must go back to the assignor to collect on the original claim. In the previous example, the creditor cannot collect the $250 from you and must therefore recover the $250 from the jeweler.

If the assignment was made as security for a debt (when, for example, the assignor owes the assignee money) and the claim is not collectible, the assignor still has the obligation to pay the money to the assignee.

> Curry owed McIntyre $500. McIntyre, who owed Ramsey $500, assigned his claim against Curry to Ramsey. Curry, who was notified of the assignment by Ramsey, was unable to pay because he was unemployed and was short of funds. Ramsey (the assignee) can collect from McIntyre (the assignor) because Ramsey took the assignment as security for a debt. ■

Summary of Important Legal Concepts

Parties to a contract may transfer their rights and obligations to other people through an assignment or delegation. An assignment involves the transfer of contract rights. A delegation involves the appointment of another to perform one's duties under a contract.

When an assignment is made, the assignee receives exactly the same rights that the assignor had before the assignment took place. This means that if the obligor has a valid excuse for not performing for the assignor under the original contract, the same excuse is also good against the assignee. Nonpersonal rights under a contract can be legally assigned without the obligor's permission, whereas rights to receive personal services may not be assigned without the consent of the person who is to perform the services. Rights also may not be transferred if the parties include a provision in their contract prohibiting an assignment, if the assignment is against public policy or otherwise illegal, or if the assignment would violate a statute.

In a delegation, only the performance of an obligation is transferred; the delegating party is still responsible for its proper performance. Duties that require a special skill, knowledge, or talent may not be delegated without permission of the person who is to receive the services.

An assignment may be oral or written, unless a written assignment is required by the terms of the contract or by state statute. Until notice of an assignment is received, the obligor can legally perform for the assignor. But once a proper notice of assignment is received, the obligor must pay or perform for the assignee. A notice of assignment may be oral or written, unless a state's statute of frauds requires that it be in writing.

Key Legal Terms to Know

Match the terms with the definitions that follow.

assignee
assignment
assignor
delegation
obligor

1. A transfer of contract rights from one person to another
2. A person obligated to pay money or to complete an act for another person under a contract
3. A person to whom a right under a contract is transferred
4. A person who transfers a right under a contract to another person
5. A transfer of the performance of one's duty under a contract to another person

Questions and Problems to Discuss

1. Why do you think that there are state statutes limiting wage assignments?
2. What is the difference between an assignment of rights and a delegation of duties?
3. Zeigler prepared a document that said: "In consideration for firewood and household supplies sold to me for my cabin on credit, I hereby transfer to Nimoy my right to receive $150 owed to me by Bader." (a) Who is the assignor? (b) Who is the assignee? (c) Who is the obligor?
4. LeBaron was a CPA (certified public accountant) hired by Rochester Copier, a small retail business that sold office equipment, to examine its financial records and make recommendations to the owners. LeBaron discovered that, due to several other commitments, the examination could not be completed for several months. Therefore, without consulting Rochester, LeBaron sent Yancy, an equally competent CPA, to examine Rochester's records. Must Rochester accept the services of Yancy?
5. On January 1, Pratt signed a five-year contract to work as a chemist for the Bausch Co. After two years, Bausch sold the business to the Itel Company. Included in the sale to Itel was Pratt's contract to work for Bausch. When Pratt learned that her work contract had been transferred to Itel, she resigned and accepted a job with a competing company. Did Bausch have the legal right to transfer Pratt's work contract to Itel? May Pratt continue to work for the competing company?

6. To settle a debt she owed to Fonti, Leary transferred to Fonti her right to $1,000 owed her by Lazarre. Fonti notified Lazarre by telephone, but Lazarre refused to pay Fonti. Lazarre claimed that Leary could not transfer the debt without her consent. Is Lazarre correct?

7. Cancho assigned to Plonski the right to collect $500 from Pitt. Pitt, who was not notified of the assignment, paid the $500 to Cancho. Can Plonski collect the $500 from Pitt?

8. Forman, a star player for a major league baseball team, was engaged to speak at a sports banquet sponsored by a veterans' organization in a large city. One week before the banquet, Forman learned that he was scheduled to make a television appearance on a major network on the same night as the banquet. Forman offered to send an equally well-known player from his team. The veterans' club refused to permit this substitution and canceled the sports banquet. Could the organization legally cancel the banquet and sue Forman for breach of contract?

9. In a written contract Salim, owner of Modern Home Co., agreed to install aluminum siding on Haag's house for $6,000. When Salim had finished half the job, he assigned his right to collect the $6,000 to Austen. Salim, however, never finished the job and Haag refused to pay Austen the $6,000. Is Austen legally entitled to the $6,000 from Haag?

10. Bangor, an attorney, was killed in an airplane crash while on a business trip to Europe. At the time of her death, several wealthy clients owed her legal fees totaling $50,000. Were these legal fees canceled when Bangor died?

11. Egan owed Terry, a pilot, $500 for flying lessons. Terry assigned his claim against Egan to Ross. Before Ross had notified Egan of the assignment, Egan paid Terry $250 on account. May Ross still recover the $500 from Egan?

12. Penny purchased a new car from Bramar Motors and agreed to pay for it in monthly payments over a period of three years. Four months after purchasing the car, Penny decided that he could not afford to keep the car and sold it to Mitchell. Mitchell agreed to continue making the monthly payments until the car was paid off. If Mitchell fails to make payments as agreed, can Bramar Motors hold Penny liable for these payments?

Cases to Decide

1. Mack, a dealer, sold Hudgens a used car on credit. At the time of the sale, Mack fraudulently informed Hudgens that the car was in good condition; in fact, the car needed extensive repairs. When Hudgens attempted to return the car to Mack within the thirty-day guarantee period, Mack refused to take the car back. In the meantime, Mack had assigned Hudgen's contract to Universal CIT Credit Corp. When Hudgens refused to pay on the contract, Universal CIT sued him. Hudgens's defense was that he had the right to set aside the contract based on fraud. Was Hudgens correct? (*Universal CIT Credit Corporation* v. *Hudgens*, 356 SW 2d 658)

2. Siler agreed to complete a project for Mountain Bell. To finance the project, Siler borrowed money from First National. As security for the loan, Siler assigned to First National his right to collect from Mountain Bell upon completion of the project. First National never notified Mountain Bell of the assignment. Consequently, Mountain Bell did not pay First National when the money was due but instead paid Siler. First National then sued Mountain Bell for that same payment. Is Bell obligated to pay First National after it has already paid Siler? (*First National Bank of Rio Arriba* v. *Mountain States Telephone & Telegraph Co.*, 571 P. 2d 118)

3. Pizza, owner of six pizza restaurants, entered into a contract with Virginia Coffee Service to install cold-drink vending machines in each of its restaurants and to maintain the equipment. One year later, Macke bought out Virginia Coffee Service and the six contracts with Pizza were assigned to Macke. Pizza claimed that the contract was not assignable because when it contracted with Virginia Coffee, it relied on Virginia's skill and reputation in the field. Is it correct? (*Macke Co.* v. *Pizza of Gaithersburg, Inc.*, Md 270 A2d)

4. Greer purchased property from Lancaster. Greer made a cash payment and entered into a credit contract with Lancaster for the remainder of the purchase price. Greer assigned this contract to someone else and Lancaster sued to have the assignment invalidated. Was the contract assignable? (*Lancaster* v. *Greer*, Tex 572 SW 2d 787)

5. Mr. and Mrs. Ehrens separated. According to the separation agreement, Mr. Ehrens was to pay his

wife support payments of $600 per month. Mrs. Ehrens assigned the right to receive the money to Elkin. Mr. Ehrens stopped making the support payments, claiming that the right to receive the money could not be assigned. Elkin sued. Was Elkin legally entitled to the money? (*Elkin* v. *Ehrens*, 43 Misc 2d 493, 251, NYS 2d 560)

6. Basic Construction Co. signed a contract to build some buildings for the State University of New York. Basic hired Stone as supervising architect. One of Stone's duties was to personally arbitrate disputes that might arise between Basic Construction Co. and the state of New York. A subcontractor sued both Basic and Stone on a dispute that had been arbitrated by someone other than Stone. Stone claimed that he could not be held liable because the decision had been made by a person to whom Stone had delegated his duties as arbitrator. Is Stone liable? (*John W. Johnson, Inc.* v. *Basic Construction Co.*, 292 F Supp 300)

7. National Commercial Bank issued a credit card to Mr. and Mrs. Eldridge. Mrs. Eldridge used the credit card to make a purchase at Malik's store and by mistake left the card at the store. Before Mrs. Eldridge could return for the card, it disappeared from Malik's possession and was used to make unauthorized purchases of over $3,000. Mr. and Mrs. Eldridge then assigned to the National Commercial Bank all claims that they had against Malik for negligence on the part of Malik in letting the card fall into someone else's hands. Malik claimed that since the Eldridges could be held liable for only $50 for unauthorized use of the credit card, the bank as assignee could also be held liable for only $50. Is Malik correct? (*National Commercial Bank and Trust Co.* v. *Malik*, NY 72 Misc 2d 865)

Chapter 13

The Termination of Contracts: Discharge

CHAPTER PREVIEW

11/16

Contracts end (terminate) in either of two ways: discharge or breach of contract. Termination by breach is the subject of Chapter 14. Chapter 13 discusses the most important ways in which contracts are discharged. Prior to a discharge of their contract, the parties to a contract may be in one of the following positions: the parties may be in a position where, by law, they must accept slightly less than they agreed to under the terms of the contract. Or, by choice or circumstances, they may decide to discharge their original contract and enter into a new agreement with different terms. If the parties wish to, they may simply call off the contract because they want to, because the contract is impossible to perform, or because one of the parties to the contract was dishonest. All of these options are discussed in this chapter.

HOW CONTRACTS END

Eventually, a valid enforceable contract comes to an end and the rights and duties that existed under the contract are no longer in effect. A contract ends (terminates) either because one or both parties are discharged from any further obligation under the contract or because one of the parties breached the contract and thus incurred liability to the other party in damages or some form of equitable relief. Breach of contract is discussed in Chapter 14. Discharge of contracts is the subject of this chapter.

DISCHARGE OF CONTRACTS

Contracts may be discharged in one of the following ways: performance, agreement of the parties, impossibility or impracticability of performance, and alteration of a written contract.

Performance

A contract is usually discharged by performance—that is, the parties have fulfilled the terms of the agreement. Performance must take place at the time and place stated in the contract. If no time is stated, the contract by law must be completed within a reasonable time. As is often the case, the definition of "reasonable" is sometimes left to the courts to decide.

Performance on the due date or at the end of a reasonable time usually is not so vital that a party will forfeit all rights because performance is late. Rather, a court will hold that the entire contract has not been forfeited but that the injured party has the right to recover damages caused by the delay.

Performance may be the doing of an act or the paying of money. The offer to perform what is required is called a **tender of performance.** If the other party refuses to allow the tendering party to perform the act required, the contract is generally discharged.

The Ruben Asphalt Company signed a contract to blacktop Carpenter's driveway. Carpenter, who questioned the quality of the blacktop materials being used, refused to let the company do the work. This refusal by Carpenter discharged the contract; the company was no longer obligated to perform. ■

When the tendering party (the debtor) is required to pay a sum of money, and the other party refuses the debtor's offer to pay, the refusal does not discharge the contract. The refusal does, however, excuse the debtor from paying any interest charges or court costs in the event of a lawsuit. The debtor, however, must be ready to pay the money at any time.

Legal Tender   A tender of money is good only if the debtor offers the exact amount of money due, on the due date, and in legal tender. **Legal tender** is the form of money—coins and currency—that is accepted as lawful payment of debts in the United States. The creditor may refuse to accept payment that is not in legal tender. A check is not legal tender and the creditor may refuse to accept it.

Brock owed you $25 for repairing a lawnmower. She offered you a check but you refused because you preferred cash. Since a check is not legal tender, you have the legal right to refuse it. ■

If a check is accepted, the contract is not legally discharged until the check is honored by the debtor's bank.

Degrees of Performance   Full performance is the most common method by which contracts are discharged. A contract is discharged by **full performance** when both parties do all that they agreed to do under the terms of the contract.

You hired Quigley to rebuild the motor in your car for $350. Quigley satisfactorily completed the job and you paid him the $350. Since both Quigley and you had fully performed, the contract was discharged. ■

The law does not always require full performance of a contract; it will allow minor deviations. This type of performance, called **substantial performance,** is slightly less than full performance. (Courts sometimes say 95 percent or better performance.) A person who substantially performs has, in good faith, fulfilled all the major requirements of the contract, leaving only minor details incomplete. Consequently, the courts will permit the party who performed to recover the contract price less the amount needed to correct any defects in the performance. Recovery is permitted because it would be unfair to deny all payment when the performance is essentially complete. Recovery under the doctrine of substantial performance is often applied to construction contracts.

A building contractor agreed in writing to build Stern a house for $150,000. When the house was completed, Stern discovered that the front and back doors were not hung properly and that the bookcase in the family room was not flush against the wall. The contractor was not deliberately negligent but was behind schedule and failed to correct the defects. Stern hired a carpenter to make the changes at a cost of $300. Because the house was substantially completed and the defects were minor ones, the contractor can collect $150,000 less the $300 paid to the carpenter. ■

Substantial performance, however, does not apply to contracts calling for the payment of money. If you borrow $1,000 with interest for ninety days, you cannot repay $995 plus the interest. You must repay the full $1,000 plus interest.

Agreement

Some contracts state, at the time they are made, exactly when they will end. Such a contract would be discharged by mutual agreement on the specified date. In other contracts, the parties mutually agree to release each other on the happening of a certain event, even though the intended performance by one or both parties has not been completed. If the contract is completely executory, the release of one party is the consideration for the release of the other party.

■ Brody agreed in writing to act as a chauffeur for Eastman for two years. Both parties changed their minds before Brody started work and mutually agreed to cancel the contract. This executory contract was thus discharged. ■

Another way that a contract ends through agreement is that the parties may make a new agreement that will discharge or modify the obligations of one or both parties under the original agreement. The new agreement could take the form of a rescission, a novation, or an accord and satisfaction.

Rescission   The parties may decide to rescind the contract even after one or both of the parties have completely performed. To **rescind** is to mutually agree to end or cancel a contract. The parties do this by making a new agreement to discharge each other from rights and obligations under the original contract. This new agreement requires each party to return the consideration received so that they are back where they started before the contract was made.

■ You purchased a show horse from a friend for $5,000. After you paid for and received the horse, you changed your mind and asked for your money back. Your friend agreed. The contract was discharged when you returned the horse and your friend returned the $5,000. ■

Novation   After entering into a contract, the parties may agree to release one party from the obligation to perform. A new, third party would be substituted who would then assume this obligation by means of a novation. In a **novation,** the original contract is actually terminated and a new contract formed between the remaining party to the original contract and the new party. The other terms of the new contract generally remain the same as those in the original contract. This substitution requires the consent of both original parties and the new, third party.

> Just before completing law school, Vincent purchased a set of law books from the Laramie Law Book Company. Vincent signed a contract to make monthly payments over a two-year period. Six months later, Vincent discovered that he could not keep up the monthly payments. Washington, Vincent's college roommate, agreed to assume responsibility for the payments. The Laramie Law Book Company agreed to cancel its contract with Vincent and enter into a new contract with Washington. This substitution of parties is a novation. ■

Accord and Satisfaction An **accord** is an agreement by one party in an original contract to accept from the other party performance that is different from the performance agreed on in the original contract. Actually, the old contract is breached by one of the parties, and they make a new contract. **Satisfaction** is the actual performance of the accord. An accord alone is not enough to discharge the original contract. There must be both an accord and a completed satisfaction to discharge the original contract. If the new agreement is made before the original contract is breached, this new agreement is called a **substitute contract.**

> You borrowed $300 from Santos for your college fees. When you were unable to repay the loan when it was due, Santos agreed to accept your stereo set in place of the $300 (the accord). The original agreement was discharged only after Santos received and accepted the stereo set (the satisfaction). ■

An accord and satisfaction is often used to settle an honest disagreement about the amount of money that a debtor owes to a creditor.

Impossibility or Impracticability

Under the common-law rule (which is the majority rule), a contract may be discharged and the parties excused from their contractual duties by **impossibility of performance.** The following situations generally qualify to legally discharge contractual obligations under the doctrine of impossibility of performance:

1. Destruction of the subject matter of the contract
2. Death, serious illness, or other incapacity in a personal services contract
3. Change in the law

Destruction of the Subject Matter If the subject matter that is essential to the performance of the contract is destroyed through no fault of either party, the contract is discharged. If the contract had been partly performed before the impossibility arose, the courts usually permit recovery for work performed up to the time of the impossibility.

> The Detrex Company contracted to paint the exterior of Lunt's house for $900. After Detrex had applied one coat of paint, the house was destroyed by fire. The contract was discharged. Detrex could, however, recover for labor and paint used before the fire occurred. ■

Death or Serious Illness   A personal services contract (a contract involving a person who has special skills and talents, for example a rock star) is discharged if the person obligated to perform that personal service dies or becomes seriously ill or disabled.

> Hind, a country music star, was rushed to Rock Memorial Hospital after collapsing from severe stomach pains in his hotel room two hours before his scheduled concert at Arlan College. Hind's serious illness discharged this personal services contract. ■

Change in the Law   Sometimes a law is passed after a legally constituted contract is made that makes performance illegal. In this case, the contract is discharged. This law could be a local ordinance, a state statute, a court decision, or a government regulation.

> Ibsen contracted to sell Hilton ten cases of fireworks for use at a July 4th celebration. Because of the increasing number of accidents resulting from the use of fireworks, the state passed a law making the sale of fireworks illegal. Since performance of this contract was made impossible by the passage of the state law, the contract was discharged. ■

Occasionally, unforeseen circumstances arise after the contract has been formed, making performance unreasonably (extremely) difficult. Although these situations do not discharge a contract under the common-law doctrine of impossibility unless there is a contingency clause in the contract, modern law (that is, case law and the UCC, section 2-615) has departed from this harsh rule and allows a discharge under the doctrine of **commercial impracticability.** This doctrine recognizes those unanticipated events in which performance (while still possible) would be extremely burdensome and would create a hardship for the party obligated to perform. Consequently, performance is excused and the contract is discharged. Although modern law deliberately refrains from listing all possible unanticipated occurrences, the doctrine has been cautiously applied to events that radically alter the original performance in certain cases, for example those involving severe shortages of raw materials due to an act of God, a war, an embargo, a local crop failure or an unforeseen shutdown of major sources of supply. These factors must either have caused a marked increase in price quite disproportionate to what would reasonably have been contemplated (e.g. ten times more than an original estimate), or have precluded the seller totally from obtaining the supplies necessary to his or her performance.

> Alco Oil Co. agreed to supply 3,000 barrels of jet fuel to Monsoon Airlines. However, Alco's supply of crude oil (the source of jet fuel) from Alaska was cut off because the destruction of equipment used to obtain the oil resulted in a severe shortage. The destruction was caused by a sudden series of earth tremors (act of God). To fulfill the terms of the contract with Monsoon Airlines, Alco would have to obtain oil from other sources at a price at least ten times the original cost. In these circumstances Alco may be excused from performance. ■

Relief on grounds of impracticability is unavailable if a party seeking to be discharged did not employ all due measures to ensure that his or her source would not fail, that he or she willfully did something to cause the event to occur, failed to foresee at the time the contract was made that the event could happen (negligence), or agreed in the contract to assume an obligation to perform despite impracticability.

The common-law rule is opposed to the concept of commercial impracticability, claiming that it weakens the stability of a contract. Furthermore, the risks against which this new concept protects could have been guarded against by including a *contingency clause* in the contract stating that the contract is discharged and performance excused for circumstances beyond the control of the parties. Take the following example as an illustration of the common-law rule:

■ The McCracken Garment Company, a manufacturer of clown suits, contracted in writing to make and ship 150 clown suits to the Royal Uniform Company by June 1. A prolonged breakdown of factory machinery caused an interruption in production. McCracken informed Royal that it could not fulfill the terms of the contract until August 1. McCracken is not discharged from the contract because of the breakdown in machinery. ■

In this example, McCracken could have obtained the clown suits from another company. This would have been more costly for McCracken, but it was necessary to avoid a breach of contract.

Alteration of a Written Contract

If one party to a contract deliberately makes a material change in its terms without the permission of the other party, the contract is discharged. This change in the terms of the contract is called **alteration.** An alteration is material if the rights or duties of the parties are changed.

■ You signed a contract with CompuWorld to take a computer programming course at a cost of $1,200. The admissions counselor at CompuWorld did not give you, nor did you ask for, a copy of the contract. Because the counselor received a commission for each signed contract, she changed the cost on your contract to $1,500. When you discovered the alteration, you had the legal right to terminate the contract and could not be sued for breach of contract. ■

Summary of Important Legal Concepts

Contracts come to an end (terminate) in either of two ways: discharge or breach of contract. When a contract terminates, the rights and duties that existed under the contract are no longer in effect. This chapter concentrated on a termination of contracts by discharge.

Contracts may be discharged by performance, agreement, impossibility or impracticability, and alteration. Performance may be either complete or substantial. Substantial performance is slightly less than full performance. (Some courts demand 95 percent or better). If the parties agree to a discharge at a certain time, the time will generally be stated in the contract, or the parties may instead agree to a discharge through release (at a stated time or upon the happening of a certain event), rescission, novation, or accord and satisfaction. The law excuses the parties from their performance under a contract because of legal impossibility. Unforeseen and unpredictable hardships that occur after the contract is made and simply make performance more difficult do not meet the legal definition of impossibility. A contingency clause would have to be placed in a contract to discharge it for such hardships. The law recognizes only the following situations as reasons to discharge a contract because of impossibility: destruction of the subject matter; death, serious illness, or other incapacity in a personal services contract; and change in the law. Finally, if a court finds evidence that a contract has deliberately been changed in any material way by one party without the consent of the other party, it will excuse performance by the nonconsenting party, based on the legal concept of alteration.

Key Legal Terms to Know

Match the terms with the definitions that follow.

accord
alteration
commercial impracticability
full performance
impossibility of performance
legal tender
novation
rescind
satisfaction
substantial performance
substitute contract
tender of performance

1. Performance in good faith of all but minor details of a contract
2. An agreement to accept performance different from that agreed upon in the original contract

3. The performance of the terms of a new agreement reached as the result of an accord
4. A material change in the terms of a contract deliberately made by one party without the consent of the other party
5. Performance by both parties of all they had agreed to do under the terms of a contract
6. Offer to perform the obligations of a contract
7. To cancel a contract by mutual agreement
8. A new contract entered into to replace an original contract before a breach occurs
9. The substitution of a new party for one of the original parties to a contract
10. The form of money accepted as lawful payment of debts in the United States
11. Recognizes that unanticipated events, while making a contract extremely burdensome and creating a hardship for the party obligated to perform, nevertheless discharge the contract
12. A common-law rule that excuses parties from their contractual duties as long as there is proof that the contract could no longer be performed by either party

Questions and Problems to Discuss

1. In relationship to contracts, what does the term *rescind* mean?
2. In what circumstances will a court allow a contract to be discharged because of impossibility?
3. If a contract calls for the performance of an act, what effect does a refusal of tender of performance have on the contract?
4. What is the difference between a novation and an accord and satisfaction?
5. You were having a house built. Upon completion, you discovered that the building contractor did not perform every detail. Are you released from your obligation to pay?
6. If a debtor tenders money to the creditor in payment of a debt but payment is refused by the creditor, is the debt discharged?
7. In what circumstances may unforeseen hardships that occur after the contract is made discharge the contract under the common law?
8. Kristy signed up to take private flying lessons from Stull for six months at the rate of $100 per month. After one month, Stull became seriously ill with a terminal disease and could not continue

with the lessons. Is Stull released from the contract under the common law?

9. Trotter entered into a written contract to sell his clothing business to Wolpert for $50,000. Before Wolpert took control of the business, both parties changed their minds and agreed to cancel the contract. Is the contract discharged under the common law?

10. Arma contracted to put aluminum siding on the exterior of Woodley's house. Before Arma began work, but after obtaining the siding at a cost of $1,500, the house was destroyed by a tornado. Is the contract discharged under the common law?

11. The Blue Knights Community Club made a contract with Wayne, a well-known rock star, to perform in concert on a certain date. The day before the concert, Wayne was stranded in Europe because of an airline strike. Is his contract with the Blue Knights Community Club discharged under the common law?

12. The Arco Construction Co. contracted in writing to build an addition on Wheeler's house. Before performance of the contract was to begin, the company workers went out on strike. Rosaire, the owner of Arco, suggested that Wheeler contact another company to complete the job, since it appeared the strike would go on indefinitely. Wheeler agreed, released Arco from the contract, and made a new contract with Beauty Lines Construction Co. to complete the job. The Arco strike ended quickly, however, and Arco insisted on completing the job according to the terms of the original contract. Must Wheeler permit Arco to complete the job?

13. Ross signed a contract with the Revere Home Center to redecorate the interior of her home. The decorator went to Ross's home, made recommendations for Ross to consider, and set a date for the home specialists to begin work. However, when the specialists arrived to begin work, Ross refused to let them proceed, claiming that she wanted first to check on the reliability of their company. Was Revere's obligation to Ross ended by Ross's action?

14. Josten, a contractor, agreed in writing to build a warehouse for Blanda according to specific plans. Josten deliberately and without Blanda's consent deviated substantially from the plans. As a result, Blanda refused to pay Josten any money due under the terms of the contract. Josten, claiming substantial performance, contended that he was entitled to the contract price less the amount needed to correct any defects in the performance. Was Josten correct?

15. A contractor was hired to demolish several old buildings to make way for a shopping mall. The contractor entered into a contract with a refuse hauler to remove the debris from the demolition area. A dispute arose over how quickly the refuse hauler was required to remove the debris. The hauler contended that, since no time was stated in the contract, he could remove the debris from the area at any time. Was the hauler correct?

Cases to Decide

1. Grevas entered into a contract with the Surety Development Corporation to have a prefabricated house built for $16,385. A completion date was set but, according to Grevas, the house was not ready for occupancy on that date. As a result, Grevas refused to pay the balance due. Surety Development then sued for the money, claiming substantial performance. According to testimony at the trial, the house was actually far from finished on the morning of the date it was to be completed. But Surety Development Corporation initiated a crash program, with workers all over the place doing whatever was necessary to complete the house by the end of that day. In fact, by day's end, the house was finished and ready for occupancy, with only minor details to be completed. Grevas, who had taken a tour of the premises early in the morning of the completion date set in the contract, remarked that the house could not possibly be completely finished and ready for occupancy by the end of the day. Consequently, he never returned later in that day to inspect the premises. Was the Surety Development Corporation entitled to the balance due on the house? (*Surety Development Corp.* v. *Grevas*, 192 N.E. 2d 145)

2. Deive signed a contract for membership in a physical fitness program. The contract provided that he was obligated to make payments whether he participated in the program or not. Deive had a lung ailment when he signed the contract but never mentioned it to the operators of the program. After he had signed the contract, Deive's

doctor told him that participation in the program would be dangerous to his health. Deive tried to cancel the contract and refused to pay his fees. The plaintiff sued for breach of contract. Can Deive cancel the contract based on impossibility of performance? (*Trans-State Investments, Inc.* v. *Deive*, 262 A2d 119)

3. The LaCumbre Golf and Country Club contracted to extend membership privileges, including use of its golf course, to guests of the Santa Barbara Hotel for $300 per month. When the hotel was totally destroyed by fire and no longer able to take in guests, it stopped making monthly payments on a contract it had with the country club. LaCumbre then sued the hotel to recover the balance owed on the contract. During a court trial, the hotel contended that the destruction of its building excused further performance of its responsibilities under the contract. Is the hotel correct? (*LaCumbre Golf and Country Club* v. *Santa Barbara Hotel Co.,* Calif 271 P 476)

4. Sugarhouse sued Anderson for nonpayment of a promissory note and obtained a judgment against him for $2,423.86. For two years, Anderson had financial difficulties and couldn't pay the judgment. When he learned that he could get a loan to help him pay a portion of the judgment, he reached an agreement with Sugarhouse to pay $2,200 in full settlement of the judgment. Anderson then gave Sugarhouse a check for $2,200. Before the check was cashed, however, Sugarhouse found out that Anderson had some property that he was about to sell. Sugarhouse then refused to go through with the settlement. Anderson asked the court to enforce the settlement agreement he had made with Sugarhouse. Will Anderson succeed? (*Sugarhouse Finance Co.* v. *Anderson,* Utah 610 P2d 1369)

5. Bergman, a contractor, sued Parker, a builder, for breach of their contract to construct an apartment building. Parker contended that the contract was terminated by impossibility because he was unable to obtain a building permit. He refused to go ahead with the construction. At the trial, how-

ever, Bergman introduced evidence to show that Parker could have obtained a building permit by making modifications, which were acceptable to Bergman, to his building plans. Should Bergman's suit be successful? (*Bergman* v. *Parker*, DC 216 A2d, 581)

6. Joseph Goldberg, Inc., a builder, contracted to build a theater for Fisher. The U.S. Fidelity and Guaranty Co. guaranteed completion. After work had been started on the building, it was stopped by order of the Commissioner of Buildings because of a local ordinance that prohibited the construction of a theater within 200 feet of a church. Fisher then sued U.S. Fidelity as guarantor for breach of contract. U.S. Fidelity contended that the contract was terminated because of an impossibility to perform. Is U.S. Fidelity correct under the common law rule? (*Fisher* v. *United States Fidelity and Guaranty Company*, 212 Ill App 66, 39 NE 2d 67)

7. Northern Corporation contracted with Chugach in August 1966 to make repairs to Cooper Lake Dam in Alaska. Northern was required by the contract to secure rock from a quarry at the opposite end of the lake and to transport the rock to the dam across the ice on the lake during the winter of 1966 at a time when the lake was frozen sufficiently to permit heavy vehicle traffic on it. In December 1966, Northern prepared the water on the lake for deep freezing, but thereafter water overflowed the ice, preventing the use of the road. Although Northern claimed that it was unsafe to travel on the lake ice, Chugach insisted on performance. Northern tried again, but after several of its trucks broke through the ice, in two instances causing the death of the driver, Northern ceased operations, notified Chugach that it would make no more attempts to haul across the lake, and declared that it considered the contract terminated. Chugach claimed breach of contract. Is the contract legally terminated so that Northern has no liability to Chugach for breach of contract? (*Northern Corp.* v. *Chugach Electrical Association* 518 P2d 76.)

Chapter 14

The Termination of Contracts: Breach of Contract

CHAPTER PREVIEW

CHAPTER HIGHLIGHTS The first part of this chapter discusses breach of contract, the second way in which a contract ends. The discussion includes a definition of *breach,* the types of breach that may occur, and the various remedies available to an injured party who is the victim of a breach of contract.

Sometimes parties breach their contracts and offer one of many defenses for not performing. The second part of this chapter deals with these defenses. You will learn that a party who raises one of these defenses successfully is released from blame or responsibility in a breach of contract suit.

BREACH OF CONTRACT

Another way in which a contract ends is by breach. An **actual breach** occurs when one party fails to perform the obligations required by a contract. Contracts are usually breached after the performance date. Sometimes, however, a contract is breached before the performance date. This is called **anticipatory breach.** Before the time for performance stated in the contract, one party says, "I'm not going to perform." When this happens, the injured party may immediately declare the contract ended and sue for any damages caused by this breach. Legally, the injured party does not have to wait until the performance date has passed to sue but may choose to do so, hoping that the breaching party will undergo a change of mind and perform the contract on schedule. For any breach, the injured party has certain remedies.

REMEDIES FOR BREACH OF CONTRACT

A **remedy** is a course of action available to a party (the party hurt by the breach) to obtain satisfaction, in court if necessary, for an injury caused by breach of contract. A remedy may be either legal or equitable. In a legal remedy, the injured party is awarded money damages. When money alone does not provide satisfaction to the injured party, courts will provide an equitable remedy (discussed later in the chapter). Money damages are the usual remedy for breach of contract.

If the breach is material, the injured party may treat the contract as ended and thereby be relieved from her or his duty to perform. The injured party may also sue for money damages for this breach. A **material breach** is one that occurs, for example, when one party refuses to perform or deliberately prevents or hinders the other party from performing. In either case, the injured party is deprived of a substantial benefit because of the breach.

Metzinger signed a contract to work for a marketing research company beginning June 1. On June 1, the company refused to allow Metzinger to begin work. By preventing Metzinger from beginning work, the company created a material breach. The contract was discharged. In addition, Metzinger may sue the company for money damages for breach of contract. ■

Whether a breach is material is often a matter to be decided by a court. Most breaches of contract, however, are minor breaches. If a breach is minor, the contract is not ended. Both parties must still perform, but the injured party may sue for damages.

> Munson, a mechanic, agreed to replace parts on Tracy's motorcycle by June 10. Completion of the work, however, was delayed until June 20. Since the delay amounted to a minor breach, the contract remains in force, but Tracy may sue for any damages incurred because of the later completion date. ∎

The injured party may waive his or her rights when the other party breaches the contract. A **waiver** is the voluntary surrender of a given right. As a result of this waiver, the contract is canceled. To be on the safe side, the breaching party should ask for a written release. The written release, however, must be supported by consideration, except in those states where an agreement in writing needs no consideration.

Legal Remedies

Once a contract has been breached, the injured party, as noted above, has the right to sue for money damages. Damages, determined either by the parties to a contract or by a court, are awarded to compensate the injured party financially for her or his loss. Sometimes the injured party attempts to make a profit from the breach of contract. This is unfair. The money damages awarded should, by law, place the injured party in the position she or he would have been in if the contract had been carried out.

Damages may be compensatory, liquidated, nominal, or punitive.

Compensatory Damages   Damages awarded to the injured party as compensation for an actual loss or injury caused by the breach of contract are called **compensatory damages.** The amount of compensatory damages awarded can be determined by the courts with reasonable certainty.

As soon as the breach occurs, the injured party has a duty to **mitigate the damages.** That is, the injured party must make a reasonable effort to hold down the amount of damages and prevent them from increasing. Mitigation is required to assure that the damages awarded do not exceed the amount necessary to compensate the injured party.

> Groves had a one-year contract to work as a manager for Modern Hotels, Inc., at a salary of $50,000. After six months, Groves was fired for no legal reason. She did not try to find another job but instead sued Modern Hotels for $25,000, the remainder of her salary due on the contract. Modern Hotels claimed that Groves had made no effort to find another job and was not entitled to the $25,000. ∎

In the example, Groves would be entitled to damages but not to the full $25,000. She had a duty to mitigate the damages by searching for another position similar to the one she had held with Modern Hotels. If she had found another job, the court would have awarded Groves damages of $25,000 less her earnings from the new job. Groves would receive the full $25,000 only if she could not find a similar job. Because Groves did not even try to find other employment, the amount of damages awarded would be decided by a court.

In addition to damages, the losing party also pays court costs (for example, witness fees and filing fees). Each party pays her or his own attorney's fees.

Liquidated Damages   The amount of damages to be awarded to an injured party in case of a breach may be determined by the parties in advance and stated in the contract. This amount is called **liquidated damages.**

> Kerry signed a lease renting an apartment for one year from Snider. A clause in the lease stated that the security deposit of $250 would be forfeited as liquidated damages if Kerry gave up the apartment before the end of the lease. ■

A liquidated damages clause will be enforced if the court determines that the amount is a reasonable forecast of the loss that may result or does result from the breach. In the example, the $250 is the amount needed by Snider to prepare the apartment for new tenants.

A court will not enforce a liquidated damages clause if the amount appears to be a penalty. The court will ignore it and instead award whatever compensatory (actual) damages could be proven.

Nominal Damages   The court awards **nominal damages,** usually a very small amount such as 10¢ or $1, when an injured party establishes that a contract has been breached but fails to prove that he or she has suffered actual damages.

> Samuels, owner of the Uptown Automotive Station, made a contract to buy twenty cases of motor oil from the Apex Wholesale Company at $25 per case. When Apex breached the contract and did not deliver the motor oil, Samuels purchased the same number of cases at $21 per case from another wholesaler. Since Samuels suffered no actual loss, only nominal damages would be awarded in a suit against Apex. ■

Nominal damages may also be awarded to an injured party who has sued in order to establish a court decision (precedent) concerning her or his rights in a dispute that may occur in the future.

Punitive Damages   Money damages awarded to the injured party in the contract to punish the breaching party for wrongful conduct and to deter similar future conduct by that party are called **punitive damages** (or exemplary damages). Punitive damages are generally not awarded in breach of contract suits. However, the modern trend is for state statutes to allow punitive damages when evidence shows that the breaching party maliciously or fraudulently caused the breach, for example an insurance company that willfully refuses to pay a known claim.

Equitable Remedies

As noted earlier in the chapter, equitable remedies are allowed by courts when money damages will not adequately compensate the injured party for her or his loss. Equitable remedies include rescission of a contract, specific performance, or an injunction.

Rescission   When a breach occurs, the injured party may choose to rescind (terminate) the contract and end further performance. If a contract is rescinded, both parties must return any consideration received under the contract. The injured party usually rescinds the contract if the other party commits a material breach. Rescission is also used as a remedy when the breaching party induced the injured party to enter into the contract by fraud, duress, or undue influence; when the breaching party wished to exercise her or his right as a minor to rescind; or the parties voluntarily agree to call off the contract for whatever reason (as discussed on page 198 of Chapter 13). Rescission must be accomplished promptly so that both parties can be restored as nearly as possible to their original positions.

Specific Performance   When money damages will not adequately and fairly compensate for a loss and rescission is not the proper remedy, the injured party may sue for specific performance. **Specific performance** is a court order forcing the breaching party to carry out the contract according to its original terms. Specific performance is generally granted only if the subject matter of the contract is rare or unique and an identical item cannot be purchased elsewhere. For example, a contract for the sale of real property will generally be enforced because each piece of land is considered to be unique and unlike any other piece. Specific performance will also be granted in contracts for the sale of such personal property as rare paintings and books, antiques, relics, and heirlooms. It is difficult to put a value on a priceless work of art or an heirloom.

> Marx entered into a contract to sell the original manuscript of a book to Bartel, a rare-book collector. Marx then changed his mind and refused to deliver the manuscript. Bartel could sue for specific performance. The court would force Marx to carry out the terms of the contract by selling the manuscript to Bartel. ∎

The courts will not order specific performance in a personal services contract (one involving a person who has special skills and talents). A person cannot be forced to perform against her or his will. For example, a musician who has played with a band and who refuses to continue with that band cannot be forced to remain even though under contract. The musician, however, could be sued for damages for breach of contract.

Injunction   In special cases where damages, rescission, and specific performance will not adequately compensate for a breach of contract, the court may grant an injunction to the injured party. As you recall from page 71, an **injunction** is a court order that forbids a person from doing a certain act.

■ Bermudes, a professional baseball player, signed a two-year contract to pitch for the Panthers, a major league baseball team. The manager of the team and Bermudes frequently disagreed on strategies to be used during the games and often quarreled. Before the end of the first year of the contract, Bermudes quit the Panthers because he was dissatisfied with the manager and because he had a better offer from another team. Bermudes could be prevented, by an injunction, from playing for another team until the original contract expired. ■

DEFENSES FOR A BREACH OF CONTRACT SUIT

When a breach of contract occurs, the injured party has a right to sue the party who broke the contract. The breaching party (the defendant in the lawsuit) may offer one of many defenses for not performing on the contract. **Defenses** are reasons offered by a defendant (the party being sued) that are meant to release her or him from blame or responsibility. In a breach of contract suit, the defenses offered are intended to excuse the breaching party from further liability under the contract.

You have already learned of some actions that affect the performance of the terms of a contract (lack of competency, impossibility, illegal purpose, and lack of proper form). These actions may be used as defenses. Other defenses are fraud, duress, undue influence, mistake, bankruptcy, and the statute of limitations.

Fraud

A person who persuades another to enter into a contract by making a false statement about a material fact or by concealing a material fact is guilty of **fraud.** Such a contract is voidable by the victim of the fraud. That is, the victim may refuse to go through with the contract and may use fraud as a defense if sued for breach of contract. All of the following elements are necessary to establish fraud.

1. A false statement or concealment of a material fact must be made.
2. The false statement or concealment must be deliberate.
3. The false statement or concealment must have caused the victim to act.
4. The victim must offer proof of damages.

False Statement or Concealment of a Material Fact   The false statement, oral or written, must be about a material fact. A material fact is one that is important enough to influence another's decision. A mere statement of opinion is not fraud. For example, a salesperson's statement that "this TV set is the best you can buy for the money" is one of opinion (called sales puffing) not fact. But a statement such as "with this mower you can cut an acre of lawn on less than a gallon of gasoline" is a statement of fact, one that can be tested.

A person who conceals a material fact is also guilty of fraud. The conceal-ment must prevent the victim from discovering the truth about material facts.

> Jessie offered to sell her car to Arby for $1,000. Before accepting, Arby asked if the car was in good mechanical condition. Jessie stated that she had just had the engine overhauled. Arby accepted the offer and agreed to pay for the car in thirty days. A week later Arby discovered that Jessie had filled the engine with heavy grease to keep it from knocking. Arby refused to pay for the car and offered to return it. Jessie sued for breach of contract. Since Jessie concealed an important fact about the engine, Arby may claim fraud as a defense. ■

Generally, silence is not fraud. A person does not have to volunteer all the details to the other party. Although in a sense this is concealment, the law allows it as part of the bargaining process. However, if a person's silence creates a false impression about certain facts, that person has a duty to speak out.

Deliberate Misstatement or Concealment The speaker must know that what is being said or done is false and must deliberately intend to mislead the victim.

> Arden, an automobile tire dealer, sold four new tires to Limrick. In order to make the sale, Arden told Limrick that the tires were guaranteed for 50,000 miles. Actually, Arden knew that the average life of that brand was only 20,000 miles. When Limrick discovered the truth, he would not go through with the purchase and tried to return the tires. Arden refused to accept them and sued Limrick. Since Arden had deliberately lied about the tires, Lim-rick can use fraud as his defense. ■

Fraud also occurs when a person who should have known the facts of a situation carelessly makes a statement without really knowing whether it is true or not.

> Kotch, a door-to-door salesperson for the Home Utility Company, sold Arnold an expensive set of kitchen utensils. Arnold made the purchase because Kotch told her that the utensils were solid copper. As it turned out, the utensils were only copper plated. The salesperson did not know that the utensils were only copper plated and never checked with the company to find out. Since Kotch should have checked with the company, Arnold may claim fraud as a defense in a breach of contract suit. ■

Reliance on False Statement or Concealment The victim of fraud must actually rely on the false statement or concealment and suffer a loss or injury. There is no fraud if the victim is not deceived because he or she makes an independent investigation but enters into the contract anyway. There has been no reliance on the false statement or concealment.

> Delmar, an automobile dealer, received in trade a car that had been damaged in an accident. He explained to Tinker that the car had been thoroughly

repaired and many parts had been replaced. When Tinker took the car for a trial run, she had it examined by a mechanic. The mechanic told Tinker that the frame had been badly bent and that the repair job had not completely straightened it. Nevertheless, because of its low price, Tinker bought the car. Since Tinker did not rely on Delmar's statement, she cannot claim fraud if she later tries to get out of the contract. ■

Victim Must Offer Proof of Damages   The victim of fraud is entitled to bring a lawsuit. However, unless the victim has suffered actual legal damages (compensatory damages) as a result of the fraud and can offer proof of these damages, a court would award only nominal damages.

Duress

Valid contracts are made by persons who enter into them of their own free will. **Duress** occurs when a person compels another to enter into a contract through physical force (such as pointing a gun at a person or taking a person's hand and making the person sign a written contract) or by other improper threats. Because it involves the use of physical force or improper threats, duress destroys a person's free will to decide whether or not to enter into a contract. This type of duress is rather uncommon, but it renders the agreement voidable by the victim. Under modern law, threats include economic pressure if it is wrongful.

■ Duff, owner of an apartment complex, wrongfully threatened to terminate Romano's present lease and to initiate eviction proceedings against her if she refused to sign a new three-year lease at a much higher rent. Duff did this knowing that Romano was physically handicapped and bedridden. Since Duff's actions amounted to duress, Romano, who signed the lease, can cancel if she wishes. ■

The threat by one person to bring a lawsuit against another person to enforce a legal claim is not duress. Assume, for example, that a friend owed you money but refused to pay. If you threatened to sue your friend in small claims court unless payment was made, your friend could not refuse to pay claiming duress. You have a right to use whatever legal means are available to collect the debt.

Undue Influence

Undue influence is the power or dominance that one person has—and uses for personal advantage—over another person. No force or threats are used, as in duress. However, the stronger-minded person can exercise so much influence that the victim ends up doing whatever the other person wishes. A contract entered into because of undue influence is voidable by the victim.

Undue influence is often difficult to determine. Mere persuasion is not undue influence. The victim must be incapable of using her or his own free will. Undue influence may arise when the parties have a close confidential or personal relationship. Examples of such relationships are those between lawyer and client, doctor or nurse and patient, parent and child, or husband and wife.

> Paton, an elderly woman, lived with her son, who was Paton's only child and sole support. The son persuaded Paton to sell him some land worth $150,000 for $50,000. Shortly before the transfer of title, Paton discovered that her son was going to resell the property to Vestel for $175,000 for construction of an apartment complex. The mother refused to go through with the sale. In the breach of contract suit that followed, the court found that the son had taken advantage of his mother's trust in him to persuade her to sell the land. Paton could avoid the contract. ∎

Mistake

People often attempt to back out of a contract because they claim that they made a mistake (misunderstood, misinterpreted, or drew a wrong conclusion) about certain facts in a contract. However, not all mistakes will allow them to avoid the contracts they made. A mistake made by one party is called a **unilateral mistake.** A mistake by both parties about the facts is called a **mutual mistake.** Most mistakes are unilateral. A unilateral mistake may be caused by ignorance, forgetfulness, poor judgment, or carelessness. As a general rule, a unilateral mistake has no effect on a contract.

> By mail, Farley offered to sell Sprinkler, a medical student, a set of medical encyclopedias for $195. Sprinkler immediately mailed a letter of acceptance. When she received the acceptance, Farley discovered that she had typed $195 instead of $295, as she had intended. Farley refused to mail the books to Sprinkler, who sued. Since this mistake by Farley was due to her carelessness, it had no effect on the contract. Sprinkler could enforce the contract for $195. ∎

As mentioned, unilateral mistakes have no effect on the validity of contracts. However, in the example, if Sprinkler believed that Farley had made an error but did not mention it, the contract would have been voidable by Farley, the injured party. One person is not allowed to take unfair advantage of another's mistake.

Certain types of mutual mistakes can serve as defenses in breach of contract suits because they show there has been no meeting of the minds. They are mutual mistakes about the existence of the subject matter and mutual mistakes about the identity of the subject matter.

Mutual Mistake About the Existence of the Subject Matter   The subject matter must exist at the time the contract is made. If it does not, there can be no contract. The offeror cannot offer to sell something that doesn't exist. Likewise, the offeree cannot accept an offer for something that no longer exists.

> You made a contract to sell a friend your motorboat, which was stored at a marina near your summer home. Unknown to both of you, the marina and the boat were destroyed by fire two days earlier. In spite of this, your

friend, who had spent a lot of money building a boathouse, sued for damages. Because the boat had been destroyed, you can claim mutual mistake as a defense. ■

Mutual Mistake About the Identity of the Subject Matter   If both parties are mistaken about the subject matter that is the basis of the contract, there can be no meeting of the minds and, therefore, no contract.

■ Rapp owned two racehorses, one younger than the other but both named Pogas Song. Rapp offered to sell her racehorse to Peters. In making the offer, Rapp had the older horse in mind. Peters accepted, thinking he was buying the younger horse. Learning of the error, Peters sued to force Rapp to sell him the younger horse. Rapp, because of the mutual mistake about the identity, cannot be forced to sell Peters the younger horse. ■

If one or both persons make a mistake (unilateral or mutual) about the value or quality of the subject matter, this mistake in judgment will not excuse either party from carrying out the contract.

■ You sold your friend an old ring for $10, neither of you knowing its true value. Later you discovered that the ring was considered a piece of antique jewelry worth $500. You demanded the return of the ring. Your friend is entitled to keep the ring. ■

Bankruptcy

A person who is hopelessly in debt may resort to bankruptcy to be relieved of many, but not all, of those debts. Bankruptcy technically does not discharge a debt. It simply prevents a creditor from suing to collect the money from a person who has more debts than money to pay them. Bankruptcy is discussed in Chapter 41.

Statute of Limitations

All states have a **statute of limitations,** which fixes a time limit within which a lawsuit must be filed after a contract has been breached. This time limit varies from state to state, but in most states it is six years (see Table 14.1). After the time limit has passed, any action for breach of contract is outlawed, or barred, by statute. The contract is not discharged, but the legal means to enforce the contract is lost. The person responsible for the breach may, after the right of action is outlawed, choose to fulfill the contract but is not legally obligated to do so.

It is important to determine when the contract is legally breached. In the case of money owed, the time of the breach is figured from the due date of the debt.

■ Your doctor charged you $150 for a physical examination made on March 3, 1984. She requested full payment within thirty days (by April 2, 1984). The doctor tried to collect from you and then, on July 1, 1990, finally sued you to recover the money. The statute of limitations in your state was six

TABLE 14.1 Limitations for Civil Actions for Breach of Ordinary Contract*

State	Time Limit (years)	State	Time Limit (years)
Alabama	6	Montana	8-W; 5-O
Alaska	6	Nebraska	5-W; 4-O
Arizona	6-W; 3-O	Nevada	6-W; 4-O
Arkansas	5-W; 3-O	New Hampshire	3
California	4-W; 2-O	New Jersey	6
Colorado	6	New Mexico	6-W; 4-O
Connecticut	6-W; 3-O	New York	6
Delaware	3	North Carolina	3
District of Columbia	3	North Dakota	6
Florida	5-W; 4-O	Ohio	5-W; 6-O
Georgia	6-W; 4-O	Oklahoma	5-W; 3-O
Hawaii	6	Oregon	6
Idaho	5-W; 4-O	Pennsylvania	6-W; 4-O
Illinois	10-W; 5-O	Rhode Island	10
Indiana	10-W; 6-O	South Carolina	3
Iowa	10-W; 5-O	South Dakota	6
Kansas	5-W; 3-O	Tennessee	6
Kentucky	15-W; 5-O	Texas	4
Louisiana	10	Utah	6-W; 4-O
Maine	6	Vermont	6
Maryland	3	Virginia	5-W; 3-O
Massachusetts	6	Washington	6-W; 3-O
Michigan	6	West Virginia	10-W; 5-O
Minnesota	6	Wisconsin	6
Mississippi	3-W; 3-O	Wyoming	10-W; 8-O
Missouri	10-W; 5-O		

W = Written O = Oral
*Does not include sales contracts under UCC §2-725

years. Since the doctor had only until April 1, 1990, to collect from you, she is barred from suing you after that date. ∎

If the borrower makes a voluntary part payment after the due date, the time limit under the statute starts all over again from the date of this part payment.

∎ Maytag borrowed $325 from Ziegler on September 4, 1982, and promised in writing to repay the loan in full one year later (by September 4, 1983). Maytag, who was unemployed, failed to repay the loan on the due date. He did, however, make a part payment of $125 to Ziegler on September 4,

1984. Because of the part payment, Ziegler had until September 4, 1990, to file a lawsuit to collect the $200. ◾

If the borrower makes a part payment on a debt or promises in writing to repay a debt barred by the statute of limitations, the creditor's right to collect this debt is legally reinstated. In this case, the statute starts over again as of the date of the part payment or written promise.

◾ On September 8, 1987, one of your debts for $200 was outlawed by the six-year statute of limitations in your state. You paid the creditor $50 on December 31, 1987, and promised to pay the remainder of the debt ($150) in three weeks. When you failed to pay the balance as promised, the creditor sued. The $50 payment on December 31, 1987, reinstated the right of the creditor to collect the balance of $150 until December 31, 1993. ◾

If the party to be sued leaves the state (for example, by entering the armed forces or transferring to a new job) or is under a disability (for example, by being confined to a prison or mental institution), the time spent away from the state or under the disability is not counted in determining whether the debt is outlawed by a statute of limitations. The statute begins to run again when and if the debtor returns to the state or is no longer under the disability.

◾ Galvin retained an attorney to represent him in a lawsuit. The lawyer submitted her bill for $500 on April 1, 1981, payable immediately. Galvin paid the attorney $75. On April 10, 1981, Galvin moved out of the state to begin a new job. When the attorney later discovered that Galvin had returned to the state on May 8, 1987, she brought an action to collect the balance due her of $425. Galvin refused to pay, claiming that the debt had been outlawed. Because the time between April 10, 1981, and May 8, 1987, did not count, the debt was still legally collectible. ◾

The statute of limitations is sometimes unfair to creditors. Borrowers legally owe the money and creditors are entitled to be paid. On the other hand, an unreasonable delay in bringing legal action makes it more difficult for a borrower to prove the facts. Evidence may be lost or destroyed and witnesses may have relocated to another state or may have died.

The Uniform Commercial Code, section 2-725, provides a four-year statute of limitations for contracts involving the sale of goods. (This topic is discussed in Chapter 15.)

REMEDIES FOR FRAUD, DURESS, AND UNDUE INFLUENCE

Fraud, duress, and undue influence make a contract voidable. The victim of one of these acts also has remedies. The victim may either rescind or ratify the contract.

If the contract is rescinded, the victim must return any consideration received and is entitled to recover anything given as consideration, by a lawsuit if necessary. The victim may also sue for damages.

If the victim chooses to ratify, the contract is as valid as if no fraud, duress, or undue influence had occurred. As with rescission, the victim may sue for damages for actual loss or injury suffered.

■ You were induced to purchase a used car through fraud. Before you purchased the car the dealer stated that the engine had recently been rebuilt. Actually it had not. After you bought the car, you had engine troubles and the car stopped running. ■

In this example, if you wanted to keep the car, you could choose to ratify the contract and sue the dealer for damages. In this case, damages would be the cost of repairing the engine.

Summary of Important Legal Concepts

In addition to discharge, another way in which a contract ends is by an actual breach. This type of breach occurs when one party fails to perform an obligation according to the terms of the contract. Although breaches of contract usually occur after the date for performance, some take place before the performance date. This type of breach is called an anticipatory breach.

For any breach, the injured party has a course of action called a *remedy*. Remedies available to the injured party are either legal or equitable. In a legal remedy, the injured party is awarded money damages. Money damages, the most common remedy for breach of contract, are awarded to compensate the injured party financially for her or his loss. Money damages may be compensatory, liquidated, nominal, or punitive. Equitable remedies are provided by a court when money does not adequately compensate the injured party for his or her loss. Equitable remedies include rescission, specific performance, and injunction.

A material breach—that is, one that is substantial—usually ends a contract, and the injured party no longer needs to perform. In addition, the injured party can sue for damages. A minor breach does not end a contract. Both parties must still perform, but the injured party may sue for damages. As soon as a breach occurs, the nonbreaching party has a duty to mitigate the damages, that is, to make a reasonable effort to hold down the amount of damages. Instead of suing, the injured party may elect to waive his or her rights (not sue) when the other party breaches the contract.

The defendant in a breach of contract suit may claim such defenses as fraud, duress, undue influence, and mutual mistake. These four acts make a contract voidable by the victim. In some cases, they make the contract void and excuse the victim from further liability under the contract.

Other defenses for a breach of contract suit are bankruptcy and the statute of limitations. In both cases, creditors are prohibited from bringing court action against the borrower to recover a debt. A victim of fraud, duress, or undue influence may either rescind the contract and recover any consideration given or ratify the contract and sue for actual damages suffered.

Key Legal Terms to Know

Match the terms with the definitions that follow.

actual breach
anticipatory breach
compensatory damages
defenses
duress
fraud
injunction
liquidated damages

material breach
mitigate the damages
mutual mistake
nominal damages
punitive damages
remedy
specific performance
statute of limitations
undue influence
unilateral mistake
waiver

1. A court order that prohibits a person from doing a certain act
2. Damages awarded as compensation for an actual loss or injury
3. A court order requiring a party to carry out a contract according to its original terms
4. Power or dominance used to make a person enter into a contract against his or her will
5. A course of action an injured party may take to obtain satisfaction for a breach of contract
6. An error made by both parties to a contract
7. Damages awarded when a breach of contract occurs but there is no real loss or injury
8. Damages determined in advance by the parties and stated in the contract
9. An error made by only one party to a contract
10. Reasons offered by a defendant in a lawsuit for being relieved of responsibility
11. Making a reasonable effort to hold damages down after a breach of contract has occurred
12. Forcing a person to enter into a contract by using violence or threats of violence
13. Intentionally misleading a person into making a contract either by making material false statements or by concealing material facts
14. A breach of contract that occurs before the stated time of performance
15. The failure to perform the obligations required by a contract
16. Money damages awarded to the injured party as punishment for the breaching party's wrongful conduct
17. A law fixing a time limit within which a lawsuit for breach of contract must be started
18. The voluntary surrender of a legal right
19. A violation of contract that allows the injured party to end the contract and sue for damages

because he or she has been deprived of a substantial benefit

Questions and Problems to Discuss

1. When may an injured party sue for specific performance rather than for money damages?
2. Briefly describe the types of money damages that may be awarded to an injured party for breach of contract.
3. Describe the defenses that a breaching party may offer for not performing on a contract.
4. Dunes called the Sauna Resort Hotel and made a reservation for his family of four for July 6–12. A letter of confirmation signed by the hotel manager stated, "This is to confirm your reservation for the period July 6 to July 12 inclusive. The rate for the Fernwood Cottage No. 10 Accommodation (American Plan) you requested is $600. A $100 deposit is required in advance to guarantee this accommodation. Please sign the original of this confirmation letter and return it to this office with the required deposit. Keep the other copy for your files." Dunes immediately signed and returned the letter along with a certified check for $100. In settling Dunes's account at checkout time, the manager discovered that a typing error had been made in the quoted price of the accommodation listed in the confirmation letter. The quoted price should have been $700, not $600. Dunes refused to pay the additional $100 when requested to do so by the hotel manager. Can the Sauna Resort Hotel require Dunes to pay this additional amount based on the hotel's error?
5. Deveney, who had been hired by Rollins Community College as a marketing instructor, was asked to provide the college with a copy of his MBA (master of business administration) degree, which he did. Six months after Deveney began teaching, the director of personnel discovered that Deveney had no MBA of his own as required by the college. Deveney had instead "borrowed" a retired person's MBA diploma and had cleverly removed the retired person's name and inserted his own. What action can the college take?
6. The seniors at Washington College booked their Graduation Ball at the Washington Plaza Hotel for June 1. The student activities director signed the contract and sent a deposit of $500 to the

hotel as required to guarantee the booking. Two weeks before the ball, the seniors decided instead to hold the affair at the new convention center just down the street from the Washington Plaza Hotel. The student activities director went along with the change and signed another contract with the manager of the convention center. The student activities director then called the Washington Plaza Hotel and canceled. What action, if any, can the hotel take?

7. The Arbor Construction Company entered into a written contract with the BMI Investors Group to construct a new shopping mall. The contract called for the job to be completed within a one-year period. One clause in the contract provided for damages of $2,000 per day for each day's delay in completion. Due to errors on the part of the contractor, work was finished one hundred days after the original completion date. BMI sued Arbor for $200,000 ($2,000 for each day's delay) claiming that, because of the delay, approximately $1 million in sales had been lost. Will BMI be successful in its lawsuit? Why or why not?

8. Strouse bought a used motorcycle from Biker's World and agreed to pay for it in monthly installments. When Strouse asked about mileage, the salesperson stated that the motorcycle had been driven only 4,000 miles, had never been raced, and needed no major engine repairs. In fact, the motorcycle had been driven over 6,000 miles, had been entered in several racing contests, and needed major engine repairs. Strouse soon discovered the salesperson's misrepresentations, returned the motorcycle, and refused to make any more payments. In a breach of contract suit, can Strouse claim fraud as a defense?

9. A door-to-door salesperson offered to sell you a freezer plan that included the freezer and a six-month supply of meat. The salesperson stated that only top-quality meat would be provided. Before deciding, however, you investigated and discovered that lesser-quality meats were actually provided. Nevertheless, because of the good price, you entered into a contract to buy the plan. Shortly before the freezer was delivered, you tried to avoid the agreement, claiming that the salesperson lied to you. Can you avoid the contract for the freezer plan?

10. Zigmont and her husband opened a factory in Dallas, Texas, to manufacture Santa Claus suits

and accessories. The factory was the only one of its kind in the country. While in Baltimore on a business trip, Zigmont contracted to sell one hundred Santa Claus suits to Garson Brothers, a chain of costume stores in the Baltimore area. The costumes were to be manufactured at the Dallas factory. Unknown to the parties, the factory in Dallas had been destroyed by a fire the day before the contract was signed. Can Garson Brothers recover damages if Zigmont fails to deliver the costumes?

11. Barnaby offered to sell you her house for $100,000. Barnaby said she paid $50,000 for the house ten years ago but that it was worth three times that amount today. Relying on this statement, you accepted Barnaby's offer to sell the house for $100,000. Later you discovered that Barnaby did pay $50,000 but that the house was not worth $150,000 according to a bank appraisal. You refused to buy the house, and Barnaby sued. Can you claim fraud and break your contract to pay Barnaby the $100,000?

12. One of Hope's debts was outlawed under the statute of limitations. Later, after inheriting a large sum of money, Hope wrote to the creditor and promised to repay the debt. Two months later the creditor, who had not yet received any money, sued Hope for collection. Should the creditor succeed?

13. Benson, a homeowner, made a contract with a roofer to repair her roof, which had begun to leak slightly. Several months after the contract was made, the roofer still had not come to do the job, nor had Benson contacted him to ask when he was coming. In the meantime, the condition of the roof deteriorated to the point where heavy rains severely damaged the interior of Benson's house. Benson then sued the roofer for breach of contract, claiming that since he (the roofer) did not show up to repair the roof, he should be liable for the interior damage caused by the heavy rains. Is Benson correct?

14. Montrello, a professional baseball pitcher, signed a three-year contract to play for the Los Angeles Stars for $1,500,000. He was to receive $50,000 as a sign-on bonus and $500,000 a year for the term of the contract. Montrello did receive the $50,000 sign-on bonus but, because the Los Angeles team was having financial difficulties, he did not receive the $500,000 at the end of the first year of

his contract. Can Montrello break his contract with Los Angeles? Explain.

Cases to Decide

1. Robert and Sandra Bell hired McCann to build a house for them at a contract price of $45,000. McCann then changed his mind and refused to build, claiming that he would make no profit. The Bells then advertised for bids from other contractors. The lowest bid was $54,500, which the Bells accepted. They then brought suit against McCann for the difference between the original contract price and the market price ($54,500 − $45,000), less the extras of $4,562 that were discussed but had not been included in the contract. Thus, the Bells were awarded $4,938 in damages by the trial court. McCann appealed, claiming that the trial court applied an improper measure of damages. Do you agree with McCann? (*Bell* v. *McCann* 535 P. 2d 233)

2. Watts Construction Co. was awarded a construction contract with Cullman County to complete a County Water Works Improvement Project. One section of the contract provided that it would not become effective unless and until approved by a certain federal agency, namely the Farmers Home Administration, U.S. Department of Agriculture. The agency's approval was delayed, which in turn delayed the initiation of the project. In response to this delay, Watts Construction Co. requested a 5 percent increase in the contract price due to seasonal and inflational price increases. In his letter to Cullman County, Watts stated, "If this is not agreeable with you, please consider this letter a withdrawal of our bid." Cullman County refused to pay the additional 5 percent and hired another company to take on the project. Watts then informed the county that he was willing to perform the contract at the original price (without the 5 percent price increase) but with certain modifications. The county refused and Watts sued for breach of contract. Should he be successful? (*Watts Construction Co.* v. *Cullman County* 382 So. 2d. 520)

3. Beckman signed a contract with the Vassall-Dillworth Lincoln-Mercury dealer for the purchase of a Lincoln Continental at an agreed-upon price. When Beckman inquired about the car four weeks later, he was told that the agreement had been lost and, as a result, that the car had not been ordered. The dealer told Beckman that he could place his order again, but at a higher price than the price originally agreed upon. Instead, Beckman sued the dealer for specific performance (delivery of the original car at the quoted price). Is this an appropriate remedy? (*Beckman* v. *Vassall-Dillworth Lincoln-Mercury*, Pa 468 A2d)

4. Parker, a well-known actress, had a contract with Twentieth Century Fox to act in the musical motion picture *Bloomer Girl*, where she would use her talents as a dancer as well as an actress. The musical was to be filmed in California and she was to receive $750,000. However, *Bloomer Girl* was canceled and Parker was offered a straight dramatic role in *Big Country, Big Man*, a western that was to be filmed in Australia. Parker refused the replacement role, claiming that it was a different as well as an inferior role. Instead, she sued for payment on the *Bloomer Girl* contract. Twentieth Century Fox contended that Parker failed to mitigate the damages by not taking the role in *Big Country, Big Man*. Is its contention correct? (*Parker* v. *Twentieth Century Fox Film Corporation*, 89 Cal Rptr 737)

5. Knutton, owner of a music company, entered into a contract with Cofield, a restaurant owner, in which a jukebox was to be installed in Cofield's restaurant, with the parties sharing the receipts. The contract provided that if Cofield discontinued using the jukebox before the expiration of the contract, Cofield would pay Knutton a sum of money for the unexpired term of the contract based on the average of the amount paid from the time the jukebox had been installed. Prior to the expiration of the contract, Cofield disconnected the jukebox and installed one belonging to another company. Knutton sued for damages for breach of contract. Cofield, however, claimed that the damages being sought were a penalty and not liquidated damages. Was Cofield correct? (*Knutton* v. *Cofield*, 273 NC 355)

6. Burns and his wife bought a new car from a dealer and financed it through the Manhattan Credit Co. The finance company assured Burns that it would take care of the insurance but in fact did not arrange for enough coverage. A few months after the car was purchased, the car was damaged beyond repair, and the insurance wasn't enough to cover the damage. Burns and

his wife sued to cancel the contract of sale because of the false statements made by the finance company regarding the insurance coverage. Can the sale be legally canceled? (*Manhattan Credit Co.* v. *Burns*, 230 Ark 418, 323 SW2d 206)

7. Palmer was a retail florist. He sold his business to Flower Haven and agreed not to engage in the retail florist business in his city for five years. Before the end of the five years, Palmer went back into the business and Flower Haven sued for an injunction. Can Palmer be stopped from going into the flower business again before the end of five years? (Assume that five years is reasonable.) (*Flower Haven, Inc.* v. *Palmer, Colo* 502 P2d 424)

8. Kennedy gave a promissory note (a promise to pay money) for $20,000 to Ragsdale, the president of Onslow Livestock Corp., in order to purchase shares of stock in the corporation. Ragsdale had told Kennedy that the corporation was a "going concern." In reality the company was losing money, had many debts, and generally was "going under." Ragsdale attempted to obtain a judgment against Kennedy when Kennedy failed to pay the promissory note. Does Kennedy have a defense for not paying the promissory note? (*Ragsdale* v. *Kennedy*, 286 NC 130)

Atlas Manufacturing Company developed a new line of inexpensive solar calculators. It decided to advertise the calculators in a unique way: by dropping leaflets from a plane offering the calculators for sale for $9.99. By mistake, the leaflets were printed showing a sale price of $3.99; thousands of the leaflets were dropped over a nearby city.

When Atlas realized a mistake had been made, it decided to revoke the offer. To do so, it sent up a plane over the same city and dropped thousands of leaflets containing a notice revoking the offer.

Castle, who had picked up one of the first leaflets, placed an order by mail for one of the calculators, sending a check for $3.99 as payment. Atlas returned Castle's check with a letter stating that the offer had been revoked. Castle, who had not received the leaflet revoking the offer, brought suit to force Atlas to sell her a calculator for $3.99.

The Trial

During the trial, the owner of Atlas testified that $3.99 was an unreasonably low price to pay for a calculator and that anyone receiving the original leaflet would know that an error had been made. The owner also testified that the precise area of the city over which the original leaflets had been dropped was known and that the leaflets revoking the offer were dropped over the same area.

Castle's attorney produced testimony to the effect that solar calculators were sold with varying discounts throughout the city and that $3.99 was a common price for a calculator of similar quality.

The Arguments at Trial

During the trial, Castle's attorney argued that it was absurd to revoke an offer by dropping leaflets and expecting them to reach the same people who had received the original offer. The attorney further argued that the proper way to have revoked the offer would have been to place advertisements in all of the local newspapers advising the public that the price was incorrect and that the offer had been revoked. Because Castle had not received a proper revocation of the offer, Atlas was bound by the offer and was obligated to sell the calculator for $3.99.

Atlas's attorney argued that it was established law that a valid revocation of an offer had to be made in the same manner that the original offer had been made. Since the revocation had been done properly in this case, Castle was bound by the notice of the revocation.

Questions to Discuss

1. If Atlas's attorney has correctly stated the law regarding revocation of offers, shouldn't the judge or jury automatically decide in Atlas's favor?
2. If you were the judge or jury hearing the case, for whom would you decide? Why?
3. Can you think of any other methods that Atlas could have used to revoke the offer?
4. What do you think the law should be regarding methods used to revoke an offer?

PURCHASE AND SALE OF GOODS UNDER THE UCC

After studying Part III, you should be able to

1 Apply the provisions of the Uniform Commercial Code (UCC) to the following situations: merchants dealing with merchants; merchants dealing with nonmerchants; and nonmerchants dealing with nonmerchants.

2 Point out the ways in which the UCC has changed the common-law rules of contracts, especially as they relate to offer and acceptance, consideration, and the writing requirements for contracts under the statute of frauds.

3 Determine the point at which risk of loss (and in some cases, title) passes from buyer to seller in the various types of sales contracts.

4 Summarize remedies available to the buyer and the seller for breach of the sales contract.

5 Explain product liability and three well-recognized theories of product liability available to injured parties as the bases for personal injury lawsuits.

Chapter 15

The Sales Contract: Key Concepts

CHAPTER PREVIEW

This chapter is the first in a unit of four chapters (Chapters 15, 16, 17, and 18) dealing with contracts for the sale of goods—tangible movable items—under Article 2 of the Uniform Commercial Code (UCC). The UCC, also commonly referred to as the Code, is a group of laws governing commercial transactions (including the sale of goods) throughout the United States. You will discover that the study of the law of sales (sale of goods) is a continuation of the study of basic contract law except in those cases modified by the Code.

Chapter 15 is an introductory chapter that defines terms you will encounter when dealing with the law of sales. The chapter also discusses many of the key modifications that Article 2 of the Code has made in basic contract law (common-law principles) to accommodate the needs of people dealing with each other contractually in a modern business world.

The contract essentials of offer and of acceptance and consideration are areas in which some of the greatest modifications have been made by the Code, and they are examined and explained. The chapter also discusses other key modifications made by the Code that impact the sales contract.

THE LEGAL SETTING FOR A SALE OF GOODS

Of all business transactions, by far the most common is the sale of goods—clothing, computers, building materials, auto parts, food, boats, cars, office equipment, raw materials, and similar things. This unit of four chapters examines contracts for the sale of goods under Article 2 of the UCC. In a sense, the study of the law of sales is a continuation of the study of the common-law principles of contracts (basic contract law) discussed in Chapters 6 through 14 of this text. A **sale** is a contract that transfers title to (ownership of) goods from the seller (vendor) to the buyer (vendee—also known as the purchaser) for a consideration (price). The price can be money, other goods, services, or real estate.

The sale of goods is one of many commercial transactions governed by a group of laws known as the **Uniform Commercial Code (UCC).** The UCC is statutory law that modernizes the common-law principles in many areas including contracts. Common-law principles in these areas are outdated; and the rules are rigid, formalistic, and technical. The UCC is national in scope (followed throughout the country), having been adopted in whole or substantially by all states. (The state of Louisiana has adopted only parts of Article 2.) The UCC defines **goods** as tangible personal property. *Tangible* means physically in existence; *personal property* refers to movable property—property other than land and things permanently attached to land, which are called *real property.* The courts, however, have found the definition of the term *goods* troublesome, and other items that deviate somewhat from the term *movable* have been included in the definition of goods. Goods include the items mentioned in the first paragraph above because those items fall under the definition of movable property. Among the other items that are defined as goods are growing crops and timber to be cut; minerals (including gas and oil); and structures, such as a shed, if severance (removal) is to be made by the seller. Also defined as goods are money that is bought and sold as a commodity (for example, Confederate dollar bills), the unborn young of animals, and items specially manufactured for a buyer (special orders).

An item that is attached to real property may be considered goods and sold separately from the real estate if the item can be easily removed without doing material harm. For example, a portable heater attached to a wall only by means of bolts could be considered goods, whereas a bathtub would be considered a part of the real property because its removal would do substantial damage to the walls and floor.

The term *goods* does not include intangible (not physical) personal property (such as shares of stock or *rights* to real property). An example of intangible property would be your right to the income from a trust fund that had been set up to provide money for you to go to college.

Even though a sale of services may supply goods, a sale of services is not governed by the UCC. The Code applies only when the sale of goods is the *primary* purpose of the transaction.

> Farley had her hair dyed and set at a beauty parlor. Farley received a service (beauty treatment); the hair coloring (which could be classified as goods) was incidental to that service. ■

The UCC, Article 2, applies to all sellers and buyers of goods, whether they are merchants or nonmerchants. However, in a few limited provisions of Article 2, some special rules apply solely to sales contracts between merchants (that is, transactions in which both the seller and buyer are merchants). A **merchant** is a person who either deals regularly in the sale of goods involved in the sales contract (such as a retailer, a wholesaler, or a manufacturer) or professes by occupation to have specialized knowledge of these goods (as, for example, a purchasing agent for a large corporation would have). In short, the merchant is a professional, a commercial expert so to speak, as compared with the **nonmerchant,** who is an occasional or casual seller.

> Underwood, owner of a retail clothing store, purchased fifty suits from Best Suits, a clothing manufacturer. Underwood and Best Suits are both merchants, because as retailers they both deal regularly in the sale of goods. ■

> Underwood sold a used video recorder to a friend. In this case, Underwood is a nonmerchant or occasional seller. ■

It should be kept in mind that the provisions of the UCC are not mandatory. That is, freedom of contract is a basic principle of the Code as stated in §1-102: "The effect of provisions of this Act may be varied by agreement except as otherwise provided in this Act. . . ."

THE SALES CONTRACT

A sales contract must contain the same essential elements as other contracts: offer and acceptance, consideration, competent parties, and legal purpose.

In general, the rules that apply to basic contract law also apply to sales contracts; in some areas, however, the UCC modifies those rules as they relate to sales of goods. The individuals who developed the UCC believed that the "old law" no longer met the needs of modern business practices.

In effect, the Uniform Commercial Code has relaxed the rules relating to sales transactions by removing many of the technical requirements found in basic contract law. Under the UCC, it is now far easier to form a binding sales contract. For example, the "mirror-image" rule discussed on page 122 in Chapter 7 no longer applies under the Code. The mirror-image rule, under basic contract law, states that the acceptance of an offer cannot legally add, alter, omit, or change any terms in the offer. This rule, which tended to obstruct the formation of a contract, has been replaced by a rule that is more practical and reduces delay in forming a contract. This change alone is better suited to the special needs of merchants who are in the daily business of trading in goods. More important, however, the Code allows a contract to be enforced as long as the parties really intended to make the contract, even in cases in which essential terms—such as those specifying price, quantity, place and time for delivery, and terms of payment—are for some reason missing. The Code states that the contracting parties can add these terms at a later time. If the parties do not add the necessary terms, other provisions of the Code will determine a fair price or the proper place for delivery and payment. The UCC rules are so practical that many courts have even applied some of these modern principles to nonsales transactions.

To offset these relaxed rules, the Code insists upon two conditions. First, the parties to the contract must perform their obligations in good faith (honestly), without manipulating contract terms to take advantage of another party, especially when misunderstandings arise or when unforeseen events occur. Second, if the parties to the contract are of unequal bargaining power— as, for example, in a contract between a merchant (a professional) and a consumer (a nonprofessional or inexperienced person, who may know very little about the goods being purchased)—the dominant party must avoid being unfair in dealings with the other party. If unfairness occurs, a court could refuse to enforce the contract because it is unconscionable. Unconscionable contracts were discussed in Chapter 10.

The sections that follow and the remaining chapters in this unit will point out in more detail the important areas in which the UCC has modified basic contract law. (References to Code sections are in parentheses.)

Offer and Acceptance

Under the UCC, a sales contract will not fail for indefiniteness even if some of the terms (such as price or quantity) are left open (§2-204). The key to this rule, however, is that the contract must be definite enough for the court to identify the agreement and conclude that the parties at least *intended* to make a contract. Without such an identification, the court could neither enforce the contract nor make an appropriate award for damages if the contract is breached. If necessary, the courts will fill in the missing terms by applying the various rules found in the Code (sections §2-305–§2-311). Note that, under basic contract law, an agreement with vague or missing terms would have been thrown out by the courts.

For ordinary contracts, an offeree must pay the offeror consideration in order to keep an offer open. In some states, the offer must be in writing. Otherwise, an offer can be revoked at any time before it is accepted. The Uniform Commercial Code modifies these rules and distinguishes between merchants and nonmerchants. The UCC provides that if the offeror is a merchant and offers, in writing, to keep an offer open, the offer is firm. In other words, the offer cannot be revoked during the time stated, even if no consideration is paid by the offeree. The time stated in such an offer, however, may not exceed three months. If no time is stated, the offer remains open for a reasonable time but for no longer than three months (§2-205).

■ In a written offer signed by its president, the Lite Company offered to sell 50 dozen AAA batteries to the Beta Hardware Company for $500 and to keep the offer open for ten days. Five days later, the Lite Company sent a notice to Beta Hardware revoking the offer. Under the UCC, the Lite Company, a merchant, cannot revoke its written offer for ten days. ■

Acceptance by the offeree may be made by any means reasonable under the circumstances, unless the offeror specifies the method by which acceptance must be made. The acceptance is effective when properly sent (§2-206).

■ On February 8, the Barrons and Lippson Corporation sent a letter offering to sell Bundy, owner of Bundy's Clothing Fashion Barn, a new line of men's sport shirts at a considerably reduced introductory price. The letter stated that the offer would be good until February 20. When Bundy received the letter on February 10, he immediately sent a telegram of acceptance. However, because an employee of the telegraph company failed to send the telegram, the telegram never reached the Barrons and Lippson Corporation's home office. Because Bundy used a commercially reasonable means of acceptance, a valid contract was formed on February 10 when he sent the telegram. If Bundy wished (provided he had proof that the telegram was sent), he could legally demand that Barrons and Lippson send the merchandise according to their offer. ■

As mentioned on page 227, the UCC eliminates the mirror-image rule and replaces it with a rule that is more practical because of the way merchants do business in today's business world. Agreements are made by exchanges of written forms: the offeror spells out his or her needs in a purchase order, while the offeree accepts the order and promises delivery with a confirmatory memorandum. Each business drafts its own form in terms that are in its own best interests. The terms on the separate forms, however, often do not agree. Hence the "battle of the forms." To resolve this battle, the Code provides us with Section 2-207, which focuses upon the intent of the parties. This section states that if the offeree's response indicates a definite acceptance of the offer, adding new or different terms does not destroy the acceptance. Between merchants, additional terms will automatically become part of the contract without further assent by the offeree unless (1) the offer expressly limits acceptance to the terms of the offer, (2) the new terms materially alter the contract, or (3) the offeror rejects the new terms and so notifies the offeree within a reasonable time.

> The Livilla Equipment Company offers to sell Condor, a retail hardware merchant in the same city, several lawnmowers at a special price. Condor sent a memo to Livilla confirming the order but specifying that the lawnmowers were to be disassembled and loaded onto Condor's trucks when the trucks arrived at Livilla's warehouse and that the cost of loading was to be charged to Livilla. Condor (the offeree) definitely accepted Livilla's offer when he sent a confirming memo. Therefore, since Condor and Livilla were both merchants, the terms Condor added relating to the disassembling and loading of the trucks automatically became part of the agreement. ∎

If one or both parties are nonmerchants, the Code states that additional terms will not prevent acceptance by the offeree but that these terms will not *automatically* become part of the contract. When requested by a nonmerchant, the terms are mere proposals, which would have to be agreed to by the offeror. If the offeror accepts the proposals, they are part of the contract; if not, the contract simply remains silent on these matters.

The UCC states that an offer to buy goods (the buyer initiates the offer) can be treated as though a unilateral contract offer has been made. The seller can accept such an offer either by shipping the goods to the buyer or by treating the offer as a bilateral contract offer and promptly communicating to the offeror a promise to ship the goods (§2-206). This section of the Code resolves the problem caused by an ambiguous offer in which the offeree was unable to determine whether the offeror wanted a return promise or an act. The Code now says that the offeree can use either method of acceptance.

The Code goes one step farther and states that the seller, if he or she chooses, may promise to ship or actually ship *conforming* or *nonconforming* (substitute) goods (§2-206). A shipment of nonconforming goods is simultaneously regarded both as an acceptance (and therefore results in a contract) and also as a breach of contract for which the buyer may pursue appropriate remedies. However, the seller may state to the buyer that the shipment is nonconforming and that it is offered only as an accommodation to the buyer. In this case, the shipment constitutes only a counteroffer, and the buyer is free to accept or reject the goods. If the buyer decides to use the nonconforming goods, there is a contract.

> Wiggins, the owner of Lasting Treasures, a craft store, ordered one hundred 36-inch grapevine wreaths from Star Vineyards. Star Vineyards shipped one hundred 40-inch wreaths, the only size in stock, knowing that Wiggins needed wreaths immediately for an upcoming craft show. Star then notified Wiggins that the 40-inch wreaths were sent as an accommodation. This shipment of 40-inch wreaths is not an acceptance but a counteroffer. A contract will result only if Wiggins accepts the 40-inch wreaths. ∎

In the above example, if Star Vineyards ships one hundred 40-inch wreaths instead of one hundred 36-inch wreaths and fails to notify Wiggins that a substitute was made as an accommodation, Star Vineyard's shipment acts as both an acceptance of Wiggins's offer and a breach of contract. Wiggins now has the right to sue Star Vineyards for an appropriate amount of money damages.

Under basic contract law, an offeree who is required to accept by completing the act requested (unilateral request) must notify the offeror of performance only if the offeror would not otherwise know the act is being completed. In this context, the UCC applies a stricter rule, stating that if the beginning of a requested performance (for example, beginning to manufacture and/or ship the goods) is a reasonable method of acceptance, the offeree must notify the offeror of such beginning within a reasonable time. An offeror who is not reasonably notified of acceptance may treat the offer as having lapsed before acceptance (§2-206).

> Anderson, in New York City, placed an order for parts for his car with the Zee-Bart Co. in Boston, Massachusetts. Three months went by, but Anderson did not hear from Zee-Bart. Anderson then bought the parts elsewhere. Finally, after the fourth month, the parts arrived from Zee-Bart. At this point, Anderson would have the right to reject the parts Zee-Bart sent; four months generally would be considered an unreasonable length of time. ■

Consideration

Under contract law, a change in an existing contract must be based on consideration. Under the UCC, an agreement modifying a contract for the sale of goods needs no consideration to be binding. The Code treats the change in the contract as a matter of good faith rather than a matter of consideration. That is, the court considers what is fair to the parties involved. However, if the statute of frauds requires the contract to be in writing, any modifications without consideration made to that contract must also be in writing to be enforceable (§2-209).

Statute of Limitations

Under ordinary contract law, an action for breach of contract must be brought within six years of the time of the breach. However, under the UCC, an action for breach of a sales contract must be started within four years of the breach. The parties to a sales contract may agree to reduce this period to as little as one year, but it may not be extended beyond four years (§2-725).

Statute of Frauds

A contract for the sale of goods may be oral or written. However, the statute of frauds provision of the UCC states that when the sale price of goods is $500 or more, the sales contract must be in writing to be legally enforceable in a court of law (§2-201). The party who is liable for performance of the contract must sign it, although it is a good idea for both parties to sign.

■ Bray signed an order for a $600 microwave oven from Modern Kitchens Appliance Store, to be delivered the next day. When the oven was delivered, Bray refused to accept it, claiming he had changed his mind. Since the agreement was in writing as required, and signed by Bray, Bray is legally obligated to accept and pay for the microwave. ■

The UCC has greatly relaxed the statute of frauds requirement of the written memorandum as evidence of a sale. There is only the requirement of "some writing"—a check, a letter, an invoice, an order blank and so on—as evidence that a contract for the sale of goods has taken place. One essential term of the sale—the *quantity*—must be in the writing. The contract is not enforceable beyond the quantity shown in the writing. In case of a lawsuit, other essential terms of the transaction (price, for example, or the time and place of payment or delivery) that are in dispute but that are not included in the writing can be proved by oral testimony.

Enforceable Oral Sales Contracts

In some cases, oral contracts for the sale of goods for $500 or more will, if proved, be enforced (§2-201). These situations are described in the following sections.

Buyer Receives and Accepts the Goods   An oral contract will be enforced if the buyer both receives and accepts all of the goods. "Receipt of goods" means that the buyer physically takes possession of them. "Acceptance of goods" means that the buyer indicates, by words or actions, an intention to become the owner.

■ Johnson made an oral contract with a dealer to buy a used tractor for $1,500. The tractor was to be delivered on a Monday, and Johnson was to pay for it on Thursday. The tractor was delivered on Monday as agreed, and Johnson accepted it but then refused to pay for it on Thursday, claiming he was not bound by the oral contract. Because Johnson received and accepted the goods, he is liable. ■

An oral contract will also be enforced if the buyer receives and accepts part of the goods. The oral contract will be enforced only for the portion of the goods actually received and accepted by the buyer. If the goods cannot be separated, the entire contract is unenforceable.

■ Baylor read in the newspaper that Rudnick Furniture Store was having a summer furniture sale. She telephoned the store and ordered a patio table and chairs for $800 and two family room chairs for $350 each, for a total of $1,500. She had looked at these items in the store a few days earlier. Rudnick agreed to deliver the items. When the items arrived, Baylor decided to accept and pay for only the patio table and chairs. Baylor is legally obligated to pay for only the patio table and chairs. ■

Buyer Makes Full Payment   The entire oral contract is enforceable if the buyer makes full payment for the goods under the terms of the sales contract.

Cobb orally agreed to purchase a used snowmobile from the Arctic Cat Snowmobile Company and paid $700 cash. When the snowmobile was delivered the next day, Cobb refused to accept it and demanded the return of her $700. She claimed that because the agreement was not in writing, she was not bound to accept the snowmobile. Cobb was liable, however, because she had paid for the snowmobile in full. ■

Buyer Makes a Part Payment on the Goods   An oral contract is binding if the buyer makes a partial payment on the goods. The contract is enforceable, however, only for those goods covered by the part payment. If the goods cannot be separated, the oral contract cannot be enforced against the buyer.

Bono made an oral contract to purchase a stereo system from Sound-Com for $600. The system included a receiver, $235; a turntable, $130; and speakers, $190. She made a part payment of $235, the cost of the receiver. The turntable and speakers were temporarily out of stock, but Bono did take the receiver at the time of the sale. Bono later changed her mind and decided to use her old turntable and speakers and keep only the receiver that was already paid for. Sound-Com insisted that Bono was obligated to take the entire stereo system. Since the contract was oral, Bono was liable only for the receiver that she had already paid for. She was not liable for the price of either the turntable or the speakers. ■

The courts have ruled that an oral contract for the sale of goods consisting of a single item is binding when the buyer makes a down payment (*Lockwood* v. *Smigel* 96 Cal. Reptr. 289).

Sacco offered to sell her used Rolls Royce to Ruff for $20,000. Ruff accepted the offer and paid Sacco $1,000 as a down payment. The balance was to be paid upon delivery of the car. Sacco never delivered the car but instead sold it to someone else. Ruff sued for damages for breach of an oral contract. Sacco would be liable. ■

Specially Manufactured Goods   An oral contract for goods to be specially manufactured for the buyer is enforceable. The contract is enforceable, however, only if (1) the goods to be manufactured are not suitable for resale to others in the regular course of the seller's business and (2) the seller, before receiving notice that the buyer did not want them, made a substantial beginning on the manufacture of the goods or made commitments for the manufacture of the goods. This rule protects the seller, who would have to absorb the loss if the buyer did not take the goods. Goods made to a buyer's specifications or imprinted with the buyer's name generally cannot be resold to others.

Boddin, an insurance agent, made an oral agreement to purchase several hundred calendars from the Riga Printing Company for $600. The calendars were to contain Boddin's name, the name of the insurance company, and certain advertising designed by Boddin for each page of the calendar. When the calendars were nearly completed, Boddin contacted Riga to cancel the contract. The company refused. Boddin claimed he was not liable because the contract was made orally. Nevertheless, Boddin is liable; the calendars were made especially for him and could not be sold to anyone else. ■

An oral contract is not enforceable if the contract is completely executory—that is, if the terms of the contract have not been carried out—when notice of revocation is received from the buyer. If Boddin had canceled the order before Riga had started to manufacture the calendars, the oral contract would not be enforceable.

Admission in Court of an Oral Contract   If a person being sued admits in court (on the witness stand) that an oral contract for the sale of goods was in fact made, the contract will be enforced. Enforceability, however, is limited to the quantity of goods admitted.

> You orally agreed to buy a set of encyclopedias for $800 from the Educational Book Company. Delivery of the books by the company and payment by you were to take place on a certain date. On that date, the books were delivered but you refused to accept them. The company could not win in a suit against you unless you admitted in open court that the oral contract for the encyclopedias was actually made. ■

Written Confirmation Between Merchants   This is one of the few special rules within Article 2 of the UCC that applies to the sale of goods only between merchants. The rule states that if two merchants make an oral agreement, the statute of frauds requirement is satisfied if one of them sends a written confirmation of the oral agreement to the other merchant. The merchant receiving the confirmation must give written notice of objection to this confirmation within ten days after receiving it. If the receiving merchant does not give written notice within that time, the contract will be enforceable, even though the receiving merchant has not signed anything.

> Cavanna, a North Carolina merchant who sells women's apparel, placed a telephone order for ten dozen hats from PSI, a wholesaler in New York City. PSI sent Cavanna a signed invoice for the hat order (written confirmation), giving details of their oral agreement. If Cavanna does not send PSI a written objection to the contents of this invoice within ten days of receipt of the invoice, the oral (telephone) contract will be enforceable. ■

UNCONSCIONABILITY

The doctrine of unconscionability was discussed in Chapter 10. This doctrine, which has been around for centuries, has become significantly more important under the UCC (§2-302). Because of changes in the way in which people do business in the modern business world, the ethical behavior of merchants can now be controlled more directly by courts. Under basic contract law (common-law principles), the parties to a contract were considered equals; if the contract turned out to be unfair to one party (generally the consumer) this consumer had no recourse at law. He or she had agreed to the terms and that was that. Courts of equity very often refused to grant relief of a contract that was unfair (unconscionable). A party who signed an unfair contract had to find other ways to get relief. A common device was to have the contract declared void, on the grounds that it was against public policy. Now, under the Code, courts, using normal legal processes, can deal directly with such problems and can exercise discretion that traditionally belonged to equity courts. Under the UCC, courts have expanded powers to deal with unfairness and to ensure that all contracts seem perfectly ethical. Nevertheless, only contracts that are so extremely unfair to one of the parties as to "shock the conscience" of the court have been found unconscionable. Typically, the courts have held unconscionable contracts that involve uneducated consumers who are placed in a position of having unequal bargaining power—contracts in which the seller is in a position to impose his or her will on a consumer who would not have contracted if he or she had known all the facts. Too often this consumer is a person who speaks little English and cannot read, let alone understand the language of a standard form contract. This person often pays an excessive price (two or three times greater than the average retail price elsewhere) or agrees to waive certain basic rights such as the right to sue in the event of dissatisfaction with a product.

THE PAROL EVIDENCE RULE

Recall that the parol evidence rule was discussed in Chapter 11. According to this rule, when a contract has been put in writing as the final expression of agreement between the parties, parol evidence—evidence of an oral agreement made prior to or at the time of signing the written agreement—cannot be presented in court to change or add to the terms of the written contract. Parol evidence can be presented to give meaning or add clarity to unclear language. The UCC reaffirms this basic contract law rule, along with the exceptions noted in Chapter 11. But the Code goes beyond these exceptions. It further states that when a written sales contract made in today's modern business world is in dispute, the contract should be interpreted in light of surrounding circumstances. Evidence is allowed from three sources: course of dealing, course of performance, and usages of trade (§2-202). A **course of dealing** refers to any conduct that took place between the parties prior to the present dispute (such as a series of agreements showing a pattern of dealings between the parties) and that can be followed to interpret their wording in the present disputed agreement (§1-205). A **course of performance** refers to the way in which a particular transaction has been carried out (§2-208). Repeated acts—such as the acceptance without objection of several deliveries of goods that do not technically meet the requirements of the disputed contract—may be sufficient to help a court decide what the parties actually intended. A **usage of trade** refers to a standard custom or a widely accepted practice in a particular occupation that can be applied to the disputed contract (§1-205). For example, customary practice in the farm produce business may be to state in the sales contract a reasonable estimate rather than an exact number of each fruit and vegetable to be purchased.

Summary of Important Legal Concepts

Laws relating to the sale of goods (sales law) have their origin in the common-law principles of contracts (basic contract law). However, Article 2 of the Uniform Commercial Code (UCC), which governs sales law, had made changes that meet the needs of merchants and consumers who deal with each other contractually in a modern business world. In effect, the UCC has relaxed the rules relating to sales transactions by removing many of the technical requirements found in basic contract law. Under the UCC, it is now far easier to form a binding sales contract. In fact, a sales contract may be made in any manner sufficient to show that the parties intended to be bound—even though essential terms such as price, quantity, place and time for delivery, and terms of payment are missing. These missing terms can be added later by the parties or supplied under other provisions of the Code. To offset these relaxed rules, however, the Code does insist that the parties perform in good faith (honestly) and that the dominant party deal fairly with the other party to the sales transaction.

The UCC defines a sale as a contract that transfers ownership of goods from the seller (vendor) to the buyer for a price. Under the UCC, goods are defined as tangible personal property—that is, something movable. The term *goods* also includes other items, such as growing crops and timber to be cut; minerals (including gas and oil) and structures—if severance is to be made by the seller; money bought and sold as a commodity; the unborn young of animals; items specially manufactured for a buyer; and items that are attached to real property and can easily be removed without doing material harm. The term *goods* does not include intangible (not physical) personal property, such as shares of stock.

Article 2 generally applies to all sellers and buyers, whether they are merchants or nonmerchants. In a few limited provisions of Article 2, some special rules apply only to sales contracts between merchants. A merchant is a professional. He or she either sells goods of the type involved in the sales contract (for example, a retailer) or has specialized knowledge of these goods by virtue of his or her profession (for example, a purchasing agent for a big company). A nonmerchant is a casual seller.

Article 2 of the UCC has made substantial modifications to basic contract law in the areas of offer and acceptance and consideration. Moreover, an action for breach of contract under the Code must be brought within four years of the breach. Under the UCC statute of frauds, most contracts for the sale of goods costing $500 or more must be in writing to be enforceable. In some cases, however, oral contracts for more than $500 are enforceable. Under the Code, courts can now deal directly with unconscionable contracts—that is, contracts that are unfair in a court of law. Before the Code, the unethical behavior of merchants, which is the basis of unconscionability, was handled in an indirect way in equity court.

The Code reaffirms the parol evidence rule and its exceptions. This rule states that after a contract has been reduced to writing as the final expression of agreement between the parties, oral evidence cannot change or add to the terms of the written contract. The exceptions to the parol rule permit evidence that will clarify the written document but not change its terms. The Code broadens the type of evidence that may be introduced to help interpret (but not change) disputed contracts. It allows evidence based on widely accepted practices in a particular occupation and on dealings between the parties at various times either before or after the disputed contract was made.

Key Legal Terms to Know

Match the terms with the definitions that follow.

course of dealing
course of performance
goods
merchant
nonmerchant
sale
Uniform Commercial Code (UCC)
usage of trade

1. Tangible personal property
2. A casual or occasional seller

3. A professional who deals regularly in the sale of goods or who has a specialized knowledge of these goods

4. A contract that transfers ownership (title) in goods from the seller to the buyer for a price

5. A group of laws governing commercial transactions

6. Any conduct that takes place between the parties such as a series of previous agreements showing a pattern of dealings that can be followed to interpret the meaning of parties in a present contract dispute

7. The way in which a particular transaction has been carried out, for example repeated acts used to interpret the meaning intended by parties involved in a contract dispute

8. A standard custom or a widely accepted practice in a particular occupation that can be applied in a contract dispute

Questions and Problems to Discuss

1. Is it true that before there can be a legally binding sales contract, the parties must first agree upon price, the terms of payment, and the place and time of delivery?

2. The UCC relaxes the technical rules for sales transactions, but the UCC does insist upon two things when parties enter such contracts. What are these two things?

3. What effect does the Uniform Commercial Code have on consideration as it relates to the modification of contracts?

4. The Chewy Candy Co., a large candy retail outlet store, sent a purchase order to the Bitter Sweet Manufacturing Co. for several thousand candy bars. Bitter Sweet accepted the offer, but with the condition that any disputes over the contract would be settled out of court by arbitration, not by a lawsuit. Did Bitter Sweet's condition prevent a contract from being formed with the Chewy Candy Co.?

5. Bilco Overhead Door Co. made an oral contract to sell 100 garage doors at $150 each to Cartright, a building contractor. It was agreed that twenty doors would be shipped immediately and the remaining eighty doors shipped one month later. Cartright received and accepted the first twenty doors but canceled the remaining order, claiming that the same door could be purchased elsewhere for less money. When Bilco sued, Cartright claimed it was not obligated by its oral contract to accept the remaining eighty doors. Is Cartright correct?

6. Stereo Discounters entered into a contract to sell equipment to Marx for $475. Because of sudden changes in the market price, Stereo Discounters notified Marx that it could no longer deliver the equipment at $475 but would have to charge $500. Marx at first agreed to pay the $500 but then changed her mind and refused to pay more than $475. Was Marx bound by her promise to pay the $500?

7. Clift, who planned to build a fence around his yard, ordered $475 worth of lumber by phone from the Maine Lumber Company. When the lumber was delivered, Clift refused to accept it, claiming he got a better price from another company. Maine Lumber claimed that Clift was bound by this contract even though it was not in writing. Is that correct?

8. Under an oral agreement, Nash, a lawn-care specialist, purchased two hundred bags of Triple Z fertilizer from the Brighton Nurseries at $20 per bag. Nash made a part payment of $1,000 (the cost for fifty bags) and agreed to pay the balance upon delivery. Shortly before the delivery date, Nash notified Brighton that she would not accept the shipment because she was not bound by the oral contract. Is Nash correct?

9. Vogel, a used-car dealer, made an oral contract to sell a used car to Frank for $750. Frank paid the $750 at the time the contract was made, and Vogel agreed to deliver the car the next day. When Vogel failed to deliver the car, Frank sued, claiming breach of contract. Vogel claimed that because the contract was oral, it was not enforceable. Is Vogel correct?

10. Cole, a retail auto parts dealer, needed some parts quickly. He sent a telegram to Veterans Wholesale Auto Parts, requesting that the necessary parts be sent immediately. Two days later, Cole followed up with a telephone call to Veterans. Five weeks later the parts arrived, but Cole rejected them, claiming they arrived too late. Cole had made other arrangements. Veterans sued Cole for breach of contract. Was Cole liable for breach of contract?

11. The Cellular Garment Company of Atlanta, Georgia, a manufacturer of men's clothing, wrote a letter to the London Men's Shop of Albany,

New York, offering to sell fifty leather jackets at a special low price of $1,800. The letter, which London received on June 15, stated that the offer was firm. On September 30 of the same year, London accepted Cellular's offer by telegram. London specified that delivery was to be made in two installments of twenty-five jackets each, one installment to be delivered immediately and the second installment to be delivered by December 1. Due to increased costs of production, however, Cellular refused to ship the jackets. London sued Cellular for breach of contract. Is the Cellular Garment Company liable?

12. The Crown Oak Co. contracted by telephone to manufacture fifty Revolutionary War costumes especially designed for the Royal Clothing Store. Royal planned to donate these costumes to a local bicentennial committee for use in an upcoming celebration. The agreed-upon price per costume was $75. When the costumes were completed, Royal refused to accept or pay for them because the local bicentennial committee had canceled the celebration. Crown Oak sued for breach of contract. Royal claimed that the contract could not be enforced because there was no writing that satisfied the statute of frauds. Way Royal correct?

Cases to Decide

1. Ralston Purina contracted to buy soybeans from McNabb. Poor weather damaged most of the soybeans, making it impossible for McNabb to deliver his crop by the deadline date. Ralston Purina agreed to modify the contract, without additional consideration, to allow delivery at a later date. When McNabb still could not deliver by the new deadline date, Ralston Purina sued for breach of contract based on the new deadline date. McNabb admitted damages but claimed that Ralston Purina, an experienced purchaser of soybeans, was not acting in good faith when it modified the contract, knowing that the price would rise as the result of the crop failure. McNabb contended, therefore, that the modification was not good and that the measure of damages claimed by Ralston Purina should be based not on the price as of the new deadline date but on the price of soybeans as of the date McNabb originally agreed to furnish the soybeans but

failed to do so. Do you agree? (*Ralston Purina Co. v. McNabb*, 381 F. Supp. 181)

2. Auburn Plastics sent a letter to CBS offering to manufacture molds that CBS used to make parts for toys. The letter offer stated that CBS had fifteen days to accept or the option would lapse and that if CBS did accept the offer and required delivery of the molds, there would be a 30 percent charge for services. CBS waited four months to respond to the offer. It sent a purchase order for the molds but included a condition that it (CBS) had the right to demand delivery of the molds from Auburn Plastics at any time without payment of the service charge. Auburn accepted the offer through an acknowledgment form but stated that the service charge would apply. When CBS demanded immediate delivery of its order, Auburn refused to deliver the molds unless CBS paid the 30 percent charge for services. CBS then obtained an order directing the sheriff to seize the molds. Did CBS have the right to do this? (*CBS, Inc. v. Auburn Plastics, Inc.*, 413 NYS 2d 50)

3. Skinner purchased an airplane from Tober Motors under a written installment agreement providing for monthly payments of $200. Before the first payment was due, the plane developed engine trouble. Tober orally agreed to install a new engine and to reduce the payments to $100 a month for the first year. After a few months Tober changed its mind and raised the monthly payments back to $200. Skinner objected, but Tober claimed that its oral promise to reduce the payments to $100 for the first year was not enforceable because Skinner did not give any consideration for the promise. Is Tober correct? (*Skinner v. Tober Foreign Motors*, 187 NE2d 669)

4. Mrs. Whitehurst received nine pints of blood while she was a patient in the Tucson Medical Center Hospital. The charge for each pint of blood was $5.20, of which $4.95 was reimbursed to the Red Cross. From this transfusion, Mrs. Whitehurst contracted homologous serus hepatitis. She brought an action against the American National Red Cross for damages for the sale of goods under Article 2 of the UCC. Was the furnishing of blood by the Red Cross a sale? (*Charles R. Whitehurst and Lucille Whitehurst v. The American National Red Cross*, Ariz 402 P2d 584)

5. Barron owned and operated a sod farm. Edwards orally agreed to purchase Barron's entire sod crop for $300. Before the sod was removed, Barron

notified Edwards that he had changed his mind and further stated that, because the sod was part of the real estate, the oral agreement was invalid under the statute of frauds. Edwards sued for breach of contract, stating that the sod was personal property (goods) because it could easily be removed without doing damage and that the oral contract was valid. Was Edwards correct? (*Barron v. Edwards,* 45 Mich App 210)

6. Lewis orally agreed to sell Hughes a house trailer for $5,000 cash. Shortly after the oral agreement was made, Hughes informed Lewis that he would not pay the full $5,000 in cash. He wanted to pay it over a period of time or to pay Lewis $3,500 immediately in full settlement. Lewis sued for breach of the oral contract. Hughes contended that an oral contract for a sale of goods of $500 or more was not binding under the statute of frauds unless it was in writing. During the trial, however, Hughes repeatedly testified that he had informed Lewis that he would purchase the mobile home for $5,000 cash. In these circumstances, should Lewis be awarded damages suffered as a result of the breach of the oral contract? (*Lewis v. Hughes,* 276 Md 247, 346 A2d 231)

Chapter 16

The Sales Contract: Transfer of Title and Risk of Loss

CHAPTER PREVIEW

11/18

Chapter 16 concentrates primarily on the rules that determine the point in time when risk of loss passes from seller to buyer after the contract is made and the goods have been damaged, destroyed, or lost while being delivered. The chapter also spells out the rights of third parties, who may acquire goods from the buyer under various circumstances. You will learn that although title, or legal ownership, of goods is a very important concept, it is not as important under the Uniform Commercial Code (UCC) as it was in the past. Early in the chapter, some very important terms are defined. A knowledge of these terms will give you a better understanding of the concepts and principles discussed in the chapter.

RELEVANCE OF TITLE AND RISK OF LOSS IN SALES LAW

A problem that frequently arises in sales law is who suffers the loss if goods are damaged, destroyed, or lost after a sales contract has been signed. Ideally, the parties to a contract determine when the title, or ownership, of goods passes from seller to buyer. The parties also determine when the risk of loss of goods—the placement of loss for goods that have been damaged, destroyed, or lost—passes from the seller to the buyer. Typically, however, most lawsuits involve situations in which (1) goods are damaged, destroyed, or lost after the contract is made and (2) both the seller and the buyer claim they are not at fault. If the contract does not specify when title and risk of loss pass from buyer to seller, the courts will use the rules set out in Article 2 of the Uniform Commercial Code to determine liability.

The primary emphasis in this chapter is on the UCC rules for shifting risk of loss rather than on the rules that determine when title passes. The reason for this emphasis is that the UCC rules for shifting loss are more important than the rules for passing title. Title does not determine who bears the loss if goods are damaged, destroyed, or lost, although title is important in other contexts. Title, for example, prevents the seller's unpaid creditors from claiming goods when the title to those goods has passed to the buyer. Title also determines whether goods are the subject of a present sale or simply a contract to sell. We shall return to this topic in the next section.

Before we begin that discussion, however, you should note that, under UCC rules, the decision about who will suffer risk of loss depends on whether the sales contract had been breached at the time the loss occurred. If either party has committed a breach of contract, the risk of loss usually falls totally or in part on the party who committed the breach (§2-510). Such cases are not discussed in this chapter; we examine only those situations in which no breach of contract has taken place and both parties to the sales contract are silent as to who bears the risk of loss.

PRESENT SALE VERSUS CONTRACT TO SELL

A contract for the sale of goods involves either a *present sale* or a *contract to sell*. When a **present sale** of goods is made, title passes from the seller to the buyer at the time the parties make the contract. Title passes immediately because the goods are both physically in existence and identifiable. A cash sale is a present sale, as is a credit sale of identified goods.

Goods become **identified goods** when the seller and the buyer decide on (single out) the exact goods to be sold. Thus, when you select a *particular pair* of skis at a sporting goods store, the goods become identified.

Even though title to goods cannot pass from the seller to the buyer until the goods are in existence and have been identified, the parties may nevertheless enter into a contract to sell. In a **contract to sell,** the seller promises to sell future goods and to transfer title at a later time. **Future goods** are goods not yet in existence and not yet identified.

> You placed a special order for a new car with a car dealer. The car was to be manufactured to your specifications. This was a contract to sell. Title will not pass to you until the car is in existence and has been identified as the car you ordered. ■

The seller and the buyer may not always agree on the exact time at which identification took place. Identifying the skis for purchase in the sporting goods store noted in the above example was relatively easy. Very often, however, identification will take place between merchants after the contract has been made. At the time the contract is made, the merchant seller simply agrees to furnish a specified number of items from his or her general inventory. Then, at a later time, the merchant seller will separate the specific items specified in the contract. It is at this point that a disagreement may arise. In such cases, the Code contains detailed provisions to establish when identification takes place (§2-501). There could not, of course, be a present identification of future goods.

RISK OF LOSS

Article 2 of the UCC takes a very practical view of who should bear the risk of loss in the event that goods are destroyed, damaged, or lost. The rules under the UCC are discussed below and illustrated in Table 16.1. Keep in mind that, as indicated earlier in the chapter, these rules apply only if the seller and the buyer, for whatever reason, have failed to state in their agreement who will bear the risk of loss.

The Code places the loss on the party who is most likely to insure the goods as they move to their destination point, or on the party who seems to be better able to prevent a loss of these goods. If the seller legally must bear the risk of loss, he or she cannot recover the price of the goods from the buyer; if the buyer has already paid the price, the seller is obligated to

TABLE 16.1 **Rules for Passage of Risk of Loss from Seller to Buyer Under the UCC**

Contract Terms	Risk of Loss Passes to Buyer
Sale made by merchant at merchant's place of business	On receipt (physical possession) of goods by the buyer
Sale made by nonmerchant at nonmerchant's location	When the seller notifies the buyer that the goods are available
Sale made by merchant FOB shipping point (goods delivered to carrier)	When goods are properly delivered to an independent (for-hire) carrier at the shipping point
Sale made by merchant FOB destination (location designated by buyer)	When goods are properly tendered (offered) to the buyer after reaching the destination point
Sale on approval	When the buyer accepts goods in his or her possession by approval, whether by words or by conduct
Sale or return	At the time of the sale
Auction Sales	When the auctioneer indicates that an item is sold

return it. If the buyer legally must bear the risk of loss, he or she is liable for the price of the goods, even if the price has been paid but the goods have not been received.

Sale by Merchant at Merchant's Place of Business

When a sale is made by a merchant seller to a consumer buyer at the merchant's place of business, risk of loss passes when the buyer actually receives (takes physical possession of) the goods. Until then, it is the merchant who suffers any loss. This rule applies even if the buyer has made full payment. The UCC tends to place the risk of loss on the merchant because the merchant is a professional seller and would probably have insurance to cover loss or damage to the goods.

■ Marny purchased a waterbed for $450 from World of Water. The waterbed had been selected (identified) and placed in the shipping room to be delivered by the store's truck to Marny's home. The day before the delivery, fire destroyed the store and all the merchandise, including Marny's waterbed. Because Marny never received the waterbed, risk of loss never passed to her. World of Water must suffer the loss. ■

Sale by Nonmerchant at Nonmerchant's Location

When the seller is a nonmerchant (casual seller), risk of loss passes to the buyer on the seller's tender (offer) of delivery. A proper tender consists of the seller's notifying the buyer that the goods are available.

(§2-326). In the meantime, while the buyer has the goods, creditors may lay claim to them.

> You bought seventy-five packages of flower seeds from the Marx Flower Seed Company on a ninety-day, sale-or-return basis. At the end of the ninety days, you had ten packages of flower seeds left and decided to return them to the company. However, before you could return the seeds, you accidentally dropped them into a tub of water, and the paper packaging disintegrated. Because the seeds have been damaged, you cannot return them to the company and must bear the loss yourself. ∎

If is often difficult to determine from the facts of a particular transaction whether the buyer and seller intended a sale on approval or a sale or return. In such cases, the UCC considers the transaction to be a sale on approval if the delivered goods are primarily for use (rather than for resale). This provision keeps the risk of loss from passing to the consumer buyer. The transaction is considered to be a sale or return if the delivered goods are primarily for resale. The risk of loss then falls on the commercial merchant buyer (§2-326).

AUCTION SALES

Under the UCC, auction sales generally follow the ordinary rules of contract law discussed in Chapter 7. One modification, however, requires that a sale of goods of $500 or more must comply with the statute of frauds. Title and risk of loss pass from seller to buyer when the auctioneer indicates an item is sold.

BULK TRANSFERS

A **bulk transfer,** or bulk sale, occurs when a merchant sells all or a "major part" of the materials, supplies, merchandise (goods available for resale to customers), or other inventory (such as equipment) at one time and not during the ordinary course of the merchant's business. Although the term "major part" of the inventory is not defined, most courts have interpreted the term to mean greater than 50 percent of the total value of the inventory.

Generally, suppliers of merchandise on credit expect the merchant to pay them as the inventory is sold to customers in the ordinary course of business. If the merchant-debtor does not pay, the suppliers have the right, as creditors, to obtain a judgment and seize the merchandise and then sell it to obtain their money. Occasionally, however, a merchant will sell an entire business without notifying or paying creditors, and will then pocket the money and disappear. Under ordinary circumstances, the creditors (suppliers) would be unable to recover money or any part of the sold inventory from the bulk-sale buyer unless they can show that the intent of the sale was to cheat the creditors. (If the buyer has paid a fair price, the sale is not fraudulent.) The only alternative creditors have is to try to locate the merchant-debtor and hope that they will be able to collect their money.

The bulk transfer law under Article 6 of the UCC offers creditors another option. It gives them the right to void a bulk sale (within a six-month period) if the buyer does not notify them at least ten days before the sale takes place—that is, ten days before the buyer takes possession of the property transferred in bulk. By voiding the sale, creditors can disregard the sale, seize the goods as if the merchant still owned them, and have the goods sold to satisfy claims of money owed to them.

> ■ Karpinski sold her entire computer software business—merchandise, office furniture, and equipment—to Harvey. DeLuth, a creditor to whom Karpinski owed $5,000, sought to have the sale declared void on the grounds that Karpinski provided no notice of the sale. DeLuth was legally entitled to have the sale set aside. ■

Some states have repealed UCC Article 6, on the grounds that modern business methods make it difficult for a debtor to defraud his or her creditors. For example, credit-reporting technology now enables creditors to determine quickly the debtor's credit history and to discover liens against the debtor's assets. Some other states who still desire continued bulk sales regulation have adopted a Revised Article 6. This revision offers improved creditor protection while reducing the obstacles to good faith sales. Under Revised Article 6, noncompliance does not render the sale void, nor does it otherwise alter the buyer's rights in or title to the inventory. Rather, a noncomplying buyer is simply liable for money damages to any creditor who is injured as a result of the buyer's failure to comply. Also, a noncomplying buyer may escape liability completely by proving that he or she made a good faith effort to comply with Article 6 or in good faith believed that Article 6 did not apply to the sale.

COD SALES

Unless the seller has agreed to extend credit, payment is due when the buyer receives the goods. The seller who permits the buyer to take possession of goods under the terms of a cash sale before payment has been made loses the right to possession. Thus, in a cash-only sale, the seller can retain possession by sending goods **COD**, or "collect on delivery." In a COD sale, the carrier delivering the goods will not give possession of the goods to the buyer until the price and any delivery charges are paid. Title and risk of loss, however, pass as if the sale had been made without the COD terms. For example, if the goods are shipped COD with shipping terms of FOB shipping point, title and risk of loss pass to the buyer when the goods are delivered to the carrier at the shipping point. In addition, in a COD sale the buyer loses the right to inspect the goods before paying for them.

RIGHTS OF THIRD PARTIES

A purchaser in good faith—one who has no knowledge that anything is wrong with a transaction—can acquire ownership of goods in spite of the claims of prior owners, except when the goods were stolen.

Stolen Goods

Generally, a buyer obtains no better title to goods than the seller had. A person who has no title cannot pass a legal title to someone else. Thus, a thief cannot pass a legal title on to a good faith purchaser.

> Baker stole a compact disc player from Lennert's car and sold it to Wood for $200. Wood received possession but not title to the disc player because, as a thief, Baker received no title from Lennert. As the legal owner, Lennert has the right to demand the return of the compact disc player from Wood and does not have to pay Wood $200, even though Wood had no knowledge of the theft. ■

Before making a purchase, the buyer can require the seller to produce evidence of ownership of the goods. A **bill of sale** is written proof of such ownership. It is written evidence that title to personal property has been transferred from a seller to a buyer. If the bill of sale has been stolen or forged, the buyer obtains no title.

The bill of sale may be an informal written document, such as a sales slip from a department store, or it may be a more formal document, which is sometimes used for large purchases. A formal bill of sale describes the item, gives the name of the buyer, states the price of the item, and contains the signature of the seller. In an informal bill of sale, usually only the price and the item are given. (See Figure 16.1.)

> Morrison purchased a portable television set from the Amart Department Store and received a bill of sale signed by the manager of the store. Six months later, Morrison decided to get a floor model TV and advertised the portable set for sale in the newspaper. Arons offered to buy the portable TV but wanted proof that the set legally belonged to Morrison. Morrison produced the bill of sale from Amart. Arons can request a new bill of sale showing the transfer from Morrison to Arons. ■

The general rule that a buyer obtains no better title to goods than the seller had is subject to at least two exceptions under the UCC: (1) where the seller had a voidable title or (2) where a merchant was given temporary possession of goods and unlawfully sells them (§2-403).

Where the Seller Had a Voidable Title

A buyer with a voidable title can transfer a valid (good) title to a third party who obtained the goods for value and in good faith. Under the UCC, value

MC

COMMUNICATIONS

535 West Side Drive, Pontiac, MI 15432 (101) 555-1888
"YOUR CAR STEREO, CELLULAR TELEPHONE, AND ELECTRONICS STORE"

CUSTOMER'S ORDER Feb. 10 19 96

NAME Mark Ash

ADDRESS 13 Birch Crescent
Pontiac, MI 15432

QUAN.	DESCRIPTION	PRICE	AMOUNT
1	Car Stereo		$395.00
		TAX	27.65
		TOTAL	422.65

	CLERK	CASH	C.O.D.	CHARGE	ON ACC'T.	MDSE. RET'D.	PAID OUT
100306	RN	X					

Figure 16.1
Informal Bill of Sale

is any consideration that will support a simple contract. As mentioned at the beginning of this section, a good faith purchaser is a person who is not aware that anything is wrong with the transaction.

■ Riley purchased a used station wagon from a used-car dealer. The car dealer accepted Riley's older car as part of the purchase price. Riley said the car had been driven only 50,000 miles. A check of the odometer confirmed this statement. A short time later, however, a mechanic who was preparing the car for resale for the used-car dealer discovered that the car had actually been driven over 100,000 miles. ■

In the example, Riley had a voidable title to the station wagon since it was obtained from the dealer through fraud. The dealer in this case could rescind the contract and recover the station wagon. If, however, Riley sold it to Bacon, a third party who was unaware of the fraud, Bacon would receive a valid (good) title and could keep the station wagon. The seller's only recourse would be to sue Riley to recover damages for fraud.

Where a Merchant Was Given Temporary Possession

Often people give a merchant temporary possession of goods they own—for example, when the goods need to be repaired. The merchant might, without the permission of the owner, sell these goods to a buyer in the ordinary course of business. A **buyer in the ordinary course of business** is one who purchases goods in good faith from a seller who normally deals in the goods requested by the buyer. In this case, the buyer has no knowledge that the goods do not really belong to the merchant and legally becomes the owner of the goods. In other words, the buyer receives a valid title. The original owner would, however, have the right to sue the merchant for money damages resulting from the loss of ownership of the goods.

> Gifford left her computer to be repaired by a merchant who both sells and repairs computers. The merchant sold the computer to Jarvis. Jarvis received a valid title to the computer because he purchased it without knowledge that the computer belonged to Gifford. Gifford can hold the merchant liable for the value of her computer. ■

Summary of Important Legal Concepts

The parties to a sales contract do not always specify in the contract when title and risk of loss are to pass from seller to buyer. In such cases, rules set down under Article 2 of the UCC will apply.

Under the Code, the rules for shifting risk of loss are more important than the rules for deciding when title passes. Although significant in many respects, title has lost some of its importance. Deciding who suffers risk of loss depends on whether a sales contract has been breached at the time of the loss. This chapter dealt with risk of loss only in situations in which no breach of contract had taken place.

In a sale by a merchant to a consumer at the merchant's place of business, risk of loss passes to the buyer when the buyer takes physical possession of the goods. If the seller is not a merchant, the risk of loss passes when the seller has tendered delivery.

If the seller is to ship the goods (FOB shipping point), risk of loss passes from seller to buyer on proper delivery to an independent (for-hire) carrier. If the seller is to deliver the goods (FOB destination), risk of loss passes a reasonable time after the buyer has been given notice that the goods are available for pickup at the destination point.

In a sale on approval, risk of loss and ownership remain with the seller until the buyer accepts the goods by approval. A sale or return is a present sale in which the buyer accepts risk of loss and ownership of the goods at the time of the sale; both the risk and title will revert to the seller if the buyer returns the goods.

A bulk transfer (bulk sale) is the sale of all or a "major part" of the stock of merchandise, materials, supplies, or other inventory at one time and not during the ordinary course of business. The bulk-transfer law protects creditors by giving them the right to void a bulk sale (within a six-month period) if the bulk-sale buyer does not notify them at least ten days before the sale takes place.

Auction sales involving goods costing $500 or more must be in writing. In a cash-only sale, the seller may retain possession of the goods until they are paid for by sending them to the buyer COD (collect on delivery).

A buyer generally obtains no better title to goods than the seller had. A person who has no title cannot pass a title on. Thus, a thief cannot pass legal title on to a good faith purchaser. The UCC allows at least two exceptions to this general rule: (1) a buyer with a voidable title can transfer a valid title to a third party who obtained the goods for value and in good faith; (2) any merchant who is given temporary possession of goods can transfer a valid title to those goods to a buyer in the ordinary course of business.

Key Legal Terms to Know

Match the terms with the definitions that follow.

bill of sale
bulk transfer
buyer in the ordinary course of business
COD
contract to sell
FOB destination
FOB shipping point
future goods
identified goods
present sale
sale on approval
sale or return

1. A present sale in which the buyer may return the goods after a set or reasonable time
2. Collect on delivery
3. Written proof of ownership of goods
4. A sale in which title to goods passes from the seller to the buyer at a future time
5. A transaction in which goods are delivered to the buyer for trial purposes
6. Terms that indicate the seller has title and risk of loss until the goods are given to the carrier for shipment to the buyer
7. Goods not yet in existence or identified
8. Terms that indicate the seller has title and risk of loss until goods are actually delivered to the point where the buyer is located.
9. The exact goods being sold that have been decided upon by the seller and the buyer
10. A sale in which title to the goods passes from the seller to the buyer at the time the parties make the contract
11. The sale of all or a major part of a merchant's stock of merchandise, supplies, materials, and other inventory at one time
12. One who purchases goods in good faith from a seller who normally deals in the goods

Questions and Problems to Discuss

1. What is the significance of "identification of goods?"
2. When goods are shipped by an independent (for-hire) carrier, how does the UCC treat the agreement if the FOB terms are not mentioned?
3. What does the term *risk of loss* mean under the UCC?
4. Johnson purchased a television set on thirty days' credit from Martinson & Kelly TV Sales and Service Center. While filling out the credit application, Johnson made false statements about his credit rating. Shortly after the purchase was made, Johnson moved to another city without paying for the set. Before moving, however, he sold the TV set to Carvel, who knew nothing of the fraudulent transaction. Martinson & Kelly traced the sale of the TV to Carvel and demanded the return of the set. May Martinson & Kelly legally recover the TV set from Carvel?
5. Weyman bought a washer and dryer from Carlson Appliance on a fifteen-day approval basis. Before the fifteen-day period expired and before Weyman gave an approval, the washer and dryer were destroyed by a fire in her home. If she was in no way responsible for the fire, must Weyman pay for the washer and dryer?
6. Heinrich purchased a fur coat from the Boston Fur Company, terms thirty days' credit. Before the coat was delivered, thieves broke into Boston's warehouse and stole many of the furs, including the coat purchased by Heinrich. Does the loss fall on Heinrich?
7. Venuso, a wholesale home appliance dealer in Bangor, Maine, ordered a dozen microwave ovens from the Benton Manufacturing Company of Albany, New York, for $1,800, terms FOB Albany. The microwave ovens were damaged in transit. Benton sent Venuso a bill for the full price. Venuso refused to pay, claiming that the risk of loss or damage to the microwaves was on Benton. Is Venuso's claim correct?
8. Which of the following situations is a present sale and which is a contract to sell?
   a. You purchased a new computer at Computer Land on thirty days' credit.
   b. You placed a special order for a new sailboat (to be manufactured to your specifications) with the Anchor Marine Company.

9. Wynn sold his entire appliance business (merchandise and fixtures) to Kirk. Benny, a large creditor of Wynn, sought to have the sale declared void on the grounds that Wynn failed to notify her of the sale. Will Benny succeed?

10. Doser sold a radar detector to Erdle. Doser had stolen the detector from a local electronics store, but Erdle did not know this. May the owner of the store recover the radar detector from Erdle?

11. King, of Dayton, Ohio, purchased a car for $8,000 from the Corbett Car Agency of Detroit, Michigan. The car was to be shipped to Dayton, FOB destination. Before the car was delivered to the Midwest Transportation Company to be shipped, it was destroyed by fire. Must Corbett suffer this loss?

12. McKnight obtained a computer on approval from the Ace Computer Center. The store agreed to let him take it home, try it out, and—if he liked it—pay $2,250 for the computer. Otherwise, McKnight would return it within three days. McKnight kept the computer for five days, at the end of which time one of his children damaged the screen extensively. Must Ace bear the loss?

13. Harkness purchased a calculator from BBL Calculator Company on a sale-or-return basis on February 1. No time for return was specified. On August 5 Harkness returned the calculator, claiming he had changed his mind. BBL refused to take the calculator back, however, claiming that Harkness had kept it beyond a reasonable time. Was BBL correct?

14. Garner purchased for cash an expensive and unique gown from Jacquelyn's Dress Shop. She left the gown with the dress shop for minor alterations. When Garner returned for the dress two days later, she discovered that someone in the dress shop had mistakenly sold the dress to another customer, Wilkins, for her daughter. However, when Wilkins purchased the dress she had no idea it belonged to Garner. Garner contacted Wilkins about returning the gown, but Wilkins refused. Can Wilkins keep the gown?

Cases to Decide

1. Clark, a merchant, sold a boat to Chatham, a consumer buyer, for cash. The sale took place at the Parkside Marina, Clark's place of business. Chatham, however, was about to go on a business trip and asked Clark to keep the boat at the marina until his return. A severe storm struck soon thereafter. When he returned, Chatham could not take delivery of the boat because it had sunk as the result of the storm. Nevertheless, Clark refused to refund the cash price to Chatham, claiming that, because a present sale had been made, risk of loss passed to Chatham, thereby making Chatham liable to absorb the cost of the boat. Is Clark correct? (*Chatham* v. *Clark's Food Fair, Inc.* 127 S.E. 2d 868)

2. Hughes purchased a new Lincoln Continental from Al Green Motors for $30,490 and made a down payment of $2,490. The balance due was financed through a local bank. Hughes took immediate possession, but it was agreed that she would return the car to the dealership for normal new-car preparations. On the way home, Hughes was in a car accident that, through no fault of hers, caused extensive damage to the car. Regardless of the damage, the car dealer issued a certificate of title (ownership) to her after receiving a check from the bank where she financed the car. Hughes now claims that Al Green Motors had no right to issue her a certificate of title because the car, having been damaged, was not the car she bargained for—an undamaged Lincoln Continental. Al Green Motors claimed it had every right to issue the title because it was not responsible for the damage to the car. Is Al Green Motors correct? (*Hughes* v. *Al Green, Inc.* 418 N. E. 2d 1355)

3. Harrison, the owner and operator of a men's clothing store in Westport, Connecticut, ordered a variety of clothing items from Ninth Street East, a clothing manufacturer in Los Angeles, California. Harrison was notified that the terms of the sale were FOB Los Angeles. When the truck carrying the goods arrived at Harrison's store, Harrison's wife insisted that the goods be placed inside the door, but the carrier refused. The dispute was not resolved, and the carrier kept the merchandise and left the store premises. The merchandise was subsequently lost by the carrier. Harrison notified Ninth Street East of the nondelivery of the goods. Many attempts were made to locate the merchandise, but without success. Ninth Street East then sued Harrison for

the purchase price of the goods. Harrison refused to pay. Is Ninth Street East entitled to payment? (*Ninth Street East, Ltd.* v. *Harrison*, Conn 259 A2d 772)

4. While he was a soldier in the U.S. Army during World War II, Lieber found some of Hitler's personal effects. Twenty-two years later, while Lieber was living in Louisiana, his chauffeur stole the collection and sold it to a dealer, who then sold it to Mohawk. Mohawk had no knowledge of the background of the collection and bought it in good faith. When Lieber learned that Mohawk had the collection, he demanded its return. Must Mohawk return the collection to Lieber? (*Lieber* v. *Mohawk Arms, Inc.*, 64 Misc 2d 206, NYS 2d 510)

5. On November 7, 1960, Crosby purchased a tractor and plow for $3,000 from Lane Farm Supply, Inc., on an approval basis. The length of time of the trial period was not definitely stated. After the purchase, when questioned about payment, Crosby indicated that he would pay for the equipment after a big deal had been completed. Crosby used the tractor and plow until the tractor was burned in his barn on January 1, 1961. Lane Farm Supply insisted that since Crosby owned the equipment, he was responsible for the loss. Was Lane Farm Supply correct? (*Lane Farm Supply, Inc.* v. *Crosby*, 243 NY2d 725)

6. B&B Parts Sales, Inc., delivered merchandise to a store owned by Collier. The bill that accompanied the merchandise had the words "Sold to" printed on it, followed by Collier's name and address. The agreement was that any equipment not sold would be picked up in ninety days by B&B Parts. While the merchandise was in Collier's store and before the ninety days were up, the store was burglarized and most of the merchandise got stolen. Collier claimed that the risk of loss was on B&B Parts. B&B Parts claimed that the sale was on a sale-or-return basis. Was B&B correct? (*Collier* v. *B&B Parts Sales, Inc.*, Tex 471 SW2d 151)

7. Medico Leasing Company gave possession of a car to Smith, a merchant engaged in the used-car business. It was agreed that Smith would sell the car for Medico. Smith sold the car to Wessell Buick Co. but kept the money. Medico sued Smith. Since Smith had no money, Medico then tried to recover the car from Wessell Buick. Wessell Buick claimed that they had purchased the car from Smith, a merchant, in good faith and had every right to keep the car. Was Wessell Buick entitled to keep the car? (*Medico Leasing Company* v. *Smith*, 457 Okla 2d 548)

8. Crump bought a TV antenna and tower from Lair for $900, payable in monthly installments of $7.50. The set was installed and Lair agreed to maintain it, but the contract was silent about insurance or repairs. Nine months later, the set was struck by lightning and badly damaged. Who was responsible for the loss? (*Lair Distributing Co.* v. *Crump*, 48 Ala App 72, 261 S2d 904)

Chapter 17

The Sales Contract: Performance, Breach, and Remedies for Breach

CHAPTER PREVIEW

The first part of this chapter focuses on performance of the sales contract—that is, what is legally expected of the seller and the buyer in order for them to discharge their obligations under the contract.

The second part of the chapter details options (remedies) available to the buyer and the seller if one or the other breaches (fails to perform) the contract. The discussion covers first the remedies available to the buyer and then those available to the seller.

As you study the rules in the chapter relating to performance and breach, remember that they apply only to cases in which the seller and buyer have failed to specify in the sales contract how they will fulfill their obligations.

PERFORMANCE OF THE SALES CONTRACT

The seller performs a sales contract by delivering the goods called for in the contract. The buyer then performs by accepting and paying for these goods according to the terms of the contract (§2-301). All the obligations of the seller and the buyer associated with performance are contained in the sales contract. If disputes arise because the contract is unclear, either the Uniform Commercial Code (UCC) or customs of the trade fills in the gaps. Both parties are required under the Code to perform their contractual obligations in good faith (§1-203). As mentioned in Chapter 15, good faith in the case of a merchant means honesty and fair dealing (§2-103). Neither party should, for example, attempt to manipulate the contract terms or to delay performance for an unreasonable period of time.

Delivery of Goods

The seller's first obligation is to tender (offer) **conforming goods**—that is, goods that meet the requirements of the contract. Second, after properly notifying the buyer that the goods are ready for delivery, the seller must make the goods available to the buyer. How delivery is accomplished will depend on the arrangements to which the seller and buyer agreed. Often the goods are made available to the buyer at the seller's place of business or, if there is no place of business, at the seller's residence. Delivery, in this sense, does not require the seller to move the goods to the buyer's place of business or residence; it simply means making the goods available to the buyer.

If the goods are in a place different from the seller's place of business or residence (such as in a warehouse), then that is the place for delivery. If the seller is required to ship the goods, a proper delivery occurs when the seller places the goods in the possession of an independent (for-hire) carrier and notifies the buyer that the goods have been shipped. If the contract requires the seller to deliver the goods to a particular destination, a proper tender of delivery occurs when the goods are delivered to the destination point and the buyer is notified of their arrival. If the seller does not notify the buyer and an unreasonable delay or loss results, the buyer may reject the shipment.

In all cases, if no definite time for delivery is set, the seller must give the buyer a reasonable time to accept delivery. If, for example, goods are immediately ready for delivery, a reasonable time would be very short.

Inspection of Goods

The buyer has the right to inspect the goods (at any reasonable place and time and in any reasonable manner) before accepting delivery, to determine if they conform to the contract (§2-513). If the seller is required to ship the goods to the buyer, inspection may be made at the place of arrival. The goods are usually inspected before the buyer pays for them, but if they are sent COD (collect on delivery) or the contract requires it, the buyer must pay for the goods before inspecting them. However, payment in these circumstances does not constitute acceptance of the goods. The expenses of inspection must be borne by the buyer but can be recovered from the seller if the goods do not conform and are rejected.

Acceptance and Payment

If there has been a proper delivery and if an inspection reveals that the goods conform to the contract, the buyer has a duty to accept the goods and pay for them according to the terms of the contract (§2-607). If either the goods or the delivery fails to conform to the contract, there is no duty on the part of the buyer to pay; but if the correction is relatively simple, the seller has the right to correct the defect in the performance so as to avoid being held in breach. This correction, or **cure,** is permitted only if the seller notifies the buyer of the intention to correct the defect and the cure is relatively simple. The seller must then deliver conforming goods (which the buyer must accept) before the time for performance expires (§2-508). This right of cure prevents a buyer from rejecting goods merely because he or she wished to back out of a deal that was not profitable.

Sometimes, however, the seller for some reason does not exercise the right of cure, or is not allowed to exercise the right because it would be a complicated process, or the defect may be so serious that the buyer cannot receive what was initially bargained for. In such cases, the seller is in breach of contract and the buyer is allowed to reject the goods (§2-601). If the buyer rejects the goods, he or she must do so within a reasonable time and must notify the seller of this intention. Rejection allows the buyer to treat the contract as ended (canceled), make other arrangements to purchase the goods, recover the purchase price from the seller if it has already been paid, and collect any damages suffered.

A buyer who rightfully rejects a delivery after taking possession of the goods must hold the goods with reasonable care for a time sufficient to allow the seller to remove them but has no further obligation concerning them. If the seller fails to give instructions after notification of rejection, the buyer (merchant or nonmerchant) may either (1) place the rejected goods in storage; (2) ship them back to the seller; or (3) resell them, with the proceeds going to the seller. In all cases the buyer is entitled to reimbursement for expenses. (§2-602; §2-604)

As in any contract, after the buyer accepts the goods, (having had a reasonable opportunity to inspect them and having offered no objection), the buyer may no longer reject them even though they are nonconforming goods—that is, different from those ordered.

BREACH OF THE SALES CONTRACT

Most sales transactions are concluded without problems. The sales agreement is made, the seller transfers the goods to the buyer, and the buyer either pays cash or asks for credit. Sometimes, however, a situation occurs that causes the seller or buyer, or both, to refuse to carry out her or his part of the sales agreement.

As with other types of contracts that are breached, the wronged party may take action against the other party to obtain justice. In a sales contract, the seller and buyer may, in the sales agreement, provide for remedies in the event of a breach of the contract by one party or the other. If they do not, the remedies provided in the UCC will apply (§2-703; §2-711; §2-714). This chapter discusses these UCC remedies. The purpose of the UCC remedies is to return the injured party to status quo—the same position he or she would have been in if the other party had not breached the contract. Therefore, the Code provides that remedies for breach are cumulative. That is, the selection of one remedy does not bar the injured party from pursuing another remedy. Keep in mind that certain remedies will be available at some times; other remedies at other times. The facts of each case determine the remedy that is available and whether more than one remedy is available to the injured party. (Table 17.1 on page 262 summarizes these remedies.)

REMEDIES FOR BREACH AVAILABLE TO THE BUYER

If the seller breaches the sales contract, either by failing or refusing to deliver the goods or by sending nonconforming goods, the buyer may (1) sue for breach of warranty, (2) cancel the contract and cover, (3) cancel the contract and sue for damages, or (4) sue to obtain the goods.

Sue for Breach of Warranty

A buyer who receives nonconforming goods may accept them anyway and then recover damages from the seller for breach of warranty. A warranty (to be discussed in greater detail in Chapter 18) is a guarantee by the seller that the goods are not defective and that they are suitable for the use for which they are intended. An action for breach of warranty usually occurs when the nonconformity could not be discovered on inspection and, because the goods have been accepted, rejection is no longer possible. The buyer may sue for breach of warranty only after notifying the seller that the goods do not conform to the contract.

> Marcus, owner of J & S Engine Performance Center, ordered three dozen batteries from a sample presented to him by a salesperson for the Excel Battery & Tire Company. When the batteries arrived, Marcus accepted them and paid $600, the amount due. One week later a customer who had purchased one of the batteries returned it to Marcus because it had gone dead. By testing the batteries still in his possession, Marcus discovered that they were of inferior quality and did not conform to the sample. Marcus notified Excel of his findings. Because the batteries were not as warranted, Marcus is entitled to sue Excel for breach of warranty. ■

If a breach of warranty is proved, the buyer may recover damages from the seller. Damages are generally the difference between the value of the goods accepted and their value had they conformed to the warranty. Damages also include expenses incurred by the buyer because of the breach of warranty. In addition, damages may include money for any bodily injury or property damage that resulted from use of the nonconforming goods.

> You purchased a used car from the Quansit Used Car Agency for $2,000. During a conversation with a salesperson, you asked if the car had good brakes. The salesperson replied, "They're brand new." The day after you purchased the car, the brakes gave out and you were injured when the car ran into the side of a building. Damages for breach of warranty would be the difference between $2,000, the price you paid for the car, and the amount the car was actually worth. In this case, damages would also include money for hospital and medical bills, as well as for pain and suffering. ■

Cancel the Contract and Cover

A buyer who rightfully rejects nonconforming goods (thereby causing a breach of contract by the seller) may cancel the contract, obtain any part of the purchase price already paid, and then cover the purchase. To **cover** means to buy substitute goods elsewhere to replace those originally due from the seller. This remedy permits the buyer to obtain without delay the goods needed for use or for resale. The buyer who exercises the right to cover and suffers a loss is permitted to recover the difference between the cost of cover and the contract price of the original goods, plus any expenses, such as transportation expenses, necessary to obtain the substitute goods. A buyer who chooses cover does not have to obtain the goods at the cheapest price available. All that he or she has to do is act reasonably and in good faith. The right to cover applies both to merchants who buy from manufacturers and wholesalers and to consumers who purchase from merchants.

> Mandrin Drug Store contracted with the Superior Pen Company to purchase 1,000 ballpoint pens to be sold at a special back-to-school promotion. The pens, which cost $1 each ($1,000 total), were to be delivered within one month.

One week before the delivery date, Superior refused to deliver the pens, which other companies were then selling for $1.10 each. Since the pens were needed for the special promotion, Mandrin could purchase them from another company at $1.10 each ($1,100 total) and then sue to recover damages from Superior in the amount of $100 ($1,100–$1,000). Mandrin could also recover from Superior the amount of any expenses required to get the pens from another company. ■

The option to cover is also available to a buyer when the seller repudiates the contract or fails to deliver the goods.

Cancel the Contract and Sue for Damages

The buyer has no duty to cover if the seller breaches the contract by sending nonconforming goods. The buyer may instead cancel the contract, obtain any part of the purchase price paid, and sue for damages for nondelivery. If a seller repudiates the sales contract or fails to deliver the goods, the buyer can also sue for damages. In either case, damages would be the difference between the contract price and the market price at the time the buyer learns of the breach, plus any expenses. **Market price** is the price at which goods are currently bought and sold in the business world. In a period of inflation, market prices may change fairly quickly.

■ Joplin, owner of a jewelry store, purchased fifty electronic watches from the LCD Precision Watch Company, paying one-fourth of the total price as a down payment. When the wrong watches were sent, Joplin refused to accept them and demanded the return of her down payment. Because the wrong watches were sent, Joplin had the right to have her down payment returned and to sue LCD for damages. ■

If the buyer does not suffer actual (or real) damages, he or she is entitled to nominal damages, such as a dollar, for a technical breach of contract. The buyer's purpose in bringing a lawsuit under these circumstances would be to show in the court records that a cause of action existed and that he or she was successful.

Sue to Obtain the Goods

In some circumstances, if the seller breaches the contract, the buyer may demand that the seller deliver the goods described in the sales agreement (§2-716). This action, you may recall, is called *specific performance*. To obtain specific performance, the buyer must be unable to find substitute goods (to cover) because the goods contracted for are unique (such as works of art, antiques, custom-made products, or goods considered to be one of a kind) or because there are no suppliers of equal quality. It should be noted that under the UCC, the term *unique* as it relates to specific performance has been broadened and goes beyond what was considered unique in Chapter 14.

Examples of unique goods under the UCC include goods that cannot be obtained elsewhere because there are spot shortages or because sellers have discontinued offering them as being unprofitable.

> The United Metals Corporation made a contract to deliver several units that fit into the interior of blast furnaces owned by the Kostic Blast Furnace Company. The units, made of nickel, were hard to obtain on the open market because of a temporary shortage of nickel. Knowing this fact, United Metals refused to deliver the units unless Kostic Blast Furnace paid more money. Since these units could not be obtained elsewhere, Kostic would be forced to shut down its operations. In these circumstances, Kostic could be granted specific performance by the courts. ■

Another remedy exists for the buyer of goods that are not unique and that are originally identified and ordered but wrongfully detained by the seller. If the buyer, after a reasonable effort, cannot buy these goods elsewhere (cover), the buyer can exercise the right of **replevin** to obtain the goods (§2-716). To exercise the right of replevin, a buyer must obtain a court order that orders the seller to deliver the goods to the buyer.

> Riggins, who designs and makes furniture, entered into a contract with Arnold, the owner of a local sawmill, to purchase twenty oak logs. Riggins personally selected the logs and made arrangements with Arnold for a delivery date. However, before the delivery date, the market price of oak rose considerably. As a result, Arnold refused to deliver the logs to Riggins at the contract price. Since the logs had been identified to the contract, and since he could not cover after making a reasonable effort to do so, Riggins could exercise his right to replevy the logs under the UCC (after first obtaining a court order). ■

REMEDIES FOR BREACH AVAILABLE TO THE SELLER

The UCC also provides remedies for the seller if the buyer breaches the sales contract. A buyer generally breaches the contract by refusing to go through with the contract, by wrongfully refusing to accept or keep the goods, or by failing to pay for the goods. If the buyer breaches the contract, the seller may (1) cancel the contract, (2) resell the goods and sue for damages, (3) sue the buyer for the purchase price, (4) sue the buyer for damages for nonacceptance, (5) withhold delivery of the goods, or (6) reclaim the goods from the buyer.

Cancel the Contract

A seller who is notified that the buyer will not go through with the contract may simply cancel (rescind) all performance due the buyer under the contract. If the seller cancels the contract, he or she may then, in addition, choose any of the other remedies that the UCC makes available to the seller for breach of contract. These remedies are discussed below.

■ The Clover Pool Company ordered seven above-ground pools from the Waterlaken Manufacturing Company for a total of $3,000. Clover agreed to pay $1,500 as a down payment before delivery of the pools and the balance over a five-month period. Clover did not make the down payment as agreed. The Waterlaken Company could cancel all performance due the Clover Pool Company under the contract and sue for an additional remedy. ■

Resell the Goods and Sue for Damages

The seller who has possession of goods, either because delivery was withheld or because the buyer refused to accept them, may resell the goods if there is a market for them and may then sue the buyer for damages. The amount of damages would be the difference between the resale price and the original contract price, plus any expenses necessary to resell the goods. The resale may be at either a public auction or a private sale.

■ On November 15 Blevins, who owned a retail clothing store, placed a special order for ten dozen shirts of assorted colors and sizes from Smith-Gormly Wholesalers. Because Blevins had planned to have a pre-Christmas sale, she asked Smith-Gormly to rush the shipment. Smith-Gormly notified Blevins that the merchandise would be shipped on November 28. On November 27 Blevins notified Smith-Gormly that she had changed her mind, no longer wanted the merchandise, and would not accept the shipment. In these circumstances, Smith-Gormly could resell the goods to someone else and sue Blevins for damages. ■

Sue to Recover the Purchase Price

A seller who still has possession of the goods but is unable to resell the identified goods elsewhere may choose to hold the goods for the buyer and sue for the purchase price. This remedy, however, could prove to be a burden because it requires the seller to hold the goods for the buyer until the goods are paid for. The seller must then deliver the goods to the buyer.

■ A department store received a special order from a local hotel for draperies of a special size and design for the entire hotel. The hotel owner later refused to accept the draperies or to pay the purchase price of $15,000. Since the draperies were made specifically for the hotel and would therefore be difficult to resell in the normal course of business, the department store may sue to collect the purchase price from the hotel and then turn the draperies over to them. ■

Sue to Recover Damages for Nonacceptance

If the buyer refuses to accept the goods, the seller may choose to sue the buyer for damages for not accepting the goods. This remedy is usually selected if the seller is unable to sell the goods or prefers not to sell them. Damages in this case are the difference between the market price of the goods at the time and place they were to be delivered to the buyer and the unpaid contract price, plus any expenses caused by the buyer's breach of contract.

> ■ A novelty shop ordered several boxes of novelties from the Ruoff Novelty Corporation totaling $1,500 but then wrongfully rejected the shipment. If the market price at the time the novelties were rejected by the buyer was $1,200, Ruoff could sue for damages of $300, plus any other expenses caused by the breach. ■

Withhold Delivery of the Goods

The seller may legally withhold delivery of the goods purchased on credit if the seller discovers before delivery that the buyer is **insolvent** (unable to pay debts that are due) or has failed to make a requested payment before the date set for delivery. The seller may withhold delivery even though ownership (title) of the goods has passed to the buyer. By exercising an **unpaid seller's lien** the seller may retain these goods until the buyer pays the purchase price in cash. If the purchase price is not paid within a reasonable time, the seller may cancel the contract and either resell the goods or cancel and sue for money damages for nonacceptance. The lien is lost, however, if the seller delivers possession of the goods to the buyer.

The seller may discover that the buyer is insolvent only after the goods have been delivered to a carrier for shipment to the buyer or after the goods have arrived at their destination and are being stored in a warehouse until the buyer picks them up. In either case, the seller should notify the carrier or the warehouse operator not to deliver the goods to the buyer. If the seller is successful in preventing delivery of the goods—referred to as **stoppage in transit**—the seller's right to withhold the goods until paid for continues. The UCC also permits an unpaid seller to stop goods in transit when the buyer is guilty of fraud in making the contract.

> ■ On March 9, Rusk, owner of Skate Town, a popular roller skating rink, ordered fifteen dozen pairs of roller skates from the Ball Bearing Company. Ball Bearing was to ship the skates on March 11 and Rusk was to pay for them on March 13. The Ball Bearing Company shipped the skates on schedule but Rusk failed to pay as agreed. Ball Bearing immediately checked on Rusk's credit and found that he was a poor credit risk. Ball Bearing then notified the carrier not to deliver the skates. Because Rusk was unable to pay, Ball Bearing had the right to stop delivery. ■

Reclaim the Goods from the Buyer

The seller who sold the goods on credit may not discover the buyer's insolvency until after the buyer has received the goods. At that point it would obviously be too late to withhold the goods or to stop them in transit. The UCC, however, permits a seller who loses possession of goods to reclaim them upon discovering a buyer's insolvency if a demand is made within ten days after the buyer has received the goods (§2-702). If the buyer has resold the goods to a good faith purchaser (a person not aware that anything is

TABLE 17.1   Remedies for Breach of Sales Contract

Remedies of Buyer	Remedies of Seller
Sue for breach of warranty.	Cancel the contract.
Cancel the contract and cover.	Resell the goods and sue for damages.
Cancel the contract and sue for damages.	Sue to recover the purchase price.
Sue to obtain the goods.	Sue to recover damages for nonacceptance.
	Withhold delivery of the goods.
	Reclaim the goods from the buyer.

wrong), the seller may not reclaim the goods but may sue the buyer for damages. In the case of perishable goods, the seller will usually not choose to reclaim the goods.

> Five days after selling and delivering fifteen microwave ovens to Johnson, Rubin Wholesalers discovered that Johnson was insolvent. If Rubin acts before ten days have expired, it can demand that Johnson return the microwave ovens. ■

The ten-day limitation on recovering goods from an insolvent buyer does not apply if the buyer has made false statements in writing about her or his solvency within three months of the delivery. The three-month period starts with the date on which the false statement was given to the seller.

Summary of Important Legal Concepts

The seller performs the sales contract by delivering conforming goods; the buyer performs by accepting and paying for these goods, assuming of course, that there has been a proper delivery by the seller and an inspection reveals that the goods do conform to the contract. If goods are delivered COD, the buyer must pay for them before an inspection can be made. The UCC governs performance unless the seller and the buyer make other arrangements in the sales contract. If either the goods or the delivery does not conform to the contract, the seller has the right to cure (correct) the defect in certain circumstances. If the seller does not cure, or is not allowed to, then the buyer may reject the goods, in effect canceling the contract. If after a reasonable inspection the buyer accepts nonconforming goods, however, he or she may no longer reject them.

Most sales contracts are concluded without problems—that is, both seller and buyer meet their obligations as required. In case of a breach by one party or the other, however, there are remedies provided by the UCC or in the sales agreement. Remedies available to the buyer for breach of the sales contract by the seller are (1) suing for breach of warranty, (2) canceling the contract and cover, (3) canceling the contract and suing for damages, and (4) suing to obtain the goods. The buyer may exercise more than one of these remedies, depending on the individual case. Remedies available to the seller if the buyer breaches the sales contract are (1) canceling the contract, (2) reselling the goods and suing for damages, (3) suing the buyer to recover the purchase price, (4) suing the buyer to recover damages for nonacceptance, (5) withholding delivery of the goods, and (6) reclaiming the goods from the buyer.

Key Legal Terms to Know

Match the terms with the definitions that follow.

conforming goods
cover
cure
insolvent
market price
replevin
stoppage in transit
unpaid seller's lien

1. Right of an unpaid seller to notify a carrier or warehouse operator not to deliver goods to an insolvent buyer
2. Unable to pay debts that are due
3. Right of an unpaid seller to retain goods sold to an insolvent buyer until the goods are paid for in cash
4. The price at which goods are currently bought and sold in the business world
5. The buyer's right to purchase substitute goods elsewhere if the seller fails or refuses to deliver the goods required by the contract or sends non-conforming goods
6. Allows the buyer to obtain through a court order goods that are not unique and that were originally ordered but wrongfully detained by the seller
7. Goods that meet the requirements of the contract
8. The right of the seller to correct a defect in goods sold to the buyer

Questions and Problems to Discuss

1. What is the basic obligation of the seller and the basic obligation of the buyer under the UCC?
2. Recall the remedies that this chapter states are available to the seller if the buyer breaches the sales contract. Which of these remedies would in all likelihood be the easiest for the seller to accomplish?
3. Why might a buyer demand specific performance if the seller breaches the sales contract?

4. Why could the remedy of cover be important to the buyer?
5. McDonald, owner of Sports Craft, a sporting goods store, contracted to purchase 200 footballs for $2,000 from the Pro Manufacturing Co. With no explanation, Pro Manufacturing shipped 100 footballs instead of the 200 called for in the contract. McDonald had already prepaid $1,000 on the purchase. What sales remedy or remedies could McDonald pursue?
6. BonTon, a merchant and owner of a fabric store, ordered fabric from Lanny, a wholesaler. Lanny sent the goods specifically ordered by BonTon. When the rolls of fabric arrived, BonTon did not take time to inspect them. She simply signed the order, which included a statement certifying that the goods were acceptable; paid the transportation company the amount due for the goods; and returned a copy of the signed order to Lanny. Later BonTon discovered several imperfections in the material. What rights, if any, does BonTon have in these circumstances?
7. The Industrial Disposal Corporation sold truck parts to Heberle, owner of a disposal service, on thirty days' credit. Before the parts were shipped, Industrial learned that Heberle had become insolvent. What right does the Industrial Disposal Corporation have?
8. VanCola Manufacturing Company sold auto supplies on credit to Joel, the owner of Palmetto Auto Supply House. The goods were delivered to the carrier for shipment. VanCola then learned that Joel was insolvent and made arrangements with the carrier not to deliver the goods to the buyer. Does VanCola have the right to withhold goods already in transit?
9. Projansky, owner of a retail leather goods store, entered into a contract to purchase luggage from the Likely Manufacturing Company for $2,000. Likely later refused to deliver the luggage at that price, claiming that inflation had caused the price of luggage to rise 15 percent since the contract with Projansky was made. Projansky then purchased the luggage from another company for $2,400 and sued Likely for $400. Should Projansky recover?
10. Salim entered into a contract to build a custom-made sailboat for McGregor for $8,000. On the delivery date, McGregor told Salim that he had changed his mind and no longer wanted the sailboat. Salim tried to sell the boat elsewhere but

couldn't because of its special features. Salim then sued McGregor for the purchase price. Should Salim recover damages from McGregor?

11. Siegel, the owner of a gasoline station, made a contract to purchase 100 cases of 30-weight motor oil (each case containing 25 cans) from the Lube Oil Company. Because of a temporary oil shortage that developed after the contract was made, the Lube Oil Company decided not to send the 100 cases. The company, however, had the required amount on hand. Can Siegel demand that the Lube Oil Company deliver the oil as required by the contract?

12. Weatherwax owned a driveway coating and resurfacing business. She ordered 500 gallons of driveway sealer on September 1 from Mr. Blacktop Company at a special end-of-season rate of $3.75 per gallon. According to the contract, delivery was to be made by September 15.

   On October 1, because it had no sealer of the quality ordered by Weatherwax, Mr. Blacktop delivered a different quality of sealer. Weatherwax refused the shipment. A new shipment of the correct sealer could not be obtained before October 30 from any other company. Other companies were selling the same quality sealer ordered by Weatherwax for $4.50 per gallon. Because any new shipment would be delivered much too late to service her customers on the waiting list, Weatherwax decided to cancel the contract and sue Mr. Blacktop for damages. Weatherwax determined that she lost $700 worth of business by not having the correct driveway sealer by October 2. How much could Weatherwax receive in damages from Mr. Blacktop?

13. Kutsher's Culinary Shop purchased a large quantity of kitchen equipment from Kitchens Unlimited, with terms of cash on delivery. When the goods arrived, the owner of Kutsher's demanded to inspect the goods before she paid for them. Is she entitled to do this?

Cases to Decide

1. Scampoli, a merchant, sold and delivered a new TV set to Wilson. When Wilson discovered that the set did not work properly, he asked Scampoli to correct the problem. Scampoli's repairperson, however, could not fix the set at Wilson's house and stated that the TV set would have to be taken back to the store and dismantled in order to determine the cause of the problem. Wilson refused to let the set go; instead, he demanded that Scampoli deliver a new TV or else refund his money. Scampoli said no to the refund and insisted that he be given the opportunity to correct the problem with the TV before returning the purchase price. Does Scampoli have the right to attempt to cure the problem? (*Wilson* v. *Scampoli*, 228 A.2d 848)

2. Ray-O-Vac made a contract to sell certain of its products on credit to Daylin, Inc. After making the delivery, Ray-O-Vac was informed that Daylin was insolvent. Within ten days after making the delivery, Ray-O-Vac demanded the return of the goods and Daylin refused. Can Ray-O-Vac recover its goods? (*Ray-O-Vac* v. *Daylin, Inc.*, 596 F2d 853)

3. Hisaw ordered 3,000 sacks of seed potatoes from Ingram at a price of $2.10 per cwt (hundredweight). Hisaw had permission to select the potatoes he wanted from the total of some 21,000 sacks owned by Ingram. Hisaw did select the potatoes he wanted, but before delivery he refused to go through with the contract or to pay for the potatoes. Ingram resold the 3,000 sacks refused by Hisaw on the open market and sued Hisaw for the difference between the contract price of $2.10 per cwt and $1.85 per cwt, the market price. Is Ingram entitled to collect the difference from Hisaw? (*Ingram* v. *Hisaw*, 94 Idaho 751)

4. Neff purchased from the Hanna Lumber Company prefabricated wooden trusses, which were manufactured according to pre-engineered specifications. Although the truss system was represented as structurally sound, it collapsed the day after its installation. The collapse occurred when a weak and defective truss broke, causing the remaining truss system to collapse. An inspection of the system following its delivery to Neff would not have revealed the flaw in design or material that caused the collapse. Neff sued for breach of warranty, asking for damages caused by failure of the truss system. Can Neff recover? (*Neff* v. *Hanna Lumber Company*, 579 SW2d 95)

5. Flavorland Industries, Inc., entered into a contract to sell Schnoll a load of goose necks (bottom round cuts of beef) at a stated price with delivery to be completed on October 6 or October 7.

Flavorland, unable to make the delivery, notified Schnoll before the delivery date and tried to make a further agreement on the delivery. After advising Flavorland that it could not accept a different delivery date, Schnoll purchased other beef to cover the original order. The cost was $2,438.61 higher than the original contract price. Can Schnoll recover from Flavorland the amount of its cover? (*Schnoll Packing Corporation* v. *Flavorland Industries, Inc.*, 167 NY Super 376)

6. Downing purchased a TV set from Wood Radio and TV Service and put $100 down on the purchase price. He agreed to pay the balance and take the set when his new home was furnished. When Downing went to pay the balance and accept delivery of the TV set, he was informed that the set had been sold to a third party. Can Downing purchase another TV set elsewhere and sue Wood Radio and TV Service to recover his down payment and any difference in cost of the TV set? (*Downing* v. *Arnold Wood Radio and TV Service*, 243 Ark 137)

Chapter 18

Product Liability: Negligence, Warranties, and Strict Liability

CHAPTER HIGHLIGHTS

This chapter focuses on product liability—the liability that manufacturers and other sellers have to buyers and users of products for physical injury and property damage caused by defective products they place on the market.

The chapter opens with some background on the shift in law in recent years surrounding the protection of the public from harmful products placed on the market. The remainder of the chapter is devoted to three well-recognized theories of liability—negligence, breach of warranty, and strict liability—that a buyer may use as the basis for recovery if he or she is injured by a defective product. Similarities and differences among these theories are noted. Some discussion in the chapter revolves around the Magnuson-Moss Warranty Act, a federal law that Congress passed to help prevent deceptive practices in the field of warranties (guarantees) made by sellers of products.

WHAT PRODUCT LIABILITY IS

Product liability refers to the liability that manufacturers and sellers have to buyers, users, and other persons for physical injury or property damage caused by defective products they place on the market or for the failure of these products to perform adequately. Lawsuits involving product liability have become very common, and the development of case law in this area has been rapid. Product liability lawsuits have been filed for such items as portable hair dryers, floor wax, football helmets, automobiles, medications, food, soft drinks, soap powder, television sets, health equipment, sunglasses, eyedrops, electric toothbrushes, and barbecue grills.

There has been a significant shift in the law in recent years. This shift has increased protection for the public by expanding the liability of manufacturers and sellers. The rule of **caveat venditor,** or "let the seller beware," now prevails. This rule reflects the view that the seller should bear the burden of determining that goods conform to certain standards. The rule of **caveat emptor,** or "let the buyer beware," has practically been abandoned by the courts. In the past, buyers were expected to examine goods they were buying and to rely on their own judgment about whether these goods were of suitable quality and free from defects. This rule assumed that both seller and buyer were in an equal position to bargain. In today's high society, however, the seller has more product knowledge and the consumer possesses far less bargaining power than the seller.

The trend in modern court cases is to allow anyone who is harmed by a product to sue whoever is in any way responsible. At one time, it was not possible for anyone except the ultimate consumer to sue. Even the ultimate consumer was limited to suing the immediate seller, with whom the consumer had a contract. This type of suit was generally not successful because harm from the defective product was seldom the fault of the retailer (the immediate seller), who had neither designed nor manufactured the product.

Today, product liability cases may be based on any one of three well-recognized theories of liability: negligence, breach of warranty, or strict liability. A buyer who is injured and elects to sue may do so using one or all of these theories as the basis for recovery in the same suit. (See also Table 18.1 on page 278.)

In view of the seller's increased liability, there has been a great proliferation of product warnings.

NEGLIGENCE

Negligence, a tort, was defined in Chapter 4 as the failure to act carefully. The ultimate purchaser of a product (the plaintiff) suing under this theory of product liability must prove that somebody's negligent conduct caused a defective product to be placed on the market and that this defective product caused the purchaser to suffer personal injury or property damage. A question arises: Whom does the ultimate purchaser sue to recover damages? This question was answered by the court in the landmark case of *MacPherson* v. *Buick Motor Co.* (111 N.E. 1050). This famous New York Court of Appeals case established beyond question that the manufacturer or any other seller in the chain of distribution (for example, a wholesaler or retailer) responsible for placing the defective product on the market is liable. This case further established that others (such as innocent bystanders) who were harmed by the defective product could also sue. Negligent conduct very often relates to a manufacturer's improper design of the product, a failure to inspect the product properly for defects after it leaves the assembly line, a failure to test the product adequately, or a failure to warn of a known danger related to the product.

> ■ Gardner purchased a doll for her three-year-old daughter from the Appian Department Store. While playing with the doll, the daughter easily removed its head. Attached to the head of the doll was a pin that, when inserted into the body of the doll, held the head in place. The daughter pushed this pin into her eye, causing a severe eye injury. Gardner could sue the manufacturer for negligence. ■

Suing under the negligence theory of product liability is often an unsatisfactory remedy for the injured plaintiff to pursue because proving specific acts of negligence on the part of the defendant is difficult. For example, it may be hard to prove that the manufacturer was careless in designing the product or that he or she failed to test the product after it came off the assembly line. Determining negligence in this case may involve a visit to the manufacturer's plant to examine the facilities and processes used to produce and test a product. Acquiring information in this fashion could be costly and futile.

WARRANTY LIABILITY

As part of their sales contracts and as an inducement to buyers, sellers guarantee that the products they sell will conform to certain qualities, characteristics, or conditions and that they are suitable for the use for which they are intended. This guarantee by a seller is called a **warranty.** If a warranty is false, the seller has committed a breach. If the buyer suffers harm as a result of the breach, he or she may bring an action for damages.

Article 2 of the Uniform Commercial Code (UCC) applies to much of the law of warranty, including an action based on the product liability theory of breach of warranty, which is discussed later in this chapter. This theory is in contrast to the product liability theories of negligence and strict liability, which are both tort actions and are ordinarily governed by common law.

There are two types of warranties made by sellers: express warranties and implied warranties.

Express Warranties

An **express warranty** is an oral or written guarantee given by manufacturers and sellers. Exactly what they promise in their express warranties is entirely up to them. A manufacturer's express warranty is generally in writing, either on a separate card or as part of the instructions packed with the product. Warranties made by sellers, such as retailers, may be oral or written. Under the UCC, a seller's express warranty may arise in several ways (§2-313). The seller may make a factual statement or a promise, orally or in writing, about the product. The seller may also describe the goods to the buyer or show the buyer a sample of the item that is being sold. To constitute an express warranty, the statement, description, or sample must be part of the basis of the sale—that is, it must be one of the reasons that the buyer purchased the goods.

Statement of Fact or Promise   Any oral or written statement of fact or any promise made to the buyer by the seller relating to the goods creates an express warranty.

> You went to Martin's to purchase an air conditioner and saw a model you liked. When you asked the salesperson if the unit needed 220-volt wiring, she said, "Standard house current is adequate." You then purchased the air conditioner. ■

In the example, the salesperson's statement is an express warranty. You bought the air conditioner not only because you liked it but also because of the salesperson's guarantee that "the standard house current was adequate." The salesperson did not actually use the word "warranty" or "guarantee," but this is not necessary. Under the UCC, her statement would be taken to mean, "I guarantee (promise) that the standard house current is adequate." The salesperson could argue in court that she did not intend to give a warranty. But a court of law would follow the UCC and would probably say she did. It is not necessary that a seller intend to make a warranty. If what is said or done induces the person to buy the product, under the Code, an express warranty is created.

A seller's written statement or promise may be expressed in the written contract of sale or in a separate document. Manufacturers and sellers can even create warranties through their advertisements in newspapers, brochures, and TV commercials. For example, because a TV commercial by the manufacturer said it was safe to drive on mountainous terrain at high rates of speed, you purchased a pickup truck with four-wheel drive. Courts have ruled that if you are injured while trying to do what the ad said the truck could do, a breach of an express warranty has occurred for which you may file an action for damages.

Sellers often make a variety of statements about their products. As a buyer in the marketplace, the law holds you responsible for determining which of these statements are warranties and which are simply puffing. **Puffing,** or statements by salespersons expressing their opinions about the goods they sell, does not form an express warranty (a statement of fact). The statement, "This is the best used-car value in town," made to you by a salesperson as an inducement to purchase the car is not an express warranty. It is merely the salesperson's opinion.

Since an express warranty is considered part of the sales contract, part of the purchase price is consideration for the warranty. If there is a breach of warranty by the seller, the buyer may recover damages, but the sales contract remains in force.

Under the UCC, it is not essential that a warranty be given by the seller at the time of the sale. A warranty, oral or written, given by the seller following the transaction becomes a part of the original sales contract without additional consideration (§2-209). An oral warranty is enforceable even though the original sales contract was in writing. As a practical matter, however, the buyer must be able to prove the existence of an oral warranty or it will not be enforced by the courts.

> Harkness purchased a guitar from the House of Music without any warranty. About a week after Harkness made the purchase, she expressed some concern about a guarantee and talked to the owner of House of Music about it. The owner said, "I guarantee all musical instruments I sell against all defects for one year." This oral warranty, although made after the sale of the guitar, was binding. ■

Description of the Goods If the buyer purchases goods after they are described by the seller, either orally or in writing (including drawings), there is an express warranty that the goods obtained by the buyer will conform to the description. If you purchase goods after reading a description in a catalog or on the label of a can or box, an express warranty of description is also created.

> You purchased a can of Quick-Sun at a drug store because the words on the label stated that the contents, when applied, would give you a deep tan within fifteen minutes. This description on the can is an express warranty. ■

Sample of the Goods Sometimes the buyer purchases goods after inspecting a sample or model of these goods. In this case, there is an express warranty that the goods delivered to the buyer will conform to the sample or model.

■ The local jeweler was taking orders for class rings. Before you ordered a ring, the jeweler showed you a sample of the ring you intended to buy. The jeweler, by showing you the sample, made an express warranty that the ring delivered to you would be like the sample. ■

Implied Warranties

An **implied warranty** is an obligation the law imposes on a seller. An implied warranty is not in writing. When a sale of goods is made, however, certain warranties become part of the sale even though the seller may not have intended to create them. These implied warranties protect the buyer when there is little or no opportunity to inspect the goods or the seller does not expressly warrant the goods. Breach of the implied warranty is grounds for a suit for money damages if injury or damage results from use of the product. In some cases, disaffirmance of the contract is also grounds for a lawsuit for breach of warranty. The UCC has established two types of implied warranties: the implied warranty of merchantability and the implied warranty of fitness for a particular purpose (§2-314; §2-315).

Merchantability   If a sale of new or used goods is made by the merchant who ordinarily deals in these goods, there is an implied warranty that the goods are merchantable. **Merchantable goods** are goods that are fit for the purpose for which they would ordinarily be used. If you purchase a pocket calculator, you have the right to expect that it will perform the functions (such as addition and subtraction) indicated on the calculator.

■ You purchased a portable typewriter from Orion Copier. The first time you used the typewriter, a defect caused the motor to burn out. Since the typewriter was not merchantable, Orion was liable for breach of the implied warranty of merchantability. ■

The implied warranty of merchantability also applies to the sale of food or drink that is consumed on the premises (as in a restaurant) or elsewhere (such as food purchased from a store and eaten at home). In this case merchantability means that the food is fit for human consumption.

■ A doughnut you bought at the Lively Doughnut Shop contained a human fingernail. The doughnut was not merchantable. ■

An implied warranty of merchantability exists whether a merchant is selling to another merchant or to an ultimate consumer. However, no implied warranty of merchantability exists in a sale of goods by a nonmerchant. For example, if you sell two snow tires at a garage sale there is no implied warranty of merchantability.

In addition, merchantable goods are of average quality, are adequately packaged and labeled, and conform to the promises or statements of fact on the label.

Fitness for a Particular Purpose   An implied warranty that goods will be fit for a particular purpose arises if, at the time of making the contract, the seller has reason to know the buyer's purpose, and the buyer relies on the seller's skill or judgment to select something suitable. (This warranty cannot be applied when the buyer and seller have equal skill and knowledge.) This warranty applies to both merchants and nonmerchants.

> ■ Preston told Hunter, the owner of a retail paint store, that he wanted to paint the exterior of his brick house. Hunter recommended Clean Gloss Shingle and Shake paint and told Preston how to apply the paint. Preston followed the instructions carefully and applied six gallons. Three months later, most of the paint had peeled, flaked, or blistered. Hunter is liable for breach of an implied warranty of fitness for a particular purpose. ■

Goods recommended by the seller under their trade name continue to give the buyer protection under the implied warranty of fitness for a particular purpose as long as there was actual reliance on the seller's judgment.

> ■ Carp went to Auto Finishers and asked for a cleaner that would remove spots from the cloth upholstery in her new car. The seller recommended "Easy Clean," the trade name of a new product on the market. When applied, however, the cleaner discolored Carp's upholstery. When Carp discovered that several other people had had the same experience with Easy Clean, she had the cleaner professionally tested at a laboratory. The lab report indicated that the chemicals in the cleaner were too strong. The store was liable for breach of the implied warranty of fitness. ■

If the buyer does not rely on the seller's judgment but personally selects the goods, including brand-name items, or describes to the seller the type of goods he or she needs, the implied warranty of fitness for a particular purpose does not apply.

Warranty of Title

In every sale of goods under the UCC, there is an implied warranty of title by the seller—both merchant and nonmerchant (§2-312). In other words, the seller guarantees that he or she owns the goods (has good title) and has the right to sell them.

> ■ Heinz sold a radio, which she had stolen, to Vance. Vance was unaware that it had been stolen. McAllister, the true owner, identified the radio to the police by the serial number and it was returned to him. Vance can sue Heinz for breach of the implied warranty of title. ■

The warranty of title is an implied warranty. To distinguish it from those implied warranties that may be excluded from a sales contract, however, it is not designated as such under the UCC.

Exclusion of Warranties

Under the UCC the seller may exclude certain express and implied warranties (§2-316). A statement in a contract that excludes a warranty is called a

disclaimer of warranty. If a disclaimer is used, the seller must use specific language set forth in the UCC to eliminate these warranties.

Express Warranties   The seller may exclude an express warranty as part of a sales contract by being careful not to induce a person to buy the goods by making factual statements or promises, by describing the goods, or by producing a sample or model of the goods. The seller may also exclude an express warranty by using clear, specific language. For instance, the following warranty is legal and binding: "The goods sold under this agreement are warranted from defects in workmanship and materials for ninety days. No other express warranty is given and no affirmation by the seller, by words or actions, shall constitute a warranty."

Sometimes a sales contract includes an express warranty by the seller and also includes a statement that no express or implied warranties exist. In this case, the sentence eliminating the warranties is not binding. Take, for example, the following statements made by a seller in a sales contract: "Your Super Permanex trash container is made of thick-wall, high-molecular-weight, high-density plastic. Its rugged handles can lift up to 250 pounds. The seller makes no express warranties of this product." The sentence stating that there are no express warranties has no effect. The statements made about the trash container amount to an express warranty even though the word *warranty* or *guarantee* was not used.

Any oral warranties made by the seller, before or at the time of the sale, that are contrary to the terms of the written warranty given with the goods are not binding. Where a written warranty exists, only the terms stated in that written warranty are enforceable.

> Marcus purchased a refrigerator from a local appliance dealer and, at the time of the sale, received a written manufacturer's warranty stating in part that, "For 90 days from date of delivery, Roncone Refrigeration (manufacturer) will remedy any defect or replace any part or parts found to be defective." The salesperson told Marcus that, "Roncone will remedy any defects free of charge for 120 days even though the written warranty says 90 days." Since the salesperson's oral warranty is contrary to the written warranty, the oral warranty is not binding. ■

Implied Warranties   If, before entering into the sales contract, the buyer has examined a sample or model of the goods or has refused to examine them after being given the opportunity to do so by the seller, there is no implied warranty as to defects that were or should have been obvious. This is the rule of caveat emptor, and as noted on page 267, it has practically been abandoned by the courts. This rule applies as long as there is no fraud on the part of the seller, such as concealing obvious defects.

> You purchased a used car from the A-1 Car Company. At the time of purchase you inspected the car but failed to notice that the two front tires were bald. Any attempt by you to cancel the contract with A-1 should fail. Bald tires constitute an obvious defect. You should have discovered this defect when you inspected the car. ■

The expressions "as is" and "with all faults" make it clear that no implied warranties exist and that the buyer takes the risk as to the quality of the goods.

■ Lloyd purchased a blender for cash from Cole's Department Store, which was running a special sale. A large sign at the counter next to the blenders read: "Prices as marked and all merchandise purchased 'as is.'" Later, when Lloyd attempted to use the blender, she found that it did not work properly. The store was not liable under an implied warranty of merchantability because the sign identified the sale of the blender as an "as is" sale. ■

The expressions "as is" and "with all faults," or similar expressions, will not exclude an implied warranty of title. The warranty of title is excluded only if the seller specifically states that no warranty of title is given or when the circumstances of the sale indicate that the seller does not have a clear title to the goods being sold.

■ The student government of Geneva University took charge of lost and found articles. In order to raise money for underprivileged children, the student government officers had a Christmas sale of the lost and found articles in their possession. Given the circumstances of the sale, it should be clear to any buyer that the student government does not have clear title to the goods being sold. ■

The implied warranty of merchantability may be excluded either orally or in writing, but the word *merchantability* must be used. If the exclusion is in writing, the clause excluding merchantability must be conspicuous. According to the UCC, a term or clause is conspicuous when it is written so that a reasonable person would notice it. The following clause, written in large, bold print, excludes the warranty of merchantability: **SELLER MAKES NO WARRANTY OF MERCHANTABILITY WITH RESPECT TO THE GOODS SOLD UNDER THE TERMS OF THIS AGREEMENT.**

The implied warranty of fitness for a particular purpose can be excluded only in writing. While the writing must be conspicuous, no specific language need be used. The language used in the following example is sufficient: **WE MAKE NO OTHER WARRANTIES, EXPRESS OR IMPLIED, BEYOND THE WARRANTY EXPRESSED IN THIS AGREEMENT.**

Breach of Warranty

Breach of warranty is a second basis for suing under the theory of products liability. Under this theory, the plaintiff must prove that (1) a warranty existed, (2) there has been a breach of the warranty, (3) the breach of warranty caused a loss or injury, and (4) notice of the breach was given to the seller. It is not necessary for the plaintiff to prove that the defendant was in any way negligent. The buyer must give notice of the breach within a reasonable time after he or she has discovered or should have discovered that the goods were not as warranted. If the buyer fails to notify the seller of any breach within a reasonable time, he or she is barred from any remedy against the seller. (§2-607)

Originally, since a warranty was part of a sales contract, a lawsuit for breach of an express or implied warranty was based on whether the buyer had entered into a contract of sale for a product with the seller. Parties who have contracted with each other are said to be in **privity of contract.** When privity of contract is required, only the buyer can sue for breach of warranty and can sue only the immediate seller.

> Atkinson purchased from the Ace Drug Store two bottles of Sun-Pro lotion, which was guaranteed by the manufacturer, the Altra Corporation, to protect a person's skin from sunburn. Atkinson gave a bottle to his sister to use. After they applied some of this lotion, their skin was severely sunburned. ■

Under the privity of contract rule, only Atkinson could sue; and he could sue only the Ace Drug Store, with whom the contract for the purchase of Sun-Pro was made.

The privity requirement as to who can sue for breach of warranty has been either eliminated or significantly reduced under the UCC and in the courts (the decision in the *MacPherson* case cited on page 268 was a landmark decision in the abolition of the privity requirement), thus allowing people other than the buyer to sue. Various alternatives are allowed under the Code (§2-318). The most popular of the alternatives, which has been adopted in a majority of the states, extends the right to sue the immediate seller to any member of the buyer's family or household or a guest in the buyer's home who suffers personal injury while using or consuming the product. Applying this rule to the previous example, Atkinson's sister may also sue the immediate seller. The UCC also offers another alternative, which has been adopted in some states. This alternative further relaxes the privity requirement, primarily by extending the right to sue the immediate seller to anyone who is harmed by the product.

The UCC is neutral on relaxing the privity requirement that deals with the issue of who can be sued for breach of warranty. Under the UCC, the immediate seller remains as the person against whom a lawsuit may be directed. It is left to the courts to decide on a case-by-case basis if anyone beyond the immediate seller can be sued. As a result, modern courts, with the impetus of the landmark case *Henningsen* v. *Bloomfield Motors, Inc.* (32 NJ 358), have dropped the privity requirement and now permit all individuals harmed by a product to sue not only the immediate seller but also all parties in the chain of distribution. This chain may include not only the retailer but also the manufacturer and the wholesaler. Again referring to the example given earlier, both Atkinson and his sister could, under case law, sue the manufacturer for their injuries.

There are some disadvantages to suing for breach of warranty. Failure to properly notify the seller of the breach within a reasonable time after he or she discovers or should have discovered the breach will bar the buyer from suing for the breach (§2-607). As the injured party, the buyer would then have to seek another remedy. Recall also that sellers, as they are entitled to do under UCC Section §2-316, may and often do disclaim express and implied warranties. If a seller does give an express warranty, it often contains restrictions and limitations. Another drawback relates to an inspection of the goods. If the buyer inspects the goods but fails to discover "noticeable" defects or for some reason refuses to inspect the goods, then he or she waives any benefits from implied warranties against defects that an inspection reasonably should have detected.

Magnuson-Moss Warranty Act

The federal **Magnuson-Moss Warranty Act** was passed by Congress in 1975 to protect purchasers of consumer goods (those goods used for personal, family, or household purposes). The purpose of the act is to make available to consumer purchasers adequate information about warranties. This act has not replaced UCC warranty law, but in certain cases it imposes additional standards and remedies.

Under this act, the terms of any warranty must be disclosed in simple and readily understood language. The law does not require manufacturers and sellers to give written warranties. But if they choose to give a warranty and that warranty is written, and if the warranted goods cost more than $10, the warranty must be prominently labeled as either a "full" warranty or a "limited" warranty. In addition, if the cost of the goods is more than $15, the Federal Trade Commission requires that certain additional information in the nature of disclosures be made fully and conspicuously in "readily understood language." Such disclosures include, but are not limited to, the parts that are covered by the warranty, the length of the warranty period (such as "full ten-year warranty"), a step-by-step explanation of the procedure the consumer should follow to obtain performance of any warranty obligation, and whether the enforceability of the written warranty is limited to the original buyer or is extended to every buyer who has owned the goods during the term of the warranty period. Furthermore, if a written warranty is given, the implied warranties cannot be eliminated by the manufacturer or seller. (Under most state laws, a manufacturer could eliminate its obligation under implied warranties simply by providing the buyer with a written disclaimer of these warranties.)

A *full warranty* gives the buyer much more protection than the limited warranty. It requires a defective product to be repaired within a reasonable time at no cost to the owner. If it cannot be repaired, the "lemon clause" of the act requires the manufacturer or seller to refund the buyer's money or to replace the product. *Limited warranties* have more restrictions than full warranties. For example, with a limited warranty the buyer is not guaranteed a refund or a replacement if the product cannot be fixed. Most limited warranties cover parts but not labor. An example of a limited warranty is shown in Figure 18.1.

ONE YEAR LIMITED WARRANTY

1. Your new KRONOS Watch is warranteed by the NEWBOS WATCH REPAIR SERVICE.
2. This warranty is valid only at the NEWBOS WATCH REPAIR SERVICE and not at the place of purchase.
3. NEWBOS WATCH REPAIR SERVICE warranties your new watch movement for one year from the date of purchase against defects in material and workmanship.
4. This warranty does not cover watch case, watch bracelet, straps, glass, or battery.

   NEWBOS WATCH REPAIR SERVICE disclaims any liability for consequential damages for breach of any written or implied warranty of this watch. Some states do not allow the exclusion or limitation of consequential damages, thus this exclusion or limitation may not apply to you. This warranty gives you specific legal rights, and you may have other rights which vary from state to state.
5. This warranty is good only in the U.S.A. If your KRONOS watch should require service during the period of warranty, mail or express this watch along with the following material:
   - $5.00 to cover processing, handling, and return.
   - This original warranty, filled in as required.
   - Your original bill of purchase to validate the date of purchase.

   Package this watch carefully, enclose necessary documents and return to:

   NEWBOS WATCH REPAIR SERVICE
   P.O. Box 1066
   Boston, Massachusetts 02106
6. This warranty will no longer be valid if this watch has been tampered with, taken apart, wet or repaired by anyone but ourselves. In the case of water resistant watch cases, cracking of the crystal glass or loosening of the watch case back cover, will invalidate the warranty.

Figure 18.1
Limited Express Warranty

To help consumers make better informed decisions, warranty information about a product must be readily available in the store for customer inspection. Provisions in the act provide formal and informal procedures for settling claims for breach of warranty. One significant feature allows consumers to recover attorney's fees if a lawyer is needed to enforce a warranty.

STRICT LIABILITY

Strict liability is the third and final theory of products liability presented in this chapter that a buyer may choose as the basis for recovery if he or she is injured by a defective product. This theory, based on tort law, has developed rapidly in recent years and is now the prevailing basis for lawsuits in most states. The rapid growth of this theory of liability can be traced to the fact that the injured party does not have to prove negligence (fault) and need not show the existence of a warranty, which, you may recall, can be disclaimed by a seller.

The word *strict* in this term means that there is no need to prove fault. Under the rule of strict liability, the ultimate consumer must show that at the time it left the manufacturer or another seller in the chain of the sale, the product was defectively designed or manufactured, was unreasonably dangerous because of a defect (the defect contains a danger beyond that which an ordinary consumer would contemplate), and was responsible for causing personal injuries or damage to the user's property. The injured party does not need to show who caused the defect or why or in what manner the product became defective. The average consumer can presume that the product is not unreasonably dangerous and harmful if, for example, there are no warnings in the instructions that come with the product and if there are no other references to danger on the product label. The manufacturer or seller cannot claim as a defense that reasonable care was used to discover defects in the manufacture of the product, that reasonable care was used to prepare and sell the product, or that there was no privity of contract.

TABLE 18.1 **Theories on Which Product Liability Cases Are Based**

Theory of Liability	Legal Action Based on	Degree of Proof Required	Who Can Sue	Who Can Be Sued
Negligence	Tort	Defective product. Negligent conduct (fault) must be established. Product defect caused buyer's injury.	Anyone harmed.	All parties in chain of distribution.
Warranty	Contract	Existence and breach of warranty. Breach caused buyer's injury. Notice of breach given to seller.	Under the UCC in most states: the buyer, members of the buyer's family, household guests. According to modern case law, anyone harmed.	Immediate seller. All parties in chain of distribution.
Strict liability	Tort	Product was defective when it left the manufacturer or other seller in the chain of distribution. Product defect caused buyer's injury.	Anyone harmed.	All parties in chain of distribution.

The effect of the strict liability theory in most states, therefore, is to make the manufacturer, seller, or whoever is in any way responsible for the harm liable without question for the safety of the product. It allows not only the buyer to sue but also other persons who used the goods and suffered injury or damage because of the defect.

> ■ Marty, age ten, was excited on Christmas morning when he went to open his presents. One of them was a toy gun called "Blast Out," which his parents had purchased as a gift for him. The toy gun was advertised by the manufacturer as "absolutely harmless." When Marty fired the gun, however, it ignited his clothes and he was severely burned. A legal action may be brought on Marty's behalf against the manufacturer. ■

MISUSE OF PRODUCT BY INJURED PARTY

In many product liability lawsuits, manufacturers and sellers raise the improper conduct of the buyer as a defense to lawsuits by injured buyers. They claim that the buyer used their product either knowing that it was defective or in a manner not contemplated by the seller, as, for example, in the case of a teenager who mounts a lawnmower motor onto a bicycle and is then thrown from the bike while riding because the motor stalls and "dies out." While manufacturers and sellers may generally have good cases, courts still offer some protection to the buyer by applying the comparative negligence doctrine (see page 74) or limiting a seller's defense by requiring that the buyer's misuse of a product not be foreseeable by the seller.

Summary of Important Legal Concepts

A buyer injured by a defective product may sue (as the plaintiff) a manufacturer and other sellers in the chain of distribution (as defendant or defendants) under one of three well-recognized theories of liability: negligence, breach of warranty, or strict liability. (A summary of theories on which product liability cases are based appears in Table 18.1.) The trend in modern court cases is to allow not only the buyer of the defective product but also anyone who is harmed by this defective product to sue, and to sue whomever is in any way responsible.

The buyer who sues for negligence must prove that the defendant's negligence caused a defective product to be placed on the market and that this defective product caused the buyer to suffer personal injury or property damage. Negligence, however, is often an unsatisfactory remedy because it is hard to prove. If the buyer chooses to sue for breach of warranty, he or she must establish the existence and breach of a warranty, an injury resulting from the breach, and the fact that notice of the breach was given to the seller. It is not necessary to prove that the defendant was negligent. There are disadvantages to suing for breach of warranty, most notably that the buyer will have no basis for a lawsuit if the seller exercised his or her right under the Code to disclaim express and implied warranties. The most popular theory of liability under which to sue is strict liability.

This theory, like negligence, is based on tort law. But unlike negligence, the buyer does not have to prove that anyone was negligent. In other words, it is a no-fault approach. The buyer must only show that, at the time it left the manufacturer or another seller in the chain of the sale, the product was defectively designed or manufactured, was unreasonably dangerous because of a defect, and caused injury or damage as a result. Unfortunately, strict liability has not been adopted in all states, and serious injury cases caused by defective products must often be settled under the warranty theory. If you recall, in certain cases the basis for a breach of warranty lawsuit requires that a contract exist between the person suing and the person being sued.

Congress passed the federal Magnuson-Moss Warranty Act to help prevent deceptive warranty practices. This act has not replaced warranty law but rather imposes additional standards and remedies.

In many product liability lawsuits, manufacturers and sellers offer as a defense to lawsuits by injured buyers the improper conduct of the buyer.

Article 2 of the UCC provides for two types of warranties made by sellers: express warranties and implied warranties. Express warranties arise in several ways. The seller may make a factual statement or a promise about the product, may describe the goods to the buyer, or may show the buyer a sample of the item being sold. To constitute an express warranty, the statement, description, or sample must be part of the basis of the sale. The two types of implied warranties are the implied warranty of merchantability and the implied warranty of fitness for a particular purpose. Another type of implied warranty exists under the Code but is not designated as such: the implied warranty of title. Express warranties can be excluded from sales contracts by using clear, specific language that meets the requirements of the UCC, or simply by refraining from using language, descriptions, or samples that induce people to purchase the goods. The expressions "as is" and "with all faults" exclude all implied warranties except the implied warranty of title. The implied warranty of title is excluded only if the seller specifically states that no warranty of title is given or if the buyer realizes or should realize that the seller does not own the goods. If the buyer examines the goods, sample, or model or has refused to do so after a demand by the seller, there is no implied warranty as to the defects that were or should have been obvious.

Key Legal Terms to Know

Match the terms with the definitions that follow.

caveat emptor
caveat venditor
disclaimer of warranty
express warranty
implied warranty
Magnuson-Moss Warranty Act
merchantable goods
privity of contract
product liability
puffing
warranty

1. "Let the seller beware."
2. A guarantee that goods will conform to certain qualities, characteristics, or conditions and are suitable for the use intended
3. An obligation imposed upon the seller by law
4. Liability of manufacturers and sellers to persons harmed by defects in their products
5. "Let the buyer beware."
6. A contract relationship
7. Statement in a contract excluding a warranty
8. Goods that are fit for the purposes for which they would ordinarily be used
9. Statements made by salespersons expressing their opinions about the goods they sell
10. The manufacturer's or seller's oral or written statement of fact, promise, description of the goods, or sample or model that a buyer relies upon when purchasing goods
11. A law that prevents deceptive warranties and that requires the terms and conditions to be clear and understandable

Questions and Problems to Discuss

1. A person injured by a defective product placed on the market may sue the manufacturer or seller under any one of three theories of liability. Name these three theories.
2. What is the difference between an express warranty and an implied warranty?
3. The county of Ontario, New York, ordered twenty-three cell doors for the new wing of the

Ontario County Jail. The vice president of the company that was to manufacture the doors told the jail superintendent that he (the vice president) knew exactly how the cells should be constructed; the jail superintendent relied on the vice president's statement. When the cell doors were delivered, the bars were so far apart that prisoners could wriggle through them. Instead of the standard 5 inches, the bars were 5¾" apart. What warranty has been breached? What is the basis for this breach of warranty?

4. Marc was thrown off his motorcycle when he hit a deer. At the time of the accident, he was riding within the speed limit. A rivet from the helmet he was wearing was driven into his brain, causing Marc to be paralyzed for life. An investigation of the accident revealed that the helmet contained a design defect that made it dangerous to use. Marc wished to sue the company that manufactured the helmet. What theory of recovery would be best suited to his claim? What should be the result?

5. Rice purchased a purse with a shoulder strap. She put things in the purse that normally would be placed in a purse of that kind. A week later, however, the strap pulled away from the purse and also pulled part of the purse loose. Would there be any breach of warranty on the part of the store that sold Rice the purse?

6. Russ purchased a camera, not knowing that it had been stolen. If the camera is reclaimed by the rightful owner, does Russ have a claim against the seller?

7. Dayton purchased a rug from Max Floor Covering because the owner stated that the rug was "a genuine Oriental rug." Could this statement be considered an express warranty?

8. Yang purchased a used car from the Better Used Car Agency on the basis of a salesperson's statement that the car was "a real bargain and a tremendous buy." Shortly afterward, Yang found that the car did not give the performance that he had expected. Can Yang legally return the car on the grounds of the salesperson's statement?

9. The Jacobson Appliance Company entered into a written contract to sell and install some new appliances in Lopez's home. After the appliances were installed, Jacobson warranted them in writing against all defects for one year. Three months later, one of the appliances failed to work because of a defect in its motor. Could Lopez enforce the warranty?

10. Darling ordered a tote bag after seeing a description in Rem's Discount Catalog. When the bag arrived, Darling discovered that it did not conform to the description given in the catalog. Was there a breach of warranty by the Rem Company?

11. Jason and several members of her college soccer team purchased team jackets after seeing a sample shown to them by a salesperson from the Champion Sportswear Company. When the jackets arrived and Jason found that hers was quite different from the sample, she returned the jacket to the company. The company refused to take it back. Did Jason have the right to return the jacket? (Assume that Jason is an adult.)

12. Lutz purchased an electric circular saw for cash from Draper's Discount Store. The sales tag attached to the saw read as follows: "$49.99 reduced from $59.99, sale 'as is.'" Later, while attempting to use the saw, Lutz found it was defective and unusable. May Lutz sue Draper's Discount Store for breach of implied warranty of merchantability?

13. Zachary purchased a package of frozen peas at Walman's Food Market. While eating the peas, Zachary suffered a cut on the inside of his mouth. When he examined the empty container that the peas came in, Zachary found several small bits of glass. Is Walman's liable to Zachary for breach of an implied warranty of merchantability?

Cases to Decide

1. Flippo was trying on a pair of slacks in Mode's store and was bitten by a poisonous spider concealed in the slacks. Flippo became sick and was hospitalized for three days because of the spider bite. Was Mode liable for breach of the implied warranty of merchantability? (*Flippo* v. *Mode O'Day Frock Shops of Hollywood*, 298 Ark Reports 1, 449 SW2d 692)

2. The Stones entered into a contract to purchase a mobile home from Mobile Housing, Inc. Mobile took the Stones through the model on display on one of its lots and informed them afterwards that the one they purchased would be like the model. The one delivered, however, was very different

from the model. Mobile refused to do anything about it, and the Stones sued to rescind the contract and recover the payments they had already made. Did the Stones have a legal claim? (*Mobile Housing, Inc.* v. *Stone*, 490 SW2d 611)

3. Balch purchased a dog for $800 from Newberry, who operated a kennel. Before the sale Balch informed Newberry that he wanted a male dog for breeding purposes. Newberry stated that the dog had the ability to produce pups of pedigreed quality. Balch relied on this fact when he purchased the dog. After the purchase, Balch discovered that the dog was sterile and therefore of no value to Balch for breeding pups. Could Balch demand the return of his $800 after returning the dog? (*Balch* v. *Newberry*, Okla 253 P2d 153)

4. Hook sold two milk trucks, together with two milk routes, to Janssen. At the time of the sale, Hook told Janssen that the trucks were in good condition. Janssen, however, had inspected the trucks before purchasing them. He was aware that the trucks needed repairs and were in generally poor condition. After purchasing the trucks, Janssen spent a considerable amount of money for work done on the trucks. He then brought a lawsuit against Hook for the amount spent, claiming that the statement by Hook that the trucks were in good condition amounted to a breach of an express warranty. Is Janssen correct? (*Janssen* v. *Hook*, 272 NE2d 386)

5. Henningsen purchased a brand new Plymouth automobile from Bloomfield Motors and gave it to his wife as a gift. While driving the new car Henningsen's wife crashed into a brick wall and was injured because a defect in the steering wheel caused her to lose control of the car. She sued Bloomfield Motors for her injuries under the breach of the implied warranty of merchantability. Bloomfield Motors claimed that there was no privity of contract between them and Mrs. Henningsen and that she could not recover. Can Mrs. Henningsen recover from Bloomfield Motors? (*Henningsen* v. *Bloomfield Motors*, NJ 161 A2d 69)

6. Swenson, a farmer, planted corn and then, to control rootworm, applied an insecticide called Ortho Bux Ten Granular, manufactured by the Chevron Chemical Co. About two months after he applied the insecticide, he discovered severe corn rootworm damage, although each bag contained a statement that the insecticide would control rootworm. Swenson then sued Chevron, claiming that this statement on each bag was an express warranty. Is Swenson correct? (*Swenson* v. *Chevron Chemical Co.*, So Dakota 234 NW2d 38)

7. Husted purchased a used car from Reed Motors and obtained a loan through the First National Bank. The car broke down and could no longer be used. Husted refused to pay the balance due on the car. At the time the car was purchased, the contract signed by Husted contained a conspicuous clause stating that the buyer accepted the car in its present condition. The contract also contained other language indicating that the car was sold "as is." Was Husted responsible for paying the balance due on the car? (*First National Bank of Elgin* v. *Husted*, Ill 205 NE2d 780)

8. Maritime entered into a contract to purchase a helicopter from Fairchild. Among the relevant provisions typed into the agreement in normal size, lowercase print on a regular printed form was a clause stating that the sale was to be made "as is" and that the seller gave no express or implied warranties except the warranty of title. Maritime had problems with the helicopter and sued Fairchild for an implied warranty, claiming that the helicopter was not merchantable. Fairchild defended, saying that the clause in the contract, which stated that no warranties were given with the sale of the helicopter, acted as a disclaimer of the implied warranty of merchantability. Is Fairchild correct? (*Fairchild Industries* v. *Maritime Air Services, Ltd.* 333 A.2d 313)

9. While shopping at a grocery store, Embs suffered a leg wound from broken glass when a Seven-up bottle exploded near the counter where she was standing. She was taken to a hospital and treated for this wound. Later, Embs sued Pepsi-Cola Bottling Company, which bottled the Seven-up for distribution locally; the owners of the Seven-up Co.; and the local distributor of Seven-up. She sued for strict product liability, basing her claim on the injury received from the broken glass caused by the exploding bottle. The three defendants claimed that they had no liability to Embs, an innocent bystander, because they were not in privity of contract with her. Were the defendants liable to Embs despite lack of privity? (*Embs* v. *Pepsi-Cola Bottling Co. of Lexington Kentucky, Inc.* 528 S.W. 2d 703)

The Ridgeway Theater purchased a large air-conditioning system from Blair Manufacturing Co. The system was purchased and installed in May, prior to the start of the summer season. The sales contract contained a statement that the system would provide sufficient cooling for 1,500 people to a maximum temperature of 72 degrees. The statement further said, "The seller makes no express warranties for this product." At the beginning of June, it became apparent to Ridgeway that the system did not work properly; it provided cool air, but not enough to enable patrons to be fully comfortable. Ridgeway complained to Blair about the air-conditioning system and withheld payment but continued to use the machine during the summer months because there was not enough time to order another system; without any air conditioning at all, the theater would have had to close down. All efforts to repair the system failed, and at the end of the summer Ridgeway demanded that Blair take the machine back. Blair refused to accept the machine and brought suit against Ridgeway for the purchase price.

The Trial

Ridgeway testified that the temperatures during the summer in the area where the theater was located were extremely warm and that air conditioning was absolutely essential to enable customers to feel comfortable during the showing of movies. The theater stated that it relied on the wording in the sales contract that the system would produce sufficient cooling. It further stated that it could not return the air-conditioning system immediately after delivery because the theater would have had to close down and lose its costumers for the entire summer. The theater also stated that returning a large system involved a great deal of effort and expense and that it did not want to return the system until it had obtained significant use from it.

The Arguments at Trial

Blair's attorneys argued that the specific wording in the sales contract disclaiming any express warranties prevented Ridgeway from claiming that the system was defective. They further argued that the theater should have returned the system immediately when it discovered that the system was faulty. They also argued that when the theater used the system for three months and received many benefits from it, it automatically gave up its right to rescind the contract and return the system.

Ridgeway's attorneys argued that because of the size and weight of the system and the costs involved in returning it, Ridgeway had a legal right to use the system for a reasonable amount of time and then return it. They further argued that the statement in the sales contract that the system would produce sufficient cooling outweighed the importance of the statement that there were no express warranties. The theater also argued that by keeping the machine and getting some benefit from it, it was able to mitigate its damages. Otherwise, the theater could have held the manufacturer responsible for the loss of profits.

Questions to Decide

1. Who has the stronger arguments, Ridgeway or Blair? Why?
2. If you were the judge or jury hearing the case, for whom would you decide on the question of the warranty? Why?
3. If you were the judge or jury hearing the case, for whom would you decide on the question of the right to rescind the contract? Why?
4. What do you think the law should be with regard to a problem of this nature involving something that is not easily returnable?

PART IV

COMMERCIAL PAPER

After studying Part IV, you should be able to

1 Relate the various types of commercial paper and distinguish among the various parties involved.

2 Describe the requirements necessary to make commercial paper negotiable.

3 Explain the process of negotiation—that is, how negotiable instruments are transferred from one party to another.

4 Explain the meaning of the term indorsement and name five types of indorsements.

5 Restate the holder in due course (HIDC) concept and explain the significance of one's having the status of an HIDC.

6 Explain the liabilities of the primary and secondary parties for payment of commercial paper.

7 Describe the legal effect of personal and real defenses on a holder in due course.

8 Summarize the rights and responsibilities that banks and their customers have to each other.

9 Trace the path of a check through the check-collection and payment channels.

10 Explain what has been done to improve check-processing procedures.

11 Discuss the impact of the electronic funds transfer system (EFTS) on the payments and collections procedures used in the business world.

Chapter 19

Nature and Types of Commercial Paper

CHAPTER PREVIEW

The purpose of this chapter is to introduce you to commercial paper—written documents that may be used either as a substitute for money (such as checks) or as a way to extend credit (promissory notes, for example). Commercial paper is the subject of this and the next three chapters.

The current chapter, Chapter 19, identifies the types of commercial paper available in the business community and the basic features of each type. Specimen documents that appear in the chapter will help you better understand these basic features. The chapter also introduces the concept of negotiability (transferability), a key feature of commercial paper, and examines the language that must be used to make commercial paper negotiable.

Article 3 of the Uniform Commercial Code (UCC) now governs commercial paper. This article, as pointed out in the chapter, substantially updates earlier rules governing commercial transactions.

WHAT COMMERCIAL PAPER IS

Commercial paper (which includes promissory notes, certificates of deposit, drafts, and checks) refers to written instruments (documents) that can be used either as a substitute for money or as a credit device (a means of extending credit). When a person pays a bill by check, the check substitutes for money. When a person buys a used car and gives the dealer a promissory note agreeing to pay for the car in thirty days, the note is a credit device. The seller has actually extended thirty days' credit to the buyer.

The use of commercial paper developed because the modern concept of business demands quicker, safer, and more efficient ways to carry on transactions with large as well as small businesses and with consumers.

Payments made by checks far exceed payments made with cash, particularly when large transactions are involved. By using checks, people need not carry large amounts of money on their person. The use of checks also lessens risk of loss or theft when payments are sent through the mail. In addition, using commercial paper as a means of payment provides a receipt and a record for tax purposes.

Article 3 of the UCC governs commercial paper. The 1952 version of this article, which resulted in a substantial updating of the earlier rules governing commercial transactions, has been adopted in every state. This version was updated extensively in 1990, but many of the changes simply clarify old sections. As of today, some states still follow the original 1952 version of Article 3, while other states have adopted the 1990 version. The material presented in this chapter generally reflects the provisions of the 1952 version (unless otherwise noted), which, at this time, is the majority rule.

TYPES OF COMMERCIAL PAPER

There are two types of commercial paper: *promises to pay* and *orders to pay*. Promissory notes and certificates of deposit are promises to pay. Drafts, including checks, are orders to pay.

A **promissory note** is a written promise by one party, the **maker,** to pay a certain amount of money to another party, the **payee.** The money may be payable either on demand or at a specified time. A promissory note is used to obtain goods and services on credit or to borrow money. For example, Figure 19.1 shows that Ross Gerble borrowed $500 at 13% interest from Ann Rearden for thirty days.

A **certificate of deposit** (commonly known as a CD) is a specialized form of promissory note issued by a bank to a depositor with that bank, acknowledging that money was placed on deposit. The bank promises to repay the money to the depositor with interest after a certain period of time. The certificate of deposit shown in Figure 19.2 is an acknowledgment by the Columbia Savings Bank (the maker) that it received $5,000 from Darlene Weaver (the depositor-payee) on July 1 (date of issuance), and that the $5,000 will be repaid with interest at the rate of 7 percent per year.

A **draft** (also called a bill of exchange) generally involves three parties. It is a written order by one party, the **drawer,** to a second party, the **drawee,** to pay a sum of money to a third party, the **payee,** on demand or at a definite future time. (A note has two parties—one party promises to pay another.) The draft has many uses. For instance, suppose that Catherine Karshick owes William McKinney $500 and Clair Arden owes Karshick $500 and Karshick is transferring her right to receive $500 from Arden to McKinney. Assume also that McKinney and Arden live in the same city and Karshick lives in another city. It would be possible for Karshick to draw a draft for $500 naming Arden as the drawee and McKinney as the payee. Karshick could send the draft to McKinney, who would then present it for payment to Arden. Figure 19.3 represents the draft Karshick would send to McKinney in this situation.

A **check,** the most common form of commercial paper, is a specialized type of draft drawn on a bank and payable on demand (immediately). The drawee is always a bank and the drawer is the depositor. The payee is the person to whom the check is made payable. A check is the most common

Figure 19.1
Promissory Note

Payee

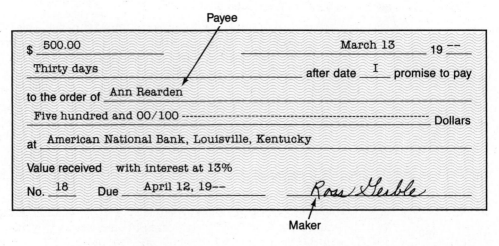

Maker

Payee

CSB Columbia Savings Bank
1200 North Street
Columbia, South Carolina

CERTIFICATE OF DEPOSIT

Date: July 1, 1996

This acknowledges that there has been deposited with the

undersigned, the sum of $ _5,000.00_____

Five thousand and 00/100------------------------------ Dollars

which is payable to the order of ____Darlene Weaver____ on the

_1st_ day of ____January____, 19_97___, upon presentation and

surrender of this certificate, and bears interest at the rate of

___7%___ per annum calculated and credited at maturity. No payment

may be made prior to, and no interest runs after, that date.

COLUMBIA SAVINGS BANK

By __*Michael Henry*_____

Vice President

Member F.D.I.C.

FEDERAL REGULATIONS PROHIBIT THE COMPOUNDING OF INTEREST
DURING THE TERM OF THE DEPOSIT.

Maker

Figure 19.2
Certificate of Deposit

Figure 19.3
Draft

Payee

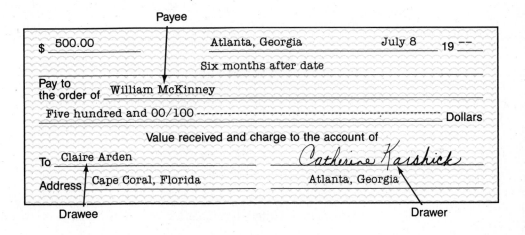

$ _500.00_____   Atlanta, Georgia   July 8   19 _--_

Six months after date

Pay to
the order of ___William McKinney_____

Five hundred and 00/100------------------------------------- Dollars

Value received and charge to the account of

To _Claire Arden_____   *Catherine Karshick*

Address | _Cape Coral, Florida____   Atlanta, Georgia

Drawee   Drawer

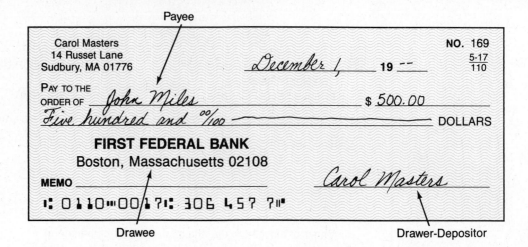

Payee

Carol Masters
14 Russet Lane
Sudbury, MA 01776

NO. 169

5-17
110

December 1, 19 --

PAY TO THE
ORDER OF John Miles $ 500.00

Five hundred and 00/100 ——————————————— DOLLARS

FIRST FEDERAL BANK
Boston, Massachusetts 02108

MEMO _____   Carol Masters

⑈ 0110⬛00/17⑈ 306 457 7⬛

Drawee   Drawer-Depositor

Figure 19.4
Check

way of making payments. In Figure 19.4, Carol Masters, who has money in a checking account at First Federal Bank, made out a $500 check payable to John Miles. First Federal would be required to pay the $500 when the check was presented for payment at the bank by John Miles. Of course, Carol Masters would have to have at least $500 on deposit at the First Federal Bank.

A check can also be drawn by a bank on another bank. This instrument is known as a *bank draft.* (Revised Article 3 of the UCC defines a bank draft as a "teller's" check.)

COMMERCIAL PAPER AS A NEGOTIABLE INSTRUMENT

Commercial paper can be negotiable or nonnegotiable. If an instrument is **negotiable,** it can be transferred freely from one person to another, and each person who receives the instrument will obtain a special privilege. This special privilege is discussed in Chapter 21.

Instruments that meet the requirements for negotiability are subject to the rules of Article 3 of the UCC in determining the rights and liabilities of the parties to these instruments. Under Article 3, to qualify as a *negotiable instrument,* commercial paper must (1) be in writing, (2) be signed, (3) contain a promise or order to pay, (4) contain a promise or order that is unconditional, (5) be payable in a sum certain in money, (6) be payable on demand (or at sight) or at a definite time, (7) be payable to order or to bearer, and (8) designate a drawee (in the case of a draft) with certainty. These elements are illustrated in the check in Figure 19.5.

Written Form

To promote certainty and prevent fraud, commercial paper must be in writing—either printed, typed, or handwritten. There is no such thing as an oral

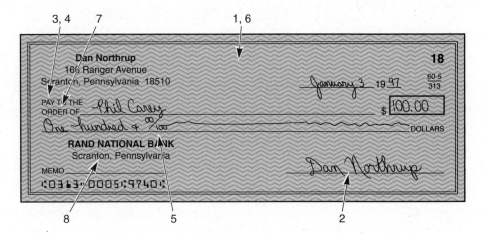

Figure 19.5
Elements of Negotiability

note or check. If handwritten, pen or pencil may be used, although ink is preferable to prevent someone from altering the written paper.

Signature

The signature on the instrument must be that of the maker (for a promissory note or a certificate of deposit) or drawer (for a draft or a check) or their authorized agents. The signature, which may appear in the body of the instrument (as, for example, "I, Merle Hanley, promise to pay . . ."), generally appears in the lower right-hand corner and may be handwritten, typed, printed, stamped, in the form of a symbol (usually an "X"), or even a thumbprint.

■ The Atlas Company paid its employees by check each week. Since the company issued a large number of checks, it printed the signature of its treasurer on each check rather than having the treasurer sign each check personally. This printed signature in no way affects the negotiability of the checks. ■

Promise or Order to Pay

A promissory note or certificate of deposit must contain words indicating a promise to pay. The words "I promise to pay" in Figure 19.1 clearly indicate that a promise has been made. On the contrary, a phrase such as *IOU, Joan Hartman, $50.00* merely acknowledges that a debt exists; it does not contain a promise to pay and therefore is not negotiable.

To be negotiable, a draft or check must order the drawee to pay. For example, the word "pay" that is printed upon a draft or check (see Figures 19.3 and 19.4) constitutes this order. It is a demand upon the drawee by the drawer to pay a third party, the payee.

Unconditional Promise or Order

The promise or order to pay must be payable without any conditions attached (it must be unconditional). Otherwise, the instrument is nonnegotiable.

■ Darcy (the maker) gave Archer (the payee) a promissory note for $500. The note contained a statement that it was "payable only upon Archer's graduation from college." Since the note was payable only upon the happening of a certain event (graduation from college), which may not occur, it was nonnegotiable. ■

Added promises or orders will also destroy negotiability. For example, a note in which the maker promises to pay money and to perform services or deliver goods is nonnegotiable.

The requirement of an unconditional promise or order to pay is a practical one. No one would accept commercial paper if the right to recover was conditional. After all, people do not want to spend time and money investigating whether or not the conditions stated in commercial paper will be met.

A Sum Certain in Money

The requirement that the instrument be payable in a sum certain in money is designed to make it easy for the taker of the instrument to know the exact amount that will be received. The taker must be able to compute this amount from the instrument itself. A note or check payable in merchandise or anything other than money, such as services, is not negotiable. Furthermore, "money" does not require payment in U.S. currency. A note or check payable in a foreign currency that is the legal currency of that foreign country is fully negotiable. Thus, a sum payable in German marks, French francs, or Japanese yen would not hinder negotiability. Unless specified otherwise in the instrument, if the instrument is payable in foreign currency, §3–107 provides that payment may be made in the equivalent amount of United States dollars.

■ Albert, of Pittsburgh, Pennsylvania, gave Hanson, who lived in the same city, a note promising to pay "one ounce of platinum." Since platinum is not legal currency in the United States, Albert's note is not negotiable. ■

The amount stated on an instrument is still certain even though a sum is to be paid with interest. Thus, a $200 note payable with 10 percent interest is still negotiable. If the person who is required to pay the instrument has an option of paying something in addition to money or paying something other than money, the instrument is not negotiable.

■ Rickets gave Bellini a promissory note that read, in part, "I (Rickets) promise to pay Bellini two hundred dollars ($200) or one used stereo set." This note is not negotiable. ■

Under the UCC, if there is a discrepancy between the amount written in words and the amount indicated in figures on an instrument, the amount written in words would be paid. However, if the words are not clear, the figures will control. For example, if the words on a check are "One hundred dollars" and the figures are "$1,000," the check would be for $100. But if the words read "Seven fifty-five dollars" and the figures "$7.55," the check would be for $7.55.

Payable on Demand or at a Definite Time

"Payable on demand" means payable at the time when the payee presents the instrument for payment to the person obligated to pay it. It is not necessary that the obligated party know ahead of time when the demand will be made. A check is a good example of an instrument payable on demand because no time of payment is stated on the instrument (see Figure 19.4). The words *at sight,* which mean payable on demand, are used for drafts.

An instrument can also be payable at a definite time, usually in the future. Thus, an instrument payable on, before, or after a specified date, such as "payable on or before January 13, 1996" or "payable sixty days after date," meets the requirement of a definite time for payment. On the other hand, an instrument "payable ten days after my death" is not negotiable. While the fact of death is certain, the time when death will actually occur is not certain. If nothing is said about the due date, it is demand paper.

The importance of the requirement that a negotiable instrument be payable on demand or at a definite time is that the holder of the instrument must know when the note must be presented for collection and whether it is current or overdue. If an instrument were payable upon the happening of an event in the future, the holder would not know when that event occurred and would not know when to present the note for payment. This would destroy the whole reason behind negotiability—easy transfer of commercial paper.

Payable to Order or Bearer

The words *order* and *bearer* are words of negotiability—that is, by using these words in the instrument, the maker or drawer states that the instrument is payable to the original payee or to someone else designated by the payee. An instrument is **payable to bearer** if it is to be paid to anyone who has possession of it. For example, the phrase *Pay to Henry Ling or bearer* means that the instrument is payable to Henry Ling or to anyone else who bears (possesses) it. An instrument is **payable to order** if it is to be paid to a specific person or to anyone that person designates. For example, the phrase *Payable to the order of Martha Mandry* means that the instrument is payable to Martha Mandry or to whomever Martha Mandry orders the paper to be paid. An instrument made payable to "Cash," "To the order of cash," "Myself," or "To the order of bearer" is considered payable to the bearer. Without the word *order* or *bearer,* payment of the instrument would be restricted to the original payee. Some courts hold an instrument nonnegotiable without the magic words *order* or *bearer,* even if the instrument states on its face "this instrument is negotiable."

> ■ Bendix borrowed $2,000 from his friend Burr and gave Burr a promissory note that read: "One year after date, I promise to pay Adam Burr two thousand dollars ($2,000) with interest at 12.5% (signed) William Bendix." Since this note does not contain either of the words of negotiability ("pay to the *order*" or "pay to the *bearer*"), the instrument is not negotiable. Adam Burr cannot legally transfer this promissory note to another person. ■

Revised Article 3 provides that a check that meets all of the requirements of being a negotiable instrument except that it does not include the words *to the order of* is nevertheless a negotiable instrument. This revised rule does not apply to instruments other than checks.

Drawee Named with Certainty

In the case of a draft or a check, the drawee must be named in the instrument with certainty. This rule permits the payee, or any individual who receives the instrument from the payee, to know the person who is responsible for payment.

ADDED LANGUAGE AND OMISSIONS NOT AFFECTING NEGOTIABILITY

The UCC does not prevent instruments from being negotiable because information is lacking or because certain information is added. The date of issue on a note or check may be important, but it does not affect negotiability if it is omitted. An undated instrument is considered to be dated as of the date it is delivered. That date may be filled in by the person who receives the instrument. A postdated check (a check dated after its actual date of issue) is also fully negotiable. It is like a note payable in the future and will be paid on or after the date appearing on its face.

For notes it is common to insert information regarding the place of payment of the instrument, such as "Payable at First Federal Bank of Boston, Massachusetts." The words *Value received* are often inserted on the face of the note, meaning that consideration was given for the instrument. This information does not affect payment and, if omitted, does not make an instrument nonnegotiable. Finally, the sum in figures, which is generally included, has no effect on negotiability if not included as part of the instrument.

As noted above, Revised Article 3 provides that a check is nevertheless negotiable even though it does not contain the words *to the order of.*

Summary of Important Legal Concepts

Commercial paper is governed by the provisions of Article 3 of the UCC and consists of written instruments (documents) that are available in the business community and that can be used as either a substitute for money or a means of extending credit. There are two types of commercial paper: promises to pay and orders to pay. Promissory notes and certificates of deposit are promises to pay. Drafts and checks are orders to pay. Notes have two parties. The maker is the person making the promise to pay, and the payee is the person to whom the note is payable. Drafts and checks have three parties. The person issuing the draft or check is the drawer, the person ordered to pay is the drawee, and the person to whom the draft or check is payable is the payee. A check is a type of draft in which the drawee is always a bank and the drawer is the depositor. Instruments that serve as commercial paper may be either negotiable or nonnegotiable, depending on the language used in the instrument.

To be negotiable, commercial paper must meet the following requirements: it must (1) be in writing, (2) be signed, (3) contain a promise or order to pay, (4) contain an unconditional promise or order to pay, (5) be payable in a sum certain in money, (6) be payable on demand (or at sight) or at a definite time, (7) be payable to order or to bearer, and (8) designate a drawee (in the case of a draft) with certainty.

Certain language that is added, such as the place where the instrument is payable and the words *Value received,* has no effect on negotiability. Certain information that is lacking, such as the date of issue of the instrument, the place of payment, and the sum in figures, likewise has no effect on the negotiability of the instrument; and neither does the practice of postdating a check. Finally, under Revised Article 3, a check lacking the words *to the order of* is still negotiable.

Key Legal Terms to Know

Match the terms with the definitions that follow.

certificate of deposit
check
commercial paper
draft
drawee
drawer
maker
negotiable
payable to bearer
payable to order
payee
promissory note

1. Words directing an instrument to be paid to the person possessing it
2. The party to a check or draft who is ordered to pay the payee
3. Written instruments that may be used either as a substitute for money or as a credit device
4. A term indicating that commercial paper may be transferred from one person to another
5. An instrument by which a drawer orders the drawee to pay a certain amount of money to the payee
6. A promise by a bank to repay to a depositor an amount left on deposit for a certain period of time
7. An instrument by which one party promises to pay a sum of money to another party
8. The party who signs a check or draft ordering the drawee to pay the payee
9. A type of draft in which the drawee is always a bank
10. The party who receives payment on a check, draft, or promissory note
11. The party who makes out and signs a promissory note, promising to pay a sum of money to the payee
12. Words directing an instrument to be paid to a named payee or to whomever the payee orders the paper to be paid

Questions and Problems to Discuss

1. What are the two major uses of commercial paper?

2. Commercial paper is negotiable if it contains certain essential elements. What are they?
3. Explain the differences among a note, a check, and a draft.
4. Study the check in Figure 19.6 and then answer the following questions:
   a. Who is the drawer? the drawee?
   b. Who is the payee?
   c. Is this check payable on demand or at a future time?
5. Is the instrument in Figure 19.7, dated January 5, in the handwriting of Renee Cartwright considered a negotiable instrument?
6. You received an instrument, dated March 15, that stated, "I promise to pay to the order of the bearer one thousand dollars ($1,000) on demand. (Signed) Myron Hatch." The signature was placed on the instrument with a signature stamp. Is this instrument negotiable? (Assume that all other essentials of a negotiable instrument not specifically mentioned are present.)
7. "Ninety days after date, I promise to pay to the order of Philip Vance five thousand dollars ($5,000) worth of New York State bonds. (Signed) Catherine Maxwell." Is this a negotiable instru-

ment? (Assume that all other essentials of a negotiable instrument not specifically mentioned are present.)
8. "On March 14, 1996, I promise to pay to Melvin Dell, three hundred fifty dollars ($350). (Signed) R. Horn." Is this a negotiable instrument? (Assume that all other essentials of a negotiable instrument not specifically mentioned are present.)
9. On January 4, 1996, Martinez wrote out in ink, in longhand, the following: "IOU, Carolyn Edwards, one hundred dollars ($100). (Signed) James Martinez." Is this instrument negotiable?
10. Why does the promissory note in Figure 19.8 fail to meet the requirements of negotiability?
11. Would the promissory note in Figure 19.9 be negotiable in the following circumstances (state a reason for your answer):
    a. If the words *Value received* had been omitted?
    b. If the date July 1, 1997 was omitted?
    c. If Ronald Brown had written the note in his own handwriting as follows: "I, Ronald Brown, promise to pay to the order of Alexis Smith, five hundred and 00/100 dollars or one used car"?
12. Andrea Nesson made out a check payable to

Figure 19.6

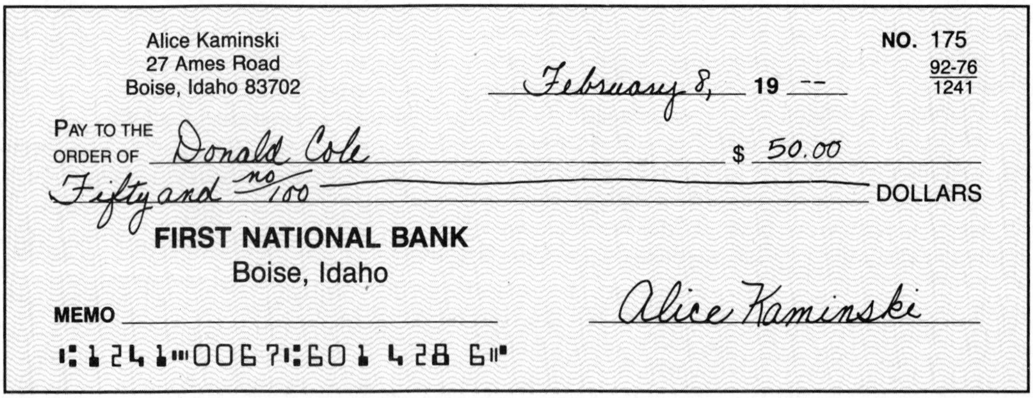

Alice Kaminski
27 Ames Road
Boise, Idaho 83702

February 8, 19 --

NO. 175

92-76
1241

PAY TO THE
ORDER OF Donald Cole $ 50.00

Fifty and no/100 ————————————————————— DOLLARS

FIRST NATIONAL BANK
Boise, Idaho

MEMO _____

Alice Kaminski

⑈1241⑈0067⑈601 428 6⑈

Figure 19.7

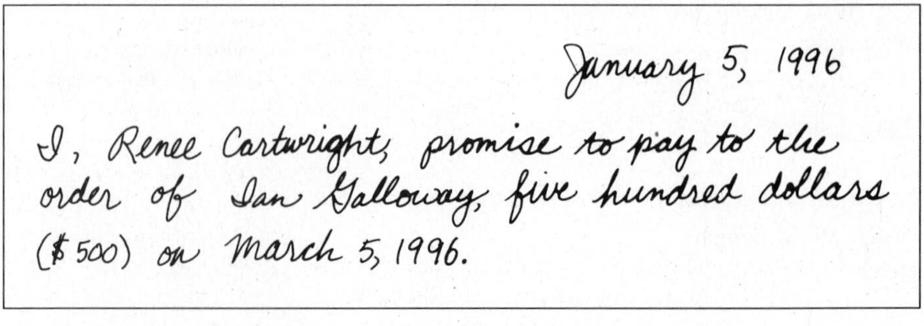

January 5, 1996

I, Renee Cartwright, promise to pay to the order of Ian Galloway, five hundred dollars ($500) on March 5, 1996.

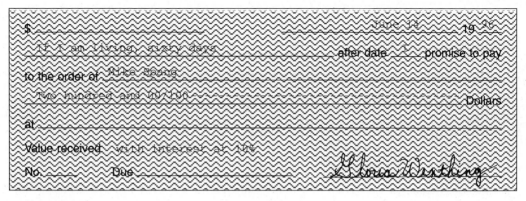

Figure 19.8

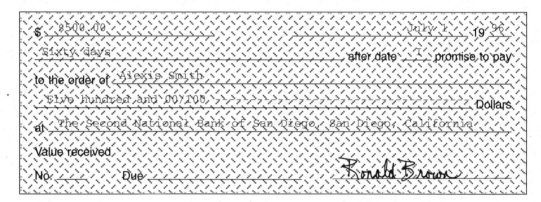

Figure 19.9

"Cash." Assuming that all other essentials of a negotiable instrument were present, would the fact that the check was made payable to "Cash" prevent the instrument from being negotiable?

13. A check written and signed by William Frank (drawer) was made payable to Jennifer Rhinestone. The check contained the written words "Five hundred dollars," but the amount in figures written on the face of the instrument was "$50.00." Under the UCC, what amount of money would be paid?

Cases to Decide

1. Zimmerman gave a note to Homecraft Company as payment for some remodeling work. The note did not contain a due date for the payment and the wording regarding monthly installments was left blank. Homecraft sued immediately on the note, but Zimmerman claimed that the note was not a demand note, even though the date for payment was missing. Was Zimmerman correct? (*Master Homecraft Company* v. *Zimmerman,* 208 Pa Super 401)

2. Lindsay signed a note to Clements that stated, "On or about five years from date, I promise to pay Bonnie M. Clements $25,000 without interest." When Lindsay failed to pay the note, Clements sued. Lindsay claimed that the note was invalid because it did not contain any fixed or determined future time for payment. Will Clements recover on the note? (*Clements* v. *Lindsay,* Louisiana 320 So 2d 608)

3. Mr. and Mrs. Hinphy borrowed money from De-Rouin and signed a document stating, "I have this day borrowed $12,000 from David DeRouin to be paid on demand. (Signed) Mrs. W. Hinphy and W. Hinphy." More than three years later, DeRouin sued the Hinphys for failing to pay the amount due. The Hinphys claimed that the document was not a note, but was only an acknowledgment of indebtedness that was no longer valid because of a three-year statute of limitations. Are the Hinphys correct? (*DeRouin* v. *Hinphy,* Louisiana 209 So 2d 352)

4. Norwood was in possession of a document that read as follows:
   AUDITOR CONTROLLER'S GENERAL WARRANTY
   COUNTY OF LOS ANGELES
   The treasurer of the county of Los Angeles will pay to the order of John Norwood $5,000.
   Could this document be considered a check? (*People* v. *Norwood* 103 Cal Rptr 7)

5. Fabacher gave a promissory note to Hoss. At the top of the note the date was given, as well as the figure $6,002.19. The body of the note read, "Pay to the order of." The name of the payee was never inserted, nor was any amount. Was the note enforceable? (*Hoss* v. *Fabacher,* Texas 578 SW2d 454)

6. Andersen gave the following undated, handwritten promissory note to the Great Lakes Nursery Corporation for the purchase of 65,000 trees: "Robert Andersen promises to pay to Great Lakes Nursery Corporation at Waukesha, Wisconsin, six thousand four hundred twelve dollars with interest at 7% per annum." Great Lakes Nursery, in payment of a debt, transferred the note to the First Investment Co., which questioned its negotiability. Is this note negotiable? (*First Investment Co.* v. *Andersen,* Utah 621 P2d 683)

7. Robinson had purchased a certificate of deposit (CD) from a bank and had the instrument made payable to him. On its face, the instrument stipulated that if Robinson was deceased at the time the instrument was to be paid, that payment should be made to his stepdaughter, Wygant (payee). Before the note was due, Robinson remarried and changed the name of the payee from Wygant to that of his new wife. When Robinson died, Wygant claimed the proceeds from the CD. Her contention was that the CD was a negotiable instrument that required her to sign it before it could be transferred to Robinson's new wife. Was Wygant correct? (*West Grely National Bank* v. *Wygant and Robinson* 650 P. 2d 1339)

Chapter 20

Issue, Transfer, and Discharge of Commercial Paper

CHAPTER PREVIEW

CHAPTER HIGHLIGHTS

Chapter 20 deals with the negotiation (transfer) and discharge of commercial paper. The first section discusses the concept of negotiability—how promissory notes, certificates of deposit, checks, and drafts are transferred to third parties by the payee—and the rights these third parties acquire after negotiation. One issue that is crucial in determining the rights that third parties have after the negotiation of commercial paper is whether the transferred instrument is an order instrument—one payable "to the order" of a named person—or a bearer instrument—one payable to anyone who possesses it. The chapter points out the differences between order instruments and bearer instruments. Two other topics covered are the various ways in which people sign their name (called an indorsement) to an instrument they wish to negotiate and the effect an indorsement has on the instrument being negotiated. The remainder of the chapter examines ways in which commercial paper can be discharged—that is, the circumstances that will take away the liability a person has on the instrument.

THE ISSUE AND TRANSFER OF COMMERCIAL PAPER

The circulation of commercial paper begins when either the maker or the drawer prepares an instrument (a note or check, for example) and transfers (delivers) this instrument to the payee. This first transfer of the instrument to the payee is called an **issue.** Once issued, the payee is entitled to collect payment on the instrument or transfer it (pass it on or deliver it) to a third party. One way to pass it on is by **negotiation.** (Only an instrument meeting the requirements of negotiability discussed in Chapter 19 can be negotiated.) The third party who takes possession of the instrument by negotiation becomes, like the original payee, a **holder.** The third party may even become a *holder in due course* and acquire more rights than the original payee had. Holder in due course will be discussed in Chapter 21. Keep in mind that an instrument may be negotiated many times before it is finally presented for payment. How an instrument is negotiated depends on whether it is an order instrument or a bearer instrument.

Negotiation of Order Instruments

An order instrument (one payable "to the order of" a named payee) may be negotiated only by indorsement and delivery. (This procedure is outlined in Figure 20.1.) An **indorsement,** a signature that usually appears on the back of the instrument, transfers ownership of commercial paper. It may also appear on an attached sheet of paper (an *allonge*) when there is no more room on the instrument itself. The signature may be handwritten, typed, or stamped. An indorsement must be proper, which means that the signature must be that of the rightful holder, and not, for example, that of a thief or finder; delivery by the rightful holder must be voluntary.

Figure 20.1
**Negotiation of
Order Paper**

| Maker or drawer issues order instrument to | → | Payee (Holder) indorses instrument and delivers to | → | Third party (Holder) |

A check is shown in Figure 20.2. The first negotiation of this check occurs when Walter Archer (the payee) indorses it (signs it) and then voluntarily delivers it to the third party. The third party obtains legal ownership of the note only by the payee's indorsement and voluntary delivery. After receiving the instrument by negotiation from Walter Archer, the third party, now a holder, may again negotiate the instrument, once more indorsing it and delivering it to another person. This other person also becomes a holder and could in turn negotiate the instrument (the check) by indorsement and delivery. This process continues until the holder in possession of the check decides to present the instrument to the party responsible for payment. (The question who is responsible for payment will be discussed in Chapter 21.)

For an instrument to be properly negotiated, the entire amount must be transferred. You as payee cannot negotiate part of the amount.

Figure 20.2
Indorsed Check

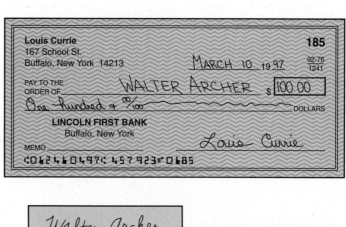

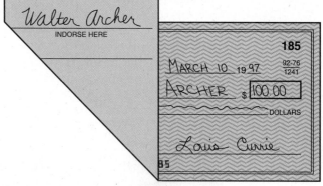

Negotiation of Bearer Instruments

A bearer instrument is one that is payable to anyone who has possession of it. A check payable to "Cash" is an example of a bearer instrument. These instruments may be negotiated by a voluntary delivery alone. This procedure is outlined in Figure 20.3.

> ■ O'Leary owed Jenkins $100 and gave him a check payable to "Cash" (bearer) in the amount of $100. Jenkins wanted to buy some parts for his car and gave the owner of the parts store the same check. The check was negotiated to the parts store owner by delivery. ■

No indorsement is required to transfer ownership of a bearer instrument. A thief or a finder legally cannot obtain a bearer instrument by negotiation because the delivery to him or her was not voluntary. But a thief or finder can negotiate the bearer instrument by voluntarily delivering the instrument to a subsequent innocent purchaser, who will then become a holder of the instrument. Consequently, there is danger in using a bearer instrument.

Although bearer paper can be negotiated by delivery alone, in practice, banks normally require the bearer to indorse the paper so as to impose the liability of an indorser. The indorsement is not required by the UCC. (Indorser liability is discussed in Chapter 21.)

TYPES OF INDORSEMENTS

As discussed on page 300, both indorsement and delivery are required to negotiate an instrument payable to "order." There are four basic types of indorsements: blank, special, restrictive, and qualified indorsements. Each type has a specific purpose.

A **blank indorsement,** shown in Figure 20.4, consists only of the signature of the indorser (the first indorser is the payee) on the reverse side of the instrument. An **indorser** is a person who signs an instrument, usually for the purpose of transferring it to a third party. A blank indorsement makes the instrument payable to the bearer and similar to cash—it may then be transferred by delivery alone without further indorsement. An instrument with this type of indorsement should not be sent through the mail. As noted earlier in this chapter, anyone in possession of bearer paper, including a thief or finder, can negotiate it.

A **special indorsement** specifies the person to whom the indorser intends to make the instrument payable—that is, the name of the indorsee. An **indorsee** is the person who receives an indorsed instrument. This type of indorsement consists of a statement that the instrument is being transferred

Figure 20.3
Negotiation of Bearer Paper

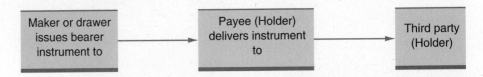

| Maker or drawer issues bearer instrument to | → | Payee (Holder) delivers instrument to | → | Third party (Holder) |

Figure 20.4
Blank Indorsement

to a particular (named) person, followed by the signature of the indorser. (See Figure 20.5.) Such phrases as "Pay to the order of Roberta Fisk (signed) R. Folger" or simply "Pay to Roberta Fisk (signed) R. Folger" are acceptable forms of a special indorsement. It is not necessary to use the word "order" or "bearer" in the indorsement. The instrument is still negotiable and may be further negotiated. This type of indorsement, often referred to as a full indorsement, is used to prevent an instrument such as a check from being cashed by an unauthorized person. Unlike a check with a blank indorsement, a check with a special indorsement may not be transferred by delivery alone. Further negotiation requires the signature of the person to whom the instrument was transferred. For protection, it is legal for a person who has a negotiable instrument containing a blank indorsement to change this indorsement into a special indorsement by writing above the blank indorsement words such as "Pay to the order of" and then the name of a specific person.

A **restrictive indorsement** limits or restricts the rights acquired by the indorsee (the party to whom the instrument is transferred). In other words, the indorsement states what that party may do with the instrument. A person receiving a check, for example, might wish to make sure that the check is deposited in her or his account. A restrictive indorsement, such as the "For deposit only" shown in Figure 20.6, would accomplish this. The bank (indorsee) receiving the check would be restricted to depositing the funds in the account of the indorser. People often use a restrictive indorsement to safeguard a check mailed to a bank because a thief or finder of the check cannot then cash it. Sometimes a person paying for services with a check might want to make sure that the work was done properly before payment

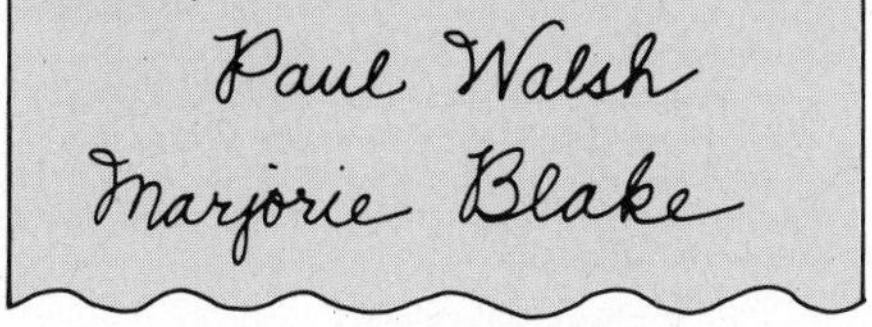

Figure 20.5
Special Indorsement

pay to the order of
Paul Walsh
Marjorie Blake

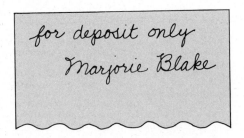

Figure 20.6
Restrictive
Indorsement

was made. That person could write a restrictive indorsement such as "Pay to the order of Dan Mooney upon satisfactory completion of the construction of my garage." UCC §3-206 states that a restrictive indorsement does not destroy the negotiability of an instrument. An instrument negotiable on its face cannot be rendered nonnegotiable by subsequent indorsement. Thus, after the directions are carried out, the instrument may be further negotiated.

A **qualified indorsement,** illustrated in Figure 20.7, limits the liability of the indorser. A qualified indorsement may be used by an indorser who wants to transfer an instrument but does not want to be held liable if the instrument is not paid by the maker or drawee when due. To accomplish this, an indorser can put words limiting liability in the indorsement such as "without recourse," which means not liable as an indorser.

In addition to the four basic types of indorsements, there is a type of indorsement known as an accommodation indorsement. An **accommodation indorsement** is an indorsement placed on an instrument by a person to help out (accommodate) another person whose credit rating is in doubt or not yet established and who is, as a result, unable to cash a check or borrow money. An accommodation indorser generally receives no money for the indorsement but signs in order to add her or his liability on the instrument as an indorser. In essence, the accommodation indorser guarantees payment should the person primarily liable fail to pay.

■ Welch wanted to borrow money from a bank but was a minor and had not yet established credit. The bank agreed to lend Welch the money provided his mother would be responsible if Welch didn't pay. Welch's mother agreed and indorsed the loan instrument as an accommodation to her son. ■

Figure 20.7
Qualified Indorsement

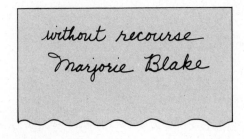

Commercial paper may be discharged in several ways, including payment, alteration, the statute of limitations, bankruptcy, and cancellation.

Payment

When the party who is liable for payment (maker, drawer, indorser) pays the amount of the instrument to the holder, this payment will normally discharge commercial paper. This is the usual way of discharging liability on a negotiable instrument. Although payment is generally in money, the party to whom payment must be made may agree to accept a different consideration of equal value, such as merchandise or personal property.

Alteration

If the holder of commercial paper alters it in any significant and fraudulent manner, that alteration will discharge the obligation of any party whose liability is changed by the alteration. This is to protect innocent parties who take the instrument without knowing it has been altered. What constitutes a significant and fraudulent alteration depends on the facts in each case. An alteration may consist of an addition, a substitution, a deletion, or an unauthorized completion of an incomplete instrument. For example, a change in the written amount and the amount in figures on commercial paper from $1,000 to $10,000 with an intent to deceive is both significant and fraudulent.

Statute of Limitations

If commercial paper is not paid on time, a state's statute of limitations begins to run from the due date of the instrument. If a suit is not brought within the statutory period (usually six years), the instrument is discharged.

■ Kraig gave a promissory note to Melvin on March 8, 1988, payable in ninety days. Kraig did not pay the note when due. Seven years later Melvin brought suit against Kraig to collect on the note. Melvin would not succeed because the note was discharged by the statute of limitations on June 6, 1994, six years from the due date. ■

Bankruptcy

If a party to commercial paper becomes bankrupt and a debt for which the instrument has been given is discharged, the commercial paper is also discharged.

Cancellation

A cancellation is any act that indicates that the underlying obligation is ended and the paper is discharged. Cancellation by the holder may be accomplished by deliberately destroying or defacing the commercial paper or by marking it "paid," "void," or "canceled." Delivery of the note back to the maker will also cancel it.

> Wyler wrote a promissory note payable to Richards, who was a close friend, in return for a $100 loan. When the note became due, Wyler was unable to repay the loan. Richards then canceled the note by tearing it up and telling Wyler to forget about making the $100 payment. ■

Summary of Important Legal Concepts

The circulation of commercial paper begins when the maker or the drawer issues an instrument to the payee. The payee is then entitled to collect payment on the instrument or to pass it on to a third party. One way to pass it on is by negotiation. This is possible as long as the instrument meets the requirements of negotiability. The third party who takes possession of the instrument by negotiation becomes, like the original payee, a holder. How commercial paper may be negotiated depends upon whether the instrument is an order instrument or a bearer instrument. Order instruments are negotiated by indorsement and delivery. Bearer instruments are negotiated by delivery alone. There are four basic indorsements: blank, special, restrictive, and qualified. A blank indorsement, which consists only of the signature of the indorser, makes an instrument payable to the bearer. A special indorsement names the person who will receive the instrument and includes the signature of the indorser. A restrictive indorsement limits what the party to whom the instrument is transferred may do with the instrument. For example, a check presented to a bank with the indorsement "For deposit only" restricts the bank to depositing the funds in the account of the indorser. A qualified indorsement ("without recourse") frees the indorser from liability if the negotiable instrument is not paid by the maker or drawee when due. In addition to the four basic indorsements, an accommodation indorsement can be used to guarantee payment of an instrument. Commercial paper can be discharged by five means: payment, alteration, the statute of limitations, bankruptcy of a party, and cancellation.

Key Legal Terms to Know

Match the terms with the definitions that follow.

accommodation indorsement
blank indorsement
holder
indorsee
indorsement
indorser
issue
negotiation
qualified indorsement
restrictive indorsement
special indorsement

1. An indorsement directing payment to a specified person
2. An indorsement that limits what a transferee may do with the instrument
3. An indorsement guaranteeing payment of an instrument
4. One to whom an order instrument is negotiated by indorsement and voluntary delivery
5. An indorsement limiting the indorser's liability
6. An indorsement consisting solely of the signature of the indorser
7. A person who is in possession of commercial paper that has been properly issued or transferred to him or her
8. The writing of a person's name on the back of a negotiable instrument for the purpose of transferring ownership of the document

9. The person who negotiates an order instrument by indorsement and voluntary delivery to another person
10. The transfer of commercial paper by one person to another person
11. The first transfer of a commercial instrument by the maker or drawer to the payee

Questions and Problems to Discuss

1. Following his uncle's death, Merz inherited several promissory notes made out to his uncle as payee. Merz's attorney advised him that these notes were no longer valid. Based on this advice, Merz burned the notes. Six months later, when it was determined that the notes had actually been valid, Merz demanded payment of the notes from each of the makers. Was Merz entitled to payment?

2. You wish to deposit through the mail a check indorsed to you by means of a blank indorsement. How could you further indorse the check to protect yourself against its loss or theft?

3. Welk's credit rating was poor. To obtain a loan from the First Federal Bank, Welk needed the signature of someone who had a good credit rating. Farber, therefore, indorsed a $1,000 promissory note that Welk gave to the bank. On the due date, Welk failed to pay and the bank sought to recover from Farber, the indorser. Farber claimed that because he received nothing for his signature, he could not be held liable. Is Farber correct?

4. Hoyt negotiated a check that she had received from a friend by indorsing the check as follows: "Pay to the order of Suzanne Rapp (signed) Lillian Hoyt." What type of indorsement did Hoyt use?

5. Edgar was treasurer of the local Rotary Club. At each dinner meeting, many members paid for their meals by check. Before depositing the money in the local bank, Edgar indorsed each check on the back with a rubber stamp as follows: "For deposit only—Eastridge Rotary Club." Is an indorsement with a rubber stamp proper or must it be handwritten?

6. Armond wrote a check payable to Gaston. Gaston negotiated this check to Wright using a blank indorsement. Fearing she would lose the check before she got to the bank, Wright converted the blank indorsement into a special indorsement by writing the words "Pay to the order of Wilma Wright" over Gaston's signature. Was this legal?

7. O'Neill wrote a promissory note payable to the order of Donnelly. What must Donnelly do to negotiate this instrument properly?

8. Weymouth wrote a $500 check to Rhodes. Before cashing the check, Rhodes changed the written amount and the amount in figures from $500 to $5,000. Is Weymouth discharged from her obligation to pay Rhodes?

9. Berra made out and signed a promissory note payable to the order of Streb. Streb placed a blank indorsement on the note and gave it to Harder. Harder in turn transferred the note by delivery alone (no indorsement) to Bell. Does Bell become a holder?

10. Kagel, who owed money to Ryan, offered Ryan a check signed by Shepherd as the drawer and payable to "Bearer." Ryan asked Kagel to add his signature as indorser, claiming that otherwise ownership of the instrument would not pass to her. Was Ryan correct?

11. McGrattan was the maker of a promissory note due on March 13. The payee, Simpson, tried to collect the amount owed on the due date, but McGrattan was unable to pay. For how long is McGrattan liable for the amount due on this note?

12. Anchor was the maker of a $500 promissory note payable to Carter. Carter transferred the note to Petty using a qualified indorsement. What advantage did Carter gain by using a qualified indorsement?

13. Herd used a blank indorsement on a check payable to his order and left it on his desk at work. Rammage stole the check and voluntarily delivered it to Guard, to whom he (Rammage) owed money. Was the check properly negotiated to Guard?

Cases to Decide

1. As office manager for the Palmer & Ray Dental Supply Company, Mrs. Wilson did the daily banking, which included depositing checks in the company account at a local bank. She used a rubber stamp to indorse each check before deposit. The rubber stamp consisted of a blank in-

dorsement rather than a restrictive indorsement. The company discovered that Mrs. Wilson had been cashing the checks at the local bank and keeping the money instead of depositing them in the company account. Palmer & Ray sued the First National Bank, contending that the bank should not have allowed Mrs. Wilson to cash the checks but should have accepted the checks only for deposit in the company account. The bank claimed that the rubber stamp, although only a blank indorsement, was nevertheless authorized by the company and that the bank was therefore not responsible when Mrs. Wilson, an authorized company agent, decided to cash the checks and keep the money. Was the bank legally correct? (*Palmer & Ray Dental Supply of Abilene, Inc.* v. *First National Bank,* Texas App 477 SW2d 954)

2. Four Seasons Country Club Caterers issued twelve promissory notes payable with interest. Keybro became a holder of the notes. When the notes became due, Four Seasons paid the principal amount but did not pay the interest due. Keybro accepted this amount and returned the notes to Four Seasons. It then sued Four Seasons for the interest. Is Four Seasons liable? (*Keybro Enterprises* v. *Four Seasons Country Club Caterers, Inc.,* New York 25 AD2d 307)

3. Baugh gave a promissory note to the bank that was payable with interest at a rate of 9.5 percent per year. After the note was executed, the bank sent Baugh a letter stating that the interest rate was being increased. The decision to raise the interest rate was a business decision and there was no evidence of fraud. When Baugh didn't pay the note, the bank sued. Baugh claimed that the note had been discharged by alteration. Is Baugh correct? (*New Britain National Bank* v. *Baugh,* New York 31 AD2d 898)

4. Hargrove sold cars that were financed by loans to his customers from the First National Bank. Three customers signed promissory notes payable to the bank, and Hargrove wrote his own name on the reverse side of the notes. When the customers failed to pay the notes, the bank sued Hargrove, claiming he had indorsed the notes. Was Hargrove's signature an indorsement? (*First National Bank of Atlanta* v. *Hargrove,* Texas 503 SW2d 856)

5. Barnes was the payee of a $5,088.70 check drawn by Portland Cement Association. Barnes indorsed the check, "J. Y. Barnes, for deposit only," and placed the check for mailing in a cooperative mailing rack in the lobby of a building in Denver. The envelope containing the check was stolen by Woodward, who passed himself off as Barnes and opened a checking account in Cherry Creek National Bank in the name of Jack Y. Barnes. Woodward deposited the check into the account and the check was paid by Cherry Creek. Barnes than sued Cherry Creek to recover the money, claiming that the check had been restrictively indorsed and could be paid only to the real Jack Barnes. Will Barnes succeed? (*Barnes* v. *Cherry Creek National Bank of Denver,* Colorado 432 P2d 471)

6. Gold signed a promissory note payable to her stepfather as evidence of a loan from him and from her mother. When she did not pay the amount due on the note and her stepfather sued her for the balance due, Gold claimed that her mother had canceled the obligation. There was proof that her mother had in fact orally canceled the note. Must Gold pay the balance due? (*Community National Bank & Trust Company, Executor of Michel Thorgevski* v. *Mary J. Gold,* New York 45 AD2d 947)

Chapter 21

Rights and Duties of Parties to a Negotiable Instrument; Holder in Due Course Status

CHAPTER PREVIEW

The first part of this chapter identifies the parties who have liability for payment of a negotiable instrument, describes the extent of their liability, and summarizes what the holder of a negotiable instrument must do to hold these parties liable for payment.

The second part of the chapter describes the concept of holder in due course, points out how a person qualifies to be one, and discusses the legal defenses that are good or not good against a holder in due course attempting to collect on a negotiable instrument.

The concluding pages of the chapter explain how, in certain transactions, a ruling of the Federal Trade Commission deprives holders from acquiring holder in due course status. These pages also briefly outline the liability of accommodation parties—those who sign instruments for the purpose of lending their names and credit to other people.

LIABILITY OF PARTIES TO A NEGOTIABLE INSTRUMENT

Parties to a negotiable instrument who have liability for payment of the instrument are classified as either primary parties or secondary parties. **Primary parties** are those who are first obligated to pay the instrument. Examples of primary parties are the maker of a promissory note and the drawee who agrees to pay a draft (accepts the draft) at the request of the drawer.

By accepting a draft, the drawee becomes primarily liable for payment to the payee or any other holder of the draft. After accepting the draft, the drawee is known as the **acceptor.** Acceptance, which must be in writing, usually consists of the word *Accepted* stamped or written on the face of the instrument, the signature of the drawee, and the date it was accepted. The refusal of the drawee to accept the draft amounts to a dishonor of the instrument.

The liability of primary parties is unconditional. That is, the maker or acceptor agrees to pay the instrument according to its terms whenever it is presented for payment, even if it is presented for payment many months or even years after the due date. The only exception to this liability is for an instrument that is not presented for payment before the statute of limitations runs out.

■ Melrose (payee), who held Carpinski's $300, three-month promissory note dated October 15, presented it to Carpinski on January 25 and demanded payment. Carpinski refused to pay it, claiming that presentment had not been made on the proper date. Because Carpinski is primarily liable for payment, Melrose can still legally collect the $300 even though the due date (January 15) had passed when the request for payment was made. ■

Secondary parties are those who are obligated to pay only if the holder of the instrument cannot collect payment from the primary party. Examples of secondary parties are drawers of checks (or drafts) and indorsers of commercial paper. In contrast to the unconditional liability of primary parties, the liability of secondary parties is said to be conditional. Secondary parties would be liable only if the holder of the paper takes the following steps: (1) presenting the instrument for payment to the primary party, (2) having the primary party dishonor the instrument (refuse or be unable to make payment), and (3) giving notice of dishonor to the secondary party. An indorser may limit her or his secondary liability by using a qualified indorsement, using such words as "without recourse." If this is done, the indorser is not liable for nonpayment of the instrument by the primary party even if the conditions of presentment, dishonor, and notice of dishonor are met.

The secondary liability of drawers differs from that of indorsers. Perhaps an example will help clarify this difference. In the example, we will use a check, where the drawee is always a bank.

Assume that McCall has an account at Midtown Bank. McCall (the drawer) writes a check on that account and makes it payable to Wright (the payee). Wright (now the indorser) indorses the check to Feinstein, who becomes the holder. Assume also that Midtown Bank refuses to pay the check when Feinstein presents it at the bank. (Technically, under the Uniform Commercial Code (UCC), a bank can for good reason refuse to pay an ordinary check—but not a certified or cashier's check—to a holder on presentment because the bank never signed the check. The Code states that "no person is liable on an instrument unless his/her signature appears thereon" [§3-401].)

Because of the UCC rule, Feinstein cannot complain to Midtown Bank. The burden of paying Feinstein is then placed on McCall, the drawer, who is the secondary party. Moreover, McCall must pay even if the conditions of presentment, dishonor, and notice have not been met. If Feinstein wanted to collect from Wright, the indorser, a different set of conditions would apply, as noted above. Feinstein would have to present the check to Midtown Bank for payment, have Midtown dishonor the instrument, and then give notice to Wright that Midtown had dishonored the check. Only then would Wright be liable for payment and only if Wright had not used a qualified indorsement.

Presentment for Payment

Presentment is a demand for payment or acceptance made by or on behalf of a holder of commercial paper. Presentment may be made by mail, in person, or through a bank. To be effective, presentment must be made within a proper time and at a proper place. When an instrument is due on a certain date (as, for example, a promissory note), presentment must be made on that date or, if the due date is not a full business day, on the next full business day.

Demand instruments (such as checks) must be presented within a reasonable period of time after the secondary party signed the instrument. What is "reasonable" depends on the type of instrument and the customs of a particular bank or particular business. Under the UCC, the holder of a check has thirty days after the issue of a check to present it for payment; after that time, the drawer will not be liable for payment (§3-503). If the check is presented more than seven days after it has been indorsed, the indorser is no longer liable for payment.

Presentment must also be made at the proper place. Most instruments indicate where presentment is to be made. If there are no such directions, presentment should be made at the business office or the residence of the primary party.

If presentment is late or is improper, the liability of the secondary parties to an instrument may be discharged. Exceptions to this rule are the death of a party to the instrument or the existence of an agreement by all parties to the instrument to waive the need for proper presentment.

Dishonor of Instrument

Dishonor of an instrument is the refusal of the primary party to pay or to accept an instrument (in the case of the drawee of a draft) when it is presented for payment. The instrument is considered dishonored if it is not paid or accepted by the close of the next business day following presentment.

Notice of Dishonor

If a primary party dishonors an instrument, **notice of dishonor** must be given to the secondary party by the holder in order to hold the secondary party liable for payment. If notice is not given, or is given improperly, the secondary party may be released from any obligation to pay. Notice of dishonor may be given orally or in writing. To be effective, the notice must be given within three business days after dishonor by the primary party.

■ Carey was the maker of a sixty-day promissory note for $250 due on July 8. When Phillips, a holder, presented the note to Carey on July 8, Carey dishonored it. On August 1 Phillips gave Marvel, an indorser, notice of the dishonor and requested payment of the note. Marvel is not liable for payment of the instrument, however, because notice of dishonor was not given within three business days after Carey dishonored the note. ■

Indorsers of commercial paper are generally liable in the order in which they indorse the instrument. An indorser who is required to pay can recover from a prior indorser, provided that the prior indorser has been notified.

■ Martin issued a promissory note payable to the order of Perkins. Perkins indorsed the note to Armish; Armish indorsed it to Bello; Bello indorsed it to Harter. When Harter, the last holder, promptly and properly presented the note to Martin for payment, Martin refused to pay. Harter then notified Bello and collected the amount due. In order to collect, Bello must notify Armish. If Armish wishes to collect, she must notify Perkins. ■

A delay in both presentment and notice of dishonor may be excused in certain circumstances. For example, if a holder cannot present a note for payment because a snowstorm has made travel impossible, the holder would be excused until a reasonable time after the storm, when travel is again possible.

Presentment and notice of dishonor may also be waived by the parties. Many lenders provide for such waivers in their loan agreements and loan documents because it speeds up the process of collection of commercial paper.

If a bank incorrectly or wrongfully dishonors an instrument, it can be held liable to the wronged party. The bank is liable for all damages actually resulting from its actions. For example, a bank's refusal to honor a check could result in a loss of business or a bad credit rating for the drawer.

HOLDER IN DUE COURSE STATUS

A payee to whom a negotiable instrument has been issued may, as noted in Chapter 20, transfer the instrument to a third party by negotiation; that third party becomes a holder. Each succeeding party who receives the instrument by negotiation also becomes a holder. If certain conditions are met, a holder may become a holder in due course. A **holder in due course** is a holder who gains a special privilege—the privilege of enforcing payment of the negotiable instrument in spite of the fact that certain reasons for not paying, called personal (limited) defenses, are introduced in court by the party obligated to pay. Personal (limited) defenses are discussed later in the chapter. The reason for establishing the holder in due course rule is to give commercial paper a high degree of marketability—that is, to encourage people to use commercial paper like money by giving them some assurance that the instrument will be paid when presented to the proper person.

If an instrument is not negotiable and therefore does not meet the requirements of negotiation, the transfer by the payee is considered an assignment. Consequently, the person receiving the instrument under these circumstances becomes an **ordinary holder** and has the legal rights of an assignee of a simple contract (see Chapter 12). Unlike a holder in due course, an ordinary holder does not gain the privilege of enforcing payment of the instrument when personal defenses are raised by the party obligated to pay.

Holder in due course status is not presumed, which means that a holder must *prove* he or she is a holder in due course. To qualify as a holder in due course, the holder must take the instrument (1) for value, (2) in good faith, (3) without knowledge that the paper might be overdue or dishonored, and (4) without knowledge that some other person has a defense against it.

For Value

To qualify as a holder in due course, a holder must give value (something in payment) for the instrument. A person who receives a negotiable instrument as a gift cannot be a holder in due course because he or she has given nothing in payment. The usual consideration for an instrument is money, although the amount need not be equal to the amount written on the face of the instrument. Under the provisions of the UCC, a holder is considered to have taken an instrument for value when he or she takes the instrument in payment of a prior debt.

> ■ Your uncle indorsed and delivered to you as a gift for your birthday a promissory note made by Salvatore. The note, payable to the order of your uncle as payee, was originally obtained from Salvatore for a debt owed to your uncle. ■

In this example you received the note by negotiation (indorsement plus delivery). However, since it was a gift and you gave no value for it, you became an ordinary holder, not a holder in due course.

In Good Faith

A holder who acts honestly and does not take an instrument under suspicious circumstances takes the instrument in good faith. Good faith is hard to define. The courts would need to look at the experience, intelligence, and judgment of each individual when deciding whether the individual acted honestly.

> ■ Keil bought a promissory note with a face value of $10,000 for a payment of $100. It should have been obvious to Keil that the person transferring the note had either found or stolen it. In this case, Keil would not qualify as a holder in due course. ■

Without Knowledge of Overdue or Dishonored Paper

To qualify as a holder in due course, a person who accepts a negotiable instrument must have no knowledge that the instrument is overdue or has been dishonored by a maker or drawee. A person is considered to have knowledge if, as a reasonable person of average intelligence, he or she can conclude from the information received that something may be wrong with the instrument. A person who takes an instrument after its maturity date has actual knowledge that the paper is overdue. The person should suspect that something may be wrong with the instrument.

> ■ A promissory note due and payable on January 20 was negotiated to you on February 1. Although you obtained the overdue note by negotiation, you are an ordinary holder, not a holder in due course. ■

Without Knowledge of Defenses

To become a holder in due course, a person can have no knowledge of any defenses the party obligated to pay may have against the instrument. For example, if there is evidence on the face of the instrument that the signature has been forged or the paper has been altered in some way, a person accepting that instrument cannot become a holder in due course. A reasonable person would have questioned whether the instrument was valid.

> Gerard made out a promissory note, written in ink, for $1,000. The note was payable to Monroe Business School. The owner of the business school, who needed money to keep the school going, erased the $1,000, inserted the figure of $2,000, and negotiated the note to the bank, a creditor of the school. ■

In this case, the bank was not a holder in due course. Evidence of the alteration (for example, rough spots on the paper where the erasure was made) should have alerted the bank to a possible alteration. Because the note had been altered, Gerard would not have to pay the $2,000 when the bank presented the note for payment. Gerard would, however, be liable for the original amount of the note—$1,000.

DEFENSES AGAINST HOLDERS OF NEGOTIABLE INSTRUMENTS

In relation to negotiable instruments a *defense* is a legal reason offered by a primary or secondary party for not paying a holder the amount due on an instrument. Defenses may be classified as either personal (limited) defenses or universal (real) defenses. **Personal (limited) defenses** are not good against holders in due course but as indicated on page 313, are good against ordinary holders. As discussed above, a holder in due course may collect on the instrument in spite of any personal (limited) defenses offered by a party obligated to pay. **Universal (real) defenses** are good against all holders, including holders in due course. A party having a real defense against a holder of commercial paper is not liable for payment of that instrument.

Personal (Limited) Defenses

Personal (limited) defenses, which may arise either before or after an instrument has been negotiated, include (1) fraud in the inducement, (2) lack of consideration, (3) payment at or before maturity, (4) lack of delivery, (5) unauthorized completion of an incomplete instrument, and (6) slight duress.

Fraud in the Inducement The defense of fraud in the inducement arises when a person is persuaded to sign an instrument because of false statements by another person. The person is fully aware that he or she is signing a negotiable instrument but is not aware that the other party has misrepresented a material fact concerning the transaction in order to persuade this person to sign the paper.

> You wished to buy a used car from Whalen, who was very eager to sell the car. Whalen told you that she had recently had the motor overhauled.
> You relied on this statement and agreed to buy the car, signing a promissory note for $2,000 to pay for the car. Shortly thereafter, you discovered that Whalen had lied about having the motor overhauled. ■

In this example, you could refuse to pay the note because, as one of the immediate parties, you have a good defense against the instrument: fraud in the inducement. However, if Whalen had negotiated the note to another person, who would be a holder in due course, you would be liable for payment to that person. The defense of fraud in the inducement is not good against holders in due course. You could, of course, sue Whalen for damages suffered from the tort of fraud.

Lack of Consideration   As in any contract, consideration makes a promise to give a negotiable instrument binding. Lack of consideration is a defense between the immediate parties to an instrument, but it is not a defense against a holder in due course.

> Jenkins purchased a minicomputer from Raven. When Raven told Jenkins that the computer would be delivered in a few days, Jenkins made out a promissory note to Raven and delivered the note to her. The minicomputer was never delivered to Jenkins. In the meantime, Raven negotiated the note to Harris as payment for a debt. Harris became a holder in due course. ■

In this example, the lack of consideration was a personal defense that Jenkins could raise against Raven. However, because Raven negotiated the note to Harris, a holder in due course, the defense of lack of consideration is not valid against Harris. Harris could collect on the note from Jenkins, who could then sue Raven.

Payment at or Before Maturity   A person who pays the amount due on a negotiable instrument should take actual possession of the instrument. The same is true for an instrument that is canceled before the due date by mutual agreement. If this paid-up or canceled instrument is not retrieved, it may either deliberately or accidentally fall into the hands of a third party through negotiation. That party would be a holder in due course.

> You borrowed $100 from Heinz to make a down payment on some ski equipment. You gave Heinz a thirty-day promissory note. At the end of fifteen days, you paid off the note but did not ask Heinz for its return. ■

In this example, if Heinz negotiated the note before its maturity date to a person who becomes a holder in due course, you must pay the note again on the due date.

Lack of Delivery   An instrument may unintentionally be transferred (delivered) from one person to another, for example through loss or theft. Even in these circumstances, lack of delivery is not a valid defense against a holder in due course. It is, however, a valid defense between the two immediate parties to the instrument. Lack of delivery may involve either a complete or an incomplete instrument.

A *complete instrument* is one on which all important blanks have been filled in, including the signature of the maker or drawer.

■ You made out a check payable to "Cash" and left it on a table in your family room. A burglar who entered your house stole the check and negotiated it to a holder in due course. The holder in due course could collect the amount of the check from you, but the burglar could not. ■

An *incomplete instrument* is one lacking information because all the blanks have not been filled in by the maker or drawer. If, through carelessness or theft, the instrument is negotiated to a holder in due course, the maker or drawer does not have a valid defense against that person.

■ Jerome made out a promissory note and signed it, but he did not write in the name of the payee. Jerome lost the note. Adler found the note, filled in his own name as payee, and negotiated it to Black, a holder in due course. Although Adler could not collect from Jerome, Black could. ■

Unauthorized Completion   In certain circumstances, a signed instrument may be transferred to another person with some of the blanks not filled in. The maker may authorize this person to complete the instrument according to the maker's instructions. However, if the blanks are completed in an unauthorized manner, the maker does not have a valid defense against a holder in due course.

■ Raleigh, who was in the specialty food import business, gave his agent a blank check and authorized the agent to fill it in for the correct amount of a purchase he was asked to make. The agent instead filled it in for a larger amount and then cashed the check. Raleigh would have to pay the full amount of the check to a holder in due course. Raleigh would not, however, have to pay the agent the larger amount. ■

Slight Duress   "Slight duress" refers to threats that prevent a person from exercising her or his own free will. A person forced to give a negotiable instrument under slight duress will not be liable on the instrument to the person who actually committed the duress. However, the defense of slight duress cannot be used against a holder in due course. If the person who acquired the instrument through duress has already collected, the maker can recover damages if he or she finds the guilty person.

■ Bulin was a professor at Finger Lakes Community College. Inya, another professor at the college, was in desperate need of money and threatened to tell the personnel office that Bulin had a criminal record unless Bulin gave him $200. Bulin did not have the cash, but Inya agreed to take a check payable to him. He indorsed the check and cashed it at a local grocery store. As a holder in due course, the owner of the grocery store could collect the amount of the check from Bulin. ■

Universal (Real) Defenses

Universal (real) defenses make a negotiable instrument void from the time of its creation. These defenses include (1) fraud in the execution, (2) forgery, (3) minority, (4) material alteration, (5) illegality, and (6) serious duress.

Fraud in the Execution   Fraud in the execution of an instrument occurs when one person obtains a negotiable instrument from another person through fraud or trickery. The maker in this case could avoid payment to all parties, including a holder in due course, because there was never an intent to create the instrument.

> Lutz, who was selling magazine subscriptions in an apartment building, told a customer that besides being a salesperson, he also was a handwriting analyst. He told the customer to sign her name on a piece of paper, which he handed to her. After leaving the apartment building, Lutz wrote a promissory note above the signature and then indorsed the "note" to Gimbel, a holder in due course. Gimbel could not legally collect on this instrument. The magazine customer could raise the real defense of fraud in the execution because she never intended to create a note. ■

Forgery   A person whose name is forged to an instrument has a universal (real) defense against all holders. Even a holder in due course cannot collect from the maker or drawer.

> Karlan, a holder in due course, presented a promissory note for payment to Cato, whose name appeared as the maker. Cato proved her signature had been forged. Karlan cannot collect from Cato. ■

Minority   Minors can avoid liability on negotiable instruments in the same manner that they can avoid liability on simple contracts. Even holders in due course cannot collect on an instrument signed by a minor as a maker, drawer, or indorser (except for necessaries).

> As payment for a stereo, Langdon, a minor, wrote a ninety-day promissory note for $200 to Arnold, the payee. The note was negotiated to Marvin, a holder in due course, who demanded payment from Langdon. As a minor, Langdon may refuse to pay Marvin. ■

Material Alteration   A material alteration made in a fraudulent manner is a universal (real) defense that is valid against all holders. An alteration is material when the rights and obligations of the parties are changed, such as when the amount of the instrument is increased or the due date is changed. The defense of material alteration is good against a holder in due course only for the changes made in the instrument. That is, a holder in due course can enforce the instrument for the amount before the alteration.

> Carson, the payee of a check, changed the amount of the check from $100 to $1,000 and then negotiated it to Spicer, a holder in due course. Spicer could legally demand that Carson pay $100. ■

Illegality   Whether illegality may be used as a universal (real) defense or a personal (limited) defense against a holder in due course depends upon state statute. If the transaction for which a negotiable instrument is given is illegal or void by state statute, then illegality is a universal (real) defense that is good against even a holder in due course. If, however, the transaction for which a negotiable instrument is given is not void by state statute, illegality is a personal (limited) defense and is not good against a holder in due course.

> ■ Perkins gave Engle a note in payment of a gambling debt. Engle negotiated the note to Heller, a holder in due course. Perkins refused to pay Heller the amount of the note when it was properly presented to her (Perkins). In Perkins's state, gambling was illegal. Therefore, the note Perkins gave Engle was void and Heller, even as a holder in due course, could not collect. ■

Serious Duress Serious forms of duress, such as forcing a person to sign an instrument or threatening a person at gunpoint, are considered universal (real) defenses and are good against all holders, including a holder in due course.

> ■ Comfort was physically forced by LaGrange, a known organized crime figure, to sign a promissory note for $1,000. LaGrange negotiated this note to O'Hara, a holder in due course. O'Hara could not legally collect from Comfort, even as a holder in due course. ■

Figure 21.1 summarizes the types of personal (limited) and universal (real) defenses.

Defense of Consumers Against Holders in Due Course

In 1976 the Federal Trade Commission (FTC), which has the authority to prohibit unfair business practices, ruled that the holder in due course concept cannot be used against ultimate consumers when they buy goods or services

Figure 21.1
Defenses Against Holders of Negotiable Instruments

Classification of Defenses	Types of Defenses
Personal (limited) defenses Good against ordinary holders but not against holders in due course	1. Fraud in the inducement 2. Lack of consideration 3. Payment at or before maturity 4. Lack of delivery 5. Unauthorized completion 6. Slight duress
Universal (real) defenses Good against all holders, including holders in due course	1. Fraud in the execution 2. Forgery 3. Minority 4. Material alteration 5. Illegality 6. Serious duress

on credit from a merchant-seller. (This ruling overrides the UCC provisions.) The FTC declared that if a consumer gives a seller a negotiable instrument (such as a promissory note) and the seller negotiates the instrument, the party taking the instrument (such as a bank or a finance company) cannot become a holder in due course. Rather, this party is placed in the position of an assignee and takes the instrument subject to all claims and defenses that the buyer could assert against the seller.

> ■ Sanders purchased a $600 microwave from Kitchens Unlimited and gave Kitchens Unlimited a negotiable instrument for that amount. A salesperson for Kitchens Unlimited had made false statements about the appliance (fraud in the inducement) to induce Sanders to make the purchase. The appliance turned out to be defective. In the meantime Kitchens Unlimited negotiated the instrument to the First National Bank, which presented the note to Sanders for payment. ■

Under the old rule, fraud in the inducement is a personal defense that is not good against a holder in due course. Thus, in the example, even though Kitchens Unlimited lied and even though the appliance turned out to be defective, the First National Bank, not being a party to the fraud, could still collect from Sanders. Sanders's only recourse would be to try to collect from Kitchens Unlimited. In such cases, recovery is difficult and frequently impossible.

Under the FTC ruling, however, the First National Bank was not considered to be a holder in due course. Sanders could assert the defense of fraud in the inducement against the bank and withhold payment of the instrument until the seller corrects any deficiencies.

Each consumer credit transaction must now contain the following clause in at least 10-point, boldface type. The type as shown here is 10-point boldface:

NOTICE
ANY HOLDER OF THIS CONSUMER CREDIT CONTRACT IS SUBJECT TO ALL CLAIMS AND DEFENSES WHICH THE DEBTOR COULD ASSERT AGAINST THE SELLER OF GOODS OR SERVICES OBTAINED PURSUANT HERETO OR WITH THE PROCEEDS HEREOF. RECOVERY HEREUNDER BY THE DEBTOR SHALL NOT EXCEED AMOUNTS PAID BY THE DEBTOR HEREUNDER.

The FTC rule, however, does not apply when a consumer purchases goods or services and pays by check. The party to whom a check has been negotiated may qualify as a holder in due course.

LIABILITY OF ACCOMMODATION PARTIES

As you learned in Chapter 20, accommodation parties are those who sign instruments for the purpose of lending their names and credit to other people, either as a favor or for some consideration. Some accommodation parties sign as co-makers, others as indorsers. The liabilities of accommodation co-makers and indorsers differ. Co-makers have primary liability, while indorsers have secondary liability. The liability of accommodation indorsers, in whatever capacity they sign, extends only to subsequent holders and not to the person accommodated.

Banks and others extending credit often require an accommodation party to guarantee payment. The words "payment guaranteed" or similar words on an instrument make the accommodation party a guarantor and primarily liable along with the maker of the note.

Summary of Important Legal Concepts

Parties liable for payment on negotiable instruments are classified as either primary parties or secondary parties. Makers of notes and acceptors of drafts are primary parties. Drawers and indorsers are secondary parties. A primary party has unconditional liability for payment of the instrument according to its terms, whereas the liability of secondary parties is conditional. To hold a secondary party liable, the holder of the paper must (a) present the instrument for payment to the primary party, (b) have the primary party dishonor the instrument, and (c) give notice of dishonor to the secondary party. Generally, the drawer as a secondary party has to pay even if the conditions of presentment, dishonor, and notice are not met.

To qualify as a holder in due course, a holder must take the instrument for value, in good faith, and without knowledge that the paper might be overdue or dishonored or that a party may have a defense against it. A holder who does not qualify as a holder in due course is considered an ordinary holder and is in the same legal position as an assignee of a contract. Defenses against holders of negotiable instruments are classified as personal (limited) defenses and universal (real) defenses. Personal (limited) defenses are good against ordinary holders, assignees, and the immediate parties to commercial paper, but, they are not good against holders in due course. Universal (real) defenses are good against assignees and all holders, including holders in due course. Personal (limited) defenses include (1) fraud in the inducement, (2) lack of consideration, (3) payment at or before maturity, (4) lack of delivery of a complete instrument, (5) unauthorized completion of an incomplete instrument, and (6) slight duress. Universal (real) defenses consist of (1) fraud in the execution, (2) forgery, (3) minority, (4) material alteration, (5) illegality, (6) serious duress.

Under a ruling by the Federal Trade Commission, if a consumer who buys on credit gives a seller a negotiable instrument and the seller negotiates the instrument, the person taking the instrument cannot become a holder in due course. The FTC rule, however, does not apply when a consumer purchases goods or services and pays by check. The party to whom a check has been negotiated may qualify as a holder in due course.

Sometimes, as a favor or for some consideration, people lend their names and credit to other people as an accommodation. Some accommodation parties sign instruments as co-makers, others as indorsers. The liabilities of co-makers and indorsers differ.

Key Legal Terms to Know

Match the terms with the definitions that follow.

acceptor
dishonor
holder in due course
notice of dishonor
ordinary holder
personal (limited) defenses
presentment
primary parties
universal (real) defenses
secondary parties

1. A holder who holds an instrument subject only to real defenses
2. A holder who does not qualify as a holder in due course and is subject to both universal (real) and personal (limited) defenses
3. Parties who are first responsible for payment of an instrument.
4. Parties who are responsible for payment of an instrument only if the person who is first responsible fails to pay
5. Notice given to a secondary party that a primary party has refused to pay an instrument
6. A demand for payment of a negotiable instrument made by the holder of the instrument
7. The refusal of a party to pay or to accept an instrument
8. Defenses that arise after the instrument has been negotiated and that cannot be used against a holder in due course
9. Defenses that arise at the time negotiable instruments are created and that can be used against all holders
10. A drawee who agrees to pay a draft

Questions and Problems to Discuss

1. What are the requirements for becoming a holder in due course?
2. What effect do personal (limited) defenses have on a holder in due course? What effect do universal (real) defenses have on such holders?
3. Franklin signed a contract and a negotiable promissory note for $8,500 payable to Rankin, the merchant-owner of Style House, for the installation of vinyl siding on his house. To induce Franklin to sign the contract and the note, Rankin had promised that a high-quality vinyl would be used, that the house would serve as a show house for advertising purposes, and that Franklin would receive $100 for each contract sold in a specific area of his town. When the vinyl siding was installed, however, Rankin did not use a high-quality vinyl or use Franklin's house as a show house. His promises had been falsely made simply to induce Franklin to sign the contract. In the meantime, Rankin negotiated the note to the Cordial Finance Company. When Cordial presented the note to Franklin for payment, Franklin refused to pay, claiming fraud in the inducement. Cordial claimed that, as a holder in due course,
it could collect in spite of that defense. Is Cordial correct?
4. Stern purchased merchandise for $300 from a local merchant and gave a sixty-day promissory note as payment. The note was payable at Stern's bank. On the due date, the merchant forgot to present the note. One week later the merchant presented it for payment. Stern claimed to be no longer liable for the note. Is Stern correct?
5. Keaton accepted Maxwell's promissory note for $150. Keaton then changed the amount on the note to $1,500 and negotiated it to Dixon, a holder in due course. When the note matured, Dixon properly presented the note, but Maxwell refused to pay. Was Maxwell liable to Dixon for $1,500?
6. Sampson's name appeared as a maker of a $500 note. On the due date, Robbins, a holder in due course, presented the note to Sampson for payment. Sampson proved the signature to be a forgery and refused to pay. Can Robbins legally collect from Sampson?
7. Green found a piece of paper on which Carey's signature was written and wrote a promissory note above the signature. Green indorsed the note to Friedman, a holder in due course. Can Friedman recover from Carey?
8. Metzler made a note payable to Gardner, her attorney. Because of a dispute over the amount actually owed, Metzler never gave Gardner the note. On a visit to Metzler's office, Gardner saw the note and took it. Gardner then negotiated the note to Cohen, a holder in due course. Could Cohen collect from Metzler?
9. Monroe made a note payable to Barnard for $900, which had a due date of August 13, 1991. Monroe did not pay Barnard when the note was due. Since Barnard needed money, he indorsed the note and gave it to Rumpkin, a creditor. In the meantime, Monroe discovered that she had a case of fraud against Barnard. When Rumpkin sued Monroe for the amount due on the note, could Monroe claim fraud against Rumpkin?
10. Karr was the maker of a two-month promissory note dated April 9 and due June 9. Rogers, a holder in due course, presented the note to Karr on June 15 and demanded payment. Unable to collect from Karr, Rogers notified Brown, a regular (not a qualified) indorser and requested payment from her. Is Brown legally obligated to pay the note?
11. Sagamore borrowed $200 from Copp, to whom she gave a promissory note due and payable on

January 15. One week before the note was due, Sagamore met Copp at a local bank and paid him the $200. Copp promised to mail the note to Sagamore the next day. Instead, Copp made a gift of the note to his nephew. Could the nephew collect the amount of the note from Sagamore?

12. Brant indorsed a note "without recourse." On the maturity date of the note, Jones, the holder, failed to receive payment from the maker because the maker's name had been forged. Jones then sued Brant for payment. Brant stated that because she signed with a qualified indorsement, she is not liable on the note. Is she correct?

13. Coe needed money and threatened Doer with violence if he did not write a promissory note for $500 payable to Coe. Doer yielded and wrote the note. Coe negotiated the note to Fitch, a creditor, who knew how Coe had obtained it. On the due date Fitch properly presented the note for payment to Doer, who refused to pay. Is Fitch entitled to payment?

Cases to Decide

1. Biggs, owner of a drive-in restaurant, bought a communication system from Cunningham. As payment for the system, Biggs gave Cunningham a promissory note and a chattel mortgage, which included certain warranties and a service contract. Howard bought the note from Cunningham. When Biggs did not pay the amount due on the note, Howard brought suit against Biggs. Biggs's defense was that the equipment had not been serviced and could not be used by him. Was this a valid defense? (*Howard*, v. *Biggs*, 378 P2d 306 Okla)

2. Mr. and Mrs. Dorsey gave a promissory note to U.S. Homes as payment for home improvement work. The day after the note was signed, New Jersey Mortgage bought it from U.S. Homes. When the Dorseys did not pay, New Jersey Mortgage brought an action against them to collect the amount due. The Dorseys' defense was that they did not know that they were signing a note and thought it was a credit application. They claimed that this was fraud and a valid defense against a holder in due course. Is this a valid defense? (*New Jersey Mortgage and Investment Co.* v. *Dorsey*, 158 A2d 7112)

3. Barnes received a promissory note from Park Place in the amount of $34,400, payable on or before January 1, 1973. Three officers of the corporation indorsed the note as individuals. Barnes apparently felt he was not going to be paid and wrote each indorser on December 7, 1972, to say that he would sue if the note was not paid. The note was not paid on January 1, 1973, and Barnes presented the note for payment on March 20, 1973. Nine days later Barnes sent out a notice of dishonor to each indorser. If Barnes sues the indorsers on the note, can he succeed? (*Barnes* v. *Park Place Homes, Inc.*, Louisiana 289 So 2d 859)

4. Locke gave a promissory note to Consumer Foods, Inc. The note read, in part, "Buyer agrees to pay to Seller." Consumer Foods assigned the note to Aetna Acceptance Corporation. When the note wasn't paid and Aetna brought an action against Locke, Locke's defense was that the note was not negotiable because it was not payable to order or to bearer. As a result, Aetna was not a holder in due course and was subject to personal defenses that Locke had. Is Locke correct? (*Locke* v. *Aetna Acceptance Corp.*, Fla 309 So 2d 43)

5. Middle Georgia Livestock Sales bought cattle at an auction, paying by check. A couple of days later, Middle Georgia discovered that they had purchased stolen cattle and put through a stop-payment order on the check. Commercial Bank, however, cashed the check without knowledge of the stop-payment order. When the drawee bank refused payment, Commercial Bank sued the maker of the check. In this state a transaction involving stolen goods is illegal and void. Can Commercial Bank collect from the maker? (*Middle Georgia Livestock Sales* v. *Commercial B & T Co.*, Georgia 182 SE2d 533)

6. The Paddocks hired Harper Realty to sell their hotel. The Paddocks agreed that if Harper sold the hotel, they would pay Harper a commission of $15,000, with $3,000 down and the balance in monthly installments. The Paddocks gave Harper a note for the $12,000. Harper negotiated the note to McLean, a holder in due course. When the payments were not made, McLean sued the Paddocks. The Paddocks' defense was that they were induced to sign the note because of a false representation by Harper that the note was required, when in fact it was not. Is this defense valid against the claim? (*McLean* v. *Paddock*, New Mexico 430 P2d 392)

Chapter 22

Checks, Electronic Fund Transfers, and the Banking System

CHAPTER PREVIEW

depositor's reputation resulting from a bad credit rating or from being arrested and prosecuted. A depositor, however, has the responsibility of proving the wrongfulness of the dishonor and that the dishonor was the cause of the injury. The usual reason for a bank to dishonor a depositor's check is that there are insufficient funds in the account to cover the check. However, if the bank thinks that there are insufficient funds in a depositor's checking account but is in error, the bank is liable.

> Nichols made out a check payable to Lark for $250 for a used motorcycle. Lincoln National Bank, the bank on which the check was written, refused to pay Lark, stating that there were insufficient funds in Nichols's account. Actually, the bank's records were incorrect because of an error in bookkeeping. Lincoln National Bank would be liable for any damages suffered by Nichols. ■

A bank may also legally refuse to honor a depositor's check for other reasons: the check may lack a necessary indorsement; the check may be stale; the depositor may have stopped payment; the check may contain a material omission (such as lack of an amount); or the bank may be suspicious of either the check or the holder.

A bank that dishonors a check has no liability to a holder even though the bank's refusal to pay was improper. A holder who wishes to recover under these circumstances must proceed against the drawer and other secondary parties. However, the holder must first notify these parties of the dishonor.

Postdated Checks

A check that is dated after its actual date of issue is called a **postdated check.** It is perfectly valid and is often used in the same way as a promissory note—to pay for something in the future. Postdating a check has no effect on negotiability. A person who takes a postdated check therefore may become a holder in due course.

The problem is that a bank has no obligation to pay a postdated check until its due date. The bank can be held liable to a drawer if it does pay a postdated check before it is due and such action causes harm to the drawer. This might occur if other checks prepared by the same drawer are dishonored because of insufficient funds resulting from premature payment of a postdated check. In a few states, a bank is not liable for the premature payment of a postdated check unless the drawer notifies the bank that the check is postdated.

> You wanted to give your parents an anniversary gift at a party to be held in their honor. The party, however, was going to be held on June 21, one week before you got your next paycheck. A friend of yours, who owned the Swiss Clock Shop, agreed to take a check dated June 28 (seven days later) in payment of an unusual clock you wanted to buy for your parents. This is a postdated check. ■

Stop-Payment Order

The drawer of a check may wish to prevent the check from being deposited or cashed. For example, you might want to stop payment if a check you wrote has been lost or if merchandise you purchased turned out to be defective and you were trying to get the payee to do something about this merchandise before you made payment. If you discovered fraud in a transaction, you might also wish to revoke the transaction by stopping payment on the check. Payment on a check is stopped through a **stop-payment order.** This is an instruction by a depositor to the bank to refuse payment on a particular check when it is presented for payment. The bank is bound by this stop-payment order. If the bank pays the check by mistake over a valid stop-payment order, it is liable to the depositor and must credit the depositor's account for the amount of the check. The bank, however, must receive the order in the proper way and within a reasonable time.

A stop-payment order may be either oral or written. The UCC provides that an oral (usually by phone) stop-payment order is binding on the bank for only fourteen days after the request is made unless the order is confirmed in writing and that a written stop-payment order is effective for six months unless it is renewed in writing (§4-403). Most states have adopted the UCC rule permitting oral stop orders. In some states, only a written stop order is binding, but the bank may honor an oral stop order if it wishes to do so. The most important requirement is that the order be given to a bank as soon as possible after the need for it arises.

> You made out a check payable to "Cash" and put the check in your wallet. While shopping you lost your wallet. You could request your bank to stop payment on the check. The bank is obligated to do so if you notify them promptly. ■

OBLIGATIONS OF A DEPOSITOR

If you have a checking account with a bank, you have certain obligations to that bank. First, as a depositor you have the obligation to keep enough money in your checking account to cover the checks you write. Writing checks without enough money in an account could lead to accusations of writing bad checks. A **bad check** is one written by a drawer who knows there is not enough money in the checking account to cover it. The drawer knows that the drawee bank will refuse payment.

Writing a bad check is a criminal act that could lead to the arrest of the drawer. Before starting criminal proceedings for passing a bad check, however, the bank generally must notify the drawer to place funds in the account to cover any bad checks. Under the statutes of many states the law presumes that if the drawer does not deposit these funds within a specified time, this is evidence of an intent to defraud the holder. A drawer who writes a check that a bank dishonors for lack of funds remains liable to the holder.

The depositor's second obligation is to examine the monthly statement of bank transactions and to advise the bank promptly of any mistakes.

A third obligation of a depositor is to report check forgeries and check alterations to his or her bank within a reasonable time after they are discovered or should have been discovered.

SPECIAL TYPES OF CHECKS

There are special types of checks that perform different functions. These include certified checks, money orders, cashier's checks, and traveler's checks.

Certified Checks

Payment of a regular check depends on the availability of funds on deposit in the drawer's account. A **certified check** is a personal check that a bank guarantees to pay. In effect, the bank guarantees that there is enough money in the drawer's account to cover the check and promises to pay (honor) the check any time after it is issued (see Figure 22.1). A certified check is considered to be as dependable as cash. Certification is accomplished by either the drawer, the payee, or a subsequent holder taking the personal check to the bank on which the check is drawn. If the drawer's account has sufficient funds to cover payment, those funds are set aside for payment of the check and the check is then marked "Certified."

■ Bak (payee) received a check for $100 from Abba (drawer) that was certified by Abba's bank. A few days later Bak presented the check for payment at Abba's bank. The bank, however, would not cash it, claiming Abba had closed her account. Since the check had been certified, Abba's bank was obligated to honor it. ■

Figure 22.1 **Certified Check**

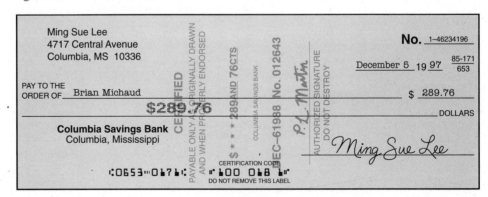

A certified check is commonly used in important commercial and personal transactions, such as a down payment on the purchase of a business or a home. In these cases, large sums of money are involved, and the seller wants to be certain that the buyer's check is good.

If a drawer has a check certified, the drawer is still secondarily liable for payment of the check if for some reason the certifying bank cannot or does not honor the check when it is presented for payment. If the payee or a subsequent holder has the check certified, the bank becomes the only party liable for payment and the drawer and any indorsers prior to certification are completely discharged (released from liability).

Payment of a certified check cannot be stopped. A certified check becomes a promise to pay by the bank and not by the depositor. The drawer of a certified check has no legal right to force a bank to stop payment on a certified check.

Money Orders

A **money order** is a draft issued by a bank, a private company, or the U.S. Postal Service that is used to transfer funds to a named payee. A *bank money order* is a check even though it bears the words "money order." Money orders are often used by persons who do not have checking accounts or who wish to send a payment by mail and do not wish to send a check (see Figure 22.2). Money orders may be purchased in various amounts, although there is usually a maximum amount.

Cashier's Checks

A **cashier's check** (sometimes called a bank check) is a check that a bank draws on its own funds, payable to a certain party (see Figure 22.3). As with

Figure 22.2 **Money Order**

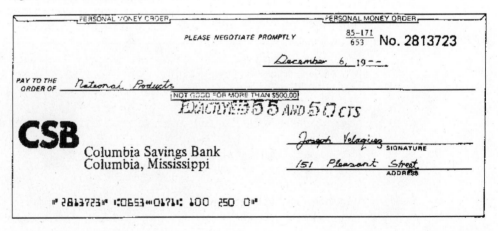

Figure 22.3

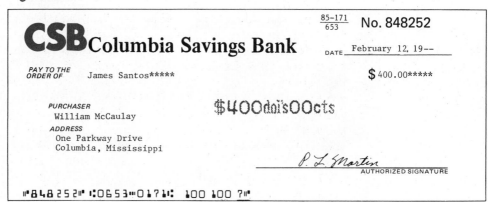

CSBColumbia Savings Bank

$\frac{85-171}{653}$ No. 848252

DATE February 12, 19--

PAY TO THE
ORDER OF James Santos*****

$ 400.00*****

PURCHASER
William McCaulay

$400dols00cts

ADDRESS
One Parkway Drive
Columbia, Mississippi

P. L. Martin
AUTHORIZED SIGNATURE

⑆848252⑈ ⑆0653⑈017⑉ 100 100 7⑈

Figure 22.3 **Cashier's Check**

a certified check, the bank promises to pay the amount of the check to the holder. Unlike a certified check, a cashier's check is drawn on the bank's funds.

In practice, a person who wants a cashier's check pays the issuing bank the amount of the check, and the bank issues its own check. A cashier's check, like a money order, is used when a person either does not have a checking account or does not want to go through the procedure of having a check certified. In fact, cashier's checks are used more often, primarily because many banks no longer certify checks.

Traveler's Checks

A **traveler's check** is a popular type of cashier's check issued by banks and private companies (see Figure 22.4). It is used primarily by tourists who want a safe method of carrying funds while traveling. A traveler's check differs from a cashier's check in two ways: it is purchased in denominations such as $20, $50, and $100, and it is issued with the name of the payee omitted.

Purchasing traveler's checks is a simple matter. The buyer pays for the checks in the requested denominations and pays a service charge to the issuing bank. When the checks are issued, the traveler writes her or his name on each check in the presence of the person issuing the check. When the check is used to pay for goods or services, the traveler signs the check a second time—in the presence of the person receiving the check. At this point the check becomes either bearer paper or order paper (by inserting the name of a payee).

Traveler's checks have two primary advantages. They are readily accepted all over the world. In addition, the traveler can recover the value of the checks quickly if they are lost or stolen, provided notice of the theft or

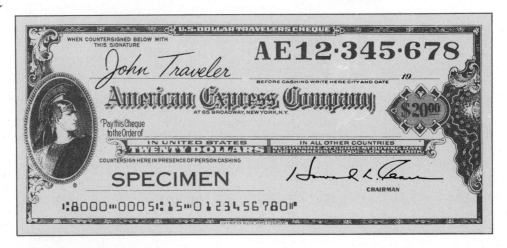

Figure 22.4 **Traveler's Check**

loss is given to the issuing company as soon as possible. Whether checks are lost or stolen, the traveler is protected even if her or his signature is forged and the checks are cashed.

BANK'S LIABILITY FOR WRONGFUL PAYMENT OF A CHECK

A bank's liability to the drawer is affected by the following circumstances: (1) alteration of a check, (2) forgery of the drawer's signature, (3) forgery of an indorsement, (4) missing indorsement, and (5) death of the depositor (drawer).

Alteration of a Check

If a bank pays a check that has been materially altered, the bank is liable to the drawer for the amount of the alteration. A material alteration usually involves raising the amount—both the figures and the words—on the face of the check. A bank is held responsible for failing to detect the alteration because it has both the opportunity and the expertise to examine the check before honoring it. However, the bank may charge the drawer's account for the original amount of the check. In addition, the bank may sue the person to whom the amount on the altered check was paid.

> Given made out a check payable to Davis for $42. Before cashing the check, Davis raised the amount to $420. The bank paid Davis the $420 and charged this amount to Given's account. Given can recover $378, the amount of the alteration, from the bank. ∎

There are some exceptions to the rule regarding a bank's responsibility for an altered check. A drawer whose negligence contributes to the alteration may not be able to hold the bank responsible. For example, leaving blank spaces on a check so that the amount can be raised easily may relieve a bank from liability. This is especially true if the bank takes reasonable precautions to examine checks before honoring them. Another exception is a failure by the drawer to notify a bank of alterations within one year from the time the altered, canceled check is returned to the depositor. Failure to give notice within this time may relieve a bank from liability for paying an altered check, even though the bank was negligent.

Forgery of Drawer's Signature

A bank is liable to a drawer-depositor if it pays a **forged check**—one in which the drawer's signature is made without authorization. The bank must return to the drawer's account any money paid out as the result of the forgery. The bank has a duty to pay out funds according to the drawer's order. A check with a forged signature is not prepared and paid according to that order; therefore, a forged signature on a check has no legal effect as the signature of a drawer. The drawer must report the forgery within one year after the canceled check has been returned. In reality, however, the drawer must act promptly, which means within a reasonable time. It makes no difference whether the bank was or was not negligent. A bank has the drawer's signature on file and assumes the burden of knowing that signature. (As noted earlier in the chapter, a bank requires a signature from each customer who opens a checking account.)

> Lester forged Cataldo's name on a $100 check payable to herself. She then indorsed the check for value to Matties, who was unaware of the forgery. Matties presented the check to Cataldo's bank and received payment. Cataldo discovered the forgery when he received his next bank statement and immediately notified his bank. ■

In this example the bank must restore the $100 to Cataldo's account. The bank, however, cannot collect from Matties, who took the check in good faith and for value. By paying the check, the bank admits the genuineness of the drawer's signature. The bank is considered to have greater knowledge and experience than an indorser in detecting forgeries and is therefore liable for the loss.

As with the alteration of a check, a drawer whose negligence contributes to a forgery may not be able to collect from the bank. An example of such negligence would be a drawer who signs checks in different ways from that shown on the bank's signature card. Such practices make it much harder for a bank to detect a forgery. Another example of negligence is the failure of a business owner to keep a check writer (used to sign checks) or signature stamp in a safe place so that unauthorized people do not have access to it. Still another example is the depositor's failure to examine his or her monthly statement of account and canceled checks returned by the bank to discover if any entries on the statement seem out of line or if any of the signatures on the checks are forgeries.

Forgery of an Indorsement

A bank is liable for paying a check on which the payee's indorsement or the indorsement of a subsequent holder has been forged. The forgery must be reported within three years from the time the canceled check with the forged indorsement is returned to the depositor. The bank is liable to the drawer for paying the check but may in turn recover from the holder who presented the check to the bank.

A forged indorsement on bearer paper has no effect on the validity of the paper. Bearer paper is negotiable by delivery alone and an indorsement is not required.

If the name of a fictitious payee is put on a check and that name is then indorsed, the bank is not liable. In this situation, it is presumed that the drawer has been negligent. Thus, the drawee bank will not be responsible as long as it used reasonable care in accepting and cashing the check.

■ At a Chamber of Commerce dinner, Savage introduced herself to Rickles as "Dr. Vera Ralston," a noted authority on cancer. She claimed to be raising money for the Cancer Foundation. Rickles donated $1,000 by writing a check payable to the order of "Dr. Ralston." Savage indorsed the check as "Dr. Ralston" and cashed it at the Taylor National Bank. The bank is not liable to Rickles. ■

Missing Indorsement

A bank may be liable for any loss that results from its cashing a check that lacks an indorsement. Failure to indorse a check is considered improper presentment, and the person presenting the check is not a holder.

■ Genovese, a teacher, lost his paycheck. A finder presented the check for payment to the bank on which the check was drawn. A new teller at the bank cashed the check without an indorsement. The bank is liable for improperly paying the check. ■

Death of the Depositor

A depositor (drawer) may deposit checks in or draw checks on his or her account shortly before death. A check is an order to pay, and death revokes that order. However, a bank may not be notified immediately of the drawer's death. UCC §4-405 protects banks in this situation by providing that a bank may pay or certify checks until it has knowledge of the drawer's death and has had reasonable time to act. Even with knowledge of the death, the bank may continue to pay or certify checks drawn against the account for a period of ten days after the date of the drawer's death. This rule allows holders of checks issued shortly before death to cash them without having to file a claim against the deceased drawer's estate. Filing a claim, which in effect is a mere formality, could be burdensome on the bank. Without this provision, banks would constantly be required to check and see if their depositors are still living.

> ■ On August 8 Marin gave Sikes a personal check for $500 drawn on the Midland Bank. Marin was killed in an accident on August 9. On August 10 Midland Bank cashed the check for Sikes, not knowing of Marin's death. Even though the bank was unaware of Marin's death, it had the authority to honor the check. ■

THE COLLECTION PROCESS

Generally, the check collection process begins when a person deposits a check with his or her bank. A typical collection process is shown in Figure 22.5. Calvin Turner of Rochester, New York, issues a check to Ace Hardware Store (the payee-holder) of Cleveland, Ohio, in payment for an electric drill he purchased while visiting his parents. At this point, Ace Hardware, if it wished, could present the check to Central Trust of Rochester, New York (Turner's bank), for payment. This is not only an impractical but also an unnecessary step, because the instrument is easily transferable. As a holder of the check, Ace Hardware can negotiate it. What typically happens is that Ace Hardware will deposit the check in its own bank (in this case, Chase Manhattan of Cleveland, Ohio) and let this bank, as agent for Ace Hardware, collect the amount of the check.

Chase Manhattan, called a depositary bank (meaning that it is the first bank to which the check is transferred for collection), will provisionally (temporarily) credit the account of the payee (Ace Hardware). Chase Manhattan will forward Turner's check to a series of intermediate banks, usually Federal Reserve Banks, that collect checks for other banks. Each intermediate bank provisionally credits the account of the prior bank. (As a "collecting bank"—a sub-agent—it must forward the check to the next bank no later than midnight of the banking day following the day of receipt.) The check will eventually reach Central Trust, Turner's bank.

When Turner's check reaches Central Trust, upon which it was drawn, the bank debits (charges) Turner's (the drawer's) account (provided there is enough money to cover the check). Central Trust then authorizes a Federal Reserve Bank to credit the amount of the check to Chase Manhattan's account in Cleveland, Ohio, which in turn credits Ace Hardware's account. When the check is paid (honored), that is the end of the transaction. If the check is not paid (dishonored, in this case by Central Trust), each bank in the collection process revokes the provisional credit it gave, and the unpaid check is returned to the depositor (in this case Ace Hardware).

Each bank has an obligation to use ordinary care in performing its collection operations. This involves forwarding checks and sending out required notices correctly and within the time period mentioned above. Failure of a bank to use ordinary care in a collection process may subject it to liability for any losses suffered.

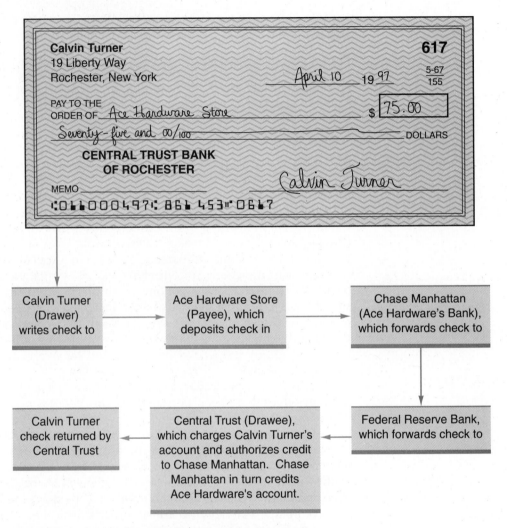

Figure 22.5 **How a Check Is Processed for Payment**

CHECK PROCESSING

In 1987, Congress passed the Expedited Funds Availability Act to improve check-processing procedures. One purpose of the act was to reduce the "float period"—the period between the time that a customer deposits a check and the time that the bank makes available to the depositor the funds represented by the check. Until this law was passed, consumer groups charged that Americans were losing millions of dollars annually because banks were freezing funds for undue amounts of time. They were making customers wait until the check had been honored by the payor bank. This delay sometimes took two weeks, even though 99 percent of the time the banks were getting credit for the money within two days.

The Expedited Funds Availability Act now limits the number of days banks can place holds on checks that customers deposit in their accounts. It also requires banks to disclose to depositors their policy as to when funds deposited are available for their use. Individual banks may set their own "float" time as long as they stay within the guidelines set by the federal law. In broad terms, the law requires that all local checks of less than $5,000 be cleared by the bank by the second business day after the banking day of deposit. (Every day except Saturday, Sunday, and a federal holiday is a business day.) A *local check* is one deposited in a bank located in the same metropolitan area or within the same Federal Reserve check-processing region as the payor-drawee bank. Nonlocal checks of less than $5,000 must be available no later than the fifth business day after the banking day of deposit. A *nonlocal* check is one deposited in a bank located in a different Federal Reserve check-processing region than the payor-drawee bank.

The law allows funds you deposit by check to be delayed for a longer ("reasonable") period beyond those stated above if (1) you deposit checks totaling more than $5,000, (2) you have overdrawn your account repeatedly, or (3) the bank believes that a check you deposit will not be paid. An extension of up to four business days is considered a reasonable period. The bank has the burden of proving that any longer extension is reasonable.

ELECTRONIC BANKING

Today we are living in a virtually "cashless" society. For a host of reasons, including crime, cash has lost much of its utility as a medium of exchange. Most money obligations are now settled by the use of checks. Advanced technology has brought about an electronic revolution, which in turn may eventually lead to a "checkless" society. A system of electronic transfers called **electronic funds transfer system** (EFTS), with the computer at the heart of the system, allows money to be transferred electronically from your bank account to that of a creditor or into the account of a store where you made a purchase. In many cities you can even buy groceries via EFTS. You stop at a grocery store and buy groceries costing $100. You hand the clerk a plastic card (called a debit card) with a secret code number. The clerk inserts the card into a device linked to your bank's computer. The computer is then given instructions to deduct the amount of your purchases from your bank account and to add that amount to the store's bank account. The entire process takes only a few minutes. Because the transaction took place at the "point of sale," it is referred to as a POS transaction. With such a system, no money or checks change hands. POS systems have already sprung up in several cities around the country, and they offer the following advantages: consumers can carry less cash; check-out time is quicker, especially when compared with the time it takes to have a check approved; and the "float" time (the time between writing a check and having the check clear at the bank) is eliminated.

Many banks now have the equipment to handle some other electronic transactions. At automated teller machines (ATMs), people can receive "instant cash" from their checking or savings account by inserting a plastic identification card into an electronic terminal and entering a personal identification number (PIN). People can also deposit to an account, transfer funds between savings and checking accounts, pay credit card charges and utility bills, and even make mortgage payments. These ATMs are conveniently located in shopping centers, at grocery stores, at branch banks, and at other key locations in large cities. Pay-by-phone—another type of electronic transaction—permits customers to pay bills by calling their bank and requesting that funds be transferred from checking to savings (or vice versa) or that money be transferred from either a savings or checking account to a designated third party, such as a department store.

Electronic transfers eliminate a feature of the current system people have grown used to: the recordkeeping advantages of checks. The canceled check is a convenient and universally recognized proof of payment.

Some problems have arisen with the advent of the EFTS. One is the opportunity for dishonest individuals to use other people's lost or stolen plastic cards in an unauthorized manner. Such usage could create problems for bank customers who are liable to the bank in varying degrees for these lost or stolen cards.

Legal questions have also been raised concerning EFTS. For example, a bank customer cannot initiate a stop-payment order because there is no check. This question and others will have to be solved if EFTS is to be entirely effective.

Summary of Important Legal Concepts

A check is the most frequently used negotiable instrument for doing business in this country. Its use is governed by the UCC. A debtor-creditor relationship exists between a bank and its depositor. After a depositor puts money in a bank, the bank owes that sum to the depositor and promises to pay the money either to the depositor or to someone else at the depositor's order. The bank is always obligated to honor the depositor's checks if there are sufficient funds to cover them and if the check is not stale—that is, more than six months old. If a bank wrongfully dishonors a check, it is liable in damages to the depositor. A drawer may stop payment on his or her check by giving the bank a stop-payment order either orally or in writing. If the bank disobeys a stop-payment order and pays the instrument, it is liable to the drawer for any loss resulting from its failure to ob-

serve the order. Depositors have obligations to keep enough money in their checking accounts to cover checks written; to examine the monthly bank statement they receive and promptly advise the bank of any mistakes; to report check forgeries and alterations to the bank; and, above all, not to write a bad check—that is, one written when there is an insufficient amount of money in the checking account to cover it.

There are special types of checks that perform different functions. These include certified checks, money orders, cashier's checks, and traveler's checks.

The bank may not charge the depositor's account where there is an alteration, a forgery, or a missing indorsement—assuming of course, that the drawer was not negligent in the transaction. A bank may pay a check after the death of a drawer until it receives notice of the death or for ten days after the drawer's death.

Congress passed the Expedited Funds Availability Act in 1987 to improve check-processing procedures. One purpose of the act was to reduce the "float period," the period between the time that a customer deposits a check and the time that the bank makes the funds represented by the check available to the depositor. Until this law was passed, banks were freezing checking account funds for undue amounts of time.

The electronic funds transfer system (EFTS) allows money to be transferred electronically from the accounts of depositors to accounts of creditors or stores where the depositors have made purchases.

Key Legal Terms to Know

Match the terms with the definitions that follow.

bad check
cashier's check
certified check
electronic funds transfer system
forged check
money order
overdraft
postdated check
stale check
stop-payment order
traveler's check

1. A check used primarily by travelers; its main feature is security against loss or theft
2. A personal check, payment which is guaranteed by a bank
3. A check for which there is not enough money in an account to cover the amount of the check
4. A check on which the drawer's signature is made without authorization
5. A check that is dated after its actual date of issue
6. An order to a bank to refuse payment of a check
7. A check drawn by a bank on its own funds
8. A check written by a drawer without sufficient funds on deposit to pay the check but that will be paid by the bank
9. A type of commercial paper that may be purchased from any post office, from banks, or from private companies

10. A system allowing depositors to transfer money from their accounts to accounts of creditors and stores where they have made purchases
11. A check that is more than six months old

Questions and Problems to Discuss

1. What is a bank's liability for payment of an altered or forged check?
2. Saxon died April 12. His sister-in-law immediately filed a claim against Saxon's estate for $500, the amount of a check issued to her on August 18 (eight months earlier) by Saxon for her services as an accountant. Liability was denied by the person in charge of Saxon's estate, who claimed that, since the check was more than six months old, it was void. Does a check become void because the payee failed to cash it within a six-month period?
3. Davidson, who owed Perry $150, gave her a personal check as a payment. Perry took the check to Davidson's bank and had it certified. Perry then negotiated the check to Severt, to whom she owed $150. When Severt presented the check to Davidson's bank, the bank refused to pay. Severt then demanded payment from Davidson. Is Davidson liable for payment of the check?
4. Howard drew a check on City Bank made payable to Goldberg's Catalog House for some stereo equipment. Since Goldberg's would not accept personal checks, Howard had the check certified. When Goldberg's presented the check at Howard's bank, the bank refused payment, claiming that the account had a zero balance. Is the bank wrong in refusing to pay?
5. A burglar entered Bowie's house and stole, among other things, some blank checks from a checkbook. Bowie did not realize that the checks were missing. When Bowie received her bank statement, she found a canceled check for $50 on which her signature had been forged. She immediately notified her bank. Will the bank be liable to Bowie?
6. Simpson, who had $1,500 in his account at Banker's Trust, wrote a $500 check payable to Hanson. When Hanson presented the check for payment, Banker's Trust refused to honor it, claiming (in error) that there were not sufficient funds in Simpson's account. Simpson was charged with issuing a bad check. The bank later discovered

its error, and the charges against Simpson were dismissed. Can Simpson take any action against the bank?

7. Price wrote a check on the Carthage National Bank for $250 payable to Lotus. When Lotus tried to cash the check, Carthage Bank refused to pay, claiming that Price did not have sufficient funds to cover the check. Can Lotus legally recover from the bank?

8. Whitcomb paid his telephone bill with a personal check. Shortly thereafter, the check was returned to the telephone company marked "Insufficient Funds." The bank then notified Whitcomb to place sufficient funds in his checking account to cover the check for the telephone bill. Whitcomb made no effort to do this. Can the bank file a criminal complaint against Whitcomb?

9. Marcus purchased a one-week package deal to a summer resort area through a travel agency. Since the price had to be paid in advance, Marcus sent the travel agency a certified check for $900 drawn on the Citizens National Bank. The next day he decided to cancel his trip and requested the bank to stop payment on the check. Could Marcus order the bank to stop payment on the certified check?

10. At a book fair on August 15, Lee, an encyclopedia salesperson, talked Tanaka into purchasing a set of encyclopedias for $450. Tanaka gave Lee a check for $450. Later in the day Tanaka changed her mind about purchasing the books and issued an oral stop-payment order to her bank. On September 1 Tanaka went to the bank and signed a written stop-payment order, but the bank had already honored the check on August 31. Tanaka demanded that the bank return the money to her account. Must the bank comply with Tanaka's demand?

11. Martin paid a $100 debt to Adler with a personal check drawn on her account at the Arvac National Bank. Before properly negotiating the check to Chives, Adler raised the amount of the check to $1,100. Chives then cashed the check at the Arvac National Bank, obtaining $1,100. When Martin received her canceled checks and discovered the alteration, she asked the bank to return the $1,000 to her account. If Martin was not negligent, must the bank comply with her request?

12. Payne, an employee of China Tea Company, lost his payroll check on the way to the bank. Ritter found the check, forged Payne's signature on the back, and negotiated the check to Carpentier, who had no knowledge of the forgery. Carpentier cashed the check at the bank on which the check was drawn. Payne had notified the China Tea Company, which in turn notified its bank, of the loss of the check. Is the bank liable to China Tea Company?

Cases to Decide

1. Darwin, who was a partner in both Rancho Village Partners Ltd. and Settlement Ltd., had full authority to manage the funds of both partnerships. He indorsed a $300,000 money order payable to Rancho Village Partners with the restrictive indorsement "Deposit to the account of Rancho Village Partners Ltd. Only." Darwin then desposited the money order in the bank account of Settlement Ltd., the other partnership. The bank teller accepted the deposit in spite of the restrictive indorsement. Shortly thereafter, Darwin illegally withdrew the money from the Settlement Ltd. account. The other Rancho Village partners sued the bank for ignoring the restrictive indorsement and accepting the $300,000 for deposit to the wrong account. Is the bank liable for payment to Rancho Village Partners? (*Rutherford* v. *Darwin*, NM App 622 P2d 245)

2. Tally's personal secretary, who managed his Washington, D.C., law office, swindled him out of $52,825. In seven instances she had signed his name on bank withdrawals from the American Security Bank. As custodian of Tally's bank records, the secretary had avoided detection for over four years. Tally brought action against the American Security Bank to recover the $52,825. Is the bank liable to Tally? (*Tally* v. *American Security Bank*, 355 UCCRS 215, US District Court, DC)

3. Jerman brought several cashier's checks, payable to named payees, from a bank. The checks were cashed with forged indorsements, and Jerman lost her money. She sued the bank that issued and paid the checks. Is the bank liable? (*Jerman* v. *Bank of America National Trust & Savings Assn.*, 87 Cal Rptr 88)

4. Stewart received a check as a payee drawn on the Citizen's Bank. The bank refused to pay the check even though there were sufficient funds in the drawer's account. Stewart sued the bank on the check. Is Stewart entitled to collect from the

Citizens' Bank? (*Stewart* v. *Citizens' and Southern National Bank*, Georgia 138 GA App 209)

5. A certified check for $16 payable to Sam Goody was altered (after it had been certified) to $1,600. The check was then used to pay for merchandise costing $1,600 that had been ordered from Goody. The drawee bank refused to honor the check because of the alteration. Is the bank liable to Goody for the $1,600? (*Sam Goody, Inc.* v. *Franklin National Bank of Long Island*, New York 57 Misc 2d 193)

6. Cook sold and delivered traveler's checks for $25,000 to Mr. and Mrs. Kochton. Mr. Kochton signed half the checks, but Mrs. Kochton failed to do so. The checks were stolen while she and her husband were on a trip to Tahiti. Ashford, who lived in Tahiti, bought the checks from someone who appeared to be an agent of Cook. When Ashford tried to cash the checks, they were dishonored. Who should bear the risk of loss resulting from the theft? (*Ashford* v. *Thomas Cook & Son*, Bankers, Ltd., Hawaii 471 P2d 530)

7. Siniscalchi wrote a check on his account in the Valley Bank of New York and then negotiated the check on to a holder. He placed a stop-payment order on the check with his bank two days after the holder had cashed the check. Siniscalchi, however, was unaware that the check had been cashed. Upon checking its transactions, the Valley Bank discovered that Sinscalchi's check had been cashed and charged his account. Siniscalchi sued the bank, claiming that Valley Bank ignored his stop-payment order. Is the bank liable in damages to Siniscalchi for violating the stop-payment order? (*Siniscalchi* v. *Valley Bank of New York* 359 NYS 2d 173)

8. Kendall Yacht Corporation was running into financial problems. Its owners, Lawrence and Linda Kendall, obtained permission from its bank, United California, with which it had corporate accounts, to write overdrafts from this account temporarily. Because the account became so badly overdrawn, the bank dishonored a number of their checks. The Kendalls then brought suit, charging that the bank's wrongful dishonor of the checks damaged their reputation. They offered proof that several civil and criminal proceedings had been brought against them for writing checks against insufficient funds. Do the Kendalls have a legitimate cause of action against United California Bank? (*Kendall Yacht Corporation* v. *United California Bank* 50 Cal App 3d 949)

The Case of the Forged Checks

Helen Calder had a business checking account at the Globe National Bank. She kept a supply of blank checks in her desk drawer at her office, together with the signature stamp that she used to sign each check. She usually left her drawer, as well as the door to her office, unlocked.

One day, an employee stole some checks out of the drawer, used Calder's stamp to sign the checks, and wrote in his name as the payee. The employee then cashed the checks at Argus Bank. Argus paid the checks and forwarded them to Globe National Bank for collection. Globe paid the checks and charged Calder's account. Calder didn't know that the checks had been stolen until she received her monthly bank statement. She immediately notified the bank and then brought suit to prevent Globe from charging her account.

The Trial

During the trial, Calder testified that it was her custom to keep both her desk drawer and the door to her office unlocked. She kept the checks in the office desk because it was convenient, since she used them quite often. She also testified that she used the signature stamp on all checks and did so with the bank's approval. Calder stated that she rarely examined her blank checks and didn't notify the bank until three weeks after the incident because she had not yet received her monthly statement.

The Arguments at Trial

Calder's attorneys argued that the bank was absolutely liable for paying a check with a forged signa-
ture, regardless of whether Calder was negligent and regardless of whether the bank was negligent. They further argued that the use of the signature stamp made no difference in the circumstances, since a signature stamp is an acceptable way to sign checks.

The bank's attorneys argued that the bank should not be held liable because of Calder's negligence. They claimed that Calder should not have kept blank checks and the signature stamp in an open drawer that was accessible to all sorts of people. They also argued that there is no way that the bank can know that the signature is forged when a signature stamp is used.

Questions to Discuss

1. Based upon your reading of the text, what law applies in this situation?
2. Who do you feel has the stronger argument, Calder or Globe National Bank?
3. If you were the judge or jury deciding this case, for whom would you decide? Why?
4. What do you think the law should be when a bank pays a check on which the drawer's signature has been forged?
5. What could Calder have done to prevent this situation? What could the bank have done to avoid the situation?

PART V

AGENCY, EMPLOYMENT, AND LABOR LAW

After studying Part V,
you should be able to

1 Name the federal and state laws that guarantee rights and benefits to employees and state what these rights and benefits are.

2 Point out the distinguishing features between the employer-employee and principal-agent relationships.

3 Describe the ways in which employer-employee and principal-agent relationships may be created.

4 List the duties of an employer or principal and an employee or agent within the relationship.

5 Explain the liability of the employer or principal and the employee or agent within the relationship.

6 Name the ways in which employer-employee and principal-agent relationships may be terminated.

Chapter 23

Employer-Employee Relationship

CHAPTER PREVIEW

The employer-employee relationship is one of the most common legal relationships. This chapter begins with a description of how the relationship is created and how it is affected by labor-management relations when there is a labor union present.

As parties to an employment agreement, employers and employees both have certain rights and obligations. The chapter discusses the duties that each has to the other and what each may expect from the other. The liability of an employer for the torts of an employee is also described.

There is a great deal of legislation, on both the state and federal levels, that affects relations between employers and employees. The chapter describes and discusses some of the more important federal and state statutes, including those dealing with wages and hours, discrimination in employment, safety and health, and provision for the retirement and disability compensation of employees.

The chapter ends with a discussion of the change in the way the courts have treated the termination of the employer-employee relationship. It describes the many circumstances under which courts have been changing the traditional rule that an employer may terminate the employment of an employee at any time and regardless of cause.

THE EMPLOYMENT PROCESS

An employer-employee relationship exists when one person, the **employee,** is hired to work, usually under the direction and control of another person called the **employer.**

The employment process generally begins with the completion of an employment application form. Most application forms ask for such basic information as your name, address, Social Security number, previous employment history, education, school activities, and salary or wages expected. Most forms also ask for personal references or for the names of people who can provide background data on you.

The Civil Rights Act, which was passed in 1964, prohibits hiring practices that discriminate against applicants because of sex, race, religion, or nationality. Questions relating to these factors may not be asked on the application form. Obviously, since these questions cannot be asked, an employer cannot take these factors into consideration when hiring you. For example, if a French restaurant is hiring a chef, a female applying for the job may not be turned down simply because the employer feels that chefs are traditionally male or because the employer considers female chefs less qualified than male chefs. Of course, if the employer can show that a specific female applicant is not as well qualified as a male applicant, then it is not a violation of the Civil Rights Act to hire the male.

CREATION OF THE EMPLOYER-EMPLOYEE RELATIONSHIP

The employer-employee relationship is most often created by contract, either orally or in writing. However, if the contract is to last for more than one year from the date it is made, it must be in writing to satisfy a state's statute of frauds.

> Mendelson, a computer specialist, entered into a contract to work for Computer Net for a period of two years. This two-year contract between Computer Net and Mendelson must be in writing to be enforceable. ■

The employer and the employee can include any terms they desire in the contract so long as the terms are not unlawful. Employment contracts for top-level positions, such as a president of a company, generally are in writing. These contracts include such terms as the length of time the contract will run, the amount of pay, fringe benefits, and a brief description of the position. Terms that are not discussed or not included as part of a written contract are implied or assumed to exist because of state and federal regulations applying to the employer-employee relationship.

RIGHTS OF EMPLOYERS

Employers and employees have certain expectations of each other in their working relationship. Some of these expectations are determined by the contract of employment, some are implied by law, but most are imposed by federal and state statutes.

Employers have the right to expect that employees who have stated that they have certain skills actually have those skills. Employers also have the right to expect certain performance levels from their employees. That is, employees are expected to achieve a reasonable amount of work. In addition, employers have the legal right to tell employees not only what tasks are to be performed but also how those tasks are to be performed.

An employee owes an employer the obligation not to reveal trade secrets or confidential information learned on the job. Whether a discovery or invention of the employee belongs to the employee or the employer depends on the nature of the invention, the terms of any agreement between them relating to inventions, and whether the employee was hired to work on certain processes leading to inventions.

> You were employed in the personnel office of the Alliance Printing Company. A friend, who owned a competing printing business, asked you to obtain a list of Alliance's customers. Your friend intended to use this list to try to take customers away from Alliance. If you gave the list to your friend and your employer discovered what you had done, you could not only be fired but could also be held liable for any damages caused by your disloyal act. ■

Employees have an implied agreement to work exclusively for the employer during the hours of employment. They cannot, for example, do personal tasks or carry on the activities of a private business venture on company time. Employees are expected to follow reasonable instructions and to abide by company rules. An employee who fails to follow instructions can be fired.

> ■ You were hired as a stock clerk in the warehouse of a large department store. Your supervisor called you into her office and reminded you that you had been coming in late for work every day. You also took more time away from your job than the normal fifteen-minute breaks allowed each morning and afternoon. If you refuse to arrive at work on time and continue taking long breaks, you could be fired. ■

RIGHTS OF EMPLOYEES

The rights of an employee are regulated to a great extent by legislation, discussed in detail later in this chapter. However, an employer had certain obligations to employees in common law that still exist today, though many of them have been enacted into statute law.

Employees hired by a company must be paid for the work that they do. If the employee belongs to a union, wages may be controlled by a collective bargaining agreement with workers who are in the same classification and who have the same skills and receive similar wages. Most companies offer varying levels of **fringe benefits,** that is, nonwage extras that are paid for by the company. Examples of fringe benefits include life insurance, a pension plan or retirement plan, health and dental insurance, and paid sick days and vacations. Employees have the right to receive the same fringe benefits as others in their job classification.

An employee has the right to expect a reasonably safe workplace and safe tools and appliances. What is considered "reasonably safe" depends on the type of industry, the type of job being performed, and other similar factors. An employer may be held liable to an employee for failure to exercise care if that failure causes injury to the employee.

Whenever hazardous work is involved, an employee has the right to expect that the employer will provide a sufficient number of skilled workers to perform the job. This right includes a duty on the part of the employer to provide sufficient explanations to prevent injury resulting from lack of instruction.

Access to Personnel Records

Employers keep many records regarding their employees. Some—such as payroll records, tax information, pension records, and information regarding illness and injury—are required by law. Some—such as reference and credit checks, job performance reports, and disciplinary action records—are kept for internal purposes.

All of these records are important from the point of view of both employers and employees. An employer who fails to keep required information may be penalized for that failure. An employer who keeps information that is inaccurate or harmful to an employee may face legal action by the employee, since an employee's right to privacy and to present and future employment may be seriously affected by incomplete, inaccurate, or harmful information in his or her personnel record.

Four basic questions govern an employee's right to privacy:

1. What information may an employer maintain about an employee?
2. When does an employee have the right to examine his or her personnel records?
3. In addition to the employee, who else may examine an employee's personnel records?
4. When is an employer required to correct inaccurate information or delete harmful information?

In general, in addition to information that must be maintained by law, an employer should keep only the information about an employee that relates to his or her ability to perform a job or to actual job performance.

Most states have laws covering an employee's right to inspect his or her personnel records and the procedures to be followed in such cases. Except for reference letters (the disclosure of which might violate the privacy of the writer) and information related to a criminal investigation, an employee may examine all other information in a personnel file.

Most state laws regulate procedures to be followed in examining a personnel file. These laws cover the method of making a discovery request, the place and time of the examination, where and when it is held, and the persons who may or must be present when the examination occurs.

In most cases, access to personnel records by someone other than the employee is determined by the employer and not by state law. Because of potential lawsuits for invasion of privacy, libel, or slander, most employers severely restrict access to personnel records and maintain strict security in keeping such records confidential. Access to medical records is specifically and severely restricted by the Americans with Disabilities Act, which regulates how medical records must be maintained and who has access to them.

Approximately eleven states have laws permitting an employee to request the removal or correction of inaccurate information from a personnel file or the insertion in the file of an explanation by the employee of any disagreement with the data. In other states, correction or removal of inaccurate data is at the employer's discretion.

Labor-Management Relations

For many employees, the employer-employee relationship is affected by a **labor union,** an organization of employees formed to promote the welfare of its members. Union members generally select leaders to negotiate a contract with the company for which the members work. The contract between the employer and the union is arrived at through a series of discussions known as

collective bargaining. The resulting contract is called a **collective bargaining agreement.**

In the collective bargaining process, union leaders, usually led by a chief negotiator, meet and discuss issues with representatives of the employer. Issues that may be discussed include working conditions, wages, hours to be worked, fringe benefits, retirement benefits, job security, promotion and layoff procedures, a grievance procedure for what are considered violations of the contract, and any other concerns management and union members may have. When agreement is reached by both sides, the union leaders must get approval of the contract from the union members they represent. If the members vote to approve the contract, a written contract is prepared, incorporating all the points on which both sides have agreed. Both the employer and the union are governed by this contract for the term of the contract.

If the union members do not approve the contract, the union leaders and company representatives must go through the collective bargaining process again in another attempt to reach an agreement the union members will accept.

■ Sweeney was hired as a machinist for the R&R Tool Company. All employees of the company were covered by a union contract, which outlined specific duties for each job classification in the company. One day Sweeney's immediate supervisor ordered him to help unload some heavy crates from a truck. He refused, because this work was not in his job classification. The supervisor attempted to fire Sweeney, but because Sweeney was not required to perform tasks not included in his job classification (as outlined in the collective bargaining agreement), he could not legally be fired. ■

TERMINATING THE EMPLOYER-EMPLOYEE RELATIONSHIP

If an employment contract states a specific term for employment, the contract is terminated either at the end of the term or upon the occurrence of a specific event, such as improper conduct. However, if the employment contract (oral or written) does not state how long the agreement is to last, the traditional view is that in such circumstances, employment is at will. **Employment at will** means that in the absence of a contract, or collective bargaining agreement, the employer or employee may terminate the relationship at any time for any reason whatsoever.

■ You were hired, on an oral agreement, by the manager of a fast-food restaurant at the minimum hourly wage. After three months, the manager discharged you from your job because the owner ordered a cutback in personnel. The owner has the legal right to discharge you and not be liable for damages. ■

The termination of an employment contract at will by an employer has occasionally resulted in injustice and hardship. Consequently, the at-will doctrine is gradually being eroded and modified in most states. The courts and state legislatures are accomplishing this by laws and decisions providing exceptions to the at-will rule, indicating a growing acceptance of the requirement that an employee's discharge must be justifiable.

Some of the best-recognized exceptions to the at-will rule are (1) discharges in violation of law, (2) any discharge of an employee that goes against some well-defined public policy, (3) a discharge of an employee when there is an implied contract for a period of time, and (4) discharges that violate stated employee policies and practices.

Termination in Violation of Law

Certain laws prohibit discharging an employee even if the employee is considered "at will." The Civil Rights Act of 1964, Title VII (see page 352) prohibits discharge of an employee because of race, color, gender, age, religion, marital status, national origin, and handicap. Under the Occupational Safety and Health Act (see page 356), an employee may not be discharged for complaining that an employer has violated the health and safety requirements of the act. The Fair Labor Standards Act prohibits discharging an employee who complains that an employer has violated the wage and hour provisions of the act.

Termination That Goes Against a Well-Defined Public Policy

Many state legislatures have enacted laws known as **whistle-blower laws,** which prevent an employer from firing an employee if the sole reason for termination was that the employee filed a worker's compensation claim or reported a labor law violation by the employer. Some of the statutes also prohibit firing an employee solely because the employee reports violations that may endanger the welfare of the employees or the public. A number of courts have approved of exceptions to the at-will rule even in the absence of specific statutes.

Most states prohibit an employer from firing an employee who refuses to perform an act that is illegal or violates public policy.

Termination Prohibited Based on an Implied Contract Term

Many courts have attempted to find an implied duration of an employment term even though such a term is not specifically stated in an employment contract. Rather than looking at any one fact to conclude that the contract was for a specific time, the courts will examine many factors. One of these is the circumstances in which a person was hired, such as the fact that the employee always served for a specific period of time in prior jobs. Another is the type of work performed by the employee—the more executive the position, the more a court is inclined to imply a specific duration for the employment.

The factor most often considered by the courts in determining whether the duration of an employment term may be implied is whether the employee's pay is stated in terms of a specific time period. Although the majority of courts do not follow the rule, a minority of courts have held that an employment contract that states the employee's compensation in terms of a specific period of time creates a presumption that the employee was hired for a specific period of time. Under this rule, the statement that an employee's salary is $10 per hour would not create any such presumption. However, a statement that the employee's salary is $20,800.00 per year (based on $10 per hour for a 40-hour week) would create such a presumption in those states in which the courts follow the minority view.

Discharge Affected by Employee Policies and Practices

Although many employees have neither written nor oral contracts, the companies for which they work often have employee policies and practices that are distributed to them in written form. Many of these practices and policies outline the steps that management must take before firing an employee.

In attempting to soften the results of the employment-at-will doctrine, courts in a number of states are holding that the right of an employer to fire an employee at will is restricted because of the existence of company employment policies outlining the procedures that must be followed before an employee can be fired. The basis for this reasoning is that such policies imply a contract between the employer and the employee regarding termination, even though there was no specific agreement to this effect. Of course, courts must still consider such factors as whether the policies were in existence when the employee was hired, whether the employee knew of these policies, and whether the employer had the right to change the policies at any time.

■ Lerner was hired to run a riveting machine by Acme Company on an hourly basis. Two months after she was hired, Acme distributed a book to all employees containing the company's personnel practices, one of which dealt with firing procedures. Lerner is entitled to the benefit of these procedures if she is fired. ■

Regardless of whether the employment-at-will doctrine applies in a specific state, there is no doubt that an employer who can show good cause can discharge an employee and not be liable for breach of contract.

■ Thompson signed a one-year contract as an accounting instructor at a local community college. Shortly after Thompson signed the contract, college officials discovered he had lied about being capable of teaching accounting. In this case, even though Thompson had a written contract for one year, the college officials could discharge him immediately. ■

An employee has similar rights and may quit before the time stated in the contract if he or she has good reason. An example of good reason would be an employer's failure to pay the employee the salary agreed upon in the contract. In this case, the employee could also recover damages for breach of contract by the employer.

There are four areas of federal and state regulation of employer-employee relations: (1) labor-management, (2) employment discrimination, (3) employee protection, and (4) hiring of aliens.

Labor-Management

The collective bargaining process is governed by rules established under the National Labor Relations Act (Wagner Act) of 1935 and amended by the Labor Management Relations Act of 1947 (often called the Taft-Hartley Act). The National Labor Relations Act protects union growth and activities from unfair interference by employers. For example, employers may not prevent employees from organizing a union, nor may employers fire or discriminate against those employees who do join a union.

It is also sometimes necessary to protect employees from unfair activities by a union. The Taft-Hartley Act prohibits a **closed shop,** a situation in which a company requires union membership as a prerequisite to employment. Also, under the Taft-Hartley Act and the Landrum-Griffin Act of 1959 (also an amendment to the National Labor Relations Act), when a union and an employer have an **open shop** arrangement, an employee cannot be forced to join a union as a condition of being hired or of keeping a job. Neither can the union force an employer to discriminate against an employee who is not a union member. An employer may, however, agree to have a **union shop.** Under this arrangement, employees need not be members of a union when they are hired, but they must join the union within a certain period of time, usually thirty days. Union shops are not permitted in states that have laws known as "right to work" laws. The Landrum-Griffin Act also protects employees by regulating union elections, business procedures, and use of funds.

Employment Discrimination

Legislation, regulations, and judicial decisions now protect employees and unions, reversing the previous situation in which employers and unions were free to establish any conditions of employment they desired. With few exceptions, these laws apply to companies with fifteen or more employees.

Civil Rights Act (Title VII)   The Civil Rights Act of 1964, as amended by the Equal Employment Act of 1972, prohibits discrimination by employers on the basis of race, national origin, color, gender, or religion in the hiring, discharge, compensation, promotion, or training of employees. The Equal Employment Opportunity Commission (EEOC) was established to deal with employment discrimination cases. The EEOC has the power to stop unfair practices by seeking a court injunction if necessary or, as a final resort, by suing in court for damages.

The EEOC requires those employers that contract to provide products or services to the federal government to file an affirmative action plan with the government. **Affirmative action** is an effort by employers to recruit women and members of minority groups for the higher positions within their organizations that have traditionally been occupied by white males. Employers must first provide statistics relating to the breakdown of their employees into categories of race, religion, color, gender, and national origin. They must also study the surrounding area from which they intend to recruit employees, paying regard to the same categories. Employers must then submit a plan designed to increase the numbers of female and minority group employees. The federal government has the right to cancel a contract with an employer who fails to comply with a plan submitted.

Civil Rights Act of 1991   This law expanded protection against discrimination and in particular enables women and handicapped persons to obtain more damages as a result of discriminatory practices than were available under prior laws. Those bringing suit under this law can, if successful, receive punitive damages in addition to compensatory damages and expert witness fees.

Formerly, it was the employee claiming that a particular employment practice was discriminatory who had the burden of proving that it was unnecessary for the competent performance of the employee's job. Under the Civil Rights Act of 1991, it is now the employer who has the burden of proving that the particular practice complained of is in fact necessary for competent performance.

> Sally applied for a job on an oil well drilling team. The company refused to hire her, claiming that a woman would not have sufficient strength to perform the job properly. Under the Civil Rights Act of 1991, the employer would have the burden of proving that a certain degree of strength was necessary for the proper performance of this job. ■

Age Discrimination in Employment Act   Congress passed the Age Discrimination in Employment Act in 1967 (amended in 1978) to encourage the employment of persons between the ages of forty and sixty-five. Employers cannot discriminate against people in this age group when they are interviewing and hiring applicants for a job. Neither may employers discriminate against them in promotions on the job or in any other way modify or change their conditions of employment.

There are many different forms of discrimination; some are obvious, some subtle. The various civil rights acts and regulations prohibit many types of discrimination, including the following:

1. Disparate treatment. This occurs when an employer treats an individual differently from other employees without good reason, as, for example, when a woman is paid less than an equally qualified man who performs the same job. To prove this type of discrimination, a plaintiff must show that he or she (a) is a member of a protected group (because of race, sex, etc.); (b) is being treated differently from other employees who do the same or similar work; and (c) is being treated differently solely because of race, sex, religion, etc.

2. Disparate impact. This occurs when a company policy or rule, nondiscriminatory on its face, works to the detriment of a protected group. The defense to this type of discrimination is that there was a valid reason for it.

> Ajax Motor Co. had a rule limiting employment of car salespersons to those over 5'10" tall. This would exclude most women and would be considered discriminatory, as there could be no valid business reason for such a rule. A professional basketball team having the same requirement, however, would not be found to be discriminatory. ■

3. Perpetuating discrimination. This occurs when an employer actively discontinues a discriminatory practice but continues it in subtle ways through conduct.

> The Crowe Company had a rule restricting employment to white persons. It then rescinded the rule but adopted a policy that all new employees must be related to existing employees. This seemingly neutral policy would discriminate against African-Americans and would be prohibited. ■

Sexual Harassment

Like other forms of discrimination, sex discrimination is prohibited by federal and state civil rights laws. Recently, sexual harassment has become the most widely publicized and discussed form of sex discrimination.

There are obvious types of sexual harassment, such as unwelcome advances or conduct indicating that submission to such advances is a condition of continued employment or promotion. The courts have had little difficulty with this type of case, provided adequate proof of such harassment is shown. Where such harassment is proved, a court may award damages, back pay, and/or reinstatement.

The most difficult cases in which sexual harassment is charged involve a more subtle form of harassment—the creation of a "hostile working environment" that unreasonably interferes with the employee's job performance. A coworker or supervisor who makes unwanted physical contact, tells offensive jokes and stories, or makes comments about an employee's physical appearance would be guilty of creating such an environment. It is often difficult to prove this type of harassment, however; not every physical contact is considered sexual, and a joke may be offensive to one person but not to another. The courts have generally adopted the following tests to determine whether the conduct complained of can be deemed sufficiently severe to have created a "hostile working environment":

1. The harassing conduct must be part of an ongoing general practice, not just an isolated incident.

2. The harassing conduct must interfere with the performance of the employee's job when seen from the point of view of a reasonable employee in the plaintiff's position.

3. When the conduct complained of is that of a supervisor or coworker, it must be proven that the employer knew of the offensive conduct, or should have known of it, and yet failed to take prompt and sufficient measures to prevent it.

> Blair complained that her supervisor was making unwanted sexual advances toward her and offered proof of it. Her employer said that he would investigate the matter within sixty days and send a letter to the supervisor requesting an end to this type of conduct. This would be deemed insufficient remedial action; and Blair's employer could be held liable for damages for sexual harassment. ■

It is important to know that Title VII of the Civil Rights Act of 1964 and other laws also protect job applicants and employees from discrimination because of their "sexual orientation." These laws provide protection for bisexuals and homosexuals.

Equal Pay Act   The Equal Pay Act of 1963 (amended in 1972) makes it unlawful for employers to discriminate in the payment of wages because of gender. Where performance on the job requires equal skill and responsibility, men and women must be given equal pay. For example, a female soccer coach must be paid the same wages as a male soccer coach if both coaches perform the same duties under similar working conditions.

Americans with Disabilities Act (ADA)   This act, passed in 1990, prohibits discrimination in employment because of a potential employee's disabilities. It covers employers with more than fifteen employees. It also protects employees after they have been hired. The term *disability* is broadly defined—it covers both physical impairment (including AIDS) and mental impairment (including learning disabilities). The law is designed to prohibit discrimination against a potential or actual employee solely because of the disability; the employer has the burden of proving that the disability prevents the potential employee from performing the job properly.

> Jones, a deaf person, could not be denied employment as a television repairperson solely because of her disability. Jones, however, could be denied employment as a piano tuner, because that job can be performed properly only by a person with excellent hearing. ■

The Americans with Disabilities Act covers more than discrimination in employment. It prohibits discrimination on the basis of disability by private entities in places of public accommodation. It also requires that both existing and new buildings and other facilities be modified and designed to make them easily accessible to and usable by disabled persons. Examples of this would be adding braille control panels in elevators, making store aisles wide enough to accommodate wheelchairs, and installing entrance ramps in front of buildings.

Remedies   Not all of the antidiscrimination laws discussed above provide for the same remedies for violations, but the remedies available under all of these are (1) job reinstatement, (2) payment of back pay, (3) injunction against future violations, (4) damages, and (5) legal fees.

Defenses

Employers have certain defenses in discrimination suits even though the practices complained of appear to be discriminatory. The defenses that are available depend on the law involved and on whether the alleged discrimination is direct or indirect. Direct discrimination involves obvious discrimination, for example, giving male employees a longer work break than that given to female employees. Indirect discrimination involves practices that have an unintended discriminatory effect, for example, giving employment interviews and tests only on a day when certain groups might be unable to participate because of religious requirements.

The basic defenses are as follows:

1. Seniority. Awarding promotions based on an existing, fair seniority program is a valid defense to a suit claiming discrimination.

2. Business necessity. If a company can show that it has a sound business reason for a certain practice that appears discriminatory, that reason will be a sufficient defense to a discrimination suit. The ability to read would be a valid requirement for a position as a book reviewer, for example; it would not be a valid requirement for a job as a refuse collector.

3. Bona fide occupational qualifications (BFOQ). This defense is available to an employer who can show that a job requires specific traits or characteristics. The courts tend to limit this defense to cases of alleged gender discrimination. An airplane manufacturer could not refuse to hire a female as a test pilot solely because of her gender, for example. Gender would be a good defense, however, for a play producer who refused to hire a female for the role of Hamlet in Shakespeare's play.

Note that many states have enacted laws that supplement, and often offer greater protection than, federal legislation. In addition, Congress and the states have enacted many laws protecting employees' health and privacy in general and the disabled, the retired, and the unemployed in particular.

Health and Safety

Occupational Safety and Health Act   The Occupational Safety and Health Act, a federal statute passed in 1970, requires most employers to meet certain health and safety standards, issued by the Department of Labor. Employers are required to provide employees with safe working conditions in the buildings where they work. Employers must also ensure that the machinery and equipment that employees use for their work are safe and that employees have the proper training necessary to operate machinery and equipment safely. In addition, the employee has the right to choose not to perform his or her assigned task because of a reasonable fear of death or serious injury. The employer may not discharge an employee because of this fear. The employee also has the right to inform the Occupational Safety and Health Administration (OSHA), a division of the Department of Labor, of any workplace condition that is immediately threatening and dangerous and to request that OSHA inspect that condition. An employer may be fined up to $1,000 for each violation reported by an employee or discovered during an OSHA inspection. An employer is also subject to a fine of up to $1,000 per day for each day that a serious violation is not corrected. In certain cases criminal penalties may be imposed. Employees who report violations to OSHA are protected in the event that employers attempt to fire them. OSHA inspections of the workplace must be announced, in keeping with the Constitution's protection against unreasonable searches.

> ■ Radcliff was employed by a company that processed and bottled baby food. While Radcliff was working at a conveyor belt, the feeder failed to operate because of a short circuit in the primary electrical unit that operated the system. Radcliff notified her employer, who failed to correct the situation. A short time later the conveyor belt stopped again. Radcliff pushed a switch in the emergency electrical unit to get the conveyor started and was nearly electrocuted. ■

The company just described violated the Occupational Safety and Health Act by not providing safe working conditions for its employees. In addition, because of the company's failure to correct the situation, a fine and possible criminal penalty could be imposed if Radcliff reports the employer to an OSHA inspector or if the inspector discovers the electrical defect on an inspection of the plant.

Privacy

Legislation has been enacted and constitutional provisions have been evoked to prevent harassment of employees and invasion of their privacy.

Many employers require their employees to take lie detector tests as a condition of recruitment or continued employment. Because the admissibility of these tests in evidence is usually prohibited, the imposition of such a test is considered harassment and an invasion of privacy. Some states have enacted legislation to protect employees. In 1988, Congress enacted the Employee Polygraph Protection Act. With certain exceptions (such as government employers) employers are prohibited from requiring such tests, using the results, or penalizing an employee either for refusing to take one or because of its results. In certain situations tests are permitted, such as when a theft or embezzlement has occurred. Because the use of drugs and alcohol affects job performance, many employers want to test their employees periodically. Both federal and state constitutions and regulations have been invoked to either permit or prohibit drug and alcohol testing of employees. So far the courts have tended to decide each case on its own merits rather than adopting broad rules. If an employee's work involves national security or potential injury to the employee or to others, drug and alcohol testing are usually permitted. In general, such testing will be permitted if it is found to be accurate and is being used to detect current or recent drug use rather than past use.

Note that the Americans with Disabilities Act specifically excludes as a disability the current use of illegal drugs.

Employee Protection: The Disabled, Retired, and Unemployed

Workers' Compensation Laws   All states have **workers' compensation** laws (there are no federal workers' compensation laws). These laws provide benefits to employees who are injured or who become seriously ill on the job as a result of their work conditions, regardless of whether the employer or the employee was at fault. Some states cover employees who acquire what is known as an occupational disease, such as an illness contracted by a nurse as a result of exposure to a patient. The cost of workers' compensation is borne by the employer alone.

Employees who are covered by workers' compensation are entitled to receive (1) medical treatment, (2) a certain percentage of their regular wages if they will be away from their jobs recovering from injuries or illness, and (3) periodic payments for a permanent disability (such as the loss of an arm or a leg). Benefits are also paid to dependents of deceased employees. In those states where employees are not covered by state laws, employers may provide workers' compensation benefits through private companies.

> Velasquez was employed in a factory that manufactured small tools. One day he was injured when a toolbox full of tools slipped from his hands and fell on his foot. He was unable to work for several weeks and incurred costly medical bills for treatment of the injury. ■

In this example Velasquez would not be personally responsible for the medical bills. Those would be covered under workers' compensation. In addition, Velasquez, while unable to work, would be entitled to some income in place of the wages he normally received as an employee.

Workers' compensation entitles an employee to recover for work-related injuries regardless of whether the injuries were caused by the employee's ordinary or gross negligence. However, most workers' compensation laws deny benefits to employees if they were injured while acting outside the scope of their employment, injured themselves intentionally, or were injured or died as a result of using alcohol or other drugs.

Social Security Act   The Social Security Act of 1935 and its amendments provide a continuing (but limited) income to those employees whose earnings are covered by the act. The Social Security system is actually a social insurance program. It provides benefits to employees or families whose earnings stop because of retirement or death or are reduced because of illness or any other physical disability.

Almost all persons in the United States are covered by Social Security. In fact, nine out of every ten workers in the United States are covered, including self-employed persons. Federal government employees, who are covered by a separate plan, are the largest single group of people not covered by Social Security. Employees of state and local governments and religious and nonprofit organizations may choose to be covered. Special eligibility rules apply to farm workers, students, and those who work outside the United States.

The costs of the Social Security program are financed by contributions from both employees and employers. Employers must automatically deduct a certain amount from their employees' paychecks, contribute an equal amount, and send both contributions to the Internal Revenue Service. The amount of the employee's contribution is fixed by Congress and is stated as a certain percentage of annual wages. For example, for the year 1994 an employee had to contribute 6.2% on all wages up to $60,600, plus 1.45% on all wages without limit; the employer had to contribute a similar amount. Self-employed individuals are required to send in their own contributions, which are 12.4% of net earnings from self-employment up to a maximum of $60,600, plus 2.9% of net earnings without limits.

The major types of insurance provided under Social Security are old age, survivors', and disability insurance; Medicare; and unemployment insurance. *Old age insurance* provides benefits to qualified workers who retire after age sixty-five. *Survivors' insurance* provides payments to the dependents of a wage earner who dies. *Disability insurance* provides a monthly income to a wage earner who is under sixty-five and unable to work because of sickness or injury.

The *Medicare* program offers health insurance to people age sixty-five and over, as well as to those persons under 65 who have been disabled for two years. Part A, Hospital Insurance, which is premium-free, provides coverage for a limited time for inpatient hospital care, inpatient care in a skilled nursing facility following a hospital stay, and home health care. Part B, Medical Insurance, which requires premium payments by the insured, covers doctors' services, outpatient hospital care, diagnostic tests, medical equipment, and ambulance services.

The federal *unemployment insurance* system provides temporary compensation to persons who lose their jobs through no fault of their own. It is a substitute for a portion of the wages lost. The unemployment insurance program is financed by taxes paid by employers only. As a rule, benefits paid are a percentage of the worker's previous weekly earnings. However, there is a minimum and maximum amount payable and a maximum length of time for which an unemployed person may receive benefits.

> Cranshaw worked as a clerk in a steel warehouse one mile from her home. Her employer went out of business, and Cranshaw applied for unemployment insurance benefits. Cranshaw was told that a similar job was available in the area, but she refused to take it because it was five miles from her home. Cranshaw's refusal to take a similar, available job would prevent her from receiving any unemployment benefits. ■

Pension Protection

Many employers have established pension plans for their employees. Because of the need to protect employees who depend on pension benefits for their retirement, in 1974 Congress enacted the Employee Retirement Income Security Act (ERISA). ERISA controls the length of time an employee must work before becoming entitled to pension plan benefits, the management of pension funds, and reporting requirements for employers.

Wages, Hours, and Minors

Fair Labor Standards Act   The federal Fair Labor Standards Act, also known as the Wage and Hour Law, requires certain employers to pay their employees a legal, minimum hourly wage, plus at least one and a half times their regular hourly wage for all hours worked over forty hours in a week. The minimum hourly wage is determined by Congress and is periodically revised. The Wage and Hour Law also contains provisions dealing with the employment of minors. It regulates the minimum age for employment, the hours minors are allowed to work, and occupations for which minors may and may not be hired.

THE HIRING OF ALIENS

Certain aliens are prohibited from accepting employment in the United States. The U.S. Immigration and Nationality Act of 1903, as amended by the Immigration Reform and Control Act of 1986, prohibits the recruitment or employment of aliens known to be unauthorized to accept employment. Immigrants, those aliens lawfully admitted for permanent residence in the United States, may be employed. Nonimmigrants, aliens who have been granted temporary admission for a specific purpose such as tourism or business, may not be employed.

A prospective employer must question a prospective employee and examine certain documents to determine his or her eligibility for employment before hiring the person. An employer who fails to comply and who hires an ineligible alien is subject to both civil and criminal penalties.

Summary of Important Legal Concepts

The employer-employee relationship is usually created by a contract, either oral or written. For many employees, the relationship is affected by a collective bargaining agreement, a contract between a labor union and management covering the terms of employment for employees who are union members.

Many federal and state statutes govern employer-employee relations. Some federal laws that affect this relationship are the Fair Labor Standards Act (wages, hours, and minors), the Civil Rights Act (prohibiting discrimination on the basis of race, color, gender, religion, or handicap in the hiring, discharge, compensation, promotion, or training of employees), the Occupational Safety and Health Act (to provide healthy and safe conditions on the job), and the Social Security Act (old age, survivors', and disability insurance; Medicare; and unemployment insurance). Two other federal laws protecting employees are the Employment Retirement Income Security Act (pension plan protection) and the Americans with Disabilities Act (discrimination because of disability.)

Most states also have laws that protect employees who are either ill or are injured on the job as a result of work conditions. These laws include workers' compensation laws and disability benefits laws.

The general rule has been that either an employer or an employee may end an oral or written contract at will if the contract fails to specify the length of the employment period. Recent court decisions, however, have watered down this rule by recognizing certain exceptions to the general rule, including discharges in violation of law, discharges that go against public policy, discharges that constitute a breach of an implied contract, and discharges that violate stated employee policies and practices.

Key Legal Terms to Know

Match the terms with the definitions that follow.

affirmative action
closed shop
collective bargaining
collective bargaining agreement
employee
employer
employment at will
fringe benefits
labor union
open shop
union shop
whistle-blower laws
workers' compensation

1. A person who hires another to work for him or her
2. The duty of employers to recruit women and members of minority groups for higher-paying positions within an organization that have traditionally been occupied by white males
3. An organization of employees formed to promote the welfare of its members in relation to their working conditions
4. Advantages other than wages received by an employee from an employer
5. State laws that provide benefits to most employees who are injured or become seriously ill on the job
6. An arrangement whereby new employees must join the union within a certain period of time after they are hired
7. A series of discussions between union leaders and representatives of the employer that are designed to reach agreement on issues of concern to both parties, such as working conditions, wages, and hours worked
8. A business where employees are not required to join a union as a condition of employment
9. A contract negotiated between union leaders and company representatives
10. A person hired to work, usually under the direction and control of another
11. Legislation that prohibits an employer from firing an employee because the employee reports that the employer has violated certain laws
12. The right of an employer to fire an employee at any time for any reason whatsoever
13. A company that requires union membership as a prerequisite to employment

Questions and Problems to Discuss

1. What is the trend in the law with regard to the employer's right to fire employees at will?

2. What are the rights and obligations of employers? What are the rights and obligations of employees?

3. Ten construction workers fell to their deaths when the bridge they were building collapsed. An on-site investigation concluded that the accident occurred because the scaffolding used by the workers collapsed. The construction company knew that the scaffolding was unsafe because some of the workers had filed a complaint with an agency. The company, however, did nothing to correct the situation. What agency would be charged with the investigation of this accident? What are possible outcomes for the construction company's failure to correct a dangerous situation?

4. When Mannix applied for the position of law clerk at the firm of Huxley, Huxley, Banner, and Rains, she indicated that she had completed law school, a major requirement for the position. A few months after Mannix was hired, one of the partners in the law firm discovered that she had lied about completing law school. Mannix had actually left law school after two years, without graduating. The law firm immediately discharged her. Mannix sued for breach of contract, claiming that she had signed a two-year contract with the firm and that only seven months had passed. Is the law firm liable for breach of contract?

5. The West End Auto Paint and Repair Shop was required by state law to provide certain ventilating equipment for the protection of its workers. Because this equipment was not installed, one employee developed lung congestion and was unable to work for several months. Is the employee entitled to benefits under the workers' compensation laws?

6. Angie was employed by Reed's TV Repair Service to pick up and deliver appliances in need of repair. While removing a television set from the company truck at Marsh's house, Angie dropped the set and completely destroyed it. Could Marsh hold Reed's liable?

7. The Tri-City Optical Company advertised in local newspapers for supervisory personnel to take charge of various departments within the company. The advertisement listed the qualifications desired and specified that all applicants must be male. When Blaze, a female with all the qualifications listed in the ad, applied for the job, she was refused an interview. Could Tri-City legally refuse to interview Blaze?

8. Fingold, who was employed by the Rolf Tool and Die Company as a supervisor, called a meeting of all employees in the plant to discuss organizing a union. When the plant manager discovered what Fingold had done, she fired him. Was the plant manager's action legal?

9. Kraft, a nurse, was hired by Genesee Hospital at a beginning salary of $15,000 per year and assigned to the surgical ward. A short time later, Timmons, also a nurse, was hired and assigned to the surgical ward to perform the same duties as Kraft. However, his salary was only $12,000. When Timmons discovered the difference in pay, he complained to the administrator who had hired him. The administrator claimed that nursing was traditionally a job for women. They performed better on the job and therefore should be paid more. Can Timmons force the hospital to pay him the same salary as Kraft?

10. You were hired under an oral agreement by the Metro Repair Shop as a mechanic. Soon after you were hired, you were involved in a car accident and lost the use of your right hand. As a result, you could not perform your job properly at the repair shop. Could you legally be discharged from the job?

11. Preston interviewed for a job at the Drake Soup Company, which had a union shop. The company was located in a state that has no right-to-work law. When told that she would have to join the union if she wanted a job, Preston indicated that she was against unions. She felt that she had the right to work for Drake without joining the union. Is she correct?

12. Filbert was a lathe operator for the Bausch Manufacturing Company. One day during her lunch hour she got "high" on drugs. After returning to work she injured her hand while operating the lathe. Is she entitled to workers' compensation for her injury?

13. Arrow was hired as the business manager of the Harmon Central School District under terms specified in a five-year, written contract. After two years at Harmon, Arrow was offered a position as business manager in another school

district. Can Arrow legally break his contract with Harmon Central School District without being liable for breach of contract?

14. Johann was admitted to the United States to study engineering. Soon after he arrived, he ran out of money and applied for a job at a local supermarket. The supermarket manager did not ask him about his status in the United States and did not examine any of his immigration documents. Are the supermarket owners liable for penalties under the Immigration and Nationality Act?

Cases to Decide

1. At a Whirlpool manufacturing plant, overhead conveyors moved appliance components throughout the plant. To protect employees from the components and the debris that occasionally fell from these conveyors, the company installed a wire mesh screen 20 feet above the plant floor. Maintenance employees were required to step onto this screen each week to remove any fallen objects. Several employees had fallen partly through the screen. A number of employees reacted to this accident by discussing the unsafe conditions with their foreman. Following the latest accident, in which one maintenance worker was killed after falling completely through to the plant floor, the employees took their concern to the plant manager. In spite of the accidents and the employer-employee talks, the maintenance workers were instructed to continue with their jobs as usual until a new, heavier wire mesh screen was installed. Two maintenance workers refused and notified OSHA of the dangerous situation. The Personnel Department then placed a letter in each of their employment files reprimanding them for refusing to continue doing their jobs. Did the Whirlpool Company have the legal right to reprimand the two employees for refusing to continue working in a dangerous situation? (*Whirlpool Corporation* v. *Marshall* 445 US 1, 100 S Ct 883, 63 LEd 2d 154)

2. Schoneberg, a female, held a certificate for teaching elementary education and for teaching children with learning disabilities. The principal told Schoneberg that her learning disabilities classes would be combined with others because of declining enrollment and that, as the last learning disabilities teacher to be hired, she would be let go at the end of the current school year. Schoneberg learned, however, that a fourth-grade position would be available the following year. As she had an elementary teaching certificate and was therefore qualified to teach fourth grade, she formally applied for the job. The principal, however, said that he preferred a male teacher and that "it was an educational advantage to have a strong male influence in the environment." The position remained open until a male teacher was hired. Does this action by the principal constitute sex discrimination? (*Schoneberg* v. *Grundy County Special Education Cooperative & Board of Education No. 54*, 385 NE2d 351)

3. Salomon, a white, full-time associate professor, taught African studies at the State University College at New Paltz, New York. He was notified early in the school year that because of budget cuts there would be no course offerings in African history during the upcoming year and that because of his low seniority in the African Studies Department he would not be rehired. There was, however, a position open in the Black Studies Department teaching courses in Introduction to Black Studies, History of Slavery in the Americas, and Black History I. Salomon had no expertise in these areas. The position went to a black, part-time instructor with a master's degree in black studies. Salomon claimed he was not hired because he was white. Was Salomon a victim of discrimination? (*Salomon* v. *N.Y. State Human Rights Appeal Bd.*, 417 NYS2d 805)

4. Thomas was an employee of Hollingsworth, a dairy farmer. Her duties included driving cows from the field to the barn and milking them. Thomas's right eye was injured when she was hit in the face by a cow's tail while hooking up a milking machine. A hair on the cow's tail cut the cornea of her eye, allowing bacteria to get into the wound. The resulting infection caused a 95 percent loss of vision in that eye. Thomas sued Hollingsworth for the eye injury, claiming that, as the employer, Hollingsworth did not provide a safe place to work because he did not provide clamps or other safety devices to secure a cow's tail during milking. At trial, however, Thomas presented no evidence to show that such a device existed, nor did she present an expert's opinion to show that one was necessary for the safe operation of a dairy. Evidence was presented

by Hollingsworth, on the other hand, to show that all his equipment on the dairy farm was the newest and most modern available and that he had never seen a clamp for restraining a cow's tail when he visited other dairies. Has Hollingsworth violated the law by not providing Thomas with safe working conditions? (*Thomas* v. *Hollingsworth*, 250 SE2d 791)

5. When Corning Glass Works of Corning, New York, introduced automatic production equipment, it began a night shift. For night inspector positions the company selected male employees from among its male day workers. The male employees so transferred received wages higher than those paid to women inspectors on the day shift, although the inspectors on the day and night shifts performed the same tasks under the same working conditions. In addition, the tasks required the same skill, effort, and responsibility. Did Corning violate the Equal Pay Act by paying male inspectors more just because they worked at night? (*U.S. Supreme Court Reports*, 417 US 188, 41 LEd 2d 1, 94 S Ct 2223)

6. Nathan, a twenty-two-year-old nurse, worked in the surgical ward of the Presbyterian Hospital in New York City. She was exposed for a period of about twelve days to a patient who had tuberculosis. As a result she contracted tuberculosis in her right lung and had to leave work until she was cured. Was Nathan covered for payment under workers' compensation? (*Nathan* v. *Presbyterian Hospital in the City of New York*, 411 NYS2d 419)

Chapter 24

Principal-Agent Relationship

A principal-agent relationship is an extremely common one that is used for both personal and business transactions. The chapter begins with a discussion of the concept of agency and the nature of the principal-agent relationship. There are many ways in which an agency may be created and there are many different types of agents. The chapter examines the different ways in which an agency may be created and the difference between general agents and special agents.

The principal-agent relationship involves a great deal of trust, and each party has obligations and duties toward the other. The chapter discusses the obligations of the agent to the principal, including such implied duties as obedience and loyalty. Because of their relationship, the principal also has obligations to the agent, including compensation and reimbursement, and the chapter discusses these.

Like the employer-employee relationship, the principal-agent relationship may be terminated in many ways. The chapter describes the different ways in which a principal-agent relationship may be terminated, including fulfillment of purpose, mutual agreement, and operation of law.

Because the principal-agent relationship involves dealings with third parties, the question arises as to what notice must be given to third parties when an agency is terminated. The chapter ends with a discussion of the requirements for notifying third parties of the termination of the agency and the results if such notice is not given.

THE AGENCY CONCEPT

A principal-agent relationship is created when one person, called the **principal,** grants authority to another person, called the **agent,** to act in place of and bind the principal in dealing with third parties. The relationship is outlined in Figure 24.1

Although the principal-agent relationship may be used for personal purposes, its primary use is for business transactions. Many businesses can operate effectively only through the use of agents. This is particularly true for businesses organized as partnerships and corporations. In a partnership, each partner is an agent of the partnership and, as such, has the authority to bind the partnership in transactions related to the partnership business.

Figure 24.1 **The Principal-Agent Relationship**

PRINCIPAL	AGENT	THIRD PARTY
Person for whom the agent acts.	Person who acts for principal in business transactions with third parties.	The person the agent deals with on behalf of the principal.

A corporation, as an entity separate from its owners, can do business in its own name. As such, it must depend on natural persons, such as the officers and employees, to act as agents for the corporation. Partnerships and corporations are discussed in greater detail in Chapters 26 and 27.

A principal who appoints an agent gives the agent **authority,** the power to perform acts on behalf of the principal and for the principal's benefit. Generally, whatever a person may do personally, he or she may do through an agent. However, an agent may not do anything that would be harmful to the principal or that would be illegal. An agent cannot perform acts that are too personal to be performed by an agent, such as voting, serving on a jury, or making a will for the principal.

> Wurz appointed a friend to act as his agent to handle his finances. Wurz's agent does not have authority to make a gift of his money to Wurz's other friends. ■

CLASSIFICATION OF AGENTS

General Agents

There are two types of agents, general and special. A **general agent** has the authority to perform acts that relate to all business matters of the principal. The general agent is considered to be in complete charge of the principal's business affairs.

> You appointed Mitchell, an attorney, to represent you in all matters relating to your business affairs. Mitchell is a general agent. ■

Mitchell can do all the things you would do if you were personally taking care of your business affairs. For example, if you owned apartment buildings, Mitchell could collect the rents from tenants and authorize all repairs to the apartments. Mitchell could also draw money out of your bank account to pay your bills. Mitchell could even sell your company car if there was a good reason.

Special Agents

A **special agent,** in contrast with a general agent, has the authority to perform one type of act or a limited number of acts relating to the principal's business. A real estate salesperson is a good example of a special agent.

> A friend gave you written authorization to sell her tractor. You are considered a special agent for that transaction and your authority is limited to selling the tractor. ■

Gratuitous Agents

Agents do not always receive pay for the services they perform. Agents who do not receive compensation are called **gratuitous agents.**

> A friend handed you $15 and asked you to purchase two tickets for her to an upcoming rock concert at Holander Stadium. Your friend is the principal, you are the agent, and the person who sells you the tickets is the third party with whom you deal on behalf of your friend. ∎

A gratuitous agent who agrees to act for the principal has the same power to bind the principal as an agent who is paid. Since no consideration is given to the gratuitous agent in return for a promise to perform for the principal, however, the gratuitous agent cannot be forced to carry out an action for the principal.

WHO MAY SERVE AS PRINCIPAL AND AGENT

Principals who appoint agents must first be legally competent to act for themselves. In most states, minors may appoint agents. This is not advisable from the agent's point of view, however, because the contract appointing the agent is voidable by the minor principal. Moreover, any contracts made by the agent for the minor are voidable unless the contracts are for necessities.

> Robert, a minor, hired Vogue, an adult friend, as an agent to sell his (Robert's) motorcycle. Vogue sold the motorcycle to Hernandez but Robert changed his mind and refused to deliver the bike to Hernandez. Since Robert, the principal, was a minor, he had the legal right to cancel the contract. ∎

Because agents act not for themselves but for their principals, anyone can legally be appointed an agent. Thus, minors and other incompetents who lack the legal capacity to act for themselves may nonetheless act as agents. As agents, they may bind their principals to such business transactions as contracts. In some states a person who has legally been declared insane may not be appointed an agent.

> Sandburg, an adult, hired Noble, a minor, as the general manager of her service station. Noble entered into a contract to purchase supplies for the station from the Seneca Supply Company. When Sandburg discovered that Noble had purchased too many supplies because he overestimated the amount needed, she refused to be bound on the contract, claiming that Noble was a minor. Nevertheless, because Noble made the contract as Sandburg's agent, Sandburg was bound to pay Seneca for the supplies, despite the fact that Noble was a minor. ∎

Both principals and agents may be either individuals, partnerships, or corporations.

RELATIONSHIPS SIMILAR TO AGENCIES

There are other relationships that are similar to the principal-agent relationship but that can be distinguished from it. Two of these are the employer-employee relationship and the independent contractor relationship.

Employer-Employee

The major difference between the principal-agent relationship and the employer-employee relationship is the degree of control exercised. An employee is not authorized to act in place of the employer. An employee is hired primarily to work under the employer's direction and is subject to the employer's control. The employer controls not only what the employee does but also how it is done.

An agent is authorized to act on behalf of the principal; although an agent is told what tasks to perform, he or she is not told how to carry out the tasks.

A person may act as both an employee and an agent. For instance, as an employee, the vice president in charge of the loan department of a bank must follow bank procedures determined by the bank president and perhaps the bank's board of directors in deciding who is or is not eligible for a loan. The vice president also enters into contracts with the bank's customers when granting them loans. In this second capacity the vice president is an agent acting on behalf of the bank's president and board of directors, the principals.

Independent Contractor

A person may be hired not as an employee or an agent, but as an independent contractor. An **independent contractor** is generally hired to accomplish a specific job but, unlike an employee, is not subject to the direction or control of the hirer in completing the job. The independent contractor has complete control over the manner in which the work will be conducted. He or she decides how the job is to be done and is responsible to the hirer only when the task has been completed. An independent contractor does not represent the hirer in dealings with third parties. Masons, plumbers, electricians, TV repairers, and physicians are examples of independent contractors.

> You hired Ripkin, a mason, to build a fireplace in your livingroom according to a plan you selected. Since Ripkin is an independent contractor, you would rely on his skill and would not tell him how to build the fireplace or in any way control decisions regarding the methods to be used to build the fireplace. ■

CREATION OF THE PRINCIPAL-AGENT RELATIONSHIP

A principal-agent relationship may be created by a contract, by appearance, by ratification, or by necessity.

By Contract

A principal may legally appoint an agent by means of an oral or written contract. Most states require that the appointment of the agent be in writing.

Warren was leaving for a winter vacation in Florida. She orally engaged Zaks to act as her agent to handle all matters relating to an apartment building that she owned and rented to several tenants. This oral appointment of Zaks was legal. ■

To prevent any misunderstandings between the principal and the agent (or between the agent and third parties) regarding the agent's authority, an agent should be given written authority. Written evidence of authority to act could be an informal instrument, such as a letter written by the principal to the agent containing all the essential elements of a contract. It could also be a formal written document such as the **power of attorney** shown in Figure 24.2. A power of attorney may be general or special. A general power of attorney gives the agent the authority of a general agent—that is, the power to do every act that can be lawfully performed by the principal. A special power of attorney gives the agent very restricted authority, the authority of a special agent.

In some cases, the statute of frauds must be satisfied. If the contract between the principal and the agent is for more than one year, the contract creating the agent's authority must be in writing. Likewise, if an agent is given the authority to sell real estate, the agent's authority must be in writing because a contract for the sale of real estate is required to be in writing.

By Appearance

If third parties are led to believe that a person is an agent because an appearance of a principal-agent relationship exists, an **agency by estoppel** is created. In this case, the so-called principal is *estopped* (prevented) by law from denying the relationship. Otherwise, the third parties would unjustly suffer damages or loss.

■ Southworth, a friend who owned a service station, asked Habbab to watch the station while Southworth went to lunch. He told her not to deal with any customers but simply to inform them that he would return in one hour. While Southworth was gone, a customer requested some automotive parts. Habbab sold the parts but guessed at the prices because no price list was available. When Southworth returned from lunch and discovered that Habbab had undercharged by $20, he called the customer to ask for the additional money. He explained that Habbab was not employed at the station and consequently had no knowledge of what prices to charge. The customer refused to pay the additional $20, claiming that she thought Habbab worked at the station and sold the parts at the correct price. ■

By leaving Habbab alone at the station, Southworth created the impression in the customer's mind that Habbab had the authority to deal with customers. The law now prevents Southworth from claiming that Habbab had no right to charge the prices she did. Since he allowed her to watch the station, Southworth must suffer the consequences of her act and cannot legally collect the additional $20. To allow otherwise would be unfair to the customer, who might not have purchased the parts if she had known their true price.

```
                        POWER OF ATTORNEY

           KNOW ALL PERSONS BY THESE PRESENTS, that I, WILLIAM P. TEDESCI,
      638 Fernwood Avenue, Topeka, Kansas, have made, constituted, and
      appointed, and by These Presents do make, constitute, and appoint
      KARA HIGGINS, my true and lawful attorney for me and in my name,
      place, and stead, to enter into any contract or contracts for the
      sale of premises owned by KARA HIGGINS and me in Newton, Missouri,
      on such terms as she shall in her discretion elect, and to execute
      in my behalf any deed or other conveyance of said premises, and to
      receive and deliver to me my share of the proceeds of any such sale,
      also giving and granting unto my said attorney full power and
      authority to do and perform all and every act or thing whatsoever
      requisite and necessary to be done in and about the premises,
      including obtaining of financing with regard to said premises, as
      fully to all intents and purposes as I might or could do if personally
      present, with full power of substitution and revocation, hereby
      ratifying and confirming all that my said attorney, or her substitute,
      shall lawfully do or cause to be done by virtue thereof.

           IN WITNESS WHEREOF, I have hereunto set my hand and seal the
      5th day of January, 19--.

                                         William P. Tedesci

      STATE OF KANSAS    )
      COUNTY OF SHAWNEE  )  SS:

           On this 5th day of January, 194-, before me, the subscriber,
      personally appeared WILLIAM P. TEDESCI, to me personally known to
      be the same person described in and who executed the foregoing
      instrument, and he acknowledged to me that he executed the same.

                                         Luella M. Wolff
```

Figure 24.2
Power of Attorney

By Ratification

If one person attempts to act as an agent for another and this other person approves the unauthorized act of the assumed agent, a principal-agent relationship arises by ratification (approval). Approval of the unauthorized act by the so-called principal has the effect of authorizing the agency.

Geary, your best friend, knew that you had a ten-speed bike for sale. Without your permission Geary, representing herself as your agent, sold the bike to Morrow for $100. Morrow made a $25 deposit on the bike. When Geary handed you the $25 and explained that she had sold the bike to Morrow, you accepted the money. By accepting the money, you ratified Geary's act of selling the bike and created a principal-agent relationship. You cannot now legally change your mind and refuse to sell the bike to Morrow. ■

By Necessity

An emergency situation may require a person to act as an agent and thus may create a principal-agent relationship by necessity.

A chartered bus taking a group of senior citizens to a large city on a three-day excursion trip broke down just outside the city. The bus driver made arrangements to have the necessary repairs made. Although not generally authorized to act as an agent for the bus company (the principal), the bus driver had authority by necessity in this case because of the emergency. ■

If time permits and the principal is available, the agent must consult with the principal about a possible solution to the emergency. Furthermore, the agent receives no greater authority than that necessary to resolve the problem.

When a man and woman marry, the marriage relationship does not automatically give each person the authority to act as an agent of the other. The authority to act for each other develops naturally over a long period of time as, for example, when the wife as the wage earner willingly pays her husband's bills. Under these circumstances, the husband has the authority to continue to buy items and charge them to his wife's account.

On the other hand, under the domestic relations laws of most states, a husband and wife are responsible for furnishing each other and their minor children with the necessaries of life. If either fails to do so, the other may then purchase these necessaries and charge them to the other spouse's account (agency by necessity). For non-necessaries, each spouse is liable only if an agency relationship can be established.

OBLIGATIONS OF THE AGENT TO THE PRINCIPAL

The duties of an agent to a principal are usually spelled out in the agency contract. In addition to the duties expressly mentioned, certain other duties are implied by law, based upon the special relationship of trust and confidence. The usual implied duties are obedience, loyalty, reasonable skill, and accurate accounting. The agent also has a duty to communicate all pertinent information to the principal. A failure to live up to these obligations gives the principal the right to fire the agent. The principal may also recover damages for any loss suffered, which includes the right not to compensate the agent.

Obedience

The agent must follow all lawful instructions given by the principal. Failure to obey these instructions is grounds for dismissal and makes the agent liable in damages for any loss that results. Of course, if an emergency arises and the principal cannot be contacted, the agent is permitted to change the instructions as required by the situation and to use her or his own judgment. Any material change in the agent's original duties may amount to a breach of the agency contract.

> Ossen owned a shoe store and instructed her salespeople not to sell shoes to customers at discount prices. Redman, a salesperson who worked on commission, sold several pairs of shoes at discount prices. Redman would be liable to Ossen for any loss as the result of disobeying instructions. Redman could also be denied any commissions due. ■

Loyalty

An agent is always expected to be loyal and to act in the best interests of the principal, and not in the agent's own interest or in the interest of another. In fact, the relationship is a **fiduciary relationship,** a relationship of trust and confidence. An example of a breach of loyalty by an agent is failing to turn over all money received for the principal while acting as an agent, including all secret profits such as gifts, bonuses, or commissions. The principal is entitled to this money and may demand it from the agent upon discovering that it was paid to the agent. Personally benefiting from a business deal or getting involved in conflict-of-interest situations (such as working for two principals or owning a competing business unknown to the principal) are also examples of breach of loyalty.

> Talbot was employed as a full-time salesperson for the Spartan Wholesale Jewelry Company. Talbot was also employed as a part-time salesperson for a competing firm, the Blair Jewelry Company. Neither company was aware that Talbot worked for the other. ■

In this case Talbot violated the duty of loyalty and is not entitled to collect compensation from either company. It is difficult, if not impossible, for an agent to work for two competing principals and to act in the best interests of both. This arrangement would be permissible, however, if Talbot received the consent of both companies to work full time for one and part time for the other.

When not doing business for a principal, an agent is free to engage in any business so long as it is not a competing one.

Reasonable Skill

An agent is usually hired because he or she possesses some special knowledge or skill. In performing required tasks for the principal, the agent is expected to exercise the degree of skill he or she claims to possess. Of course, the agent must exercise at least reasonable skill. Reasonable skill is the degree of skill that average individuals would use in performing the same tasks for themselves. An agent who does not exercise the required skill is liable to the principal for any loss that results.

■ Nash, who recently inherited $25,000 from an aunt, hired Walker as an agent to invest this money in stocks to produce a stable income. Walker studied the stock market for several weeks and consulted several investors before buying stocks for Nash. Nevertheless, shortly after Walker invested the $25,000, the stocks went down in value because of a world crisis that affected the entire stock market. Walker could not be held liable for Nash's loss since at least reasonable skill was used in the purchase of the stocks. ■

Accurate Accounting

The agent must keep accurate, up-to-date records of all business transactions affecting the principal-agent relationship. Money collected on behalf of the principal should be turned over to the principal as soon as possible or, if the principal desires, placed in a bank account. The bank account should be opened in the principal's name, not the agent's. If money belonging to the principal is placed in the agent's account and it cannot be determined what amount belongs to the agent and what amount to the principal, the entire amount may be claimed by the principal.

■ Poore agreed to represent Frost, the owner of a small retail clothing store, by collecting payments due from Frost's credit customers. Poore placed the money in a personal bank account. Because Poore kept inaccurate records, there was no way of knowing what part of the money belonged to Frost. Poore could legally be required to turn over all the money in the bank account to Frost. ■

Communication

By law, a principal is understood to know any information the agent obtained from third parties while acting in the scope of authority, even if the principal does not actually receive this information. Since the agent represents the principal, what the agent knows, the principal knows. Therefore, the agent has a duty to communicate to the principal all matters coming to the agent's attention that would affect the principal's relationship with third parties.

■ Able offered to sell Corbett some electrical equipment through her agent, Melville, and gave Corbett three days to decide. Corbett accepted the offer within one day by informing Melville, but Melville did not tell Able of Corbett's acceptance until after the three days had expired. Able would be liable on the contract even though Melville did not inform her of Corbett's acceptance. ■

OBLIGATIONS OF THE PRINCIPAL TO THE AGENT

Principals likewise have certain fiduciary obligations to their agents. These obligations, imposed by contract or implied by law, are compensation, reimbursement, indemnity, safe working conditions, and cooperation.

Compensation

An agent who is not a gratuitous agent is entitled to compensation for work done according to the terms agreed on in the contract. If the agent's fee is not provided for by contract, the agent can expect to be paid a reasonable sum for the services performed. The principal must compensate the agent even when the principal-agent relationship arose because the principal ratified an unauthorized act. Sometimes compensation is on a contingency basis, such as when the agent earns a commission only after the sale of a product is concluded. In this case, the agent cannot collect the compensation from the principal until the contingency has occurred, which in this case is the completion of the sales transaction.

Reimbursement

The principal must reimburse (repay) an agent, even a gratuitous agent, for all necessary expenses the agent incurred in carrying out the principal's business. Usually the agent pays the expenses connected with the agency from personal funds and then submits a bill to the principal. Reimbursable expenses include meals, lodging, airfare (or car mileage), entertainment expenses, and some incidental expenses such as telephone calls.

> Gerold, manager of Copy King Printing Company, attended a three-day business conference at a resort hotel to learn about new methods and techniques in the printing field. Gerold submitted an expense statement for airfare, $250; hotel room, $165; meals, $50; telephone calls to the company, $15; and cab fares, $25. ∎

These expenses would probably be paid by Copy King because Gerold incurred them while on company business. An agent is not entitled to be reimbursed for expenses that are personal in nature or that were incurred as the result of the agent's misconduct or negligence, such as a speeding ticket.

> Blanchard, a traveling salesperson, spent a week in Florida on a business trip for the Ruston Restaurant Supply Company. After completing the business, Blanchard stayed three additional days at a neighboring resort hotel for a personal vacation. Blanchard could not ask for reimbursement from Ruston for these three days. ∎

Business expenses that are unreasonable in view of what the agent was asked to accomplish for the principal are also not reimbursable.

Indemnity

The principal must indemnify the agent (protect the agent by making payment) for any personal loss incurred by the agent when the agent becomes liable to third parties while following the principal's lawful instructions. If the loss was incurred because of negligence or the agent's own misconduct, the principal is not bound to indemnify the agent.

■ Chen was hired by the Beauty Mark Company to sell beauty products house to house in a certain town. Unknown to either Chen or Beauty Mark, an ordinance required all salespersons to register at the local town hall before selling any products in town. Chen, who was arrested and required to pay a $100 fine for failing to register, should legally be able to recover the money from Beauty Mark ■

Safe Working Conditions

Just as an employer has a duty to provide an employee with reasonably safe working conditions, so too does a principal have an obligation to exercise the same degree of care for an agent. Failure to do so may make the principal liable to the agent for any injuries that the agent suffers. This obligation has been increased by statutes and regulations.

Cooperation

A principal has a duty to assist the agent in every way possible and to cooperate with the agent in the performance of the agent's duties. A principal may not, for example, bypass an agent and deal directly with a third party in an attempt to avoid paying a commission to an agent.

TERMINATION OF THE PRINCIPAL-AGENT RELATIONSHIP

A principal-agent relationship may be terminated by (1) fulfillment of purpose, (2) mutual agreement, (3) revocation of authority, (4) renunciation by the agent, (5) operation of law, or (6) subsequent destruction or illegality.

Fulfillment of Purpose

If the agent has authority to accomplish a specific act, the agency ends as soon as that act has been accomplished. For example, the authority of a real estate agent hired to sell your house ends when the house is sold. If an agent is hired for a specific period of time, such as six months or one year, the agency ends when this time period expires.

Mutual Agreement

The principal and the agent may mutually agree to end their relationship at any time.

Revocation of Authority

A principal may generally revoke an agent's authority at any time and thus terminate the principal-agent relationship with or without cause at any time. Actually, the principal discharges the agent. If the discharge is for a good reason, such as a failure to follow instructions, the agent may not recover damages for breach of contract. Instead, the agent may have to pay money damages to the principal for causing the breach.

> Bush, a scout for a professional baseball team with authority to hire, was told not to sign contracts with any more players because the team was already overstaffed. Nevertheless, Bush signed a pitcher he thought would be an asset to the team. Bush could be discharged and made to pay damages for any loss caused by his act. ■

If an agent has been wrongfully discharged, the agent can collect unpaid compensation up to the time of discharge and, in addition, recover damages for the wrongful discharge.

> Volpe, a civil engineer, signed a two-year contract to design and oversee the construction of an office complex for Reed at a salary of $75,000 per year. Reed was pleased with Volpe's work but, when a personality conflict developed between the two at the end of the first year, Reed fired Volpe. ■

In the example, Volpe could recover damages because of the wrongful discharge before the expiration of the two-year contract. Volpe, however, is not entitled to the full $75,000 salary for the second year. The law generally requires the wrongfully discharged agent to seek other employment and to deduct any income for such work from the damages sought. Thus, Volpe would be entitled to $75,000 less any income from another job.

The authority of an agent may not be revoked unilaterally by the principal when the agent has an interest in the subject matter of the agency in addition to his or her compensation. In this case, the agency is said to be an **agency coupled with an interest** and the agent must consent to the termination. This type of principal-agent relationship is not terminated even by events that normally end agencies by operation of law, such as the death or bankruptcy of the principal.

> Drake left the United States to work with a firm in Europe. Before he left, he gave McIntyre permission to sell his car. McIntyre advanced Drake $1,000 with the understanding that McIntyre would be reimbursed out of the proceeds of the sale of the car. Before McIntyre had a chance to sell the car, Drake decided to revoke McIntyre's authority. ■

In the example, since McIntyre was to get the $1,000 lent to Drake back from the proceeds of the sale of the car, this was an agency coupled with an interest. Drake could not terminate the agency unless McIntyre consented to the termination. McIntyre could sell the car in spite of Drake's attempted revocation.

Renunciation by the Agent

An agent may refuse to continue to work for the principal. Of course, an agent who quits without just cause breaches the agency contract. The agent could be held liable for any loss suffered by the principal.

> ■ Partridge had a contract with the Rundall Tool and Die Company to act as an agent to negotiate a new contract for the company with its employees. Halfway through the negotiation process, Partridge became dissatisfied with the way the negotiations were proceeding and quit. Rundall hired a substitute at a higher salary to complete the negotiations with the employees. Since Partridge breached her contract by wrongfully quitting the job, she was liable to Rundall for the additional salary paid to her substitute. ■

Operation of Law

By operation of law, certain situations will terminate a principal-agent relationship immediately. Among these situations are the death or insanity of either the principal or the agent, bankruptcy of the principal, and in some cases bankruptcy of the agent.

> ■ Goode was employed by Carey, owner of Talent Unlimited, to book bands to play at high school proms and other school dances. Goode booked a band to play at a local high school, unaware that Carey had died earlier in the day. ■

In the example, the principal-agent relationship terminated with Carey's death. Consequently, the contract Goode made with the school was void. An agent cannot make a contract for a deceased principal.

A bankruptcy petition filed by the principal to liquidate the business usually terminates the principal-agent relationship. The filing of a bankruptcy petition by the agent generally will not terminate the principal-agent relationship unless the purpose of the agency was affected. For example, if you are acting as a financial adviser to clients of your principal, who is a stockbroker, your filing of the bankruptcy petition would terminate the relationship because your credibility as a financial adviser would be destroyed.

A principal-agent relationship also terminates by operation of law when the subject matter of the agency is destroyed or when the performance of the agent's duties becomes impossible.

> ■ Clemens was hired under a two-year contract to manage a Houston, Texas, branch of Prep Tax, a nationwide chain that prepared individual income tax forms. Six months later, the state of Texas passed a law requiring all income tax preparers to pass a licensing examination. If Clemens fails to pass the test, it would be illegal for him to continue as manager. The principal-agent relationship will be terminated by impossibility. ■

Subsequent Destruction or Illegality

A principal-agency relationship established for a specific purpose will end if the purpose becomes illegal, or prohibited by law, making the agency meaningless.

> You appointed Jergens as your agent to manage an industrial plant for you. If the zoning law changes and prohibits operation of such a plant in that area, the agency relationship will terminate. ■

A principal-agency relationship established to deal with specific property will also end if the property is destroyed, also making the agency meaningless.

> Russell appointed Adelman as her agent to sell her car; Adelman would have received a commission based on a percentage of the purchase price. If the car is destroyed in an accident before it is sold, the agency will terminate. ■

NOTIFYING THIRD PARTIES OF THE TERMINATION

The agent's actual authority ends when the principal tells the agent that authority has been revoked. Third parties with whom the agent deals may not always know this. Consequently, there is a general rule that third parties, unless otherwise notified by the principal, may presume that a principal-agent relationship continues to exist. Thus, the principal will continue to be bound by the agent's acts until third parties have been notified.

Third parties who have dealt regularly with the agent must be notified by the principal of the termination of the agent's authority, either personally or in writing. For all other third parties, a public notice, such as in a newspaper circulated in the area where the agent has been operating, is sufficient even though a third party may not actually read the notice.

> Cooley was the manager of Racquet, a sporting goods store. As manager, Cooley purchased merchandise for the store on credit. The merchandise would then be paid for by Syms, the owner of the store. Syms sold the store to Cooley, who continued to buy merchandise from the same creditors. When Cooley did not pay the bills, one creditor sued Syms. ■

In the example, Syms failed to give creditors actual notice, personally or in writing, that Cooley was no longer an agent for the store and Cooley therefore still had apparent authority to purchase merchandise in Syms's name. The creditor had a legal right to recover from Syms even for merchandise purchased by Cooley as the new owner of the store. Of course, Syms could then sue and recover damages from Cooley.

When a principal-agent relationship is terminated not by the principal but rather by operation of law (such as by death, insanity, or bankruptcy), notice to third parties is not necessary. Third parties generally become aware of the termination through publicity officially given these matters in newspapers, official records, or by other means.

Ordinarily, notice is not required to revoke the authority of a special agent, since most people do not deal with such agents on a continual basis. If, however, the principal has led third parties to believe that the special agent has unusual authority as, for example, authority granted under a special power of attorney, then actual notice of termination is required.

Summary of Important Legal Concepts

A principal-agent relationship is created when an agent is asked to enter into transactions, usually business transactions, with third parties and to act in place of and at the request of the principal. Agents make independent decisions and exercise judgment as if they were making the transactions themselves. Their authority may be very broad, in which case they are called general agents, or may be very narrow, in which case they are called special agents. Agents who do not receive compensation for their services are called gratuitous agents.

A person may be hired as an employee rather than as an agent. The difference is that an employee acts under the direct control and supervision of the employer, but an agent makes independent decisions. A person may also be hired as an independent contractor rather than as an employee or an agent. The independent contractor also makes independent decisions and exercises judgment but does not deal with third persons on behalf of the hirer.

Principals who appoint agents must be legally competent. In most states, minors may appoint agents. Because agents act not for themselves but for their principals, agents are not required to be legally competent. Minors and incompetents who are not prohibited by state law may act as agents.

A principal-agent relationship may be created by an oral or written contract, but it may also be created by appearance, by ratification, or by necessity.

An agent owes the principal certain duties based upon their special relationship of trust and confidence, including the duties of obedience, loyalty, reasonable skill, accurate accounting, and communication. The principal owes the agent the obligations of compensation, reimbursement, indemnity, safe working conditions, and cooperation.

A principal-agent relationship may be terminated by fulfillment of the purpose of the agency, by mutual agreement, by revocation of the agent's authority, by renunciation by the agent, by operation of law, or by subsequent destruction of the subject matter or illegality of the purpose.

As a general rule, third parties, unless otherwise notified by the principal, may presume that a principal-agent relationship continues to exist. The principal will continue to be bound by any acts that the agent performs in the apparent scope of authority until the principal gives notice of termination of the agency.

Key Legal Terms to Know

Match the terms with the definitions that follow.

agency by estoppel
agency coupled with an interest
agent
authority
fiduciary relationship
general agent
gratuitous agent
independent contractor
power of attorney
principal
special agent

1. An agent who has the authority to perform one type of act or a limited number of acts relating to the principal's business
2. A situation in which one party creates the appearance that another person has the authority to act as her or his agent
3. An agent with authority to perform acts that relate to all business matters of the principal
4. The power to act for someone else
5. One hired to perform a task for another, but not subject to the direction or control of the hirer
6. An agent who represents another in business transactions without receiving compensation
7. One who represents another in making business transactions
8. A formal, written document giving an agent the authority to act
9. A relationship based on trust and confidence
10. One who authorizes another to act for her or him in making business transactions
11. Principal-agent relationship in which the agent has an interest in the subject matter of the agency

Questions and Problems to Discuss

1. Why is the agency concept so important to the conduct of business transactions?
2. What third parties should be notified when a principal-agent relationship is terminated? How should these third parties be notified?
3. Margolis gave Frey a power of attorney as follows: "I, William R. Margolis, appoint Amanda Frey to represent me in my business, Eddy Meat Packing Company, and in my name to write checks and other such instruments, and do all such matters in reference to the business as may be required to lawfully conduct this business."
   a. Who is the principal?
   b. Who is the agent?
   c. What type of agency has been created: general or special?
4. Wardlow, a school social worker in the Laura Linda school district, was a permanent member of the district committee for the handicapped. One purpose of this committee was to review the cases of students having academic and emotional problems in school and to make recommendations for placement of these students, if necessary, in special programs where they could meet success. Wardlow and two other members honestly voted against placing Aresti, a tenth grader at Laura Linda High School, in a special educational program. Since Wardlow was the most vocal committee member on the denial of placement, Aresti's parents sued Wardlow. Does the Laura Linda school district have any responsibility toward Wardlow, an agent of the school district, if Aresti's parents are successful in their lawsuit?
5. Rinere, a used-car dealer, hired Masters, a minor, as a salesperson. Masters sold a car to Duncan, an adult, for the wrong price. Rinere (an adult) sought to break the contract and recover the car from Duncan on the grounds that Masters was a minor and was legally incompetent. Is Rinere entitled to recover the car?
6. Hickman, the night custodian at Central High School, discovered a crack in the pool wall during his rounds. Water was slowly overflowing into a room where expensive gymnastics equipment was stored. Hickman could not reach the school's business manager, who was the only person permitted to authorize repairs. To prevent further damage, Hickman called a repair service. Tempo-

rary measures were taken to stop the leak. When the repair bill was sent to the school, the business manager refused to pay it, claiming that the cost of the repairs was too high and Hickman did not have authority to authorize the repairs. Is the school liable for the cost of the repairs?
7. Cohen, while driving on business for her principal, was fined $50 for speeding. Is the principal legally bound to reimburse Cohen?
8. Russ was hired by the Atrium Car Agency as a new-car salesperson on a commission basis. She was told by Atrium, her principal, that the sale of any new car must be approved by the owner of the agency. Russ did not follow these instructions and approved the sale of a new car on her own. The sale price was not acceptable to the principal. Russ tried to collect her commission on the sale, but the principal refused to pay. Could the principal deny Russ her commission?
9. Seitz orally appointed March as his agent to sell some farm equipment for $400. Seitz agreed to pay March a 20 percent commission when the equipment was sold. March sold the equipment to Hays, but Seitz then changed his mind and refused to go through with the contract. When Hays insisted on obtaining the equipment, Seitz claimed that the contract was not valid because March did not have the written authority to act as agent. Was Seitz right?
10. Price had worked for several years as a purchasing (general) agent for the Zeif Company. In this capacity, Price had often purchased material from the Enright Supply Company. After he was discharged by Zeif, Price made a purchase for himself from Enright Supply but charged it to Zeif. Enright had no knowledge of Price's dismissal. Could Enright hold Zeif liable for this last purchase by Price?
11. Wheeler, who was about to enter the Marine Corps, engaged Worthy Auto Sales to sell his automobile for a commission. Worthy advanced Wheeler $300 with the understanding that it was to get the $300 back from the proceeds of the sale. Three weeks later, before the automobile was sold, Wheeler changed his mind and acted to terminate the agency. Would Wheeler be successful in terminating the agency?
12. Voorhis signed a one-year written contract to manage Ravin's University Motel. After Voorhis had worked for Ravin for two months, Ravin

decided to fire Voorhis because business was not doing well enough to have a manager. Voorhis claimed that Ravin could not fire her because she (Voorhis) had a contract to manage the motel for one full year. Is Voorhis correct?

Cases to Decide

1. Fields granted permission to the Clayton County Water Authority to construct a sewer line across his property. The Water Authority in turn subcontracted the actual construction of the sewer to the B&B Pipeline Company. No directions or control over the method, manner, or means of the construction to be done by B&B was exercised by the Water Authority. During construction, the B&B Company damaged some trees on Field's property. Fields sued the Water Authority for damages, claiming that the Water Authority, as principal, was responsible for the damage. Is the Water Authority liable as a principal in this case? (*Fields* v. *B&B Pipeline Company, Inc.*, 147 Ga App 875)

2. Brenner, an agent of the Western Electric Company, was responsible for awarding a contract to the J. L. Williams Company to construct a building for Western Electric. For his efforts, Brenner demanded and received $50,000 from the J. L. Williams Company. Western Electric discovered that Brenner had received $50,000 from the J. L. Williams Company and demanded that the money be turned over to them. Is Western Electric entitled to the $50,000? (*Western Electric Company* v. *Brenner*, 41 NY2d 291)

3. The Levines planned an overseas trip. They purchased airline tickets on British Overseas Airways Corporation (BOAC) through Comet Travel Agency. Before the flight the Levines canceled the trip and returned their tickets directly to BOAC for a refund. BOAC mailed the refund to the Comet Travel Agency. When the Levines were unable to obtain the refund from Comet because the manager of the agency stole the money, they sought to recover the money from BOAC. BOAC refused payment, claiming that, because the refund was sent to Comet, the Levines' authorized agent, they must collect the refund from Comet. The Levines claimed that their agency relationship with Comet Travel ended when the tickets were purchased and that BOAC was liable for the mistake in sending the refund to Comet Travel. Are the Levines correct? (*Levine* v. *British Overseas Airways Corp.*, 66 Misc 2d 766, 322 NYS2d 119)

4. Valley View Cattle Company sued Iowa Beef Processors for 259 head of cattle, claiming that Heller purchased the cattle as an agent for Iowa Beef. Iowa Beef claimed that Heller was an independent contractor and that Valley View should sue and recover the price of the cattle from Heller. At the trial it was determined that Heller was bankrupt, but that Heller had been purchasing cattle for Iowa Beef for eight years, that Heller received daily instructions from Iowa Beef about the price and quantity of cattle to buy, and that Iowa Beef placed money in Heller's account to pay for cattle purchased. It was also shown that Iowa Beef gave Heller some discretion as to the area in which Heller could buy cattle to be shipped to Iowa Beef. Is Iowa Beef liable to Valley View for the price of the 259 head of cattle? (*Valley View Cattle Company* v. *Iowa Beef Processors, Inc.*, 548 F2d 1219)

5. Prince (an agent) was under contract to work for Sportswear by Revere, Inc. (the principal), selling and obtaining orders for sweaters, sportswear, and other products offered for sale by Revere. Under the terms of the contract, Prince was to receive a commission for the goods only after they were sold and actually delivered. Prince sold certain goods but died before they were actually delivered. Kowal, who became responsible for Prince's business affairs after Prince died, sued for the commission due on the goods Prince sold just prior to Prince's death. Is Kowal entitled to the commission? (*Kowal* v. *Sportswear by Revere, Inc.*, 222 NE2d 778)

6. Stewart signed a two-year contract with Seco Chemicals, Inc., to sell Seco's lines of electroplating processes. His sales were not as good as the company expected and Seco discharged him, although the two-year contract period had not expired. Stewart, who was unemployed for about two months, sued Seco for wrongful discharge and asked for damages for those two months. Is Stewart entitled to damages for wrongful discharge? (*Stewart* v. *Seco Chemicals, Inc.*, 349 NE2d 733)

7. Vowels contracted for dancing lessons from an Arthur Murray Studio in Birmingham, Michigan. The contract, entered into in September 1961,

called for 139.5 hours of lessons for a total of $1,393. In September 1961, the Birmingham studio went out of business. Vowels sued the parent company for breach of contract, claiming that the local studio had acted as an agent for the parent company. The contract and other documents showed that the contract had been made with the Birmingham branch. A statement sent to Vowels had the name *Arthur Murray Studios* on the letterhead and the parent company's address. The owner of the Birmingham studio gave his title as "manager." Can Vowels hold the parent company responsible for breach of contract? (*Vowels* v. *Arthur Murray Studios of Michigan*, 163 NW2d 35)

Chapter 25

Principal-Agent, Employer-Employee, and Third-Party Relationship

CHAPTER PREVIEW

CHAPTER HIGHLIGHTS

Chapter 24 covered the obligations that a principal owes to an agent and that an agent owes to a principal. This chapter discusses the liability of the principal and the agent and the employer and the employee to third parties with whom the agent and employee deals. It describes the liability of a principal to third parties when the agent enters into contracts with them on behalf of the principal. It also describes in detail the effect of the different types of authority that an agent may have. The chapter examines the liability of the principal and employer for torts committed by the agent or employee while acting within the scope of the purposes of the agency or the scope of employment. It then discusses the circumstances in which a principal and employer can be held liable toward a third person.

Like the principal or employer, the agent and employee may also be liable to third parties. The chapter continues by focusing on the liability of an agent to third parties for contracts that the agent makes without obtaining authority from the principal or without disclosing the existence of a principal. The agent's and employee's liability to third persons for torts he or she commits is also discussed.

The chapter concludes with a brief discussion of the liability of both principal and agent and employer and employee for criminal acts committed by an agent or employee.

LIABILITY OF PRINCIPAL AND EMPLOYER TO THIRD PARTIES

The principal is legally liable to third parties for contracts an agent makes as long as the agent operates within the authority given to her or him. A principal may choose to be bound by ratifying (approving) an unauthorized contract. The principal would then be liable on the contract as if it had been authorized in the first place.

In addition to contract liability, the principal may be liable to third parties who are injured as the result of torts committed by an agent who was legally acting for the principal.

Contract Liability of Principal

An agent has the authority to enter into contracts with third parties on behalf of the principal. Generally, the principal is bound by these contracts if the agent acts within the scope of authority. **Scope of authority** refers to the extent of the agent's authority and generally includes express, implied, and apparent authority.

Express authority is the authority the principal actually gives the agent either orally or in writing. A power of attorney is an example of express authority.

Implied authority describes the authority of an agent to perform duties not expressly given by the principal but understood as necessary to carry out the purpose of the agency. The principal does not usually list in writing every duty expected of the agent. If, for example, you are a professional manager and are hired to run a ski shop, the principal will probably not discuss with you every detail of running the shop. It is understood that you will do such things as pay utility bills, order proper merchandise, and keep an account of what you have sold.

Another type of implied authority is known as **emergency authority.** This is the authority that an agent has to act in the event of an emergency if the agent is unable to contact the principal for express authority to act. In such circumstances, the principal will be bound by the act of the agent.

> Green appointed Burt as his agent to collect rents from tenants in an apartment that Green owned. While visiting with a tenant, Burt observed that the tenant was extremely ill and required medical attention immediately. Burt would have implied authority to call an ambulance for the tenant, even though Burt has no express authority from Green to do so. ■

Apparent authority is the authority that an agent has because a principal leads third parties to believe that the agent possesses such authority when, in fact, the agent does not. If a third party reasonably believes, from the principal's words or conduct, that the agent has such authority, the principal will be bound. However, the agent will be liable to the principal for disobedience in making an unauthorized contract for which the principal is liable.

> Gibbons, a salesperson for Monumental Used Cars, was told not to sell cars on credit in the future but to sell for cash only. Nevertheless, he sold a used car to Tucker on credit so that he would not lose the commission on the sale. Tucker had purchased used cars from Gibbons on credit in the past and knew of other customers who had purchased cars from Monumental on credit. Because Gibbons had the apparent authority to sell cars on credit, a binding contract resulted between Monumental, the principal, and Tucker, the third party. Of course, Gibbons disobeyed instructions and would be liable in damages to his principal if Tucker failed to pay for the car. ■

Sometimes an agent performs an act that is outside the scope of her or his authority. As mentioned earlier, if the principal ratifies (approves) the agent's unauthorized act, the principal is as liable as if the act had been authorized in the first place. Ratification of an unauthorized act may be either express or implied. *Express ratification* occurs when the principal approves of the transaction either in writing or orally. *Implied ratification* occurs when a principal knows that an unauthorized act has taken place but decides to accept it and keep its benefits.

Tort Liability of Principal and Employer

Both a principal and an employer may be held liable for torts committed by an agent or an employee. They may both be liable although they were personally not at fault, a theory known as **vicarious liability;** in the case of an employer, this liability is more specifically called **respondeat superior.**

The rules governing the vicarious liability of a principal and employer for the wrongful acts of an agent and an employee are the same.

It would be unfair to hold a principal or employer liable for every wrongful act of an agent or employee. The law is that a principal is generally liable to third parties for torts committed by an agent only when the agent is carrying on the principal's business, known as the **scope of the agency.** The same holds true for an employer's liability to third party—liability exists only when the employee acts within the *scope of employment.*

It is often difficult to determine whether an agent was acting within the scope of authority, or whether an employee was acting within the scope of employment, when a tort occurred. In general, if an act is committed in furtherance of the principal's or employer's business, it will be considered to be within the scope of the agency or employment.

If an agent or employee commits a tort while pursuing his or her own interests, the tort is not within the scope of the agency or employment, and neither the principal not the employer would be liable.

> Block, an employee of Granite Marble Co., drove the company truck to a movie theatre one night. While driving too fast for existing road conditions, his truck struck Allen and injured him. Granite would not be liable for Block's negligence because at the time of the accident, Block was pursuing his own interest and was not on company business. ∎

If an agent or employee maliciously commits an intentional tort (such as assault and battery) on a third party, the courts have interpreted such an act as a turning away from the principal's business or the employer's business and have held neither the principal nor the employer responsible. They could be held liable, however, if the agent or employee who committed the intentional tort did so in the belief that the intentional act would further the business of the agent or principal.

LIABILITY OF AGENT AND EMPLOYEE TO THIRD PARTIES

As long as an agent has the authority to act, the agent has no personal liability on a contract. The law does not recognize the agent who acts within her or his authority as a party to a contract. However, when an agent who has no authority to do so makes a contract, he or she is bound by the contract, but the principal is not.

Contract Liability of Agent

The agent is liable to third parties if (1) the agent enters into a contract without authority, (2) the agent does not disclose the principal's identity to third parties, (3) the agent is careless in signing a contract, (4) the agent voluntarily agrees to become liable on a contract, or (5) a person pretends to be an agent.

Agent Acts Without Authority   When a third party deals with an agent, the third party is in fact dealing with the principal. As a result, the law does not recognize the agent as a party to the contract when he or she acts within the scope of authority. Sometimes, however, an agent attempts to enter into a contract with a third person on behalf of the principal but lacks the authority to do so. If the principal does not ratify the transaction, the agent becomes personally liable to this third person. The agent's liability is based on an implied warranty that the agent has the authority to act as an agent on the principal's behalf.

> Farmer, an automobile insurance agent, authorized Block, whose car had been damaged in an accident, to have the car repaired at a collision shop. Farmer had no authority to permit such repairs without authorization from her insurance company. Since Farmer exceeded her authority, she would be personally liable to Block if the insurance company did not approve her unauthorized act. ■

Agent Acts for Undisclosed Principal   An agent sometimes enters into a contract in the agent's name without disclosing the name of the principal. Individuals and businesses sometimes prefer to keep secret from third parties their connection with a particular transaction, and they ask an agent to contract in the agent's own name. When third parties dealing with an agent in such circumstances are unaware of the existence of a principal, the principal is known as an **undisclosed principal.** An agent who contracts for an undisclosed principal is as liable on the contract as if the agent were the principal.

> Manger purchased office buildings as investments. To maintain secrecy, he hired Rupp as an agent to purchase several office buildings in Rupp's name from Troy, owner of the buildings. Rupp is personally liable on this contract with Troy even though Rupp was authorized to enter into the contract. Rupp's liability to Troy stems from the fact that Troy may have entered into the contract only because of the confidence Troy had that Rupp would perform the contract. If Manger refuses to go through with the contract, Troy may hold either Rupp or Manger liable, but not both. If Troy elects to enforce the contract against Rupp, Rupp may then recover the amount of the liability from Manger. ■

The undisclosed principal, once discovered, may hold a third party to a contract made with the agent even though this third party did not realize that the agent was acting for an undisclosed principal.

> Pierson hired Wilshire to purchase an antique car from Rogers. Wilshire did not reveal that she was buying the car for Pierson but signed the contract in her own name. Rogers discovered that Wilshire was purchasing the car for Pierson and refused to go through with the deal because they were on unfriendly terms. Pierson, as the now-disclosed principal, may sue Rogers for breach of contract. ■

Agent Is Careless in Signing   If the agent is acting for a disclosed principal, the agent should be careful to sign the principal's name to a written contract first and then sign her or his name as agent. For example, an agent should sign the contract "Billie Holmes (principal) by Nancy Ling, Agent." By signing in this way, the agent makes clear that the contract is between the principal and the third party and that the agent is not a party to the contract. If the agent neglects to include the principal's name on the contract, only the agent is bound by the contract.

Agent Agrees to Personal Liability   Sometimes a third party, for one reason or another, is not willing to deal directly with the principal but will deal with the agent. For example, the principal may have an unknown or bad credit rating but the agent has a strong credit rating. The principal, therefore, may ask the agent to sign the contract as a coprincipal. By doing this, the agent assumes equal liability with the principal on the contract. This situation frequently occurs when the agent and third party are well established locally but the principal is located out of town.

This same situation may also occur when an agent agrees to become personally liable on the contract to induce the third party to enter into the contract.

Person Pretends to Be an Agent   A person who pretends to be an agent of another is personally liable for any contracts made with a third party.

Beamer and several individuals decided to form a social club. Before the club could legally open its doors to members, it had to be officially registered with the state as a club. Before the club was officially registered, however, Beamer purchased some equipment for the clubhouse, claiming to be the club's treasurer. The state later refused to recognize the club. Beamer, who had claimed to be an agent for a club that legally did not exist, is personally liable on the contract for the equipment. ■

Tort Liability of Agent and Employee

An agent acting within the scope of the agency or an employee acting within the scope of employment is personally liable for torts committed against a third person even though the principal and employer are also liable. Actually, the third party may sue either the principal or the agent, the employer or the employee, or both jointly. The agent or employee is liable as the person who actually committed the tort. The principal or employer is liable because a benefit is derived from the agent's or employee's work and also because the principal or employer has the right of control over the agent or employee. In many cases, the third party sues the principal and the agent or the employer and the employee jointly.

If the third party elects to sue only one person (either the principal or the agent or the employer or the employee) and receives compensation for the tort in a court of law, that third party is then barred from suing the other party. Of course, if a successful legal action is brought against the principal or employer, the principal or the employer can then sue the agent or employee for the wrongful act.

> Flynn was a salesperson in the toy department at the Daw Department Store. During the Christmas rush, Flynn became angry and pushed a customer, causing the customer to fall to the floor and injure his back. The customer sued the store owner and received money damages for his injuries. Since the customer collected money damages from the store owner (the principal), he cannot also sue Flynn (the agent) for his injuries. ∎

CRIMINAL LIABILITY OF PRINCIPAL, AGENT, EMPLOYER, AND EMPLOYEE

Generally, neither a principal nor an employer is liable for criminal acts committed by the agent or employee. The agent or employee is personally liable.

> Weir was a sales representative for Amco Manufacturing Company. While driving a company car to a company meeting in an intoxicated condition, Weir hit and killed Tydings, a pedestrian. ∎

In the example, Weir would be criminally liable, but Amco would not. Amco would, however, have tort (civil) liability for damages (along with Weir), since Weir was acting within the scope of the agency.

A principal or employer may be held criminally liable (in addition to the agent and employee) if he or she authorizes the criminal act. Furthermore, a statute sometimes places criminal responsibility on a principal or employer such as a corporation. As an artificial person and a recognized separate legal entity, a corporation may commit crimes only through its human agents and employees.

Summary of Important Legal Concepts

A principal is liable to third parties for contracts that an agent makes if the agent is acting within the scope of the agent's express, implied, emergency, or apparent authority. An agent who makes an unauthorized contract with a third party does not bind the principal unless the principal chooses to ratify the contract.

The agent is liable for contracts made if (1) the agent acts without authority and the principal does not ratify the transaction, (2) the agent acts for an undisclosed principal, (3) the agent's name is placed on a contract in a way that binds the agent rather than the principal, (4) the agent agrees to be personally liable on a contract made on behalf of the principal, or (5) the person is not really an agent.

The principal is liable to an injured party for a tort that the agent commits while acting within the scope of the agency and while carrying out the principal's business.

An employer is also liable to an injured party for a tort that the employee commits while acting within the scope of employment and while carrying out the employee's business.

An agent acting within the scope of the agency, or an employee acting within the scope of employment, is personally liable for torts committed against a third person even though the principal or employer is also liable.

A principal is not liable for the criminal acts of

the agent unless he or she authorized the act. The agent is personally liable. The same holds true for an employer and an employee.

Key Legal Terms to Know

Match the terms with the definitions that follow.

apparent authority
emergency authority
express authority
implied authority
respondeat superior
scope of the agency
scope of authority
undisclosed principal
vicarious liability

1. Authority an agent is understood to possess to carry out the purpose of the agency
2. A principal whose identity is not known to third parties with whom the agent deals
3. The extent of the agent's authority to carry out the principal's business
4. Authority that a principal leads third parties to believe the agent possesses because of words or conduct of the principal
5. The extent of an agent's duties in carrying out the principal's business
6. Authority specifically given to the agent by the principal, either orally or in writing
7. An agent's authority to act when the agent cannot contact the principal to receive express authority
8. The liability a person has for the acts of another
9. An employer's liability for the torts committed by an employee

Questions and Problems to Discuss

1. Compare the contract liability of the principal and the agent (a) when the agent acts within the scope of authority and (b) when the agent acts without authority or does not disclose the principal's identity to third parties.
2. What are the differences between the three types of authority that an agent has?
3. Jensen was called home to California because of an emergency but did not have enough money to purchase the airline ticket. A ticket agent for Munster Airlines offered Jensen a reduced rate on the trip from New York City to California but did not get approval from corporate headquarters as required. Jensen was later billed for the additional amount but refused to pay. Can the ticket agent be held liable for the additional payment?
4. Moss was employed by the West Marlan School District as a teacher's aide in one of the elementary schools. Without any authorization, Moss permitted Drew to take her place from time to time when Moss was ill. One day while Drew was in the classroom, Kemp, a third grader, was injured through no fault of his own. Kemp's parents sued the school district. The school district denied liability, claiming that Moss, its employee, was not in the classroom at the time of the accident. Kemp's attorney proved that the school district knew and accepted the fact that Drew occasionally filled in for Moss. In addition, the school district authorized the business manager to pay Moss her full salary for the pay period following the accident without deducting for the days Drew filled in. Should Kemp be permitted to recover damages for his injuries from the West Marlan School District? Why or why not?
5. Munz, a paraplegic, was being flown from Houston, Texas, to a clinic in Rochester, Minnesota, for treatment. As Track Airlines personnel were carrying her hurriedly and roughly aboard in a special chair for wheelchair-bound people, they dropped her on the plane's stairwell. As a result, she suffered bruises and muscle spasms and experienced a substantial period of pain and suffering. Munz sued Track Airlines, claiming negligence by its agents. Is Track Airlines liable?
6. Nugent purchased a ticket for an African safari tour from Solomon, owner of the Comfort Travel Agency. The travel agency did not tell Nugent or any of the other clients booked for the African trip that it was a special agent for the tour sponsor, World Trek. During the course of the trip, the tour itinerary had to be changed. Comfort Travel Agency failed to contact Nugent, and as a result, Nugent was stranded in Egypt for one week. Nugent sued Comfort Travel Agency for damages. Comfort Travel claimed it was not liable because it was merely an agent for World Trek and World Trek was the proper party to the

lawsuit. Is the Comfort Travel Agency correct?

7. Buckner was employed by the Green Valley Bakery Company as a route salesperson. Under the terms of his employment he made calls to retailers along a designated route and brought the company car back to the company garage for overnight storage. One day, after completing his calls, Buckner drove the car 35 miles to a family picnic instead of returning it to the garage as required. On the way home from the picnic, Buckner was negligent in operating the car and hit McCracken, who was riding her bicycle on the proper side of the road. McCracken sued the Green Valley Bakery Company for her injuries. Did McCracken have a valid cause of action? Why or why not?

8. Galvin, while employed as a real estate agent for Appleton Real Estate, got into an argument with a client about Galvin's commission. He struck and injured the client, who required hospital treatment. Is Appleton liable to the customer for the injuries that resulted?

9. Buckholz, who was in charge of Carmen's Dance Studio, had been instructed to advertise weekly on a local television station. In response to the increased costs of television advertising, Carmen told Buckholz to stop advertising on TV and to switch to newspaper and radio. Feeling she would get better results, Buckholz continued the television advertising. When the bill for the television advertising arrived, Carmen refused to pay, claiming that Buckholz no longer had the authority to advertise on Television. Was Carmen liable for payment of this bill?

10. Arlis, an agent for Potts, an undisclosed principal, made a contract for Potts with Ting. Arlis signed the contract in her own name without revealing that she was an agent for Potts, whom Ting disliked. Ting, who later learned that Arlis was acting as an agent for Potts, the principal, then sued for breach of contract. Is Ting entitled to damages?

11. Doody, an agent for Hart, bought a racehorse from Zinn, making a down payment of $1,500. The balance was to be paid to Zinn after the horse was examined and found to be healthy. Although the horse was found to be healthy, Zinn was not paid the balance due. Does Zinn have the legal right to sue either Doody or Hart?

12. Krezmer, manager of Sullivan's Department Store, had a customer arrested, honestly believing that the customer was shoplifting. The charge was eventually dismissed by the judge of a local court and the customer sued the owners of the department store for false arrest. The owners denied liability, claiming that Krezmer was liable because they had not given Krezmer the authority to have suspected shoplifters arrested. Were the owners correct?

Cases to Decide

1. Schoenberger accepted a job with the Chicago Transit Authority (CTA) at a salary of $19,300, with the understanding that he would receive a $500 raise within a year. The Placement Department told Schoenberger that they would investigate this possibility but made no promises. During the interview process, ZuChristian, the senior communications analyst in the department where Schoenberger was to work, had taken it upon himself to tell Schoenberger that the increase would be given at the first performance evaluation review in about six months. Schoenberger relied on what ZuChristian said and took the job. When ZuChristian's superiors heard what he had done, they immediately informed him and Schoenberger that his act was unauthorized. When the increase was not given, Schoenberger resigned and sued CTA. At the trial, CTA showed that ZuChristian had no authority (express, implied, or apparent) to promise Schoenberger a $500 increase. CTA also proved that it did not ratify ZuChristian's unauthorized act. Was Schoenberger entitled to the additional $500 raise? (*Schoenberger* v. *Chicago Transit Authority*, 84 Ill App 3d 1132, 39 Ill Dec 941, 405 NE2d 1076)

2. Como, an accountant, was looking for employment in the state of Montana. Rhines, president of Sound West, Inc., agreed to hire Como. After Como moved and settled his family, Rhines told him there was no job. Como found a job elsewhere and sued Rhines for lost wages and moving expenses for breach of an employment contract. In court, Rhines argued that he was acting as an agent for Sound West; therefore, he was not personally liable to Como. Como argued that Rhines never disclosed that he was an agent for Sound West but rather gave the impression that he owned and managed the business. The

principal-agent relationship (between Sound West and Rhines) was actually disclosed during the trial. Was Rhines liable to Como for damages resulting from breach of the employment contract? (*Como* v. *Rhines*, 645 P2d 948)

3. Clarke and Manko, both agents of Reserve Insurance Company, attended a convention relating to their work, although their attendance was not required by the company. While at the convention, Clarke and Manko met Jones, a former agent of Reserve Insurance. Following one of the convention meetings attended by all three, a fight developed between Clarke and Jones over a book, which Jones contended Clarke had not returned to him. Jones, who was injured in the fight, sued the Reserve Insurance Company, claiming that the company was liable for the tort of assault and battery committed by one of its agents, Clarke, who was acting in the scope of the agency. Can the Reserve Insurance Company be held responsible for Clarke's behavior? (*Jones* v. *Reserve Insurance Co.*, 253 NE2d 849)

4. Laccoaree ran a grocery store and employed his son part time in the store. Laccoaree asked his son to pick up supplies for the store in the nearby town of Roseburg. While returning to the store with the supplies, the truck the son was driving negligently struck a vehicle driven by Stanfield. Stanfield sued Laccoaree for damages to the car. Is Laccoaree liable for the accident in which the son was involved? (*Stanfield* v. *Laccoaree*, Oregon 588 P2d 1271)

5. The Bradleys, who were black, were interested in purchasing a house. They noticed a FOR SALE sign in front of one house that was listed with the Brabham Agency. When the Bradleys contacted the agency to inspect the house, Pate, a salesperson, refused to show it to them, claiming he was not interested in selling to blacks. The Bradleys sued the Brabham Agency for damages under the Fair Housing Act, which makes it illegal for a salesperson to refuse to show a house for racial reasons. The Brabham Agency claimed it was not responsible for Pate's actions. Is Brabham correct? (*Bradley* v. *John M. Brabham Agency, Inc.*, SC 463 F Supp 27)

Susan Royal, an employee of the Wilson Tool & Die Company, was a model of efficiency and a stickler for detail. She became convinced that her employer was not complying to the fullest extent with the safety regulations of the Occupational Safety and Health Act (OSHA). She would call a representative of the agency to complain about every alleged violation of the act, even reporting minor incidents or problems that were not potential hazards to any employees. Susan's supervisor discovered that Susan was making these calls and asked her to stop making them, on the grounds that they were disruptive to the work that was being done at the tool and die company. Susan continued to make the calls, however, and she was finally told by her supervisor that if she continued to do so, her employer would consider firing her.

Believing that she was going to be fired, Susan voluntarily resigned from the company and then submitted a claim for unemployment compensation. She was denied compensation on the grounds that she had terminated her employment voluntarily. Susan decided to appeal the decision.

The Trial

During the trial Susan testified about the various alleged violations of the OSHA rules. She stated that she was concerned about the safety of her fellow employees and that she felt that it was her duty to complain about such violations. On cross-examination, she admitted that she had never complained about the alleged violations to her supervisor, or indeed to anyone else in the company, but had reported the alleged violations only to OSHA.

A safety expert testified at trial that the violations were minor and in no way constituted a hazard to the employees. A company executive testified that it was standard procedure at the company for employees to report infringements of safety regulations to their immediate supervisors so that steps could be taken to correct the violations.

The Arguments at Trial

Susan's attorney argued that as an employee, Susan had the right and perhaps the obligation to report safety violations to the proper officials. The attorney further argued that Susan was convinced that she was going to be fired. Rather than have a discharge appear on her record, therefore, she had voluntarily resigned. In these circumstances, she should be treated as if she had been wrongfully discharged.

Wilson Tool & Die's attorney argued that Susan's first obligation was to report any alleged violations to the company so that actions could be taken to correct them. The company's attorney further argued that Susan's action constituted insubordination, which would have entitled the company to fire Susan. The attorney further argued that while Susan might have believed that she was going to be fired, she was not in fact dismissed, and her voluntary resignation was unnecessary and premature.

Question to Discuss

1. Based on the facts presented here, who do you think should prevail on appeal, Susan or the company? Why?
2. Are there any other factors that would make it easier to decide who has the better argument on appeal?
3. How do you feel the appellate court should decide this appeal? Why?
4. Aside from the question of Susan's entitlement to unemployment compensation in this case, do you think she would have a good case against her employer for unlawful termination? Why or why not?

PART VI

BUSINESS ORGANIZATION AND REGULATION

After studying Part VI, you should be able to

1 Describe the three major forms of business organization.

2 List advantages and disadvantages of the sole proprietorship, the partnership, and the corporation.

3 Describe the rights, duties, powers, and liabilities of partners to each other and to third parties.

4 Describe the two types of stock issued by a corporation.

5 Identify the two kinds of powers a corporation has and distinguish between them.

6 Describe the rights, duties, powers, and liabilities of stockholders, directors, and officers of a corporation.

7 Describe several ways in which government regulates business.

Chapter 26

Sole Proprietorships and Partnerships

CHAPTER HIGHLIGHTS

This chapter discusses the two most common forms of business organization in the United States, the sole proprietorship and the partnership. It describes the advantages and disadvantages of each type of organization. It outlines the methods used to form each type and discusses the various types of partners a partnership may have.

How a partnership is operated, what the rights and duties of partners are, and how a partnership may be terminated are all important matters examined here. The limited partnership, another form of business organization being used with greater frequency, is discussed—its advantages and disadvantages, how one is formed, the liability of partners, and how it may be terminated. The chapter concludes with a discussion of other forms of business organization.

FORMS OF BUSINESS OWNERSHIP

Many of you may decide to go into business. You may work for yourself or for others. Whatever business you enter will have a distinctive type of ownership. Although there are a variety of ways in which businesses may legally organize, the three most common forms of ownership are the sole proprietorship, the partnership, and the corporation. Corporations are discussed in Chapter 27.

THE SOLE PROPRIETORSHIP

Most businesses in the United States are owned and operated by individuals. This form of business organization is known as the **sole proprietorship.**

There are no formalities required to establish a sole proprietorship. It is the most easily started of the three major types of business organization. Anyone who wants to start a business and has the money to do so may start a sole proprietorship. Any person starting a business must comply with all government rules and regulations that apply to businesses in general and to that person's business in particular. This compliance may include obtaining a license for a certain type of business or profession, such as operating a taxi or practicing medicine. It will also usually include registering as a collector of state and local sales taxes. In most states, a person using a business or trade name different from her or his own name must register that name in a public office. The owner of the business must also be identified. This enables consumers to know with whom they may be dealing.

> ■ Hardy decided to open a pizza restaurant under the name Hardy's Pizza. Hardy would not be required to register the name. However, if Hardy used the name "A-1 Pizza" instead, she would have to register the name and identify herself as the owner so that the public would know they were dealing with Hardy when buying pizza at her restaurant. ■

In a sole proprietorship, the owner has the full responsibility for managing the business. Generally the owner supplies all the capital (money and other property) needed to start and operate the business, although additional money may be borrowed. The income from a sole proprietorship goes entirely to the owner, but so do the losses. The owner of a sole proprietorship receives no special tax advantages. Income the owner receives from the business is added to whatever income the owner may have from other sources; all of the owner's income is taxed at the same rate.

As with any form of business organization, the sole proprietorship has both advantages and disadvantages. One advantage is that the sole proprietorship is a very flexible form of business organization, allowing the owner to manage the business as he or she likes. In addition, no special legal formalities are required to set up a sole proprietorship, other than minor requirements such as purchasing a business permit or paying licensing fees.

The sole proprietorship also has disadvantages. Many small business owners go out of business every year, some of them because they do not have enough capital to continue to operate the business. The risk of not being successful and losing all or most of the money invested in the business must be borne by the owner alone. The owner, and only the owner, is liable for all the debts of the business. Another disadvantage is that the sole proprietorship ceases to exist when the owner dies or retires. The business may continue, often under the same name, but the ownership changes.

THE PARTNERSHIP

The Uniform Partnership Act contains most of the laws relating to the formation, operation, and dissolution of partnerships. It has been adopted in all states except Louisiana. The Act defines a **partnership** as "an association of two or more persons to carry on as co-owners a business for profit." The persons who are associated in the business are known as **partners.**

People who join together for some activity are not always considered to be associated in a partnership. The Uniform Partnership Act specifically refers to people joining together in a *business,* and this means the sharing of investment, management, and work. The Act would not include as a partnership the joint ownership of property where no management would be involved. It would also not include joint efforts of nonprofit organizations or unincorporated associations that were formed for charitable or recreational purposes.

> Doctors Varga and Dale formed a nonprofit clinic to provide medical care for needy persons. Their organization would not be considered a partnership because it was not formed to earn a profit. ■

Like a sole proprietorship, partners using a business or trade name different from their own names must register the partnership name and their own names in a public office. Identification of the partners is required so that the public may know with whom they are dealing.

Under the Uniform Partnership Act, a partnership is treated as a legal entity. It can buy, hold title to, and sell real estate in its own name. It can also make bank deposits and purchase securities. It is also treated as a legal entity for accounting purposes.

In some states, a partnership may sue or be sued in its own name. The title of a suit brought by a partnership, for example, would be "John Doe and Richard Roe, doing business as Doe and Roe, a partnership," and not "Doe and Roe." In other states, actions by or against a partnership must be brought in the names of the partners.

A partnership is not a legal entity for tax purposes. There is no such thing as an income tax on partnerships. The partnership acts like a funnel, pouring profits and losses into the hands of the partners. The partners must include on their personal income tax returns their individual shares of the partnership profits and losses. Partnerships are required, nevertheless, to file informational returns for federal and state tax purposes.

The advantages of operating a business as a partnership are the ease of organization and dissolution, informality in management, and lack of a partnership income tax. The disadvantages are the unlimited liability of partners for partnership debts and torts, the difficulty of settling disputes among the partners, the difficulty in transferring a partnership interest, the lack of continuity, and the danger of dissolution if a partner withdraws or dies. As will be seen in the next chapter, the advantages and disadvantages of a partnership are the opposite of the advantages and disadvantages of a corporation.

Types of Partners and Partnerships

Partnerships are often classified according to their purpose and the extent of the partners' liability. A **trading partnership** is an association for commercial purposes, such as a manufacturing, wholesale, or retail business. A **nontrading partnership** is an association for professional purposes, such as a law firm.

Partnerships may also be classified as general or limited partnerships. A *general partnership* is the customary partnership in which all partners share equal liability for the debts and torts of the partnership. A **general partner** is a fully active partner.

There are many other types of partners in addition to general partners. A **silent partner** is inactive in a general partnership but is known to the public as a partner. A **secret partner** is active in the partnership but is not known to the public as a partner. A **dormant partner** is neither active in the partnership nor known to the public as a partner.

Another type of partnership that is recognized in most states is the limited partnership. A *limited partnership* has both general partners and limited partners. A **limited partner** contributes cash or property to the business but may not take part in its operation and thus has limited liability for partnership obligations. The limited partner is not bound by the obligations of the partnership and is not subject to any personal liability beyond the investment made in the business. A limited partner who does participate in the operation of the business will take on the same liability as the general partner. Often, however, limited partners have different roles in management and control of partnership operations.

Forming a Partnership

A partnership results when two or more persons decide to form one. Like other commercial arrangements, it arises from an express agreement or by implication from the acts of the parties.

As with other contracts, a partnership agreement, to be valid, must meet the usual tests of legal capacity of the parties and the absence of fraud and/ or duress in the formation of the contract.

Express Agreement An express agreement establishing a partnership may be either oral or written. If the term of the partnership will be greater than one year, however, the statute of frauds applies and the agreement must be in writing to be enforceable. But, in any instance, to avoid any disputes among the partners, a written contract is advisable.

The written agreement creating the partnership is usually called the **partnership agreement,** or the articles of copartnership. An example of a partnership agreement appears in Figure 26.1. It should include the name of the partnership, its main office, and the names and addresses of the partners. It should also state the term of the partnership, the initial investment of each partner, and a formula for sharing profits and losses. It is advisable to include provisions for settling disputes, for the death or retirement of a partner, and for the purchase of the interest of a withdrawing partner.

Implication A partnership may also arise by implication from the acts of the partners. Two or more persons often join together in a business and conduct it as a partnership without formally agreeing that it is a partnership. It is treated as a partnership by the partners and by any third parties who deal with them.

A partnership will be implied only when the partners conduct their business in a manner typical of formal partnerships. This includes sharing profits and losses, sharing control over the business, sharing an interest in the partnership property, and showing the intention to have a partnership. If any of these factors is missing, the relationship is not a partnership.

▪ Vanderver and Stern were partners operating a small department store. They brought in Lewis as a general manager and agreed to pay her 20 percent of the profits of the store for her services. Even though she shared in the profits, Lewis was not a partner because the other elements of a partnership were missing, such as sharing an interest in the partnership property and having an equal voice in controlling the business. ▪

PARTNERSHIP AGREEMENT

This agreement, made June 20, 19--, between Penelope Wolfburg of 783A South
Street, Hazelton, Idaho, and Ingrid Swenson of RR 5, Box 96, Hazelton, Idaho.

1. The above named persons have this day formed a partnership that shall
   operate under the name of W-S Jewelers, located at 85 Broac Street, Hazelton,
   Idaho 83335, and shall engage in jewelry sales and repairs.

2. The duration of this agreement will be for a term of fifteen (15) years,
   beginning on June 20, 19--, or for a shorter term if agreed upon in writing
   by both partners.

3. The initial investment by each partner will be as follows: Penelope
   Wolfburg, assets and liabilities of Wolfburg's Jewelry Store, valued at a
   capital investment of $40,000; Ingrid Swenson, cash of $20,000. These
   investments are partnership property.

4. Each partner will give her time, skill, and attention to the operation of
   this partnership and will engage in no other business enterprise unless
   permission is granted in writing by the other partner.

5. The salary for each partner will be as follows: Penelope Wolfburg, $40,000
   per year; Ingrid Swenson, $30,000 per year. Neither partner may withdraw
   cash or other assets from the business without express permission in
   writing from the other partner. All profits and losses of the business will
   be shared as follows: Penelope Wolfburg, 60 percent; Ingrid Swenson, 40
   percent.

6. Upon the dissolution of the partnership due to termination of this agreement,
   or to written permission by each of the partners, or to the death or
   incapacitation of one or both partners, a new contract may be entered into
   by the partners or the sole continuing partner has the option to purchase
   the other partner's interest in the business at a price that shall not exceed
   the balance in the terminating partner's capital account. The payment shall
   be made in cash in equal quarterly installments from the date of termination.

7. At the conclusion of this contract, unless it is agreed by both partners to
   continue the operation of the business under a new contract, the assets of
   the partnership, after the liabilities are paid, will be divided in
   proportion to the balance in each partner's capital account on that date.

Penelope Wolfburg   _Ingrid Swenson_
Penelope Wolfburg   Ingrid Swenson

June 20, 19--   _June 20, 19--_
Date   Date

Figure 26.1
Partnership
Agreement

Operation of a Partnership

A partnership operates according to the provisions of the partnership
agreement and the Uniform Partnership Act. Principles of the law of contracts
and agency also apply. To a great extent, a partnership operates according
to custom, the nature of the business, and the relationship between the
partners. All partnerships share one thing in common—the partners have
rights, duties, powers, and liabilities to each other and to nonpartners.

Rights of Partners   The first important right of partners is to participate in management. Unless the partnership agreement holds otherwise, all partners have a right to participate in management on an equal basis, regardless of how the profits and losses are shared. The partners may and usually do give certain partners more responsibility than others. Partners may also be given different types of responsibilities depending on their education, skills, and experience.

As in other business organizations, decisions in a partnership on most matters are decided by majority vote. If there are only two partners and they cannot agree, the dispute will be resolved according to the provisions included in the partnership agreement. If the agreement contains no provisions for settling disputes, the partners will have to go to court or dissolve the partnership.

Certain decisions are so important that they affect the existence of the partnership. In such a case, the decision must be unanimous. A unanimous vote is required, for example, when the partners wish to amend the partnership agreement so that there is a material change in the nature of the business. A unanimous vote is also required to change the contributions of the partners, start a new business, or admit other partners.

> Zivan had a 10 percent interest in a partnership that operated a stereo shop. If the partners decide to change the business to a bakery store, they cannot do so without Zivan's consent. ■

The second important right of a partner is to share in the profits (and losses) of the partnership. The partners may and usually do divide up the profits, by agreement, according to their individual investments in or contributions to the partnership. In actual practice, some partners are more active than others in the operation of a partnership. They may receive a salary in addition to a share of the profits.

> Jasper was one of three partners in a bicycle repair business. The partnership agreement did not have a provision about sharing the profits. If Jasper does only 5 percent of the work involved in operating the partnership, she is still entitled to one-third of the profits. ■

A third important right is to share in the property of the partnership. Unless the partnership agreement provides otherwise, a partner has an equal interest in the property owned by the partnership and used for partnership purposes. The interest is not in a specific piece of property but only in all partnership property in general, including real property, accounts receivable, goodwill, and so forth. A partner cannot use specific partnership property for personal purposes and cannot transfer an interest in specific property.

A fourth important right is that of inspecting the books and records of the partnership. Any partner has the right to know how the business is being conducted. To accomplish this, a partner may examine any and all records kept by the partnership. The partner may also make copies of them. The records must be kept in a stated place and must be available for inspection at reasonable hours.

A fifth important right is that of an accounting. Under the Uniform Partnership Act, a partner has a right to an accounting of partnership assets and liabilities to determine the value of each partner's shares when:

1. The partnership agreement provides for it.
2. The other partners wrongfully exclude a partner from management and/or inspection of the partnership records.
3. Another partner withholds profits or benefits that rightfully belong to the partnership.
4. It is just and reasonable under the circumstances.

A court can compel an accounting, usually upon a dissolution of a partnership by court order.

Duties of Partners   A partnership is a relationship based on trust and confidence. Partners usually work closely together and certain duties are imposed upon them because of the personal nature of the relationship. These include the duties of loyalty, use of reasonable care, and accounting for actions taken.

Loyalty in a partnership means acting in good faith and in the best interests of the partnership. Whether dealing with the other partners or with outsiders, a partner may not obtain a personal benefit or take any action that harms the partnership. In addition, a partner may not participate in any activity that either competes with the partnership or interferes with the expected performance of duties.

■ McVee and Carter were partners operating a drug store. McVee had an opportunity to buy an interest in another drug store one block away. McVee is not entitled to buy the interest because it would mean competing with his own partner. If McVee does go ahead and purchase the interest, he must account to Carter for a share of the profits from the second store. ■

A partner must use reasonable skill and care in conducting partnership business. Regardless of other obligations or participation in other businesses, a partner must devote time and skill to the partnership or the relationship is considered breached.

A partner is required to account to the other partners for actions taken and any benefits obtained. This means that a partner is liable to other partners for breach of the duties of loyalty and use of reasonable care. It also means accounting for and sharing any advantages obtained that arise from the partnership business.

■ Albertson and Posniak were partners in a used-car business. Albertson learned that a valuable antique car was for sale at a reasonable price. She bought the car and resold it at a large profit. Posniak is entitled to a share of the profit because the transaction concerned partnership business. ■

Powers of Partners   Just as a partnership may be created by express agreement or by implication, the powers of a partner may be either express or implied. The source of express powers is the partnership agreement as well as the Uniform Partnership Act. The sources of implied powers are the oral agreement among the partners, the nature and customs of the business, and the general laws of agency. These powers include the power to make contracts, to buy and sell partnership property, to borrow money, and to hire employees and agents. The general rule is that a partner has the power to do all of these things and bind the other partners as well, provided what is done is carried out in the ordinary course of partnership business.

One partner may enter into binding contracts for the business, provided the contract is made in the ordinary course of partnership business and the partner has the apparent authority to enter into the contract. This is often determined by what is customary in the business in question and in the type of business in general.

A partner may buy and sell goods and services, including real property, in the ordinary course of business. A partnership is bound by purchases made by a partner and must pay for them. It is also bound by sales made by a partner in the ordinary course of business and must execute any documents required to transfer title.

A partner may receive or borrow money for the business. When a bank agrees to lend money to a partnership, or a creditor is willing to extend credit, it wants to make sure that the partnership is bound by the loan or credit agreement. The general rule is that a partner may borrow money and obtain credit for the partnership and bind it, as long as the borrowing is in the ordinary course of business.

> Morton was a partner in a company that manufactured fencing. She wanted to borrow money to finance the purchase of a new boat for her family. At the bank's request, she signed a promissory note on behalf of the partnership and received the money. The partnership is not bound by the note because the loan was not in the ordinary course of the partnership business. ■

A partner may hire and fire employees and agents. Hiring is often the responsibility of one of the partners. As long as the employees or agents are hired for the usual and ordinary work of the business, the partnership is bound by the contracts of employment.

Liability of Partners   Partners have obligations to each other and to outsiders. A breach of those obligations may impose liability on all the partners. A partner is liable to other partners for a breach of duty, such as benefiting at the expense of the partnership or defrauding the other partners. Just as partners share profits, they also share losses. A partner is liable to the other partners for her or his share of the partnership's debts and obligations. A partner who pays a higher share of partnership debts has a right to be reimbursed by the other partners.

Partners are liable to outsiders for contracts made by other partners and for torts and crimes committed by other partners, provided they occur within the apparent scope of the business of the partnership. Personal assets of the partners, as well as the partnership property, may be taken to satisfy debts.

If a partner enters into a verbal agreement on behalf of the partnership, all partners are jointly liable on the contract. If a partner commits a tort for which the partnership is liable, such as fraud or negligence, all of the partners are jointly and severally liable. **Joint and several liability** means that the wronged party may sue all the partners in a single legal action or any one of the partners individually. If a partner commits a crime in the course of the partnership operations and a fine is imposed, the partners are jointly liable for payment of the fine.

> Barker, Crone, and Dobbs were partners in a car rental business. Crone rented a car with faulty brakes to a couple, who were injured in an accident caused by brake failure. The couple may sue Barker, Crone, or Dobbs, or all three together, for their injuries. ■

A judgment obtained against a partnership is satisfied first out of partnership assets. If those assets are insufficient, a judgment creditor may then proceed against the personal assets of the individual partners. A creditor with a judgment against a partner (as distinct from a judgment against the *partnership*) may not attempt to collect the judgment from partnership assets—only from a partner's interest in the partnership. A partnership may also file in its own name for protection under the bankruptcy laws.

New partners and retiring partners may also be liable for certain partnership actions. Under the Uniform Partnership Act, a new partner is liable for the obligations of the partnership arising before he or she joined the partnership. But the personal assets of the new partner may not be used to satisfy any of those obligations. Retiring partners are also liable for obligations created while they were members of the partnership, until those debts are paid. Retiring partners are also liable for obligations of the partnership arising after their retirement until a certificate showing the change of partnership members is filed in the appropriate office.

Termination of the Partnership

The termination of a partnership is known as **dissolution.** Dissolution may occur for several reasons, such as expiration of the partnership term, agreement among the parties, a change in the members of the partnership, death of a partner, bankruptcy, or court order.

Many partnership agreements provide for a specific term for the life of the partnership. When that term ends, the partnership is dissolved. The partners may, if they wish, renew the partnership. If the agreement does not set a time for the partnership to end, the partnership continues until it is dissolved for other reasons. Partners may, by agreement, dissolve the partnership at any time. The vote to dissolve must be unanimous, and the rights of creditors of the partnership must be respected.

If a partner retires from a firm or a new partner is added, the relationship among the other partners is considered changed to such an extent that the partnership is dissolved. Most agreements provide that the partnership will continue despite the admission of a new partner or the retirement or withdrawal of an old one, provided the other partners agree to the change.

If a partner withdraws from a partnership in violation of the partnership agreement, that partner may be liable to the other partners for breach of contract. If the partnership agreement is silent about withdrawal, there will be no liability unless the suddenness of the withdrawal causes severe damage to the partnership.

> Jones and Gray, a partnership formed to paint office buildings, had a contract to paint the state capitol. Jones withdrew from the partnership in the middle of the job without any advance warning. The state then canceled the contract and the partnership was forced into bankruptcy. The partnership agreement was silent about withdrawals, but Jones may be liable to the partnership for damages caused by his actions. ■

The death of a partner usually results in the dissolution of the partnership. Most partnership agreements provide for the purchase of the deceased partner's interest in the partnership, allowing the partnership to continue. Many partnerships carry insurance on each partner's life to finance the purchase of a deceased partner's interest in the business.

Under the Uniform Partnership Act, the transfer by sale or gift of a partner's interest in a partnership, or the sale of a partner's interest to satisfy a judgment does not automatically cause the dissolution of the partnership. The remaining partners may permit the partnership to continue or may ask for dissolution of the partnership because of changed circumstances.

The bankruptcy of the partnership itself or of an individual partner will dissolve the partnership. A dissolution may also occur by court order. This happens when a partner asks the court to dissolve the partnership for one or more reasons, including inability to continue in business, insanity of a partner, or a deadlock that prevents agreement from being reached.

> Cannon and Swartzell were partners in a stock brokerage business. They could not agree on the best way to borrow money for the partnership. A loan was needed to permit the company to remain in business. Cannon could seek a court order dissolving the partnership because of the inability to reach agreement. ■

Dissolution does not mean the immediate termination of the partnership. Certain steps must be taken to wind up the partnership affairs. After those steps are taken, the partnership either ends or starts up again under a new agreement.

One step involved in winding up the partnership is to give notice of the dissolution to creditors. This protects creditors who have first claim on the partnership assets. Another step is to prepare an accounting of the partnership assets and liabilities. The final step is to distribute the partnership assets. Creditors are paid first, then partners who have lent money to the partnership. Any funds remaining are paid to the partners according to the partnership agreement. Until all these steps are completed, the partners continue to have authority to bind the partnership.

LIMITED PARTNERSHIP

In recent years, the limited partnership has become a popular form of business organization. It is typically used for the syndication of real estate purchases, the formation of leasing companies, and the financing of movies and plays. Unknown at common law, limited partnerships are the creatures of state law; all states have enacted laws permitting limited partnerships.

A limited partnership is in effect a hybrid—a partnership form that contains many elements of a corporation. It was designed to enable investors to put capital into a venture in a form that would have the advantage of operating as a partnership but in which liability would be limited, as in a corporation. A limited partnership has both general and limited partners. The general partner invests in the partnership and is completely responsible for its management. The limited partner also invests but has no management role.

The law that governs limited partnerships is the Uniform Limited Partnership Act (ULPA) adopted by all states except Delaware and Louisiana. A number of states have also adopted a Revised Uniform Limited Partnership Act. These Acts cover the formation of limited partnerships, the rights and duties of general and limited partners, and dissolution of the partnership.

Forming a Limited Partnership

The UPLA contains specific requirements for the formation of a limited partnership. There must be a minimum of two partners. They must execute a certificate that states the partnership's name, purpose, duration, and location of its principal place of business; the name and address of each general and limited partner; and the amount of capital each invested. The certificate must be filed in a designated public office. In many states, notice of filing and a summary of the provisions of the certificate must be published in an official newspaper, a newspaper designated by a government body to carry official notices.

Role and Liability of the Partners

The general partners in a limited partnership are completely responsible for managing the partnership; they are also personally liable for the partnership's debts. The limited partner may not participate in management, must contribute cash or property and not services, and cannot have his or her name as part of the partnership name. In return for these concessions, a limited partner's liability for partnership debts is limited to the amount of capital he or she contributed.

As is the case with regular partnerships, a limited partner has the right to inspect the books and records of the partnership, the right to an accounting, and the right to participate in the dissolution of the partnership and the distribution of its assets.

Dissolution

A limited partnership may be dissolved for the same reasons and in the same manner as a regular partnership with a few exceptions. It will be dissolved when its term ends; it may be dissolved by agreement among the general and limited partners. The bankruptcy of a general partner dissolves a limited partnership, but the bankruptcy of a limited partner does not.

LIMITED LIABILITY COMPANY

Since 1977, thirty-eight states have enacted legislation authorizing a new type of business ownership, the **limited liability company** (LLC). Like the limited partnership, the LLC is a hybrid of the corporation and the partnership. It is taxed like a partnership, enabling investors to take advantage of losses and to avoid the double taxation of corporations. Like the corporation, investors have limited liability—only the business assets, not the personal assets of the investors, are subject to judgments resulting from business lawsuits.

The LLC is very similar to a limited partnership but with two added advantages. Recall that in a limited partnership, only the limited partners, not the general partners, have limited liability. In an LLC, all members have limited liability. In a limited partnership, limited partners are prohibited from any active management of the business. In an LLC, all members may participate in active management and still enjoy limited liability.

More states will probably enact legislation permitting the formation of LLC's. This is expected because in 1988, the Internal Revenue Service issued a ruling confirming that an LLC organized in Wyoming would be treated as a partnership for income tax purposes.

For an LLC to obtain the tax benefits of a partnership under IRS regulations, the LLC must be set up in such a way that it lacks at least two of the following characteristics of a corporation: (1) limited liability, (2) centralized management, (3) continuity of life, and (4) free transferability of interests. An LLC that possesses three or more of those characteristics will be treated as a corporation for federal income tax purposes.

OTHER FORMS OF BUSINESS ORGANIZATIONS

In addition to the more common forms of business organizations, there are other less common forms that are used for special purposes. These include the joint venture, the syndicate, and the cooperative.

Joint Venture

A **joint venture** is a business arrangement in which two or more separate persons or business organizations join together to work on a project that each would be unable to handle separately. The project may be too large, too expensive, or too complicated for one of them but manageable if they work together. A joint venture may be treated as a partnership or a corporation, depending on how it is formed and how closely the parties are tied together.

Syndicate

A less formal type of joint venture is called a **syndicate.** This form is often used by individuals to purchase assets such as real estate, franchises, and racehorses. Depending on how it is formed, it may be either a corporation or some form of partnership.

Cooperative

A **cooperative** is a nonprofit (often called not-for-profit) arrangement set up to provide certain benefits to its members. The members wish to pool their resources and talents to accomplish what they could not do individually. Some cooperatives are formed just for purchasing—to enable members to buy goods and services at reduced prices because of group volume. Some, such as farm cooperatives, are organized to market products in order to get the benefit of controlling supply and prices and qualify for reduced shipping rates.

Cooperatives may be treated as partnerships or corporations, depending on how they are formed and on state laws. Their business operations, powers, and liabilities will be determined by their form of organization.

Summary of Important Legal Concepts

The sole proprietorship is the most common form of business organization. It is also the easiest type of business to form, operate, and dissolve. The owner has sole responsibility for managing the business, receives all profits, and is responsible for all losses.

The operation of a partnership is governed by the partnership agreement and the provisions of the Uniform Partnership Act. Partners can agree on their respective shares of management, profits, losses, and partnership property. Unless otherwise stated in the partnership agreement, they share equally.

A partnership is treated as a legal entity—it can hold title to real estate in its own name and, in some states, may sue or be sued in its own name. It is not a legal entity for tax purposes, however, and there is no such thing as an income tax on partnerships.

Partnerships come into existence either by agreement or by the acts of the partners. After a partnership is formed, partners have the right to participate in management, to share in the profits (and losses), to share in the property of the partnership, and to receive an accounting. A partner also has obligations to the other partners. These include loyalty, use of reasonable care, and accounting for actions taken. A partnership may be bound by the contracts, torts, and crimes of a partner if they are done with apparent authority and in the ordinary scope of partnership business.

A partnership may be dissolved because of expiration of its term, agreement, change in membership, death of a partner, bankruptcy, or court order.

The advantages of operating a business as a

partnership are the ease of organization and dissolution, informality in management, and the lack of a partnership income tax. The disadvantages are the unlimited liability of partners for partnership debts and torts, lack of continuity, and dissolution if a partner withdraws or dies.

A limited partnership is permitted by law in every state. This form of organization is a hybrid of a corporation and a partnership. The limited partnership is treated as a partnership for income tax purposes, avoiding the double taxation of corporations. At the same time, the limited partners enjoy the limited liability of stockholders—they are not personally liable for the partnership's debts. In return for these advantages, however, a limited partner may not participate in management. A limited partnership is formed and dissolved in much the same way as a regular partnership, except that with a limited partnership the formation and registration requirements are much more complicated.

Other forms of business organization are the limited liability company, the joint venture, the syndicate, and the cooperative. The limited liability company is a recent form of business organization permitted in some states. It is similar to a limited partnership, with the added advantage that all partners have limited liability and all may participate in management.

Key Legal Terms to Know

Match the terms with the definitions that follow.

cooperative
dissolution
dormant partner
general partner
joint and several liability
joint venture
limited liability company
limited partner
nontrading partnership
partner
partnership
partnership agreement
secret partner
silent partner
sole proprietorship
syndicate
trading partnership

1. A partner whose liability is limited to the amount of capital invested
2. Termination of partnership existence
3. A business owned and operated by one person
4. Written agreement that creates a partnership
5. A partner known to the public but inactive in management
6. A partner unknown to the public and inactive in management
7. An association of two or more companies engaged in a common project
8. Liability of partners as a group or individually
9. A partner unknown to the public but active in management
10. A partner fully active and known to the public
11. A partnership doing business for commercial purposes
12. An association of two or more persons to carry on, as co-owners, a business for profit
13. Persons who are co-owners of a business
14. A partnership doing business for professional purposes
15. An informal type of joint venture
16. A nonprofit business arrangement for the benefit of members
17. A limited partnership that permits all partners to participate in management

Questions and Problems to Discuss

1. Explain the differences among general, silent, secret, and dormant partners.
2. What are the advantages and disadvantages of the partnership form of business organization?
3. Huntley and Dodge were partners in a dry cleaning business. While making deliveries one day, Huntley went the wrong way down a one-way street and injured a pedestrian. Is Dodge liable for the pedestrian's injuries?
4. Flores and Luke were partners in a florist business, Flores owning a 70 percent interest and Luke a 30 percent interest. If a creditor obtains a judgment against the partnership, is Luke liable for only 30 percent of the amount due?
5. Freymann worked for Craft as a clerk in Craft's store. Freymann's monthly pay was 20 percent of the net profits of the business for that month. Freymann followed Craft's orders, making no management decisions. Are Freymann and Craft partners?

6. O'Connell, Russ, and Lerner owned and operated a 600-acre farm as partners. O'Connell who had a large personal debt, wanted to deed to his creditor his interest in 200 acres of the farmland. Russ and Lerner claimed that O'Connell couldn't do this. Are they right?

7. Mace and Singh, partners in the Realworth Company, owned land in the firm's name. Mace sold the land to Salem without telling Singh. Mace signed the deed "Realworth Company, by Mace, Partner." Realworth Company was not in the business of selling land. Salem did not know that Mace was selling the land without Singh's knowledge. Can Salem get clear title to the land?

8. Hurley, Ling, and Holt were partners in a bowling alley. Hurley and Ling decided they wanted to change the percentage of profits that each partner was to receive. Can they do so without Holt's consent?

9. Mill and Nolan operated a drugstore as partners. Mill became tired of the business and wanted to withdraw from the partnership. Nolan did not want her to withdraw. If the partnership agreement says nothing about leaving the partnership, may Mill do so?

10. Landrum decided to open a sandwich shop and call it "The Eatery." Is she required to register that name in a public office?

11. Barnes and Brooks operated a bookstore for ten years. They had no partnership agreement but divided the profits and management equally. The name Barnes and Brooks was on the store, its sales slips, and its purchase orders. If the partnership is held liable for Barnes's negligence, can Brooks avoid liability because there was no partnership agreement?

12. Curry owned 2 percent of an oil and gas drilling partnership. He wanted to examine the partnership records to learn the nature of the expenses of the partnership. The partnership officers denied Curry the right to examine the records on the grounds that his ownership interest was too small. Is this correct?

Cases to Decide

1. Brodsky, a lawyer, acted as general manager and attorney for a theatrical production produced by Stadlen. Brodsky's compensation was a fixed weekly salary and 2 percent of the gross profits. He also lent money to Stadlen but was not responsible for any losses. Brodsky claims he is a partner in the production business. Is he correct? (*Brodsky* v. *Stadlen*, NY, 138 App Div 2d 662-No. 7).

2. Plastex sold merchandise worth $9,900 to a company called "Central Pump and Supply Company." Central paid only part of the amount due and Plastex sued for the balance. Plastex brought suit against Johnson and another person, naming them as partners "doing business as Central Pump and Supply Company, a partnership." Johnson claimed he was not a partner, even though he owned the property in which the business was located, his signature appeared on the bank card for the partnership, and he wrote a letter asking for credit for the partnership. Can Johnson be held liable as a partner? (*Johnson* v. *Plastex Company*, Oklahoma 500 P2d 596)

3. Lewis and Dinkelspeel opened up a furniture business as a partnership. They purchased furniture, fixtures, and merchandise together. They agreed that the profits would be divided equally and that Dinkelspeel would be in charge of running the business. While Lewis was supposed to raise funds and provide space for the business, Lewis's interest was not to be disclosed to the public. When the partnership failed to pay for certain goods and was sued, Lewis denied liability as a partner. Is he liable? (*International Association Credit Men* v. *Lewis et. al.*, 50 Wyo 380)

4. Lavin, Dillworth, and Ehrlich were partners in a tax preparation business, located in a store. Ehrlich served notice that he wished to dissolve the partnership, then proceeded to buy the store, and refused to renegotiate a lease with the partnership. His partners claimed that this was a breach of his duties as a partner. Were they right? (*Lavin* v. *Ehrlich*, New York 80 Misc 2d 247)

5. Rice and Campbell were doing business as partners. They entered into an agreement with Travelers to write money orders. The partnership sold some of the money orders but failed to send the money to Travelers. To secure the debt, the partnership gave a promissory note to Travelers, with a guaranty by Campbell. When the note wasn't paid, Travelers sued both partners. Rice claimed that he was liable only if Campbell didn't pay. Was Rice correct? (*Rice* v. *Travelers Express Company*, Texas 407 SW2d 534)

6. Moser and Williams were partners in a land development business. By agreement, title to the

land was placed in Williams's name. Williams had contracted to sell the land to another for a much higher price. When Williams sold the land, Moser brought suit to have Williams account to him for his share of the profit. Will he succeed? (*Moser* v. *Williams*, Missouri 443 SW2d 212)

7. Roberts and Hunt were partners in a law practice. A client asked them to attempt to collect the proceeds due on a promissory note and gave the partnership the authority to settle the claim. The partners obtained a judgment and ultimately settled the claim, with Hunt collecting $75 as the settlement. Hunt, however, kept the money and left the state. Was Roberts, the remaining partner, liable to the client for the sum collected? (*Powell* v. *Roberts*, 116 Mo App 629)

Chapter 27

Corporations and Franchising

CHAPTER PREVIEW

CHAPTER HIGHLIGHTS This chapter describes the nature, formation, financing, operation, and termination of corporations. It covers both profit and nonprofit types of corporations. The steps that must be taken to form a corporation are outlined. When a corporation is formed, financing must be obtained to carry out the organization's business operations—both equity and debt financing are discussed.

A corporation is owned by its stockholders and managed by its directors and officers. The chapter describes the rights, liabilities, and powers of stockholders, directors, debtors, and officers. The corporation portion of the chapter concludes with a discussion of the ways in which a corporation may be terminated and the advantages and disadvantages of the corporate form of organization.

Finally, the chapter discusses franchising—what it is, its advantages and disadvantages, and how it is regulated by government.

NATURE OF A CORPORATION

A **corporation** is an artificial legal entity created by permission of the state or federal government. It is an entity in itself, separate from its owners. It is an artificial person and does business in its own name. Among other things, it can buy and sell property, sue and be sued, and borrow money all in its own name.

Corporations are usually classified as either public or private corporations. Public corporations are chartered by the state or federal government to carry out governmental purposes. Among the most common public corporations are state hospitals, state universities, and public utility companies. There are two types of private corporations: profit and nonprofit.

Profit Corporations

A **profit corporation** is one organized to make money. It is the typical type of business enterprise used to operate manufacturing, financial, and service businesses. Most of the material in this chapter will be concerned with profit corporations.

Professional Corporations   There is a special type of profit corporation known as a **professional corporation,** or professional association, as it is called in some states. This is a corporation organized to operate a professional practice, such as that of a physician, attorney, or accountant. It is similar to a typical business corporation except that its directors and stockholders must be licensed to practice the profession for which the corporation has been created. In addition, stockholders may be individually liable for torts relating to professional activities, such as malpractice, but not for torts unrelated to the professional activities.

■ Smith & Smith Law Firm, P.C. practices law as a professional corporation. If one of the stockholders assaults someone, the corporation and the one who commits the assault may be held liable but the other stockholders will not. ■

Close Corporations   Many private corporations operate as **close corporations.** A close corporation is one in which the stock is held by a few people, often members of the same family. Although a close corporation is formed in the same manner as all other private corporations, many states have simplified the way in which such corporations may be managed. This is done in recognition of the fact that close corporations are managed as if they were partnerships rather than corporations. These laws restrict the number of stockholders and the transfer of stock.

Subchapter S Corporations   Just as a limited partnership is a hybrid business organization, so too is a Subchapter S corporation. A **Subchapter S corporation** is a private corporation that elects what is called Subchapter S status under the U.S. Internal Revenue Code. Provided certain requirements are met, a Subchapter S corporation is treated as a partnership for tax purposes but as a corporation for all other purposes. One advantage is that corporate income taxes are avoided; only the stockholders are taxed and only on their distributions from the corporation. Another advantage is that losses are passed along to the stockholders, enabling them to deduct them from their income—a benefit usually available only to sole proprietors and members of a partnership.

The requirements for qualifying as a Subchapter S corporation are many, but the most important ones are that there must be thirty-five or fewer stockholders, and that the corporation cannot derive more than 5 percent of its gross income from investments in which no active management takes place (passive investment income).

Corporations are also classified as either domestic or foreign corporations. Each state has its own laws for creating corporations. A business incorporated in one state is considered a domestic corporation in that state and a foreign corporation in all other states where it does business. Foreign corporations are permitted to do business outside their state of incorporation with permission and proper registration.

Nonprofit Corporations

A **nonprofit corporation** is a corporation organized not to earn money but to provide educational, charitable, or social services. This includes religious organizations, private colleges, hospitals, and veterans' organizations.

■ The Great Woods Corp. was formed to provide camping experiences for disabled children. Even though the corporation may receive more than it spends (may earn a profit), it is a nonprofit corporation because its primary purpose is a social one. ■

FORMING A CORPORATION

While some corporations are chartered by the federal government, most are incorporated under state law. Each state has its own laws regulating the formation of corporations. These laws differ in certain respects, but the basic steps in all states are signing and filing the articles of incorporation and setting up the corporate structure.

Articles of Incorporation

Once a decision is made to conduct business under the corporate form of organization, the first step is to prepare the application for incorporation. This is known in most states as the **articles of incorporation.** The articles normally include the name of the corporation, its purpose, its term of existence, the location of its principal business office, and the names and addresses of the incorporators. The articles must also include a description of the investment makeup of the corporation, known as **capitalization.** This description includes a statement of the number of shares of stock the corporation is authorized to issue. **Stock** is the ownership interest in a corporation. The articles of incorporation indicate whether the stock is to have a stated value or no stated value. Stock with a value printed on it is known as **par stock;** stock with no printed value is known as **no-par stock.**

An important part of the articles of incorporation is the corporate name. Most states have laws limiting the types of names that may be used. The name must usually indicate that the business organization is in fact a corporation so that the public knows with whom it is dealing. The word "Corporation" or some abbreviation such as "Corp.," "Inc.," or "Ltd." is often used. To avoid confusion, the name must not be similar to an existing name. And the name cannot mislead the public by appearing to indicate that the organization has some official status.

> Barnes and Selwin decided to form a corporation using the name "U.S. Treasury Dept. Bonds, Inc." They would not receive permission to use the name because it would mislead the public. ■

The name of the corporation is also important because of its advertising value. It is often considered a valuable asset of the corporation. In most states an examination is made of state records to determine the availability of a corporate name before the articles of incorporation are prepared.

After the articles of incorporation are signed, they are sent to the appropriate state office for filing. There is usually an incorporation fee plus a tax on the number and value of shares of stock that the corporation is authorized to issue. When the articles are approved, a notice of approval is sent to the applicants, the corporate charter is issued, and the corporation begins its existence. Two additional steps are required—obtaining for the corporation a tax identification number from the Internal Revenue Service and preparing the bylaws.

Bylaws are rules for managing the internal affairs of a corporation. They cover such matters as the number of officers and directors, the duties and powers of corporate officers, and the time and place of corporate meetings.

OWNERSHIP OF A CORPORATION

A corporation is owned by its **stockholders.** Each stockholder owns one or more shares of stock in the corporation. The document that indicates the ownership of a corporation's stock is called a **stock certificate** (see Figure 27.1). The certificate lists the name of the stockholder and the number of shares of stock owned. Each certificate is registered in the corporate records. When a stockholder sells her or his shares of stock, the certificate is returned to the corporation and canceled, and a new certificate is issued to the new owner.

RIGHTS OF STOCKHOLDERS

Stockholders have specific rights granted by state statute and protected by court decisions. In practice, the extent to which these rights are claimed depends on the size of the corporation and the number of stockholders.

In larger corporations, the stockholders have a tendency to permit the officers and directors to exercise complete control over corporate affairs. A stockholder is entitled to vote on matters that require stockholder approval. Voting usually takes place at annual meetings of stockholders. A stockholder who cannot or does not wish to attend a meeting may vote by proxy. A

Figure 27.1 **Stock Certificate**

proxy is a written authorization by a stockholder allowing another person to cast her or his vote. Most large corporations have so many stockholders that many votes are cast by proxy. The stockholder who votes by proxy may vote on specific issues or may give certain officers or directors the right to vote on the issues as they choose.

Most voting is done on a one-vote-per-share basis. In a few states, however, a stockholder may cast a number of votes equal to the number of shares owned multiplied by the number of directors to be elected at an annual meeting. This type of voting is known as *cumulative voting*. It enables stockholders holding large blocks of stock to split their votes among several directors or to cast all of the votes for one director. As such, it is a means of exercising control.

Another right of stockholders is to share in profits. If profits are earned and paid out as dividends, a stockholder is entitled to a share of them based on the number of shares owned.

The right to obtain a stock certificate as evidence of ownership is another important right. The certificate not only proves ownership but is used to transfer the ownership interest to others.

A stockholder has a right to inspect the books and records of the corporation and to copy them. This right is subject to reasonable rules and regulations to prevent harassment of a corporation or improper use of its records. The inspection must be for a reasonable purpose related to the business of the corporation. It must be done at a reasonable time and must not involve release of corporate secrets or confidential information that might harm the business.

> Anderson, a stockholder in an automobile company, demanded to see price lists showing the profit made on each car sold. Since this information could harm the corporation if competitors obtained it, Anderson is not entitled to see such records. ■

Unless eliminated by the articles of incorporation or the bylaws, whenever a corporation issues new shares, current stockholders have a right to purchase these shares before they are offered to the public. This is known as the **pre-emptive right** and enables stockholders to maintain their proportional interest in the corporation.

The right to share in the assets of the corporation upon dissolution is another important right. Creditors, however, have first claim against the assets, followed by bondholders and then preferred stockholders. The common stockholders receive the remainder.

LIABILITIES OF STOCKHOLDERS

State laws vary on the liability of stockholders. Unlike partners, stockholders have **limited liability.** Their liability for the debts of a corporation is limited to the amount they have invested in the corporation through the purchase of stock. In certain states, however, certain stockholders owning the largest number of shares are liable for wages due employees who are not paid by the corporation.

A corporation needs capital for its operations, both at the time it commences business and later on when it wishes to expand. The two most common forms of financing are known as equity (consisting of stocks) and debt (consisting of borrowed funds such as loans and bonds). **Equity** represents ownership of the corporation; **debt** represents borrowing by the corporation.

Equity—Stock: Common and Preferred

The two types of stock issued by corporations are common stock and preferred stock. **Common stock** is the ordinary stock of a corporation. It gives the owner the right to vote at stockholders' meetings and to share in the profits of the corporation according to the number of shares owned. A common stockholder receives a share of the profits only if the company earns a profit and votes to return a portion of those profits to stockholders. This share of the profits is called a **dividend.** The amount of the dividend depends on the profits earned by the corporation.

Common stockholders have the lowest priority when it comes to a claim on earnings. Various taxing authorities, employees, lending institutions, bondholders, and preferred stockholders are all entitled to be paid before common stockholders receive anything. On the other hand, common stockholders have the greatest chance to see their investments appreciate in value.

Preferred stock has a preferred, or prior, claim to dividends over other categories of stock. A preferred stockholder is entitled to receive a specific dividend for each share owned. It is only after all preferred dividends are paid that a corporation may pay dividends on the common stock. Preferred shareholders usually do not have the right to vote on corporate matters unless a dividend is not paid.

There are many types of preferred stock issued by corporations. **Convertible preferred** may be exchanged for common stock of the corporation at the option of the stockholder, usually within a given period of time. **Cumulative preferred** requires that any preferred stock dividends not paid when due be accumulated and paid before any common stock dividends may be paid. **Callable preferred** is stock that may be redeemed by the corporation and bought back at a certain price, usually at any time but sometimes during a given period of time. **Participating preferred** enables the holder to share in the profits of the corporation, in addition to the preferred dividend payable.

Debt—Bonds and Loans

Instead of selling interest in a corporation in the form of stock, many corporations borrow money. Sometimes the money is borrowed from private investors or even from the stockholders themselves. A promissory note is given as evidence of the debt, and the loan is repayable over a fixed period of time (or sometimes on demand) and at a fixed rate of interest. Many corporations borrow larger sums of money from banks or insurance companies. Such loans are usually secured by a pledge of some or all of the corporation's assets.

The most common form of corporate debt financing is the bond. A **bond** is an obligation of a corporation to repay a loan to it over a fixed period of time at a fixed interest rate. Bonds are sold to the public or to institutions and are traded on the various stock exchanges.

As with preferred stock, there are many different types of bonds. **Mortgage bonds** and **equipment bonds** are secured by specific pieces of real or personal property. If the corporation defaults in making payments, the specific property may be seized and sold and the proceeds used to pay the debt. A **debenture** is a bond that is unsecured and protected only by the general assets of the corporation. There are also **convertible bonds,** which may be converted into common stock of the corporation, and **callable bonds,** which the corporation may redeem and pay off at a given price within a given period of time.

Bondholders are entitled to be paid before any dividends are paid to common and preferred stockholders. They also have first claim against the assets of a corporation in the event of dissolution or bankruptcy; they have no voting rights and cannot participate in management.

MANAGING A CORPORATION

Stockholders, directors, officers, and employees all play a role in the management of a corporation.

The stockholders, the owners of a corporation, have the following powers:

1. To elect and remove directors
2. To vote on basic changes such as amending the bylaws, merging or consolidating, and selling all or a major part of the corporation's assets

Directors manage a corporation at the highest level—they make policy decisions for the corporation. They set the basic policies, make major financial decisions, and appoint and remove corporate officers and other high-ranking employees. Their terms, powers, and duties are established by the articles of incorporation, the bylaws, and state law. The **board of directors** of most corporations delegates power to an executive committee and to corporate officers to handle day-to-day operations.

The officers actually run the corporation. They are employees who manage the corporation on a daily basis and are accountable to the directors and the stockholders. The officers in turn hire the other employees of the corporation, who handle the details involved in the corporate business.

Powers of a Corporation

A corporation's powers may be either express or implied. The express powers are those contained in the corporate charter, the bylaws, or in state corporation statutes. The implied powers are those a corporation must have to be able to function properly and to carry out its express powers. If a corporation does anything that goes beyond its express or implied powers, its actions are said to be **ultra vires.** The stockholders can invalidate an ultra vires act unless the act has been completely performed by all parties. Such an act is fully enforceable, however, by the parties to the act.

■ The president of Hightop Corp. signed an agreement to lend money to another corporation, an ultra vires act. Before the loan was completed, the stockholders brought suit to cancel the loan. They would succeed in their suit. Neither the lender nor the borrower, however, would be able to cancel the transaction on their own. ■

The most important powers of a corporation are to have a name and corporate seal, to enjoy perpetual existence, to sue and be sued in its own name, to acquire and dispose of real property needed for the proper conduct of the business, and to borrow money for any proper corporate purpose.

Powers and Duties of Directors

Directors have the power to direct corporate policies. They may do whatever is reasonable to accomplish this, limited only by statute or bylaws. The board of directors must act as a group; individual directors cannot bind the corporation.

Directors may be liable for contracts and for negligence and other torts. They must act in the best interest of the corporation and are liable for intentional acts of negligence that harm the corporation. Directors are usually liable only to the corporation and not to third parties. However, directors who commit fraud or intentionally deceive third parties dealing with the corporation are liable for their actions.

■ Curran was a creditor of the Barnes Corporation. The directors of the corporation were negligent in carrying out a corporate project, and the corporation had to file for bankruptcy. Curran would not be able to hold the directors liable for negligence. ■

Powers and Duties of Officers

Officers have the responsibility of managing the corporation on a day-to-day basis. Like the directors, their powers are derived from the bylaws and state statutes. Their liability is usually only to the corporation and then only for negligence or intentional torts. However, officers, like directors, are liable to third parties for such intentional torts as deceit or fraud.

TERMINATING A CORPORATION

Unlike partnerships, corporations do not terminate when there is a change of ownership. Corporate existence ends only when the term of the corporate charter ends, when the corporate charter is revoked, or when there is a consolidation or merger.

The charters of most corporations provide for perpetual existence. Other charters provide for a specific term, such as fifty years. When the term ends, the corporate existence terminates. A corporation may also be dissolved when the stockholders agree to end the corporate existence.

The state may dissolve a corporation and revoke its charter under certain limited conditions. Examples of this would be failure to pay corporate taxes or continuous violation of state statutes regulating corporations.

Corporate existence often ends with consolidation or merger, usually because a corporation wants to expand its business. In a **consolidation,** two or more corporations join together to form a new corporation, with the old corporations disappearing. The obligations and liabilities of the old corporations are assumed by the new corporation.

In a **merger,** one corporation buys another corporation. The buying corporation stays in existence, obtaining all of the assets and assuming all of the obligations and liabilities of the selling corporation; the selling corporation then ceases to exist.

> The Brant Corporation made an offer to purchase all of the stock of the Deke Corporation. The stock was purchased, and the Deke Corporation ceased to exist. This is an example of a merger. ■

All states have laws regulating merger and consolidation procedures. They usually require approval by the directors and stockholders of all corporations involved, as well as the filing of a merger or consolidation plan with the Department of State in each state involved.

Suppose a stockholder does not agree with the merger or consolidation plan? The law in most states permits a dissenting stockholder to have the value of his or her shares determined as of the date of the merger or consolidation and to receive payment for those shares. The basic procedures may vary among the states, but they basically provide for the giving of notice by the dissenting stockholder and for an appraisal process to determine the value of the shares.

PURCHASE OF ASSETS AND STOCK

Corporations often expand by purchasing the assets or stock of another corporation. The method of acquisition depends on many factors, including tax consequences.

Purchase of Assets

Some corporations prefer to acquire the assets, rather than the stock, of another corporation. One advantage is that this step does not require approval by the stockholders of the acquiring corporation. Another advantage is that except in unusual circumstances, the acquiring corporation does not have to assume the obligations of the selling corporation. The disadvantage is that the assets must be valued, an often expensive and time-consuming process.

Purchase of Stock

A corporation can expand by buying a controlling interest in another corporation through the purchase of stock. The advantage is that only an overall purchase price for the stock has to be determined, rather than the value of individual assets. The disadvantages are that the acquiring corporation must receive stockholder approval for such an acquisition and must also assume all the debts and liabilities of the selling corporation.

There are many different methods of purchasing stock to obtain a controlling interest in another corporation. One method is the use of a tender offer. A **tender offer** is a public offer to the stockholders of a corporation to purchase all or a portion of their shares at a stated price. The offering group may offer to pay for the shares so acquired by cash or its own stock.

Another method is known as a **leveraged buy-out** (LBO). In an LBO, a group of investors (usually managers or employees) buys all of the outstanding stock of a corporation held by the public, acquires control of the corporation, and turns it into a private rather than a public corporation. The acquisition is usually financed by obtaining a loan on the corporation's assets. Sometimes, an LBO turns a formerly unprofitable business into a profitable one, and the private investors then sell stock in the corporation and turn it back into a public corporation. It is often the case that the LBO places such a heavy debt load on the business that it fails; bankruptcy or reorganization is then required.

ADVANTAGES AND DISADVANTAGES OF CORPORATIONS

Operating as a corporation has its advantages and disadvantages. These are usually the exact opposite of those for a partnership. A comparison of the sole proprietorship, the partnership, and the corporate forms of business organization is shown in Table 27.1.

Unlike the partnership, a corporation continues its operations despite changes in ownership. The death of an owner (stockholder) rarely results in the termination of a corporation, unless it is a one-stockholder corporation.

Another advantage of the corporation is ease of transfer of ownership. To transfer stock, a stockholder need only sign the stock certificate and transfer it to the new owner. Transfer of a partnership interest usually requires a complicated contract and the approval of the other partners.

Centralized management is another advantage of corporations. In a partnership, all partners have a right to participate in management and they usually take part. This can cause dissension and make management unwieldy. In a corporation, management functions are delegated to a small group of officers who can act on behalf of a large group of owners.

An important advantage of the corporate form is the availability of many fringe benefits. These include tax-saving devices such as pension and profit-sharing plans. In addition, a corporation that provides its employees with

TABLE 27.1   Comparison of Forms of Business Organization

	Advantages	Disadvantages
Sole proprietorship:	• Flexible method of business organization • Profits taxed as owner's personal income • No special legal formalities required to begin business • Opportunity for close personal contact between owner and customers	• Large initial capital requirements • Business risk is unlimited and must be borne by owner alone • Business ceases to exist when owner dies or retires
Partnership:	• Simple to organize • Profits taxed as partners' personal income • Minimum government regulation • No restrictions of powers	• Unlimited liability • May have conflicts over management • Business may be dissolved by change or death of a partner • Ownership is difficult to transfer
Corporation:	• Limited liability • Centralized management • Continuity of business (perpetual existence) • Ease of transferring ownership	• Expensive to organize • Double taxation • Extensive government regulation • Restrictions on powers

disability insurance, term life insurance, medical and dental plans, and education benefits can deduct the cost from corporate income.

The most important advantage of the corporate form is limited liability. A stockholder is shielded from liability for corporate losses or judgments for any amounts in excess of the stockholder's investments in the corporation.

The exception to the benefit of limited liability may occur when a court finds out that the corporation or its stockholders is using the corporate form solely to avoid liability or to commit a fraud against potential creditors. If a court finds this to be that case, the court may do what is known as "pierce the corporate veil" and make stockholders fully liable for debts or losses of the corporation.

Courts may hold that a certain corporation is a sham if the business is run more like a partnership than a corporation. Failure to hold corporate meetings, keep minutes, and file corporate tax returns is evidence of an intent not to operate a business as a corporation. Mixing personal assets with corporate assets and using corporate funds to pay personal obligations constitute further evidence. Another indication of abusing the corporate form is "thin capitalization"—having too few or no assets in a corporation to pay creditors or judgments that may be imposed against it. If a court finds thin capitalization to be the case, it may ignore the corporate shield and hold the stockholders personally liable.

Reynolds and Blaine were stockholders in Algin Corp. They each invested $100 in the corporation and then proceeded to buy $50,000 worth of inventory. If the corporation defaults in paying for the inventory, a court may hold Reynolds and Blaine personally liable on the grounds that they purposely failed to provide the corporation with sufficient assets to secure payment for purchases and were therefore operating the corporation as a sham. ■

One disadvantage of corporations is the expense and complication involved in incorporating and operating. A partnership is easy to form and requires little expense. Establishing a corporation takes time and involves the expense of incorporating, the issuance of stock to raise capital, recordkeeping for and payment of taxes, and so forth. Operating a partnership is relatively easy. The corporation must keep complicated records, take minutes of meetings, maintain employee records, and file different types of tax returns.

Another disadvantage of corporations is the double taxation that shareholders pay. Corporations, unlike partnerships, are considered to be legal entities, separate from their owners. As a result, they pay income taxes at the corporate level. In addition, the stockholders are taxed on the dividends they receive from the corporation.

State and federal regulation is another disadvantage of corporations. Partnerships are relatively free from government regulation and control. Corporations are subject to much control, including the filing of reports, issuance of stock, payment of dividends and so forth.

Investor Protection

Investors in corporations, at the time of incorporation and during the corporation's existence, require extensive protection. This is provided by both law and regulations and is discussed in Chapter 28.

FRANCHISING

One of the most common types of business arrangements in existence today is the franchise. A **franchise** is basically an agreement in which:

- A franchisor (the person who grants the franchise) gives a franchisee (the operator of the franchise) the right to use the franchisor's name, trademark, and logo.
- The franchisor gives the franchisee know-how, assistance, and training and exercises a measure of control over the franchisee's operations.
- In return for these rights, the franchisee pays the franchisor an initial franchise fee and/or a fee based on gross sales, and/or must purchase inventory and equipment from the franchisor.

■ Owens entered into an arrangement with Ultra Vacuum Cleaner Co. to distribute its vacuum cleaners. The arrangement was that Owens would open a store called Ultra Vacuums and would sell cleaners sent to him on consignment. Owens was to be paid a commission based on a percentage of the sale price. This is not a franchise because Owens is not controlled by Ultra and pays no fee for the right to be a distributor. Owens is considered a consignee and an independent contractor. ■

It is important to note that a distributor may or may not be a product franchisee, depending on the relationship between the distributor and the supplier of the merchandise.

There are two basic types of franchising. One is *product franchising*, in which the franchisee sells a product manufactured or distributed by the franchisor. Gas stations, auto dealers, and soft-drink bottlers are examples of product franchising. The second type is *business plan franchising*, in which a service or business plan is the main element. Fast-food restaurants, equipment rentals, tax preparation companies, and motels are examples of business plan franchising.

There are many advantages of the franchise system for both franchisors and franchisees. The franchisor can expand, using the franchisee's capital instead of its own; can obtain a large network of distributors without having to set up its own network, thereby saving time and money; and can have a larger base of operations than it would normally have, which enables it to buy merchandise at lower cost and to borrow money on better terms.

The franchisee benefits as well. The franchisee can get into business with less capital and less experience than would normally be required. The franchisee also gets the advantage of using a well-known name, trademark, and logo that it ordinarily would not have access to. And, finally, the franchisee gets training and supervision to enable it to conduct its business successfully.

However, franchising has not been worry-free. As franchising has become so popular, many problems have emerged from this type of arrangement. Two major abuses have arisen.

Some franchisors fail to disclose to the franchisee all of the risks involved in the franchise system and all of the details of the proposed franchise relationship. As a result, many franchisees make poorly informed decisions to purchase a franchise.

In other cases, franchisors have not made proper provisions for a default by the franchisor or the improper termination of the franchise. In both cases, the franchisee may be left holding the bag, burdened by a large capital investment.

Extensive laws and regulations have been enacted on both federal and state levels to protect franchisees. Congress has passed laws to regulate franchises in certain industries. The Petroleum Marketing Practices Act and the Automobile Dealers' Franchise Act both protect franchisees from improper or arbitrary termination of franchises. Both acts enable franchisees to sue franchisors in federal court for improper termination of franchises. It is important to note that these laws apply only in the case of improper or arbitrary terminations. They do not affect the franchisor's right under most agreements to cancel or refuse to renew a franchise if the franchisee fails to purchase the required amount of inventory, to meet certain sales quotas, to meet certain health or safety standards, and so on. The Federal Trade Commission has also adopted regulations that regulate all franchise offerings in the United States. Most of these regulations are concerned with the need for making proper disclosure to potential franchisees. They make a franchisor subject to both civil and criminal penalties for failure to make proper disclosure or for making false representations.

In addition, many states have enacted laws and regulations that govern the sale of franchises and certain elements of the franchise such as financing, renewal of the franchise agreement, and termination of it. Some states even require the registration of franchises before they may be sold within the state.

Summary of Important Legal Concepts

A corporation is a legal entity created under state law. It can hold title to property in its own name and may sue or be sued in its own name. Corporations are classified as either public or private corporations. Public corporations, such as state hospitals and public utility companies, carry out public functions. Private corporations are either profit or nonprofit. Private corporations are organized to make money. Nonprofit corporations are organized to provide educational, religious, charitable, or social services.

A corporation begins to exist on filing articles of incorporation and with the issuance of a charter by the state. The articles of incorporation and the bylaws provide the corporate name, term, corporate purpose, internal organization, and the financial makeup of the organization.

A corporation is owned by its stockholders. They have the right to vote for directors and on other major issues, to share in profits, and to inspect the books and records of the corporation, subject to reasonable rules and regulations.

They usually have the right to purchase new issues of stock before an offer is made to the public and the right to share in the assets of the corporation upon its dissolution. Stockholders enjoy limited liability—their liability for debts of the corporation is limited to their investments.

Corporations may be financed in many ways. Often, it is through debt—either bank loans or issuance of corporate bonds. Usually, it is through the issuance of stock, which may be either common or preferred.

Directors of a corporation establish general policies for corporate operations, hire officers, and declare dividends. The officers are responsible for day-to-day operations. Both directors and officers are liable to the corporation for negligence and intentional torts such as fraud. They are usually liable to third parties only for deceit and fraud.

Most corporations have perpetual existence; some have specific terms. Corporate existence ends when the term expires, by agreement of the stockholders, on revocation of the charter by the state, or on a consolidation or merger.

The advantages of the corporate form of doing business are continuity, ease of transfer of ownership, centralized management, availability of tax-deductible fringe benefits, and the limited liability of stockholders. Limited liability, however, may be unavailable if the corporate form is used solely to defraud potential creditors.

The disadvantages of corporations are the expense involved in incorporating and operating, double taxation, and extensive state and federal regulation.

Franchising is a common type of business arrangement in which a franchisee, for a fee, obtains know-how, products, management skills, and a logo (or trademark) from a franchisor. Both the state and federal governments have passed laws regulating the registration and sale of franchises and the disclosure of vital information to potential franchisees.

Key Legal Terms to Know

Match the terms with the definitions that follow.

articles of incorporation
board of directors
bond
callable bond
callable preferred
capitalization
close corporation

common stock
consolidation
convertible bond
convertible preferred
corporation
cumulative preferred
debenture
debt
dividend
equipment bond
equity
franchise
leveraged buy-out
limited liability
merger
mortgage bond
no-par stock
nonprofit corporation
par stock
participating preferred
pre-emptive right
preferred stock
professional corporation
profit corporation
proxy
stock
stock certificate
stockholders
Subchapter S corporation
tender offer
ultra vires

1. Persons who own a corporation
2. The group that sets corporate policy
3. Acts of a corporation now permitted under its express or implied powers
4. Corporate profits paid to stockholders
5. The application for permission to incorporate
6. A document indicating an ownership interest in a corporation
7. Joining two corporations to form a new one
8. A corporation organized to earn a profit
9. A separate legal entity created by permission of government
10. Written permission given by stockholders for someone else to vote their shares of stock
11. The joining of two corporations with one corporation surviving
12. Stock having a prior right to receive a stated dividend
13. A corporation organized primarily for non-business purposes
14. The ordinary stock of a corporation
15. Stock that has a stated value printed on the stock certificate
16. The investment makeup of a corporation
17. Stock that does not have a value printed on the stock certificate
18. The right of stockholders to buy new stock in a corporation prior to a sale to the public
19. Ownership interest in a corporation
20. A corporation organized to operate a professional practice
21. The liability of a stockholder for the debts of the corporation
22. A corporation treated as a partnership for tax reasons
23. A corporate bond that may be exchanged for common stock in the same corporation
24. A corporate bond secured by specific pieces of corporate real property
25. An unsecured corporate bond
26. Preferred stock that shares in corporate profits in addition to preferred stock dividends
27. A bond that a corporation may redeem and pay prior to maturity
28. Preferred stock that may be exchanged for common stock of the same company
29. Preferred stock that a corporation may redeem and buy at its option
30. Corporate obligation to repay a loan
31. Preferred stock upon which dividends must be paid before common stock dividends are payable
32. Corporation in which stock is held by only a few people
33. Borrowed funds, such as loans and bonds
34. Financing through the issuance of stock
35. Business arrangement between a franchisor and a franchisee
36. A public offer to stockholders to buy their stock
37. Acquiring control of a corporation by buying stock and financing the purchase with a loan on the acquired corporation's assets
38. A corporate bond secured by specific pieces of corporate personal property

Questions and Problems to Discuss

1. Name six rights of stockholders.
2. What are the advantages and disadvantages of the corporate form of business organization?

3. Explain the double taxation of corporate earnings that shareholders pay.

4. Abby was a preferred stockholder of the Ajax Corporation. Although the corporation had paid dividends on her stock each year, Abby was concerned and upset because the corporation had decided to merge with another corporation. Is Abby entitled to vote on the merger when it comes up for discussion and a vote at a stockholders' meeting?

5. Stetson owned 100 shares of the common stock of Blair Corp. For three years in a row, the corporation lost money and paid no dividends. Stetson sued to force the corporation to pay dividends on his stock. Will he succeed?

6. Sill formed a corporation to manufacture electronic parts. The corporation owed money to a supplier and the supplier brought an action against Sill for payment of the debt. Is Sill liable?

7. Bills and Jason tried to set up a new corporation under the name "The Group." The state government agency in charge of incorporations refused to issue a corporate charter on the grounds that the name was improper. Can the state refuse to issue a charter?

8. Zebra Corp. was organized to operate gas stations. After a few years, it had an earnings surplus and used the money to purchase and operate a chain of bowling alleys. A stockholder claimed that this was an ultra vires act. Is the stockholder correct?

9. Bison owned stock in the North Corporation. When the corporation was dissolved, all of its assets were used to pay its debts. Bison claimed that he was entitled to a share of the assets before the debts were paid because he had invested in the corporation. Is he correct?

10. Garcia was a stockholder in the Atlas Corporation. She wanted to get a list of stockholders so that she could write them about her dissatisfaction with the management of the corporation. Is she entitled to obtain this list?

11. Poor business judgment by the directors of the Bakersfield Corp. forced it into bankruptcy. A creditor sued the directors for negligence. Are the directors liable?

12. Grey, a director of Magna Corporation, entered into a contract on behalf of Magna to purchase supplies from the Lade Company. Magna then suffered financial reverses and could not go through with the contract. Lade sued Grey for breach of contract. Is Grey liable for damages?

13. Berman owned 52 percent of the stock of Alligood Corporation. He needed money for a new business venture and sold his stock to raise funds. Would the sale of his majority interest dissolve the corporation?

Cases to Decide

1. A group of shareholders of Manganese sued the corporation and four officers who were also directors. The group claimed that the officers and directors had negligently caused the assets of the corporation to drop from $400,000 to $30,000 in less than two years. Are the officers and directors liable for such losses? (*Selheimer et al.*, v. *Manganese Corporation of America et al.*, 423 Pa 563)

2. Free Baptist Church, a religious corporation, rented liquor-dispensing equipment from Southeastern. When Free Baptist defaulted on the lease, Southeastern sued the church for the rental due. Free Baptist claimed as a defense the fact that the leasing of such equipment from Southeastern was an ultra vires act. Is the defense a good one? (*Free Baptist Church* v. *Southeastern Beverage Co.*, 218 SE 2d 169)

3. Jervis Corporation was organized under the laws of the state of Michigan. It wanted to do business in New York State under its name and applied for permission to do so. At the time the application was made, there existed a New York corporation named Jervis Limited. To avoid confusion, the New York Secretary of State refused to permit the Michigan corporation to use the name Jervis Corporation. Was the secretary of state correct? (*Jervis Corporation* v. *Secretary of State*, New York 43 Misc 2d 185)

4. Pillsbury bought one share of stock in Honeywell for the sole purpose of getting a list of the stockholders and advising them of his concern that Honeywell was supplying munitions for the Vietnam war. Honeywell refused to turn over the lists. Was it correct? (*State ex rel. Pillsbury* v. *Honeywell, Inc.*, 291 Minn. 322)

5. Keser operated an auto sales company and gave cars to an auction corporation operated by Klockner to sell at auction. The auction corporation paid Keser with checks that turned out to be invalid due to insufficient funds. Keser sued Klockner and others as directors and officers of the auction corporation for fraud. Are the

directors and officers liable? (*Klockner* v. *Keser,* 29 Co App 476, 488 P2d 1135)

6. Steelmasters sold merchandise to Eisenrod, an officer of Household Corp. Steelmasters believed it was dealing with Eisenrod, but all of the invoices, letters, and purchase orders were in Household's name. When Household didn't pay what was due, Steelmasters sued Eisenrod individually as an officer of Household. Can it collect from him? (*Steelmasters, Inc.* v. *Household Mfg. Co.,* New York 40 AD2d 963)

Chapter 28

Government Regulation of Business

CHAPTER PREVIEW

CHAPTER HIGHLIGHTS

Government regulation of business has become a way of life in the United States. This chapter discusses why government regulation is needed and how such regulation protects the rights of business owners as well as consumers, employees, and stockholders.

Under our constitutional form of government, the government must be supplied with the authority to regulate business. This authority comes from many sources, which are described in this chapter. There are many areas in which government seeks to regulate business and these areas are described in detail, with particular emphasis on the area described as "Preserving the General Welfare and the Environment."

Regulations are meaningless unless they can be enforced. The chapter concludes with a discussion of the ways in which government regulations are enforced and the agencies responsible for such enforcement.

THE NEED FOR GOVERNMENT REGULATION

Businesses in the United States operate on the private enterprise system. This means that private businesses compete in the marketplace, and their success is determined by the quality and price of goods and services they offer. For this system to work, the rights of individual businesses must be protected and guaranteed.

Government regulation is designed to accomplish this. Regulation protects the rights of each business owner so that competition is maintained. It also protects the rights of consumers, employees, and, in the case of corporations, stockholders.

THE AUTHORITY OF GOVERNMENT TO REGULATE BUSINESS

The authority of government agencies to regulate business may be derived from statutes passed by Congress or state legislatures. It may come from court decisions that interpret the statutes passed. It may also arise from regulations or decisions of administrative agencies created to apply the statutes regulating business.

Because business affects the life of almost every person, both state and federal governments have exercised great powers to control and regulate it. Under our federal system, state and local governments have a basic power to provide for the general welfare of the public, known as the **police power.** From this comes the power to regulate business activity to promote the public interest. There are only two limitations on this power. The regulation must be needed, and it must be reasonable. In addition, state and local governments may regulate only the business activity conducted solely within that government's boundaries. Such business activity is known as **intrastate commerce.**

Moreover, state and local governments may not regulate areas of business already regulated by the federal government.

> If Congress passed a law prohibiting the employment of persons under fourteen years of age, a state may not then pass a law prohibiting the employment of persons under sixteen years of age. The congressional act has priority. ■

The federal government regulates business activity conducted in more than one state, known as **interstate commerce.** The power to regulate interstate commerce comes from what is called the commerce clause of the U.S. Constitution: "Congress shall have the power to regulate commerce with foreign nations, *among the several states,* and with the Indian tribes." As a matter of practice and because of various court decisions, Congress has almost unlimited authority to control business. However, that control must still be needed, must be reasonable, and must not violate anyone's constitutional rights.

AREAS OF GOVERNMENT REGULATION

Both the federal and state governments (including local governments) regulate almost every aspect of business activity. The regulation we discuss in this chapter affects business itself, and its ultimate goal is the protection of the public by maintaining competition and free trade. The most important areas of regulation are preventing monopolies, maintaining fair competition, taxation, regulating crucial industries, securities regulation, and preserving the general welfare and environment.

Preventing Monopolies

A **monopoly** is a condition in which competition is suppressed by act or agreement. If permitted to exist, a monopoly harms the public as well as individual businesses. Both the state and federal governments have enacted laws to prevent monopolies. These laws are known as **antitrust laws.**

Most of the antitrust activity is at the federal level and is based on the Sherman Act, passed by Congress in 1890. This law prohibits any monopolies or any acts that might lead to a monopoly. The Clayton Act, enacted in 1914, prohibits a merger of corporations in interstate commerce if it would tend to create a monopoly.

Not every monopoly is prohibited, only those that arise from unlawful or unreasonable acts.

> Richards Trucking Corp. operated in three states. Because it was efficient, had good customer relations, and was cost-conscious, it took over more than 90 percent of the business from its competitors. This resulted in a monopoly, but not one that was prohibited. ■

Maintaining Fair Competition

Unfair competition hurts small businesses and results in higher prices for consumers. Many laws and regulations have been passed to prevent unfair competition or any activity that might prevent the private enterprise system from functioning.

The Sherman Act prohibits any contract, combination, or conspiracy in restraint of trade. Its purpose is to prevent businesses from combining their efforts to hurt competition and increase their share of the market. One of the most common practices that the act seeks to prevent is price fixing. Businesses often try to control the market by setting common prices for goods and services. Price fixing is a violation of the Sherman Act, regardless of whether the prices set are fair or unreasonable.

The act also prohibits an indirect form of price fixing called **market allocation.** In this situation, competitors divide a market based on geography, population, product type or potential customers and agree not to compete with each other in those markets.

> Ace Bicycle Co. and Zebra Bicycle Co. agree that Ace will have an exclusive right to sell bicycles in California, while Zebra will have similar exclusive rights to sell in Texas. This is an illegal practice under the Sherman Act. ■

There are certain exceptions to the coverage of the Sherman Act. These take the form of exempting certain businesses from application of the antitrust laws because of certain policy considerations. Labor unions, agricultural organizations, and baseball teams are all exempt. Professionals—such as doctors, lawyers and accountants—used to be exempt from antitrust regulation, but these exemptions are being eroded by judicial decision and government regulations.

The Clayton Act also prohibits certain practices that might lessen competition. Among these are price discrimination and mergers or acquisitions of another corporation's assets or stock that might create a monopoly or lessen competition. The act also seeks to prevent tying arrangements and exclusive dealing arrangements that might lessen competition. A **tying arrangement** is an agreement in which a seller of products requires the buyer to handle additional products of that company as a condition of the sale. An **exclusive dealing arrangement** is an agreement in which a seller of a particular product requires a buyer to agree not to purchase a similar product from a competitor.

The Robinson-Patman Act of 1936, an amendment to the Clayton Act, prohibits specific types of price discrimination, such as selling goods and services at prices designed to eliminate competition.

> Adams owned a chain of department stores in several states. To attract customers and harm his competitors, he began to sell all furniture at cost. This is unlawful because it is an unreasonable act designed to eliminate competition. Smaller stores could not do the same thing and remain in business. ■

Other unfair methods of competition are prohibited by the Federal Trade Commission Act of 1914. One prohibited method is business defamation, such as spreading a damaging rumor about a competitor to lessen competition. Malicious competition is also prohibited. This involves acts done solely to eliminate a competitor.

Government also maintains fair competition by making the public aware of prices of merchandise so that comparisons can be made among competing products or businesses. Local governments often require labels and/or signs that are clearly marked to indicate the total and unit costs of various products. As long as the regulations are reasonable, they will be upheld.

Taxation

Another important area of government regulation is taxation of businesses. Taxation involves every aspect of business and affects business decisions on every level.

One important tax is the income tax. Whether a business operates as a sole proprietorship, a partnership, or a corporation, a tax on income limits the amount the business may spend or may return in the form of profits. Many business decisions are based on the tax consequences.

Government also regulates by means of the sales tax. Although this tax is passed on to the consumer, its presence affects sales and therefore also affects the profits of the business producing or selling the item that is taxed. Similarly, payroll taxes also lessen profits and have an important effect on spending and other business decisions.

Regulating Crucial Industries

Some industries are subject to unusual government regulation because their products and services are crucial to the public welfare. By necessity, these companies are allowed to operate as monopolies. Public utilities, such as electric and gas companies, are one such example; it would be impractical to have three electric companies operating in the same city. In return for their status as monopolies, public utilities are regulated very closely at the federal and state levels. Areas of regulation include rate charges, profits, advertising, and environmental effects.

Other industries, such as transportation and communication companies, are considered semi-monopolies and are also subject to extensive governmental regulation. Their services are crucial for our well-being, and, at the same time, only a limited number of them can operate in a given area at any one time. For economic and safety reasons, for example, only a certain number of flights can operate at the same time in the same area. The radio wave spectrum is limited and can accommodate only a limited number of radio and television stations. Some deregulation has taken place. Although the airline, motor carrier, and railroad industries—which operate interstate— have been deregulated with regard to rates and routes, they are still subject to regulation in the areas of passenger safety, advertising, and prevention of monopoly practices.

Securities Regulation

The securities industry is one of the most heavily regulated industries in the United States. The need to protect the public is so great that both the original issue of securities and their subsequent transfer are regulated at both state and federal levels of government. State laws do help to protect buyers, but they are not as effective as federal legislation. State laws are not uniform and fraudulent promoters can move from state to state to avoid compliance. To prevent this sort of abuse and to achieve some degree of uniformity, many states have adopted the Uniform Securities Act. This act requires full disclosure to prospective purchasers of all relevant information regarding a security. It also requires securities salespersons to register and obtain a license, and provides for injunctive relief and criminal penalties for those who engage in fraudulent sales of securities.

It is at the federal level, however, that the most effective regulation takes place. The stock market crash in 1929 emphasized the need for uniform securities regulation on a national basis. In response, Congress enacted the Securities Act of 1933. The Securities Exchange Act of 1934 was passed to offer additional protection.

The 1933 act was designed to ensure that a prospective investor will receive the information she or he needs to make an informed decision on whether to buy a specific security. The act also prohibits fraud and misrepresentation in the sale of securities. It covers only initial issues of securities; it does not cover subsequent trading.

The main purpose of the 1934 act is to protect the buyer after the initial issue of a security. It requires registration of a security prior to an offer to sell. It also requires annual reports containing all relevant information about a company and its securities, including the sale of major assets, management changes, and litigation by and against a company. The 1934 act also established the Securities and Exchange Commission (SEC), the independent regulatory body charged with enforcing the provisions of both the 1933 and the 1934 acts.

Not all securities are regulated by these laws. It would be too cumbersome and expensive to have small-volume issues subject to this type of regulation. In addition, regulation is not necessary when the investors involved are extremely knowledgeable about the securities being issued. For this reason, there are a number of situations in which the sale of certain securities is exempt from the provisions of the 1933 and 1934 acts. These include securities of corporations with limited assets, a limited number of stockholders, stockholders who all reside within the same state, and securities offerings with a value below a certain amount.

The main purpose of government regulation is to provide full disclosure of information and to prevent fraud and misrepresentation. The SEC is responsible for setting standards for disclosure, investigating fraud, regulating the activities of brokers and dealers, and regulating the trading of securities. Regulation does not provide an evaluation of the securities themselves. It is up to the individual investor to decide whether it is worthwhile to buy a certain security.

In recent years, the SEC has been increasingly involved in regulating insider trading. Insider trading is trading in securities by those who, because of their position in a corporation, possess information not available to the public that may affect the value of its stock. The Securities Exchange Act of 1934 makes liable those corporate officers, directors, stockholders, and others who use inside information for their own benefit when trading in the securities of their corporation. Under this act and subsequent legislation, those found to have traded using inside information may be assessed civil penalties, fined, and receive jail terms.

In addition to the federal government, all states have laws regulating the sale of securities, known as "blue sky" laws. Like the federal laws, state laws also regulate the actions of brokers and dealers and are designed to prevent fraud. Unlike federal legislation, state laws apply only to securities sold or offered for sale solely within a single state.

Private organizations also exert control over the securities industry. The major exchanges, such as the New York Stock Exchange and the American Stock Exchange, as well as the National Association of Securities Dealers, have enacted regulations to protect investors.

Preserving the General Welfare and the Environment

Based on the constitutional power given to Congress to provide for the general welfare, government has become increasingly involved in regulating business. The courts have interpreted the term *general welfare* in such a broad manner that almost any type of regulation is considered permissible. Regulation is considered to be the price any business pays for the privilege of serving the public. It occurs at all levels of government—federal, state, and local.

One form of regulation is the licensing of certain businesses and professions. Most states require licensing of automobile repair persons, real estate brokers, attorneys, doctors, accountants, and so forth. The objective is to make sure that only qualified persons serve the public in areas where qualifications and competence are important. Usually a person must meet minimum educational standards or have a certain amount of experience, or a combination of both, before she or he may obtain a license.

Another form of regulation controls the products a business may sell and the times it can sell them. Pharmacies, for example, may not sell certain products without a prescription. Other products, such as cigarettes and alcoholic beverages, may not be sold to minors. One of the most common regulations of this type is the prohibition against selling certain items on Sunday. These laws, known as Sunday laws, were passed to provide a day of rest in which business would be limited. Sunday laws vary from state to state but have been upheld by the courts as being a proper exercise of a state's police powers. In actual practice, they are gradually being repealed or ignored.

The need to protect the environment has affected every aspect of the operations of many businesses. Regulations control where businesses may be located, how they may dispose of wastes, and what they may use for energy. A company may be prohibited from locating in an area if the noise from its machines will affect its neighbors or if disposing of its wastes will harm wildlife in the vicinity. Certain fuels may create a pollution nuisance as they are burned. All of these factors have an effect on the environment and are subject to government review and regulation.

> ■ Acme Music Company wanted to build a factory near an airport. Because the noise from the planes could seriously affect the hearing of Acme's employees, Acme could be denied permission to build in that area. ■

For centuries, common law provided many remedies to control harm to the environment. Suits for negligence or nuisance prevented pollution or provided damages payable by the offender. However, as the amount and types of pollution increased, statutes were needed to provide protection against all types of pollution.

Many states have enacted legislation dealing with zoning problems, waste recycling, noise and visual pollution, and waste disposal. On the federal level, Congress and the regulatory agencies have passed laws regulating air and water quality, toxic waste disposal, and radiation control.

Some of the most significant federal legislation includes the Federal Water Pollution Control Act (for the control of the discharge of polluted matter into our nation's navigable waterways), the Atomic Energy Act (to regulate and control radiation from nuclear facilities), and the Clean Air Act (to regulate and limit air pollution).

Many federal agencies, such as the Nuclear Regulatory Agency and the Food and Drug Administration, are responsible for protecting special aspects of our environment. The Environmental Protection Agency, created in 1970, has the overall responsibility for protecting our environment and coordinating the environmental protection efforts of all federal agencies.

Visual pollution also affects the environment, and it is becoming a more important subject of government regulation. Federal, state, and local governments regulate the size and location of commercial signs, particularly signs near state and federal highways and residential districts. Such regulations have been upheld by the courts as long as they were reasonable and applied on a nondiscriminatory basis.

Other areas of government regulation include health and safety, consumer protection (Chapter 40), and employment practices (Chapter 23).

HOW GOVERNMENT REGULATIONS ARE ENFORCED

Regulations are meaningless unless there is a way to enforce them. Business regulation is considered so important that three different groups have the power to enforce compliance. These are administrative agencies, courts, and the public.

Administrative agencies are government bodies created by Congress or a legislature to act in the public interest. They have legislative, executive, and judicial powers. In the legislative area, agencies make rules, set rates, and establish standards. Under their executive power, they enforce their own rules. In the judicial area, they determine whether their rules have been violated and impose penalties for any violations discovered. They have full power to have investigations and call witnesses.

Administrative agencies exist at all levels of government. Examples at the local level are zoning boards, tax assessment review boards, and bridge and tunnel authorities. At the state level, there are public utilities commissions, professional licensing boards, and transportation authorities. At the federal level, administrative agencies are part of larger government units. For example, the Occupational Safety and Health Administration (OSHA) is a part of the Department of Labor.

The most active and powerful agencies are the independent regulatory agencies created by Congress. These agencies have unusual power because they are independent of Congress and do not have to account to anyone unless they exceed their powers. Their decisions affect almost every aspect of business, including rates, health and safety standards, right to merge, territory of operations, and business practices. Examples of such agencies are the Federal Communications Commission (television, radio, telephone), Federal Reserve Board (banks and money supply), and the Securities and Exchange Commission mentioned earlier.

Regulatory agencies can enforce compliance with their regulations in many ways. They may impose fines for violations of rules or get a court order to stop such violations. They may revoke a business's license or refuse to renew its license for failing to comply with the regulations.

> TV station GROW was required by its license from the FCC to broadcast four hours of public-interest programming each week. If GROW fails to provide this type of programming, the FCC could impose a fine or refuse to renew GROW's license to broadcast. ■

The courts play an important role in enforcing compliance with regulations controlling business. Recall that the Sherman Act prohibits conspiracy in restraint of trade. A business that violated the act could be found guilty of committing a federal crime, punishable by fines and imprisonment. Government can go into court and seek to have a fine imposed or to obtain an order preventing such violations (an injunction).

Members of the public who have been harmed by a violation of government regulations may enforce those regulations by suing the business that is responsible. To make sure that the public is represented, the attorney general of a state may bring suit on behalf of its citizens for violation of regulations. In certain cases, the victim(s) may recover three times the amount of damages sustained. This amount is known as **treble damages,** a form of punitive damages.

A railroad was permitted to charge only $.06 per mile for transportation on its lines. It violated the regulation and charged $.13 per mile. The attorney general of the state in which the railroad does business could sue the railroad on behalf of its citizens and seek treble damages for the excessive and unlawful rate charged by the railroad. ■

Licensing and Liability of Professionals

Professionals—such as doctors, lawyers, accountants, and architects—occupy a distinct position in society. Limited in number because of examination and licensing requirements, they therefore enjoy something of a monopoly. To protect the public, all states require the licensing of professionals. In addition, most states require the licensing of other trade practitioners, including electricians, plumbers, real estate brokers, and stockbrokers. In some states, unlicensed persons or businesses may be fined. In other states, an unlicensed professional or businessperson may be unable to enforce an otherwise valid contract.

Most states, through statutes and judicial decisions, also protect the public by making professionals liable to their clients or customers for negligence and breach of contract.

Professionals may be held liable to clients for negligence in the performance of their services under the common-law principles of negligence discussed in Chapter 4. This includes the existence of a duty to act carefully, proof of a failure to act carefully, and proof that damage resulted from the negligence. A person damaged by improper or negligent services performed by a professional may sue for malpractice, the term for professional negligence.

Professionals may also be liable to clients for improper performance of services through breach of contract. Like parties to other types of contracts, professionals who fail to perform under the terms of the contract for services may be liable for damages for claims under that contract. Claims against professionals for breach of contract are subject to different standards of proof and time limitation periods than those in a negligence suit. In most cases, those who sue professionals claim both negligence and breach of contract in their suits.

In addition to being subject to common law, professional conduct is governed by state statutes, judicial decisions, and codes of professional conduct. Professional organizations, such as state bar associations and the American Bar Association, establish standards of conduct by which professional performance is evaluated. Violations of those standards may result in suspension or dismissal. Certain standards are also set by state and federal agencies. A violation of the standards is often proof of negligence on the part of professional in malpractice cases.

Summary of Important Legal Concepts

Government regulation of business is needed to maintain competition, which protects the rights of business owners, their employees, and their customers. Regulation is also needed to protect the rights of consumers, employees, and stockholders.

Both the state and federal governments have the power to regulate business. A state's power is known as the police power and is concerned with intrastate (within one state) commerce. The federal government's power comes from the commerce clause of the U.S. Constitution.

There are certain industries, such as public utilities and transportation companies, whose services are so crucial to the public that they are subject to unusual government regulation. In return such businesses enjoy monopoly status. Areas of regulation include passenger safety, advertising, and prevention of monopoly practices.

The securities industry is one of the most heavily regulated industries in the United States. Although regulation occurs at both the state and federal levels, the most effective regulation takes place at the federal level. The Securities Act of 1933 regulates the initial sale of securities; the Securities Exchange Act of 1934 regulates subsequent transfer of securities. Both acts are designed to prevent fraud and misrepresentation and to protect potential buyers of securities. Not all securities are subject to the provisions of the 1933 and 1934 acts.

Government has become increasingly involved in regulating business under the power given to Congress to provide for the general welfare. Such regulation occurs at all levels of government and includes the licensing of certain businesses and professions, controlling what products a business may sell and when it may sell them, and protecting the environment against pollution.

Government regulations may be enforced by administrative agencies, the courts, and the public. The means of enforcement include injunctions, fines, revocation of licenses to operate, and private lawsuits.

Key Legal Terms to Know

Match the terms with the definitions that follow.

administrative agencies
antitrust laws
exclusive dealing arrangement
interstate commerce
intrastate commerce
market allocation
monopoly
police power
treble damages
tying arrangement

1. Business activity solely within one state
2. Punitive damages awarded for violation of some government regulations
3. Power of a state to protect the welfare of its citizens
4. Laws that prohibit monopolies
5. A condition in which competition is limited by act or agreement
6. Government bodies created to act in the public interest
7. Business activity conducted in two or more states
8. An agreement by competitors not to compete in certain markets
9. An agreement between a buyer and a seller requiring the buyer to refrain from buying a similar product from a competitor
10. An agreement between a buyer and a seller requiring the buyer, as a condition of the sale, to buy other of the seller's products

Questions and Problems to Discuss

1. What are the six important areas of government regulation of business activity?
2. Acme Manufacturing Co., a producer of paints, was disposing of waste chemicals in a river that flowed behind its plant. The attorney general of the state in which it was located went into court to prevent a violation of regulations prohibiting such disposal. May the attorney general bring an action on behalf of the citizens affected by such disposal?
3. Describe the ways in which compliance with government regulations may be enforced.

4. Congress passed a law setting a maximum speed of 65 mph on all highways. May a state legislature enact a law setting the maximum speed at 70 mph for all roads solely within its borders?

5. Allen Corp. and Excelsior Company were competitors in the manufacture of bicycles. Allen made an offer to buy out Excelsior, a merger that would give Allen 90 percent of all the bicycle business in the United States. If the government brings suit to prevent this, is the fact that the merger may result in increased efficiency and lower costs to the consumer a complete defense to the suit?

6. Copyrite Carbons sold carbon paper throughout the country. To increase its sales in one part of the country, it offered to sell carbon paper to local dealers at a rate lower than the rate charged to dealers in other parts of the country. May it do so?

7. Four companies manufacturing paint were concerned about new government regulations affecting their industry. They decided to join forces and form an association for the purpose of keeping track of and affecting new legislation. Would this be an unlawful combination in restraint of trade?

8. Herrand decided to build a restaurant in a residential area. The local zoning board brought suit to stop her, claiming the area was not zoned to permit the operation of a restaurant. Herrand claimed that she has a right under the Constitution to engage in business in any location. Is she correct?

9. Grable was arrested for keeping his shoe repair shop open on Sundays in violation of a local Sunday law. May Grable claim as a defense that this law violates his constitutional rights to do business as he sees fit?

10. The city of Briggs passed an ordinance prohibiting the sale of cigarettes within the city limits on the grounds that cigarettes are harmful to the health of its residents. Does the city have the power to pass such a law?

11. The Doan Co. and the Dean Co. manufactured typewriters. They got together and agreed that they would sell their typewriters to stores at the same price. This agreed-upon price was lower than that charged for comparable typewriters of other manufacturers. Would this lower price be a defense to an antitrust action?

12. Garth bought a valuable piece of land for the construction of an industrial plant. She decided to build a paper mill but city officials refused to permit this on the grounds that the mill would pollute nearby streams and the city's water supply. Does the city have the right to do this?

13. The *Daily Planet* newspaper and the Watercress Restaurant were both owned by the same partnership. To lessen competition from other restaurants, the newspaper refused to accept any restaurant ads except those of Watercress. Is this a violation of law?

Cases to Decide

1. David Findlay and Walstein Findlay were brothers who were in the art business together. After they split up, David operated a store in New York under the name "Findlay Galleries" for over twenty-five years. Walstein, who had been in business in a different state, bought the premises next door to his brother and opened a gallery under the name "Wally Findlay Galleries." David sued to stop him from using the family name in the art gallery business. Should he succeed? (*David B. Findlay, Inc.* v. *Findlay*, 18 NY2d 612)

2. To protest high municipal taxes in the city of Rye, New York, the Stovers hung tattered clothing, rags, and scarecrows on lines in their front yard in a residential neighborhood. The city of Rye passed an ordinance prohibiting the practice without a permit and then refused to grant the Stovers a permit. The city then brought action against the Stovers. Was the statute and its use a valid exercise of the police power? (*People* v. *Stovers*, 12 NY 2d 462, 191 NE2d 272)

3. Police Conference of New York was a group interested in securing more effective law enforcement. Metropolitan Police Conference started a group to engage in the same work. Police tried to stop Metropolitan from using that name on the grounds it was likely to deceive the public. Is Police entitled to an injunction against Metropolitan? (*Police Conference of New York* v. *Metropolitan Police Conference of Eastern New York*, 66 AD2d 441)

4. Engle and Showell conducted a business that the city of Phoenix considered to be a public nuisance. Without a trial or public hearing, officials of the city of Phoenix sought to end the business. Engle and Showell sought an injunction from the

court to prevent such action. Are they entitled to the injunction? (*Hislop* v. *Rodgers,* 54 Ariz 101, 92 P2d 527)

5. An automobile dealer association printed and distributed to its dealers a retail price list. The association was indicted and charged with a conspiracy to control the retail price of Plymouth cars. The association claimed it could not be found guilty unless prices were actually fixed as a result of the lists. Is this a good defense? (*Plymouth Dealers Association of Northern California* v. *United States,* 279 F2d 128)

6. Prior to 1920, DuPont acquired a large block of stock in General Motors. General Motors then bought large amounts of auto paints and fabrics from DuPont instead of from other suppliers. The federal government brought suit under the Clayton Act to force DuPont to give up its ownership of the GM stock, claiming that the stock ownership decreased competition. Should the federal government succeed? (*United States* v. *E. I. DuPont de Nemours & Co.,* 353 US 586)

7. Klors operated a retail store in San Francisco. Broadway-Hale operated a chain of department stores, including one next door to Klors. They competed in the sale of appliances. Klors charged that Broadway-Hale, using its buying power, influenced appliance manufacturers to refuse to sell to Klors. Klors sued Broadway-Hale and the manufacturers under the Sherman Act, claiming it was the object of a group boycott that tended to create a monopoly. Broadway-Hale claimed that the public was not affected because people could buy from other retailers in the neighborhood and only one small retailer was affected. Is this an adequate defense? (*Klors, Inc.,* v. *Broadway-Hale Stores, Inc.,* 359 US 207)

8. Monroe County, New York, passed a local law requiring a sign on each fuel pump at a filling station showing the price, taxes, and octane rating. The law was passed to prevent fraudulent practices in the sale of gas. It also allowed one additional sign, but the sign could not exceed 18 inches by 18 inches. A gas station owner claimed that the portion of the law controlling the size of the sign was unconstitutional because it exceeded the police power of the municipality. Is the owner correct? (*Stubbart* v. *County of Monroe,* 58 AD2d 25)

Barbara Bolton, Ann Rogers, and Beth Wright were partners in a real estate development company. They bought apartment houses and shopping centers that were in need of repairs or that were experiencing financial problems. After making improvements and increasing rents, they would sell the properties they had acquired at a considerable profit.

One day, Bolton learned of a shopping center that was in trouble and could be purchased at a very low price. Wishing to keep this property for herself, she later purchased the property in her own name, developed it, and sold it for a profit of $500,000.

Rogers and Wright brought an action against Bolton, claiming that she had taken for herself what should have been a partnership opportunity. They sued for their share of the profits from the sale.

The Trial

Bolton testified during the trial that she had bought properties for herself on many occasions before the partnership was created and that she saw no reason why she should not continue. The other partners testified that during the time the partnership was in existence, they had never purchased properties on their own behalf. The partnership agreement was introduced in evidence; it contained no clause relating to the purchase of properties by the partners in their individual names.

The Arguments at Trial

During the trial, Bolton's attorney argued that if the partnership agreement was silent, there was no reason why Bolton couldn't buy properties for herself. The partners had always bought many non-real estate investments in their own names—why not real estate?

The attorney for Rogers and Wright argued that a partnership implies the sharing of investment opportunities and that this does not have to be stated specifically in the partnership agreement. They further argued that if the partners are in a real estate business, it is implied that they should share real estate opportunities even though it is expected that they will not share non-real estate investments.

Questions to Discuss

1. Who do you feel has the stronger argument: Bolton or the other two partners? Why?
2. If you were the judge or jury hearing the case, for whom would you decide? Why?
3. Would it make any difference if the three partners had been simply joint tenants and had not been in the real estate business?
4. If you were an attorney drafting a partnership clause to cover this problem, what terms would you insert?

PART VII

REAL AND PERSONAL PROPERTY

*After studying Part VII,
you should be able to*

1 Distinguish between real and personal property.
2 Describe the various ways in which real property and personal property can be acquired.
3 List the characteristics of the various forms of ownership of property.
4 Explain the restrictions placed on owners of real property.
5 Describe the important terms generally found in a lease.
6 List the steps involved in buying a house.
7 Name and describe the three most common types of deeds used to transfer title to real property.

Chapter 29

Basic Legal Concepts of Property

CHAPTER PREVIEW

This chapter discusses the nature of real and personal property. It describes the manner in which each type of property may be acquired. Both real and personal property are usually acquired by purchase, gift, or inheritance. In addition, the chapter describes how real property may be acquired by law through adverse possession, accretion, or condemnation by a public authority. Personal property may be acquired through taking control of abandoned or lost property. Valuable rights and personal property may also be acquired through one's intellectual efforts, including patents, trademarks, and copyrights. The chapter describes how these rights are acquired and for how long such rights exist.

Title to property may be taken in many different ways, including various types of tenancies, community property, cooperative and condominium ownership, and time sharing.

The chapter concludes with a discussion of the ways in which the use of real property may be restricted. This includes private means, such as restrictive covenants, easements, and wills; and public means, such as zoning and building regulations.

THE NATURE OF PROPERTY

Property is defined by law as the right to possess, use, and dispose of something under the protection of the law. We commonly use the term to refer to the "something" that is subject to those rights. Property is generally classified as personal property or real property.

Personal Property

Personal property consists of movable property, such as motor vehicles, furniture, books, and so forth. It may be tangible—capable of being seen, felt, or touched—such as merchandise and livestock. Or it may be intangible and be a *right* to something of value, such as a patent, a promissory note, or a stock certificate.

Real Property

Real property consists of land, anything permanently attached to the land, and certain interests in land. Land includes the surface, what is below the surface, and the air space above the surface. Grass, trees, rock, minerals, and liquids are all included within the definition of land.

If buildings are permanently attached to the land, they are considered real property. A temporary structure, such as a trailer or a mobile home, is personal property. A garage is permanent, and therefore real property, even if it can be removed easily.

A **fixture** is any item of personal property that is attached to real property in such a way that it is treated as real property. It becomes a part of the real property to the extent that its removal would damage the real property. Elevators, built-in stoves, bathroom fixtures, and lighting fixtures are all considered fixtures.

> Armand sold his home to Farber. Before the transfer of the home, Armand removed a built-in shower stall, claiming it was not part of the sale. Farber can insist that the shower stall be put back because it is a fixture. ■

Fixtures are a part of the real property and are included as part of the sale of real property. Items of personal property may or may not be included in a sale of real property, depending on any agreements between the buyer and the seller.

The decision as to whether an item is a fixture or personal property is usually determined by the following rules:

1. An agreement between the parties concerning the items will govern the decision.

2. In the absence of an agreement, the law will make the decision based on the nature of the property, the intent of the parties, and the extent to which removal of the item would damage the real property.

> The Hanover Company operated a department store in a building owned by Acorn. Hanover installed a central air-conditioning system and adjustable shelving throughout the store. The lease was silent regarding ownership of fixtures. At the end of the lease term, Hanover was entitled to remove and keep the shelving but not the air-conditioning system. ■

Easements, Licenses, and Profits

Rights to use the land of others are common and are often valuable. Such rights include easements, licenses, and profits.

An **easement** is a right to use the land or a portion of the land of another for a specific purpose and is either perpetual or for a specific period of time. For example, a public utility company may obtain an easement (sometimes called a right-of-way) across an owner's property for the purpose of installing a gas line. The owner of a landlocked parcel of land is entitled to an easement across the land of a neighbor in order to be able to get to the property, provided the two parcels of land were purchased from the same seller. Adjoining homeowners may give each other easements so they can build and share a common driveway. Most easements are transferred to the purchaser when the land subject to the easement is sold. An easement must be in writing to be enforceable.

> Janeway gave Manley an easement across her property so that Manley could build a road from her property to the main highway. When Janeway sold her property, the buyer purchased it subject to the easement; the road would remain in existence. ■

A **license** is similar to an easement except that it is usually temporary and binds only the person who gives it. Unlike an easement, a license does not bind successive owners of the property. An example of a license would be permitting a neighbor to park a car on your property for a certain period of time.

A **profit** is the right to remove water, natural gas, minerals, or wood from another person's land. An example of a profit would be the right to cut down and take trees from someone's land.

ACQUIRING REAL AND PERSONAL PROPERTY

Real and personal property may be acquired in similar ways—for example, by purchase, gift, or inheritance. Personal property may also be acquired when it is found after being abandoned or lost. Real property may also be acquired through adverse possession, accretion, or condemnation.

Purchase

Real and personal property may be purchased, or sold, under a contract of sale. (The contract of sale is discussed in Chapter 31.) Real property is always purchased or sold under a written contract of sale because the statute of frauds requires it. Personal property may be purchased or sold under a written or oral contract, depending on the purchase price of the property involved. Under the Uniform Commercial Code (UCC), a contract for the sale of goods costing $500 or more must be in writing to be enforceable. A purchase of a vacuum cleaner from a friend probably would not be in writing.

The formal document transferring title to real property is known as a **deed.** The various types of deeds are discussed in Chapter 31 in relation to buying real property.

Personal property may be transferred simply by delivery. If it is transferred by means of a formal document, the document is known as a bill of sale. A formal bill of sale is shown in Figure 29.1.

Gift or Inheritance

Real and personal property may be acquired and transferred by gift. A gift of real property is made by transferring title with a deed. A gift of personal property may be made by a document describing the gift or by delivery alone.

A person may also acquire title to real and personal property through a will or, when there is no will, through inheritance (discussed in Chapter 38).

Abandonment

Personal property may be acquired by taking control of lost or abandoned property. In many states, however, certain procedures must be followed before title may be obtained. Property that is found may have to be turned over to the police or other authorities. Often, a notice of lost or abandoned

Figure 29.1
Formal Bill of Sale

Know all Men by these Presents,

That JASON M. MILLER, 1721 Long Street, Brookville, Arkansas,

party of the first part, for and in consideration of the sum of FOUR THOUSAND AND 00/100-------------------- --- Dollars ($ 4,000.00) lawful money of the United States, to the party of the first part in hand paid, at or before the ensealing and delivery of these presents, by

LAVERNE E. NEWTON, 28 Mainland Avenue, Brookville, Arkansas

party of the second part, the receipt whereof is hereby acknowledged, has bargained and sold, and by these present does grant and convey unto the said party of the second part, the heirs, executors, administrators, successors and assigns thereof.

One (1) Martin Hi-Power Tractor, Model X-47, Serial Number XY4296H

To Have and to Hold the same unto the said party of the second part, the heirs, executors, administrators, successors and assigns thereof forever. And the party of the first part does covenant and agree to and with the said party of the second part, to **Warrant and Defend** the sale of the said goods and chattels hereby sold unto the said party of the second part, the heirs, executors, administrators, successors and assigns thereof, against all and every person and persons whomsoever.

Whenever the text hereof requires, the singular number used herein shall include the plural and all genders.

In Witness Whereof: the party of the first part has duly executed this bill of sale on the

6th **day of** March 19 -- .

In Presence of

Jason M. Miller _____(L. S.)
Cornelia T. Ames _____(L. S.)
_____(L. S.)

property must be published in a local newspaper. If the owner does not claim the property after a certain period of time, the finder may keep the property or sell it and keep the proceeds. If property is abandoned, there must be proof that the former owner intended to abandon it.

■ Hazelton was sitting on a bus next to Jordan. Hazelton had a camera with her. When the bus got to her stop, Hazelton got off the bus in a hurry and left the camera behind by mistake. Jordan could not claim title to the camera because Hazelton never intended to abandon it. ■

Escheat is the process by which a state government obtains title to property that is abandoned or unclaimed. Many bank accounts, dividends, interest payments, and refunds are never claimed by their rightful owners. Most states have statutes providing that, after a public notice is published and a certain period of time passes, abandoned or unclaimed funds or property escheat to the state. The real property of a person who dies without a will or heirs also escheats to the state.

Lost Property

Abandoned property is property with which its owner parted purposely. **Lost property** is property with which its owner has parted involuntarily.

A person who finds lost property can claim good title to it as against anyone else except its true owner. A finder of lost property who knows its true owner must return it to the owner or may be held liable for the tort of conversion. If the finder does not know who or where the true owner is, the finder must take certain steps to locate the owner, such as notifying the police and/or advertising in a local newspaper. In many states, a finder of lost property who takes the proper steps to locate its true owner may, after a certain period of time, obtain good title to the property if its true owner cannot be located.

Mislaid Property

Mislaid property is property whose owner has temporarily placed it somewhere and forgotten its location. The finder becomes an involuntary bailee and cannot keep the property or obtain title to it.

> By mistake, Reynolds left her umbrella at the home of a friend. The property is considered mislaid, and Reynolds's friend must keep it until Reynolds returns to claim it. ∎

Adverse Possession

Real property belonging to another may be acquired by occupying it without the owner's consent for a long period of time. Title obtained in this manner is known as title by **adverse possession.** Not only title to land but also rights in land such as easements may be obtained in this way. Rights in land obtained through adverse possession are obtained by **prescription.** Public property—property owned by a federal, state, or local government—may not be acquired by adverse possession.

Strict rules apply before title may be obtained by adverse possession. The first is that the possession must be actual. The person claiming possession must actually and physically occupy the property in question. The second rule is that the possession must be exclusive. The person claiming possession cannot occupy the land together with the owner, or a third party, and claim title. The third rule is that the property must be occupied under a claim of ownership that is hostile (opposed) to that of the owner. Mere possession is not enough. The claimant must actually occupy the land and claim ownership against all others, including the recorded owner. This rule applies even if the occupant is mistaken about the claim of title.

The fourth rule is that the possession must be continuous for a certain period of time. The period of time required to gain title by adverse possession varies from state to state; ten, fifteen, and twenty years are the most common time periods.

■ Heller owned a home next door to Cromwell. A driveway he built between the homes was actually on Cromwell's land. He believed it was on his land and maintained and repaired the driveway. After the required period of time in his state had passed, Heller could claim ownership of the driveway land. ■

Possession sufficient to acquire title by adverse possession does not require that the occupation be by only one owner. As long as all the rules just outlined are met, periods of occupancy by various owners may be added together to reach the required time period. This practice is known as **tacking.**

■ Worthy occupied land for six years, meeting all the conditions required to obtain title by adverse possession. Worthy then sold the land to Blaine, who occupied it for fourteen years in a state in which a period of twenty years is required for adverse possession. At the end of fourteen years, Blaine could claim title to the land by adverse possession. ■

Accretion

Land that borders water may be increased in size by the flow of that water. When this occurs, the owner of the land acquires title to the additional land by **accretion.** Accretion may occur when waters recede, exposing land that was previously under water. Additional land may also be acquired when waters wash up soil or sand that remains in place and gradually builds up.

Condemnation

Federal, state, and local governments often require property for public use. They may need the property for a highway, school, airport, bridge, or urban renewal project. Government may take land for these purposes under the power of **condemnation,** or *eminent domain* as it is often called.

While the power of condemnation is practically unlimited, there are two restrictions on its use. The first is that the condemnation must be for the public welfare. The second is that the owner of the land must receive fair compensation for the property taken.

ACQUIRING RIGHTS IN PERSONAL PROPERTY

Artists and inventors acquire interests in property as a result of their labors. The product of their work is often an exclusive and valuable right to property.

This right is protected by Congress under the patent, trademark, and copyright laws.

Patents

A **patent** is the grant to an inventor of an exclusive right to manufacture, sell, and license others to make and sell an invention. The term of the patent is seventeen years for most patents, and it is not renewable. Without the patent, anyone can make, use, or sell a similar product without the permission of the inventor. A patent, therefore, is a valuable property right.

To obtain a patent, an inventor must prove that the invention or design is unique, useful, and not clearly obvious based upon existing technology. Obtaining a patent often involves considerable time and expense.

Trademarks

A **trademark** is a word or symbol used to identify products or businesses. Because of the effect of advertising, a trademark can be a very valuable property right. The right to a trademark derives from proper identification and use of the mark. Additional protection is granted by registering the trademark with the U.S. Patent and Trademark Office. Registration, which gives the holder an exclusive right to use the trademark for a period of twenty years plus unlimited renewal terms, provides a relatively speedy way to enforce trademark rights and to prevent others from infringing on the trademark. Like a patent, a trademark must be unique and distinctive. Once a trademark is granted, its owner may sue anyone who uses it without permission.

Copyrights

A **copyright** is a grant by Congress of an exclusive right to own, produce, sell, and license artistic and intellectual works. For works copyrighted after January 1, 1978, the grant is for the author's lifetime plus an additional 50 years after the author's death. For works copyrighted before January 1, 1978, the term of copyright is 28 years, with the right to renew for an additional 47 years.

Copyright claims are classified into nondrama literary works, works of the performing arts, works of the visual arts, and sound recordings. A copyright may be obtained for such things as paintings, books, computer software, musical works, and plays. Like patents and trademarks, copyrights are granted only for original works and only for those that involve an expression of ideas rather than the ideas themselves.

■ Darien had an idea for a motion picture. It involved a modern version of many Bible stories. Darien submitted the idea to the Copyright Office and applied for a copyright. A copyright was not granted because Darien's work involved an idea and not the actual expression of that idea. ■

Under the Trademark Revision Act of 1988, an applicant may apply for a trademark on the basis of (1) the existing use of the trademark or (2) an intent to use the trademark in the future. An applicant who intends to use a trademark in the future must put the trademark into use within six months after the application has been filed and must show that no one has opposed the application. The six-month period can be extended under certain circumstances.

Protection Against Infringement

A person who makes a product without the consent of the inventor may be charged with infringement of the patent. The same applies when a person uses the trademark of another or copies someone else's copyrighted material.

An injunction may be obtained to stop such infringement. In addition, penalties may be imposed—including fines, actual damages, and punitive damages.

There are exceptions, however, and not every use of another's invention or material is considered an infringement. Using some parts of a patented process but not all of them, for example, is not considered an infringement. Copying portions of a book for use in a literature class would also be permissible and not considered an infringement. What is or is not considered an infringement depends very often on who uses the material, to what end, and whether the use is for nonprofit or commercial purposes.

FORMS OF OWNERSHIP OF PROPERTY

There are many different forms of ownership of property. These include tenancy, community property, cooperative, and condominium.

Tenancy

Tenancy is the interest one has in the ownership of property. There are different types of tenancy, including sole tenancy, tenancy in common, joint tenancy, and tenancy by the entirety. The type of tenancy affects the rights of ownership and survivorship.

A **sole tenancy**, which is often called a tenancy in severalty, is ownership by one person.

A **tenancy in common** is a form of multiple ownership in which each co-owner's interest may be sold, given as a gift, inherited, or subject to sale by a judgment creditor. On the death of a tenant in common, the deceased tenant's interest passes to the person named in the tenant's will or to the tenant's heirs. It does not automatically pass to the surviving tenants. If a tenant in common sells her or his interest, the new owner becomes a tenant in common with the other tenants. This tenancy ends only when all interests are sold, when one tenant acquires the interest of the others, or when the property is physically divided among the tenants.

> Berger and Teele bought a home as tenants in common. Five years later, Teele bought Berger's interest in the house. This ended the tenancy in common; Teele became a sole tenant. ■

Today these forms of ownership apply to both real and personal property, but it is rare to see multiple ownership of personal property referred to as a tenancy in common or as a tenancy by the entireties.

In most states, if property is transferred by deed or by will to two or more persons without any statement as to the type of tenancy, it is to be presumed that it is a tenancy in common.

A **joint tenancy** also involves multiple ownership. It differs from a tenancy in common in that it has a feature known as the **right of survivorship.** This means that if a joint tenant dies, her or his interest passes directly to the surviving tenants. The deceased tenant's interest does not pass according to the deceased tenant's will or to the deceased tenant's heirs. The last remaining joint tenant becomes sole tenant of the property.

> Alvarez and Laredo had a joint bank account. When Alvarez died, she left her interest in the account to her children. This provision in her will would not be upheld. At her death, Alvarez's interest passed directly to Laredo as the surviving joint tenant. ■

Joint tenants own equal shares of the property; tenants in common may own unequal shares. If a joint tenant sells an interest, the joint tenancy ends and becomes a tenancy in common.

A **tenancy by the entirety** is a tenancy consisting of a wife and husband. It is similar to a joint tenancy, with one important exception. Neither the husband nor the wife may transfer her or his interest without the consent of the other. Such an attempted transfer would be void. Upon the death of one spouse, title passes to the survivor. If the husband and wife divorce, the tenancy changes to that of a tenancy in common. In some states, transfer of property to a wife and husband automatically creates a tenancy by the entirety. In other states, specific language must be used to set up this tenancy or no such tenancy is created.

> The Halls bought a home and took title as tenants by the entirety. Mr. Hall sold the home and gave a deed to the buyer. The deed would be invalid unless Mrs. Hall consented to the sale. ■

Community Property

In some states co-ownership of property may arise by operation of law under a system known as community property. **Community property** is a system in which the wife and husband are considered to own equal and undivided interests in all property acquired by either spouse during marriage, excluding property received by gift or inheritance. Also excluded is any property owned prior to the marriage. Those states having community property laws are Arizona, California, Idaho, Louisiana, Nevada, New Mexico, Texas, Washington, and Wisconsin. Community property cannot be sold in those states without the consent of both spouses.

Cooperative Ownership

A special type of ownership, usually of an apartment house, is known as a cooperative. A **cooperative** exists when two or more persons form a corporation to purchase and manage the apartment house or building in which they live. Each person receives stock in that corporation. The individual stockholder does not own the apartment he or she resides in (real property) but owns only a share of stock in the corporation (personal property). The stock entitles its owner to occupy a specific unit in the apartment house for as long as the stock is owned. The stock may be sold, usually only with the consent of the other stockholders. All stockholders share the expense of repairing, maintaining, and operating the building. Major decisions are made by a majority vote of the stockholders. Management is usually handled by a board of directors elected by the stockholders and carried out by professional management personnel. If a stockholder fails to meet her or his financial obligations—payment of taxes, utilities, and so forth—the corporation is liable for payment.

> The Walters purchased a share of stock in a cooperative apartment building. A majority of the stockholders voted to construct a swimming pool and to charge each stockholder a proportionate share of the cost. The Walters are bound by a majority vote of the other stockholders and may not object that they do not swim and do not wish to share the cost. ■

Condominium Ownership

Another special type of ownership is the condominium, which is similar to a cooperative with one major difference. In a **condominium** each person owns a specific unit or apartment in a building rather than a share of stock in a corporation. The owner receives a deed to the unit, which is recorded like a deed to any other type of real estate. Within limits, the owner has complete control over the unit she or he owns and can sell or mortgage it without the consent of the other unit owners. The owner is also responsible for the real estate taxes, the maintenance, and any repairs for her or his own unit.

A condominium owner also has an ownership interest in areas of the building shared by all owners, such as the sidewalks, grounds, parking area, and so forth. Each owner pays a monthly maintenance fee for the upkeep of these areas. If an owner fails to pay this fee, the other owners may bring an action in court to collect the amount due. Any judgment entered becomes a lien on the unit and must be paid before the unit may be sold.

> Schultz bought a condominium unit as a summer home. She failed to pay the taxes on the unit for three years and local officials sued to collect. The other unit owners would not be obligated to pay the taxes owed by Schultz. ■

Decisions involving the condominium as a whole are usually made by majority vote of all the owners. Generally, a condominium association is formed to meet periodically to decide matters of mutual interest. The owners may also elect a board of managers to make major management decisions.

Time Sharing

In recent years, a new form of ownership known as **time sharing** has developed. This form of ownership is similar to condominium ownership. The owner purchases the right to use a certain property, usually a resort condominium, for a specific period of time each year. In some cases, the time share is limited to a certain number of years. In other cases, the time share is perpetual, and the right to use the property may be sold or transferred by agreement or by will. Time-share owners can often trade with other owners for a different time of the year or trade for time in a different property or location.

State laws regulate the sale, financing, and operation of time-share investments, particularly investments that are purchased on credit.

RESTRICTIONS ON THE USE OF REAL PROPERTY

Most property owners believe their right to use their property is unlimited. This belief arose from the early history of our country, when people were free to use their land as they saw fit, provided they did not disturb their neighbors.

In recent years, however, an expanding population combined with an increase in environmental concerns have prompted a need for increased control over the way owners use their property. Property owners do have the right to the exclusive use of their property, and they have the right to dispose of it. Beyond these rights, however, their use is often limited by both private and public means.

Restrictive Covenants

Use of property may be limited by a restriction, known as a **restrictive covenant,** in a deed. Restrictive covenants are used to maintain the appearance and value of a neighborhood, usually residential neighborhoods. They accomplish this by prohibiting owners from using their property for other than residential purposes and by regulating the size, cost, and location of dwellings. They may even prohibit such things as roof antennas and outdoor clotheslines. Some restrictive covenants require property owners to obtain approval before constructing dwellings or putting up fences. Other persons subject to the same restrictive covenants may sue in court to prevent a property owner from violating a restrictive covenant or to collect damages resulting from such a violation. A restrictive covenant becomes so much a part of a piece of property that it is referred to as being "attached" to the land. A person who buys a piece of property subject to a restrictive covenant is held to be aware of the restriction at the time of purchase and is bound by it. When the property is transferred, succeeding owners are also bound by the restriction, regardless of whether the restriction is cited in the deed.

> Hertz bought some land that had a restriction prohibiting its use for commercial purposes. Hertz sold the land to Ryan, but nothing was said in the contract of the sale about the restriction. Nevertheless, Ryan is bound by the restriction because it is attached to the land and cannot be changed by agreement. ∎

Because restrictive covenants limit the use of the land and the rights of landowners, courts do not favor them. Often, courts will not enforce such covenants if they can find a public policy reason, such as change of circumstances, to support their decision.

> Berger bought a piece of land that was subject to a seventy-five-year-old restrictive covenant preventing the use of the land for commercial purposes. If Berger decided to build a store on the property, and if all of the surrounding properties are used for commercial purposes, a court would probably not enforce the covenant. ∎

Easements

The use of land may also be restricted by previously granted easements that "attach" to the land, such as access easements and public utility rights-of-way. Once an easement is granted and recorded, subsequent owners of the land are bound by the terms and conditions of the easement.

> Barnes owned some land over which he gave a neighbor the right to cross to gain access to a street. This right was contained in a recorded easement. When Barnes sold the land to Lebow, Lebow became bound by the same easement. ∎

Zoning Laws and Regulations

Government may restrict the use of land through zoning laws and regulations. Typically, a city or town establishes districts throughout the municipality for residential, commercial, and industrial purposes. In each district, only certain uses are permitted, and specific rules govern the uses of structures and their cost, design, and location. Zoning laws and regulations often set restrictions on the size, height, and set-backs of buildings and requirements for minimum parking space. In certain cases, a literal application of the zoning laws would produce economic hardship. In such cases, a property owner may apply for a **variance,** an exception to the strict requirements of the zoning ordinance, which may be granted if severe hardship can be shown.

The use of land may also be restricted for health or environmental reasons. As our population increases, there is a greater awareness of health, safety, and environmental problems and the need to solve them. Most municipalities regulate methods of constructing structures and the materials, such as asbestos fibers or other potentially hazardous substances, that are used in them. Codes may regulate plumbing, heating, air conditioning, and electrical systems. Waste disposal, air and water purity, and noise pollution are also regulated by city and town ordinances.

Wills

Land use may also be restricted through a will. For example, an alumnus may donate his property to the college he graduated from and include a condition that it be used for a certain purpose, such as a science library. This restriction prevents the college from using that land for any other purpose, such as a new gym.

Summary of Important Legal Concepts

There are two types of property, personal and real. Personal property consists of both tangible and intangible property, such as furniture, cash, stocks and bonds. Real property consists of land, anything attached to the land, and certain interests in land, including easements, licenses and profits.

Both real and personal property may be acquired by purchase, gift, and inheritance. Personal property may also be acquired through abandonment and escheat, by finding it, and by creative efforts, including patents, trademarks, and copyrights. Real property may also be acquired by adverse possession, accretion, and condemnation.

Title to real property is transferred by deed. Title to personal property may be transferred either by delivery or by delivery and bill of sale.

There are five common forms of ownership of real property: sole tenancy, tenancy in common, joint tenancy, tenancy by the entirety, and community property.

There are three special types of ownership, the condominium, the cooperative, and the time share. They involve either individual ownership of a property unit, ownership of stock in a corporation that owns the property, or ownership of a right to use a unit for a specific period of time. In all three cases, there is a right to use areas shared by all residents of the property in which the units are located.

The use of property is not unlimited; it is often restricted for value-maintenance reasons or for health and safety purposes. Restrictions may be imposed by property agreement, operation of law, or statutes and regulations. The most common examples of private restrictions are restrictive covenants, easements, and wills. The most common examples of public restrictions are zoning laws, health and safety regulations, and environmental control laws.

Key Legal Terms to Know

Match the terms with the definitions that follow.

abandoned property
accretion
adverse possession
community property
condemnation
condominium
cooperative
copyright
deed
easement
escheat
fixture
joint tenancy
license
lost property
mislaid property
patent

personal property
prescription
profit
real property
restrictive covenant
right of survivorship
sole tenancy
tacking
tenancy by the entirety
tenancy in common
time sharing
trademark
variance

1. A restriction in a deed limiting property use
2. Obtaining title to property as a result of the movement of water
3. Movable property, tangible or intangible
4. The right of a government unit to take private property for public use
5. Obtaining title to another's property by occupying it for a long period without the owner's consent
6. Ownership of land deeded to a husband and wife
7. Ownership and occupancy of property with others through the purchase of stock
8. A grant of an exclusive right to make, sell, or license others to make and sell an invention
9. A temporary right to use land belonging to another
10. Obtaining an easement by adverse possession or use
11. The right of wife and husband to share equally in property acquired during the marriage as provided by laws in certain states
12. Adding periods of occupancy to determine if title has been obtained by adverse possession
13. Ownership of a dwelling unit that is one of many, plus a common interest in property used by all unit owners
14. Ownership by two or more persons that passes at death to the surviving tenant(s) rather than to heirs or beneficiaries
15. Ownership by two or more persons that passes at death to heirs or beneficiaries rather than to surviving tenants
16. A right, granted in writing, to use the land of another for a specific purpose
17. Property consisting of land, rights to land, and anything permanently attached to the land

18. Personal property attached to land or a building in such a way as to be considered real property
19. A word or symbol used to identify a product or business
20. The right of the state to claim abandoned or unclaimed property
21. A grant of an exclusive right to own, produce, sell, and license artistic and intellectual works
22. Ownership by one person
23. A right assuring that ownership interest passes to a surviving joint tenant rather than to the heirs of the deceased joint tenant
24. A formal document transferring title to real property
25. The right to remove water, natural gas, minerals, or wood from another person's land
26. An exception to a zoning-ordinance requirement
27. The right to use a property for a specific period of time each year
28. Property with which its owner has parted involuntarily
29. Property that has been temporarily misplaced by its owner
30. Property with which its owner has parted purposely

Questions and Problems to Discuss

1. Describe the various ways by which real and personal property may be acquired.
2. Explain the differences among the various types of tenancies of real property.
3. Adams donated land to a university with the stipulation that it always be used for recreational purposes. Fifty years after Adams's death, the university needed the land to build a library. May it build the library on the land Adams donated?
4. Feller owned land in a residential area that was zoned to permit two-family homes. The deed for Feller's land contained a restrictive covenant prohibiting the construction of any buildings other than one-family residences. If Feller tries to build a two-family house, can his neighbors prevent him from doing so?
5. Polk owned a valuable piece of land that she planned to sell to a shopping center developer. The state condemned half the land for the construction of a highway. Can Polk prevent the state from taking this land on the grounds that she believes the highway should be built in a different location?

6. Harrison bought a building lot in order to construct a new home. The deed contained a restriction limiting the height of the home to one story. If Harrison decides to build a two-story home on the lot, can his neighbors prevent him from doing so?

7. Grant owned some land directly under the flight path leading to the airport. Zoning regulations in his area prohibited the construction of any residences under the flight path. May Grant ignore the regulations and build a home in that area?

8. Harding died, leaving his home by will to his three sons. One son decided to sell his interest in the home to a friend. His brothers tried to stop him, claiming that he could not sell his interest to another without their consent. Were they correct?

9. Wilson and Jackson owned land as joint tenants. Wilson died, leaving all her property to her sister. What interest in the land did her sister receive under the will?

10. Johnson owned a farm next to a highway. He orally gave his neighbor permission to cross the farm to get to the highway. No time limit was set and no specific path was agreed upon. The neighbor used the path for thirty years. Johnson sold the land to his uncle, who then refused to permit the neighbor to use the path. Was Johnson's uncle legally entitled to do this?

11. Adams owned a tract of land upon which she built a home. She gave an easement to the local water company to construct and maintain a pipeline across the property. Adams died, leaving the property to her daughter in her will. The daughter knew nothing about the easement. Can the daughter disregard the easement because she was not aware of its existence.

12. Granby died, leaving all his personal property by will to his daughter, Sarah. Granby owned an apartment cooperative. Will Sarah receive the cooperative under the will?

13. Duell bought property on which there was a large hole that had been dug for a swimming pool. Duell decided not to build a pool and to leave the hole. Can city officials force Duell to fill in the hole?

14. Mr. and Mrs. Allen owned a home as tenants by the entirety. Mr. Allen decided that after he died, it would be advisable to have the house owned by his children so he left the home to them in his will. Upon Mr. Allen's death, will his children receive title to the home?

15. Argent bought land in a subdivision which was subject to a restrictive covenant that prohibited the construction of a television antenna on the roof of any residence. Neither the deed to Argent nor the deed to the person who sold Argent the property contained the restrictive covenant, but prior deeds contained it. If Argent decided to build an antenna on his roof, would his neighbors be able to stop him?

16. Bates owned a home that was located next door to his son's public school. For twenty-two years, Bates planted a garden in a 10- by 120-foot strip of land located on the border between his home and the school property. The town subsequently discovered that the land Bates was planting had originally belonged to the school district that operated the public school. A twenty-year adverse possession statute exists in the state in which the property is located. Is Bates entitled to claim title to the strip of land?

Cases to Decide

1. Prior to Kitchum's death, Kitchum and Cundaro received title to a piece of property in the names of "Kitchum and his wife, as tenants by the entirety." Kitchum and Cundaro were not married when they received the deed. Place, who was administering Kitchum's estate, brought suit, claiming that Kitchum's interest passed to his estate and not to Cundaro. Was Place correct? (*Place* v. *Cundaro*, New York 34 AD2d 698)

2. Mr. and Mrs. Conwell owned a lot next to Allen's property. They planted grass in an area that appeared to be between the two properties but actually belonged to Allen. After the statutory period had passed, the Conwells claimed that this was sufficient notice of their interest to obtain title by adverse possession. Allen brought suit to determine who has title to the land. Decide. (*Conwell* v. *Allen*, 21 Ariz App 383)

3. Bucella went to the recording office to register his title to a piece of land. Agrippino and others before him had used this land for over 20 years for a passageway for access and to remove ashes and garbage. Agrippino objected to Bucella's attempt to register the title, claiming he had an easement by prescription. Is Agrippino correct? (*Bucella* v. *Agrippino*, 257 Mass 483)

4. Redman and Kidwell bought adjoining parcels of land from the same seller. Redman was unable

to build a house on his land because he had no access to a public road except over Kidwell's land. Is Redman automatically entitled to an easement for access over Kidwell's land? (*Redman* v. *Kidwell*, 180 So 2d 682)

5. Martin owned land in a subdivision and planned to construct two apartment buildings on the land. When the land was purchased, it contained a covenant restricting any building to one-story residences. Lidke and others, who lived in the subdivision, brought a suit to stop construction of the apartment buildings. Martin's defense was that the construction was permissible because the zoning regulations allowed it. Is this a good defense? (*Lidke* v. *Martin*, 500 P2d 1184)

6. Cottrell and others bought lots in a subdivision from Nurnberger. The seller told them, at the time they purchased their lots, that a certain piece of land in the subdivision was to be reserved for recreational and playground purposes. Later, Nurnberger sold the land to a developer for the construction of a hotel. Cottrell sued to prevent construction of the hotel, claiming a violation of a restrictive covenant. Is Cottrell correct? (*Cottrell* v. *Nurnberger*, W. Virginia 47 SE2d 454)

7. Stromberg and others owned land in a subdivision that was subject to a restrictive covenant that provided that "the premises may be used only for residential purposes for one family." Stromberg built a one-family home on his lot but then decided to construct a second home on the same parcel. Thrun and others brought suit to prevent the construction of the second home, on the grounds that the restrictive covenant prohibited the construction of a second single-family home on the property. Is Thrun correct? (*Thrun* v. *Stromberg*, 136 AD 2nd 543 #13, NY)

8. Martin and others owned land in a subdivision subject to a restrictive covenant that restricted buildings to one-story residences. The zoning of the property permitted the construction of apartment buildings. Martin and others decided to erect two apartment buildings on the land. Lidke and others brought suit to prevent the construction of the buildings, on the grounds that the restrictive covenant prohibited the construction of apartment buildings, regardless of what the zoning regulations permitted. Was Lidke correct? (*Lidke* v. *Martin*, 500 P2nd 1184)

Chapter 30

Renting Real Property

CHAPTER PREVIEW

The landlord-tenant relationship is one of the most common business relationships. This chapter discusses the nature of that relationship and of many different types of tenancies, including tenancies that are for a specific period of time and tenancies that are open ended.

The landlord-tenant relationship is based on a lease. This chapter describes the essential information each lease should contain. It also discusses the rights and duties of both landlord and tenant—rights and duties contained in the lease or imposed by law. The chapter also discusses the many ways in which a lease may be terminated.

The landlord and the tenant have rights and duties between them, and they may also have obligations toward third parties, such as visitors on the premises. The chapter concludes with a discussion of the nature of those obligations.

THE LANDLORD-TENANT RELATIONSHIP

At some point in your life, you will probably rent real property—an apartment, an office, a summer cottage, and so on—from another person. The person who owns the property and rents or leases it to you is a **landlord.** When you occupy the property, you will be the **tenant.** You and your landlord will have some sort of agreement of rental, which will be your **lease.** The lease will exist for a length of time known as the **term** and will specify the amount of money, the **rent,** that you will pay for the use of the property.

A lease may be oral or written. Under the statute of frauds, a lease for a term of more than one year must be in writing or it will not be enforced by the courts. Oral leases are often used, but it is better to have a written lease that outlines the rights and duties of the landlord and the tenant.

> Dodge told Allen that she could rent Dodge's cottage for two years at a rent of $200 per month. A written lease was never signed. Just before Allen was to move in, Dodge changed his mind and canceled the lease. Allen cannot force Dodge to rent the property to her, because the lease was not in writing. ■

TYPES OF TENANCIES

A tenant acquires from the landlord an interest in the real property being leased. That interest is known as a *tenancy.* Note that a tenancy may be by ownership of specific property, as discussed in Chapter 28, or by lease of the property.

Tenancies by lease are classified by the length of the lease term: a tenancy for years, a periodic tenancy, a tenancy at will, and a tenancy at sufferance.

Tenancy for Years

The most common type of lease is a **tenancy for years.** You, as tenant, lease the property for a fixed period of time, such as one year. You may be given an option to renew the lease by giving the landlord notice of an intent to renew.

Periodic Tenancy

A **periodic tenancy,** like a tenancy for years, is a tenancy for a specific period of time. Unlike a tenancy for years, a periodic tenancy automatically continues for periods of time equal to the original lease term until canceled by either the landlord or the tenant. A periodic tenancy may be a tenancy from month to month or from year to year, depending on the original term of the lease.

> You leased an apartment from Clarke for one year as a periodic tenant. Because the lease was renewable for its original term, the lease will continue for another year unless you or Clarke gives notice of cancellation. ∎

Tenancy at Will

A **tenancy at will** is a lease for an indefinite period of time. It may be canceled at any time by either the landlord or the tenant. Most tenancies at will are created by oral agreement.

Tenancy at Sufferance

A **tenancy at sufferance** comes into existence when a lease ends and the landlord allows the tenant to remain on the premises. Such tenancy usually lasts for as long as the original term of the lease. If the original lease was for one year, the landlord, by accepting additional rent payments, has agreed to continue the lease for another year. If the tenant does not vacate the premises on the last day of the lease term, the landlord has the right to hold the tenant to another year's lease.

NATURE AND ELEMENTS OF A LEASE

A lease is a form of contract, and to be valid, it must satisfy the usual requirements for a valid contract: offer and acceptance, consideration, competent parties, and lawful purpose.

There is no such thing as a required form for a lease or required language. All that is needed is language that expresses the agreement reached between the landlord and the tenant. It is important, however, that a lease be as complete as possible and contain all the elements agreed upon by the landlord and the tenant. This avoids arguments and lawsuits arising out of the relationship. The essential elements of a lease are factual information and a listing of the rights and duties of the landlord and the tenant. An example of a formal, written lease is shown in Figure 30.1.

Unconscionability

The doctrine of unconscionability, which was discussed in Chapters 10 and 15, applies to leases as well as to other types of contracts. Courts can invalidate a lease or any of its provisions because of unconscionability when they determine that the provisions are unfair based upon the circumstances

This Agreement *BETWEEN*

UNITED PROPERTIES, INC., 180 14th Avenue, New York, New York

as Landlord

and MINTON DRAPERY COMPANY, 429 Curtis Street, New York, New York

as Tenant

Witnesseth: *The Landlord hereby leases to the Tenant the following premises:*

The building at 1642 Draper Avenue, Brooklyn, New York

for the term of one (1) year

to commence from the 1st *day of* June *19 -- and to end on the* 31st *day of* May *19 -- to be used and occupied only for*

the manufacture and sale of curtains and draperies

upon the conditions and covenants following:

1st. *That the Tenant shall pay the annual rent of* SIX THOUSAND DOLLARS ($6,000.00)

said rent to be paid in equal monthly payments in advance on the 1st *day of each and every month during the term aforesaid, as follows:*

FIVE HUNDRED DOLLARS ($500.00) per month

2nd. *That the Tenant shall take good care of the premises and shall, at the Tenant's own cost and expense make all repairs* necessitated by tenant's use of premises

and at the end or other expiration of the term, shall deliver up the demised premises in good order or condition, damages by the elements excepted.

3rd. *That the Tenant shall promptly execute and comply with all statutes, ordinances, rules, orders, regulations and requirements of the Federal, State and Local Governments and of any and all their Departments and Bureaus applicable to said premises, for the correction, prevention, and abatement of nuisances or other grievances, in, upon, or connected with said premises during said term; and shall also promptly comply with and execute all rules, orders and regulations of the New York Board of Fire Underwriters, or any other similar body, at the Tenant's own cost and expense.*

4th. *That the Tenant, successors, heirs, executors or administrators shall not assign this agreement, or underlet or underlease the premises, or any part thereof, or make any alterations on the premises, without the Landlord's consent in writing; or occupy, or permit or suffer the same to be occupied for any business or purpose deemed disreputable or extra-hazardous on account of fire, under the penalty of damages and forfeiture, and in the event of a breach thereof, the term herein shall immediately cease and determine at the option of the Landlord as if it were the expiration of the original term.*

Figure 30.1
Lease

involved and the difference in bargaining power between the landlord and the tenant.

Brower, a person with limited knowledge of English, signed a two-year lease containing a provision that allowed the landlord to terminate the lease at any time for any reason and keep Brower's security deposit. A court would declare such a provision unconscionable and invalid. ■

Factual Information

The important factual information of a lease includes the names and addresses of the landlord and tenant, a description of the property being leased, the term of the lease, the amount of the rent, the time and place for payment of the rent, and the signatures of the parties. Most of this factual information is so important that its absence from the lease may make the lease invalid. A lease missing the names of the landlord and tenant or the amount of rent, for example, would be considered incomplete and not enforceable.

■ Allbright leased a warehouse to James. A written lease was prepared but did not include the lease term. Neither party would be able to enforce the lease because the factual information was incomplete. ■

Rights and Duties

The most important part of a lease describes the rights and duties of the landlord and the tenant. These are known as the **covenants,** or conditions, of the landlord-tenant agreement. The number and type of covenants depend on the type of property leased. A lease for a large office building, for example, may contain extensive covenants and conditions, whereas a lease for a home may have few of them. The basic covenants cover utilities, taxes, repairs, security deposits, payment of rent, destruction of the property, condemnation, fixtures, enjoyment of the leased property, and assignment and subletting. Some covenants are controlled by state law.

Payment of Utilities   Payment of utilities, such as water, gas, and electricity, is an important factor in a lease. The lease should state who is responsible for paying the utility charges. In some cases, the tenant's premises are separately metered and the tenant pays the utility companies directly. In other cases, the landlord pays utility bills and charges the tenant for the tenant's share of the bills.

Payment of Taxes   If a lease is silent about who pays the real estate taxes assessed against the property, the landlord is responsible. In some cases, either the tenant pays the taxes or the taxes are added to and included in the rent. One practice, primarily for business leases, is to have the tenant pay any increase in real estate taxes over a base amount, usually the taxes existing when the tenant first occupied the premises. The tenant's obligation to pay the increased taxes is known as a **tax escalator clause.**

■ Coram rented a store that occupied 25 percent of a shopping center. Coram's lease contained a tax escalator clause. If the taxes for the shopping center increase by $10,000 a year, Coram will have to pay 25 percent of the increase, or $2,500. ■

Redecoration and Repairs   Another important item in a lease is the cost of redecoration and repairs, which can be very expensive. Most leases specify who is responsible for these items. In most cases, the tenant must keep the interior of the leased premises in good repair, and the landlord must make structural repairs, such as roof repairs. The landlord must also make repairs to common areas that all tenants share, such as stairs and hallways.

More and more states and municipalities are imposing repairs and other obligations on landlords regardless of what the leases state. In many states, a landlord owning residential property is deemed to have given the tenant a **warranty of habitability.** This is an implied warranty that the premises are fit for human habitation and that there are no defects or conditions that might be hazardous to the life, health, or safety of the tenant. If this warranty is broken, a court may permit the tenant to pay a decreased monthly rent or may order the landlord to use the rent to correct defects. This concept has even been applied to permit tenants to decrease their rent payments if essential services, such as heating and elevators, are interrupted.

Most leases state that the tenant must take reasonable care of the property. At the end of the lease term, the tenant must return the property, as most leases state, "in as good a condition as at the beginning of the term, wear and tear and damage by the elements excepted." This means that the tenant is not liable for ordinary wear and tear during the term but is liable for any unusual damage.

> Sunkis rented a lakeside cottage from Marple for a two-year term. The cottage was furnished with furniture and rugs. During the term of the lease, the rugs became discolored because of the sand and water coming in through the cottage door. Sunkis would not be liable for this wear and tear because it would be expected that this would occur. ■

Security Deposit   Many landlords now require a tenant to deposit a sum of money with the landlord to guarantee that the tenant will live up to the lease terms. This deposit, known as a **security deposit,** usually consists of one month's rent. The security deposit is often used to pay for any damages the tenant caused during the lease term. At the end of the term, if the tenant has fulfilled all obligations, the deposit is returned to the tenant. In some states, the landlord must deposit the money in a separate bank account, which earns interest for the tenant.

> Brandon rented an apartment and gave the landlord a security deposit of one month's rent. At the start of the last month of the term, Brandon told the landlord he was not going to pay that month's rent, because the security deposit could be used for that purpose. Brandon is not entitled to do this, because the deposit is returnable only at the end of the lease. ■

Payment of Rent   A lease generally specifies when and to whom the rent must be paid. In some cases rent is payable in advance; in other cases it is paid at the end of the rental period. Many leases allow the landlord to charge a penalty or interest charge if the tenant does not pay the rent on time.

Most leases also contain clauses outlining a landlord's remedies if the tenant does not pay the rent, usually after a certain amount of time. If a tenant fails to pay the rent, the landlord may sue her or him to collect the rent due. Another remedy is **eviction,** which is the legal action taken by a landlord to force a tenant to leave the premises. A landlord may bring a proceeding known as a summary (or dispossess) proceeding. After a hearing, the court may grant the landlord a warrant of eviction and/or a judgment for the rent due. If the tenant is required to pay taxes or other charges, failure to pay them may also result in eviction. An eviction notice is shown in Figure 30.2.

Figure 30.2
Eviction Notice

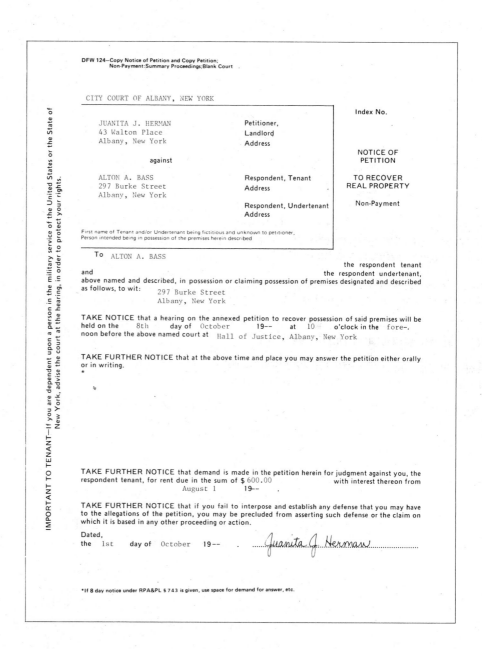

Destruction of the Property   Most leases provide that if the leased property is completely destroyed by fire or other means, the lease is terminated. The tenant is responsible only for the rent due up until the time of destruction. If the leased property is only partially destroyed, the landlord must repair the property as soon as possible. The tenant must continue to pay rent if she or he is able to stay in the premises while the repairs are being made. If this is not possible, the tenant moves out and does not have to pay rent until the premises can be reoccupied.

■ Alden rented a barber shop owned by Noschang. When the shop was slightly damaged during a fire, Alden claimed that the lease was terminated due to the fire. The lease will continue because the property was only partially damaged by the fire. ■

Condemnation   Recall from Chapter 29 that condemnation, or eminent domain, is the right of a government unit, such as a city, to take private property for public use. After following certain legal procedures, the government takes the property and pays the owner the fair value. The tenant of condemned property, who may have invested a great deal in a store and its fixtures, may lose that investment. Whether the tenant will be compensated depends on the lease. Most leases provide that if only a portion of the property is taken and the major portion is still usable, the lease continues and the tenant pays less rent. If the entire property is taken, the lease ordinarily terminates and the tenant is entitled to compensation for the remaining portion of the lease. In some cases, the tenant may be reimbursed for moving expenses.

Fixtures   A tenant often makes improvements to property by adding valuable fixtures such as lights, shelves, and so forth. Understandably, the tenant may want to take them when the term is over. The landlord, however, will want to make sure that removal of the fixtures will not damage the property. A lease usually provides that certain fixtures are considered temporary and belong to the tenant. Other fixtures are permanent and remain on the property when the lease term ends.

Permanent fixtures would include **trade fixtures** used in a business such as a restaurant soda fountain, a club's music system, or the pinsetters in a bowling center.

Use of Property   A tenant paying rent wants to make sure that he or she is able to use the property without being disturbed. In most leases, the landlord promises that the tenant will have undisturbed possession of the property. This is known as a **covenant of quiet enjoyment.** At the same time, the tenant is obligated to use the leased premises only for the purpose described in the lease. A tenant, for example, may be restricted by the lease or by a health law from having more than a certain number of people occupying the property. Some leases prohibit occupancy by pets.

A landlord usually has no right to enter the tenant's premises. Many leases, however, include a provision allowing the landlord to enter the premises in order to inspect the property, make necessary repairs, or show the property to prospective buyers or tenants. The landlord may enter the property for these purposes even if the tenant is not present.

Assignment and Sublease Many tenants find it necessary to leave the premises before the end of the term. To avoid a loss, a tenant wants to be able to have a new tenant take over and pay the rent. A lease and/or the law often gives the tenant two different ways of doing this: assignment and subletting.

As with other types of contracts, a lease may be assigned. An assignment by a tenant is a transfer to another person of all of the tenant's rights under the lease, including the entire unexpired term. The tenant is the *assignor;* the person who receives the assignment is the *assignee.* When the assignment takes place, the assignee becomes the new tenant and is bound by all the terms of the lease. Despite the assignment, however, the original tenant remains obligated under the lease and can be held responsible together with the assignee.

A **sublease** is a transfer of a portion of the lease term or a portion of the leased space. The original tenant remains as such and becomes the landlord of the new occupant of the property, known as the **subtenant.** The subtenant is not responsible to the landlord for payment of rent.

In most states a tenant may assign the lease or may sublease the premises unless the lease provides otherwise. Even where the right to assign or sublease is subject to the approval of the landlord, the law in many states is that this approval cannot be unreasonably withheld. The reason for this is to prevent hardship on a tenant forced to vacate the premises before the end of the term.

> Valor rented a store for a clothing business. Because of illness, Valor was forced to close the store six months before the end of the lease term. If the lease was silent on the matter, Valor could sublease the property and not be liable for the rent for the remainder of the term. ∎

HOW A LEASE IS TERMINATED

In the unit on contracts you learned that a contract may be terminated in many ways, depending upon the agreement between the parties or by operation of law. The same is true of leases, with some differences because of the nature of the lease agreement. A lease may be terminated by the passage of time, agreement between the parties, agreement in the lease, condemnation, destruction of the leased property, or operation of law.

A tenancy for years (a lease for a fixed period of time) expires when the fixed period is over and the notice of termination is given by either the landlord or the tenant. A periodic tenancy is terminated when either the landlord or tenant gives notice. The amount of notice required is determined by how often rent installments are paid. In a month-to-month tenancy, for example, notice must be given one month before the beginning of the last month of the lease term. If no notice is given, it is assumed that both parties wish to continue the tenancy for another month on the same terms and conditions. A tenancy at will continues indefinitely until notice of termination is sent by either the landlord or the tenant.

The death of the landlord or the tenant does not terminate the lease unless the lease provides otherwise. The estate of the deceased becomes bound by the lease.

If both landlord and tenant agree, the lease may be terminated before the end of the lease term. Early termination often occurs when the tenant is having financial problems or the landlord wants to raise the rent.

Most leases provide for termination upon the happening of certain things, usually nonperformance or breach of covenants by either the landlord or tenant. Examples of nonperformance include failure to provide heat, nonpayment of the rent, bankruptcy of the tenant, and violation of the landlord's rules.

> Tanaka rented a store for one year from McGowen. The lease terms provided that the lease would terminate if Tanaka became unable to pay the rent. When Tanaka became insolvent three months after signing the lease, McGowen had the right to terminate the lease. ■

A breach that would result in a termination of the lease must be material. For example, failure to supply heat for a few hours would not result in termination of the lease. Lack of heat for two weeks would be a material breach of the lease and could lead to termination. Such a material breach by the landlord may make the premises uninhabitable. In effect, the landlord has evicted the tenant by making it impossible for the tenant to occupy the leased premises. This is known as a **constructive eviction** of the tenant.

If the entire leased premises are condemned (taken) by a government body such as a city or state, it is impossible for the tenant to occupy the premises. The lease is therefore canceled.

Total destruction of the leased property also makes it impossible for the tenant to use the property for the purpose for which it was leased, and the lease is canceled.

Operation of law is a less dramatic but equally effective way in which a lease ends. If property cannot be used for a certain purpose because the law prevents it, a lease will be considered terminated by operation of law. Examples of this are a change in the zoning laws that prevents use of property for a certain purpose, a new safety law that prevents the property from being used for its original purpose, and so forth.

> Schwartz leased property from James in order to refine oil. A law was passed prohibiting the use of property in the area for any manufacturing that produced odors. As Schwartz was prohibited from using the property by operation of law, the lease was terminated. ■

OBLIGATIONS TO THIRD PARTIES

Both the landlord and the tenant may be liable to guests who are injured on the leased premises. They may also be liable for damage to the personal property of a guest. To what extent each is liable depends upon the covenants in the lease and upon who has possession and control of the area where the property damage or injury occurred.

Between the landlord and tenant, the lease governs who will have to pay any claim for injury or damage. The guest who suffers injury or damage, however, is not bound by the lease and may recover depending on where the injury or damage took place. A tenant who has exclusive control of a rented area, such as the interior of an apartment, is liable to guests for injuries caused by a defective and dangerous condition of the property.

> ■ Gordon was a guest at Frost's apartment for dinner. While walking into the kitchen, Gordon was injured when he slipped on a loose rug. Frost would be liable to Gordon for this injury. ■

If the injury or damage takes place in an area in which the landlord has exclusive control, the landlord is liable for injuries or damage. Such areas would include steps, elevators, halls, and stairs.

> ■ Cranshaw came to visit a friend at a boardinghouse owned by Owens. While climbing the stairs to the friend's apartment, Cranshaw fell down two flights of stairs and was severely injured. The cause of Cranshaw's fall was a faulty railing that collapsed when Cranshaw held on to it. Owens would be liable to Cranshaw for the dangerous condition. ■

Summary of Important Legal Concepts

A lease of real property is a contract between a landlord and a tenant for the rental of property for a specific time and for a specific price.

Tenancies of real property include a tenancy for years, a periodic tenancy, a tenancy at will and a tenancy at sufferance. The most important differences among them are the length of the lease and the absence or presence of an option to renew the lease.

As with other contracts, a lease of real property must satisfy the usual requirements for a valid contract. It should contain every important element, including the names and addresses of the landlord and tenant, a description of the property being leased, the term of the lease, the amount of the rent, the time and place for payment of the rent, and the signatures of the parties. In addition, the lease should include all of the terms outlining the rights and duties of the landlord and the tenant. These include the duty of repair, responsibility for payment of taxes and utility charges, the effect of destruction of the premises, and the effect of a condemnation of the property.

A tenant who wishes to leave before the end of the lease term may be able to either assign the lease or sublet the leased premises to another person. Assignment of a lease transfers the entire unexpired lease term. Subletting transfers a portion of the unexpired lease term or a portion of the tenant's rights and duties. Whether a tenant may assign the lease or sublease the premises depends on the terms of the lease and state law.

Most leases may be terminated by the lease terms, mutual agreement, breach of the lease covenants, condemnation or destruction of the leased premises, or operation of law.

Key Legal Terms to Know

Match the terms with the definitions that follow.

constructive eviction
covenant of quiet enjoyment
covenants

eviction
landlord
lease
periodic tenancy
rent
security deposit
sublease
subtenant
tax escalator clause
tenancy at sufferance
tenancy at will
tenancy for years
tenant
term
trade fixtures
warranty of habitability

1. A lease for a fixed period of time
2. A lease that automatically continues for a period equal to the original lease term until canceled by either the landlord or the tenant
3. A lease for an indefinite period of time
4. A tenancy created when a lease ends and the tenant is allowed to remain
5. The parts of a lease that list the rights and duties of the landlord and the tenant
6. A condition in a lease requiring the tenant to pay any increases in real estate taxes
7. A sum of money paid to a landlord to be applied toward any damages caused by a tenant
8. Legal action taken by a landlord to force a tenant to leave the premises
9. Property that is considered permanent and remains with the leased premises when the lease term ends
10. The right of a tenant to have undisturbed possession of leased property
11. A transfer of a portion of the lease term to another tenant
12. A person to whom a portion of a lease term is transferred
13. An action by a landlord making it impossible for a tenant to occupy leased premises
14. One who owns property and rents or leases it
15. One who occupies rented property
16. An agreement of rental between a landlord and a tenant
17. The length of time a lease is in effect
18. The sum of money paid by a tenant for use of leased property

19. An implied promise by the landlord that the property is fit for human habitation and free of any hazardous conditions

Questions and Problems to Discuss

1. Describe the important covenants that should be included in every lease.
2. Brody leased an apartment from Kroll for a two-year term under a written lease. Eight months after signing the lease, Brody died. Is Brody's estate liable for the rent for the balance of the term?
3. Jarvis rented a gas station from Kronski for a three-year term. During the second year of the lease, the village in which the station was located passed an ordinance prohibiting the operation of a gas station within the village limits. Can Kronski cancel the lease?
4. Mwangi rented a one-family house from Lang for a period of two years. Three months after Mwangi moved into the house, a fire of unknown origin totally destroyed the house. Mwangi refused to continue to pay the rent. Was Mwangi within her legal rights?
5. Clary rented an apartment from Dollinger. Dollinger required Clary to pay a $100 security deposit. At the end of the lease, Clary asked Dollinger to refund his deposit. If the lease was faithfully performed and there was no agreement otherwise, was Clary entitled to have his deposit refunded?
6. Phillips, the landlord, while inspecting the apartment being vacated by Bryon, noticed that the wallpaper had faded. He tried to hold Bryon liable. Will he succeed?
7. Reynolds rented a one-family house from Dern for one year at a monthly rental of $300. After occupying the house for six months, Reynolds notified Dern that the walls of several rooms had become soiled from wear and asked Dern to repaint them. Dern refused. Is Dern obligated to do the redecorating?
8. While Rogers worked on a construction job she leased a house from Pia on a month-to-month lease and agreed to pay a monthly rental of $400. The construction took longer than anticipated. After living in Pia's house for two years, Rogers gave Pia notice that she was moving. Pia sued for breach of contract. Should Pia succeed?

9. Wilson leased a summer cottage from Sage for three months, rent payable monthly. The following day Wilson was unexpectedly ordered to Europe on a business trip. Wilson immediately sublet the cottage to Carter with the agreement that Carter would pay the rent to Sage. After the first month, Carter moved out of the cottage and paid no further rent to Sage. Is Wilson legally liable to Sage for the rent for the remaining two months?

10. The landlord of an apartment building refused to repair the plumbing. As a result, all the apartments had an unpleasant odor. The landlord insisted that normal repairs were the responsibility of the tenant and that this was a normal repair. Was the landlord correct?

11. Harrison, a tenant, had steel cabinets installed in the house that she rented from Moss. She did not tell Moss of the installation, and the lease contained no mention of such improvements. Shortly before Harrison's lease expired, Moss learned of the cabinets and the fact that they had been securely screwed into the walls of the kitchen. Moss sent Harrison a written notice that she could not remove the cabinets when she moved. Was Moss entitled to retain the fixtures?

12. Briggs rented an apartment to Stratton on a month-to-month basis. At the end of the first month, Briggs canceled the lease without giving Stratton any reason. May Briggs do this?

13. Hynes rented a house from Jarvis under a two-year lease. The lease stated that it could be assigned only with the consent of the landlord. Six months after the lease was signed, Hynes decided to go to graduate school and asked Jarvis for permission to assign the lease to Mix, a friend of Hynes. Jarvis refused to permit the assignment under any circumstances, claiming it was her right to do so under the lease. Is Jarvis correct?

14. The Chens rented an apartment in a nearby apartment house. The lease they signed prohibited occupancy by children. Shortly after the lease was signed, Mrs. Chen gave birth and the landlord sent the Chens a notice to vacate the premises immediately. The Chens contend that their rights are being violated and that they cannot be required to vacate the premises. Are they correct?

15. Corwin rented an apartment on a month-to-month basis commencing March 1. On July 1, Corwin's landlord sent a letter to Corwin stating that the lease was being terminated and that Corwin must vacate the premises no later than July 15. Is Corwin obligated to vacate the premises by July 15?

16. Litman rented a store from Broward under a three-year lease. A clause in the lease provided that Litman was responsible for gas and electricity but was silent as to who was to pay the real estate taxes assessed against the property. Broward argues that, regardless of what the lease says, Litman is a tenant and is obligated to pay the real estate taxes. Is Broward correct?

Cases to Decide

1. Boyar leased property to Wallenberg on a month-to-month basis beginning October 1. On November 27, Wallenberg left without giving Boyar any notice. Is Boyar entitled to receive rent for the month of December? (*Boyar v. Wallenberg*, 132 Misc 116, 228 NYS 358)

2. Levine's young daughter lived with her family in a large apartment project owned by Miller. In the basement of one of the apartments, there was a large recreation room used by all the tenants. Levine's daughter was injured while playing in the room when a radiator fell on her. Is Miller liable for her injuries? (*Levine v. Miller*, 218 Md 74)

3. Genesee signed a lease with the Oatka Club for the use of Genesee's property for recreational purposes. The lease provided that the term was to be for "as long as the Club remained an active club." While Oatka was still in possession, Genesee sent a notice of cancellation of the lease, claiming the lease was a tenancy at will. Is Genesee correct? (*Genesee Conservation Foundation v. Oatka Fish and Game Club*, New York 63 AD2d 1115)

4. The state condemned land owned by Burk for a highway project. Included in the condemnation was a restaurant leased to Patzen and Winkenwerder. The lease was silent regarding who was entitled to any awards for property condemned by the state. Burk claimed that as the owner, he was entitled to the entire award. Is he correct? (*State By & Through Highway Commission v. Burk*, 265 P2d 783)

5. Milgrim rented an apartment from Cedarhurst Park Apartments. The lease provided that there could be no assignment or sublet without the

consent of the landlord, but that such consent would not be unreasonably withheld. Milgrim wanted to sublease the apartment to a husband and wife who would ordinarily be acceptable to the landlord. The landlord refused to consent, claiming that the apartment was needed by an officer of the landlord corporation. May the landlord refuse consent for that reason? (*Cedarhurst Park Apartments, Inc.* v. *Milgrim*, NY 55 Misc 2d 118)

6. Doktor Pet was a tenant in a mall owned by New Rochelle Mall. The lease contained a standard covenant of quiet enjoyment. Rioting broke out in the common area of the mall, harming the tenant's business. Doktor Pet refused to pay the rent, claiming constructive eviction because the owner had not provided security guards. The lease said nothing about the owner's obligation to provide guards. Is Doktor Pet correct that a constructive eviction has taken place? (*New Ro-chelle Mall* v. *Doktor Pet Centers Realty*, 317 NYS 2d 404)

7. Barash rented office space in an office building in New York City owned by Pennsylvania Terminal. The structure had sealed windows and was completely air conditioned, with the landlord having exclusive control over the air-conditioning system. Pennsylvania Terminal had said that the building would be open 24 hours a day, 7 days a week. At 6 P.M. one day, when Barash was in his office, Pennsylvania Terminal turned off the air conditioning. Within an hour, the office became hot and unusable. Pennsylvania Terminal refused to provide ventilation after 6 P.M. unless Barash paid extra for it. Barash refused to pay the extra amount, as well as regular rent, and sued Pennsylvania Terminal alleging constructive eviction. Is Barash correct? (*Barash* v. *Pennsylvania Terminal Real Estate Corporation*, 26 NY 2d 77, 256 NE 2d 707)

Chapter 31

Buying and Selling Real Property

There are many important considerations in buying and selling real property, particularly a home, and these are discussed in this chapter. The chapter describes the formation of a contract of sale between seller and buyer. The topic of financing the purchase is also explored. The chapter then discusses the steps taken to ensure that the buyer gets good title to the property. The chapter concludes by describing the steps involved in the closing and transfer of title, including the various types of deeds that may be used to accomplish the transfer of title.

THE BUYING AND SELLING PROCESS

The largest investment most individuals make is the purchase of their home. A real estate purchase can be a very complex matter, and both the buyer and the seller should exercise great care. The material in this chapter, although concerned primarily with houses, is applicable to the purchase of any type of real property.

The specific steps and laws involved in buying and selling a home vary from state to state. The major steps in all cases, however, are signing the contract of sale, obtaining financing, completing a title examination, and closing.

Contract of Sale

Negotiations for the sale and purchase of a home may be handled directly by the buyer and seller or through a real estate agent or broker. Many owners try to sell their homes themselves by advertising or putting up FOR SALE signs. If they reach an agreement with the buyer, they enter into a contract of sale.

The statute of frauds requires that a contract for the sale and purchase of a home must be in writing to be enforceable. The buyer and seller often verbally agree on all the terms of the transaction. Their agreement is then incorporated into a written contract of sale, which they, a broker, or an attorney, prepares.

The Listing Contract   Sellers who work through a real estate agent or broker usually sign a **listing contract** giving the agent or broker the right to sell the house in return for an agreed commission. The commission may be a fixed amount, although a percentage of the sale price is more common. The listing contract also usually states the period of time the agent has in which to sell the property.

The broker brings the seller and the buyer together and negotiates the details of the transaction, including the purchase price, date of transfer, method of financing, and so forth. Once this is done and a contract is signed, the broker's commission is considered earned. The seller is responsible for and usually pays the commission even if the seller decides not to go through with the sale.

> Willard signed a listing contract with Allen Realty for the sale of Willard's home. According to the terms stated in the listing contract, Allen produced a buyer willing to buy. Willard found another buyer willing to pay $2,000 more for the house and sold it to that person. Allen is entitled to a commission on the sale of Willard's house even though Allen was not responsible for the eventual buyer. ∎

Purchase Offer and Acceptance Some buyers and sellers arrive at an agreement through a purchase offer and acceptance. A **purchase offer** is a written offer from a buyer to a seller to purchase the seller's house (see Figure 31.1). It contains all the terms of the sale acceptable to the buyer. If the seller agrees to all the terms in the purchase offer, the seller signs an **acceptance.** The acceptance is usually at the bottom of the purchase offer. If the seller does not agree to all the terms, the seller may simply disregard the offer or may instead make a counteroffer with different terms. The buyer may agree to the new terms or may instead make a further counteroffer. When the buyer and seller finally agree on all the terms of the sale, the purchase offer and acceptance are considered a binding contract of sale.

A purchase offer and acceptance and a contract of sale are binding and enforceable agreements and may not be changed without the consent of both parties. They should contain all the terms and conditions of the sale. These include the names of the parties, the purchase price, a description of the property, the method of payment, and the date when title to the property will pass.

An important part of a contract of sale deals with certain conditions that, if not met, may void the agreement. These are known as **contingencies.** These may be inserted to protect both the seller and the buyer and are essential in any agreement. For example, a buyer may be able to purchase a house only if a bank mortgage can be obtained. The buyer will therefore insert a clause in the contract making the obligation to purchase the house contingent upon obtaining financing. Without such a contingency, the buyer is obligated to purchase the house regardless of whether financing is available. A seller may be building a new home and may not be able to move out until the new home is completed. Without a clause in the contract making the date of transfer of the house contingent on completion of the new home, the seller may have to move out even if the new home is not finished.

> Bell decided to purchase a home owned by Abel. He knew that he had to sell his own home before he could purchase Abel's. When he submitted a purchase offer to Abel, he failed to make the purchase of Abel's house contingent upon the sale of his own home. When Abel accepted the offer, Bell was obligated to buy Abel's home even if he had not sold his own home. ∎

𝔓𝔲𝔯𝔠𝔥𝔞𝔰𝔢 𝔞𝔫𝔡 𝔖𝔞𝔩𝔢 ℭ𝔬𝔫𝔱𝔯𝔞𝔠𝔱

REALTOR®

EQUAL HOUSING
OPPORTUNITY

WHEN SIGNED BY BUYER AND SELLER, THIS DOCUMENT BECOMES A BINDING AGREEMENT

COMMISSIONS OR FEES FOR REAL ESTATE SERVICES TO BE PROVIDED HEREUNDER
ARE NEGOTIABLE BETWEEN REALTOR AND SELLER

The undersigned offers to purchase the property situate in the
City or
Town of ____Homer_____, County of Monroe, State of New York,

known as Address ____42 Vestal Boulevard_____

Approx. Lot Dimensions ____150' x 200'_____ Tax Acct. # ____368942_____

Consisting of ____a 2-story frame house with attached garage_____

OTHER ITEMS: Together with and including all appurtenances, all buildings and other improvements thereon and all rights of Seller in and to any and all streets, roads, highways, alleys, driveways, easements, and rights-of-way appurtenant thereto; the following items, if any, now in or on said premises, are included in this sale and shall become the property of Buyer at closing: all heating, plumbing, lighting fixtures, flowers, shrubs, trees, linoleum, window shades, venetian blinds, curtain and traverse rods, storm windows, storm doors, screens, awnings, TV antennas, water softeners if owned, tool sheds, sump pumps, bathroom fixtures, weather vanes, window boxes, fences, flag poles, wall to wall carpeting and runners, exhaust fans, hoods, and garbage disposers, electric garage door openers and remote control devices, intercom equipment, swimming pool and pool operating equipment; also (unless such items are free standing) all cabinets, mirrors, stoves, ovens, dishwashers, shelving, fireplace screens and equipment, air conditioning (except window) units, humidifier and dehumidifier; Buyer agrees to accept such items in their present condition.

PURCHASE PRICE AND TERMS: PURCHASE PRICE: ....($60,000.00) Payable as follows:

1. $3,000.00 deposit with this offer.
2. $7,000.00 by certified check at closing.
3. $50,000.00 by my obtaining a bank mortgage for that amount for a period of 25 years at 12% interest. I shall have 21 banking days in which to obtain mortgage approval. Otherwise, this offer shall be null and void and any deposit made by me shall be returned to me.

OTHER TERMS:
1. Possession shall be given at closing.
2. Purchase price shall include draperies and stove.

ADJUSTMENTS AT TRANSFER OF TITLE: There shall be prorated and adjusted as of date of transfer of title, rentals, fuel, mortgage interest, F.H.A. mortgage insurance, water, pure water charges, sewer charges, current taxes computed on a fiscal year basis excluding embellishments in City tax bills, but including all items in the current county tax bill excepting delinquent school taxes. Buyer will accept title subject to and will pay all assessments for local improvements which are not payable as of date of delivery of deed. Seller represents that there is no additional assessment not appearing on the current tax roll. Buyer shall refund tax escrow balance to seller in the case of mortgage assumption.

SEARCH SURVEY AND COSTS: Seller shall furnish and pay the cost thereof and deliver to the attorney for the Buyer at least five (5) days prior to the date of closing, fully guaranteed tax, title and United States District Court Searches dated or redated subsequent hereto, and with a local tax certificate for village taxes, and a tape location map dated subsequent hereto. Seller shall pay for the continuation of said tax, title, United States District Court Search, local tax searches to and including day of transfer, and for the current tape location map and required tax stamp. Buyer shall pay for mortgage assumption charges, if any, recording deed, mortgage and mortgage tax.

TITLE DOCUMENTS: At the time of transfer, Seller shall tender to Buyer a Warranty Deed with lien covenant conveying good, marketable title in fee simple to said premises free and clear of all liens and encumbrances, except as provided herein; and Seller will furnish documents necessary to transfer title to other items above described, warranting same free and clear of all liens and encumbrances, except as provided herein; Buyer agrees to accept title to the premises subject to restrictive covenants of record common to the tract or subdivision provided the same have not been violated, and subject to public utility easements provided the same do not encroach on improvements.

REPRESENTATION: Seller represents that the premises and any improvements thereon are in full compliance with restrictive covenants and all statutes, ordinances, regulations, and/or other administrative enactments including but not limited to Building Codes

Figure 31.1
Purchase Offer

At the time a purchase offer is submitted or a contract of sale is signed, it is customary for the buyer to give the seller a deposit. In some areas, this deposit is known as **earnest money.** The deposit is often held by the seller or the seller's attorney or broker until the transfer of title takes place. It is then applied toward the purchase price. If the buyer fails to go through with the transaction without a good reason, either the seller or the broker may keep the deposit, depending upon the terms of the listing contract.

Financing

A buyer may be able to purchase a home without obtaining any financing. However, most people who buy homes require financing for at least part of the purchase price. Financing is usually in the form of a mortgage; in some cases, it is in the form of a land contract. A **mortgage** is a lien against the property held by a bank or whoever is lending the money as security until the loan is repaid. The person borrowing money is called the **mortgagor;** the lender is called the **mortgagee.** Financing is usually obtained through a new mortgage or by assuming an existing mortgage.

New Mortgage When a new mortgage is obtained to finance all or part of the purchase price, it is known as a **purchase money mortgage.** The typical way to finance the purchase of a home is to obtain a mortgage from a bank, savings and loan association, or life insurance company. Some mortgages are insured by the Federal Housing Administration and are known as FHA insured loans; others are guaranteed by the Veterans Administration and are known as VA guaranteed loans.

After a purchase contract is signed, the buyer submits it to a lender and applies for a mortgage. The lender will evaluate the home and check the buyer's credit references. The lender will also examine the buyer's earnings, employment history, bill-paying record, and other assets. If the lender is satisfied that the buyer is a good credit risk, it will issue an offer to give a mortgage to the buyer. This is usually known as the **mortgage commitment.**

Sometimes the seller, rather than a bank or insurance company, will agree to finance a portion of the purchase price by giving the buyer a mortgage. Instead of paying all the purchase price to the seller in the form of cash, the buyer obtains a mortgage from the seller and pays the seller back over a period of years. This is often done when the buyer has had difficulty obtaining a bank mortgage. It is also done when a seller prefers to have an investment rather than to receive a large sum of money at one time upon the sale of a house.

Existing Mortgage There is often an existing mortgage on a home that a buyer may take over and agree to pay. This is known as a **mortgage assumption.** The buyer will pay the seller in cash the difference between the balance of the existing mortgage and the purchase price. The buyer becomes a substitute for the seller and assumes an obligation that was formerly the seller's. For example, if the purchase price of a home is $40,000 and there is a mortgage on the home with a balance of $35,000, the buyer may assume the mortgage and pay the seller $5,000 at the time of transfer.

The advantage of assuming a mortgage is that it is less expensive than securing a new mortgage. Also, if interest rates rise, the interest rate in an older, assumable mortgage is usually lower than the interest rate on a new mortgage. In some cases, the consent of the holder of the mortgage (usually a bank or savings and loan) may be required before a mortgage can be assumed.

Terms of the Mortgage   Regardless of the source of the mortgage, it is important that the terms and conditions of the mortgage be clear and understood by the mortgagor. The terms include the amount of the mortgage, the interest rate, the amount of the monthly payment, and the terms of the mortgage. The borrower should understand the rights that the lender has if the borrower defaults in making payment, including the right to foreclose.

Two important rights that a borrower should try to obtain in a mortgage are a prepayment privilege and assumption. The **prepayment privilege** is the right of the mortgagor to pay the balance due on the mortgage before the end of the mortgage term. By paying off the mortgage in advance, the borrower saves on interest costs. In addition, if interest rates drop, the borrower may wish to refinance by obtaining a new mortgage at a lower interest rate.

The assumption right, referred to earlier, allows an owner to sell the property and assist the buyer in financing the purchase by allowing the buyer to assume the owner's existing mortgage. Unless the mortgage contains language that permits prepayment and assumption privileges, they may not be available. FHA insured and VA guaranteed mortgages may always be assumed without the consent of the lender.

> Byrd bought a home and financed it with a mortgage payable over a period of twenty years. The mortgage had no clause permitting prepayment. Six months after purchasing the home, Byrd inherited a large sum of money and wished to pay the mortgage in full. Byrd is not permitted to do so without the consent of the mortgage holder. ∎

Foreclosure is a proceeding by a lender to force a sale of mortgaged property to satisfy a debt. Upon completion of the foreclosure, the owner loses ownership of the property.

Land Contract   A **land contract** is an agreement in which a buyer agrees to purchase property and pay for it over a period of time. When the final payment is made, the seller transfers title to the property of the buyer.

After a land contract is executed, the buyer takes possession of the property even though the seller retains title until the purchase price is paid in full. If the buyer defaults in making payments, the seller may retake possession of the property and evict the buyer. In many such cases, the buyer may forfeit all or part of the payments made to the seller.

The major difference between a mortgage and a land contract has to do with the transfer of title. When a buyer buys property and pays for it with mortgage proceeds, the buyer obtains title to the property immediately. In a land contract, the seller retains title to the property until the purchase price is paid in full.

Title Examination

Title to real estate is the right of the owner to own it, use it, mortgage it, and sell it free from any claims of others. There are many types of claims that could affect the rights of the owner. For example, a former owner may still have a right to use the property. There may be restrictions on how the property may be used. State or local governments may have an interest in the property because of unpaid real estate taxes. A bank may hold an existing mortgage on the property.

Various methods are used to make sure that the buyer receives clear title to the property purchased. These methods vary from state to state and also by areas within the state. In many areas, the buyer's attorney examines the property records to determine whether there are any liens, mortgages, or other restrictions on the property. This is called a **title search.** In some states the title search is made by the attorney or a county clerk. In most states it is made by a private title company that specializes in title searches.

The attorney, or whoever is doing the search, generally uses an abstract of title to assist in the search (see Figure 31.2). An **abstract of title** is a copy or condensed summary of all transactions relating to a particular piece of property over a period of years. It will show deeds, mortgages, tax information, and other transactions that may affect the title to the property.

Title insurance may be purchased by a buyer to ensure that the title is good. If it turns out that the title is not clear, the insurance protects against any resulting financial loss. Title insurance is valuable because the abstract examined by the attorney may be incomplete and not show every transaction affecting the title. Or the attorney making the title search may have given a faulty opinion as to whether the title was good. Title insurance does not ensure that the buyer may keep the property if there is another claim to the title, but it does guarantee that the buyer will be compensated for any loss.

Fifteen states have adopted a system known as the **Torrens System** of registration. With this system, the court examines the title and issues a certificate that is filed in a public office. Any time a deed or mortgage affecting the property is put on record, the documents are recorded at the public office and new certificates of title are issued. The registration fees are used to pay for any loss that results from errors made by the public officials involved.

In addition to a title search, a survey is often made of the property. A **survey** is a map that shows the boundaries of a piece of land and the location of the structures on the land. If the survey is made by a surveyor and shows exact angles and distances, the survey is known as an *instrument survey* (see Figure 31.3). If measurements are taken by using a steel or cloth measuring tape and are only approximate, the survey is known as a *tape location map.*

A survey is important for many reasons. Descriptions in deeds are often inaccurate or refer to landmarks, such as trees, that may no longer exist. A buyer should know how much land is being purchased and its exact location. If the survey and the deed do not agree, the survey is accepted as correct because of its exactness. A survey is also important if an owner wishes to build structures and wants to make sure that they are built on the owner's land. Without a survey, construction may take place on a neighbor's land.

Melio bought a home from Corwin but did not have the property surveyed. Melio liked to swim and so built a large swimming pool in one corner of

```
┌─────────────────────────────────────────────────────────────────────┐
│   │                                                                   │
│10 │ Fletcher M. Hayes, Mary        Warranty Deed                      │
│   │ A., his wife                                                      │
│   │                                Dated Nov. 1, 1945                 │
│   │          -To-                  Ack. Nov. 15, 1945                 │
│   │                                Rec. Nov. 25, 1945                 │
│   │ Marcia Cole                                                       │
│   │                                Liber 69 of Deeds, page 354        │
│   │                                                                   │
│   │        Conveys, with other property, all that tract or parcel of  │
│   │                                                                   │
│   │   land situate in the Town of New Castle, New York, and described │
│   │   as                                                              │
│   │   follows:  The southeast part of lot #3, in Township #14 in the  │
│   │   7th                                                             │
│   │   Range of Phelps and Gorham's Purchase; being the same land      │
│   │   conveyed                                                        │
│   │   to Fletcher M. Hayes by John Frazer and others by deed, dated   │
│   │                                                                   │
│   │   Sept. 30, 1935.                                                 │
│   │                                                                   │
│   │  - - - - - - - - - - - - - - - - - - - - - - - - - - - - - - - -  │
│   │                                                                   │
│11 │ Marcia Cole and Richard        Warranty Deed                     │
│   │ D. Cole                                                           │
│   │                                Dated June 4, 1961                │
│   │          -To-                  Ack. same day                      │
│   │                                Rec. same day                      │
│   │ Joseph H. Cole                                                    │
│   │                                Liber 164 of Deeds, page 165       │
│   │                                                                   │
│   │        Conveys as follows:  Town of New Castle, New York, the     │
│   │                                                                   │
│   │   southeast part of lot #3 in Township #14 in the 7th Range of    │
│   │   Phelps                                                          │
│   │   and Gorham's Purchase; being the same land conveyed to Fletcher │
│   │   M.                                                              │
│   │   Hayes by John Frazer and others by deed, Sept. 30, 1935,        │
│   │   bounded                                                         │
│   │   north by the north half of said lot #3, now owned by Charles    │
│   │   Statler;                                                        │
│   │   east by lot #6, now owned by said Marcia Cole; south by the     │
│   │   highway;                                                        │
│   │   west by the southwest part of said lot #3; containing 57 acres, │
│   │   be                                                              │
│   │   the same, more or less.                                         │
│   │                                                                   │
│   │  - - - - - - - - - - - - - - - - - - - - - - - - - - - - - - - -  │
└─────────────────────────────────────────────────────────────────────┘
```

Figure 31.2
Abstract of Title

the property. After the pool was completed, Melio discovered that a portion of the pool had been built on land belonging to a neighbor. A survey would have prevented this. ■

If flaws are found in the title after a title search is made, the flaws must be corrected to the satisfaction of the buyer. If the flaws cannot be corrected, the transaction is usually called off. If there are no flaws or if they are corrected, the next step in purchasing the home is the closing.

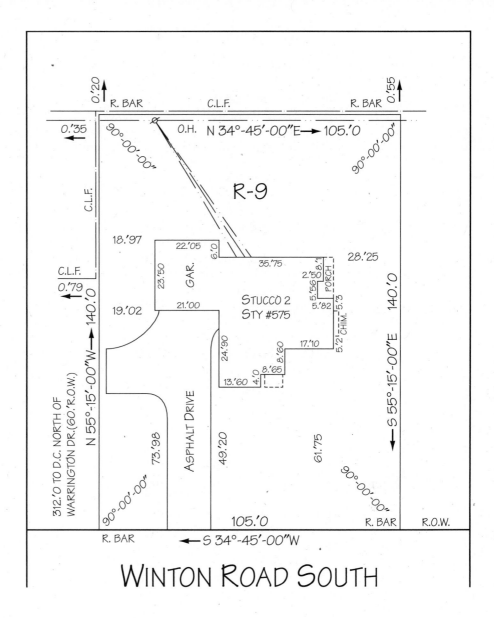

Figure 31.3
Survey

The Closing

After title is found to be good and all required documents are completed, the buyer and the seller and their attorneys meet for the transfer of title. In most states this is known as the **closing.** The closing occurs at the place and time contained in the contract of sale, unless the parties make other arrangements. If a mortgage is involved, the closing may take place at the offices of the bank or the offices of the bank's attorneys. If no mortgage is involved, the closing is usually held at the office of the clerk of the country in which the property is located. If title insurance is involved, the closing may take place at the offices of the title insurance company.

Adjustments are made at the closing for any charges paid by the seller from which the buyer will benefit. For example, the seller may have paid the annual real estate tax. If the closing takes place on July 1, the buyer will owe the seller one half of the total taxes paid. There may also be adjustments that benefit the buyer. For example, a water bill for the months of June, July, and August may not be received by the new owner until September. At the closing, the buyer is entitled to a credit for one month or one third of the total bill. A **closing statement** shows the purchase price, any adjustments made, and the expenses of the sale (see Figure 31.4).

After all adjustments have been agreed upon, the seller gives the buyer an executed deed to the property. The buyer pays the seller the purchase price plus adjustments, less any deposit given. If a mortgage is involved, the buyer signs the mortgage papers and receives a check for the amount borrowed. This amount is then turned over to the seller, and the buyer pays the seller any balance due. Payment of any balance due is usually made by certified check or cashier's check.

The buyer and seller must also pay their respective shares of the closing costs. These include transfer taxes, mortgage taxes, attorney's fees, survey costs, and other title expenses. In some cases, lenders will charge a processing fee, usually a percentage of the mortgage. Responsibility for payment of the closing expenses is determined by the terms of the contract of sale or by local custom.

TRANSFER OF TITLE

Title to real property passes to the buyer when the deed is delivered to the buyer and the purchase price is paid. The deed is a document by which real property is transferred from one owner to another. A person who transfers the title to real property is known as the **grantor.** The person who receives the title is known as the **grantee.**

To protect the buyer, the deed must be recorded in the proper public office. Recording the deed notifies the public of the transfer of title. It also protects the buyer from an unscrupulous seller who might try to sell the same property to someone else. In actual practice, the deed and the payment of the purchase price are held in trust until a final title search is made and the deed is recorded. This is known as holding in **escrow.** The attorneys or title company representatives search the records right up until the point that the deed is to be recorded. If title is still clear, the deed is recorded and the purchase funds are released to the seller. If a mortgage is involved, it is usually recorded at the same time.

There are many different types of deeds. They vary according to the interests that are being transferred. The type of deed given depends on what the contract of sale calls for and often on local custom. The most common ones are the quitclaim deed, the bargain and sale deed, and the warranty deed.

```
                S T A T E M E N T    O F    T R A N S F E R

PROPERTY:   28 Hermitage Lane, Cincinnati, Ohio
SELLER(S):  Elizabeth A. Johnson and Elliot M. Johnson
BUYER(S):   Marcia L. Jordan
DATE OF CLOSING:   July 31, 19--
___ ___ ___ ___ ___ ___ ___ ___ ___ ___ ___ ___ ___ ___ ___ ___
DUE SELLER:
      Purchase Price                                      $ 60,000.00
      County Tax Adjusted -(___mos.____days)
      City/School Tax Adj.-( 3 mos.  0  days)                  241.50
      Village Tax Adjusted
      Rents
      Escrow
      Fuel                                                 _____
                        TOTAL:                              60,241.50
CREDIT BUYER:
      Rents                                  $
      Mortgage Assumed -Interest
      City/School Tax. Adj.
      Embellishments
      Water Adjusted
      Pure Waters Adjusted
                                                          _____

      BALANCE DUE SELLER:                                 $ 60,241.50
                                                          ===========
      PAID AS FOLLOWS:
            Deposit                 $   3,000.00
            Mortgage Proceeds          50,000.00
            Mortgage Discharged
            Mortgage Assumed
            Balance                     7,241.50          $ 60,241.50
                                                          ===========
___ ___ ___ ___ ___ ___ ___ ___ ___ ___ ___ ___ ___ ___ ___ ___
CLOSING EXPENSES:
      Recording Fees               $   60.00
      Mortgage Tax -Broker's Fee     1,200.00
      Abstract Charge                   25.00
      Bank Attorney's Fee             300.00
      Bank Processing Fee             150.00
      Legal Services
      Map
      Revenue Stamps                                      $  1,735.00
TAX ESCROW ACCT. ESTABLISHED AT CLOSING:
      County Tax      ___mos.        $
      City/School Tax  3  mos.          241.50
      School Tax      ___mos.
      Village Tax     ___mos.
                                                         $   241.50
```

Figure 31.4
Closing Statement

The Quitclaim Deed

The **quitclaim deed** passes to the buyer whatever title or interest the seller has and nothing more. The seller may have good title, faulty title, or no title at all. Whatever title the seller has is the title passed through a quitclaim deed. A quitclaim deed releases the seller from any further claims against the property.

THIS IS A LEGAL INSTRUMENT AND SHOULD BE EXECUTED UNDER SUPERVISION OF AN ATTORNEY.

THIS INDENTURE, made the   7th   day of   May   1988

BETWEEN

SAMUEL SELLERS, 100 Title Way, Rochester, New York 14618

grantor

LISA BAUER, 300 East Avenue, Rochester, New York 14614

grantee

WITNESSETH, that the grantor, in consideration of
Three Thousand and-------------00/100--------------------($3,000.00) Dollars, paid by the grantee
hereby grants and releases unto the grantee, the heirs or successor and assigns of the grantee forever,

ALL   THAT TRACT OR PARCEL OF LAND situated in the City of Rochester, Monroe
County, New York, known and described as Lot #10, Genessee subdivision as shown on
a map filed in the Monroe County Clerk's Office in Liber 800 of Maps, Page 20.

Said Lot #10 is situated on the west side of Title Way and is of the
dimensions as shown on said map.

This deed is subject to all easements and restrictive covenants common to
this tract or subdivision.

TOGETHER with the appurtenances and all the estate and rights of the grantor in and to said premises.
TO HAVE AND TO HOLD the premises here granted unto the grantee, the heirs or successors and assigns forever,
AND the said grantor covenants as follows:
FIRST.—That the grantor is seized of the said premises in fee simple, and has good right to convey the same;
SECOND.—That the grantee shall quietly enjoy the said premises;
THIRD.—That the said premises are free from incumbrances;
FOURTH.—That the grantor will execute or procure any further necessary assurance of the title to said premises;
FIFTH.—That the grantor will forever warrant the title to said premises;
This deed is subject to the trust provisions of Section 13 of the Lien Law.
The words "grantor" and "grantee" shall be construed to read in the plural whenever the sense of this deed so requires.
IN WITNESS WHEREOF, the grantor has executed this deed the day and year first above written.

In presence of:

....L. S.

....L. S.
SAMUEL SELLERS

STATE OF NEW YORK, COUNTY OF   ss.:
On the   day of   19   , before
me personally came   to me known,
who, being by me duly sworn, did depose and say that deponent resides
at No.
deponent is   of
the corporation described in and which
executed, the foregoing instrument; deponent knows the seal of said
corporation; that the seal affixed to said instrument is such corporate
seal; that it was so affixed by order of the Board of Directors of said
corporation; deponent signed deponent's name thereto by like order.

STATE OF NEW YORK, COUNTY OF   MONROE   ss.:
On the   7th   day of   May   1988 , before
me personally came
SAMUEL SELLERS

to me known to be the individual   described in, and who executed
the foregoing instrument, and acknowledged that   he   executed
the same.

Figure 31.5 **Warranty Deed**

> O'Connor sold her interest in a small apartment building to Rudd. A quitclaim
> deed was executed to transfer title to Rudd. If someone in the future
> questions Rudd's title to the property, Rudd cannot go back to O'Connor
> with any claims against the property. ∎

The Bargain and Sale Deed

The **bargain and sale deed** also passes to the buyer whatever title the seller
has. In addition, the seller guarantees that she or he has possession of the

property and has done nothing to disturb or harm the title to the property. It is a personal guarantee only, relating solely to any acts the seller may have committed. The bargain and sale deed is the most common deed used when title insurance is involved.

Warranty Deed

The **warranty deed** transfers the most complete interest in property. The seller not only transfers the seller's interest in the property but also promises and guarantees certain things known as **covenants.** One covenant is a guarantee that the title is good and that the grantor has the right to sell the property. Another covenant is a guarantee that the property is free from any interests or claims of others, such as claims for taxes owed, claims of a mortgagee, and so forth. These claims are known as **encumbrances.** A third covenant is a guarantee that if any claims are made by others, the grantor will do whatever is necessary to settle the claims. If a flaw in the title is eventually discovered, the grantor is personally responsible to the grantee. An example of a warranty deed is shown in Figure 31.5.

> ■ Burns transferred title to her home to Alwin with a warranty deed. Burns had purchased the home from three owners. When the property was sold, one of the three owners failed to sign the deed of transfer and, therefore, legally still had an interest in the property. Because Burns guaranteed the title, Alwin has a claim against Burns even though the problem did not arise because of any action on Burns's part. ■

Summary of Important Legal Concepts

Buying real property usually involves four steps: signing a contract of sale, obtaining financing, title examination, and the closing. The contract of sale determines the rights and responsibilities of buyer and seller and should be examined carefully before it is signed. It should contain all of the important terms of sale, including the names of both parties, a description of the property, the purchase price, the method of payment, any contingencies, and the closing date. Once signed, the contract of sale is binding and enforceable and may not be changed except on agreement between buyer and seller.

Some homes are purchased without any financing, but most purchases are financed by means of a mortgage. This may be either a new mortgage obtained from a bank or other lender, or an existing mortgage that is assumed by the buyer. Two valuable rights a borrower should try to obtain in a mortgage are the prepayment privilege and the right to have

the mortgage assumed upon sale of the property. When a buyer buys property and pays for it with mortgage proceeds, the buyer obtains title to the property immediately.

Another form of financing is the land contract, an agreement in which the seller retains title to the property until the purchase price is paid in full.

Before a closing can take place, the seller must be able to transfer clear title to the buyer. Proof of clear title may be accomplished by a title search, title insurance or registration under the Torrens System.

Title to real property passes to the buyer at closing, upon delivery of the deed and payment of the purchase price. To protect the buyer and the lender, the deed and mortgage should be recorded in a public office.

The three most common deeds used to transfer real property are the quitclaim deed, the bargain and sale deed, and the warranty deed.

Key Legal Terms to Know

Match the terms with the definitions that follow.

abstract of title
acceptance
bargain and sale deed
closing
closing statement
contingencies
covenants
earnest money
encumbrances
escrow
foreclosure
grantee
grantor
land contract
listing contract
mortgage
mortgage assumption
mortgage commitment
mortgagee
mortgagor
prepayment privilege
purchase money mortgage
purchase offer
quitclaim deed
survey
title
title insurance
title search
Torrens System
warranty deed

1. A deposit given by the buyer to the seller for the purchase of real property
2. A system of public registration of titles using title certificates
3. A lien against property held by a lender as security for the repayment of a loan
4. An agreement on the part of a lending institution to grant a mortgage
5. A deed that conveys whatever interest the seller has
6. One who lends money used to purchase real property
7. The agreement by a seller to the terms of an offer to purchase made by a buyer
8. An examination of public records to determine if title to a piece of real property is clear or flawed
9. A summary of the transactions affecting the title to real property
10. One who borrows money to purchase real property
11. A new mortgage given for the purpose of financing the purchase of real property
12. The meeting at which title to real property is transferred from seller to buyer
13. The interest one has in real property
14. A deed that conveys whatever interest the seller has, including a promise that the seller has done nothing to disturb the title
15. A deed that guarantees clear title
16. Interests in property that conflict with the owner's title
17. An offer submitted by a buyer to a seller for the purchase of real estate
18. A statement showing the financial details of the transfer of real property
19. A type of insurance that guarantees to compensate the owner of real property for damages incurred if the title is found to be flawed
20. A map showing the location, boundaries, and size of a piece of real property
21. The person who transfers title to a piece of property to another
22. Promises made by a grantor in a warranty deed
23. The right of a buyer to take over and be bound by an existing mortgage
24. An agreement between an owner and a broker regarding the broker's rights and obligations in selling the owner's property
25. Conditions in a contract of sale of real property that may void the contract if not met
26. The right to pay the balance due on a mortgage before the end of the mortgage term
27. Holding closing documents and funds in trust until it is determined that title is clear
28. The person who receives title to the property of another
29. An agreement to buy property and pay for it over a period of time
30. The sale of mortgaged property by court order to satisfy a debt

Questions and Problems to Discuss

1. What is the difference between a quitclaim deed and a warranty deed?
2. Loeffler and White signed a contract for the sale of Loeffler's home to White. The contract stated that the purchase price included all furniture in the house. When it came time to transfer title, Loeffler realized he had made a mistake and refused to give White the furniture. May Loeffler do this?
3. After Byrd signed a contract to purchase a parcel of land from Devon, she learned that a railroad company had an easement for maintaining railroad tracks across the land. May Byrd refuse to go ahead with the purchase of the land?
4. Duke signed a contract of sale, agreeing to sell his home to Pembroke. Pembroke required a mortgage to purchase the home but nothing was said about this in the contract. Pembroke applied for a mortgage but was turned down. Is Pembroke still obligated to purchase Duke's home?
5. Clark submitted a written purchase offer to O'Reilly, offering to buy O'Reilly's home for $45,000, subject to Clark's obtaining a mortgage of $35,000. O'Reilly accepted the offer but stated that the contract would not be subject to obtaining a mortgage. Do Clark and O'Reilly have a binding contract for the sale of O'Reilly's home?
6. Richards bought a home and financed it through a mortgage obtained from Central Bank. The mortgage did not contain a prepayment privilege. Five years later, Richards took a job in a different city and needed to sell his home. Because mortgages were not available at that time, it was impossible to find a buyer who could purchase the home. Richards finally decided to sell the home and have the buyer assume the existing mortgage. Can Richards do this?
7. Smith purchased a farm from Holyoke. The deed stated that the property had an area of approximately 30 acres and extended from "the line of oaks on the west to the line of maples on the east." After Smith purchased the land, she had it surveyed and learned that the land area was only 28 acres and that the trees were no longer in existence. Which document controls—the deed or the survey?
8. Hugh sold his house to Walpole and delivered a deed to him at the closing. Walpole took the deed and placed it in his safe-deposit box, neglecting to record it. Hugh then went to a bank, obtained a mortgage on the same property, and recorded the mortgage. Is Walpole's home encumbered by Hugh's mortgage?
9. Laube bought a parcel of land from Linze without examining the title. Before the contract of sale was signed, the city in which the property was located obtained a judgment against Linze for unpaid back taxes. The city sought to enforce its lien for unpaid taxes by selling the property. Can Laube stop this from happening?
10. Monroe agreed to sell her property to Fix. They agreed on a price, the method of financing, and the date of transfer, but failed to sign a written agreement. Two days later Monroe changed her mind and told Fix that she would not go through with the deal. Can Fix force Monroe to sell her the property?
11. Dalton sold his house to Little and gave him a deed to the property. Little put the deed in a desk drawer and failed to record it. Dalton then sold the house to someone else and gave that party a deed as well. If Little sues Dalton for damages, may Dalton claim as a defense the fact that Little failed to record the deed?
12. Cedar listed her house for sale with Vance, a broker. Vance found a buyer and a contract of sale was executed. A week later Cedar decided to stay in the house and not go through with the sale. Is Cedar liable to Vance for the sales commission?
13. Goldwin rented an office in a building owned by Simon. The lease they both signed was for a two-year period. Six months after the lease was signed, Simon died and his heirs decided to sell the building. They claim that the lease was personal between Simon and Goldwin and automatically terminated when Simon died. Are they correct?
14. Glick entered into a contract to purchase Shoeman's home. After the contract was signed, Glick discovered that the closing was to take place more than sixty days after Glick needed to get into his new home. Glick went to his attorney and asked the attorney to make sure that the contract was changed so that the proper date for

possession would be inserted. Is Glick bound by the provisions in the contract of sale?

15. Lanteen purchased a home from George and the properties were transferred by a warranty deed. Lanteen discovered after the closing that there was a mortgage on the property of which he was not aware as well as unpaid real estate taxes. Does Lanteen have a valid claim against George for these encumbrances?

16. Alden failed to pay his federal income taxes for a number of years. His name appeared in a local newspaper showing that he was delinquent in making his income tax payments. Alden had entered into a contract to sell his home to Smith, but Smith, after seeing the newspaper notice, refused to go through with the transaction, claiming the unpaid income taxes were a lien on the property. Was Smith correct?

Cases to Decide

1. In a letter Hill offered to buy Bell's property. He told her to mail him a warranty deed to the property and he would send her a check for the purchase price. She agreed to sell, but wrote that she would only send Hill a quitclaim deed, as that was the only deed she had ever received. Hill sued her to transfer the property to him by warranty deed. Will he succeed? (*Hill* v. *Bell*, 111 Vt 131)

2. The Sayets agreed to buy property owned by the Cayres. They deposited $10,000 with Beekay Realty. Their contract to buy was subject to their obtaining a mortgage. The Sayets made few attempts to secure a mortgage. They were never turned down but their applications were rejected because the Sayets failed to provide the information requested. The Sayets sued to get their deposit back and to cancel the transaction. Are they entitled to do this? (*Beekay Realty Corp.* v. *Cayre*, Florida 256 So 2d 539)

3. Charter agreed to buy property at a sale in which a mortgage held by Jamaica was being foreclosed upon. Charter gave a deposit of 10 percent of the purchase price. Before closing, Charter discovered that the title was flawed because of an open judgment affecting the property. The problem could not be solved prior to closing so Charter refused to complete the transaction and asked for the return of his deposit. Jamaica sued to force Charter to complete the deal. Was Charter correct? (*Jamaica Savings Bank* v. *Charter*, New York 22 Misc 2d 569)

4. The Mitchells bought a tract of land from Brannen. They later transferred it back to Brannen by a deed that was never delivered to Brannen. Brannen then sold the property by a deed that was delivered to and then recorded by Hardeman. Mitchell claimed that the property was his and sued Hardeman to determine who owned the property. Is Mitchell correct? (*Hardeman* v. *Mitchell*, Texas 444 SW2d 651)

5. Read wanted to buy property owned by the Henzels. He sent them a letter offering to buy the property for $220,000. He suggested two different down payments and two different mortgages to finance the transaction. At the end of the letter, he stated, "This generally covers our agreement and should suffice until a more formal document can be drawn up." The Henzels returned the letter and suggested a number of changes including a mortgage with a different term and different interest rate. When the Henzels refused to go through with the deal, Read brought suit, claiming he had a valid contract to buy the property. Is he correct? (*Read* v. *Henzel*, New York, 67 AD2d 186)

Alan Boyd, a sales representative for a jewelry company, was transferred from Boston to San Francisco and decided to rent an apartment for a three-year term. He saw an apartment he liked and decided to rent it. Since the apartment needed a lot of work, the landlord Sherman Williams agreed to renovate the apartment in consideration of Boyd's signing a three-year lease. The lease was completed, the work was performed, and Boyd moved into the apartment. The written lease contained no clauses involving termination of the lease, assignment of the lease, or subletting the apartment.

One month after the lease began, the army reserve unit to which Boyd belonged in Boston was called back for active service, and Boyd was required to report for active duty one month later.

Boyd notified Williams that he was going to cancel the lease and move out. Williams then brought an action against Boyd for breach of the lease.

The Trial

Williams testified during the trial that he had spent in excess of $5,000 to renovate the property, based on the assumption that Boyd would be paying rent for the next three years. He testified that there were others who were interested in renting the apartment and that he would not have signed the lease with Boyd if there had been any doubt about Boyd's staying in the premises during the three-year period. He further testified that Boyd had never told him that he was a member of a reserve unit that might be called into active duty.

Boyd testified at trial that he did not know at the time he signed the lease that his unit was going to be recalled to active duty. He further testified that he had not told Williams about his reserve unit membership because he did not feel it was relevant to do so.

The Arguments at Trial

During the trial, William's attorney argued that as the lease was silent regarding termination in the event of being called or recalled for active duty, such termination by Boyd was not permissible. He argued that by signing a three-year lease and causing Williams to spend so much money to renovate the apartment, Boyd was in fact giving assurances that he would remain and pay rent during the three-year period. He argued that it would be unconscionable to permit Boyd to cancel the lease after Williams had spent so much money fixing up the apartment.

Boyd's attorney argued that it was not Boyd's fault that he was called to active service and that Boyd had had no way of knowing in advance that this would occur. He further argued that it would be unconscionable to hold Boyd to a lease when Boyd was terminating it solely for the purpose of protecting the safety of his country.

Questions to Discuss

1. Who do you feel has the stronger argument, Boyd or Williams? Why?
2. If you were the judge or jury hearing the case, for whom would you decide? Why?
3. Would it have made any difference if Boyd had told Williams that he was a member of a reserve unit, even without mentioning that he might be recalled to active duty? Would it have made any difference if Boyd had been a member of the armed forces, rather than a member of a reserve unit, when he signed the lease?
4. If you were an attorney drafting lease clauses to cover this problem, what terms would you insert?

PART VIII

BAILMENTS

1 Define a bailment, list the characteristics of a bailment, and identify the parties to a bailment.

2 Differentiate among the types of bailments and state the standard of care required for each type.

3 Explain the rights and duties of the parties in a given bailment situation.

4 Describe three types of special bailments.

5 State the rights, duties, and liabilities of the parties in special bailments.

Chapter 32

Nature and Creation of Bailments

CHAPTER PREVIEW

CHAPTER HIGHLIGHTS This chapter deals with one of the most common of transactions, the bailment. Initially, the chapter describes the requirements for a valid bailment. It then goes on to explain the ways in which a bailment may be created. The ways in which a bailment may be ended are also discussed. The remainder of the chapter deals with situations that are similar to bailments but not treated in the same way.

WHAT A BAILMENT IS

The word *bailment* comes from the French word *bailler* meaning to have in charge. Generally, a **bailment** exists when a person has possession or charge of personal property that belongs to someone else. Specifically, a bailment is a relationship that arises when a person takes charge of personal property that was in the possession of someone else, for a special purpose and for a limited period of time, with the understanding that the same or substantially the same property will be returned.

The following are some examples of bailments:

1. Your motorcycle doesn't work, and you borrow one from a friend for the day.

2. You enter a restaurant and leave your coat with the checkroom attendant.

3. You rent a station wagon to go on a trip.

The importance of bailments cannot be too strongly emphasized. Other than sales, most of the transactions you engage in every day are bailments. When you borrow or lend something, rent an item, store a possession, or leave something to be repaired, you enter into a bailment. It is important then to understand what a bailment is, how it is created, and how it ends.

The parties to a bailment are the bailor and the bailee. The **bailor** is the party who gives up possession of the bailed item. The **bailee** is the party who receives possession of it.

■ You have a fine collection of record albums, some of which a friend wished to borrow for a party. You agreed to lend your friend the records, provided they were returned the day after the party. You are the bailor of the records and your friend is the bailee. ■

■ Your lawn needed cutting and you rented a power mower for the day from a rental agency. You are the bailee of the mower and the rental agency is the bailor. ■

It is possible to be both a bailor and a bailee of the same property. If you rent a car from a rental agency, you are a bailee of the automobile. Upon leaving that car at a repair garage, you become a bailor of the car.

Each party in a bailment has certain rights and duties. In the next chapter you will learn what these rights and duties are.

REQUIREMENTS OF A VALID BAILMENT

The most important requirements of a valid bailment are personal property, retention of title by the bailor, possession of the property by the bailee, and return of the bailed property.

Personal Property

A bailment involves personal property only. You may recall that **personal property** is any property other than real property. Some examples of personal property are bicycles, clothing, calculators, books, and U.S. Savings Bonds. Land and buildings are examples of real property.

■ You have just found a job and rented a furnished apartment. You are the bailee of the furniture because it is personal property. You are not a bailee of the apartment because it is real property. ■

Rental of real property, such as an apartment or a house, involves the landlord-tenant relationship, which was discussed in Chapter 30.

Retention of Title by the Bailor

A bailment transfers possession only. If *ownership* of property is transferred, the transaction is not a bailment; it is a sale or a gift.

Possession of Property by the Bailee

Generally, the bailor owns the property being bailed, but ownership is not required—only possession of the property. A bailor could be an employee, a person who finds an item, or even a thief.

Property must change hands before a bailment can be created. The property may either be delivered by the bailor to the bailee or it may be found by the bailee. In either case, the bailee must accept possession of the bailed property or no bailment is created.

■ When Harper entered a store to buy some clothing, she put her coat on a nearby chair. No bailment was created if the store personnel were unaware that Harper had left her coat there and, therefore, had not accepted delivery. ■

Acceptance can be shown in many ways. It can be something said or something written. Often it occurs by some act or deed, such as picking up a lost item.

■ While walking along the street, Houston saw a set of keys on the ground. Realizing that they had been lost, Houston picked them up. By doing so, Houston accepted possession of the keys and was a bailee. ■

Return of Bailed Property

The very nature of a bailment assumes that the identical property bailed will be returned to the bailor, unless the agreement between the parties provides that the property will be returned to a third person or otherwise disposed of. The bailed property will usually be returned with little or no change.

■ You took your suit to the dry cleaners for pressing. You will get back the same suit that you took in, minus only the wrinkles. ■

Sometimes the bailed property is returned in a different condition because of alterations, repairs, or processing.

■ Ellis purchased some cloth to be made into a suit. Ellis gave the cloth to a tailor to have a suit made. The same cloth was returned to Ellis but in a different form. ■

Many bailments are contractual agreements, such as renting a car. As such, they must have all the characteristics of a valid contract: offer and acceptance, competent parties, consideration, and legal purpose.

HOW A BAILMENT IS CREATED

A bailment may be created by an express agreement or an implied agreement. Most bailments are created through an express agreement. As you learned in Chapter 6, an express agreement is one in which the agreement is stated in words, either oral or written. To be valid, such agreements must meet the test for contracts discussed in Chapter 6.

■ Gooden decided to rent a car for the weekend. At the car rental agency, Gooden discussed terms and reached an agreement on how long she could have the car, when and where it was to be returned, and the total rental cost. A rental contract was signed and Gooden took possession of the car. Gooden entered into an express written contract of bailment. ■

Bailment Implied in Fact

A bailment can also come into existence by the actions of the parties. If a bailment arises because of the acts of the parties, without any oral or written agreement, it is known as a **bailment implied in fact.** The law holds that the parties intended to form a bailment because of their actions.

■ You went into a store where all packages had to be checked. The attendant took your packages and gave you a receipt. Neither you nor the attendant spoke. You expected to have your packages held safely and to have them returned to you when you left. The store expected to return your packages when you left. This bailment was implied by your actions and those of the attendant. ■

Bailment Implied by Law

A **bailment implied by law** may also be created when a person obtains possession of another's property without any agreement at all. This bailment arises because the law requires it to promote justice and fair play.

> A stereo set purchased by Phelps was delivered to Brooks, a neighbor, by mistake. Brooks knew that the stereo belonged to Phelps and accepted delivery. By accepting delivery, Brooks agreed to hold the stereo as a bailee for the benefit of Phelps. ■

Brooks became a bailee even though there was no agreement between Phelps and Brooks. Bailments implied by law are often created when people find and take possession of lost, misplaced, or stolen property.

HOW A BAILMENT ENDS

You have already seen that a bailment exists only for a limited time and purpose; eventually it will come to an end. A bailment may be ended by the completion of the terms of the bailment agreement, mutual agreement of the parties, the acts of the parties, the destruction of the bailed property, or operation of law.

Completion

The typical bailment, created by an agreement, ends according to the terms of the agreement. If the agreement provides that the bailment will last for a specific time or purpose, the bailment will end when the time period is over or the purpose is accomplished.

> Ann's cousin borrowed Ann's copy of a current best-seller. The bailment ended when she finished reading it and returned it to Ann. ■

Mutual Agreement

Often, if there is no longer a need for the bailment, the bailor and the bailee agree to end it. It, in fact, then ends.

> You borrowed your friend's car for a week. Two days later your friend told you that his plans had changed and he needed his car back then. You agreed and returned the car to him. This terminated the bailment. ■

Acts of the Parties

If nothing specific is said or written about when the bailment is to end, either the bailor or the bailee, without the consent of the other, can end it at any time. Either party can also end the bailment if the other party does not live up to its terms.

> Lopez left his watch for repair. The jeweler agreed to repair it within ten days. If the work is not completed at the end of ten days, Lopez can reclaim his watch and end the bailment. ■

Destruction of the Bailed Property

A bailment also ends when the bailed property is lost, destroyed, or becomes worthless through damage. If the bailee's negligence causes the loss or damage, the bailee is liable to the bailor for the value of the property.

> ■ You bought your mother a present and asked your friend to keep it for you until your mother's birthday. Your friend negligently left the present in a store. When she returned for it, the present was gone. The bailment has ended, because your friend no longer has possession of the present. In addition, your friend is liable for the value of the present because of her negligence. ■

Operation of Law

A bailment implied by law ends when the need for the bailment ends.

> ■ A package belonging to your neighbor was delivered to your home because your neighbor was away on vacation. When your neighbor picks up the package, the bailment ends. ■

SITUATIONS SIMILAR TO BAILMENTS

There are other situations that resemble bailments but are quite different. Often they have some of the same characteristics. Some of these—sales and trusts—are discussed in other chapters of this book. Other situations that resemble bailments are bank deposits, safe-deposit boxes, and public lockers.

Depositing money in a bank has many of the characteristics of a bailment. Personal property (money) is delivered to and accepted by the bank for a specific purpose (storage). However, the relationship between the bank and the depositor is a debtor-creditor one. You are actually *lending* your money to the bank, which in turn promises to return the same *amount* of money to you. A bailment would occur only if the bank promises to return the identical currency that you deposited.

Many courts interpret the rental of a safe-deposit box to a customer by a bank as a bailment. However, the bank does not actually receive and accept delivery of the articles in the box. Nor does the bank have complete possession of the articles in the box. *Two* keys are needed to open the safe-deposit box: one held by the customer and one held by the bank. For these reasons, some courts rule that the relationship is that of a landlord-tenant.

The same applies to the rental of a public locker. The owner of the locker never actually receives and accepts delivery of the articles in the locker. The renter retains possession of the articles by retaining the locker key.

Summary of Important Legal Concepts

A bailment occurs when a person takes possession of property that was formerly in the possession of someone else, for a special purpose and for a limited period of time.

For a transaction to be a valid bailment, there must be a transfer of possession of personal property from one person to another and the eventual return of the property bailed. Title to property is not essential for a bailment, only possession.

Most bailments arise from an express agreement. They may also arise based on the actions of the parties, known as bailments implied in fact. They sometimes arise because justice and fair play requires it; such bailments are known as bailments implied by law.

A bailment is a temporary transaction. It may end in many ways, for example, agreement of the parties, acts of the parties, destruction of the bailed property, and operation of law.

There are many situations that are similar to bailments but that are treated differently. These include a deposit of money in a bank account, using a safe-deposit box, and renting a public locker. These are not considered bailments but either debtor-creditor or landlord-tenant relationships.

Key Legal Terms to Know

Match the terms with the definitions that follow.

bailee
bailment
bailment implied by law
bailment implied in fact
bailor
personal property

1. The transfer of possession of a person's personal property for a specific time and purpose
2. A bailment created when a person acquires possession of another's personal property without that person's consent or agreement
3. Any property belonging to a person other than real property such as land and buildings
4. One who accepts possession of another's personal property

5. One who gives up possession of personal property to another
6. A bailment created by the actions of the bailor and the bailee

Questions and Problems to Discuss

1. What are the characteristics of a bailment?
2. Explain the various ways in which a bailment may be created.
3. Kennedy entered the Riverboat Restaurant, hung his hat and coat on a hook, and sat down at a nearby table. Was this a bailment?
4. Schenk, an editor of her school newspaper, left her books in the newspaper office. She had the only key to the office. When she returned to the office the next day, her books were missing. Was the school a bailee of Schenk's books?
5. Stimson received a gift of $100 and deposited the money in an account at Prosperity National Bank. Was the deposit a bailment?
6. Would a bailment have been created if Stimson had put the $100 in a safe-deposit box?
7. DiCara left on a long trip and asked Lloyd to watch his apartment while DiCara was away. Lloyd moved into the apartment and stayed there until DiCara returned. Was a bailment created?
8. After a game of tennis, Hunt left her racket on a chair and went to get a soda. Later she picked up the racket and went home. When Hunt arrived home, she discovered that the racket she had picked up was not hers. Is she a bailee of the racket?
9. Richards stored a cord of firewood at Pauly's house. Richards told Pauly to use as much of the wood as he wanted and then return the balance. Was this a bailment?
10. Blair borrowed a hair dryer from Peppin, a friend. Peppin told Blair that she could keep the dryer for a week. Three days later, Peppin wanted the dryer back. Must Blair return the hair dryer before the end of the week?
11. Stone gave his sweater to Michaels, telling him he could keep the sweater for as long as he wanted and that he didn't have to return it. Was this a bailment?

Cases to Decide

1. Theobald entered a beauty shop operated by Satterwaite. She sat down in the waiting room until it was time for her appointment. When her turn came, Theobald left her coat on a hook in the waiting room and then went to another room for her hair care. When she returned to the waiting room, her coat was missing. She sued Satterwaite on the grounds that Satterwaite was a bailee and was negligent. Was Theobald correct? (*Theobald* v. *Satterwaite*, 30 Wash 2d 92, 190 P2d 714)

2. Gilchrist took his car in for its annual inspection. In the trunk of the car was a toolbox containing a valuable set of tools. Gilchrist did not mention the toolbox and its contents to the mechanics at the garage. The car was stolen. Did the bailment include the toolbox and the tools? (*Gilchrist* v. *Winmar J. Ford, Inc.*, NY 77 Misc 2d 847)

3. Marsh entered a railroad station and decided to store a package containing some jewelry. He found an open public locker, inserted a coin, put the package inside, and locked the door. He took the key with him and left. When he returned, the package was gone. Had a bailment been created? (*Marsh* v. *American Locker Company*, 7 NJ Super CT 81)

4. Pine Hill was in the concrete business and operated on its own land. Pine Hill sold its land and asked permission of the new owner to leave a cement mixer temporarily on the land until it could be picked up. The new owners agreed. Was a bailment created? (*Pine Hill Concrete Mix Corp.* v. *Alto Corp.*, NY 25 AD 2d 608)

5. Milo docked his boat at a marina owned by Biegler during the summer and paid $300 as a docking fee. One day the boat was stolen, the theft indicated by the fact that the mooring lines had been cut. Milo sued Biegler for $8,640, the value of his boat, claiming that, as a bailee, Biegler was responsible for the loss. Is Milo correct? (*Milo* v. *Biegler*, NY 86 AD 2nd 503)

Chapter 33

Bailments: Types, Rights, and Responsibilities

People are involved in many types of bailments in their daily lives. This chapter classifies those bailments into categories so they can be more easily identified: bailments that arise from an agreement and bailments that do not. It then discusses in detail the rights and responsibilities of the bailor and the bailee in each category. The chapter ends with a discussion of the ways in which bailees attempt to limit their liability.

CLASSIFICATION OF BAILMENTS

There are several ways to classify bailments. The most understandable way is based on whether the bailment arises from an agreement, which can be either express or implied, or without an agreement. In the first classification are *mutual benefit bailments* and *gratuitous bailments*. A **mutual benefit bailment** is a bailment in which both the bailor and the bailee benefit. It is the most common type of business bailment and is usually based on a contract.

> Rhodes rented a snowmobile for $5 an hour. As bailee, Rhodes benefited by having the use of the snowmobile; the bailor, the rental agency, benefited by being paid for the use of the snowmobile. ■

The **gratuitous bailment** is a bailment in which only one of the parties to the bailment benefits; the other does not. An example of a bailment *for the sole benefit of the bailor* is when you ask a friend, as a favor, to watch your bicycle while you are out of town. Examples of a bailment *for the sole benefit of a bailee* are letting your friend, as a favor, borrow a calculator or permitting a local library to exhibit your stamp collection free of charge.

A type of bailment in the second classification—one that does not arise from an agreement between parties—is known as a constructive bailment. A **constructive bailment** is a bailment implied by law. It occurs when a person comes into possession of another person's property without that person's knowledge or permission.

Bailments may also be classified according to the degree of care required, ordinary or special. Bailments in which an extraordinary standard of care is imposed on the bailee are known as special bailments. They are discussed in Chapter 34.

MUTUAL BENEFIT BAILMENTS

There are five types of mutual benefit bailments: renting, work and services, pledging, consigning, and storage and parking.

The standard of care required in a mutual benefit bailment is that of reasonable care. **Reasonable care** is the type of care a person would take in using her or his own property. For example, reasonable care of a rented lawnmower would include removing all the large rocks and branches from the path of the lawnmower.

Failure to use reasonable care may subject the bailee to liability for any damage that occurs to the property while it is in the possession of the bailee. The bailee may limit the responsibility to a certain amount or to certain events, provided the bailee brings the limitations to the attention of the bailor at the time the bailment is created.

Renting

This bailment, also known as leasing, is the most common type of mutual benefit bailment and often involves a contract. Any time you rent or lease an item for a period of time, you are involved in a bailment.

Bailor's Rights and Responsibilities   The bailor, the person who rents an item to someone, has the right to be paid for the use of the property, to expect that the bailee will use reasonable care, and to have the same property returned when the rental period ends.

The bailor has a duty to provide goods or equipment that are fit for the purpose of the bailment. The bailor, of course, must be familiar with the equipment and know its uses.

Work and Services

A bailment for work and services occurs when you deliver property to someone (the bailee) for repairs or servicing for a fee. The bailed property is usually returned in a changed condition, according to the agreement between bailor and bailee.

Bailor's Rights and Responsibilities   A bailee's acceptance of property for work or services is no assurance of skill. It is up to the bailor to choose a competent bailee. If the work is done poorly—if your clothes are returned from the dry cleaner's with wrinkles, for example—you have little claim against the bailee. If, however, the work is done so badly that the property cannot be used, you can insist that the work be redone, refuse to pay for the work, or demand your money back.

Johnson took some material to a tailor to have it made into a suit. The tailor mistakenly used someone else's measurements and made a suit that Johnson could not wear. The tailor was liable for the value of the material. ■

The bailor has a duty to pay for the work done and to warn the bailee of any hidden defects in the property that the bailee might not be aware of.

Your electric knife turned on when the safety switch was in the "off" position. When you take it in for repair, you have a duty to tell the repair person of this dangerous condition. If you do not, you are liable for any injuries to the bailee. ■

Bailee's Rights and Responsibilities   The bailee has the right to be paid. If the bailor does not pay, the bailee has the right to keep the property as security until paid. This right is known as the **bailee's lien.** In some states, the bailee may enforce this lien by selling the property. However, the bailee must first notify the bailor that the property is going to be sold and may keep only the amount of money to which the bailee is entitled—the amount that covers the cost of the work or services plus any expenses. Any money left over must be returned to or held for the bailor.

> DeKalb's radio was not working properly and he took it to a repair shop. When the work was done, DeKalb failed to pick up the radio and pay for having it repaired. After a certain time, the shop owner may sell the radio to recover the cost of the repairs. ■

The bailee also has certain duties. One is the duty to take proper care of the bailed property. A bailee who uses reasonable care is not responsible if the property is damaged, destroyed, or stolen.

> Lassen owned a valuable photograph, which was fading. Lassen took it to a photography studio to have it restored. In spite of the studio's alarm system, a burglar broke into the studio and stole many items, including Lassen's photograph. Lassen does not have a valid claim against the owner for the loss because the owner used reasonable care in protecting the photograph. ■

The bailee must also work on the property with the skill that a bailee of that type would normally have and must follow the terms of the bailment agreement. The bailee must not use the property without the owner's permission and must return it at the end of the bailment.

> You took your motorcycle in for repairs and asked the mechanic to give it a short road test to make sure that it ran properly. The mechanic lent it to a friend, who took it across town and damaged it in an accident. Because the mechanic lent the motorcycle without your permission, the mechanic is liable for all damages. ■

Pledging

A bailment known as a **pledge** occurs when personal property is deposited as security for the repayment of a loan or debt or the performance of a duty. A pledge is a common transaction in the business world. Pledged property may be any type of personal property, including stocks or bonds. The bailor (or debtor) is called the **pledgor.** The bailee (or creditor) is known as the **pledgee.** A pledgee may be a bank, pawnbroker, credit union, or individual lender.

> Bronson wanted a new stereo set but did not have enough money to buy it. Bronson owned a corporate bond that she didn't want to sell because of its value. If Bronson agreed to pledge the bond at a bank, she could receive a loan. When the loan is paid off, the bond will be returned to Bronson. ■

Pledgor's Rights and Responsibilities   The pledgor (bailor) has a right to get back the bailed property when the loan is repaid. If the pledgee (bailee) fails to return the bailed property after repayment, the pledgor may sue the bailee to get the property back or to recover its value.

> Price pledged a camera with a pawnbroker as security for a loan. On repaying the loan, Price learned that the pawnbroker had sold the camera by mistake. Price is entitled to get back a similar camera or an amount equal to the value of the pledged camera. ∎

The pledgor has a duty to repay the loan with interest under the terms of the pledge. If the pledgor fails to repay the loan on time, the pledgee may keep the bailed property and sell it to recover the amount of the loan. The pledgor also has a duty to make sure that he or she has the right to pledge the property. Stolen goods cannot be legally pledged. If stolen goods are pledged, the pledgee must surrender the goods to the true owner. This does not, however, relieve the pledgor of repaying the debt. The pledgor also is not relieved of repaying the debt if the property is lost, stolen, or destroyed through no fault of the pledgee.

Pledgee's Rights and Responsibilities   The pledgee (bailee) has a right to have the loan repaid under the terms of the pledge. The pledgee also has a bailee's lien and may keep the pledged property until the loan has been repaid.

The pledgee has a duty to take reasonable care of the pledged property and to return it when the loan is repaid.

Consigning

A **consignment** is a mutual benefit bailment in which the bailor, called the **consignor,** delivers property to the bailee, called the **consignee,** for purchase or sale by the consignee. Ownership of the consigned property remains with the consignor until the goods are either purchased by the consignee or sold to another person. A consignment enables a person to examine goods without having to pay for them in advance.

> Frost, a stamp collector, wanted to examine a set of stamps before deciding whether to buy them. A stamp company sent Frost stamps on consignment. Frost may keep the stamps for a certain period of time and either return them or keep and pay for them. ∎

Another purpose of consignment is to enable a retailer to keep merchandise on hand without first having to buy it from the manufacturer. The retailer saves money and can carry more merchandise in the store.

> A manufacturer sent TV sets to the Video Store on consignment. The manufacturer owns the sets until they are sold by Video Store. The store owner must pay the manufacturer when the sets are sold or return the unsold sets to the manufacturer. ∎

Consignor's Rights and Responsibilities   The consignor has a duty to provide property that is safe. The consignor must inspect the consigned property to make sure it is not dangerous and must tell the consignee if it requires special care.

The consignor has a right to have the consigned property stored under safe conditions. The consignor also has a right to have the property sold or returned within the agreed-upon period of time.

Consignee's Rights and Responsibilities   The consignee has a duty to take reasonable care of the consigned property. The consignee must either pay for the property or return it to the consignor within a reasonable time.

The consignee has a right to receive property that is safe. The consignee also has a right to keep the consigned property for the time agreed upon.

Another type of consignment involves shipments by common carrier. This type of consignment is discussed in Chapter 34.

Storage and Parking

Storing something for a fee is a common type of mutual benefit bailment. Leaving a pet at a kennel while you take a trip would be a bailment of this type. Storing a boat at a marina during the winter is another example.

The most common type of bailment for storage occurs when a bailor delivers goods to a warehouse operated by the bailee, the **warehouse operator.** The warehouse operator gives the bailor a receipt for the goods, known as a **warehouse receipt.** To get the bailed goods back, the bailor must return the receipt to the warehouse operator and pay the storage charges.

Bailor's Rights and Responsibilities   The bailor has the right to have the bailed property stored with reasonable care. The care required depends on the nature of the goods stored. Perishable goods such as fruit would require cold storage, whereas furniture might require dry storage. After turning in the receipt and paying the storage charges, the bailor has the right to get back the bailed property.

▪ You moved into a partially completed house and needed to store some furniture at a warehouse until the house was completely finished. To obtain the furniture, you must produce the warehouse receipt and pay the storage charges. ▪

The bailor must, of course, pay all storage charges. The bailor also has a duty to notify the bailee of any defects in the property or any special care required for its storage. Failure to notify the bailee of any problems or requirements may relieve the bailee of liability in the event of loss or damage.

▪ Braden owned a very valuable violin that required a high degree of humidity to prevent it from cracking. Before going on a trip, Braden arranged to store the violin but failed to tell the warehouse operator of the special care required. The warehouse operator would not be liable for any damage to the violin caused by low humidity, because Braden did not warn the operator of the special requirements. ▪

Warehouse Operator's Rights and Responsibilities   The warehouse operator has the right to be told of any special storage conditions. The operator also has the right to be paid for storing the property according to the terms of the agreement. The warehouse operator cannot use the property without the bailor's permission and must return the property at the end of the bailment period.

> The Vinson Company stored several crates of cabbage at the Granite Cold Storage Company. Granite placed the crates next to a container of fresh fish. When Vinson picked up the cabbage, it discovered that the cabbage had a fishy odor and could not be sold. Granite is liable for damages because it did not use reasonable care in storing the cabbage. ■

Some courts consider the parking of a car in a parking lot or garage to be a mutual benefit bailment. Others consider it a lease of space, which usually relieves the lot operator of liability in the event of loss or damage. What the relationship is depends on how much control the garage or lot operator has over the car. If you turn over your car to a parking lot attendant, who then parks it for you and retains the keys, you have lost control of the car and a bailment occurs. If you park the car yourself, lock it, and take the keys, a bailment does not occur. You are instead leasing space because you still have complete control over the car.

GRATUITOUS BAILMENTS

The most common type of nonbusiness bailment is the gratuitous bailment. In a gratuitous bailment only one party benefits—either the bailor or the bailee—and there is no charge for the bailment. If the bailor delivers property to the bailee and does not pay for the bailee's services, it is a bailment for the sole benefit of the bailor.

> You received a bicycle as a birthday present. You had no place to keep it and asked Carlson to take care of it for a few weeks. This is a bailment solely for your benefit as a bailor. ■

If the bailor delivers property to the bailee for the bailee's use without charge, a bailment for the sole benefit of the bailee occurs.

> During the summer Lewis earned extra money by mowing his neighbors' lawns. One day the lawnmower broke. Abel, Lewis's friend, loaned Lewis a lawnmower, free of charge, while his was being repaired. This bailment is solely for the benefit of the bailee. ■

Bailments for the Sole Benefit of the Bailor

Even though only one party benefits from a gratuitous bailment, both the bailor and the bailee have rights and duties. Many of these rights and duties are similar to those in a mutual benefit bailment. There are some differences, however.

Bailor's Rights and Responsibilities   The bailor has a right to have the bailed property stored in the agreed manner and to have the property returned at the end of the bailment.

■ Turlock asked a friend, Schneider, to store her car while she was away on vacation. Schneider let someone else use the car and it was damaged. Schneider is liable for the damages because the bailment terms did not permit the use of the car. ■

As with other types of bailments, the bailor has a duty to inform the bailee of any defects or dangers connected with the bailed property.

■ You asked a friend to repair your radio, as a favor, and delivered it to the friend's home. The radio was overheating, but you did not mention this to your friend. The radio caused a fire in your friend's home. You would be responsible for any loss that resulted. ■

The bailor must also reimburse the bailee for any expenses paid by the bailee while storing or taking care of the bailed property.

■ Marx's neighbor agreed to store his car during the winter months. She put antifreeze in the radiator to protect the car. This expense was necessary to protect the vehicle, and Marx must reimburse his neighbor for the cost of the antifreeze. ■

Bailee's Rights and Responsibilities   The bailee has a right to be warned of any defects or dangers connected with the bailed property and to have the property picked up at the end of the bailment period.

The bailee's duties are to store the property in the agreed manner and to return the goods at the end of the bailment period.

In a bailment for the sole benefit of the bailor, the bailee is doing a favor for the bailor and does not receive any benefit or compensation. Therefore, the bailee is not held to the same standard of care as in a mutual benefit bailment. The standard of care imposed on the bailee is that of *slight care,* the minimum amount of care required under the circumstances. The bailee is liable for damages or loss only if there was gross negligence.

■ White planned to go on a camping trip and asked Young to store her camping equipment for a few days. Young placed White's camping equipment on the outside porch, from which it was stolen. Young would be responsible for the loss, because even slight care would involve putting the equipment inside the house. ■

Bailments for the Sole Benefit of the Bailee

In a bailment for the sole benefit of the bailee, the bailee may use the bailor's property free of charge.

Bailor's Rights and Responsibilities   The bailor has the right to have the bailed property returned at the end of the bailment period in good condition.

The bailor also has the right to end the bailment at any time and demand the return of the bailed property.

The bailor has a duty to warm the bailee of any defects or dangers in the bailed property. If the bailor does not warn the bailee, the bailor may be liable for any injuries to the bailee.

Bailee's Rights and Responsibilities   The bailee has a right to use the bailed property as agreed and to be told of any defects or dangers. The bailee must use the property only as agreed, take proper care of the property, and return it in good condition at the end of the bailment period.

Since only the bailee benefits from this type of bailment, the bailee's standard of care is increased. The bailee in this type of bailment must use a *high degree of care.* This means that the bailee must use the property only as agreed and is liable for damages even if there was only slight negligence.

> You borrowed your friend's stereo for the day. The turntable easily held five records. You put seven records on the turntable. The reject mechanism snapped from the extra weight. You would be responsible for the cost of repairing the stereo. ∎

CONSTRUCTIVE BAILMENTS

The bailments discussed so far in this chapter come about through agreements between the bailor and the bailee. However, a person may get possession of someone else's property without an agreement or without the consent of the owner. When this happens, the person who gains possession of the property is considered a bailee, and the bailment is known as a constructive bailment.

Bailments of Lost Property

One type of constructive bailment is a **bailment of lost property.** This bailment occurs when someone finds lost property and takes possession of it. The finder is a bailee for the benefit of the bailor—the person who lost the property. The law makes the finder a constructive bailee to protect the owner's rights in the lost property.

> Evers was walking along the street and saw a purse on the ground. Evers took it home with her and notified the police. Evers is a constructive bailee of the purse until the police or the owner takes possession of the lost purse. ∎

Bailments by Necessity

Another type of constructive bailment is a **bailment by necessity.** This bailment occurs when property comes into someone's possession by mistake. The person who has possession is a constructive bailee for the benefit of the rightful owner until that owner is found.

> Granger ordered a sofa, which was delivered to Byrd's house by mistake. Byrd placed the sofa in his living room until Granger picked it up. Byrd is a bailee for the benefit of Granger. ■

Constructive bailees have certain obligations toward the owners of property. They must take reasonable care of the property, depending on the type of property and the circumstances of the bailment. In some states, the finder of the property must notify the authorities or must advertise that the property has been found.

If the true owner claims the property, the bailee must turn the property over to the owner. The bailee, however, is entitled to receive compensation for any expenses incurred in advertising or in taking reasonable care of the property. If a reward has been offered for the return of the property and the bailee knows of this reward, the bailee is entitled to collect it.

If the true owner does not appear to claim the property, the bailee is entitled to keep the property after a reasonable period of time has elapsed. The bailee may also sell the property and keep the proceeds of the sale.

LIMITING LIABILITIES—DISCLAIMERS

Many bailees attempt to avoid liability for damage to property while it is in their possession, or at least to limit the amount of that liability. They do so by inserting certain language in a ticket or receipt or posting a notice on a sign on the premises where the bailment occurs. Language typically used to avoid liability includes the statement, "Not responsible for loss or theft of property while on these premises."

Courts are increasingly finding such disclaimers to be void on the grounds that they are against public policy, particularly where public or semi-public institutions are concerned. Attempts to completely avoid liability for loss or damage despite negligence by the bailee are almost certain to be held void. However, if attempts to limit liability are reasonable and are made known to the bailor in a clear and understandable way, they are usually upheld.

Summary of Important Legal Concepts

The degree of care required in a bailment depends on the type of bailment involved. It is therefore important to classify bailments to determine the standard of care that is required. The most common classification is based on whether the bailment arises from an agreement.

The most common bailment is a mutual benefit bailment, in which both parties benefit. There are five types of mutual benefit bailments: renting, work and services, pledging, consigning, and storage and parking.

In a mutual benefit bailment, the standard of care is that of reasonable care. Failure to use reasonable care may subject the bailee to liability for any damages that may occur, unless the bailee limits its liability. In a mutual benefit bailment, the bailor has certain rights and responsibilities. The bailor has the right to be paid for the services rendered and to have the bailed property returned in good condition when the bailment ends.

A gratuitous bailment is one in which only one party benefits and in which there is no charge for services rendered. In a bailment for the sole benefit of the bailor, the bailor has a right to have the bailed property stored properly and to have the property returned when the bailment ends. The bailee has the obligation to store the bailed property with a slight degree of care and to return the property when the bailment ends. The bailor is obliged to warn the bailee of any defects or dangers connected with the property bailed.

In a bailment for the sole benefit of the bailee, the bailee must use a high degree of care in taking care of the property bailed, must use the property only as agreed and must return it when the bailment ends. The bailor has the right to have the property returned in a safe condition when the bailment ends. The bailor has a duty to warn the bailee of any defects or dangers in the property bailed.

Some bailments arise without agreement between the parties. These are known as constructive bailments. One type is a bailment of lost property. Another is a bailment by necessity, which arises when someone obtains possession of another's property by mistake. In both cases, the standard of care is that of reasonable care.

Key Legal Terms to Know

Match the terms with the definitions that follow.

bailee's lien
bailment by necessity
bailment of lost property
consignee
consignment
consignor
constructive bailment
gratuitous bailment
mutual benefit bailment
pledge
pledgee
pledgor
reasonable care
warehouse operator
warehouse receipt

1. A bailment implied by law created when a person has possession of another's property without that person's knowledge or permission
2. One who stores personal property for another for compensation
3. A bailment that occurs when personal property is deposited as security for the repayment of a loan or a debt
4. The care taken by an average person under ordinary circumstances
5. A bailment that occurs when property comes into someone's possession by mistake
6. A form issued by a bailee for the storage of personal property
7. A bailment for the purpose of purchase or sale by the bailee
8. The bailee's right to hold bailed property until paid for work or services
9. One who accepts delivery of personal property deposited as security for a loan or debt
10. A bailment that occurs when a person comes into possession of lost property
11. One who transfers possession of personal property as security for a loan or debt
12. The bailee in a consignment
13. The bailor in a consignment
14. A bailment in which both the bailor and the bailee benefit
15. A bailment in which only one party to the bailment benefits

Questions and Problems to Discuss

1. Name the types of mutual benefit bailments.
2. What is the standard of care required in a mutual benefit bailment? A bailment for the sole benefit of the bailor? A bailment for the sole benefit of the bailee?
3. Robertson borrowed Smith's movie camera to use on vacation. When Robertson packed the car to return home, he left the camera lying on the ground and it was stolen. Was Robertson liable to Smith for this loss?
4. Powers borrowed a lawnmower from a neighbor, Jackson. While mowing the lawn, Powers was injured by a defective blade on the lawnmower. Jackson had known of the defect but had failed to warn Powers. Powers brought an action for damages against Jackson. Will Powers succeed?

5. Newcomb borrowed Cole's silverware to use at a party. Thieves broke into Newcomb's home and stole many valuable articles, including Cole's chest of silverware. Newcomb had very carefully locked the silverware in a strong metal storage box. Is Newcomb liable for the loss of the silverware?

6. Rogers took a watch to a jeweler for cleaning. When Rogers returned for the watch, the jeweler told her that there was a $5 charge for the work. Rogers did not have the money with her, but told the jeweler that she would return with the money the next day. The jeweler told Rogers that he would hold the watch until the charge had been paid. Did the jeweler have a legal right to hold the watch until payment was made?

7. Motley delivered a bolt of fabric to his tailor to be used in the making of a suit. Before the suit had been made, the shop was broken into and all the fabric stolen. The shop was protected by a burglar alarm. Motley sued the tailor for the value of the fabric. Should Motley succeed in this action?

8. Andrews rented an automobile from the U-Steer-It Co. Another driver backed into the car while it was parked and the car was damaged. Is Andrews liable for the damage to the rented car?

9. To move some small household items, Young leased a small truck whose capacity was 1,000 pounds. Young told the rental agent the reason for renting the truck when making the arrangements. After moving the household items, Young tried to move some heavy steel castings for a friend and, as a result, broke the springs of the truck. Was Young liable for the damage to the truck?

10. As a favor, Martin agreed to store Duncan's winter clothes in a cedar closet during the summer. Because of Martin's negligence, moths got into the closet and damaged the clothes. Duncan sued Martin in small claims court. Is Martin liable for the damages to Duncan's clothes?

11. Jackson was permitted to keep her car in Gilman's garage for the summer months without charge. Gilman used the car one morning to drive to work, although she did not have Jackson's permission to do so. Gilman had an accident, through no fault of her own, and the car was damaged. Is Gilman liable for the damage to the car?

12. Carter rented a floor sander from a contractor, agreeing to pay $20 for one week's rental of the sander. Three days before the end of the rental period, the contractor had an opportunity to sell the sander at a substantial profit. The contractor demanded that Carter return the machine at once. Does the contractor have the right to demand the return of the sander?

13. Andrews stole a television set from a store and then deposited it in a warehouse to have it stored for a few weeks. Two days later, the set was destroyed when an electrical storm turned on the building's sprinkler system. Was the warehouse operator liable for the loss of the set?

14. Health Hospital posted a sign near the entrance stating, "This hospital is not responsible for any injuries suffered by visitors while on the premises." Will this disclaimer be upheld?

15. Coolidge decided to take a weekend vacation trip with his family. Before leaving, Coolidge borrowed a cassette tape player from a friend so that the family could enjoy music on the trip. When the car developed muffler trouble, Coolidge drove to a service station and left the car there for repairs. When he returned to pick up the car, Coolidge discovered the cassette tape player had been stolen. Is Coolidge liable to the owner of the cassette tape player for the loss of the player?

16. Goodwin took his car to the Acme Car Wash. He sat in the car as it went through the complete wash-and-dry cycle. When he checked his car after the wash was completed, he noticed that the car fenders had been damaged. Goodwin claims the car wash operator is liable as a bailee of Goodwin's car. Is Goodwin correct? Would your answer be any different if Goodwin had not accompanied the car as it went through the car wash?

17. Lennox received a shipment of plants for his plant shop. Because he did not have enough space for all the plants, he stored many of them with a local commercial greenhouse. Over the weekend, the temperature dropped below freezing during a cold spell. The owner of the greenhouse failed to turn on any heat in the building in which Lennox's plants were stored. All of Lennox's plants froze, causing a severe financial loss for Lennox. Based on these circumstances, answer the questions on the next page.

a. Is the greenhouse owner responsible for Lennox's loss?

b. Would your answer be different if there had not been a cold spell and the plants had died of no apparent cause?

c. Could Lennox collect damages from the greenhouse owner for the loss of the plants if the receipt for Lennox's plants had stated, "Not responsible for any damage or loss"?

Cases to Decide

1. Kessman owned and operated a gold, silver, and coin exchange store. In accordance with a court order issued in a nuisance action against Kessman by the city and county of Denver, the sheriff closed the store and padlocked it. While the store was in the sheriff's control, the store was burglarized. Kessman sued for damages, claiming this was a bailment. Is he correct? (*Kessman* v. *City and County of Denver*, 709 P2d 975)

2. Amerson's husband borrowed an electric drill from Howell, who had installed a new plug on the drill. Howell explained to Amerson's husband that three other people had been shocked while using the drill but had not been injured. Howell even tried the drill and was not shocked. Amerson's husband took the drill home, used it, and received a fatal shock. Amerson sued Howell for the wrongful death of her husband. Was she entitled to damages? (*Howell* v. *Amerson*, 156 SE 2d 370, 116 Ga App 211)

3. Mickey visited a Sears store to buy electrical supplies. He carried with him a regular briefcase containing $589.71. While carrying his purchases from the loading platform to his car, Mickey left the briefcase on the platform. Some Sears employees saw the briefcase, took possession of it, and returned it to Mickey the following day. The money, however, was gone. Mickey sued Sears for the loss of the money. Is Sears liable? (*Mickey* v. *Sears Roebuck & Company*, 196 Md 326, 76 A2d 350)

4. Schroeder parked his car in a parking lot operated by Allright. He received a parking ticket that had the following statement printed on it: "Loss limited to $100." Upon his return to the lot, Schroeder found that his car was gone. He sued Allright for the value of his car. Allright claimed that it was liable only up to the amount

of $100. Is Allright correct? (*Allright, Inc.* v. *Schroeder*, 551 SW2d 745)

5. England was injured when thrown from a motorized golf cart he had rented at the Fort Benning Country Club. As the cart was going downhill, England applied the brakes. The brakes didn't work, and England was thrown from the cart when it hit a bump. Proof was offered that the brakes were not working at the time of the accident but that they had been tested periodically, including the morning of the accident. England brought action against the United States, operator of the country club. Was he entitled to recover damages? (*England* v. *U.S.*, 405 F2d 862)

6. Ellish parked her car in a fenced-in parking lot at New York's JFK Airport. She received a ticket from a vending machine, drove inside the lot, found a parking space, locked the car, and took her keys with her. When she returned to the lot, her car was gone. Was this a bailment? If not, what was it? Would it make any difference if Ellish had been told to park in a certain space? (*Ellish* v. *Airport Parking Co. of America*, NY 42 AD2d 174)

7. Sealey parked her car on a monthly basis in Meyers's four-story, fully enclosed parking garage. Sealey had an assigned parking space, and she parked and locked the car herself, taking the key with her. Meyers provided a security guard for the premises and provided an attendant at a main gate who controlled any exit from the garage. One day, Sealey parked her car at 9 A.M.; when she returned at 6 P.M., she discovered that her car had been severely vandalized. Sealey claimed that Meyers was liable because a bailment relationship had been created between the parties. Is Sealey correct? (*Sealey* v. *Meyers Parking System*, NY 147 Misc 2d 217)

8. Tillman's parents owned a very valuable collection of china and pottery. After the parents died, the executor of their estate deposited 112 barrels and cartons containing the china and pottery in a warehouse owned by Lincoln in New York City. Many years later, Tillman attempted to remove the collection from storage and discovered that a substantial number of the valuable items were missing. Lincoln was unable to explain the absence of the items. Is Tillman entitled to collect for the value of the missing china and pottery? (*Tillman* v. *Lincoln Warehouse*, NY 72 AD2d 40)

Chapter 34

Special Bailments

CHAPTER PREVIEW

There are certain bailments in which an extraordinary standard of care is imposed. This chapter deals with such bailments, called special bailments. It begins with an explanation of why such a high standard of care is imposed. It then describes many exceptions to the general rule of strict liability. Finally, the chapter discusses the rights and liabilities of two groups upon whom extraordinary liability has been imposed: hotelkeepers and common carriers.

THE NATURE OF SPECIAL BAILMENTS

Chapter 33 emphasized that the type of bailment determines the standards of care imposed on the bailee. Mutual benefit and constructive bailments require reasonable care; gratuitous bailments require either slight care or a high degree of care, depending on who benefits.

There are also benefits in which an *extraordinary* standard of care is placed on the bailee. These are **special bailments,** often called extraordinary bailments. Examples of special bailees are hotelkeepers and common carriers, either of goods or of passengers.

The extraordinary standard of care required of special bailees arose out of necessity. In the days of stagecoach travel, travelers were often subject to hijacking and theft. The inns in which they stayed were quite vulnerable to robbery. Sometimes there was collusion or cooperation between the innkeepers and robbers. To promote travel and commerce and to protect travelers, special standards of care were placed on innkeepers and carriers.

Under common law the liability of innkeepers and carriers of goods was absolute. They were considered insurers—totally liable for the safety of goods left in their possession, unless loss was due to conditions beyond their control. It was thought that those who had total control over property should be completely responsible for it.

Today these bailees may still be held absolutely liable for loss of or damage to property, but this liability may be limited by law and is subject to many exceptions. In most states the rule of absolute liability has been limited by law. Unless they are negligent, hotelkeepers and common carriers are not liable for losses if the exceptions described in the following sections apply.

EXCEPTIONS TO THE RULE OF STRICT LIABILITY

Agreement to Limit Liability

Special bailees can limit their liability by agreement with bailors. Some limit the amount for which they can become liable; others limit the type of conduct for which they can be held liable.

The typical practice is to post a notice about the liability being limited or to include a statement on the receipt given to the bailor. Statements such as "liability limited to $100" and "stored at owner's risk" are examples of attempts to limit liability.

As long as the agreement is fair and the bailor is fully aware of the limitation, the limitation is effective.

Act of God

A natural disaster that could not have been anticipated, such as a flash flood, a hurricane, or an earthquake, is considered to be an **act of God.** Even a special bailee is not liable for losses due to such natural forces because the bailee could not have avoided the disaster.

> Workers for a shipping line were loading fruit onto a ship when a hurricane struck, leaving the ship marooned on dry land. The fruit was ruined by the hurricane and the delay in shipment. The shipper would not be liable; the loss was due to an act of God. ■

If the bailee can prevent or limit a loss by taking proper care and fails to do so, the bailee is held liable for losses even though a natural disaster is involved.

> A hotel stored its guests' baggage in a basement storeroom. An unusually severe snowstorm occurred. In the next few days, warm weather moved in and the snow melted. The hotel was flooded and the guests' baggage was damaged. The hotel would be responsible for the destruction of the baggage because it did not move the baggage above the flood level. ■

Act of a Public Enemy

A **public enemy** is a military or military-type force from another country. Pirates or saboteurs from a foreign country are good examples. Special bailees are not liable for losses due to the acts of a public enemy. However, mobs, rioters, strikers, and robbers are not considered public enemies.

> The Argos Company sent merchandise by ship to a foreign country. At a refueling stop, the ship was seized by a military-type force and the cargo was confiscated. The shipping line would not be liable for the loss. ■

Act of Public Authorities

A special bailee is not liable for losses that occur when goods in its possession are seized by a government authority. The bailee is not liable if, for example, public officials seize stolen goods or contaminated foods during shipment.

> While on vacation in Europe, Ingram decided to ship a carton of oranges back to her family. When the fruit reached the United States, customs officials confiscated it because fruit cannot be imported into the country. The shipping company was not liable for the loss of the oranges because the fruit was seized by a government agency. ■

Fault of the Bailor or Guest

A special bailee is not liable for losses that occur because of the actions of the bailor. The bailee is not liable, for example, if the bailor does not pack the goods properly and the carton breaks during shipment. Of course, if the defect or fault is apparent and the bailee still accepts the goods, the bailee is liable for loss.

> ■ Larson shipped a valuable clock to a repair shop by a local delivery service. The package appeared to be wrapped and sealed properly, but there was nothing inside the package to keep the clock from moving around. The clock was damaged when the truck went over a bumpy road. The delivery service is not liable for this loss. ■

Nature of the Bailed Goods

A special bailee is not liable for losses arising from the basic nature of the bailed goods. Some goods are perishable or may evaporate or ferment. Special care, such as refrigeration, may be required to prevent damage. If perishable food is being shipped, the bailee must take care to refrigerate the food properly and to ship it without delay. If these precautions are not taken, the bailee is liable for any spoilage during shipment. However, if these precautions were taken and the goods were damaged because of their perishability, the bailee would not be liable.

DUTIES, LIABILITIES, AND RIGHTS OF HOTELKEEPERS

A **hotelkeeper** is one who, on a regular basis, offers to provide living accommodations to all transients. The essential elements of a hotel or motel business are (1) regular nature of business, (2) offer to the public, (3) living accommodations, and (4) guest relationship.

The renting of rooms must be continuous and the main business activity. A hotelkeeper may operate a hotel, motel, or tourist home.

> ■ Your sister enrolled in college. Your parents, as a favor to some friends, rented her room to out-of-town visitors for a few days. Your parents would not be considered hotelkeepers, because the renting of rooms to others is not the main activity of your household. ■

Hotelkeepers must accept any person who arrives in a proper condition and who is willing to pay for the accommodations.

> ■ The Acme Corporation operated a small hotel that provided accommodations solely for its many visiting employees and business clients. The company would not be considered a hotelkeeper, because it does not serve the general public. ■

The main purpose of a hotelkeeper is to provide lodging for travelers. A hotelkeeper may also provide food and entertainment, but the main purpose is the renting of rooms.

> You entered a hotel to have dinner in the dining room. You were a patron of the restaurant, not a resident or guest of the hotel. ∎

For a hotelkeeper to be considered a special bailee, the hotelkeeper must provide lodgings for guests or **transients**—those who can stay as long as they wish and who may leave at any time.

> Simpson rented a hotel room, not knowing how long he was going to stay. Simpson enjoyed the area and stayed three weeks. While at the hotel, Simpson was a transient because he was free to leave at any time. ∎

Many people enter hotels to use the facilities but not to stay there. Some people enter the hotel to attend a social function, visit a guest, or eat in the dining room. Some have business to transact with the hotelkeeper. These people are not transients but **business guests.** A hotelkeeper is only an ordinary bailee of the property of business guests.

> Cowens was in the restaurant supply business and entered the Clearwater Hotel to demonstrate a new dishwasher for the hotel manager. On entering the hotel, Cowens left a briefcase with the desk clerk. Because Cowens is a business guest, the desk clerk must use only slight care and would not be absolutely liable for a loss of the briefcase. ∎

The relationship between a guest and a hotelkeeper begins when the hotelkeeper accepts a person as a guest. This usually occurs when that person checks into the hotel. However, a person may become a guest by giving her or his luggage to a porter or a person operating the hotel's limousine service.

A person ceases to be a guest when he or she leaves the hotel or ceases to be a transient.

> Johns checked into the Bristol Hotel for a few days while looking for a more permanent home. Johns was pleased with the hotel's accommodations and decided to become a permanent resident. Johns ceased to be a guest when she decided to live permanently at the hotel. ∎

A **boardinghouse keeper** is one who offers living accommodations to permanent residents. Unlike a hotelkeeper, a boardinghouse keeper does not have to accept everyone who applies for a room. A boardinghouse keeper is an ordinary bailee of the personal property of boarders and is not entitled to a hotelkeeper's special rights. A university dormitory is an example of a boardinghouse.

> Bartos entered college and rented a room for the school year at a college-approved, off-campus house. The owner of the house is a boardinghouse keeper because Bartos's stay is more permanent. Bartos is a roomer, not a transient. ∎

Duties of a Hotelkeeper

A hotelkeeper, by definition and by law, must receive and accommodate all those who wish to stay and who are proper guests. The Civil Rights Act of 1964 prohibits a hotelkeeper from discriminating against any person on the basis of race, color, religion, or national origin. If a hotelkeeper does discriminate for any of these reasons, the hotelkeeper could be held liable for damages, criminal prosecution, or both. The Civil Rights Act, however, does not prevent a hotelkeeper from rejecting any person who is violent, drunk, or unable to pay.

A hotelkeeper has a duty to take all reasonable precautions for the safety and privacy of guests and their baggage. Such precautions include providing protection against danger from fires and providing safe elevators, rooms, hallways, and stairs. Hotelkeepers are also liable for any actions by their employees that might endanger guests.

Liabilities of a Hotelkeeper

As mentioned earlier, hotelkeepers are absolutely liable for the safety of their guests' property. They are considered to be insurers and, like common carriers, are responsible for all losses or damages except those caused by acts of God, acts of public enemies, acts of public authorities, or the actions of the guest.

In actual practice hotelkeepers, like common carriers, may limit their liability in various ways. In many states, laws limit the liability of a hotelkeeper to a specific amount. In a few states, hotelkeepers are held liable for theft of or damage to a guest's property only if they are negligent. In other states, laws permit hotelkeepers to limit their liability by providing a safe for guests' valuables and posting a notice in rooms telling guests of this safe. (See Figure 34.1.) If a guest fails to use the safe, the hotelkeeper is no longer a special bailee and is responsible only for providing reasonable care for the guests' property.

> Kaye was a guest at the Cambridge Hotel, which posted notices in guests' rooms telling them to store their valuables overnight in the hotel safe. Kaye came back to the hotel very late one night and decided not to place her diamond earrings in the safe because of the late hour. During the night several rooms were broken into, including Kaye's. Kaye's earrings were stolen. The hotel was not liable for the loss of the earrings because Kaye had not deposited them in the safe. The hotel could be held liable only if Kaye could prove that the hotel was unusually negligent in allowing the thief to enter the hotel. ■

Rights of a Hotelkeeper

Hotelkeepers have a right to be paid for the rooms they rent. If not paid, they may keep baggage and other goods belonging to the guest until the bill has been paid. This right is known as a hotelkeeper's lien. After a reasonable period of time, the goods being held may be sold and the proceeds applied to the unpaid bill. Any money left over must be returned to the hotel guest.

Hotelkeepers also have the right to ask for payment in advance or for proof of ability to pay (usually by credit card).

NOTICE TO GUESTS

State Laws

Chapter 140, Section 10 to 13 Inclusive, Laws of Massachusetts

Section 10. "An innholder shall not be liable for losses sustained by a guest except of wearing apparel, articles worn or carried on the person, personal baggage and money necessary for traveling expenses and personal use, nor shall such guest recover of an innholder more than three hundred dollars as damages for any such loss; but an innholder shall be liable in damages to an amount not exceeding one thousand dollars for the loss of money, jewels and ornaments of a guest specially deposited for safe keeping, or offered to be so deposited, with such innholder, person in charge at the office of the inn, or other agent of such innholder authorized to receive such deposit. This section shall not affect the innholder's liability under any special contract for other property deposited with him for safe keeping after being fully informed of its nature and value, nor increase his liability in case of loss by fire or overwhelming force beyond that specified in the following section."

Section 11. "In case of loss by fire or overwhelming force, innholders shall be answerable to their guests only for ordinary and reasonable care in the custody of their baggage or other property."

Section 12. "Whoever puts up at a hotel, motel, inn, lodging house or boarding house and, without having an express agreement for credit, procures food, entertainment or accommodation without paying therefor, and with intent to cheat or defraud the owner or keeper therof; or, with such intent, obtains credit at a hotel, motel, inn, lodging house or boarding house for such food, entertainment or accommodation by means of any false show of baggage or effects brought thereto; or, with such intent, removes or causes to be removed any baggage or effects from a hotel, motel, inn, lodging house or boarding house while a lien exists thereon for the proper charges due from him for fare and board furnished therein, shall be punished by a fine of not more than one thousand dollars or by imprisonment for not more than one year; and whoever, without having an express agreement for credit, procures food or beverage from a common victualler without paying therefor and with intent to cheat or defraud shall be punished by a fine of not more than five hundred dollars or by imprisonment for not more than three months.

Proof that such food, entertainment, accommodation or beverage, or credit for the same, was obtained by a false show of baggage or effects, or that such baggage or effects were removed from any such place by any person while such a lien existed thereon without an express agreement permitting such removal, or if there was not an express agreement for credit, that payment for such food, entertainment, accommodation or beverage was refused upon demand, shall be presumptive evidence of the intent to cheat or defraud referred to herein."
Amended by St. 1965, c.490: St. 1972, c.513

Section 13. "Innholders shall post a printed copy of this and the three preceding sections in a conspicuous place in each room of their inns."

Figure 34.1 **Hotelkeeper's Notice Limiting Liability**

Aldrich arrived at the Warren Hotel and asked for a room for one night. Aldrich had no luggage and had a disheveled appearance. The hotel desk clerk legally has the right to ask Aldrich to pay for the room in advance. ∎

DUTIES, LIABILITIES, AND RIGHTS OF COMMON CARRIERS

A **carrier** is one who transports goods or people for pay. There are three types of carriers: private carriers, contract carriers, and common carriers.

A **private carrier** is owned and operated by a company for the sole purpose of transporting its own goods. The delivery trucks owned by a dairy or a department store are examples of private carriers. Private carriers are employers and are covered by the laws of employment discussed in Part V.

A **contract carrier** limits its customers and transports goods under individual contracts. A contract carrier, for example, may deliver goods only for department stores. A contract carrier is free to accept or reject customers as it chooses. Contract carriers are ordinary bailees and are covered by the laws of mutual benefit bailments and the law of contracts.

A **common carrier** transports goods and people for anyone who wishes to hire it. A common carrier is a special bailee with special rights and duties. Railroads, shipping lines, bus lines, airlines, taxis, and trucking companies are examples of common carriers. Common carriers are different from other carriers because they must accept customers without discrimination, are considered insurers of their customers' property, and are subject to government regulations because they are often public monopolies.

One who delivers goods to a common carrier for shipment is called a *consignor*. The person to whom the goods are shipped is the *consignee*. When the consignor delivers goods to a common carrier for shipment to the consignee, the consignor receives a receipt for the goods. This receipt is called a **bill of lading.** The bill of lading is not only a receipt but also a document of title and the shipping agreement between the consignor and the carrier.

Duties of a Common Carrier

A common carrier of people (passengers) has a duty to (1) accept anyone who applies for transportation, (2) provide reasonable accommodations, and (3) provide reasonable protection for its passengers.

A common carrier of goods has a duty to (1) accept and transport the lawful goods of all persons who request shipment, (2) provide adequate facilities for transporting goods and for storing goods awaiting shipment or delivery, (3) follow the consignor's shipping instructions, and (4) deliver goods to the consignee at the time and place agreed upon.

Liabilities of a Common Carrier

A common carrier is not, of course, an insurer of the safety of passengers, but it must exercise a high degree of care to protect them. A common carrier can, however, be held liable for injuries to passengers caused by the negligence of its employees. If the injuries were caused by the negligence of the passenger or by incidents beyond the carrier's control, the carrier is relieved of liability.

■ You were a passenger on a bus. As you were getting off the bus, it began to move; you fell and were injured. You can collect damages for your injuries because the driver was negligent in moving the bus while a passenger was still getting off. ■

Unless one of the exceptions described earlier applies, a common carrier of goods is absolutely liable as a special bailee for any loss or damage to the goods after the goods are delivered to the carrier and during shipment. In most states a common carrier may limit its absolute liability by contract with the consignor. Sometimes a carrier can limit its liability for damages caused by its own negligence, but the carrier cannot absolve itself from all liability.

A common carrier often limits its liability to a specific amount. However, to take advantage of this lowered liability, the carrier must give the consignor further consideration, usually in the form of lower shipping rates. The consignor must also have the option of shipping goods at the higher rate to receive higher limits of liability.

In some states a common carrier can limit its liability for losses that arise from such hazards as fire, breakage, spoilage, or the actions of rioters, mobs, and thieves.

A common carrier is liable for losses or damages caused by its failure to deliver the goods within a reasonable time. The consignor, however, must bear the loss if the delay is one that would normally occur in shipping goods.

> Carnival Chocolate Company shipped 1,000 pounds of chocolate by ship, rather than by plane. The trip took seven days because of rough seas; the chocolate was spoiled due to the longer voyage. Carnival would have to bear the loss, because the delay was one that could be expected when shipping goods by sea. ■

A common carrier's liability begins when the goods are delivered by the shipper to the carrier. The carrier's liability ends when the goods reach their final destination and the consignee takes possession of the goods. In some states, the carrier's liability ends when the consignee fails to pick up the goods after receiving notice of their arrival and availability for examination. In other states, liability is held to end when the goods are removed from the railroad cars and delivered to a warehouse.

A common carrier's liability is often limited by law or treaty. Under the Warsaw Convention, for example, an airline's liability for loss of baggage carried on an international flight is limited to a specific amount. The notice shown in Figure 34.2 appears on most airline tickets.

Rights of a Common Carrier

Common carriers are required to accept anyone who asks for service and can pay for that service. However, there are exceptions to this requirement. A common carrier has the right to refuse service to passengers who (1) require unusual attention, (2) might cause injury to the carrier or to other passengers, or (3) might be offensive to other passengers (for example, an intoxicated person).

A common carrier of goods has the right to refuse service if it is not equipped or does not have adequate facilities for transporting the particular goods. For instance, if a carrier does not have refrigerated trucks, it may refuse to transport goods that require refrigeration.

ADVICE TO INTERNATIONAL PASSENGERS ON LIMITATION OF LIABILITY

Passengers on a journey involving an ultimate destination or a stop in a country other than the country of origin are advised that the provisions of a treaty known as the Warsaw Convention may be applicable to the entire journey, including any portion entirely within the country of origin or destination. For such passengers on a journey to, from, or with an agreed stopping place in the United States of America, the Convention and special contracts of carriage embodied in applicable tariffs provide that the liability of certain carriers, parties to such special contracts, for death of or personal injury to passengers is limited in most cases to proven damages not to exceed U.S. $75,000 per passenger, and that this liability up to such limit shall not depend on negligence on the part of the carrier. The limit of liability of U.S. $75,000 above is inclusive of legal fees and costs except that in case of a claim brought in a state where provision is made for separate award of legal fees and costs, the limit shall be the sum of U.S. $58,000 exclusive of legal fees and costs. For such passengers traveling by a carrier not a party to such special contracts or on a journey not to, from, or having an agreed stopping place in the United States of America, liability of the carrier for death or personal injury to passengers is limited in most cases to approximately U.S. $10,000 or U.S. $20,000.

The names of carriers, parties to such special contracts, are available at all ticket offices of such carriers and may be examined on request. Additional protection can usually be obtained by purchasing insurance from a private company. Such insurance is not affected by any limitation of the carrier's liability under the Warsaw Convention or such special contracts of carriage. For further information please consult your airline or insurance company representative.

NOTICE OF BAGGAGE LIABILITY LIMITATIONS

Liability for loss, delay, or damage to baggage is limited unless a higher value is declared in advance and additional charges are paid. For most international travel (including domestic portions of international journeys) the liability limit is approximately $9.07 per pound for checked baggage and $400 per passenger for unchecked baggage. For travel wholly between U.S. points federal rules require any limit on an airline's baggage liability to be at least $1250 per passenger. Excess valuation may be declared on certain types of articles. Some carriers assume no liability for fragile, valuable or perishable articles. Further information may be obtained from the carrier.

Figure 34.2 **Notice on Airline Ticket Limiting Liability**

A common carrier also has the right to make reasonable rules by which it conducts its business. It may charge reasonable rates for its services and may collect those rates in advance. Because many common carriers are monopolies, rates are often regulated by the Interstate Commerce Commission or by other state and local government agencies.

If a common carrier's equipment is delayed for an unreasonable period of time by the consignee or the consignor, the carrier may make a special charge known as **demurrage.** For example, demurrage may be charged if a consignor is late in loading goods or if the consignee fails to remove goods within a reasonable time.

A common carrier has a right to be paid for its services. It therefore has a lien on goods it transports as security for payment of its charges. If the charges are not paid, the common carrier can enforce the lien by selling the goods after a specific period of time.

Summary of Important Legal Concepts

A special or extraordinary standard of care is imposed on certain bailees because of historical reasons. This special standard has been imposed primarily on hotelkeepers and common carriers. The standard of care is that of absolute liability for goods left in the possession of the bailee.

Today, the absolute liability of these bailees has been limited by law and by agreement. The exceptions to absolute liability of special bailees are (1) an agreement between the parties which is reasonable, (2) an act of God which causes the damage, (3) an act of a public enemy that causes the damage, (4) an act of a public authority that causes the damage, (5) fault on the part of the bailor, and (6) damage that occurs because of the basic nature of the goods bailed.

Hotelkeepers, defined as those who rent rooms to the public on a temporary basis, are special bailees upon whom an extraordinary degree of care is imposed. Today, however, the liability of hotelkeepers is limited by the exceptions described above. In most states, hotelkeepers may also limit their liability by posting notices to this effect or providing safe deposit boxes for their guests.

There are many types of carriers, including private and contract carriers. An extraordinary degree of care, however, is imposed only on a common carrier, a carrier that transports goods and people for anyone who wishes to hire it. This category includes airlines, railroads, trucking companies, and bus lines. Although a common carrier is not absolutely liable for injuries to passengers, it is absolutely liable for damage to goods being shipped with the carrier, unless one of the exceptions mentioned above applies. In most states, a common carrier may limit its liability to a certain amount unless the shipper pays a higher rate for the shipment.

A common carrier's liability begins when goods are delivered to it. Its liability ends either when the consignee takes possession or when the goods are removed from the carrier and delivered to a warehouse.

A common carrier has the right to refuse to service passengers who might present a special problem. It also has the right to refuse to transport goods if they are unsafe or if the carrier is not equipped to handle the goods involved.

Key Legal Terms to Know

Match the terms with the definitions that follow.

act of God
bill of lading
boardinghouse keeper
business guest
carrier
common carrier
contract carrier
demurrage
hotelkeeper
private carrier
public enemy
special bailment
transient

1. A bailment in which an extraordinary standard of care is imposed on the bailee
2. A natural occurrence that cannot be foreseen or avoided

3. One who provides living accommodations to the public for a limited time
4. One who transports goods or people for pay
5. A carrier that transports goods solely for the business that owns it
6. One who is not a permanent resident
7. A fee charged for delaying the equipment of a common carrier for an unreasonable period of time
8. A military-type force of a foreign country
9. A carrier that transports people and goods for the general public
10. A document issued to a consignor by a carrier as a receipt for the goods shipped, proof of title, and the shipping agreement
11. A carrier that transports goods or people under individual contracts for a limited number of customers
12. A person using the facilities of a hotel but not staying there
13. One who offers living accommodations to permanent residents

Questions and Problems to Discuss

1. How is a bill of lading used?
2. A railroad company notified Brooks, the consignee of a shipment of goods, that the goods had arrived and should be picked up at its freight house. Two weeks later, through no fault of the railroad, the freight house burned and the goods were destroyed. Brooks sought to hold the carrier liable for the loss of the goods on the grounds that it was a special bailee and an insurer. Is Brooks correct?
3. Johnson shipped merchandise on the Central Railway Company. A rainstorm occurred while the goods were in transit. Water leaked through the roof of the boxcar and caused extensive damage to Johnson's merchandise. Johnson sued the railroad for damages. Should Johnson recover?
4. The Pecos Manufacturing Co. delivered goods to the railroad for shipping. In transit the goods were destroyed in a fire that was caused by lightning. Was the railroad liable for the loss of Pecos's goods?
5. Ramos was a guest at the Palmer Hotel. His room was broken into and a thief took his overcoat and $200. Ramos demanded to be reimbursed for his loss. The hotel refused to pay and claimed that it was relieved of liability for the loss because

it was not responsible for thefts from its guests' rooms. Ramos sued the hotel. Should Ramos win?

6. A common carrier accepted a shipment of goods in Chicago for delivery to a buyer in Boston. While the goods were in transit between the two cities, they were destroyed by fire caused by an employee's negligence. Is the carrier liable for the destruction of the goods?

7. The Grand Moving Company was a common carrier engaged in the moving of household furniture. Alvarez asked the moving company to transport two pianos to a neighboring city. Can the Grand Moving Company refuse to transport these pianos?

8. The Empire Ceramics Co. shipped a box of vases and dishes via the Sumoto Trucking Co. Some of the dishes were broken during transit. An examination of the box showed that the damage had been caused by improper packing. Is Sumoto Trucking Co. liable for the loss?

9. Rogers was notified by the hotel where she was a guest that valuables should be placed in the hotel safe. Rogers left a ring valued at $400 with the hotel clerk for safekeeping. That night two robbers forced the clerk to open the safe and the ring was stolen. Was the hotel liable to Rogers for the loss?

10. West entered a bus depot to buy a ticket. Before she was able to buy her ticket, she tripped and fell over a mop and pail that had been left in the aisle by a cleaning person. West claimed the bus company was liable for her injury. Is she correct?

11. Peelright Banana Co. shipped four carloads of bananas on Lehigh Railroad from Los Angeles to New York City. A freak snowstorm caused a three-day delay while the bananas were being shipped. When the train arrived in New York City, the bananas were ruined because of the delay and low temperatures. Is Lehigh Railroad responsible for the loss?

12. Goode Galleries shipped a valuable painting worth $100,000 via Interstate Airlines to a Chicago gallery. When the painting was shipped, Goode told the airline what the painting was worth, but Goode also stated that it was unwilling to insure it for that amount. Goode paid Interstate an extra fee of $50 to insure the painting for $25,000. When the plane arrived in Chicago, the painting was missing, apparently stolen. For how much is Interstate liable?

13. Andrews left a fur jacket in a cloakroom at the Johnson Hotel while having lunch. The cloakroom was unattended, and there was a sign over the door saying that the hotel was "not responsible for loss or theft of personal belongings." When Andrews returned to the cloakroom after lunch, the jacket was gone. Andrews sued the hotel for the value of the jacket. Can she recover?

Cases to Decide

1. Bidlake, a guest at the Shirley Hotel, gave the keys to his car to a uniformed hotel employee and asked to have his car parked. The employee instead took the car for a "joy ride" and then left it on a public street near the hotel. When Bidlake located it the next morning, it was damaged and a number of articles that were in the glove compartment were missing. Was the hotel liable? (*Bidlake* v. *Shirley Hotel Co.*, 133 Colo 166, 292 P2d 749)

2. Marriott shipped canned goods from Kansas to Maryland on the Norfolk & Western Railroad. A severe rainstorm occurred and five inches of rain fell in four hours, something that had not happened in twenty years. The train derailed when a creek overflowed and washed out the road bed. Marriott sued for the loss of the canned goods. The railroad's defense was that the accident resulted from an act of God; thus, the railroad was not responsible. Was the railroad correct? (*Marriott Corporation* v. *Norfolk & Western RR Co.*, 319 FSupp 646)

3. The Ambassador Athletic Club was a nonprofit social club, organized to promote sports and recreational activities. It rented out a limited number of rooms to members and their guests for a fee. The state of Utah tried to collect sales tax from the club for the rental of hotel rooms. Would the club be considered a hotel? (*Ambassador Athletic Club* v. *Utah State Tax Commission*, 496 P2d 883, 27 Utah 2d 372)

4. Covington was injured when an ambulance in which she was a passenger collided with another car. The ambulance driver was speeding and had gone through a stop sign. Covington sued for damages. The ambulance's insurance company said that the ambulance was not a common carrier and was liable only for ordinary negligence.

Was the insurance company correct? (*Home Insurance Co.* v. *Covington*, Arkansas 501 SW2d 219)

5. Gillert shipped ski clothing samples on United Airlines from New York to San Francisco for an exhibition at a trade show. On the shipping document, Gillert declared that the value of the samples was $1,500. The samples did not arrive on time, resulting in a loss of current and future business and damaging Gillert's reputation. Gillert sued United for negligence, asking for $40,000 in damages. Is Gillert entitled to collect the $40,000? (*Gillert* v. *United Airlines*, 474 F2d 77)

6. Mirski shipped thousands of boxes of cherries from Yakima, Washington, to Cincinnati, Ohio, over the Chesapeake and Ohio Railroad. The cherries were in good condition when they were delivered to the railroad but they were spoiled when they arrived at their destination. There was no unusual delay while the cherries were being transported. Mirski sued the railroad for damages. Is the railroad liable? (*Mirski* v. *Chesapeake and Ohio Railroad Co.*, 31 Ill 2d 324, 202 NE 2d 22)

7. Bronson was a guest at the Delta Hotel. He left an expensive watch on the dresser in the room, locked the door, and went out for lunch. When Bronson returned, the watch was gone. It was discovered that the door lock had not been working properly and that anyone could enter the room easily. The statute in the state in which the hotel was located exempted hotelkeepers from any liability whatsoever unless guests deposited valuable objects in the hotel's safe-deposit box. Was the hotel liable for Bronson's loss? (*Walls* v. *Cosmopolitan Hotels, Inc.*, 435 P2d 1373)

Craig Wilson delivered his 28-foot sailboat to Upstate Marina for storage during the winter months. He paid the monthly storage fee in advance and left the premises.

A few hours later, the manager of Upstate, finding that the marina's storage facilities were already filled to capacity, arranged to have the boat delivered to the Genesee Marina and Storage for winter storage. Two weeks later, the boat was destroyed in a fire at Genesee. There was no evidence of negligence on the part of Genesee Marina.

Wilson brought an action against Upstate Marina for the loss of his sailboat.

The Trial

During the trial, the manager of Upstate Marina testified that it was common practice for marinas that were filled to transfer boats to other marinas. He further testified that he never notified Wilson of the fact that the boat was going to be stored in another facility. The manager of the Genesee Marina testified that his marina had taken every precaution and had installed every known safety device to protect against loss by fire. The fire that damaged Wilson's boat, and many other boats, was the result of a severe electrical storm.

The Arguments at Trial

During the trial, Wilson's attorney argued that as a bailee, Upstate Marina was absolutely liable for any damage that occurred to the boat. The attorney also argued that Wilson and Upstate Marina had a bailment contract, which was breached when the boat was delivered to another marina for storage.

Upstate Marina's attorney argued that Upstate Marina was obligated only to provide reasonable care and that it had done so. The attorney further argued that as the damage was caused by an act of God, Upstate was not responsible for the loss.

Questions to Discuss

1. Who has the stronger arguments, Wilson or Upstate Marina? Why?
2. Would Upstate have been liable for the loss if it had notified Wilson that his boat was going to be transferred to another facility?
3. If you were the judge or jury hearing this case, for whom would you decide? Why?
4. If Wilson had sued Genesee Marina instead of Upstate, would he have succeeded in obtaining a judgment against Genesee? Why or why not?

PART IX

INSURANCE

1 Explain the need for insurance.

2 Name the six most common types of property and casualty insurance and the risks covered by each type.

3 Describe the standard clauses found in most property and casualty insurance policies.

4 Distinguish among the various types of automobile insurance coverage.

5 Explain and compare the basic types of life insurance available.

6 Describe the standard clauses found in most life insurance policies.

7 Define the five basic types of health insurance.

Chapter 35

Property and Casualty Insurance

CHAPTER PREVIEW

This chapter describes the nature of insurance, with emphasis on loss of or damage to property. It discusses the ways in which insurance may be purchased and from whom.

Insurance policies are contracts and are subject to the same rules. This chapter also outlines certain conditions that are peculiar to insurance policies in general, such as when protection begins, how claims must be made, and what deductibles are. The chapter continues with a discussion of the various types of property risks for which insurance may be obtained, including fire, theft, and liability for damage to others.

The chapter concludes with an explanation of standard clauses found in all policies that insure property, including what property the policy covers, how the policy may be canceled, and how the right to assign the policy to a third person is handled.

THE NATURE OF INSURANCE

Risk and uncertainty are always with us. We are constantly exposed to the risk of accident, illness, theft, injury, and death. If we had to bear all these risks alone, we would have to keep large sums of money on hand to cover them or face financial disaster.

Insurance is a means of sharing risks with other people to limit economic loss. An insurance company sets up a fund to reimburse or repay those who suffer similar losses. This reimbursement is called **indemnification.** To join the fund, a person, the **insured,** submits an application to an insurance company, the **insurer.** If the applicant is accepted, the insurance company issues a **policy,** a written contract of insurance, to the insured. The policy describes such things as the types of risks covered, the amount of coverage (called the **face value** of the policy), and the time period of the policy. The insured pays a set amount of money, called a **premium,** for the coverage.

The amount of the premium varies depending on the amount and type of loss covered, the number of people in the fund, and the risk involved. For example, the risk of loss by fire for a wooden home is much greater than for a brick home. A fire insurance premium for a wooden home will thus be higher than for a brick home.

Insurance is based on the fact that not everyone who participates will suffer a loss at the same time. As a result, there will always be money in the fund to pay for the losses that do occur. This helps to keep premiums at a minimum.

PURCHASING INSURANCE

Insurance may be issued by insurance companies, savings banks, and government agencies. In many states, savings banks are permitted to sell life insurance, although the type and amounts of coverage are limited. The federal government provides flood insurance, crop insurance, bank deposit insurance, and health and disability insurance. In addition, it provides life insurance for members of the armed forces.

Most insurance is purchased from insurance agents or brokers. An **insurance agent** is an employee of a specific insurance company who sells insurance policies only for that company. An **insurance broker** is an independent business person who represents the insured. The broker determines the type and amount of insurance needed and secures it from one of several different companies. In most states, both agents and brokers must be licensed by the state.

A person wishing to buy insurance submits a written application to a broker or agent. Because insurance may provide a large return for a small investment, the possibility of fraud is always present. Insurance companies try to prevent fraud by learning as much as possible about the risks involved and the applicant. An application for insurance is a primary source of information. An applicant for auto insurance will be asked about age, health, occupation, address, driver training, and type of automobile. An applicant for health or life insurance will be asked about age, occupation, prior medical treatment, family history, and so forth.

Based on the information on the application and from its own investigation, the insurance company decides whether to issue the policy. The decision is usually based on the nature and extent of the risk. Any false information, concealment, or misrepresentation of information that misleads the insurance company permits the company to cancel the policy or to refuse to pay any claims, *provided* the company relied on the false information in issuing the policy and the false information was important in the decision to issue the policy.

> You applied for a life insurance policy and gave your height as 5'10" in the application. Your actual height is 5'11". Although this information is false, it would have little effect on the company's decision to issue a policy to you. The company cannot cancel this policy because you gave false information about your height. ■

False information provided by an applicant may make a policy voidable, regardless of whether the misrepresentation was accidental or deliberate. In addition, an applicant's failure to disclose important facts may make the policy voidable. The test is whether the insurance company would have issued the policy had it known of the withheld information.

> Krone applied for accident insurance and was asked if her occupation was hazardous. She answered this and other questions properly, but did not disclose her hobby of racing cars. Even though she was not asked about her hobby, failure to disclose it may allow the company to cancel the policy or refuse to pay any claims. The company probably would not have issued the policy had it known of Krone's hobby. ■

An insurance policy is similar to other types of contracts and is subject to the same rules regarding offer and acceptance, competent parties, and consideration. In addition, there are certain conditions peculiar to insurance policies.

When Protection Begins

When a policy becomes effective depends on the type of policy, its terms, and from whom it is purchased.

A policy obtained from an insurance broker does not become effective until it is accepted by a company. A broker is not an agent of an insurance company and thus cannot bind any company. In contrast, an insurance agent is an employee of an insurance company and may bind the company when an application is made. The agent may orally agree to provide insurance protection until the policy issued.

> ■ You bought a home, paying for it with a bank mortgage. To protect its interest, the bank wanted you to buy property insurance. You called your insurance agent and requested immediate coverage. If the agent orally agreed to provide that coverage, the insurance company is legally bound on the policy when its agent accepts. ■

The agent may also issue a **binder,** a temporary insurance policy. The binder is a written memorandum of the oral agreement reached. The binder is effective until the company either accepts or rejects the application. Any loss occurring during this time is covered. If a binder is not given, a policy becomes effective when it is delivered or mailed to the insured. Some policies, such as those for life insurance, become effective only when the first premium is paid. Very often a policy becomes effective according to the terms stated in the application, such as approval of the application or payment of the premium.

Many people buy insurance through the mail or from vending machines in air, train, and bus terminals. Insurance purchased by mail is not effective until the policy is signed and mailed to the buyer. Insurance purchased through a vending machine becomes effective when the insured inserts a properly completed application and a premium in the machine and receives a receipt.

Insurable Interest

A person who wishes to buy insurance must have a financial interest in the item being insured, either the life of another person or property. The policyholder must suffer financially if a loss occurs. This interest is known as **insurable interest.** For example, a person who has possession of stolen property does not have valid title to the property and would not suffer financially if a loss occurred. Therefore, that person would have no insurable interest and would not be able to obtain a valid insurance policy on the stolen property.

Without an insurable interest, a person who buys insurance is simply gambling that a loss will occur. This person may even cause the destruction of the insured property or the death of the insured person simply to collect the proceeds of the insurance policy. If there is no insurable interest, the policy is void. If a loss does occur, the policyholder may recover only the premiums paid, not the proceeds.

■ Bates owned a home that was insured against fire. She sold the house but failed to tell the insurance company that she no longer owned it. Bates continued to pay the premiums on her policy. If the house burns, the insurance company will not be liable on the policy because Bates no longer has an insurable interest in the house. However, the insurance company will have to return to Bates any premiums paid after she sold the house. ■

Exclusions

Insurance policies are very specific about the risks covered and any exceptions. An exception, or risk that is not covered, is known as an **exclusion.** An accident policy, for example, might exclude injuries suffered in a hazardous sport. An insurance company may often be very liberal in paying claims, but its responsibilities are limited by the terms of the policy.

■ The insurance policy on your home covered damage to the roof caused by ice, but excluded any additional damage. If ice on the roof caused water to leak into your home, damaging your carpets, your insurance company might indemnify you for the damage to your carpets, but it is not obligated to do so under the policy. ■

Amount of Coverage

The amount of coverage stated in the policy may be valued coverage or open coverage. **Valued coverage,** also called "actual cash value coverage," means that the insurance company will pay the original cost, less depreciation, when a loss occurs. **Open coverage,** also known as "replacement cost coverage," means that when a loss occurs, the insurance company will pay the cost of repairing or replacing the item damaged or destroyed up to the face amount of the policy, without subtracting anything for depreciation and regardless of the original cost of the item. Most property damage policies have valued coverage. For an additional premium, the coverage is changed to open coverage.

■ Grace's car was insured for $5,000 under a policy with open coverage. If it is damaged in an accident and would cost $2,500 to repair, the insurance company would pay Grace only the sum of $2,500, not the full $5,000 amount. ■

Deductible Clause

To reduce the premium amount, many insurance policies (other than for life insurance) contain a deductible clause. The **deductible** is the agreed-upon amount of the loss that the insured pays. The insurance company pays all or a percentage of the loss over and above the deductible. As most claims are small ones, the higher the deductible, the less risk for the insurance company and the lower the premiums for the insured. In effect, the insured becomes a partner with the insurance company in sharing the risk of loss.

> Bergen insured his boat for $3,000, with a $250 deductible. The boat hit a submerged log and would cost $1,000 to repair. Bergen will receive $750 from the insurance company ($1,000 minus the $250 deductible amount). ■

Claims

All insurance policies list specific procedures for filing a claim. The insured must notify the insurer of the loss, usually in writing, within a reasonable time after the loss. The insured must also provide the insurer with a sworn statement showing proof of the loss and a list of the property lost or damaged. If property is stolen, the insured must notify the police as well as the insurer. The police can then investigate the theft and perhaps recover the stolen property. If the insured does not follow these procedures, the insurer may not pay the claim.

> Martin insured her camera against theft. While on a skiing trip, the camera was stolen from her locked car. She reported the theft to the insurance company but failed to notify the police. Because Martin did not notify the police as required, the insurance company would not have to cover the loss of her camera, although it may. ■

After a claim is submitted, the insurance company will investigate and try to settle the claim. The insurance company representative who handles this settlement is called an **adjuster.** The insured should give the adjuster all the details of the claim: date and time of loss, circumstances, witnesses, damage, and any other helpful information. After investigating the loss, the company may either repair the damaged property, replace it with similar property, or pay the agreed-upon value to the insured. The company, not the insured, chooses the method of settling the claim. If the insured and the company cannot agree on the value of the damaged or lost property, they may have to go to court or arbitration to determine the value.

An insurance company often pays for a loss caused by someone other than the insured. If this happens, the company has the right to try to recover what it paid out from the person responsible for the loss. This right is known as **subrogation.**

> Cable's boat was accidentally rammed by Ford's boat. After paying for the damage to Cable's boat, Cable's insurance company can sue Ford for the amount of damages paid out. ■

After a settlement is reached, the insured will be asked to sign a release before the claim is paid. A **release** is a formal document stating that the insured has been paid for the claim and that the insurer has no further responsibility. If the claim is a small one, the release is usually on the back of the settlement check. Often, however, it is a separate document. The insured should not sign a release without being fully satisfied with the settlement and its terms.

PROPERTY AND CASUALTY INSURANCE

Property and casualty insurance protects the insured against loss or damage to real or personal property. The loss may affect the insured's property or someone else's property for which the insured is responsible. Most policies cover loss by fire, theft, windstorm, and water, but almost any peril can be insured against. Any risk or peril that is not covered is an exclusion, such as damage caused by a military invasion.

The most common types of property and casualty insurance are fire insurance, burglary and theft insurance, liability insurance, marine insurance, all-risk insurance, and multi-peril insurance.

Fire

Fire insurance protects against loss caused by fire or lightning. The loss, however, must be the result of an actual fire, by a burning or flaming fire. Scorching due to heat would not be covered.

■ You dropped a hot iron onto a plastic tabletop, melting the tabletop. Because no flame or burning occurred, this damage is not covered by fire insurance. ■

The damage must also be caused by a hostile fire. A **hostile fire** is one that is accidental and uncontrollable or that escapes from its usual place. A **friendly fire** is one that is not out of control and remains in its intended place, such as a fireplace.

■ Rupert started a fire in his fireplace one evening. He added too much wood and the fire became too hot. Sparks escaped from the fireplace and burned the nearby carpeting. Because the fire did not remain in its intended place, the damage to the carpeting was caused by a hostile fire. ■

In recent years, the hostile/friendly fire distinction has been rejected by more and more courts. Instead, "hostile" fires have been defined as those that are not related to a normal household use of fire. "Friendly" fires have been defined as those due to an intentionally lit flame, such as the pilot light in the furnace.

The fire must also be the proximate cause of the damage. **Proximate cause** means that the fire must be the direct or natural cause of the damage or loss.

■ A fire started in the basement of a restaurant when a short circuit occurred. Smoke from the fire seeped into the kitchen above, spoiling large quantities of food. The loss of the food would be covered because it was due to smoke, a natural result of the fire. ■

Every state in the United States has adopted a similar form for basic fire insurance coverage. This form, known as the **standard fire insurance policy,** insures against loss or damage from fire or lightning. For an additional premium, additional insurance coverage may be obtained and added to the standard policy. These additions are commonly referred to as riders, forms, or endorsements.

The most common rider added to the standard fire policy is an **extended coverage rider.** It insures against loss or damage from windstorm, hail, aircraft, riot, vehicles, explosion, and smoke. A burglary and theft rider is often added to insure against loss of property owned by the insured or a member of the family. This rider covers property stolen or seized after a forcible entry.

Burglary and Theft

Burglary and theft insurance covers loss of property stolen from a residence or business. It also covers property that a person has placed in a bank or warehouse for safekeeping. This insurance covers only personal belongings. It does not cover automobiles and motorcycles, which are covered under other types of policies.

Personal and Public Liability

Personal liability insurance protects against loss from claims made by persons injured as a result of the actions of the insured. Malpractice insurance is an example of personal liability insurance. **Public liability insurance** protects property owners against claims for injuries caused by the negligence or other acts of the insured, or others, on the insured's property.

Marine

Marine insurance protects against loss or damage to ships, cargo, crew, and passengers for such "perils of the sea" as sinking, bad weather, and capsizing. It is the oldest form of insurance and is often called ocean marine insurance.

All-Risk

An all-risk policy, called a **floater** (or inland marine) **policy,** insures personal property against loss from all causes except those specifically excluded. How the loss occurred, where or when it occurred, and who caused it are not important. Such policies are often carried on jewelry, furs, cameras, musical instruments, and the baggage carried by travelers.

■ You purchased an all-risk policy for your bicycle. One day you left it outside a store while you went shopping. When you returned, the bicycle was gone. It was never found, although there was no proof of theft. You are insured for this loss. ■

Multi-Peril

Since 1947 there has been a growing tendency to combine various types of coverage in a single insurance policy, called a **multi-peril policy.** The emphasis of the policy is on who is insured rather than what perils are insured against. The most common type of multi-peril policy is a homeowners policy.

The **homeowners policy** is available to those who own a one- or two-family home. It combines fire and liability insurance, provides the convenience of having one policy and paying one premium, and usually costs less than separate coverage for each peril.

A homeowners policy covers loss or damage to a house and other structures, such as garages and tool sheds. It also covers the contents of the house and personal property whether on or off the premises. A homeowners policy provides protection against claims made for damage to the personal property of guests or for injuries to them while they are on the property. An important part of a homeowners policy is the coverage for living expenses, including hotel expenses and meals at restaurants, because the insured cannot occupy her or his home because of the damage.

Special forms of homeowners policies are available for owners of mobile homes and condominiums and for renters. Special riders can even be added to cover losses due to floods and earthquakes.

There are three types of homeowners policies. The *basic form,* (also known as *HO-1*) insures against the first 11 perils in Figure 35.1. The *broad form,* (also known as *HO-2*) covers 18 listed perils. The *comprehensive form,* (also known as *HO-3*) is practically an all-risk policy.

STANDARD CLAUSES IN POLICIES

Almost all the property and casualty insurance policies described in this chapter contain provisions or clauses that are standard throughout the United States.

Coverage

Each insurance policy contains a clause describing what risks are covered. While some insurance companies are liberal when paying claims for losses, they are actually liable only for those risks mentioned in the policy. The standard fire insurance policy, for example, insures against losses caused directly or indirectly by a hostile fire. If your house catches fire, you could recover the value of the furniture destroyed in the fire—a direct loss. You

```
┌─────────────────────────────────────────────────────────────────┐
│ COMPREHENSIVE                                                     │
│ ┌───────────────────────────────────────────────────────────┐   │
│ │ BROAD                                                       │   │
│ │ ┌───────────────────────────────────────────────────────┐ │   │
│ │ │ BASIC                          Perils                  │ │   │
│ │ │  1. Fire or lightning           7. Vehicles           │ │   │
│ │ │  2. Loss of property removed    8. Smoke              │ │   │
│ │ │     from premises endangered by 9. Vandalism and      │ │   │
│ │ │     fire or other perils           malicious mischief │ │   │
│ │ │  3. Windstorm or hail          10. Theft              │ │   │
│ │ │  4. Explosion                  11. Breakage of glass  │ │   │
│ │ │  5. Riot or civil commotion        constituting a     │ │   │
│ │ │  6. Aircraft                       part of the        │ │   │
│ │ │                                    building           │ │   │
│ │ └───────────────────────────────────────────────────────┘ │   │
│ │                                                             │   │
```

12. Falling objects
13. Weight of ice, snow, sleet
14. Collapse of building(s) or any part thereof
15. Sudden and accidental tearing asunder, cracking, burning, or bulging of a steam or hot water heating system or of appliances for heating water
16. Accidental discharge, leakage, or overflow of water or steam from within a plumbing, heating,

or air-conditioning system or domestic appliance
17. Freezing of plumbing, heating, and air-conditioning systems and domestic appliances
18. Sudden and accidental injury from artificially generated currents to electrical appliances, devices, fixtures, and wiring (TV and radio tubes not included)

All perils EXCEPT: Flood, earthquake, war, nuclear accidents, and others specified in your policy. Check your policy for a complete listing of perils excluded.

Figure 35.1 **Perils Insured Against in a Homeowner's Policy**

could recover for damage to your furniture from smoke or the water used to put out the fire—an indirect loss. You could not, however, recover for furniture stolen during the fire. That loss is *too* indirect.

An insurance policy is issued for a specific amount, the face value. Generally, the insured cannot recover more than the face value of the policy for loss or damage to property. If a home is worth $30,000 and is insured for that amount, the owner will recover $30,000 if the home is destroyed. If the home is valued at $40,000 but is insured for only $30,000, the owner can recover only $30,000 if it is destroyed.

One problem with specific coverage is that, because of inflation, the same amount of protection is worth less and less. In many states you can add an inflation rider. As costs and the value of your property go up, coverage increases.

■ Gold insured her stamp collection for $5,000. Three years later, the collection, then worth $6,500, was destroyed in a fire. If Gold had an inflation rider, the insurance company would pay her $6,500 for the loss. ■

Personal property often depreciates with age and use. Under most policies, the insurance company is liable only for the actual cash value of property if a loss occurs. Actual cash value is the cost of an item less depreciation because of age, condition, and so on. In many states you can add a replacement value rider to your policy. The insurance company will then pay you the replacement value or the amount needed to replace the item in new condition.

■ Carter purchased a camera for $200. One year later, he lost the camera. At the time of the loss, the camera was worth only $150, but would cost $250 to replace. With a replacement value rider, the insurance company would pay Carter $250. ■

Removal of Property

Premiums for property insurance are based on the fact that the insured property is located in a specific place. Moving the property to a different place usually increases the risk of loss. Most policies state that coverage stops if property is moved from its normal location, unless the insurance company has consented to the move.

■ Morgan purchased a standard fire insurance policy. A week later, she had to leave for six months on a work assignment. She stored her furniture at a friend's home. In case of damage, Morgan could not collect for the loss because she did not notify her insurance company about the transfer. ■

Vacancy

Premiums are also based on the assumption that the insured property is occupied and, therefore, secure. An unoccupied property is one from which the owner or tenant is temporarily absent, leaving furniture and clothing behind. A vacant property is one that the owner or tenant has abandoned with no intention of returning.

Most policies provide that coverage stops if the residence becomes vacant for more than sixty days. When the residence is reoccupied, coverage starts again. Coverage of property that becomes unoccupied continues, but it is often reduced to cover losses only for such occurrences as vandalism or freezing of water pipes.

■ Sanger had a standard fire insurance policy on a summer cottage he owned on Cape Cod. At the end of August, he closed up the cottage and removed all his possessions. In December a fire destroyed the cottage. Because the cottage had been vacant for more than sixty days, he could not recover for the loss. ■

Pro-Rata Liability

Some people overinsure property, believing that they can collect more than the value of the property if it is destroyed. To prevent this, policies usually provide that if the same property is insured with more than one company, each company is liable only for its proportionate share of the loss. This is known as **pro-rata liability.** The insured cannot collect the full amount from both companies.

> Walters owned a boat worth $5,000. She insured it for $5,000 with Ace Insurance Company and for $5,000 with Acme Insurance Company. If the boat is destroyed, Walters could collect only $5,000—one half (or $2,500) from each company. ■

Increase in Risk

Insurance policies cover specific risks. Any increase in those risks increases the possibility of loss. Most policies provide that any increased risk caused by the insured will result in a loss of coverage. If the insurance company consents to the increased risk, however, the coverage continues.

> Leaf was planning to remove several tree stumps from his property. He bought some dynamite and stored it in the basement of his home. If the dynamite explodes, the insurance company is not liable for the damage. ■

Coinsurance

Most fire insurance and homeowners policies include a **coinsurance** clause. This clause requires that the insured carry a minimum amount of insurance on the insured property. This minimum is usually stated as a percentage of the current value of the property, normally 80 percent. If the insured carries the required amount of insurance, the insurer will pay any loss in full up to the limit or face value of the policy.

> Juarez owned a home worth $40,000. Since her insurance policy contained an 80 percent coinsurance clause, Juarez insured her home for $32,000, the required amount. A fire caused $10,000 damage to the home. Because she carried the required amount of insurance, the insurance company will pay the full loss of $10,000. ■

If the required amount is not carried, the insurer is liable only for a percentage of the loss.

> Assume that Juarez carried only $16,000 worth of insurance, one half of the required amount. If a fire caused a $10,000 loss, Juarez would collect only $5,000, one half of the actual loss. ■

Insurable Interest

As with other types of insurance, the insured must have an insurable interest in the property. The insured must suffer a financial loss if there is damage to the property. Property owners or renters have an insurable interest. A person who has a contract to buy property has an insurable interest in that property. Bailees and pledgees have an insurable interest in the property for which they are responsible.

The insurable interest must exist both at the time insurance is purchased and at the time of the loss.

> Your aunt told you she planned to leave you her home in her will. You cannot insure her home when you learn this because you do not yet have an insurable interest in the property. Your aunt could change her mind or sell her home prior to her death. ■

Cancellation and Termination

Most property and casualty insurance policies terminate either when their terms expire or when they are canceled. They do not end just because a claim is paid. Property and casualty policies are written for specific periods of time, usually one year or three years. When the time period ends, the policy terminates.

Most property and casualty policies may be canceled by either the insured or the insurer at any time. Each party must notify the other of the cancellation. If the insured cancels the policy, the cancellation is effective when the insurance company receives the notice. If the insurer cancels the policy, the insurance company must notify the insured in writing that coverage will stop within a certain number of days. The number of days' notice required varies with each policy and with state law. The most common reason for cancellation of a policy by an insurance company is nonpayment of premiums.

Insurance premiums are always paid in advance. If the policy is canceled before the end of the term, the insured is entitled to a refund. The amount of the refund depends on who has canceled the policy. If the insurance company cancels, the refund is the full amount of the unused premium. This is known as the **prorated premium.** If the insured cancels, the refund is a lesser amount and is known as the **short rate.**

> On January 1 Meadows took out a fire insurance policy on his home and paid a one-year premium of $120. The insurance company canceled the policy as of August 31. The insurance policy was in effect for eight months, two thirds of the original term. Meadows will receive a refund of one third of the premium, or $40. ■

The insurance company is liable for any damage or injury that took place while the policy was in effect, even if the claim is filed after the policy has expired.

> Talbot fell on a slippery floor in your home and injured herself. Two weeks after the accident, your policy expired. One month later, Talbot developed a limp because of the fall and made a claim against you. The insurance company that insured you when Talbot fell would be liable for her injuries. ■

Assignment

Insurance is a personal contract between the insured and the insurer. An insurance company relies to a great extent on the character of the insured. It issues a policy only to someone it has investigated and found acceptable. If the insured could transfer rights in the policy to someone else, an insurance company could be in a difficult position. To prevent this, property and casualty policies cannot be assigned or transferred before a loss occurs without the consent of the insurance company. After a loss, the insured may assign the rights to the proceeds without the consent of the insurance company. In practice, most companies freely permit assignments when insured property is sold and the buyer wishes to take over an existing policy.

Summary of Important Legal Concepts

Insurance is a means of sharing risks of financial loss among a group of people. An insurance policy is a written contract between the insurance company and the insured, the costs of which (the premium) are based on the risk involved, the amount of coverage, and the number of people insured. All insurance policies, which may be purchased from a company agent or a broker who deals with many companies, contain similar provisions. These include the term of the policy, the need for an insurable interest, what is excluded from coverage, the deductible that is paid by the insured, and the procedures for filing a claim.

Property and casualty insurance protects against loss from fire, burglary, and theft. It also covers injuries to the person insured and injuries to others. There are also special policies that insure against a variety of risks and others that cover loss from any cause whatsoever.

Property and casualty insurance policies contain standard clauses that define the legal relationship between the insurance company and the insured. These clauses state what the policy covers, what happens if property is removed from its home, and what happens if insured real property becomes vacant. Such clauses also cover what occurs if there is an increase in risk, how a policy may be canceled, and whether a policy may be assigned.

Key Legal Terms to Know

Match the terms with the definitions that follow.

adjuster
binder
coinsurance
deductible
exclusion
extended coverage rider
face value
floater policy
friendly fire
homeowners policy
hostile fire
indemnification
insurable interest
insurance
insurance agent
insurance broker
insured
insurer
marine insurance
multi-peril policy
open coverage
personal liability insurance

policy
premium
property and casualty insurance
pro-rata liability
prorated premium
proximate cause
public liability insurance
release
short rate
standard fire insurance policy
subrogation
valued coverage

1. The cost for insurance coverage
2. An independent business person who purchases insurance for the insured from one of many companies
3. A company or agency that issues insurance
4. One who settles claims for the insurer
5. Proof of the settlement of a claim
6. A financial interest in the property or life being insured
7. An agreed-upon, specific amount of insurance proceeds payable for loss or damage
8. A system of sharing the risk of loss among a group of people
9. The written contract of insurance between the insurer and the insured
10. One who purchases an insurance policy
11. The amount of proceeds payable for loss or damage based on the actual cost of the repairs
12. A temporary insurance policy
13. An insurance company employee who sells insurance only for that company
14. A risk not covered by an insurance policy
15. Reimbursement for a loss
16. That part of a loss paid for by the insured
17. The amount of coverage provided by an insurance policy
18. The right of an insurance company to recover from a person causing a loss
19. Amount of premium returned to the insured when a policy is canceled by the insurer
20. A fire that is not out of control and that stays in its intended place
21. Insurance protecting property owners against claims for injuries caused by the insured's negligence or the negligence of a guest
22. The basic insurance policy covering loss from fire and lightning

23. A clause requiring the insured to maintain a certain minimum amount of insurance
24. An all-risk policy that covers loss or damage to personal property from almost any cause
25. Insurance covering ships, crew, and cargo
26. The direct or natural cause of loss or damage
27. Additional coverage insuring against loss from windstorms, hail, aircraft, and so forth
28. A multi-peril policy insuring homeowners against many risks in the same policy
29. Insurance that protects against loss from claims made by persons injured by the actions of the insured
30. A single insurance policy combining various types of coverage with emphasis on who is insured rather than perils insured against
31. Insurance against loss or damage to real or personal property
32. A fire that becomes uncontrollable and escapes from its usual place
33. An insurance company's liability for a loss when there is more than one policy on the same property
34. The amount of the premium refunded when the insured cancels a policy

Questions and Problems to Discuss

1. What are the six most common types of property and casualty insurance?
2. Johnson applied for fire insurance on his boat. He paid a premium and received a binder that stated, "This policy not effective until the property insured is inspected and the policy is approved by the company." Before the policy was issued, the boat was destroyed in a fire. Can Johnson recover for the loss?
3. Stewart drove trucks that carried explosives. Blake, Stewart's friend, decided to buy a policy insuring Stewart's life. Does Blake have an insurable interest in Stewart's life?
4. Sanders owned a stamp collection on which she had a valued insurance policy for $1,500. The entire collection was stolen. The insurance company offered to pay Sanders $1,000, claiming that was the value of the collection at the time it was stolen. Must Sanders settle for $1,000?
5. Marshall purchased a standard fire insurance policy on his home. Marshall's policy contained

a 90 percent coinsurance clause. The home was worth $40,000, and Marshall carried $36,000 worth of insurance on it. A fire broke out in the home, causing $10,000 damage. How much can Marshall collect for the loss?

6. Farley was broiling some steaks in her kitchen. Some grease splashed on the curtains, ruining them. Can she collect for the damage under a standard fire insurance policy?

7. Clinton owned a grocery store and insured it with a standard fire insurance policy. The building was destroyed by a fire set by rioters protesting high prices. Clinton filed a claim for the loss. Must the insurance company pay for the loss?

8. Higgins and her family left their home for a six-week vacation. While they were away, thieves broke into their home and stole the television set. Would their homeowners policy cover the loss?

9. Janley came home from a movie one afternoon and could not find her diamond ring. There was no sign of any break-in, and the ring was never found. If Janley had an all-risk policy covering the ring, must the insurance company compensate her for the loss?

10. Dorn owned a valuable painting, which he sold to Craven. The painting was insured under a theft policy that Dorn assigned to Craven at the time of the sale. Neither party told the insurance company of the sale. If the painting is stolen from Craven while the policy is still in effect, is the insurance company liable for the loss?

Cases to Decide

1. On January 17 the Arleys purchased insurance on some property they owned in Nevada. At the request of the broker, the insurance company back-dated the policy five days, making it effective as of January 12. The insurance company learned that the property had been severely damaged on January 15 and refused to cover the loss. Is the company bound by the action of the broker? (*Arley* v. *United Pacific Insurance Company,* Oregon 379 F2d 183)

2. Haines Manufacturing Co. made farm equipment. A farmer was severely injured using one of the company's machines. Haines was notified of the accident. Because Haines did not believe it was responsible for the accident, Haines did not notify its insurance company even though the policy required it. When the farmer sued eleven months after the accident, Haines notified the insurance company. The insurance company claimed it was not liable. Must the insurance company cover the loss? (*Utica Mutual Ins. Co.* v. *C. L. Haines Manufacturing Co., Inc.,* New York 55 AD2d 834)

3. Moore applied for accident insurance on her husband. She paid the first premium and the insurance agent told her the policy would be issued soon. When she again asked about the policy, the agent told her she would receive the policy shortly. In fact, the application had been rejected; the policy was never issued. When her husband died in an accident, Moore made a claim under the policy. The insurance company rejected the claim on the grounds that the policy had never been issued. Moore sued the company. Can she collect? (*Moore* v. *Palmetto State Life Insurance Company,* 222 S Car 492, 73 SE2d 688)

4. Antell submitted an offer to purchase a building. At the time he made the offer, he paid a portion of the purchase price in cash and received the keys to the building from the owner. Pearl Assurance issued a fire insurance policy covering the property. A few months after the policy was issued, the building was totally destroyed by fire. Pearl Assurance refused to pay the loss, claiming that Antell had no insurable interest in the building because at the time of the loss title had not been transferred and Antell had not paid the balance of the purchase price. Is Pearl correct? (*Antell* v. *Pearl Assurance Company,* 252 Minn 118, 89 NW2d 726)

5. Miller, a jewelry dealer, gave a ring to Friedman, another dealer, to sell. Friedman in turn consigned the ring to a third dealer, Willner, whose body was subsequently recovered from the East River in New York City. The day before his death, Willner had stated that he still had the ring in his possession and was trying to sell it. The ring was never found or returned to Miller. The insurance policy covering the ring insured against all risks of loss or damage arising from any cause whatsoever. Was the insurer liable under the policy? (*Miller* v. *Boston Insurance Company,* 420 Pa 556, 218 A2d 275)

6. The Pecks owned a building in which they operated a lawn and garden supply business. Their

fire insurance policy provided that the insurance company would not be liable for loss caused by any increased hazards within the control of the insured. Three boys came into the store one day and accidentally ignited some fireworks the Pecks had for sale. A fire resulted, causing damage to the property. The insurance company would not cover the loss. Can Peck force the insurance company to pay? (*Standard Marine Insurance Co.* v. *Peck,* Colorado 342 P2d 661)

7. Feinstein bought a home in New York so that she could live near her son. Her insurance policy included a clause suspending coverage while the building was "vacant." When her son moved to New Jersey, she also moved to New Jersey, but kept the house in New York as a vacation home. Since she spent vacations and some holidays and weekends there, she kept some furniture and linens at the house for her use. While she was in New Jersey, her property in New York was vandalized. The insurance company would not cover the loss and Feinstein sued. Can Feinstein recover? (*Feinstein* v. *Reliance Ins. Co.,* New York 85 Misc 2d 819)

Chapter 36

Automobile Insurance

CHAPTER PREVIEW

CHAPTER HIGHLIGHTS Proof of financial responsibility for accidents is mandatory in every state. This chapter explains the need for such responsibility, the minimum amounts of coverage required in each state, and the most common form of automobile insurance. It continues with a discussion of the various types of insurance coverage available, including injury to others, damage to property, injuries caused by uninsured motorists, and damage to the insured's vehicle caused by a collision. The concept of no-fault insurance is explored, together with the administration of the no-fault system. Finally, the chapter ends with a detailed description of the steps to be taken in the event of an automobile accident.

THE NEED FOR AUTOMOBILE INSURANCE

Buying a car is an exciting experience, especially when it's your first car. Accidents do happen, however, and you must be prepared for them.

Persons who own or drive cars need protection in case of injury to themselves or damage to their property. They also need to protect themselves against loss for injuries to others or damage to the property of others.

All states have **financial responsibility laws.** The purpose of these laws is to ensure that the owner or driver of a vehicle involved in an accident is financially able to pay for any damage. A driver or owner must have proof of such responsibility at all times. In some states, a driver or vehicle owner must provide proof of such responsibility before a vehicle can be registered. In other states, proof must be provided at the time of an accident or within a certain period of time after one takes place. Failure to have such protection may result in a fine or the suspension or revocation of a driver's license.

The financial responsibility laws set minimum liability limits that registered vehicles must meet. Current state requirements are shown in Table 36.1. In the table, the first figure refers to bodily injury liability limits for injuries to one person, the second figure to such limits for injuries to all those injured, and the third figure to property liability.

Proof of financial responsibility may be a bond or a deposit to cover any damages, but the most common way of providing such proof is to carry vehicle insurance. In some states, vehicle liability insurance is compulsory.

In New York State, for example, an automobile owner must have insurance in the amount of $20,000 to cover injuries to one person, $100,000 to cover injuries to all persons involved, and $5,000 to cover damage to property.

TYPES OF AUTOMOBILE INSURANCE COVERAGE

A vehicle owner may satisfy financial responsibility laws by obtaining insurance with basic bodily injury and property damage liability coverage. Other types of coverage are available and are often included in a package policy. The most common types of coverage purchased are bodily injury, property damage, medical payments, and uninsured motorist. If the vehicle is new

TABLE 36.1   Automobile Minimum Financial Responsibility (1995 Summary)

State	Liability Limits (in thousands of dollars)	State	Liability Limits (in thousands of dollars)
Alabama	20/40/10	Montana	25/50/10
Alaska	50/100/25	Nebraska	25/50/25
Arizona	15/30/10	Nevada	15/30/10
Arkansas	25/50/15	New Hampshire	25/50/25
California	15/30/5	New Jersey	15/30/5
Colorado	25/50/15	New Mexico	25/50/10
Connecticut	20/40/10	New York	20/100/5
Delaware	15/30/10	North Carolina	25/50/15
District of Columbia	10/20/5	North Dakota	25/50/25
Florida	10/20/10	Ohio	12.5/25/7.5
Georgia	15/30/10	Oklahoma	10/20/10
Hawaii	35/unlimited/10	Oregon	25/50/10
Idaho	25/50/15	Pennsylvania	15/30/5
Illinois	15/30/10	Rhode Island	25/50/25
Indiana	25/50/10	South Carolina	15/30/5
Iowa	20/40/15	South Dakota	25/50/25
Kansas	25/50/10	Tennessee	25/50/10
Kentucky	25/50/10	Texas	20/40/15
Louisiana	10/20/10	Utah	25/50/15
Maine	20/40/10	Vermont	20/40/10
Maryland	20/40/10	Virginia	25/50/20
Massachusetts	20/40/10	Washington	25/50/10
Michigan	20/40/10	West Virginia	20/40/10
Minnesota	30/60/10	Wisconsin	25/50/10
Mississippi	10/20/5	Wyoming	25/50/20
Missouri	25/50/10		

or expensive to repair or replace, collision coverage and comprehensive physical damage coverage are often obtained. A portion of a page from a typical auto policy is shown in Figure 36.1.

Bodily Injury Liability

Bodily injury liability insurance protects the insured against claims for injuries to or the death of a guest in the insured's car, a pedestrian, or an occupant of another vehicle. Bodily injury insurance protects not only the insured but also members of the insured's family and anyone else who has permission to drive the insured's car. It also protects the insured and family members who drive a rented car or someone else's car with the owner's

physical damage coverages **(damage to your auto)**

COVERAGES

COMPREHENSIVE COVERAGE **We** will pay for **loss** to **your auto** not caused by collision or upset. **We** will pay for the **loss** less your declared **deductible. Loss** from contact with animals or falling or flying objects is covered. Broken glass is covered—even if caused by collision or upset—if **you** do not have Collision coverage. If **your** Comprehensive and Collision coverages have different **deductibles**, the smaller **deductible** will apply to broken glass.

Also, if **your auto** has a **loss** under this coverage **we** will:

1. pay for resulting **loss** of your clothing and luggage or that of any **relatives.** Maximum payment is $200. **We** will pay for stolen clothing or luggage only if **your auto** is stolen.
2. repay **your** travel costs after **your auto** is stolen. Maximum payment is $10 per day—not to exceed $300. These costs must be incurred within a certain time. It begins 48 hours after **you** report the theft to **us** and the police. It ends when **your auto** is returned to **you** or **we** pay for its **loss.**
3. repay **you** for the cost of travel from where **your auto** was disabled to where **you** were going. Maximum payment is $10.

COLLISION COVERAGE **We** will pay for **loss** to **your auto** caused by collision or upset. This includes broken glass. **We** will pay for the **loss** less your declared **deductible.** However, **we** will not subtract the **deductible** amount:

1. if **your auto** collides with another **motor vehicle** insured by **us**, or
2. for broken glass if **you** have full (no **deductible**) Comprehensive coverage in force.

Also if **your auto** has a **loss** under this coverage, **we** will:

1. pay for a resulting loss of **your** clothing and luggage or that of any **relatives**. Maximum payment is $200.
2. repay **you** for the travel cost to where **you** were going. Maximum payment is $10.

Figure 36.1 **Page Outlining Coverage from a Typical Automobile Insurance Policy**

permission. If the insured is found legally liable for the injuries that occurred, the insurance company will pay for the damages awarded, up to the limits of the policy. This insurance will also pay for the legal and court costs involved in defending any lawsuits brought against the insured.

It is important to note that the insurance company is responsible *only up to the limits of the policy;* the insured is responsible for any amount beyond the policy limits. This is why it is important for an owner of a motor vehicle to carry bodily injury liability insurance far in excess of the minimum coverage required by law.

Your car collided with another car, injuring that vehicle's occupants. They brought a lawsuit against you for $25,000 to recover for their injuries. Your bodily injury liability policy had a maximum coverage amount of

$10,000. The insurance company will pay any damages awarded, plus your legal expenses, up to the $10,000 limit. You are responsible for any damages and legal expenses over that amount. ■

Property Damage Liability

Property damage liability insurance protects the insured whose car damages the property of others. It also protects members of the insured's family and anyone who drives with the insured's permission. The property damaged is usually another car but may also be buildings, utility poles, or fences. In addition to covering damages, it will also pay for court costs and legal fees. It can be purchased in amounts beginning at $5,000. Most states require minimum property damage liability coverage under their financial responsibility laws.

■ While driving, Solomon swerved to avoid hitting a child and sideswiped a parked car. Solomon's property damage liability policy would cover the cost of repairing the damage to the parked car. Solomon's property damage liability insurance would not, however, pay for the damage to his own car. ■

Medical Payments

Medical payments insurance pays the medical expenses, up to the limits of the policy, for injuries suffered by anyone in the insured's car when an accident occurs. It also provides protection for the insured or members of the insured's family who are injured while riding in someone else's car or who are struck by a car while walking. Coverage is provided regardless of who was at fault. Coverage includes such expenses as x-rays, surgical expenses, ambulance charges, and hospital care. The expenses must have arisen within a certain time period after the accident, usually one year.

■ While driving to a movie one night with some friends, Klee was forced off the road and into a ditch by another car. Klee and her friends required emergency medical treatment for their injuries. All their expenses are covered by Klee's medical payments insurance in spite of the fact that another driver caused the accident. ■

Uninsured Motorists

Uninsured motorist insurance pays for injuries caused by an uninsured or a hit-and-run driver. It does not cover property damage. This insurance protects anyone in the insured's car who is injured when the accident occurred. It also protects the insured and members of the insured's family who are injured while in another person's car or while walking.

The insurance company will pay damages to those injured up to the amount of coverage required by the state's financial responsibility laws. In most areas of the United States, higher coverage can be purchased. To prevent false claims, most policies require that every effort be made to locate a hit-and-run driver.

> ■ Your car was struck by a hit-and-run driver one night and was badly damaged. Your loss would not be covered by uninsured motorist insurance because it does not cover property damage. ■

Collision

Collision insurance covers damage to the insured's car when it collides with another car or object (such as a telephone pole or fire hydrant) or when it turns over. This insurance covers the damage regardless of who was at fault. If someone else is at fault, the insured can collect from her or his insurance company immediately and need not wait to receive payment from the other driver's insurance company. Regardless of the amount of insurance carried, the insured can collect only for the actual damage to the car or for its fair market value if it is considered a total wreck.

> ■ Ritzmann lost control of his car and crashed into a tree. Damage to the car was $1,100. Ritzmann's collision insurance will cover the loss because he collided with another object (the tree); even though the collision was not with another vehicle, the collision insurance will cover the damages. ■

Collision insurance usually has a deductible clause. The deductible is that amount of the damage the insured must pay. The most common deductible amounts are $50, $100, $200, and $250. In any one accident, the insured must pay the first $50, $100, $200, or $250 worth of damages. The insurance company pays the balance. In the example, if Ritzmann had a $200 deductible, he would pay $200 and the insurance company would pay $900.

The insured can reduce the premium for collision insurance by choosing a higher deductible. The higher the deductible, the lower the premium for this coverage.

Comprehensive Physical Damage

Comprehensive insurance covers damage to the insured's car from a variety of sources other than collisions. It includes damage from theft, vandalism, falling objects, fire, flood, windstorm, earthquake, riot, and breakage of windows. Comprehensive coverage also pays for the cost of renting a car if the insured's car has been stolen. It does not pay for damage caused by mechanical difficulties or ordinary wear and tear or for the loss of the insured's personal property. It also does not cover damage to the property of others or bodily injuries.

> ■ Thieves stole your car from your garage. They had an accident and demolished your car. Comprehensive insurance protects you against the loss because the car was stolen. However, you can recover only the actual cash value of the car, not the amount you paid for it. ■

WHO IS COVERED BY AUTOMOBILE INSURANCE

Automobile insurance protects the owner of an automobile. If another person operates the car with the owner's permission, that person is also protected. This coverage is known as the **omnibus clause.**

Coverage under the omnibus clause is often a question of fact. Generally, members of an insured's family and those who drive with the insured's permission are covered under this clause. Like most other insurance policy clauses, the omnibus clause is interpreted in such a way as to protect the owner as much as possible. "Permission to drive" is often implied if the owner does not object to the operation of the car by someone else.

> ■ Chin asked for and received permission to drive Lyle's automobile. On many occasions after that, Chin drove Lyle's car and Lyle did not object. Lyle's permission to drive was implied, since she did not object when Chin used her car. ■

Most states have passed automobile **guest laws.** A guest is a passenger who rides free of charge. A passenger who shares expenses, even if a friend or relative, is not considered a guest. The guest laws relieve drivers of private vehicles of all liability to guests for injuries from an accident unless gross negligence is proven. "Gross negligence" is extreme recklessness or driving an unsafe car but failing to tell the guest that it is unsafe.

In states that have not passed guest laws, a driver may be liable for a guest's injuries if the driver is found negligent. In states with no-fault laws, the driver's insurance will protect the guest whether the driver is negligent or not. However, a guest who contributes to or knows of the negligence cannot recover for injuries even if the driver is negligent.

> ■ Crown, a passenger in Drake's car, was injured when a worn tire blew out while the car was traveling at a high speed. Crown knew about the worn tire but still went along for the ride. She cannot hold Drake responsible for her injuries. ■

NO-FAULT INSURANCE

Until the end of 1970, an automobile accident victim could collect damages for injuries only after proving that the other driver caused the accident. This system was time-consuming, often unfair, and expensive. The courts became clogged with lawsuits involving the question of fault. Delays were frequent, and accident victims often had to wait years before being compensated. Lawsuits often resulted in inconsistent decisions—victims of similar types of accidents received different amounts of compensation. The cost of this system, including legal fees and court costs, resulted in a continuous rise in insurance premiums.

To solve this problem, no-fault insurance was developed. Massachusetts was the first state to enact no-fault auto insurance legislation. Many states have followed Massachusetts's lead. It is even possible that the government may enact federal, nationwide no-fault insurance legislation.

The principle of **no-fault insurance** is that a person who was injured in an automobile accident should be compensated fully and quickly, regardless of who was at fault. In operation, an accident victim is compensated for financial loss by her or his own insurance company without having to bring a lawsuit to determine fault.

No-fault insurance laws vary from state to state, but the basic elements are as follows:

1. If an accident occurs, the injured person collects from her or his own insurance company for medical expenses and loss of income, regardless of who was at fault. An occupant of a car or a pedestrian injured by a car is paid by the insurance company that issued the policy covering the car.

2. Except in a few states, property damage is not covered.

3. The right to sue the other parties to the accident is limited to cases involving death or serious or permanent injuries. In some states, the injured person cannot sue unless medical expenses exceed a certain amount, known as the **threshold figure.**

HOW PREMIUMS ARE DETERMINED

As with other types of insurance, auto insurance premiums are based on the risk involved. The risk varies according to certain factors, such as the type of car and its use. Experience has shown that the newer the car, the safer it is. A car with low horsepower can't go as fast as a car with high horsepower and it is considered safer. Premiums are therefore higher for older and faster cars. Cars that are used only for occasional family trips have fewer accidents than those that are used for business. Consequently, the premiums for business-use cars are higher than for family-use cars. Premiums for more expensive cars, such as sports cars, are higher than for less expensive cars because of the higher cost of repairs and the difficulty of obtaining replacement parts.

The status of the driver affects premiums considerably. Experience has shown that younger drivers have more accidents than older ones, that men have more accidents than women, and that single drivers have more accidents than married drivers. Age is one of the most important considerations. Rates for drivers under twenty five years of age are often extremely high, but a discount is often given if the young driver successfully completes a driver education course. In many states a full-time student in high school or college with a good scholastic record is eligible for "good student" discount on automobile insurance rates. Drivers who have had accidents or incurred traffic violations are usually charged additional premiums for a certain period of time.

CANCELLATION OF AUTOMOBILE INSURANCE

The insured may cancel an insurance policy at any time. The insurance company has the right to cancel a policy for any reason within a certain number of days (usually thirty or sixty) after issuing it. After that time, the insurance company may cancel a policy only after giving advance notice to the insured and only for one or more of the following reasons:

1. Fraudulent statements in the insurance policy application
2. Failure to pay the premium
3. Suspension or revocation of the driver's license or revocation of the automobile registration

At the end of the policy period, both the insured and the insurance company have the right not to renew an automobile insurance policy. The insurance company is usually required, however, to notify the insured that it does not plan to renew the policy.

Because of the financial responsibility laws, cancellation or nonrenewal of an automobile insurance policy is a serious matter. If it becomes difficult to buy insurance from any company, a person may be placed in an **assigned risk pool.** Under this plan, several insurance companies combine, or pool, funds to set up a special automobile insurance fund. A person needing insurance is assigned to this plan and receives a policy for public liability only (bodily injury and property damage). Such a policy is usually limited to the minimum required by the financial responsibility laws and is very expensive.

WHAT TO DO IF YOU'RE INVOLVED IN AN ACCIDENT

An automobile accident may cause serious damage to persons and property. It is important to know what to do after an accident to minimize injuries and damage and to protect yourself if a claim is made. Certain steps should be taken at the time of the accident and after the accident.

At the Time of the Accident

If you are involved in an accident, stop at once and help anyone who is injured. Call the police and a doctor or an ambulance and make the injured person as comfortable as possible. Give first aid if you are capable of doing so. It is also important to prevent additional accidents by warning other motorists that an accident has occurred.

While this is being done, trade information with the other drivers involved in the accident. Exchange names, addresses, phone numbers, license and registration numbers, and insurance information. Get the names and addresses of any passengers. It is a good idea to write down the details of the accident while they are still fresh in your mind. Note the time, weather and road conditions, and other data. If you can, draw a diagram of what took place.

If there are witnesses to the accident, it is very important to get their names, addresses, phone numbers, and the license numbers of their cars. These witnesses may be of great help if there is a question of who was at fault.

After the Accident

Report the accident to your insurance company as soon as possible after the accident. All reports should be in writing and should contain all the details of the accident: date and time, location, vehicle information, parties involved, and circumstances. The insurance company may refuse to cover your claim if you do not notify them within a reasonable period of time after the accident.

State laws vary on when a report must be filed, with whom, and in what circumstances. All states require the filing of an accident report in the event of injury or death. If only property damage is involved, accident reports must be filed if the damage exceeds a certain amount. In most states you must file a report if the damage exceeds $100. The time limit for filing may be anywhere from five to thirty days after the accident. In most states, the report must be filed with the state's department of motor vehicles.

Filing an accident report is extremely important, since it may be used later if a claim is made. In many states failure to file the accident report is grounds for suspension or revocation of a driver's license. If necessary, your insurance company representative will help you fill out this report. You can obtain a report form at a police station, the department of motor vehicles, or the office of your insurance company or agent.

When to Consult an Attorney

If an accident produces no injuries and only minor property damage, let your insurance company handle all the details. Your company will provide and pay for legal assistance.

If you are involved in a serious accident causing injuries or severe property damage to yourself or others, consult an attorney at once. Your insurance company is responsible only to the limit of your policy; you are liable for any damages beyond that limit. Your attorney can work with your insurance company to defend you in any lawsuits brought against you or in bringing any lawsuit you may wish to file. If in doubt, consult an attorney.

Summary of Important Legal Concepts

All states have financial responsibility laws to ensure that owners and drivers of motor vehicles involved in accidents can pay for any damage for which they are legally liable. The most common way for car owners and drivers to meet these obligations is by purchasing automobile insurance.

Automobile insurance policies protect against injuries to others (bodily injury liability), damage to the property of others (property damage liability), medical expenses for injuries (medical payments), injuries caused by uninsured drivers or hit-and-run drivers (uninsured motorist), and damage to the insured's vehicle (collision and comprehensive).

Automobile insurance policies contain many standard clauses. These include who is covered by the policy, any deductible involved, and when a policy may be canceled.

No-fault insurance, which has been adopted in many states, eliminates the need to prove negligence in accidents involving nonserious injuries. The injured person's insurance company pays medical expenses regardless of who was at fault.

A person involved in an automobile accident should notify the proper public authorities and the insurance company immediately after an accident occurs. Failure to do so may result in the insurance company's refusal to honor any claim filed. Any person who has been involved in a serious accident that causes injury or serious property damage should consult an attorney.

Key Legal Terms to Know

Match the terms with the definitions that follow.

assigned risk pool
bodily injury liability insurance
collision insurance
comprehensive insurance
financial responsibility laws
guest laws
medical payments insurance
no-fault insurance
omnibus clause
property damage liability insurance
threshold figure
uninsured motorist insurance

1. Insurance that protects the insured against claims for damage to the property of others
2. Insurance for those having difficulty obtaining insurance from normal sources
3. Insurance against damage to the insured's car if it collides with a car or another object or if it turns over

4. Insurance coverage for injuries caused by a driver who has no insurance or by a hit-and-run driver
5. Insurance that protects the insured's car against damage from such perils as theft, vandalism, and falling objects
6. Insurance covering medical expenses for injuries suffered in an automobile accident
7. Insurance coverage for a person whose car injures or kills another person
8. Insurance covering bodily injuries regardless of who caused the accident
9. Laws that define responsibilities toward passengers in the insured's car
10. A state law requiring owners or drivers of cars involved in accidents to prove they can pay for any damage caused by the accident
11. Amount of medical expenses required before an injured person may sue under no-fault laws
12. Insurance coverage for members of the insured's family and those who drive the insured's car with permission

Questions and Problems to Discuss

1. What are the six types of coverage available in an automobile insurance policy?
2. Why were no-fault insurance laws passed?
3. Tree had a collision insurance policy on her car. One day Tree fell asleep at the wheel and ran into a telephone pole. The car was badly damaged and Tree filed a claim with her insurance company for the damage. Would Tree's insurance cover the damage to her car?
4. Klugman bought a car for $8,000 and insured it for that amount with a $200 deductible. Three years later, when the car was worth $3,500, Klugman demolished it in an accident. How much can Klugman collect under collision insurance?
5. Scott was involved in an automobile accident. The other driver told Scott that she would report the accident to the police. Relying on this statement, Scott did not file an accident report with the police. If Scott files a claim, can his insurance company refuse to cover it?
6. Valdez's car hit another car at an intersection, damaging both cars. When the police arrived, Valdez told them that the accident was her fault and that her insurance company would pay for all damages. She then reported the accident to

her insurance company, but the company refused to pay because of Valdez's admission. Was the company correct?

7. Adam left his car in a parking lot but forgot to lock the doors. A thief entered the car and stole Adam's leather coat, which was on the front seat. Can Adam collect for the loss of his coat under his comprehensive insurance?

8. Franz parked his car on the street each night. One night a thief stole Franz's car and was involved in an accident causing severe injuries to another driver. The injured driver sued Franz for damages. Does Franz's bodily injury liability insurance cover this accident?

9. Carmine had no-fault automobile insurance. She was involved in an accident that was not her fault. Her medical bill was $900 in a state where the threshold figure was $1,000. May Carmine sue the other driver for her injuries?

10. Greco's car was damaged when a car driven by an uninsured owner collided with it. If Greco has uninsured motorist coverage, will the insurance company pay for the damage?

11. Finkel told Harter that she could borrow Finkel's car to drive to work, but only on Mondays. One Tuesday, Harter's car wouldn't start and she borrowed Finkel's car without telling her about it. On the way to work, Harter injured another person in an accident caused by Harter's negligence. Is Finkel's insurance company obligated to pay for the injuries Harter caused?

12. Feder was arrested for going 45 miles per hour in a 30-mph zone. Because Feder had been arrested once before for the same violation, her license was suspended. May her insurance company cancel her automobile policy because of the suspension?

Cases to Decide

1. Scarola bought a car, not knowing it was a stolen vehicle. The car was then stolen from Scarola, and Scarola made a claim to his insurance company for the car's value. The insurance company refused to pay the claim, saying that Scarola had no insurable interest in the car. Is the insurance company correct? (*Scarola* v. *Insurance Company of North America*, New York 67 Misc 2d 269)

2. State Farm notified Josey that when Josey's pres-

ent automobile insurance contract expired, it would not renew it. Josey then applied for insurance to Allstate. The application blank included the question: "Has any insurer canceled or refused or given notice that it intended to cancel or refuse any similar insurance?" Because of his experience with State Farm, was Josey required to answer "yes" to the question? (*Josey* v. *Allstate Insurance Company*, 252 Md 274, 250 A2d 256)

3. Gallup's son drove his motorbike into the rear of an automobile. Gallup sued his insurance company to recover damages for his son's injuries under the medical payments provision of his auto insurance policy. The policy provided for coverage of medical payments "caused by accident . . . through being struck by an automobile." Can Gallup recover? (*Gallup* v. *St. Paul Insurance Company*, Texas 515 SW2d 249)

4. Texaco's truck was delivering fuel oil to an apartment. The fuel hose extended from the truck across the sidewalk to the apartment. Yanis, a pedestrian, was injured when she tripped over the hose while walking along the sidewalk. Yanis sued Texaco for her injuries. A question arose as to whether this came under a no-fault law as having "arisen out of negligence in the use or operation of a motor vehicle." Is this a no-fault case? (*Yanis* v. *Texaco, Inc.*, New York 85 Misc 2d 941)

5. Evans owned a car insured by Continental. The policy co red the period from March 5, 1969, to March 5, 970. In August 1969 Evans sold the car to Beese. In November 1969, Beese was in an accident in which Scott was a passenger. Scott was killed and his parents sued Continental for damages. Is the company liable? (*Scott* v. *Continental Insurance Company*, Louisiana 259 So 2d 391)

6. Mihalakis rented a van owned by Liberty Lines in order to drive to Kennedy Airport. On the way to the airport, the air conditioning failed and Mihalakis apparently suffered heat prostration. He sued Liberty Lines for injuries under the New York no-fault law. Is he entitled to recover? (*Mihalakis* v. *Liberty Lines*, NY 130 Misc 2d 241)

7. Spangenberg brought an action against Dombrowski to recover damages for personal injuries arising out of an automobile accident. Spangenberg complained of occasional shoulder and back pain. Dombrowski asked that the case be dismissed under the no-fault laws. Should Dom-

browski succeed? (*Spangenberg* v. *Dombrowski*, NY 114 AD2d 497)

8. Esterly was Heffelfinger's fiancée. Heffelfinger had permission to drive his father's car provided he let no one else use it, particularly Esterly, who had only a learner's permit. Esterly drove the car with her fiancé's permission and was involved in an accident in which Helwig was injured. Helwig sued, and the insurance company disclaimed responsibility despite an omnibus clause in the policy. Can Helwig collect under the policy? (*Helwig* v. *Esterly*, 205 Pa Super 185)

Chapter 37

Personal Insurance

CHAPTER PREVIEW

CHAPTER HIGHLIGHTS

Life insurance and medical insurance, the two most common forms of personal insurance, are discussed in this chapter. After a discussion of the need for personal insurance, the chapter describes and explains the various types of life insurance available, including whole life, term, and endowment. It explains typical clauses found in most life insurance policies, as well as rules regarding when a policy may be assigned and how premiums may be paid.

The chapter concludes with a discussion of health insurance, both private and government-sponsored. This type of insurance protects against the cost of medical, surgical, and hospital care, as well as loss of income if a person is disabled.

THE NEED FOR PERSONAL INSURANCE

Personal insurance protects the insured and the insured's family against a loss of income because of death, illness, or accident. Personal insurance may be bought either individually or as part of a group. An individual insurance policy is issued to one person and can be written to cover that person's needs. A person who buys an individual policy must satisfactorily answer a series of health-related questions and may be asked to pass a medical examination. Individual policies usually may not be canceled and must be renewed by the insurer as long as the premiums are paid.

A group insurance policy is one that insures all the members of a specific group. The group may be people who have the same employer, who are in the same profession, or who are members of the same organization. A medical examination is usually not required. Group insurance is temporary—it expires when the member leaves the group. However, the member generally has the option to convert to an individual policy after leaving the group. Group insurance is less expensive because the employer often pays for all or part of the premium. Also, because of the number of people in the group, risks are spread out and premiums are lower.

The two major types of personal insurance are life and health insurance.

LIFE INSURANCE

Life insurance is a contract between the insured and an insurance company. In return for the payment of premiums, the insurance company agrees to pay a certain sum of money (the face value of the policy) to a designated person, the **beneficiary,** when the insured dies. While there are many reasons for buying life insurance, the main one is protection—providing money after the insured's death.

If the insured does not have an insurable interest in the life that is insured, the policy is void. A person obviously has an insurable interest in her or his own life and may take out insurance naming another as beneficiary. The policy is valid regardless of whether or not the beneficiary knows of the insurance. A person also has an insurable interest in the life of someone whose relationship is such that death or accident would cause a severe financial loss. A person, therefore, has an insurable interest in the life of a spouse, a child, a parent, a business partner, and so on. For a policy to be valid, the insurable interest must exist when the insurance is purchased but need not exist when the insured dies.

There are three basic types of life insurance policies, each performing a different function: whole life insurance, endowment insurance, and term insurance.

Whole Life Insurance

Whole life insurance (often called ordinary or straight life) offers lifetime protection for the insured. The insurance remains in effect as long as the insured pays the premiums. Premiums for whole life insurance remain the same, or level, during the insured's lifetime. The premiums are based on the age and sex of the insured at the time the policy is taken out, as well as on the insured's health and occupation.

■ You purchased a whole life insurance policy when you were twenty-two years of age. The annual premium, based on the face value of the policy and your age, was $127. Your annual premium will remain at $127 for as long as you keep the policy. ■

An important feature of whole life insurance is its **cash value.** With whole life insurance, a portion of the premium pays for the cost of the insurance protection. The other portion of the premium is placed in a savings fund. The amount in this savings fund is the cash value. This amount increases with each premium payment.

There are many variations on the basic whole life insurance policy. Many people who want lifetime protection prefer to limit their premium payments. They may not wish to pay premiums after a certain number of years (such as ten or twenty) or after reaching a certain age (such as sixty-five). A form of whole life insurance known as **limited payment life insurance** provides protection for an insured's entire life, even though premiums are paid only for a certain time. This insurance is more expensive than a whole life policy with the same face value because the number of payments is limited. At the same time, the cash value for a limited payment policy increases more quickly than for a whole life policy.

■ Corot, age thirty-two, wanted life insurance but did not want to pay premiums after she retired. She purchased a thirty-year limited payment life policy. After age sixty-two, she will not pay premiums, although the insurance will still be in effect. ■

Modified life is another variation. Many people who need insurance find it difficult to pay the premiums when they first start working. The premiums for a **modified life insurance** policy start out low and increase over a period of years as the insured's income increases. After a number of years, the premium becomes fixed.

Universal life insurance, a relatively new type of insurance, permits an insured to change the policy based on changing needs. The amount of coverage may be increased or decreased by changing either the amount or frequency of premium payments, the period of coverage, or the amount of insurance. It combines term insurance (protection for a certain period of time) with an investment feature. Some versions of universal life insurance permit the insured to determine how the cash-value portion of the premium will be invested.

Endowment Insurance

Endowment insurance provides protection for a certain number of years or until the insured reaches a certain age. With an endowment policy, the insured accumulates a sum of money that will be repaid at a later date. If the insured dies during the term of the policy, the beneficiary receives the face value immediately. If the insured lives beyond the maturity date, the face value is paid to the insured.

Premiums are much higher for endowment insurance than for any other type of insurance, since the entire face value must be accumulated before the maturity date. Endowment insurance is often used to accumulate money for a specific purpose, such as for retirement or the college education of a child.

> Council wanted to make sure he had enough money when he retired at sixty-five and still wanted to protect his family should he die before that time. Council purchased an endowment policy that will mature when he reaches sixty-five. ■

Term Insurance

Term insurance provides protection for a "term" or a certain period of time. The term may be one year, five years, ten years, or until the insured reaches sixty-five. If the insured dies during that term, the beneficiary receives the face value of the policy. At the end of the term, the policy expires and coverage ends.

Term insurance can be renewed at the end of the term, but at a higher premium. The premium rate for each renewal is higher because the insured is older and the risk of death is greater. Most term insurance is not available or renewable when the insured reaches sixty-five or seventy. Term insurance may also be convertible. That is, the insured may exchange, or convert, the term policy for a whole life insurance policy.

Term insurance is much less expensive than whole life or endowment insurance because it offers only temporary protection and does not build up a cash value. Because the premiums are relatively low, term insurance offers young people the most protection for the lowest premium. It provides the maximum amount of protection when the insured's financial responsibilities are the greatest. Term insurance is often purchased to guarantee payment of a mortgage if the insured dies.

Lake bought a home, using a twenty-year mortgage loan. Should Lake die before paying off the mortgage, his family might find it difficult to make the mortgage payments. To protect them, Lake took out a twenty-year term policy. If Lake should die during the term of the policy, the proceeds can be used to pay off the mortgage. ■

Insurance for Special Purposes

Many people have needs that cannot be met by standard life insurance policies. Special policies and options have therefore been developed to provide the flexibility to meet those needs. The most common of these are the family income policy, the key-person policy, the guaranteed insurability option, and the annuity policy.

Family Income Policy   A family with young children has special needs. The head of the family needs to provide permanent protection for a spouse and to pay off debts and expenses at death. At the same time, short-term protection is needed to provide for the children until they become self-sufficient. One answer is a *family income policy,* insurance that combines whole life and term insurance. In a typical policy, the term insurance portion provides an income for the spouse and children until the children become adults. The whole life insurance portion also provides income, which continues for the spouse after the children have become adults.

Key-Person Insurance   The retirement or death of a business partner or large corporate stockholder may be disastrous for a business. The retired partner or the deceased stockholder's estate will want the business to purchase the retiree's or deceased's interest in the business. But the business may not have enough funds to do this. One answer to this problem is *key-person insurance,* a type of life insurance used to fund business buyouts. Such insurance may be purchased by partners or stockholders to insure the lives of the other partners or stockholders. In some cases, the business itself may purchase the insurance.

Guaranteed Insurability Option   For health reasons some persons cannot obtain insurance as they grow older. One insurance feature available to protect against this problem is the *guaranteed insurability option.* This plan is offered to those under a certain age who buy whole life insurance. It allows them to buy additional insurance coverage in limited amounts during their lives, even though they may be uninsurable for health reasons at the time they buy the additional insurance.

Annuity Policy   An **annuity,** which is also sold by insurance companies, provides an income for a specific period of time or for the life of the annuity owner (the *annuitant*). It is similar to whole life insurance because both accumulate cash that can be used as income later. An annuity, however, does not provide insurance protection. The entire premium goes into a savings fund, which earns interest.

An annuity differs from a life insurance policy in its purpose. Life insurance primarily provides protection for dependents if the insured dies. An annuity provides a guaranteed income to the annuity holder. Annuities are usually purchased by persons interested in providing retirement income for themselves. As a result, annuities are becoming more popular as a supplement to Social Security payments. You can purchase an annuity by making regular payments to the insurance company over a period of years or by paying one lump sum. In many cases, the proceeds of an insurance policy are used to buy an annuity and provide an income for a beneficiary.

> Flynn wanted to protect her family after her death by providing the maximum income. She purchased a whole life policy and specified that the proceeds of the policy be converted to an annuity to provide a lifetime income for her family. ■

Standard Policy Clauses

Most life insurance policies have standard clauses that outline the rights of the insured, the company, and the beneficiary. Some typical clauses are shown in Figure 37.1.

Beneficiary The proceeds of a life insurance policy are payable to the beneficiary. The beneficiary could be the insured, the insured's estate, or someone else. It could be a person or a company. It could also be more than one person, called *joint beneficiaries*. The insured has the right to change the beneficiary at any time, unless this right has been given up.

Misstatement of Age Premiums are based on the age of the insured at the time the policy is taken out. Some people misstate their age because of vanity. More often, people misstate their age in order to pay lower premiums. A misstatement about age does not void an insurance policy. Instead, the insurance company will adjust the face value of the policy to that amount of insurance the premium would have purchased if the insured's true age had been given.

> Addison bought a $10,000 life insurance policy and mistakenly gave her age as twenty-eight. She was actually twenty-nine. Since Addison was paying a lower premium at age twenty-eight than she would have at age twenty-nine, when she dies the proceeds of the policy will be adjusted to reflect the amount of insurance her premium would have bought at age twenty-nine. For example, if the premium she was paying would have bought only $9,000 of insurance, that amount will be paid to her beneficiary. ■

Incontestability Occasionally an insured may misrepresent something on the insurance application or conceal important facts. The insurance company must have the right to cancel the policy or refuse to pay the proceeds because

PREMIUMS

WHERE AND HOW PAYABLE Premiums are payable in advance at the Home Office or to an authorized representative in exchange for a receipt signed by the President or Treasurer and countersigned by the person receiving payment. A premium is due and payable on the policy date and on the day following the expiration of each premium payment period thereafter during the lifetime of the Insured until premiums for the number of full years shown in the Schedule of Premiums have been paid. Premiums may be paid for any period shown in the Schedule.

GRACE PERIOD A grace period of 31 days will be allowed for the payment of each premium after the first. The policy will continue in full force during the grace period. If the Insured dies during the grace period, the premium for the policy month in which death occurs will be deducted from the policy proceeds.

SUICIDE If the Insured commits suicide, while sane or insane, within two years from the policy date, the amount payable by the Company shall be limited to the premiums paid less any indebtedness.

INCONTESTABILITY The policy will be incontestable after it has been in force during the lifetime of the Insured for a period of two years from the policy date except for non-payment of premiums and any agreement providing waiver of premium, accidental death or loss of sight or limbs benefits.

INCORRECT AGE OR SEX If the age or sex of the Insured is incorrectly stated, the policy proceeds and all other benefits will be adjusted to the amount which the premium would have purchased at the correct age and sex.

Figure 37.1 **Clauses from a Typical Life Insurance Policy**

of these misrepresentations. At the same time, the insured should not have to worry that the policy will be challenged after her or his death, when no one may know the truth.

The **incontestable clause** provides that after a policy has been in effect for a period of time (usually two years), the insurance company cannot cancel the policy for any reason other than nonpayment of the premium.

> ■ Aragorn took out a life insurance policy. In the application, he forgot to state that his family had a history of heart disease. Aragorn died of a heart attack four years after the policy was issued. Because more than two years had passed, the insurance company cannot refuse to pay the proceeds if it learns of his misrepresentation. ■

Grace Period Premiums on all policies are payable by a certain date. But it would be unfair to the insured if a policy could expire, or lapse, because a payment was not received exactly on time. Therefore, most policies provide for a **grace period** of thirty days. The policy remains in force for thirty days after a missed premium payment.

■ Clay forgot to pay her insurance premium, which was due on January 1. She died on January 15. Because of the grace period clause, Clay's beneficiary can collect the proceeds of the policy, minus the amount of the missed premium. ■

Reinstatement   Once the grace period ends, the policy lapses. Most policies, however, include a **reinstatement clause** that gives the insured the right to put the policy back into effect. The insured must pay the overdue premiums, plus interest, and prove that he or she is in good health, often by passing a physical exam.

Double Indemnity   Most deaths are due to natural causes. For a small extra premium, most insurance companies will pay double the face value of the policy if the insured dies because of an accident. This is known as the **double indemnity clause.** Deaths from war, suicide, surgery, illegal use of drugs, or the commission of a crime are excluded. The beneficiary would receive only the face value.

■ Talbot's insurance policy had a double indemnity clause. She slipped on some ice, struck her head, and died. Because her death was a result of an accident, Talbot's beneficiary will collect double the face value of the policy. ■

Suicide   A person under great emotional strain might take out an insurance policy, pay a few premiums, and then commit suicide so that the beneficiary would collect the insurance proceeds. To protect against this, most policies contain a suicide clause. If the insured commits suicide within a certain period of time after the policy is taken out (usually two years), the insurance company only has to return the premiums actually paid. It does not have to pay the face value of the policy.

Waiver of Premium   An insured may become disabled and unable to pay the premiums. If the premiums are not paid, the policy will lapse. For a small additional premium, the insured can include a **waiver of premium clause.** If the insured is disabled and unable to work, the insurance company will waive, or do away with, the premiums either for a stated period or for life. The life insurance will still be in effect, even though the insured does not pay the premiums.

■ You purchased a life insurance policy with a waiver-of-premium clause. You were involved in an accident that left you paralyzed and unable to work. You do not have to make premium payments for as long as your disability lasts. ■

Assignment   The right to the proceeds of a life insurance policy may be transferred, or assigned, by the insured. If the insured should die before the debt is repaid, the assignee has first claim on the proceeds. The beneficiary would receive any amount remaining. To be valid, an assignment must be submitted in writing to the insurance company, signed by the insured and usually the beneficiary.

After the insured's death, the beneficiary may assign the rights to the proceeds to anyone or any group without the consent of the insurance company.

> ■ Kerner had a $25,000 life insurance policy, which named her husband as beneficiary. She borrowed $15,000 from a bank, assigning the proceeds of the policy to the bank as security for the repayment of the loan. Kerner died before the loan was repaid. The bank has first claim on the proceeds to recover the $15,000 loaned to her. The balance ($10,000) is paid to her husband. ■

Nonforfeiture Rights   People who have insurance policies often pay premiums for many years and suddenly find that they can no longer afford to pay them. To prevent the policies from lapsing, all states require whole life insurance policies to have **nonforfeiture rights,** which are ways of using the accumulated cash value to prevent a policy from lapsing. One of these rights is the *automatic premium loan.* If a premium is not paid, the insurance company lends the premium to the insured, using the cash value as security. The insured may repay the loan at any time. If the loan is not repaid, the amount is deducted from the proceeds paid to the beneficiary.

> ■ York forgot to pay a premium one month. If the cash value of York's policy is more than the premium due, the insurance company will automatically lend York the amount of the premium. The policy will stay in effect and will not lapse. ■

Another nonforfeiture right is *reduced paid-up life insurance.* If a premium is not paid, the insurance company computes the amount of insurance the current cash value of the policy would buy. This amount, always lower than the face value of the old policy, is the face value of a new, completely paid-up policy.

> ■ Towle had a ten-year-old, $10,000 whole life policy, on which he could no longer afford to make payments. The policy had a cash value of $990.
> Towle exchanged it for a paid-up whole life policy with a face value of $2,750. When Towle dies, the insurance company will pay his beneficiary the proceeds of $2,750. ■

A third nonforfeiture right is *extended term insurance.* This is similar to reduced paid-up life insurance. Instead of exchanging the old policy for one with a lower face value, it is exchanged for a completely paid-up term policy with the *same* face value. The current cash value determines the length of time the term policy is in effect.

> ■ Towle's $10,000 whole life policy in the previous example could be exchanged for extended term insurance. The $990 current cash value will purchase a $10,000 term policy that will be in effect for 15 years, 215 days. Towle does not have to pay any more premiums, but at the end of the term, the policy expires. ■

A fourth nonforfeiture right is that of cash surrender value. The insured can "cash the policy in"—surrender it to the insurance company and receive the total accumulated cash value. Of course, he or she then no longer has any insurance.

⬛ Towle's $10,000 whole life policy can be surrendered for the cash value. Towle would receive $990 from the insurance company. ⬛

Effective Date   Most life insurance policies become effective on the date of issue. Some insurance companies provide that their policies become effective for brief, trial periods upon receipt of an application and an initial premium.

How Life Insurance Proceeds Are Paid

When the insured dies, the beneficiary must notify the insurance company of the death, usually by submitting a copy of the death certificate. The insurance company will then pay the beneficiary the face value, or proceeds, of the policy.

There are several ways, called **settlement options,** in which the proceeds of the policy may be paid to the beneficiary. The insured may select the settlement option. Usually, however, the beneficiary has the right to select an option within sixty days of the insured's death. The settlement options are

1. The *lump sum option,* in which the beneficiary receives the proceeds in one lump sum.
2. The *income for life option,* in which the beneficiary receives a fixed amount at regular intervals for life.
3. The *income for a fixed period option,* in which the beneficiary receives monthly payments for a specific number of years.
4. The *fixed income option,* in which the beneficiary receives a fixed amount until the proceeds have been paid in full.
5. The *interest only option,* in which the insurance company holds the proceeds and pays the beneficiary the interest at regular intervals. The beneficiary can withdraw any amount of the proceeds at any time.

HEALTH INSURANCE

Providing for the rapidly rising cost of health care should be an important part of any personal or family financial plan. Most people feel they can handle the ordinary medical expenses. But an accident or unexpected serious illness not only deprives the family of the wage earner's income but may result in enormous medical or hospital bills. The best protection is some form of **health insurance,** which protects against the costs of medical expenses and the loss of income from illness. Today the majority of Americans have some type of health insurance.

There are six basic types of health insurance policies, all of which may be issued under either individual or group plans. These are medical insurance, surgical insurance, hospital insurance, major medical insurance, disability income insurance, and dental expense insurance. The first three—medical, surgical, and hospital—are often combined into one basic health insurance policy.

Medical, Surgical, and Hospital Insurance

Medical insurance provides coverage for emergency room costs and doctor's fees for nonsurgical services. Visits to the doctor's office are covered. Some medical insurance policies also pay for annual physicals, x-rays, prescriptions, and dental services.

Surgical insurance pays for the cost of a surgeon's operating fee, whether the operation takes place in a hospital or in a doctor's office. Only specific operations are covered, and a maximum benefit amount is set for each type of operation. In some cases the insured must pay the portion of the surgical fee that is over the amount stated in the policy.

Hospital insurance provides coverage for the expenses of a stay in the hospital, including room, board, nursing care, and charges for such things as drugs, lab tests, and x-rays. Most policies limit coverage to a maximum amount per day for a maximum number of days, such as 90 or 180.

■ Allison entered a hospital to have her appendix removed. After the surgery she received nursing care, as well as medication to prevent infection. The cost of all these services would be covered by a basic health insurance policy. ■

Major Medical Insurance

Major medical insurance protects against the very high expenses of a catastrophic illness or accident. It is used to pay those costs that exceed the coverage of the basic health insurance policy. It usually covers all types of medical expenses arising from an illness or accident. Depending on the policy, this insurance may cover expenses up to as much as $250,000. Some policies have no maximum limits.

All major medical policies have two distinguishing features: a deductible feature and a coinsurance clause. With the deductible feature, the insured must pay the initial costs in full, up to the amount specified in the policy. The deductible amount varies but may range from $250 to $500. The deductible reduces the premium by having the insured pay for smaller medical expenses. The higher the deductible, the lower the premium.

After the deductible has been paid, the coinsurance feature provides for the insurance company and the insured to share the medical costs. The insurance company usually pays 75 or 80 percent of the costs beyond the deductible amount; the insured pays the balance. This clause also reduces the amount of the premiums by discouraging unnecessary expenses and claims.

> ■ Cohen had a major medical insurance policy that paid 80 percent of any medical expenses resulting from an illness. His deductible was $100. Cohen suffered a heart attack and required medical attention. The total medical expenses were $10,000. Under the policy, Cohen would pay the first $100 plus 20 percent of the balance, or a total of $2,080. The insurance company would pay $7,920. ■

Medicare and Medicaid

Medical, surgical, and hospital insurance may be obtained from either private or public sources. Some insurance companies sell policies that cover basic needs. In most areas of the country, there are health maintenance organizations, semi-public groups that provide health services. In addition, there are government-sponsored health insurance programs known as Medicare and Medicaid.

Medicare is a federal health insurance program for people sixty-five and older or for those of any age who are disabled. The programs are administered by the Health Care Financing Administration of the U.S. Department of Health and Human Services.

Medicare has two parts: Part A, hospital insurance; and Part B, medical insurance. Part A helps pay for medically necessary services furnished by approved hospitals, nursing facilities, and home health agencies. This includes hospital room and board, general nursing, home health care, and blood transfusions.

Part B helps pay for physician's services, including diagnostic tests, therapy, home health care, and laboratory services.

Although Medicare pays a large portion of health care costs, there are gaps in its coverage. First, it does not cover custodial (nonmedical) care, outpatient prescription drugs, dental care, routine physical checkups, and medical care received outside the United States. In addition, it provides coverage only for a limited time and usually for only 80 percent of an amount approved for services provided. The patient must pay the remaining 20 percent, known as coinsurance.

Those who want to supplement Medicare coverage to fill the gaps usually obtain private insurance known as Medigap insurance. Most states have adopted minimum standards for this type of insurance. It may be purchased on either an individual or group basis.

For low-income, elderly persons, there is a federal-state program that fills the gaps in Medicare coverage. This program, known as **Medicaid,** is administered by each state. A person whose annual income is limited and who has limited access to financial resources may qualify for Medicaid assistance in paying Medicare premiums and some of the Medicare deductible and coinsurance amounts.

Disability Income Insurance

Disability income insurance provides income to an insured person who cannot work because of illness or accident. The amount of benefits paid is either a specific amount or a certain percentage of the insured's income. The length of time benefits are paid depends on whether the policy is short term (up to one year) or long term (over one year). Most policies also provide for an *elimination period*, which is a specific period of time before benefits are paid. The longer the elimination period, the less the insurer has to pay and the lower the premium.

■ Hiro had a disability income insurance policy that paid a monthly benefit of $1,000 after a fifteen-day elimination period. He was out of work for one month due to illness. Under his policy, Hiro would receive $500, or one half of one month's benefits. ■

Dental Expense Insurance

Dental expense insurance is now available on a limited basis for individuals and groups. It provides coverage for routine dental care as well as for x-rays, dental surgery, and orthodontia (straightening teeth). Many policies either have a deductible amount or require the insured to pay an amount over the policy limit.

Summary of Important Legal Concepts

Personal insurance protects the insured and the insured's family against a loss of income because of death, illness, or accident. The most common type of personal insurance is life insurance, which pays a certain sum of money to a beneficiary when the insured dies.

There are three basic types of life insurance: whole life, endowment, and term. Other policies and options are available for special purposes. Whole life and endowment offer lifetime protection, whereas term insurance provides protection for a specific period of time. Whole life and endowment insurance build up a cash value in addition to providing insurance protection; term insurance does not. The cash value allows the insured to surrender the policy for cash, purchase additional insurance, or use it as a source for a loan.

A life insurance policy may not be honored if the insured has made a material misrepresentation in the insurance application. After a policy has been in effect for two years, however, the insurance company cannot cancel it except in the case of nonpayment of premiums.

Most insurance policies contain standard clauses dealing with changing a beneficiary, a grace period in the event of late payment of premiums, assignment of the policy, and waiver of premiums for disability.

Beneficiaries may usually choose among five settlement options, ways in which the proceeds of a life insurance policy are paid.

Health insurance provides protection against high medical costs that could result from an illness or an accident. It may be purchased to cover medical expenses, surgical costs, hospital expenses, major medical expenses, loss of income, and dental expenses. Many health policies are purchased from private companies. In addition, the federal government, through its Medicare program, and the federal-state governments, through their Medicaid program, provide protection for health-related expenses.

Key Legal Terms to Know

Match the terms with the definitions that follow.

annuity
beneficiary

cash value

disability income insurance

double indemnity clause

endowment insurance

grace period

health insurance

hospital insurance

incontestable clause

life insurance

limited payment life insurance

major medical insurance

Medicaid

medical insurance

Medicare

modified life insurance

nonforfeiture rights

reinstatement clause

settlement options

surgical insurance

term insurance

universal life insurance

waiver of premium clause

whole life insurance

1. Life insurance purchased for a specific period of time
2. The portion of an insurance premium placed in a savings fund; the amount an insured will receive if a whole life policy is given up
3. Insurance that covers emergency room costs and doctor's fees for nonsurgical services
4. A contract in which an insurance company agrees to pay a sum of money to a beneficiary upon the death of the insured
5. An insurance policy clause that doubles the face value of the policy if the insured dies by accident
6. Insurance that covers surgical fees for specific operations
7. An insurance policy clause relieving an insured from having to pay premiums if disabled
8. Life insurance that is completely paid for after a specific number of payments
9. Insurance that covers fees for hospital care
10. Insurance protection against extraordinary expenses for illnesses or accidents
11. An insurance policy clause that prevents the insurance company from canceling the policy after a certain period of time for any reason except nonpayment of premiums
12. Ways in which the proceeds of life insurance policies may be paid to the beneficiary
13. Life insurance on which premiums are paid for as long as the insured holds the policy
14. A contract that provides a guaranteed income to the policyholder for a specific time or for life
15. Policy that provides income to an insured who cannot work because of illness or accident
16. Life insurance that accumulates a sum of money that will be repaid to the insured or the beneficiary at a later time
17. The person named to receive the proceeds of a life insurance policy when the insured dies
18. The period of time that a policy remains in effect after a premium payment is missed
19. Ways of using the cash value to prevent an insurance policy from lapsing
20. Insurance coverage for medical expenses and loss of income due to illness
21. An insurance policy clause allowing the insured to put the policy back into effect after it has lapsed
22. Life insurance with gradually increasing premium payments
23. Life insurance that allows the insured to change the premium payments, face value, and period of coverage
24. A government program that is administered by each state and that pays for health care for economically deprived persons
25. A federal government program that pays for health care for persons sixty-five and older and for disabled persons of any age

Questions and Problems to Discuss

1. Describe and explain the differences among the three basic types of life insurance policies.
2. Which life insurance policies are more expensive than others? Why?
3. Ames bought a life insurance policy, naming his father as beneficiary. Two years later, he married and changed the policy, making his wife the beneficiary. After he died, both his father and his wife claimed the insurance proceeds. Who is entitled to them?
4. Denton applied for a life insurance policy. On the application, Denton stated that she had not received medical treatment within five years

prior to the date of the application. Denton had, in fact, been treated for pneumonia eight months earlier. At Denton's death, five years later, may the insurance company refuse to pay the beneficiary?

5. Yamaguchi purchased a life insurance policy, naming his wife as beneficiary. He gave the insurance agent the completed application, along with the first year's premium. Before Yamaguchi could take the physical exam, he was killed in an accident. The insurance company refused to pay the policy proceeds to Yamaguchi's wife. Is the company liable on this policy?

6. Smith and Dale were business partners. Smith bought an insurance policy on Dale's life, naming herself as beneficiary. The partnership broke up two years later, but Smith continued to pay the premiums. When Dale died, Smith asked for the proceeds of the policy. Must the insurance company pay her?

7. Ryan insured his life for $100,000, naming his wife as beneficiary. One year later, Ryan was killed while attempting to rob a bank. Ryan's wife filed a claim for the proceeds. The insurance company offered to return the premiums paid but refused to pay the proceeds. Is the insurance company correct?

8. Taylor had a life insurance policy with a double indemnity clause, naming her daughter as the beneficiary. During a rainstorm, Taylor drove too fast and was killed when her car skidded off the road. The insurance company refused to pay the double indemnity amount, claiming that the accident was due to Taylor's negligence. Can Taylor's daughter collect under the double indemnity clause?

9. In applying for life insurance, Wells stated by mistake that he was twenty-three years old when he was actually thirty-four. After paying the premiums for thirty years, he died. The insurance company learned what his correct age was and agreed to return the premiums paid but refused to pay the full proceeds, claiming misrepresentation by Wells. May the insurance company refuse to pay the full proceeds?

10. Craig bought a $50,000 life insurance policy, naming his daughter as beneficiary. Craig borrowed $25,000 from a bank and assigned one half of the policy to the bank as security for the loan. When Craig died, the loan balance was still $25,000 and the bank demanded $25,000 out of the insurance proceeds. Is the bank entitled to this payment?

11. Zane had a $20,000 life insurance policy that contained a double indemnity clause. His wife was the beneficiary. One year after he purchased the policy and while under emotional stress, Zane committed suicide by driving his car off a bridge. When Zane's wife claimed $40,000 under the policy, the insurance company refused to pay it. Is the company correct?

12. Alberts paid premiums for ten years on her whole life insurance policy. When she missed a few payments, the insurance company canceled the policy, claiming it had no further obligation to Alberts. Is the company correct?

13. Metzger wanted insurance protection in the event of catastrophic illness or injury. What type of health insurance should she purchase?

Cases to Decide

1. Callicott bought a life insurance policy insuring her brother's life. She never told her brother about the policy. When the brother died, Callicott applied for payment of the proceeds. The insurance company refused to pay, claiming she had no insurable interest. Was the company correct? (*Callicott* v. *Dixie Life & Accident Insurance Co.*, 198 Ark 69, 127 SW2d 620)

2. Sambles applied for a life insurance policy. He stated on the application that he was in good health and had not been treated by a doctor within the previous five years. In fact, he had visited a doctor eleven times during a period of nine months for treatment of a heart condition. He was examined by an insurance company doctor, found to be healthy, and received the policy. He died four months after taking out the policy and his wife tried to collect the policy proceeds. The insurance company learned of his prior treatment and refused to pay. Can Mrs. Sambles collect from the company? (*Sambles* v. *Metropolitan Life Ins. Co.*, 158 Ohio 233, 108 NE2d 321)

3. LaCosta's husband was killed in an accident while driving a motorcycle. LaCosta's insurance policy covered, among other things, death from injury "while driving or riding in a private automobile." Mrs. LaCosta claimed that this wording covered her husband's accident. Is she correct?

(*LaCosta* v. *Prudential Ins. Co. of America,* 50 Cal App 3rd 526)

4. Bullis applied for life and health insurance under a group plan. The insurance agent took the signed application and the first premium. The application stated that no agent or other person except certain officers of the insurance company could bind the company. It also stated that the policy was not effective until approved by the company's home office and delivered to the insured. Before the policy was issued, Bullis was injured in an auto accident and made a claim against the company. The company denied liability on the grounds that no policy had ever been issued. Is the company liable? (*Bullis* v. *Metropolitan Life Ins. Co.,* New York 85 Misc 2d 209)

5. Falster's husband was insured under a policy with double indemnity coverage. Falster was shot and killed after going armed to meet a man with whom he had a dispute. The insurance company refused to pay the double proceeds, claiming that death was not due to accidental means. Was the company correct? (*Falster* v. *Travelers Ins. Co.,* Tennessee 390 SW2d 673)

6. Caruso was in the restaurant business with another person. He took out a $1.1 million life insurance policy on his partner, naming himself as the sole beneficiary. A few years later, his partner died and Caruso attempted to collect the proceeds of the $1.1 million policy from New England Mutual Insurance Company. The policy contained a clause stating that the policy was incontestable after two years. New England Mutual refused to pay the insurance proceeds to Caruso on the grounds that Caruso had no insurable interest in his partner's life. Assuming that it is shown that Caruso actually had no insurable interest in his partner's life, may Caruso collect on the policy? (*New England Mutual Life Insurance Co.* v. *Caruso,* 73 NY 2d 74)

Ingrid and Rosemary set up a partnership to operate a health food store. The business flourished, and after a few years they were operating twenty-five stores throughout the country. Because they were both so important to the business, they decided to take out a $1 million insurance policy on each other's lives, the benefits to be paid in the event of the death of either one. Three years later, Rosemary decided to retire; Ingrid bought out her interest in the business, paying for it in cash. Rosemary canceled the policy that she had taken out covering Ingrid's life, but Ingrid kept her policy covering Rosemary's life and continued to pay the annual premiums. When Rosemary died ten years later, Ingrid applied to the insurance company for payment of the $1 million face value of the policy. The insurance company refused to pay claiming, that Ingrid did not have an insurable interest in Rosemary's life. Ingrid brought suit to collect the face value of the policy.

The Trial

Ingrid testified that when the policies were taken out, nothing was said about the requirement of having an insurable interest at the time of the death of the insured. She also testified that during the time the policy was in effect, she had paid in excess of $50,000 in premiums.

The Arguments at Trial

Ingrid's attorneys argued that the law is clear that an insurable interest in the life of the person being insured need exist only at the time the policy is taken out and not necessarily at the time that the insured dies. They also argued that had the insurance company wanted to take this position, they should have told the applicants about it when they applied for the policies and should have inserted such a condition into the policies in a manner understandable to the average person. They further argued that because the policy had an incontestability clause, the passage of time prevented the insurance company from refusing to pay the face value of the policy.

The insurance company's attorneys argued that if the beneficiary of an insurance policy does not have to have an insurable interest at the time the insured dies, the insurance policy could then become nothing more than a gamble on another person's life and might also result in all sorts of people taking out insurance policies on other people's lives, with disasterous outcomes. They also argued that incontestability clauses should apply only in those situations where a mistake was made in the application or the coverage at the time the policy was entered into and should not apply in cases of obvious misrepresentation or the possibility of lack of insurable interest in the future.

Questions to Discuss

1. Who do you feel has the stronger argument, Ingrid or the insurance company?
2. If you were the judge or jury deciding this case, for whom would you decide? Why?
3. Based on your reading of the text, do you feel that the incontestability provision of the policy would apply in this case?
4. Do you think that the law regarding insurable interest is fair? If not, what do you think the law should be?
5. What could the insurance company have done to prevent this situation?

PART X

WILLS AND ESTATE PLANNING

After studying Part X, you should be able to

1 State the requirements of a valid will.

2 List the steps necessary to make a will valid.

3 Describe how an existing will may be changed.

4 Outline the steps that are taken upon a person's death to carry out the terms of that person's will.

5 Describe how property is distributed when a person dies without a will.

6 Point out the most important reasons for estate planning.

Chapter 38

Wills and Intestacy

CHAPTER PREVIEW

This chapter deals with the two ways in which property is distributed after death: by will or, if there is no will—a condition known as intestacy—by state law. A will provides for the distribution of property according to the wishes of the person making the will. Certain requirements must be met before a will may be declared a valid one. Certain limitations also apply to the disposition of property by will. The chapter discusses these requirements and limitations. Once executed, a will may be changed or revoked only if certain formalities are followed. Finally, the chapter discusses the steps involved in administering an estate where there is no will. In such a case, the law of the state in which the decedent resided will determine how the estate will be distributed and who has the power to administer the estate.

At death, a person's property is distributed to others. Sometimes that distribution reflects exactly what the decedent wanted to do with his or her property. In other cases, intimate friends and favorite family members receive nothing. The manner in which a person's property is distributed depends on whether the decedent died with or without a will. A person who dies and leaves a valid will is said to have died **testate,** and her or his property will be distributed according to the provisions of the will. If a person dies without a will, that person is said to have died **intestate,** and property will be distributed according to the laws of the state where the person resided. A third way in which property may be distributed upon death is through a trust; trusts will be discussed in Chapter 39.

THE PURPOSE OF A WILL

A **will** is a legal document directing how real and personal property should be distributed after the death of the person making the will, known as a **testator.** (Often the term **testatrix** is used in the case of a woman.) There are many reasons why it is important to have a will. A will enables you to dispose of property as you wish. Without a will, your estate will be distributed according to state law, regardless of your wishes. **Estate** refers to the interest that a person has in property, both real and personal. A will may eliminate a struggle over the question of who is to benefit from your estate and who is to administer it. A will may also save on estate taxes and legal costs. And a will allows you to name a guardian for minor children. If you don't have a will, the court will appoint a guardian who may or may not be the person you would have chosen. An example of a simple will is shown in Figure 38.1.

The most important part of a will is the section disposing of the property of the maker. There are many different ways of disposing of property by will. The maker's entire estate can be left outright to one or more persons. This is known as a **residuary gift.** "I give all my property to my children in equal shares" would be an example of a residuary gift. A gift of specific real property is known as a **devise.** "I give my house at 243 Elm Street to my

```
                              LAST WILL AND TESTAMENT
                                       OF
                                  SAMUEL WARREN

        I, SAMUEL WARREN, of the City of Bridgeport, County of Fairfield, and

   State of Connecticut, declare this to be my Last Will and Testament, and I

   hereby revoke all prior wills and codicils.

        First:  I devise to my wife, SHARON, the residence at 2 Elm Street,

   Bridgeport, Connecticut.

        Second:  I bequeath $500.00 to each of my children.

        Third:  I give all the rest of my estate to my wife, SHARON.

        Fourth:  I appoint my wife, SHARON, as Executrix of my Will and my son,

   JOHN, as successor executor, with full power and authority to sell and convey,

   and lease or mortgage, real estate.

        IN WITNESS WHEREOF, I have subscribed my name this 8th day of January, 1987.


                                              Samuel Warren
                                       SAMUEL WARREN


        The foregoing instrument was signed, published, and declared by SAMUEL

   WARREN to be his Last Will and Testament in our presence, and we at his

   request and in his presence and in the presence of each other, have subscribed

   our names as witnesses the day and year indicated above.

     Sanford Byrnes          residing at  32 Maple Street
     SANFORD BYRNES
                                          Bridgeport, Connecticut


     Sandra Kent             residing at  91 Mission Avenue
     SANDRA KENT
                                          Bridgeport, Connecticut


     Robert Mason            residing at  1201 Ames Avenue
     ROBERT MASON
                                          Bridgeport, Connecticut
```

Figure 38.1
A Simple Will

sister" is an example of a devise. A person who inherits property according
to the terms of a will is called a **beneficiary.**

A gift of personal property is known as a **legacy,** or a bequest. A *specific
legacy* is a gift of specific property that is easily identifiable. "I bequeath my
piano to my brother" is an example of a specific legacy. A *general legacy* is
a gift of any property of a general nature. "I bequeath $5,000 to my husband"
is an example of a general legacy.

What happens if a beneficiary in a will dies before the testator/testatrix? The gift to that person will be deemed ineffective, known as a **lapse,** unless the beneficiary was a certain kind of relative of the testator/testatrix, such as a child, grandchild, sister or brother, and provided that the beneficiary died leaving a descendant.

> Blair died in 1991, leaving a will in which his brother John and sister Alice were named beneficiaries. John, however, died three weeks before Blair, survived by his wife and two children. John's children will share whatever amount John would have received had he survived Blair. ∎

If a beneficiary or beneficaries dies before the testator/testatrix, the estate can be distributed among the surviving beneficiaries in either of two ways: through per stirpes distribution or through per capita distribution. **Per stirpes** means that the estate will be distributed to beneficiaries so that they take the share that their ancestor would have received had that ancestor survived the testator. In the above example, Blair's sister Alice survived, and she is entitled to one half of Blair's estate. Had John survived, he would have received the other half; instead, his children will share his one-half share, each receiving one quarter.

In a **per capita** distribution, each beneficiary receives an equal share. In the above example, Alice and each of John's children would receive one third of Blair's estate. The manner of distribution applied in such cases depends on the language of the will and/or the court's determination of the intent of the person who executed the will and/or state law.

REQUIREMENTS OF A VALID WILL

Every state has its own laws describing the requirements of a valid will. In most states these requirements refer to testamentary capacity; freedom from duress, fraud, and undue influence; writing; and witnesses.

Testamentary Capacity

Testamentary capacity refers to the physical and mental condition and age of a person making a will. To make a valid will, a person must be of sound mind, of proper age (usually eighteen or twenty-one, with the exceptions of Georgia and Louisiana, where the age is lower), and in fair physical condition. At the time of making a will, a person must be capable of understanding the consequences of making the will—that is, what is being disposed of and to whom. Any evidence of mental incapacity or a physical condition that prevents the maker from understanding the effects of the will may invalidate it.

> While in the hospital recovering from a serious operation, Budd decided to make a will. Budd was taking medication that caused drowsiness and made it difficult for her to concentrate. A court may not uphold the will because of Budd's physical and mental state at the time she made the will. ∎

Freedom from Duress, Fraud, and Undue Influence

To make a valid will, a person must be free from outside influences, such as threats or pressure to leave property to a certain person. If a person is defrauded into making a will benefiting another person, the will may be invalidated.

> Roderick pretended to be the son of Daniels, who had been separated from her real son when he was born. Roderick convinced Daniels that he was her real son and persuaded her to make a will leaving him all her property. The will may be declared invalid because of Roderick's fraud. ■

Written Form

A valid will must normally be in writing. An exception to this requirement is a nuncupative will, discussed later in the chapter. A will may be handwritten, typed, or printed, or any combination of the three. There are no special requirements regarding language, type, or size or type of paper. If handwritten, the will may be written with either pencil or pen.

The will must be signed by the maker. Most states require the maker's signature at the end of the document. It is also wise, but not required, for the maker to initial each page of the will. A person who is incapable of signing a will may "sign" it with an "X" and have the "X" witnessed, or the person may have someone sign the maker's name in the maker's presence and at the maker's direction and have that signature witnessed.

> Calvin lost both her arms in an industrial accident. She made a will and asked her friend Farris to sign the will for her. Farris signed in Calvin's presence and the signing was witnessed by others. This will is as valid as if Calvin had signed it. ■

Witnesses

In most states, a will must be signed in the presence of either two or three witnesses, depending on the state. In some states, witnesses must sign their names to the will in the presence of the maker and in the presence of each other. Other states have different requirements. It is best for a person making a will to determine the requirements in her or his state.

Generally, a person making a will should execute it with the greatest degree of formality possible. This means signing a will in the presence of the proper number of witnesses, telling them that the document is a will, and asking the witnesses to sign in the maker's presence and in each other's presence. The witnesses need not read the will or be familiar with its contents. A clause stating that the witnesses observed the signing of the will and were asked to witness it is usually included in the will. This clause is known as an **attestation.** An attestation is included in the will in Figure 38.1.

There are usually no specific requirements for witnesses. They need not be adults, but they should understand their role and what they are signing.

Of greatest importance is that those who are beneficiaries under a will should not also act as witnesses. In most states a witness who is also a beneficiary will not be allowed to share in the estate. However, most states allow a witness who would have received a portion of the deceased's estate if there had been no will to receive her or his share of the estate.

> Rice made a will in which he left $5,000 to his brother. The law in Rice's state required three witnesses, so he had two of his friends and his brother sign the will as witnesses. The will is valid, but Rice's brother would be disqualified from receiving the $5,000. He would, however, share in any part of Rice's estate that he would have been entitled to if Rice had not made a will. ■

SPECIAL WILLS

Special situations often arise that make it necessary to do away with the ordinary formalities involved in making a will. Many states recognize the validity of special wills, such as holographic wills, nuncupative wills, and wills of persons on active duty in the armed forces.

Holographic Wills

A **holographic will** is a will written completely in the maker's handwriting and then signed and dated. It need not be witnessed because the handwriting is considered to be sufficient evidence of who signed the document. Although the majority of states do not recognize holographic wills, there are several states that will enforce them.

Nuncupative Wills

A **nuncupative will** is an oral will. In those states in which it is permitted, it is valid only if made during the maker's final illness and in the presence of witnesses. It is usually valid only to dispose of personal property of a limited value. After the death of the maker, a nuncupative will must be put in writing and signed by the witnesses to whom it was orally made.

> Baylor became ill one day and, in the presence of her family, told them she wanted a particular friend to have her house when she died. This does not qualify as a nuncupative will because it disposes of real property and it was not made during a final illness. ■

One type of special will is that made by a person on active duty in the armed forces. It may be oral or written. If written, it need not be witnessed; if oral, it usually must be witnessed. It may be drawn and executed informally and is usually valid to dispose of personal property only. Once made, the will of a member of the armed forces is usually valid until it is revoked. The will is valid even when the tour of military service is finished.

LIMITATIONS ON DISPOSING OF PROPERTY BY WILL

Most people believe they have absolute freedom to dispose of their property by will. They do have broad powers, but most states limit these powers. A surviving wife or husband has a right to receive a certain portion of the estate of the deceased spouse. This right may not be defeated by will. If a surviving spouse does not receive by will at least as much as he or she would have received had there been no will, the surviving spouse may choose to disregard the will completely and take the portion he or she would be entitled to under state law. This limitation applies to the surviving spouse only. A person who disposes of property by will is not required to leave property, even a token amount, to any other family member.

> ■ Clemens made a will and left his entire estate to his spouse. Clemens made no provisions for his children and did not even mention them in the will. Clemens's will is valid and his children are not entitled to receive anything from his estate. ■

A person may not dispose of property in a manner that is contrary to public policy. The state will not enforce a provision in a will that violates certain accepted policies and practices. For example, a provision requiring a beneficiary to remain single to qualify for a legacy would not be enforced. A legacy to an organization for the purpose of overthrowing the government would likewise be invalid. Most states also limit the amount that may be given in a will to charitable organizations.

> ■ Baker executes a will leaving his entire estate to his daughter on the condition that she never marries. Such a provision would not be upheld because it is against public policy. ■

One of the most important limitations is that a will may dispose only of property that is solely in the name of the maker. For example, property held jointly by a husband and wife cannot be disposed of by will. On the death of one of them, the property automatically belongs to the other. The same may be true of life insurance proceeds payable to a beneficiary. Pension benefits payable to a beneficiary are also unaffected by the provisions of a will.

Finally, certain obligations must be paid upon the death of a person. These obligations cannot be avoided through a will. Debts, estate taxes, funeral expenses, and certain costs relating to the administration of the estate must be paid before beneficiaries get anything under the terms of the will.

MAKING A WILL

The making of a will generally should not be a do-it-yourself project. A will does not have to be drawn by an attorney to be valid. However, the laws relating to wills are quite complex; most people should consult an attorney to be sure they are executing a valid will.

The first step in making a will is to tell your attorney any information needed to draw up the will. The attorney will need information on your family (such as the names and ages of family members), Social Security information, a list of any assets and their value, and a list of any liabilities (debts, mortgages, loans, and so on). Information about your insurance and job benefits is also important.

The next step in making a will is to establish your goals. If you have children or other family members you want to take care of, what do you want them to receive and when? Will they be capable of handling money? Are there charities or schools to which you wish to make a gift? Whom do you wish to handle your assets? The answers to these questions should be reached after much thought and consultation with your attorney.

Once your goals have been established, your attorney will determine how they will affect your estate taxes. Often a slight change in the way in which a will is drawn may produce great tax savings.

The next step in drawing a will is to name an executor (male) or executrix (female). An **executor/executrix** (called the personal representative in some states) is the person who will administer the estate after the death of the person making the will. The executor's function is to validate the will; gather and inventory the assets; pay all debts, expenses, and estate taxes; and distribute the balance among the beneficiaries.

An executor may be a spouse, child, parent, relative, friend, attorney, or a bank. The executor should be a person who knows the maker's family situation and is competent to handle finances. It is wise to appoint an alternate executor in case the person appointed cannot or will not serve as executor. It is also important to give an executor sufficient powers to be able to deal with the estate in a flexible manner. Such powers would include the power to sell property, the power to lease a home, and so forth.

The final step in making a will is to sign the will and have it properly witnessed. The will should be kept in a safe place, such as an attorney's office or the office of the court. In addition, the maker should keep a copy of the will.

CHANGING OR REVOKING A WILL

A will doesn't become effective until the person making it dies. As a result, many people make new wills or make changes in their existing wills several times during their lives. It is a good idea to review your will periodically and change it when necessary. You may want to change your will because of a change in the tax laws, because of a change in your family situation, or because of a change in your assets or liabilities. There are five ways to change a will: by amendment, by destruction, by drawing a new one, by change of circumstances, and by operation of law.

An amendment to a will that changes one or more of its provisions is known as a **codicil.** A codicil may be either added to the will it changes or drawn on a separate piece of paper. A codicil is used when minor changes are needed. In almost all states, a codicil must be prepared with the same formalities as the will that it changes.

> Jansen made a will in which he provided funds for his daughter's college education. After she graduated from college this provision was no longer needed. Jansen, therefore, added a codicil that eliminated this provision of his will. ■

Destroying or mutilating a will revokes it, provided it is done by the maker of the will. This is usually done when a new will is drawn, so that there can be no doubt as to which will is effective. It is important to note that in most states, destroying a will makes a prior will effective.

A new will ordinarily revokes a prior one and is preferred when many changes are being made. While not required, it is best to state in a new will that it revokes any prior wills and codicils.

A will may automatically be changed by a change in circumstances. If the maker disposes of property that is named in the will and that property does not exist at the maker's death, the will provision becomes ineffective.

> You provided in your will that your children were to have your boat upon your death. If you sell the boat, that provision becomes as void as if you had changed your will and omitted the provision. ■

A will may automatically be changed by state law as a result of children born after the will was executed or of marriage or divorce. A bequest to children includes all children born after the will was executed, it being presumed that the testator/testatrix would have intended to provide for such children but simply failed to do so. In general, marriage after a will is executed changes the will because under state law, a spouse is entitled to a certain share of the estate. A bequest to a spouse is usually unenforceable if a divorce occurs after the will is executed.

ADMINISTERING A WILL

There are three steps in handling a person's estate: probating the will, administering the estate, and settling the estate.

Probating the Will

Probate is the process of proving or establishing a will's validity. The executor/executrix, usually with an attorney's guidance, files a petition with a court to declare the will valid and operative. The court is usually called a surrogate's court, probate court, or orphan's court. The petition contains information about the will and the testator/testatrix. The petition is submitted with the will, together with affidavits of witnesses to the will stating that they witnessed it. In some states the witnesses must appear in court and testify that they witnessed the signing. Probate procedures vary from state to state. Eleven states have adopted the Uniform Probate Code, a step toward uniformity throughout the United States in processing wills.

Notice of a hearing is sent to anyone who might have an interest in the will, such as persons who might have inherited property had there been no will. In some states, notice that a will has been offered for probate is published in an official newspaper. After a hearing, the court declares the will valid, and the executor/executrix named in the will receives official permission to act. The will is then said to have been probated. If a will is declared invalid, the state determines how the person's estate will be distributed. The rules governing distribution by a state will be discussed later in the chapter.

Administering the Estate

After probate, the estate of the deceased is administered. The assets of the deceased must be identified and listed. If necessary, an expert may be hired to value the deceased's land, personal belongings, and so forth. Notice is given to insurance companies and the Social Security Administration that the person has died, so that benefits may be determined. Debts of the deceased are also determined and paid.

After assets, debts, and estate expenses have been determined, estate tax returns are prepared and filed. If the assets of the estate exceed a certain value, a federal estate tax return must be filed. Some states also require a state estate tax return.

Distribution pursuant to a will may at times involve problems even though the will provisions are clear and valid. For example, after estate debts and taxes are paid, there may be insufficient funds to pay all bequests in full. Such cases result in **abated bequests,** that is the bequests are decreased according to formulas established by state law.

Suppose a will contains a bequest of a specific item, such as an automobile, but the item is sold or given away prior to death? In this event, the bequest is considered an **adeemed bequest,** that is, it is canceled.

Suppose a beneficiary named in a will predeceases the testator and there is no provision in the will for an alternate gift? **Antilapse laws** in most states provide that the bequest to the deceased beneficiary does not lapse; the children or heirs of the deceased beneficiary take the bequest to which their deceased ancestor was entitled. State laws differ on how close a relationship must have existed between the deceased beneficiary and the heirs for the antilapse provisions to apply.

Settling the Estate

The final step in administering an estate is called **settlement.** After all assets have been collected, debts paid, and taxes determined and paid, the executor/executrix distributes the remaining assets according to the instructions in the will. In addition, the executor's commissions, expenses, and legal fees are paid by the estate. Where this has been done, the estate is considered settled.

Under some circumstances an estate can be settled without court supervision. In such cases the estate property is distributed and the beneficiaries file receipts for their gifts. In other cases a court must approve of and direct the settlement.

INTESTACY

The property of a person who dies intestate (without a will) is distributed according to the laws of the state in which the person lived.

The estate of a person who dies intestate is handled in almost the same way as the estate of a person who dies with a will. One difference is that the person who manages the estate is called an **administrator** (male) or **administratrix** (female) rather than an executor/executrix. A second difference is that the administrator is appointed by the court rather than by will. Typically, the closest relative of the deceased petitions the court to be appointed as administrator. Notice of this appointment is sent to other persons who are entitled to share in the estate.

Property of a person who dies intestate is distributed to the person's heirs according to state law. **Heirs** are persons related by blood or marriage to the deceased who share in the estate of a person who died intestate. The laws of each state differ as to who are heirs and what amount each is to receive. The closer the relationship of the heir to the deceased, the greater the share that the heir receives. In most states, if the intestate leaves a spouse and no children, the spouse receives everything. If the deceased leaves children and no spouse, the children receive everything. If the deceased leaves both a spouse and children, the spouse usually receives one third of the estate and the children share the remaining two thirds. States laws vary considerably in cases in which an intestate dies without spouse or children. A typical pattern of distribution is shown in Figure 38.2.

If a person dies intestate and no living relatives (related by blood) can be found, the estate becomes the property of the state.

LIVING WILLS AND HEALTH CARE PROXIES

Until recently, health care decisions for a person unable to make such decisions for himself or herself were made by a physician or the patient's family. This situation raised many legal, medical, religious, and ethical issues.

To solve this problem, some states have enacted legislation (or some state courts have produced decisions) to ensure that a person's preferences regarding medical care would be followed in the event that the person lacked the capacity to make such decisions at the time required.

Many states now recognize two simple procedures to facilitate health care decisions: (1) the living will (see Figure 38.3) and (2) the health care proxy (see Figure 38.4).

A **living will** is a document that expresses a person's preferences regarding health care if the signer lacks the capacity to make such decisions when the need arises. Its terms may be very general or may describe specific treatments that the signer may or may not want. In those states that recognize such wills, the preferences expressed will be followed. In other states, the preferences may or may not be followed depending on many circumstances.

Person(s) Surviving	Share in Estate
A. Spouse; no children	Surviving spouse takes all
B. Spouse; one child	$5,000 and one half of the balance of the estate to the spouse; remaining balance to the child
C. Spouse and children	$5,000 and one third of the balance of the estate to the spouse; remaining balance to the children
D. Children only	Children take all and share equally
E. One or both parents	Parent, or parents, take all
F. Brothers or sisters	Brothers or sisters take all and share equally

Figure 38.2 **Distribution of the Estate of an Intestate**

A **health care proxy** is a durable power of attorney (i.e, it remains valid despite the incompetency of the signer) by which a principal appoints an agent (the proxy) to make health care decisions for the principal in the event that the principal lacks the capacity to make such decisions. The power of attorney may be very general or may give the agent specific instructions regarding the types of treatment to be given or withheld. A typical state law authorizing health care proxies is New York Public Health Law, Sec. 2980–2994. Some of its important provisions are as follows.

1. Any competent adult may apoint a health care proxy. This includes a person over eighteen or a person who is married or has a child, regardless of age.

2. The document appointing the proxy must be signed in the presence of two witnesses—it need not be notarized.

3. There are certain limitations on who can act as an agent.

4. The proxy is activated only when the principal is deemed incapable of making health care decisions.

5. The principal's attending physician determines whether or not incapability exists. In certain circumstances, the attending physician must consult with another doctor before a decision to withhold or remove life-sustaining treatment is made—both doctors must then agree on the final decision.

Living Will

INSTRUCTIONS:

This is an important legal document. It sets forth your directions regarding medical treatment. You have the right to refuse treatment you do not want, and you may request the care you do want. You may make changes in any of these directions, or add to them, to conform them to your personal wishes.

I, _____SARAH ALLEN_____, being of sound mind, make this statement as a directive to be followed if I become permanently unable to participate in decisions regarding my medical care. These instructions reflect my firm and settled commitment to decline medical treatment under the circumstances indicated below:

I direct my attending physician to withhold or withdraw treatment that serves only to prolong the process of my dying, if I should be in an <u>incurable or irreversible mental or physical condition with no reasonable expectation of recovery.</u>

These instructions apply if I am a) <u>in a terminal condition;</u> b) <u>permanently unconscious;</u> or c) <u>if I am conscious but have irreversible brain damage and will never regain the ability to make decisions and express my wishes.</u>

I direct that treatment be limited to measures to keep me comfortable and to relieve pain, including any pain that might occur by withholding or withdrawing treatment.

While I understand that I am not legally required to be specific about future treatments, <u>if I am in the condition(s) described above I feel especially strongly about the following forms of treatment:</u>

I do not want cardiac resuscitation.
I do not want mechanical respiration.
I do not want tube feeding.
I do not want antibiotics.

I do want maximum pain relief.

Other directions (insert personal instructions): _____

_____

_____

These directions express my legal right to refuse treatment, under the law of New York. I intend my instructions to be carried out, unless I have rescinded them in a new writing or by clearly indicating that I have changed my mind.

Sign and date here in the presence of two adult witnesses, who should also sign.

Signed: *Sara Allen* _____ Date: Nov 10, 1996

Witness: *John Crowley*

    Address: ___34 Market Street___

        ___Albany, New York___

Witness: *Kathleen Thompson*

    Address: ___36 Market Street___

        ___Albany, New York___

Keep the signed original with your personal papers at home. Give copies of the signed original to your doctor, family, lawyer, and others who might be involved in your care.

Figure 38.3 **A Living Will**

Health Care Proxy

(1) I,   JOHN GREEN

hereby appoint   SALLY GREEN, 152 Adams Street, Adams, Oklahoma
   405-839-4223   (name, home address and telephone number)

as my health care agent to make any and all health care decisions for me, except to the extent that I state otherwise. This proxy shall take effect when and if I become unable to make my own health care decisions.

(2) Optional instructions: I direct my proxy to make health care decisions in accord with my wishes and limitations as stated below, or as he or she otherwise knows. (Attach additional pages if necessary).

_____

_____

_____

(Unless your agent knows your wishes about artificial nutrition and hydration [feeding tubes], your agent will not be allowed to make decisions about artificial nutrition and hydration. See the preceding instructions for samples of language you could use.)

(3) Name of substitute or fill-in proxy if the person I appoint above is unable, unwilling or unavailable to act as my health care agent.

_____

(name, home address, and telephone number)

(4) Unless I revoke it, this proxy shall remain in effect indefinitely, or until the date or condition stated below. This proxy shall expire (specific date or conditions, if desired):

_____

(5) Signature *John Green*

Address   152 Adams Street, Adams, Oklahoma

Date   December 1, 1996

Statement by Witnesses (must be 18 or older)

I declare that the person who signed this document is personally known to me and appears to be of sound mind and acting of his or her own free will. He or she signed (or asked another to sign for him or her) this document in my presence.

Witness 1   *Tammy Beckett*

Address   154 Adams Street, Adams, Oklahoma

Witness 2   *Felicia Navidad*

Address   156 Adams Street, Adams, Oklahoma

Figure 38.4 **A Health Care Proxy**

6. The attending doctor must notify the principal, the principal's guardian, etc. (if one has been appointed), and the agent that the principal has been determined to be incapable of making health care decisions.

7. A health care proxy may be revoked orally, by written document, or by execution of another proxy.

The basic difference between a living will and a health care proxy is the person designated to make health care decisions if the maker of the document is unable to make such decisions. With a living will, it is essentially the doctor who makes those decisions. With a health care proxy, a designated person—usually a relative or friend—does so.

Summary of Important Legal Concepts

After a person dies, his or her property is distributed to beneficiaries according to the provisions of a will. If a person dies without leaving a will, property is distributed to heirs according to the laws of the state in which the deceased resided.

To be valid, a will must be executed by someone with testamentary capacity, who is free from fraud or duress and who observes the proper formalities. These formalities vary from state to state but usually require that a will be in writing, signed by the maker of the will and properly witnessed. Some states permit special types of wills, such as handwritten wills, oral wills, and wills made by members of the armed forces on active duty.

There are restrictions on the manner in which a maker of a will may dispose of property. The maker of a will may not dispose of property in such a way as to be against public policy, defeat a spouse's rights, or defeat the rights of creditors.

The steps in making a will are gathering the necessary information, establishing goals, determining tax problems, naming an executor/executrix, and drafting and executing the will.

An executor/executrix is the person named in a will to administer the estate of the deceased. An administrator/administratrix is the person appointed by the court to administer the estate of a person who dies without a will.

To ensure that a person's preferences regarding medical care are followed upon the incapacity of the person to make such decisions, many states now recognize the validity of living wills and health care proxies.

Key Legal Terms to Know

Match the terms with the definitions that follow:

abated bequest
adeemed bequest
administrator/administratix
antilapse laws
attestation
beneficiary
codicil
devise
estate
executor/executrix
health care proxy
heir
holographic will
intestate
lapse
legacy
living will
nuncupative will
per capita
per stirpes
probate
residuary gift
settlement
testate
testator/testatrix
will

1. A will handwritten and signed by the maker
2. An addition or amendment to a will
3. A document disposing of one's property after death
4. The person who manages the estate of an intestate
5. The person who administers the estate of a testator/testatrix
6. A gift by will of one's entire estate to one or more persons
7. A person who disposes of property by will
8. The condition of dying without a will
9. The distribution of an estate after all debts, taxes, and expenses have been paid
10. A gift by will of specific real property
11. A person who inherits property as specified in a will
12. A person who inherits property according to her or his relationship to the deceased
13. An oral will disposing of personal property
14. A gift by will of personal property
17. The interest a person has in real and personal property
18. A gift to a beneficiary that is deemed ineffective because the beneficiary has died before the testator/testatrix
19. Distribution of an estate so that beneficiaries take the share their ancestor would have received if that ancestor had survived the testator
20. Distribution of an estate so that each beneficiary receives an equal share
21. The condition of dying with a valid will
22. A document expressing one's health care preferences
23. A power of attorney giving a designated person the authority to make health care decisions
24. Laws providing for distribution of bequests if the beneficiary has predeceased the testator.
25. A bequest that becomes invalid because the subject matter of the bequest no longer exists.
26. A bequest that is decreased proportionately because of a lack of funds to pay all bequests in full.

Questions and Problems to Discuss

1. What are the four requirements of a valid will?
2. What is the difference between a holographic will and a nuncupative will?
3. What is the difference between a living will and a health care proxy?
4. Lobel executed a will and left the original with his attorney. Two months later, he wrote across his copy, "This will is revoked." Is this sufficient to revoke the will?
5. Blaine, age seventeen, made a will leaving all of her property to her parents. She died at age twenty. Will the will be upheld?
6. Howe died at age twenty-five, leaving a will that had been witnessed properly. Instead of signing the will, Howe typed in his name where the signature would normally go. Is the will valid?
7. Roland signed a will that had been prepared for him by an attorney. When he could not locate any witnesses, he mailed the will to three close friends, asking each to sign the will as a witness and return the will to him. They all did so, and the last witness mailed the will back to Roland. Would this will be admitted to probate?
8. Rigby made a will leaving all of her property to her sister on the condition that her sister remain single until the age of sixty-five. Will such a provision be upheld?
9. One year after making his will, Thomas purchased a boat. He wanted to make sure that the boat would go to his brother after his death. At the very end of his will, he inserted the following: "P.S. I have just purchased a new boat and wish to leave it to my brother upon my death." Is such a provision valid?
10. Andrew made a will leaving everything to his wife. At his death, his survivors included his wife and two children. If the will is declared invalid, who shall inherit Andrew's property?
11. Dixon, in his will, left his 1986 car to his son. Before his death, Dixon traded in the 1986 car for a 1988 car. Is the son entitled to the 1988 car under the will upon Dixon's death?
12. Dowling executed a will leaving everything to her friend, Sampson. She told Sampson and others about her will. Just before she died, Dowling destroyed the will and did not execute a new one. At her death, Dowling left two brothers. Who is entitled to Dowling's estate—Sampson or Dowling's brothers?
13. Forsythe executed a will leaving her entire estate to a country that was at war with the United States. Will the courts interfere with such a bequest?
14. Alder, age ninety-two, executed a will leaving her entire estate to her attorney and naming him executor. The attorney had drawn the will and

the witnesses were his wife and son. Can the will be declared invalid because of this situation?

15. Tower was in the hospital and asked his attorney to draw a will for him. After Tower read the will, he signed it, but there were no witnesses available at that time to witness the will. One week later, Tower asked two witnesses to witness his will. Is such a will valid?

16. Baldwin executed a will naming his wife and three of his children as beneficiaries. Two years later, one of Baldwin's children took a pen and wrote across the first page of the will, "This will is hereby revoked." Does this action actually revoke the will?

Cases to Decide

1. Golden executed a will on March 22. Before signing the will, she crossed out a paragraph that disposed of her home and wrote above it, "Omit and cancel." The notation was initialed by Golden and two witnesses. Golden died on April 21. O'Dowd, who was to have received the home, brought suit, claiming the notation was not valid. Is O'Dowd correct? (*In re Estate of Golden*, Florida 211 So 2d 234)

2. Thompson wrote a will in her handwriting on the back of an envelope. She never signed the will but five lines from the end she wrote, "I, Clara Thompson, do hereby swear that I am in very good health and sound mind." Certain heirs claimed the will was invalid. Are they correct? (*Wilson v. Polite*, 218 So 2d 843)

3. Pohndorf could understand but not read English. Her attorney prepared a will for her, read it to her in English, and explained it to her. She then signed it and her signature was witnessed. Pohndorf died shortly after signing the will. Certain relatives contested the will, claiming it was invalid because Pohndorf could not read it. Is the will valid? (*In re Estate of Pohndorf*, 11 Arizona App 29)

4. Krause executed a will and left it with his attorney. Later, during a phone conversation, he told his attorney to destroy the will. The attorney did destroy the will, but certain heirs claimed that the revocation was not effective. Are they correct? (*Matter of Krause*, New York 87 Misc 2d 492)

5. Dreyfus typed his own will and then signed and dated it in his own handwriting. Was it a valid holographic will? (*In re Dreyfus Estate*, 175 Cal 417, 165 P 941)

6. Krauss telephoned two people and asked them to come over and witness a will. When they arrived, Krauss said nothing about her own will. She simply showed the two people a folded paper and said, "Here are the pen and ink; sign it." They signed the document and left. Was the will validly executed? (*In re Krauss's Estate*, 18 CA 2d 623, 117 P2d 1)

7. Morris wrote a will that was entirely in her own handwriting. It was dated and contained her initials at the end, but there were no signatures of witnesses. Should the will be probated as a valid will? (*In re Estate of Morris*, 268 Cal. App 2d 638)

8. Barton, an undertaker, handled financial affairs for Beck, a woman over eighty years of age; he was also her financial adviser. It was proven that at a time when Beck's mind was deteriorating, Barton called in his own attorney and had the attorney draw a will for Beck. In her will, Beck left almost all of her estate to Barton. Beck's heirs contested the will, claiming that it was invalid because of undue influence. Should they prevail on this claim? (*Barton* v. *Beck Estate*, 195 A 2d 63)

9. Jefferson signed his will in the presence of his attorney, who was an attesting witness. The attorney took the will to his office and informed his partner that the will he held was Jefferson's and that Jefferson had asked that the partner act as the second witness. The partner called Jefferson by phone and verified that the will was Jefferson's. The partner then signed the will as a witness. Is the will valid? (*Matter of Will of Jefferson*, 349 So 2d 1032)

Chapter 39

Estate Planning

In this chapter, we will discuss the need for estate planning and how to accomplish it. Estate planning has a threefold purpose: providing for the proper distribution of assets, providing for retirement, and minimizing estate taxes. The chapter discusses the various means available to minimize estate taxes, including gifts, trusts, and use of the marital deduction. At the conclusion of the chapter, the various steps involved in achieving a successful estate plan are examined.

THE NEED FOR ESTATE PLANNING

Almost every person acquires assets during her or his lifetime. Most people need a plan to dispose of these assets in the most advantageous way. An **estate plan** is a program designed to protect your assets and your family by properly disposing of those assets during your lifetime and after your death.

There is no set dollar amount to measure whether an estate plan is needed. In fact, small estates often present more problems than larger ones. It would be safe to say that almost everyone needs an estate plan.

Many people have no estate or a very small one. An estate may be created by the purchase of insurance or by setting up a business pension fund. With proper estate planning, a relatively large estate may be set up easily and at a modest cost.

> After working for a few years, Clayborn purchased an insurance policy with a face value of $100,000. After the policy was issued and Clayborn had paid the first premium, she immediately had an estate of $100,000. ■

It often takes a long time and a lot of hard work to acquire assets. It is important to make sure that your assets are distributed to the right people and in the way you choose. Proper estate planning will accomplish these things.

Estate planning involves many lifetime goals, one of which is providing for retirement. Whether a person is employed or self-employed, the need to plan for retirement is very important. As early retirement in corporations becomes more common and as the average lifespan increases, the need to plan becomes more significant, particularly because of the current trend to shift the responsibility for retirement planning from the employer to the employee.

The cost of disposing of the assets you have acquired can be high. Administrative expenses, court fees, and legal fees may reduce an estate considerably. With proper planning, those costs can be minimized.

> If you die intestate, the administrator/administratrix of your estate will be required to provide a bond to the court to ensure that the estate is administered properly. The amount of the bond is based on the value of the deceased's estate and can be very expensive. Preparing a will and naming an executor/executrix can eliminate the need for such a bond. ■

Having enough cash (or assets that can be easily converted into cash) to pay taxes and expenses is a major problem in many estates. If an estate does not have enough cash, property may have to be sold. It might be necessary to sell assets that should be kept or to sell them at less than their true worth. A proper estate plan using cash, marketable stocks and bonds, and insurance can solve this problem.

As you can see, there are many reasons why an estate plan is important. The major reason, however, is to reduce taxes.

TAXES AND ESTATE PLANNING

The primary purpose of estate planning is to minimize taxes. Depending on the value of your assets, a tax problem could shrink their value considerably. The amount you save by minimizing taxes can often make a significant difference to the people you choose to be your beneficiaries. The means by which you minimize taxes must, however, fit the other goals of your estate plan.

The first goal of estate planning is to reduce income taxes. The less income tax you pay during your lifetime, the more assets you can accumulate. Making gifts is a good way to lessen income taxes. Giving gifts of property to someone who is in a lower tax bracket than you are (such as a child) results in income being taxed at a much lower rate. Putting property in certain kinds of trusts for the benefit of others can also accomplish the same thing. Of course, it is also important not to give away assets that may be needed later.

Another important benefit of estate planning is to reduce estate taxes. Both federal and state estate taxes may be considerable; proper planning will minimize them.

An **estate tax** is basically a tax on the transfer of an individual's property when she or he dies. The federal tax is assessed against the estate itself. The amount of the federal tax is a percentage of the estate, and the rates increase as the amount of the estate increases. Some, though not all, states also impose an estate tax. In any states that do impose an estate tax, the tax is similar to the federal estate tax. Other states impose a tax called an inheritance tax, which is assessed against the beneficiaries, not against the estate. The rate of inheritance tax depends on the relationship between the decedent and the beneficiary—the closer the relationship, the lower the tax. The nature and amount of tax vary from state to state.

Regardless of the nature of the tax, it is a tax on the deceased's net estate. The **net estate** consists of the assets left by an individual at death, less certain deductions permitted by law, such as funeral and administrative expenses and debts of the deceased. They also include gifts to charitable and educational institutions, in effect making such gifts tax-free. In some cases, a deduction also is allowed for property transferred to a spouse. This deduction is discussed later in this chapter.

The primary goal of estate planning is to have as low a net estate as possible. This means removing as many of your assets as possible from your estate and claiming the various deductions available. Most people need the advice of a lawyer and a tax accountant to help them achieve this goal. The most important ways to minimize estate taxes are through the use of gifts, the marital deduction, and trusts.

Gifts

Giving property as gifts during one's lifetime removes property from an estate so that at death there is less to tax. Each year you may give away $10,000 in cash or property, tax-free, to as many people as you desire. If a married couple make a gift jointly, they may give $20,000 to each recipient— $10,000 each from the wife and from the husband. If you make gifts over a period of years, you can reduce your estate considerably.

In addition to these tax-free gifts, you may make gifts that can result in a savings in estate taxes. You may have to pay a gift tax on these gifts, however. At the federal level these additional gifts would not be of much help. Federal gift and estate taxes are now coordinated so that the taxpayer pays the same tax whether the property is a gift or is part of an estate. However, at the state level, the additional gifts may be very beneficial. Only a few states have gift taxes, while most states have some form of estate tax.

Remember that, as with other types of tax-saving ideas, gifts should not be made unless thought is given to nontax considerations. One question you should ask is, "Can I afford to give the property away?" If you will need the property later, giving it away just to save on estate taxes is not a good idea.

You must also consider the *type* of property you are giving away. Many estates consist of **liquid assets,** which are assets that can be used immediately to pay debts, taxes, and so forth. Liquid assets include cash, bank accounts, marketable stocks and bonds, and insurance proceeds. Most estates also include **nonliquid assets,** which are assets that can't be used immediately. Assets such as real estate, stock in a family business, or a valuable painting are examples of nonliquid assets. Giving away a liquid asset that might be needed to pay estate debts or taxes might not be a very wise idea. A wiser idea might be to give nonliquid assets that might have to be sold in a hurry at less than their fair value if beneficiaries needed cash quickly to settle debts.

How is a gift made? Most people simply deliver the gift to the recipient or, for example, open a bank account for a person. For a gift to be valid, there must be an intention to make a gift, delivery of the gift, and acceptance and control of the gift by the person receiving it. It is best to document gifts with a letter or other written document stating the name of the **donor** (the person making the gift), the name of the **donee** (the recipient), the date of the gift, and a description of the gift. This is particularly important when the gift consists of property that is not normally listed in any recording office or in any other way, such as cash, art objects, or appliances. Unless a donor can prove that a certain gift has been made, the gift may be held to be invalid and its value included as part of the estate.

The Marital Deduction

Since 1948, married persons have had an estate tax advantage known as the marital deduction. Currently, the **marital deduction** allows all property passing to a surviving spouse to pass tax-free.

The marital deduction actually defers the federal and state estate taxes rather than eliminating them. If the marital deduction is used, the estate of the surviving spouse is increased by this amount. Estate taxes will be paid when the surviving spouse dies. The estate taxes that were deferred from the first estate by the marital deduction will be paid on the value of the second estate.

There are other advantages to using the marital deduction. Delaying payment of the estate taxes means that the surviving spouse has the use of more money during her or his lifetime. Also, the surviving spouse may be able to decrease her or his estate (and thus the potential estate taxes) by using the assets or making gifts during her or his lifetime.

> Garber left a will in which he bequeathed all of his property to his wife. As a result, there were no estate taxes on his estate. During her lifetime, Mrs. Garber spent most of her assets and gave the rest away. When she died, no estate taxes were payable. No estate taxes were paid on either estate. ∎

The marital deduction can also have disadvantages. For example, if the surviving spouse already has a large estate, the use of the marital deduction will increase that estate and make its potential estate taxes even larger.

The use of the marital deduction is a quite complicated matter. One basic idea to remember, though, is that you have a choice of whether to use it. It does not apply automatically. Another consideration is that property must be given to the surviving spouse in certain required ways for that property to qualify for the marital deduction. For example, the surviving spouse must have fairly complete control over the property transferred. Otherwise, the marital deduction will not be allowed.

> Miller left a will bequeathing a home to her husband. The will stated that he could use the home "for a period of ten years only, after which it is to become the property of our children." As her husband did not receive complete ownership or control of the home, its value did not qualify for the marital deduction. Its value would be included in the net estate and would be subject to estate taxes. ∎

The third and most important thing to remember about the marital deduction is that it is available for all types of transfers of property. It is not limited only to those that take place by will. The passing of an interest in property held jointly by a husband and wife qualifies for the marital deduction. For example, a joint bank account passes to one joint tenant on the death of the other, regardless of the existence or nonexistence of a will. Other types of property that qualify for the marital deduction are real estate held jointly, stocks and bonds held in joint names, insurance proceeds payable to a spouse on death, and interests created by trusts.

Trusts

A trust is a valuable estate planning device for many people. A **trust** is a plan by which you turn over property to someone to hold and manage for the benefit of yourself or another person. While the titles vary in different states, the person who turns over the property is often known as the **trustor.** This person may also be known as the *settlor* or the *grantor.* One who holds and manages property in trust is known as the **trustee.** Those for whom the trust is set up are the beneficiaries.

> Jones wanted to set up a trust to provide for her children's college education. She turned over $100,000 to the First National Bank with instructions to invest the money and use the interest to provide for her children's education. Jones is the trustor, First National Bank is the trustee, and Jones's children are the beneficiaries. ■

Trusts may be set up either during the lifetime of the trustor or through a provision in a will. A trust created during the trustor's lifetime is known as a **living trust** or an **inter vivos trust.** To establish a living trust, a trust agreement is drawn up between the trustor and the trustee. The property to be placed in trust is then turned over to the trustee. Living trusts may be either revocable or irrevocable. In a revocable trust, the creator of the trust can change its terms or cancel it at any time. In an irrevocable trust, the creator cannot change any of its terms or revoke it once it has been established. An irrevocable trust offers a variety of tax advantages.

A trust set up after death through a will is called a **testamentary trust.** A testamentary trust is established during the lifetime of the trustor, but the property is placed in trust only at the trustor's death.

There are many advantages to using trusts. Considerable income and estate tax savings are possible. In addition, a trust may help to keep property in the family and to prevent beneficiaries from wasting assets. The trustee is usually a professional experienced in financial matters and able to invest and manage the property in a competent way.

The main advantage of the trust is the flexibility it offers in providing income at the time it is needed. A trust also allows the trustor to determine who will get certain assets and when and how they will get those assets. The trustor can control how property is invested and used long after the trust is established.

> Henry wanted to provide for his family after his death. His children were attending college and he could not be sure what their needs would be after they graduated. If he left them an equal amount of money or property, it might not meet their individual needs. By establishing a trust, Henry could give the trustee the flexibility to distribute money and property among his children according to their respective needs. ■

There are many different types of trusts that may be used for specific needs. For example, a **standby trust** becomes effective only when one or more predetermined events occur, such as the incapacity of the trustor. The proceeds of an insurance policy may be used to set up a **life insurance trust** at the trustor's death. A trustee invests the proceeds and distributes funds according to a trust agreement that is set up during the trustor's lifetime.

A **Totten trust** is a very common arrangement in which one person opens a bank account in trust for another. It is revocable until the depositor dies; at the depositor's death, the account belongs to the beneficiary. If the depositor gives the bankbook to the beneficiary or provides some other proof of a gift during the depositor's lifetime, a completed gift will have taken place, and the trust ends. A **charitable trust** is one established to benefit charitable, scientific, educational, or humanitarian agencies.

DEVELOPING AN ESTATE PLAN

The steps involved in developing an estate plan are seeking professional help, gathering information, deciding on the plan, and executing the plan.

The first step is to seek professional help from a lawyer or an accountant. They can advise you as to what information is required, both financial and personal. If insurance is involved, they may suggest that an insurance agent be consulted. If a bank is to be an executor or trustee, a bank's trust officer should also be involved.

After the initial consultation, the next step is to gather the information needed for proper planning. A complete list of your assets and liabilities is required. The list should contain information about the nature of the assets, their value, their liquidity, and who owns them. Personal data, such as Social Security information, family history, and insurance policy information, should also be provided.

After all the required information is collected, the next and most important step is to develop the plan itself. This is a team effort, involving legal and tax professionals and the person making the plan. A frank discussion of needs, goals, and family situation is vital. The professionals involved can offer many suggestions but only if they have all the information they need.

After a plan is agreed upon, the final step is to implement it. This may involve making a will or changing an existing will. It may also involve setting up one or more trusts. Changes in the ownership of assets or in beneficiaries of an insurance policy might be suggested. With proper planning, an estate plan can be developed to meet any needs and any family situation.

Summary of Important Legal Concepts

Estate planning provides for the proper disposition of assets during one's lifetime and after one's death. The most important reasons for estate planning are to minimize taxes, dispose of property according to one's wishes, and provide for retirement.

The most important ways to minimize estate taxes are through the use of gifts, the marital deduction, and trusts. Factors to consider in the use of gifts and trusts include the need for the property later on, the need for liquidity, the type of property to be given, and to whom the disposition is to be made.

The marital deduction is a device for reducing estate taxes by transferring property to a spouse. It may be available for many types of transfers, including transfers by will, jointly held property, and insurance proceeds payable to a surviving spouse.

A trust is an estate planning tool that allows property to be transferred to a trustee and held for the benefit of either the grantor or another. A trust can be set up during one's lifetime (a living or intervivos trust) or by a provision in a will (testamentary trust). Trusts can be set up to serve specific needs.

Developing an estate plan is a group effort. It involves the person who wants it and an attorney and often an accountant, insurance agent, and bank trust officer. The basic steps in developing an estate plan are consulting with professionals, gathering information, developing a plan, and implementing the plan.

Key Legal Terms to Know

Match the terms with the definitions that follow.

charitable trust
donee
donor
estate plan
estate tax
life insurance trust
liquid assets
living (inter vivos) trust
marital deduction
net estate
nonliquid assets
standby trust
testamentary trust
Totten trust
trust
trustee
trustor

1. The person who establishes a trust
2. A trust set up during the trustor's lifetime
3. The person who manages the trust
4. A trust established according to the terms of a will
5. A plan designed to protect and dispose of one's assets
6. A tax on the transfer of property at a person's death
7. Assets that can be used immediately to pay debts, taxes, and so on
8. The assets left by an individual at death, less certain legal deductions
9. The person making a gift
10. An estate tax deduction available for tax-free transfers of property to a spouse
11. A plan for transferring and holding property for the benefit of another
12. The recipient of a gift
13. Assets that cannot be used immediately to pay debts, taxes, expenses, and so forth
14. A trust set up with the proceeds of a life insurance policy
15. A trust that comes into being by the occurrence of a certain event
16. A bank account in the name of a person in trust for another person
17. A trust established to assist nonprofit organizations

Questions and Problems to Discuss

1. Name three major reasons for developing an estate plan.
2. What are the steps involved in developing an estate plan?
3. Elder told his brother that he wanted to give him his car for a birthday gift but that he wanted to

use the car for six months before handing it over. Was this a valid gift?

4. Curran's will contained a provision leaving the income from a $50,000 trust fund to her husband for ten years, after which the fund proceeds were to be distributed to her brother. Does this bequest qualify for the marital deduction?

5. Creed died, leaving an estate valued at $1 million. She left everything to the Salvation Army. Is there any estate tax due on Creed's estate?

6. When Green died, her estate consisted of $100,000 in stocks and bonds in her name. In her will, she left all of her estate to her husband. Would there be any estate taxes payable on her estate?

7. The Halls bought a home jointly as husband and wife. When Mr. Hall died, the home was worth $50,000. What amount would be included in Mr. Hall's estate for tax purposes?

8. Greenberg wanted to provide funds to assist a sick aunt. What would be the best way to accomplish this during Greenberg's lifetime?

9. Halden gave Blaine, his uncle, some stocks and bonds. Halden told Blaine he could have the securities unless and until Halden needed them back, in which case they were to be returned. Halden died a month later. Was this a valid gift?

10. Garbis, married with two children, went to work for a company that gave each employee a $100,000 life insurance policy, payable to the employee's spouse. Garbis claims that she doesn't need an estate plan since the policy is her only asset. Is she correct?

11. Kruger owned a home jointly with her husband. She left no will, and upon her death, the home belonged to her husband by virtue of his surviving his wife. Will this situation qualify for the marital deduction?

Cases to Decide

1. Bucholz owned 360 shares of common stock. She turned her stock certificate in to the corporate stock transfer office and requested that a new certificate be prepared in the name of her minor child. The stock was transferred on the corporate books but the certificate was never delivered to the child. Bucholz argued that no gift had been made and therefore no gift tax was due. Is she correct? (*N. T. Bucholz*, 13 Tax Court 201)

2. Black transferred $1 million in bonds to his wife for her use in case of his death, but returnable to him upon demand. Was this a gift subject to gift tax? (*Black* v. *Com.*, 24 Tax Court Memo 1394)

3. LeDuc bought a government bond that was payable on his death to Darcy LeDuc, a relative. LeDuc kept the bond in his safe deposit box. After LeDuc's death the state of Michigan held that the bond was taxable as part of his estate because title had not passed to Darcy LeDuc. Was this a correct decision? (*In re LeDuc's Estate*, 5 Mich App 390)

Roger Wilson was a very wealthy man. His wife died in 1970, leaving her husband and their twenty-year-old son, James. James and his father did not get along well. Shortly after his mother's death, James left home and did not communicate with his father after that.

Wilson had a niece and nephew, the sole members of his family other than his son, James. Wilson invited his niece and nephew to move into his home on a permanent basis. He told them that if they would take care of him, he would leave his entire estate to them upon his death. For the next fifteen years, the niece and nephew took care of their uncle, attending to his every need. On several occasions, Wilson repeated his promise to leave them his entire estate.

On May 1, 1986, Roger Wilson died. In his will dated July 1, 1965, Wilson left his entire estate to his son. Wilson's niece and nephew brought an action to have the will declared invalid and to have the entire estate turned over to them.

At the Trial

During the trial, Wilson's niece and nephew testified about the services they provided for their uncle over a period of fifteen years—including cleaning the residence, purchasing and preparing food for him, paying his bills, and investing his funds. They further testified as to the number of times Wilson had promised to leave them his entire estate. The testimony also indicated that Wilson had never had any contact with James, during the entire fifteen-year period.

The Arguments at Trial

The attorney representing Wilson's niece and nephew argued that Wilson's promise to leave everything to his niece and nephew was sufficient to invalidate the will leaving everything to his son. The attorney also argued that it would be unfair to deprive the niece and nephew of what was rightfully theirs, not only because of the services they had provided for Wilson but also because Wilson had had no contact with his son over the fifteen-year period.

James's attorney argued that the will was validly executed and that regardless of the principles involved, a will takes precedence over any oral promises to leave someone something. The attorney further argued that if Roger Wilson was mentally competent when he made his will, he could have changed his will if he had wanted to prior to his death. The attorney further argued that relatives who wish to take care of the needs of other relatives do so because of the relationship and are not entitled to compensation for their services.

Questions to Discuss

1. Who has the stronger argument, James or the niece and nephew? Why?
2. If you were the judge or jury hearing this case, for whom would you decide? Why?
3. If the law favors the son, James, do you think that the law is fair?
4. What problems do you think could arise if an oral promise took precedence over a written will?

CONSUMER AND CREDITOR PROTECTION

After studying Part XI, you should be able to

1. Describe the laws passed by the federal and state governments to protect consumers.

2. Explain the plain English law.

3. Identify steps that consumers may take against sellers who violate consumer protection laws.

4. Describe the laws that govern the rights of people who borrow money or who buy goods or services on credit.

5. Explain the function of the Truth in Lending Law.

6. Identify the methods creditors may use to collect payment from debtors.

7. State the main purpose of a security agreement.

8. List a creditor's remedies if a debtor cannot or will not make payments.

Chapter 40

Protecting the Consumer and the Taxpayer

CHAPTER PREVIEW

CHAPTER HIGHLIGHTS

This chapter describes the rules and regulations that federal, state, and local governments have enacted to protect consumers. This protection enables consumers to choose among competing brands and to purchase merchandise that is safe.

These rules and regulations—and their enforcement—provide the consumer with many rights. Two of these are the rights to fair advertising and fair prices. Others enable the consumer to refuse to accept or return goods that were not ordered or to cancel contracts that were made in haste. One of the most recently developed consumer rights is the right to receive a contract written in language that is understandable by the average person.

Consumers also need product standards to ensure that the merchandise they purchase is safe. Various government agencies are responsible for making sure that products meet set safety standards and that the packaging and labeling are safe and clear. Of particular importance to consumers are the recently enacted regulations relating to the age and quality of motor vehicles they purchase.

Without enforcement, consumer laws and regulations are meaningless. The chapter therefore describes the various available methods for enforcing consumer rights.

Finally, the chapter discusses the rights of two types of persons, the air traveler and the taxpayer.

THE NEED FOR CONSUMER PROTECTION

Every person is a consumer at one time or another. A **consumer** is one who purchases goods, products, and services for personal rather than business use. In the past, government had a "hands-off" attitude when it came to protecting the consumer. This attitude, as you learned in Chapter 18, was known as *caveat emptor,* or "let the buyer beware." Government felt that a buyer knew what to buy and what price to pay and needed no protection from government. The law of supply and demand was expected to keep inferior and overpriced goods off the market.

This attitude has changed completely during recent years. Products have become more complicated, requiring greater knowledge on the part of consumers. Consumers must choose from among many different brands of goods today, requiring them to compare competing brands in order to buy the most suitable product. Modern packaging often makes it impossible to make such comparisons because consumers cannot examine a product before buying it.

To protect the consumer, many laws and regulations have been passed by state, local, and federal governments. These laws and regulations prohibit unfair business practices. They also set minimum standards of quality, weight and measurement, packaging, and labeling; and they provide procedures for correcting wrongs suffered by consumers. The group of laws and regulations that protect the consumer can be called a "Bill of Rights for the Consumer."

Enforcement of this "Bill of Rights" is the responsibility of the courts and administrative agencies. Consumers also have access to private, nonprofit organizations that can help settle complaints or grievances.

REGULATION OF BUSINESS PRACTICES

In this country consumers have the right to expect that businesses will deal with them fairly and honestly. One of the functions of government is to protect the interests of society, which includes the interests of consumers. Thus, there are a number of government agencies that protect consumers. Figure 40.1 outlines some of the responsibilities of three federal agencies charged with protecting consumers' interests. Among the business activities regulated by these agencies are advertising, pricing, and consumer rights in buying goods.

The Right to Fair Advertising

Manufacturers and sellers spend billions of dollars each year advertising their goods and services. Consumers may be influenced by such advertising without knowing whether the advertising is completely true. To protect the consumer, Congress and state legislatures have passed laws prohibiting false and misleading advertising. The agency primarily responsible for enforcing these laws is the Federal Trade Commission (FTC).

The FTC has the power to accept complaints from the public and to determine whether acts or practices of businesses are unfair or deceptive. If the FTC decides that a company is guilty of an unfair business practice, it can order the company to stop the practice.

Another way the FTC protects the consumer is by requiring certain products, and the advertisements for those products, to carry warnings to the public. For example, cigarette ads must indicate that smoking is dangerous to your health. Also, if a company makes specific claims about its products, it must make available to consumers the data that support its claims.

False Advertising One business practice the FTC tries to eliminate is false advertising. **False advertising** contains untruths or fails to include information that a consumer needs to know. The FTC can prohibit such advertising—regardless of whether or not the advertiser knows its statements are false—if the advertising has the tendency to deceive consumers.

> The manufacturer of EZ Rest mattresses advertised that sleeping on its mattresses would prevent poor posture. Since the company cannot prove this claim, the FTC can require it to remove the claim from its advertising. ∎

Advertising that a product has been endorsed by a well-known person when that person has not actually endorsed the product is another example of false advertising. The FTC can force a company using such a tactic to stop

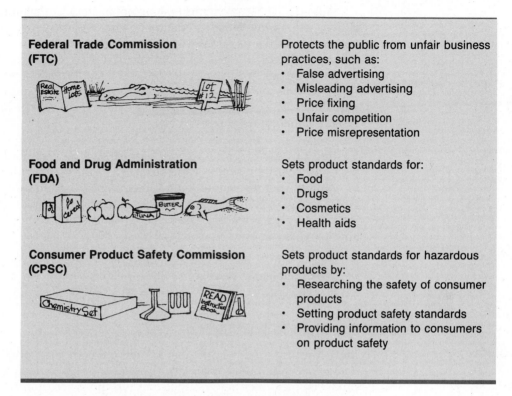

Federal Trade Commission (FTC)	Protects the public from unfair business practices, such as: • False advertising • Misleading advertising • Price fixing • Unfair competition • Price misrepresentation
Food and Drug Administration (FDA)	Sets product standards for: • Food • Drugs • Cosmetics • Health aids
Consumer Product Safety Commission (CPSC)	Sets product standards for hazardous products by: • Researching the safety of consumer products • Setting product safety standards • Providing information to consumers on product safety

Figure 40.1 **Functions of Federal Consumer Agencies**

.doing so. In addition, the company may be liable for damages to the person whose name was used without permission.

In some cases the FTC may require a company to run "corrective" advertising to inform the public that the claims made about a product in the past were untrue. Obviously this is a serious measure to be taken against a company. The majority of advertisers today do not make claims that they cannot prove.

Misleading Advertising The FTC also prohibits misleading advertising. One misleading practice is **bait-and-switch advertising.** Such advertising offers a particular product or model for sale (the "bait"), but when the consumer tries to buy the advertised item, the salesperson tries to sell the consumer another, more costly item (the "switch").

■ Alton saw an ad on television advertising a complete camera outfit for $39.95. She went to the store and was told that the camera was a good one but that it could not take flash pictures. However, for only $69.95 she could buy a camera that would take flash pictures and was of better quality. This tactic is bait-and-switch advertising. ■

Advertising for sale items that are not in stock or that are not available in sufficient quantities to meet consumer demand is also misleading advertising. Many states have passed laws requiring sellers to state in their advertising that quantities are limited. This may be done by using such phrases as "only six per store" or "while supplies last." If a store runs out of a sale item, the customer must be given a rain check. A **rain check** is a coupon or certificate that allows the customer to buy the sale item at the sale price when the item is again in stock.

Puffing   One type of ad, known as **puffing,** borders on the illegal but is perfectly legal. In this type of ad, the quality of the merchandise is exaggerated or "puffed." Because advertising something as "nature's finest" or "world's best" is merely an opinion, not a statement of fact, the ad is legal. The theory is that any person reading such an ad would know better than to rely on it and therefore will not be deceived by it.

> ■ Atlas Used Car Sales advertised a used car for sale claiming it to be "in as good condition as a new car." This is puffing, because it is an opinion and because no one would believe such a statement. ■

The Right to Fair Pricing

Most consumers have no way of knowing whether the price charged for an item is fair. Although consumers can (and should) compare prices of similar products, they often rely on their faith in the seller from whom they buy a product. Most sellers and manufacturers do price their products fairly, but some dishonest merchants use unfair practices, such as price fixing, loss leaders, and price misrepresentation.

Price Fixing   When competing manufacturers, distributors, or sellers agree to set the prices of goods at a certain level, **price fixing** occurs. Such an action eliminates competition, which generally means that the consumer pays more for the goods. Price fixing is a violation of state regulations and the federal antitrust laws.

> ■ Forest Drug Co. and Ross Pharmacy were the only drugstores in a small town. Their owners agreed to sell certain items at the same prices so they would not be competing with each other. This action is unlawful price fixing. ■

Loss Leaders   An item sold below cost or at little profit to entice a consumer into a store is called a **loss leader.** Once the consumer is in the store, the merchant tries to sell the consumer other goods at inflated prices. A loss leader may also be used as a tactic against competitors. For example, a large, successful store may be able to offer a number of loss leaders, decreasing its profits for a short time without too much damage to its financial health. A smaller, less successful competitor may not be able to match such price cuts and may lose customers to the larger store. If the smaller store loses enough customers, it may be driven out of business. This eliminates competition for the larger store, which would then be free to raise prices on all its goods to make up for the losses it suffered while its prices were so low. Most states have laws against this practice, since it harms competition.

■ Atlantic Supermarket wanted to eliminate competition from smaller food stores in its area. Since it could buy in large quantities, Atlantic bought thousands of loaves of bread and offered them for sale at 20¢ a loaf, 70¢ less than the normal price. This is a loss-leader action that is unlawful because it purposely prevents competition. ■

Price Misrepresentation Some merchants put a "regular retail price" or "suggested list price" on an item and then offer the item at a so-called discount. In many cases the item either does not have a suggested price or the discount price is higher than the regular price charged by other stores. Such a practice is called **price misrepresentation.** Most states have laws prohibiting price misrepresentation.

The Automobile Information Disclosure Act is intended to prevent price misrepresentation in the sale of automobiles. Some dealers confuse the public with references to "sticker prices," "below cost," and so forth and then misrepresent the trade-in allowances being offered. The law requires disclosure of the true list price of automobiles and what that price includes.

■ Ames Auto Sales removed the price information stickers from a group of new cars and advertised them as selling for $200 below the invoice price. This action violates the Automobile Information Disclosure Act. ■

The Right to Refuse Unordered Goods

Another unfair business practice is sending a consumer unordered goods. **Unordered goods** are goods not requested by the consumer. The goods usually arrive by mail with a notice that tells the consumer either to send them back or to keep and pay for them. Many people who receive such goods are confused and believe they must keep the goods. Others pay for the goods because they don't want to bother returning them to the sender.

In most states, a person who receives unordered goods and has no agreement with the sender may keep the goods as a gift or may throw them away without paying the sender.

■ You were sent a copy of a new book through the mail. You did not order the book and do not belong to a book club. You may either keep the book or throw it away. You have no obligation to return it to the sender or to pay for it. ■

A consumer who has an agreement with a sender, such as a book or record club, may not keep the goods as a gift or refuse to pay the sender. These agreements usually state that the monthly notice of shipment must be returned by a specific date. Failure to do so makes the consumer liable for the price of the merchandise sent.

The Right to Cancel Certain Contracts

Sometimes a consumer signs a contract in haste without giving the matter proper thought. This may happen when the consumer needs to act quickly or is faced with pressure from a salesperson. To protect consumers in such situations, both federal and state governments have passed laws allowing the consumer to cancel certain contracts after a change of mind, regardless of the reason in two situations.

First, the Federal Truth in Lending Law (discussed in Chapter 41) and Federal Reserve Board regulations permit cancellation of a contract to borrow money only when it involves a credit purchase in which the consumer's principal residence is taken as a security interest. A common example would be a "home equity loan." It does not permit cancellation of the mortgage typically obtained upon the purchase of a home.

> ■ You bought an automobile and agreed to pay for it in twelve monthly install-
> ments (payments). Two days later, you changed your mind and decided
> to return the car. The Truth in Lending Law does not apply because your
> principal residence was not taken as a security interest and you must
> fulfill your obligations under the contract. ■

The Truth in Lending Law and regulations require that the creditor give the buyer a Notice of Rescission. This notice states that the buyer may cancel the contract for any reason within three business days after the contract is signed. The buyer has only to mail the notice back to the seller within the three-day period. The contract is then canceled and any deposit must be refunded.

Second, FTC regulations also apply to door-to-door sales or sales away from the seller's place of business, regardless of whether an item is paid for in a lump-sum payment or on credit. In such a sale, a buyer must make an on-the-spot decision after hearing a fast, effective sales talk. The regulations require the salesperson to give the buyer a Notice of Cancellation form if the sale involves $25 or more. The buyer may cancel the sale within three days for any reason by notifying the seller of the cancellation. Within ten days after the cancellation, the seller must either pick up the goods or make arrangements for the buyer to return the goods to the seller at the seller's expense. If the seller fails to comply with the law, the buyer may keep the merchandise (as well as the refund) and may also sue for any damages and attorney's fees. Many states have enacted laws similar to the federal regulations.

> ■ You bought a typewriter from a salesperson, selling from a table at a school
> fair, who failed to give you the proper notice of cancellation. You gave
> the salesperson a deposit of $50 and agreed to pay the remainder in three
> monthly payments of $50 each. One week later, you decided to return the
> typewriter. Although more than three days have passed since you purchased
> the typewriter, the seller failed to give you the proper notice of cancellation
> and cannot refuse to take back the typewriter. If a seller fails to give the
> proper notice of cancellation for an installment sale, the merchandise may
> be returned for a full refund of any deposit or down payment. ■

Federal law provides that consumers who buy merchandise by mail have a right to have merchandise shipped on time. If an ad promises delivery by a certain date, the shipper must comply. If an ad contains no shipping date, the merchandise must be shipped within thirty days. A consumer has a right to cancel any order not shipped within the time stated or, if no time is stated, within thirty days.

The Right to Understandable Written Contracts

Many consumers complain that they do not understand the language in the documents they sign. The language is often complicated and understandable only by attorneys. As a result, consumers may sign contracts without really understanding what they are agreeing to. To protect the consumer, legislation has been introduced in several states and in Congress requiring that certain contracts be written so they are understandable to the average person. This legislation is known as "plain English" legislation. It is based on the common law concept that if a person signs a contract without understanding its terms, that person could not have agreed to the terms and therefore cannot be bound by them. It is also based on the practical idea that a person who understands a contract is more likely to live up to its terms.

A typical, comprehensive plain English law applies to any consumer contract involving money, goods, or services valued at less than a set amount. It requires contracts to be written in clear language using words with common and everyday meanings. It also requires that contracts covered under the law be divided into meaningful sections and that each section have a heading or caption. These headings alert the consumer to the important terms of each contract.

Consider the difference in wording in the provisions of the following two promissory notes (signed statements agreeing to repay a certain sum of money with interest at a future time).

Before the plain English law
For good and valuable consideration, the receipt whereof is hereby acknowledged, the obligor hereby acknowledges indebtedness to the obligee in the sum of $200.00, which the obligor hereby agrees to pay the obligee, together with interest on the unpaid principal balance from the day or date hereof, on such terms and under such conditions as hereinafter provided.

After the plain English law
1. BORROWER'S PROMISE TO PAY. In return for a loan that I have received, I promise to pay $200 to the Lender. The Lender is Friendly National Bank.
2. INTEREST. I will pay interest at a rate of 10% per year. Interest will be charged on that part of the loan that has not been paid. Interest will be charged starting on the date of this Note and continuing until the loan has been paid in full.

Failure to use plain English in a contract does not make a contract void or voidable. Instead, a creditor or seller who does not comply with a plain English law may be liable to the consumer for any actual damages plus $50.

Truth in Savings Accounts

Consumers often find it difficult to know exactly how much interest a bank is paying on savings accounts. Different banks compute interest in different ways, and since there is little uniformity on how this information is disclosed, it is difficult for consumers to make meaningful comparisons between competing claims of banks and other institutions in regard to deposit accounts.

To help consumers make informed decisions about deposit accounts, Congress passed the Truth in Savings Act in 1991. This law requires clear and uniform disclosure by banks and other institutions of the rates of interest paid on deposit accounts and the fees that may be charged against such accounts. Penalties may be assessed for failure to make such disclosure or for improper disclosure. The purpose of the law is to enable consumers who are about to open savings accounts to make meaningful comparisons between competing and often confusing claims of banks about interest payable.

PRODUCT STANDARDS

Consumers have a right to expect that the products they buy are of good quality and are safe when used properly and as intended. To make wise buying decisions, consumers also need to know what is in a product, such as the ingredients in a food product. Today, many products are packaged in such a way that consumers cannot examine them before making a purchase. In such cases, consumers need packaging that accurately describes the product inside the package.

The Right to Safe Merchandise

Many products either are basically dangerous or become dangerous because of the way in which they are used. Items such as poisons and insecticides are dangerous because of their ingredients. Others, such as rifles and power mowers, are dangerous if not used properly. Some products are dangerous only to some consumers and not to others, such as certain cosmetics and drugs that affect allergies.

Although the government cannot fully protect consumers from the improper use of a product, government agencies can set and enforce safety standards for most products. The Food and Drug Administration (FDA) sets standards for the preparation, manufacture, labeling, and sale of foods, drugs, and cosmetics. It regulates the conditions under which these products are prepared. The FDA requires testing of new drugs before they may be sold to the public. In addition, the FDA examines advertising and labeling to ensure that the public is properly informed about hazardous products and substances, such as cigarettes and insecticides.

The Consumer Product Safety Commission (CPSC) is the federal agency mainly responsible for product safety. It sets standards for most hazardous products, including poisons and flammable fabrics. The CPSC was established by Congress in 1972 with the passage of the Consumer Product Safety

Act. The act gave broad responsibilities and powers to the CPSC to conduct research into the safety of consumer products, to set standards of product safety, and to provide information to consumers on product safety. The CPSC may ban from the market those products that present risks of death and personal injury to consumers. It can also require manufacturers to follow strict labeling procedures to warn consumers of dangers related to their products.

■ Jason Manufacturing Company produced an electric blanket that could ignite when the temperature exceeded 100 degrees. The CPSC can require the company to warn the public of this danger. This warning would generally be placed in a conspicuous place on the product. ■

The CPSC also has the right to force manufacturers to recall hazardous items and to take corrective steps, such as replacing the item with something safer or refunding the purchase price to consumers.

■ Acme Glue Company produced Sticko Quick-Drying Cement, which was extremely flammable. Through its research the CPSC discovered that 130 Sticko users had suffered burn injuries in the past three years. The CPSC has the power to require Acme to recall Sticko from the market and either replace it with a safer product or refund the purchase price to all consumers who had bought Sticko. ■

The act is very comprehensive. It covers "any article, or component part thereof produced or distributed for sale to a consumer for use in or around a permanent or temporary household or residence, a school, in recreation or otherwise, or for the personal use, consumption or enjoyment of a consumer."

In order to compile data on unsafe products, the CPSC has set up a toll-free hotline for consumers to call and report dangerous items. Each day hundreds of calls come in from the public notifying the CPSC of such things as faulty toys or poorly constructed power tools.

The Right to Proper Labeling and Packaging

The labeling and packaging on products provide important information to consumers. Many consumers buy products solely on the basis of the information on a label. The Federal Food, Drug, and Cosmetic Act and the Fair Packaging and Labeling Act (both administered by the FDA) are laws that were passed by Congress requiring manufacturers to give consumers correct information about their products.

The purpose of these acts is to inform the consumer about the nature, quality, quantity, price, and manufacturer of a product. Labels on foods, drugs, and cosmetics must show the name and address of the manufacturer or distributor so that the consumer will know who is responsible for the quality of the product. The quantity must be shown so that the consumer may compare prices of competitive products. Labels on food products must show the ingredients for health reasons and to help the consumer compare the quality of similar products. In addition, many packaged food products must be stamped with a date, which indicates the product's freshness.

Congress has often required specific labeling and packaging to protect public safety. Since 1969, manufacturers of cigarettes and small cigars have been required to put statements on the packages that smoking is dangerous to one's health. Since 1970, manufacturers of products that might harm young children have been required to provide "childproof" caps and other opening devices.

The Right to Purchase Quality Vehicles

A car with a serious defect that can't be repaired, or can't be repaired properly, has come to be known as a "lemon." In the past, consumers who found themselves with lemons either had to replace the cars themselves or had to pay for repairs after the warranty period had expired. Because an automobile is a necessity for so many people and because it is so expensive, thirty-nine states and the District of Columbia have passed laws to protect purchasers. These laws are known as **lemon laws.**

The Magnuson-Moss Warranty Act, discussed in Chapter 18, set certain minimum standards for warranties on consumer products, including automobiles. The provisions of a warranty must be clearly listed and must state whether it is a full or limited warranty. In case of a defect, the seller must remedy it within a reasonable time. If the automobile, for example, can't be fixed after a reasonable number of attempts, the buyer has the option of getting a refund or a replacement.

Lemon laws vary from state to state, but in general they provide that the purchaser must inform the dealer of the defects in the car within a certain period of time or before a certain mileage figure is reached. The dealer must be given a reasonable opportunity to fix them. If the car cannot be repaired after a certain number of attempts or after it has been in the repair shop a certain number of days, the owner is entitled to a refund or a new car. In most states, a consumer must first submit the case to arbitration. The consumer is not usually bound by the arbitration process and, if dissatisfied, can still sue in court to get relief.

It is important to understand that lemon laws do not cover all defects. They generally apply only to defects covered by the manufacturer's warranty and those that substantially reduce the use, safety, or value of the automobile.

Some states have recently passed lemon laws that apply to the purchase of used cars. The rights and responsibilities are similar to those for the purchase of new cars but are more limited in coverage. These lemon laws apply only to sales by used-car dealers and not private individuals.

Warranties   A consumer is protected in the purchase of merchandise by warranties covering the product. These may be expressed in writing or may be implied from the transaction itself. Warranties are covered in detail in Chapter 18.

REMEDIES FOR VIOLATIONS OF
CONSUMER PROTECTION LAWS

A consumer's rights are of little value unless they can be enforced. Government agencies are primarily responsible for enforcing consumer protection laws. In addition, some laws, such as the Consumer Product Safety Act, permit a consumer to sue for violations and to recover a penalty from a manufacturer. A consumer may sue on her or his own behalf or on behalf of a group of consumers. A suit on behalf of a group of consumers is called a **class action suit.**

■ You bought a toaster that turned out to be a serious safety hazard. When you learned that other consumers had purchased the same defective toaster, you brought suit against the manufacturer on your behalf and on behalf of the other purchasers. This was a class action suit. ■

The purpose of a class action suit is to enable an individual with a complaint to obtain legal relief when the claim might otherwise be too small to warrant a separate lawsuit. A class action suit also makes it possible to settle the claims of many individuals at the same time, eliminating the need for many separate lawsuits. One or more members of a group may sue as representatives of the entire group if

1. The group consists of so many people that having all the members of the group join in the lawsuit would be impractical.
2. There are questions of law or fact that are common to all members of the group, even though the individual claims may differ.
3. Parties bringing the class action suit will fairly protect the interests of the rest of the group.

There are certain specific requirements for a class action suit. A court order must be obtained permitting the filing of the class action. The other members of the group must be notified about the suit, unless the court finds that this is unnecessary or that the cost would be prohibitive. A judgment issued in a class action suit is binding on all members of the class, thus allowing the class action to be an effective means of helping consumers and other groups.

In many states the attorney general can sue to prevent violations of consumer laws and to protect consumer rights. The attorney general may also bring a class action suit on behalf of a group of consumers.

The seller who violates consumer protection laws may be subject to both civil and criminal penalties. Civil penalties include payment of damages and seizure of products. Criminal penalties include fines and/or imprisonment.

RIGHTS OF THE AIR TRAVELER

Prior to 1978, many aspects of air travel were regulated by the Federal Aviation Administration and the Civil Aeronautics Board. In 1978, the airline industry was deregulated, and many aspects of air travel have now become contractual between the carrier and the traveler. Each passenger who purchases a ticket has in fact entered into a contract of transportation with a particular air carrier. Each ticket contains a statement, known as "Conditions of Contract" or "Terms of Transportation," which is printed on either the reverse side of the ticket or on the airline folder in which the ticket is contained. These conditions are brief and incorporate a whole variety of terms and conditions that are on file at the airport or airline city ticket office. In effect, each carrier sets its own terms and conditions, and the passenger becomes subject to these terms and conditions upon purchasing a ticket.

There are two important things to know about this system. The first is that liability of the airlines for injury to a person or death is not subject to federal law but is governed by ordinary rules of negligence. The second is that these terms and conditions represent the minimum that airlines are required to do for passengers. Airlines maintain all sorts of policies relating to travelers not specifically stated in the contract of carriage. These vary from airline to airline and often depend on the feelings of the passenger or those of the agent or supervisor in charge at any given time. These policies include compensation if you volunteer to be bumped from a flight, discounts for senior citizens, discounts for travel if there is a death in the family, and so on.

The three most important aspects of the terms and conditions relate to overbooking of flights, flight delays, and liability for loss of, or damage to, baggage.

Overbooking of Flights

Because airline flights are sometimes overbooked, there is a chance that a person who has a confirmed reservation will not have a seat available. When this situation arises, airlines usually ask for volunteers willing to give up their reserved seats in exchange for some type of compensation. If no one volunteers, some people may not be able to board. A person denied boarding will be entitled to either compensation or free air travel; the policies covering this situation vary from airline to airline. In general, an airline will provide either compensation or free air travel to a person denied boarding unless a substitute flight is provided that will get the traveler to her or his destination within one hour of the original arrival time, or the flight is canceled for weather, safety, or "operational" reasons. The compensation is usually the face value of a passenger's tickets to the destination if the airline can get her or him there within two hours after the originally scheduled arrival time. If the delay is longer than two hours, the compensation is usually doubled.

Flight Delays

More than half the contracts of carriage of the major U.S. airlines provide no specific benefits if a flight is delayed, regardless of the reason. The typical language is that the airline is not responsible for delays or for failure to make connections or to operate any flight according to schedule. Some airlines provide a meal and a free phone call if a flight is delayed for more than four hours and the delay was not caused by weather or air traffic.

If a flight is canceled or delayed for more than four hours, some airlines, as a matter of policy, offer a free meal, free transportation to a hotel, and free hotel accommodations. Whether an airline provides these benefits depends on the airline's policies, the reason for the delay, and the number of people affected by the delay.

Liability for Lost, Delayed, or Damaged Baggage

Each airline carrier establishes its own liability for lost or damaged baggage, but a typical plan provides that liability for loss or for damage to checked baggage is limited to $1,250 per passenger, for travel wholly between points in the United States, with no liability for loss of baggage that is not checked. If a higher value is declared in advance and additional charges are paid, many airlines will be held liable for any loss, delay, or damage if higher amounts are involved. In most cases, unless specific insurance protection is purchased, an airline assumes no liability for items such as money, securities, manuscripts, jewelry, furs, and works of art.

If a piece of baggage is lost or delayed, many airlines will give the traveler funds to purchase necessaries, such as clothing or shaving materials. Again, the amount depends on the airline, the reason for the delay, and other similar factors.

Liability on International Flights

Passengers on international flights are subject to provisions of the treaty known as the **Warsaw Convention,** which applies to many aspects of the flight that are not subject to an individual carrier's terms and conditions. In most cases, the liability of carriers on international flights for death of or personal injury to passengers is limited to $75,000 per passenger, regardless of negligence on the part of the carrier. For lost baggage that is checked, liability is limited to the value of 250 French gold francs (approximately $43) for each kilo (approximately 2.2 pounds) of baggage. To take advantage of this limit on liability, the airline must note the weight of the baggage on the airline ticket.

RIGHTS OF THE TAXPAYER

The Internal Revenue Service has stated that a taxpayer has the right to be treated fairly, professionally, promptly, and courteously. To make sure each taxpayer is treated fairly, the IRS has issued its Publication 1, which outlines the rights of a taxpayer. A copy of Publication 1 and an Addendum appear in Figure 40.2.

Your Rights

AS A TAXPAYER

As a taxpayer, you have the right to be treated fairly, professionally, promptly, and courteously by Internal Revenue Service employees. Our goal at the IRS is to protect your rights so that you will have the highest confidence in the integrity, efficiency, and fairness of our tax system. To ensure that you always receive such treatment, you should know about the many rights you have at each step of the tax process.

Department of the Treasury
Internal Revenue Service
Publication 1 (Rev. 10-90)

Cat. No. 64731W

Free Information and Help in Preparing Returns

You have the right to information and help in complying with the tax laws. In addition to the basic instructions we provide with the tax forms, we make available a great deal of other information.

Taxpayer publications. We publish over 100 free taxpayer information publications on various subjects. One of these, Publication 910, *Guide to Free Tax Services*, is a catalog of the free services and publications we offer. You can order all publications and any tax forms or instructions you need by calling us toll-free at 1-800-TAX-FORM (829-3676).

Other assistance. We provide walk-in tax help at many IRS offices and recorded telephone information on many topics through our *Tele-Tax* system. The telephone numbers for *Tele-Tax*, and the topics covered, are in certain tax forms' instructions and publications. Many of our materials are available in Braille (at regional libraries for the handicapped) and in Spanish. We provide help for the hearing-impaired via special telephone equipment.

We have informational videotapes that you can borrow. In addition, you may want to attend our education programs for specific groups of taxpayers, such as farmers and those with small businesses.

In cooperation with local volunteers, we offer free help in preparing tax returns for low-income and elderly taxpayers through the Volunteer Income Tax Assistance (VITA) and Tax Counseling for the Elderly (TCE) Programs. You can get information on these programs by calling the toll-free telephone number for your area.

Copies of tax returns. If you need a copy of your tax return for an earlier year, you can get one by filling out Form 4506, *Request for Copy of Tax Form*, and paying a small fee. However, you often only need certain information, such as the amount of your reported income, the number of your exemptions, and the tax shown on the return. You can get this information free if you write or visit an IRS office or call the toll-free number for your area.

Privacy and Confidentiality

You have the right to have your personal and financial information kept confidential. People who prepare your return or represent you *must* keep your information confidential.

You also have the right to know why we are asking you for information, exactly how we will use any information you give, and what might happen if you do not give the information.

Information sharing. Under the law, we can share your tax information with State tax agencies and, under strict legal guidelines, the Department of Justice and other federal agencies. We can also share it with certain foreign governments under tax treaty provisions.

Courtesy and Consideration

You are always entitled to courteous and considerate treatment from IRS employees. If you ever feel that you are not being treated with fairness, courtesy, and consideration by an IRS employee, you should tell the employee's supervisor.

Protection of Your Rights

The employees of the Internal Revenue Service will explain and protect your rights as a taxpayer at all times. If you feel that this is not the case, you should discuss the problem with the employee's supervisor.

Complaints

If for any reason you have a complaint about the IRS, you may write to the District Director or Service Center Director for your area. We will give you the name and address if you call our toll-free phone number listed later.

Representation and Recordings

Throughout your dealings with us, you can represent yourself, or, generally with proper written authorization, have someone represent you in your absence. During an interview, you can have someone accompany you.

Figure 40.2 Your Rights as a Taxpayer

If you want to consult an attorney, a certified public accountant, an enrolled agent, or any other person permitted to represent a taxpayer during an interview for examining a tax return or collecting tax, we will stop and reschedule the interview. We cannot suspend the interview if you are there because of an administrative summons.

You can generally make an audio recording of an interview with an IRS Collection or Examination officer. Your request to record the interview should be made in writing, and must be received 10 days before the interview. You must bring your own recording equipment. We also can record an interview. If we do so, we will notify you 10 days before the meeting and you can get a copy of the recording at your expense.

Payment of Only the Required Tax

You have the right to plan your business and personal finances so that you will pay the least tax that is due under the law. You are liable only for the correct amount of tax. Our purpose is to apply the law consistently and fairly to all taxpayers.

If Your Return is Questioned

We accept most taxpayers' returns as filed. If we inquire about your return or select it for examination, it does not suggest that you are dishonest. The inquiry or examination may or may not result in more tax. We may close your case without change. Or, you may receive a refund.

Examination and inquiries by mail. We handle many examinations and inquiries entirely by mail. We will send you a letter with either a request for more information

or a reason why we believe a change needs to be made to your return. If you give us the requested information or provide an explanation, we may or may not agree with you and we will explain the reasons for any changes. You should not hesitate to write to us about anything you do not understand. If you cannot resolve any questions through the mail, you can request a personal interview. You can appeal through the IRS and the courts. You will find instructions with each inquiry or in Publication 1383, *Correspondence Process*.

Examination by interview. If we notify you that we will conduct your examination through a personal interview, or you request such an interview, you have the right to ask that the examination take place at a reasonable time and place that is convenient for both you and the IRS. If the time or place we suggest is not convenient, the examiner will try to work out something more suitable. However, the IRS makes the final determination of how, when, and where the examination will take place. You will receive an explanation of your rights and of the examination process either before or at the interview.

If you do not agree with the examiner's report, you may meet with the examiner's supervisor to discuss your case further.

Repeat examinations. We try to avoid repeat examinations of the same items, but this sometimes happens. If we examined your tax return for the same items in either of the 2 previous years and proposed no change to your tax liability, please contact us as soon as possible so we can see if we should discontinue the repeat examination.

Explanation of changes. If we propose any changes to your return, we will explain the reasons for the changes. It is

important that you understand these reasons. You should not hesitate to ask about anything that is unclear to you.

Interest. You must pay interest on additional tax that you owe. The interest is generally figured from the due date of the return. But if our error caused a delay in your case, and this was grossly unfair, we may reduce the interest. Only delays caused by procedural or mechanical acts not involving the exercise of judgment or discretion qualify. If you think we caused such a delay, please discuss it with the examiner and file a claim for refund.

Business taxpayers. If you are in an individual business, the rights covered in this publication generally apply to you. If you are a member of a partnership or a shareholder in a small business corporation, special rules may apply to the examination of your partnership or corporation items. The examination of partnership items is discussed in Publication 556, *Examination of Returns, Appeal Rights, and Claims for Refund*. The rights covered in this publication generally apply to exempt organizations and sponsors of employee plans.

An Appeal of the Examination Findings

If you don't agree with the examiner's findings, you have the right to appeal them. During the examination process, you will be given information about your appeal rights. Publication 5, *Appeal Rights and Preparation of Protests for Unagreed Cases*, explains your appeal rights in detail and tells you exactly what to do if you want to appeal.

Appeals Office. You can appeal the findings of an examination within the IRS through our Appeals Office. Most

Income Tax Appeal Procedure

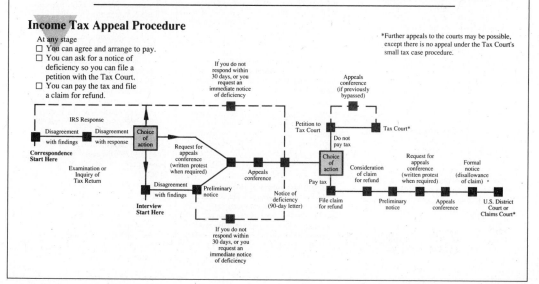

Figure 40.2 (continued)

differences can be settled through this appeals system without expensive and time-consuming court trials. If the matter cannot be settled to your satisfaction in Appeals, you can take your case to court.

Appeals to the courts. Depending on whether you first pay the disputed tax, you can take your case to the U.S. Tax Court, the U.S. Claims Court, or your U.S. District Court. These courts are entirely independent of the IRS. As always, you can represent yourself or have someone admitted to practice before the court represent you.

If you disagree about whether you owe additional tax, you generally have the right to take your case to the U.S. Tax Court if you have not yet paid the tax. Ordinarily, you have 90 days from the time we mail you a formal notice (called a "notice of deficiency") telling you that you owe additional tax, to file a petition with the U.S. Tax Court. You can request simplified small tax case procedures if your case is $10,000 or less for any period or year. A case settled under these procedures cannot be appealed.

If you have already paid the disputed tax in full, you may file a claim for refund. If we disallow the claim, you can appeal the findings through our Appeals Office. If you do not accept their decision or we have not acted on your claim within 6 months, then you may take your case to the U.S. Claims Court or your U.S. District Court.

Recovering litigation expenses. If the court agrees with you on most issues in your case, and finds that our position was largely unjustified, you may be able to recover some of your administrative and litigation costs. To do this, you must have used all the administrative remedies available to you within the IRS. This includes going through our Appeals system and giving us all the information necessary to resolve the case.

Publication 556, *Examination of Returns, Appeal Rights, and Claims for Refund*, will help you more fully understand your appeal rights.

Fair Collection of Tax

Whenever you owe tax, we will send you a bill describing the tax and stating the amounts you owe in tax, interest, and penalties. Be sure to check any bill you receive to make sure it is correct. You have the right to have your bill adjusted if it is incorrect, so you should let us know about an incorrect bill right away.

If we tell you that you owe tax because of a math or clerical error on your return, you have the right to ask us to send you a formal notice (a "notice of deficiency") so that you can dispute the tax, as discussed earlier. You do not have to pay the additional tax at the same time that you ask us for the formal notice, if you ask for it within 60 days of the time we tell you of the error.

If the tax is correct, we will give you a specific period of time to pay the bill in full. If you pay the bill within the time allowed, we will not have to take any further action.

We may request that you attend an interview for the collection of tax. You will receive an explanation of your rights and of the collection process either before or at the interview.

Your rights are further protected because we are not allowed to use tax enforcement results to evaluate our employees.

Payment arrangements. You should make every effort to pay your bill in full. If you can't, you should pay as much as you can and contact us right away. We may ask you for a complete financial statement to determine how you can pay the amount due. Based on your financial condition, you may qualify for an installment agreement. We can arrange for these payments to be made through payroll deduction. We will give you copies of all agreements you make with us.

If we approve a payment agreement, the agreement will stay in effect only if:

You give correct and complete financial information,

You pay each installment on time,

You satisfy other tax liabilities on time,

You provide current financial information when asked, and

We determine that collecting the tax is not at risk.

Following a review of your current finances, we may change your payment agreement. We will notify you 30 days before any change to your payment agreement and tell you why we are making the change.

We will not take any enforcement action (such as recording a tax lien or levying on or seizing property), until after we have tried to contact you and given you the chance to voluntarily pay any tax due. Therefore, it is very important for you to respond right away to our attempts to contact you (by mail, telephone, or personal visit). If you do not respond, we may have no choice but to begin enforcement action.

Release of liens. If we have to place a lien on your property (to secure the amount of tax due), we must release the lien no later than 30 days after finding that you have paid the entire tax and certain charges, the assessment has become legally unenforceable, or we have accepted a bond to cover the tax and certain charges.

Recovery of damages. If we knowingly or negligently fail to release a lien under the circumstances described above, and you suffer economic damages because of our failure, you can recover your actual economic damages and certain costs.

If we recklessly or intentionally fail to follow the laws and regulations

for the collection of tax, you can recover actual economic damages and certain costs.

In each of the two situations above, damages and costs will be allowed within the following limits. You must exhaust all administrative remedies available to you. The damages will be reduced by the amount which you could have reasonably prevented. You must bring suit within 2 years of the action.

Incorrect lien. You have the right to appeal our filing of a Notice of Federal Tax Lien if you believe we filed the lien in error. If we agree, we will issue a certificate of release, including a statement that we filed the lien in error.

A lien is incorrect if:

You paid the entire amount due before we filed the lien,

The time to collect the tax expired before we filed the lien,

We made a procedural error in a deficiency assessment, or

We assessed a tax in violation of the automatic stay provisions in a bankruptcy case.

Levy. We will generally give you 30 days notice before we levy on any property. The notice may be given to you in person, mailed to you, or left at your home or workplace. On the day you attend a collection interview because of a summons, we cannot levy your property unless the collection of tax is in jeopardy.

Property that is exempt from levy. If we must seize your property, you have the legal right to keep:

Necessary clothing and schoolbooks,

A limited amount of personal belongings, furniture, and business or professional books and tools,

Unemployment and job training benefits, workers' compensation, welfare, certain disability payments, and certain pension benefits,

The income you need to pay court-ordered child support,

Mail,

An amount of weekly income equal to your standard deduction and allowable personal exemptions, divided by 52, and

Your main home, unless collection of tax is in jeopardy or the district director (or assistant) approves the levy in writing.

If your bank account is levied after June 30, 1989, the bank will hold your account up to the amount of the levy for 21 days. This gives you time to settle any disputes concerning ownership of the funds in the account.

We generally must release a levy issued after June 30, 1989, if:

You pay the tax, penalty, and interest for which the levy was made,

The IRS determines the release will help collect the tax,

Figure 40.2 **(continued)**

You have an approved installment agreement for the tax on the levy,

The IRS determines the levy is creating an economic hardship, or

The fair market value of the property exceeds the amount of the levy and release would not hinder the collection of tax.

If at any time during the collection process you do not agree with the collection officer, you can discuss your case with his or her supervisor.

If we seize your property, you have the right to request that it be sold within 60 days after your request. You can request a time period greater than 60 days. We will comply with your request unless it is not in the best interest of the government.

Access to your private premises. A court order is not generally needed for a collection officer to seize your property. However, you don't have to allow the employee access to your private premises, such as your home or the non-public areas of your business, if the employee does not have court authorization to be there.

Withheld taxes. If we believe that you were responsible for seeing that a corporation paid us income and social security taxes withheld from its employees, and the taxes were not paid, we may look to you to pay an amount based on the unpaid taxes. If you feel that you don't owe this, you have the right to discuss the case with the collection officer's supervisor. You may also request an appeals hearing within 30 days of our proposed assessment of employment taxes. You generally have the same IRS appeal rights as other taxpayers. Because the U.S. Tax Court has no jurisdiction in this situation, you must pay at least part of the withheld taxes and file a claim for refund in order to take the matter to the U.S. District Court or U.S. Claims Court.

The amount of tax withheld from your wages is determined by the W-4, *Employees Withholding Allowance Certficate*, you give your employer. If your certificate is incorrect, the IRS may instruct your employer to increase the amount. We may also assess a penalty. You have the right to appeal the decision. Or, you can file a claim for refund and go to the U.S. Claims Court or U.S. District Court.

Publications 586A, *The Collection Process (Income Tax Accounts)*, and 594, *The Collection Process (Employment Tax Accounts)*, will help you understand your rights during the collection process.

The Collection Process

To stop the process at any stage, you should pay the tax in full. If you cannot pay the tax in full, contact us right away to discuss possible ways to pay the tax.

Start here

First notice and demand for unpaid tax

10 days later

Enforcement authority arises (a notice of a lien may be filed)

Up to 3 more notices sent over a period of time asking for payment

Notice of intent to levy is sent by certified mail (final notice)

30 days later

Enforcement action to collect the tax begins (levy, seizure, etc.)

Refund of Overpaid Tax

Once you have paid all your tax, you have the right to file a claim for a refund if you think the tax is incorrect. Generally, you have 3 years from the date you filed the return or 2 years from the date you paid the tax (whichever is later) to file a claim. If we examine your claim for any reason, you have the same rights that you would have during an examination of your return.

Interest on refunds. You will receive interest on any income tax refund delayed more than 45 days after the later of either the date you filed your return or the date your return was due.

Checking on your refund. Normally, you will receive your refund about 6 weeks after you file your return. If you have not received your refund within 8 weeks after mailing your return, you may check on it by calling the toll-free Tele-Tax number in the tax forms' instructions.

If we reduce your refund because you owe a debt to another Federal agency or because you owe child support, we must notify you of this action. However, if you have a question about the debt that caused the reduction, you should contact the other agency.

Cancellation of Penalties

You have the right to ask that certain penalties (but not interest) be cancelled (abated) if you can show reasonable cause for the failure that led to the penalty (or can show that you exercised due diligence, if that is the applicable standard for that penalty).

If you relied on wrong advice you received from IRS employees on the toll-free telephone system, we will cancel certain penalties that may result. But you have to show that your reliance on the advice was reasonable.

If you relied on incorrect written advice from the IRS in response to a written request you made after January 1,

1989, we will cancel any penalties that may result. You must show that you gave sufficient and correct information and filed your return after you received the advice.

Special Help to Resolve Your Problems

We have a Problem Resolution Program for taxpayers who have been unable to resolve their problems with the IRS. If you have a tax problem that you cannot clear up through normal channels, write to the Problem Resolution Office in the district or Service Center with which you have the problem. You may also reach the Problem Resolution Office by calling the IRS taxpayer assistance number for your area. If you are hearing-impaired with TV/Telephone (TTY) access, you may call 1-800-829-4059.

If your tax problem causes (or will cause) you to suffer a significant hardship, additional assistance is available. A significant hardship may occur if you cannot maintain necessities such as food, clothing, shelter, transportation, and medical treatment.

There are two ways you can apply for relief. You can submit Form 911, *Application for Taxpayer Assistance Order to Relieve Hardship*, which you can order by calling 1-800-TAX-FORM (829-3676). You can choose instead to call 1-800-829-1040, to request relief from your hardship. The Taxpayer Ombudsman, Problem Resolution Officer, or other official will then review your case and may issue a Taxpayer Assistance Order (TAO), to suspend IRS action.

Taxpayer Assistance Numbers

You should use the telephone number shown in the white pages of your local telephone directory under U.S. Government, Internal Revenue Service, Federal Tax Assistance. If there is not a specific number listed, call toll-free 1-800-829-1040.

You can also find these phone numbers in the instructions for Form 1040. You may also use these numbers to reach the Problem Resolution Office. Ask for the Problem Resolution Office when you call.

U.S. taxpayers abroad may write for information to:

Internal Revenue Service
Attn: IN:C:TPS
950 L'Enfant Plaza South, S.W.
Washington, D.C. 20024

You can also contact your nearest U.S. Embassy for information about what services and forms are available in your location.

☘U.S. GOVERNMENT PRINTING OFFICE: 1991-286-335

Figure 40.2 **(continued)**

Summary of Important Legal Concepts

As more and more products reach the market, consumers require greater knowledge to make proper choices among competing brands. Complicated products often present many safety problems. All levels of government have enacted laws and regulations to assist and protect the consumer.

A number of government agencies, such as the Federal Trade Commission, are responsible for regulating certain business practices that affect consumers. The purpose of regulation is to make sure that the products are advertised and priced fairly. Other regulations cover the right of a consumer to return unordered goods, to cancel certain contracts, and to have understandable contracts.

Other government agencies, such as the Food and Drug Administration and the Consumer Product Safety Commission, have the responsibility of making sure that certain products are safe and packaged in a safe manner. Both the federal government and many states have enacted laws regulating the sale of new and used vehicles.

Laws must be enforceable if they are to mean anything. Consumer protection laws may be enforced by government agencies or by the courts through individual or class action law suits against manufacturers and suppliers.

Certain individual rights are receiving more attention each year. Air travel, which has increased to the point where the air traveler needs greater protection, is one in which various laws and industry rules have been passed to protect the air traveler. The taxpayer also has certain rights, which are protected by Internal Revenue Service rules and regulations.

price misrepresentation
puffing
rain check
unordered goods
Warsaw Convention

1. An item sold at or below cost in order to attract customers
2. Advertising a particular product for sale but then trying to sell the consumer another, more expensive product
3. Merchandise received by a person even though not requested
4. A person who purchases goods, products, and services for personal use
5. Advertising that contains lies or omits important information
6. A coupon that allows a consumer to purchase an out-of-stock sale item at the sale price some time in the future
7. An agreement among sellers to set the price of goods at a certain level
8. Offering an item at a discount price that is higher than the regular price charged by other stores
9. A lawsuit brought by either a consumer or a state attorney general on behalf of a group of consumers
10. Laws that protect purchasers of new and used cars
11. An international treaty that regulates the liability of carriers on international flights
12. Advertising that exaggerates the quality of merchandise

Key Legal Terms to Know

Match the terms with the definitions that follow.

bait-and-switch advertising
class action suit
consumer
false advertising
lemon laws
loss leader
price fixing

Questions and Problems to Discuss

1. Why are laws needed to protect the consumer?
2. Should elimination of competition be allowed if it results in lower prices for the consumer?
3. What additional steps could government take to protect the consumer?
4. Russell joined a book club that sent monthly book selection notices to its members. If members did not want the monthly offering, they had to return the notice within two weeks. The book club sent

Russell three books she had not ordered. Must she return the books or pay for them?

5. Value Department Store advertised a typewriter for sale at 40 percent off the "suggested retail price." Actually, the manufacturer had never set a suggested retail price. Was the store's advertising false and misleading?

6. Easton Business Machines advertised calculators for sale at $3 each. When customers arrived to buy the calculators, only two were available at the sale price. Was the advertisement false and misleading?

7. Dressler owned a grocery store selling name-brand foods at discount prices. Dressler did not want customers to know the name of the manufacturer so she removed that part of the labels. Is this a violation of law?

8. Conrad wanted to increase his music store business and thus began to sell all his musical instruments at cost. Has Conrad violated the law?

9. The Jones Co. manufactured a motorcycle that was unsafe at speeds over 90 mph. Must the company warn customers of this problem?

10. Thacker saw an ad in the newspaper offering a refrigerator for $100 and went to the store to buy it. The salesperson told Thacker that he couldn't expect much for $100. But for only $300 more Thacker could buy a refrigerator that was larger and more efficient. Is the salesperson engaging in bait-and-switch advertising?

11. Coghill purchased a stereo set that proved to have a dangerous electrical problem, causing severe shock if one touched the set. Coghill learned that other sets made by this manufacturer had a similar defect. Can Coghill bring a class action suit against the manufacturer to remove the dangerous sets from the market, even though the sets sold were of different models and prices?

12. Rafferty Company advertised that its power saws were the safest on the market because of an engineering breakthrough. When a potential customer asked to see the data supporting the claim of safe design, Rafferty refused, claiming that it was a trade secret. May Rafferty legally withhold the data?

13. The Krill Corporation manufactured skis and ski equipment. It published an ad stating that the world's finest ping pong player used its skis exclusively. In reality, the ping pong player lived near the equator and had never even been on skis. Can the FTC prohibit Krill Corporation from using this advertisement?

14. A-1 Supermarket learned that a manufacturer of lightbulbs was going out of business. A-1 bought the entire stock of bulbs and then offered them for sale in its store at fifty cents less than the normal price. Would this be considered an unlawful loss leader action?

15. Which of the following statements would be considered false or misleading advertising?
    a. Key Glue is the very best on the market.
    b. Lose 60 pounds in one week with Body Shaper.
    c. Meridien is the only shirt made in the United States.

Cases to Decide

1. Charles of the Ritz sold a cream that the company claimed would restore youth to the skin, regardless of skin condition or the age of the user. The FTC ordered the company to stop the advertising, claiming it was misleading. The company argued that it wasn't misleading because "no straight-thinking person could believe that the cream would actually rejuvenate skin." Is the company correct? (*Charles of the Ritz Distributors Corp.* v. *FTC*, 143 F2d 676)

2. Clinton manufactured watches that were sold to wholesalers, retailers, and discount stores. It ticketed each watch with a tag showing a price much greater than the normal retail price. A store owner would then put a much lower price on the same tag, implying that it was a real bargain. The FTC claimed this was a misrepresentation of the retail price and was false advertising. Should the FTC succeed in stopping the advertising? (*Clinton Watch Co.* v. *FTC*, 291 F2d 838)

3. Parker advertised pens using the words "guaranteed for life." It did not advertise the fact that each time a pen was brought or sent in for repairs, a 35¢ charge was made. The FTC brought suit, saying that failure to advertise the charge was deceptive advertising. Was the FTC correct? (*Parker Pen Co.* v. *FTC*, 159 F2d 509)

4. Resort Co. used the trade name "Dollar-A-Day" for its auto rental company. When people who wished to rent cars inquired, they were told that the rental was obviously more than $1 per day. The rental company claimed that this was not

deceptive advertising because the public was informed of the actual rental cost before any rental contracts were signed. Was the company correct? (*Resort Car Rental System, Inc.* v. *FTC*, 518 F2d 962)

5. Tashoff sold eyeglasses at his store. He advertised eyeglasses "from $7.50 complete, including lenses, frames, and case." The facts showed that of 144 pairs of glasses sold during each year, fewer than 10 were sold for $7.50. The FTC argued that this was a clear example of bait-and-switch advertising. Do you agree? (*Tashoff* v. *FTC*, 437 F2d 707)

6. A supermarket owned by Abe Giles Supermarket, Inc., was cited as being in violation of the Connecticut Food, Drug, and Cosmetic Act after many inspections revealed violations and failure to remedy them. The state of Connecticut asked the court to order that the market be closed until it complied with the provisions of the act. Giles argued that the court should not close the market because fifteen employees would be out of work. Is Giles's argument a valid one? (*State* v. *Abe Giles Supermarket, Inc.*, 31 Conn Sup 242)

7. Kennir operated and controlled a private hospital. He was charged by the Internal Revenue Service with deducting certain expenditures that the IRS claimed were personal and not business expenses. At trial, Kennir tried to give testimony regarding the expenditures, but he was denied permission on the grounds that only the checks themselves could be introduced in evidence. Should Kennir have been allowed to give testimony with regard to the expenditures? (*Kennir* v. *Commissioner of Internal Revenue*, 445 F2d 19)

Chapter 41

Protecting the Borrower

CHAPTER HIGHLIGHTS

Buying goods on credit and borrowing money has become increasingly prevalent. Both federal and state governments have enacted laws and regulations to protect the consumer in this area. Under these laws, a consumer is entitled to obtain credit without regard to age, sex, and marital status, and to know what that credit will cost. The consumer also has the right to pay only those interest charges permitted by law.

Once credit has been obtained, a borrower is entitled to receive accurate bills indicating what is due and when. If bills are not paid on time and a creditor seeks to collect the amount due, the borrower is entitled to be free from harassment by the creditor.

Sometimes, a person is unable to pay debts as they come due. This chapter discusses the measures available to a person who is insolvent and who needs to be relieved from debt. These measures include protection under the bankruptcy laws and private arrangements with creditors.

THE USE OF CREDIT

Today more and more people are borrowing money to purchase homes and cars and to pay for vacations and college educations. The use of credit cards has also grown dramatically. **Credit** is the right granted to a consumer to pay for goods and services after they have been received. A person who lends money or sells goods on credit is a **creditor.** A person who borrows money for any purpose or who buys goods or services on credit is a **debtor,** or borrower.

There are a number of laws and regulations whose aim is to protect the debtor. These laws govern the availability of credit, credit information, unfair credit practices, the collection process, and remedies for debtors. The most important of these laws is the Consumer Credit Protection Act, popularly known as the Truth in Lending Law, passed by Congress in 1969. All of these laws and regulations may be termed a "Bill of Rights for the Borrower."

TYPES OF CREDIT

Credit may be obtained in a number of forms, from charge accounts to long-term bank loans. Sources of credit include banks, savings and loans, finance companies, and retail businesses. The type of credit you obtain varies, depending on what you are buying and how you want to finance (pay for) it.

There are two basic types of credit available to a consumer, unsecured and secured. **Unsecured credit** is credit that is based solely on a promise to repay. Charge accounts and credit cards represent unsecured credit. **Secured credit** is credit based not only on a promise to repay but on security—the borrower's pledge of property, which may be sold by the lender if the loan is not repaid. A home mortgage and an auto loan are examples of secured credit. (See Chapter 42, pages 648 and 649 for additional discussions.)

Three of the most-used types of credit are charge accounts, installment loans, and bank loans.

Charge Accounts

A **charge account** is an agreement between a consumer and a retail business allowing the consumer to purchase items or services now and pay for them later. Large department stores set up charge accounts and issue credit cards to their customers who qualify for credit. A **credit card** is a small card or other device that enables its holder to obtain goods and services on credit. A credit card generally may be used only in the store that issued it. Credit cards are also issued by oil and gasoline companies, airlines, and car rental agencies. Department stores and businesses usually issue their credit cards free of charge.

Banks also issue credit cards, such as MasterCard and Visa. These multipurpose bank cards may be used at many different types of businesses. You receive one bill from the bank for all your charges on the card. The bank in turn sends the proper amount to each of the businesses from which you have purchased something on credit. Banks generally charge an annual fee for the use of their credit cards. There are also companies that issue credit cards, such as American Express, Diner's Club, or Discover. These companies often charge an annual fee for the use of their cards.

There are two types of charge accounts: regular and revolving. With a **regular charge account,** you are expected to pay each bill in full when you receive it. With a **revolving charge account,** you may pay a portion of your bill. Your payment is deducted from the total bill and interest is charged on the unpaid balance. This interest charge, and the unpaid balance of your bill, will appear on the next month's statement. Usually there is a maximum amount that you may owe on a particular credit card at any one time, which is your **line of credit.**

> ■ Schertzer had a charge account at Slade's Ski Shop. He bought a pair of skis and some winter clothing for $380 and charged them to his account. Schertzer's line of credit is $500. Since he already owed the store $120 for previous credit purchases he had made, Schertzer cannot charge any other items until he has paid a portion of his now $500 bill. ■

The ease of using credit, especially with revolving charge accounts, has led to much credit abuse and has created financial difficulties for people who keep buying and suddenly find that they cannot pay for what they have bought. It's quite easy to get into the habit of paying only the minimum amount on your credit bill, until one day you find you owe several hundred dollars, a large part of which may be finance charges on your unpaid balance.

The Truth in Lending Law protects the owner of a credit card that is lost or stolen. If someone uses a credit card without consent, the cardholder is liable only for the first $50 of charges. When a credit card is issued, the issuer must tell the cardholder of this $50 limit and supply the cardholder with a form to use to notify the issuer if the card is lost or stolen. The cardholder must notify the issuer as soon as possible after the card has been lost or stolen. The law also protects a consumer from unauthorized credit card charges.

A credit card issuer who sends a card to a person who has not applied for the card is responsible for all unauthorized charges. The law prohibits sending a credit card to someone unless that person has requested it.

A new system, known as the electronic funds transfer system (EFTS), is rapidly becoming more popular and more widely used. Using a card known as a "debit card," consumers can electronically pay for goods and services or withdraw cash from their bank accounts. Unlike a credit card, a **debit card** immediately transfers funds out of the user's bank account. Today automated teller machines (ATMs), which allow consumers to do their banking twenty-four hours a day, are found in many stores and banks. Point-of-sale (POS) terminals used by businesses electronically and immediately deduct the amount of a purchase from the consumer's bank account and add it to the business's bank account.

Because of the immediate transfer feature, the owner of a debit card is subject to greater liability for the unauthorized use of the card than the owner of a credit card is. Sometimes a debit card holder is not aware of unauthorized use until he or she receives a monthly statement. If the cardholder notifies the card issuer within two business days after learning of the loss, theft, or misuse of the debit card, the cardholder is liable only for the first $50 of losses. However, if the cardholder does not notify the card issuer within two days, the cardholder is liable for losses up to $500. If an unauthorized transfer on a statement is not reported within sixty days after the statement was mailed, the cardholder is liable for *all* losses.

Installment Loans

When you buy expensive items and wish to pay for them over a number of months, you may obtain an installment loan from the store where you buy the items. An **installment loan** is an agreement to pay for an item in fixed, regular payments. An installment loan contract must be drawn up each time an item is purchased and paid for in this way. The terms of the contract apply only to that specific purchase. Usually you must make a down payment on the purchase price. The lender holds an interest in the item and may repossess it (take it back) if you do not make your payments.

Bank Loans

A bank loan is similar to an installment loan. With a bank loan, however, you apply for a loan of a certain amount of cash. A bank loan may be repaid in full at the end of the loan period or in regular installments. Bank loans are often used to finance major purchases, such as a house or a car.

A bank will generally require you to have some sort of collateral before it will lend you the money. **Collateral** is any type of asset you own that may be pledged as security to the bank in case you fail to repay the loan. For example, if you finance the purchase of a car through a bank loan, the car will serve as collateral for the bank loan. You will not have clear title to the car until your bank loan has been repaid.

THE RIGHT TO OBTAIN CREDIT

In 1974 Congress passed the Equal Credit Opportunity Act to prevent creditors from discriminating against certain people when granting loans or credit. This law states that a creditor may not discriminate against anyone because of sex, marital status, age, race, color, religion, national origin, or receipt of public assistance. The law does not mean that everyone who applies is automatically entitled to receive credit or a loan. It simply means that a person cannot be denied credit or a loan *solely* because of age, sex, marital status, and so forth. It also limits the questions a creditor may ask of potential borrowers so they will not be discouraged from applying for credit. An example of an application for credit is shown in Figure 41.1.

A credit applicant's age may be considered only if the applicant is a minor, if the creditor favors applicants age sixty-two or over, or if age affects other factors (such as future income) that are used to determine whether the applicant is a good credit risk.

■ Samuels applied for a twenty-five-year mortgage loan with a 10 percent down payment. Samuels was sixty-eight when he applied for the loan and was due to retire at seventy. The bank denied the loan because Samuel's income would be reduced two years later. In these circumstances the bank could consider Samuels's age in deciding whether to grant the loan. ■

In deciding whether or not to grant credit to an applicant, a creditor may consider such factors as the applicant's income; the amount the person wishes to borrow; the applicant's past credit history; and any other factors, such as other debts, that may relate to a person's ability to repay a loan.

When evaluating income, a creditor cannot consider an applicant's sex or marital status. It is illegal to deny credit to a woman in her own name if she has an income and otherwise qualifies for credit. The creditor may not consider the possibility that she may stop working to have a family. A creditor is also prohibited from discounting the importance of income just because it may come from part-time employment, alimony, or a pension.

■ Andrews applied for a credit card at the Sands Department Store. She was employed full time and was earning $250 a week at the time. Store officials at Sands Department Store rejected her application for credit only because of the possibility that she could leave her job to raise her children. This is a violation of the Equal Credit Opportunity Act. ■

A creditor must notify an applicant within thirty days about whether the credit application was accepted or rejected. If the application was rejected, the applicant is entitled to an explanation in writing. If the applicant was denied credit without just cause, the applicant may sue for damages.

Fast-and-Easy 4-Step Credit Application Please Fill in Sections 1, 2, 3 and 4. Print in Ink, and Sign the Agreement Inside

Employee Name			I.D. No.			Store No.	Acc't No.	
Approved By	Limit	Score	Usage	Source	Group	Type	Action	

1. About You

Your Name Mr. Mrs. M. (Optional)	First *Janice*	Middle *E*	Last *Fuentes*		Your Date of Birth	Mo. *9*	Day *7*	Year *63*
Home Address	Street No. *102 Stearns Rd.*	Apt No. *#4*	City, Town *Brookline*	State *Mass*	Zip *02146-1102*	Years There *2*	Own Rent ✓	
Home Phone	(Area Code) *(617) 272-9901*	Monthly Rental or Mortgage Payment *$450.00*		Your Social Security No. *4 0 2 9 9 7 6 3 8*				
Your Previous Address	Street No. *28 Beacon Street*	Apt No. City, Town *Boston*		State *Mass*	Zip *02107-1113*	Years There *2½*		
Name of Close Relative	Name *Maria Fuentes*	Address *19 South Street*	City *Quincy*	State *Mass*	Zip *02169-7862*	Relative's (Area Code) Phone *(617) 542-5346*		

2. About Your Work

Your Employer	Name of Company *Durkee Office Supplies*				Your Position *Office Manager*	
Your Business Address	Street No. *28 State Street*	City *Boston*	State *Mass*	Zip *02108-1204*	Other Income*	
Your Business Phone	(Area Code) *(617) 992-1188*	Your Annual Salary *$27,000*		Years There *6*	Source of Income*	
Name of Your Previous Employer		Years There —	*You don't have to tell us about alimony, child support or separate maintenance income unless you want us to consider them in approving your application*			

3. Your Other Charge Accounts and Bank Accounts

American Express Master Charge ✓ Visa (check if applicable)	Acc't No. *1002-88-09233-2*	Exact name in which account is named *Janice E. Fuentes*
Dept. Store Charge Acc't *Jordans*	Acc't No. *1-7042-9381*	Exact name in which account is named *Janice E. Fuentes*
Other Charge Account	Acc't No.	Exact name in which account is named
Savings Bank *New England Savings Bank*	Acc't No. *9901-687402*	Address of Bank *17 Janes Street, Boston*
Checking Bank *First National Bank*	Acc't No. *5301-7982*	Address of Bank *98 State Street, Boston*
Finance Co. Loan Bank Loan (check if applicable)	Name of Finance Co. or Bank	Address of Finance Co. or Bank

4. Other Information You May Want Us To Consider

Complete only if your spouse will use the account, if you are relying on a spouse's income, alimony, child support or separate maintenance payments to establish your creditworthiness or if you wish to establish a joint or co-applicant account.

Spouse's or Co-Applicant's Name	First	Middle	Last	Social Security No.		
Spouse's or Co-Applicant's Employer					Annual Salary	
Employer's Address	Street	City	State	Zip		
Position	Years There	Business (Area Code) Phone	Relationship of Co-Applicant			

Be sure to read and sign the Retail Installment Credit Agreement inside

Baron & Dubois

No. of Store Cards Requested

Name of Other Store

Figure 41.1
Application for Credit Card

THE RIGHT TO KNOW WHAT CREDIT COSTS

Using credit almost always costs something. The amount of money paid for the use of borrowed money or for credit, stated in dollars and cents, is known as the **finance charge.** This charge must be clearly disclosed to the debtor. The finance charge must also be stated as a percentage of the total amount borrowed, which is known as the **annual percentage rate.** Some lenders and creditors add other charges, such as service or carrying charges, to the actual cost of borrowing the money. The law requires that these additional charges be disclosed as such.

One aim of the Truth in Lending Law is to help consumers and debtors know what they are being charged for the use of credit. Such knowledge helps consumers compare the cost of credit from various sources and make intelligent financing decisions. An example of information that must be given to the consumer is shown in Figure 41.2.

The Truth in Lending Law applies only to certain transactions and certain lenders or creditors. It does not apply to loans made for commercial purposes, such as buying items for a business, or to purchases of property for personal, family, or household use if the amount of credit is $25,000 or over. (Financing the purchase of a home is discussed in Chapter 31.) It only protects persons and not corporations, and applies only to persons who lend money or sell on credit in the ordinary course of business.

THE RIGHT TO FAIR CREDIT INFORMATION

In 1970 Congress passed the Fair Credit Reporting Act. The purpose of this law is to enable consumers to determine whether the information in their credit records is accurate. A credit record contains the history of your use of credit. It includes information on whether you made payments on time and whether you repaid your loans in full. Credit records are kept by credit bureaus in each city. A credit bureau functions as a sort of clearinghouse of credit information for those who need access to a person's credit history. Credit bureaus obtain their information from banks, department stores, and finance companies.

Your credit record is very important because it is the basis upon which sellers or lenders decide whether to give or to deny you credit. Under the

Figure 41.2
Information Required by Truth in Lending Law

Disclosures Required Under Federal Law

1. The **FINANCE CHARGE** on a cash advance is imposed from the date such advance is posted to your cash advance account. A merchant advance becomes subject to **FINANCE CHARGE** on the first day of the billing cycle following the cycle in which the advance is first posted to your merchant advance account and will be imposed as of such date on so much, if any, of the balance of your merchant advance account as is subject to **FINANCE CHARGE.**

2. The balance subject to **FINANCE CHARGE** is the sum of (a) the total of the daily closing balances in your cash advance account during the billing cycle divided by the number of days in the cycle and (b) the total of the daily closing balances (excluding merchant advances posted to the account during the cycle) in your merchant advance account during the billing cycle divided by the number of days in the cycle, except that the balance of your merchant advance account shall be deemed to be zero for any billing cycle at the beginning of which no cash advances are outstanding and during which the total balance owed on the closing date of the previous cycle is paid in full prior to the debiting of any new cash advance. You will, therefore, incur no **FINANCE CHARGE** on a merchant advance, as distinguished from a cash advance, if it is paid in full by the end of the billing cycle following that in which it is posted to your account.

3. The amount of the **FINANCE CHARGE** is determined by applying to the balance subject to **FINANCE CHARGE** a Periodic Rate of 1½% per month (**ANNUAL PERCENTAGE RATE 18%**) to the first **$500** thereof and a Periodic Rate of 1% per month (**ANNUAL PERCENTAGE RATE 12%**) to the excess over **$500.**

4. The minimum monthly payment required will be specified in your monthly statement and will equal the total of all minimum payments previously billed and unpaid plus the greater of **$10** or that amount which equals **3%** of your total balance outstanding on the closing date of the cycle covered by the statement. Payments are applied first to **FINANCE CHARGES,** then proportionately to the closing balance in your merchant advance account as of your last previous statement date and to the current balance in your cash advance account, and then to the current balance in your merchant advance account.

Fair Credit Reporting Act, if you are denied credit because of information filed with a credit bureau, you must be notified of the rejection and must be given the name and address of the credit bureau supplying the information on which the rejection was based. You have the right to contact the credit bureau and see the information in your credit record. The law provides that if any item in your record is found to be incorrect, or cannot be proven, the credit bureau must remove the item. The credit bureau must also give you the names of any persons who have received a credit report on you within the past six months.

A credit bureau must make a reasonable effort to verify the information it receives, particularly if the information is unfavorable. Failure to do so may subject the credit bureau to liability for noncompliance with the Fair Credit Reporting Act.

■ Grady applied to a bank for a student loan. The bank refused to grant the loan, claiming that Grady had a poor credit record. Grady may contact the credit bureau that supplied the information to the bank and get a copy of his credit record file. ■

Congress amended the Fair Credit Reporting Act in 1994 to provide added protection for consumers. Among the changes in the amended act are (1) lower-cost copies of one's credit report (in certain cases, the copies will be free), (2) toll-free phone numbers for credit bureaus, (3) mandatory resolution of disputes within thirty days, and (4) liability for creditors who neglect to correct errors in one's credit report.

THE RIGHT TO ACCURATE BILLING

The Truth in Lending Law requires that users of revolving charge accounts be sent monthly statements that contain the following information:

1. The unpaid balance at the beginning of the billing period
2. The amount of additional charges during the billing period
3. Payments made by the customer during the billing period
4. The amount of the finance charge in dollars and cents
5. The annual percentage rate used to compute the finance charge
6. The unpaid balance on which the finance charge is based
7. The new balance owed and the closing date of the billing period

As buying on credit has become more frequent, so have errors in billing become more frequent. Billing errors include arithmetic errors; failure to record payments made; a charge made to the wrong account; or charges made for the wrong merchandise, an incorrect amount, or merchandise that was never delivered.

In 1974 Congress passed the Fair Credit Billing Act to enable a consumer to resolve billing errors and disputes at little cost. Under this law, a person who receives a bill and thinks it is wrong must notify the creditor in writing within sixty days after the bill was mailed. The creditor must acknowledge this letter within thirty days of receiving it. Within ninety days, the creditor must either correct the bill or state why it believes the bill is correct as it is. The notice to the creditor must contain the name and account number of the person complaining, the nature of the complaint, and the amount believed to be in error. While waiting to have a bill corrected, the consumer does not have to pay any disputed amounts. The consumer must, however, pay all charges not being disputed. The creditor may not try to collect the disputed amount of a bill or damage the consumer's credit rating during the time the dispute is being investigated.

The law also provides that if a consumer receives defective merchandise or poor services bought on credit, the consumer may withhold payment, provided he or she has attempted to return the defective merchandise or resolve the problem with the seller. The consumer will not have to pay a penalty for withholding payment until the matter is solved.

THE RIGHT TO FAIR DEBT COLLECTION

Most people pay their bills and debts on time. When they don't, creditors may take steps to collect amounts owed. Some creditors have their own collection departments; others use attorneys or collection agencies. To protect consumers against unfair collection practices, Congress passed the Fair Debt Collection Practices Act in 1977. This law covers the collection of personal, family, and household debts but does not cover business debts. One of the major purposes of this law is to control the conduct of a debt collector. A **debt collector** is a person or company whose business it is to collect the debts owed to its clients. The act specifies what methods the debt collector may use in trying to collect a debt. The law, however, does not apply to the creditors themselves or to those who are not professional debt collectors.

The debt collector has a right to contact the debtor about the debt. However, the debt collector may not contact the debtor at an inconvenient time (usually before 8 A.M. or after 9 P.M.), at an inconvenient place (such as a restaurant), or at the debtor's place of employment if the employer does not permit such contacts.

Casey stopped making payments on a VCR because of financial problems. A debt collector called Casey at work every day, even though Casey's employer objected and told the debt collector so. The debt collector violated the Fair Debt Collection Practices Act. ■

The act requires a debt collector to send the debtor written notice (within five days after initially contacting the debtor) describing the amount due, the name of the creditor, and the debtor's rights. If the debtor informs the collector in writing within thirty days that the debt is not owed, further collection efforts must be stopped until the debt collector can supply the debtor with proof of the debt.

The act also prohibits specific abusive collection tactics, such as the use of obscene language, threats of violence, and annoying or anonymous telephone calls. Misrepresentation of the collector's identity or any indication that the debtor has committed a crime by failing to pay the debt is also prohibited.

■ Carlos failed to make several payments on a car loan. A debt collector advised her that failure to make payments would result in a jail sentence. This advice was false and was a violation of the Fair Debt Collection Practices Act. ■

Debt collectors also may not issue any official-looking documents to the debtor that have any resemblance to those used by public officials or regulatory agencies.

■ Johnson was late in paying a debt owed on his motorcycle. The account was turned over to Control Collection Company. Control sent Johnson a letter that stated in part (in bold type): "YOU HAVE VIOLATED THE LAWS OF THE UNITED STATES AND ITS GOVERNMENT BY NOT PAYING YOUR DEBT. IF YOU ARE SUED, YOU WILL NOT ESCAPE FEDERAL JUDGMENT." At the top of this statement was the U.S. insignia of the bald eagle. The letter to Johnson was a violation of the Fair Debt Collection Practices Act. ■

Various state laws and court decisions also protect the debtor from unfair collection practices. Most states require certain procedures to be followed before a judgment may be taken against a debtor. In some states a debtor must be notified before a default judgment may be taken. A default judgment is a judgment entered against a debtor who fails to respond to a lawsuit brought to collect the debt. Once a judgment has been entered against a debtor, a creditor is limited in the actions it can take to collect the judgment. A creditor may ask a debtor to state, under oath, her or his assets. Certain assets may be taken to pay a debt, but some assets are exempt property under state law. **Exempt property** refers to those assets that may not be taken to pay a judgment; they include clothes, household furniture, dishes, and other personal items.

Garnishment, which is a legal means of taking part of a debtor's earnings to pay a judgment, is also limited in most states.

THE RIGHT TO LEGAL INTEREST CHARGES

Most states have laws that protect a debtor by setting a maximum rate of interest that may be charged. Most states set two rates. The **contract rate** is the maximum rate of interest agreed to by the parties and included in a credit agreement. If no interest rate is stated in a loan or credit agreement, the maximum that may be charged is the **legal rate.** In a few states the contract rate and the legal rate are the same.

An agreement requiring payment of an interest rate higher than the contract rate is illegal and is known as *usury.* (Usury is discussed in Chapter

10). In most states the penalty for usury is the forfeiture of interest by the creditor. In many states it is also a crime to charge usurious interest.

There are several situations in which usury laws do not apply. In most states, usury laws do not apply to loans to businesses or to loans under a certain dollar amount. Usury laws often do not apply to loans given by credit unions, pawn shops, and small-loan companies. The most common exception to the usury laws concerns installment loans and credit card charges. Usury laws generally do not apply to the sale of goods on credit because these transactions often involve long-term credit with a high degree of risk to the creditor. Because of this risk the creditor is permitted to charge a rate of interest that exceeds the contract rate.

> Ferris bought a new color TV and agreed to pay for it on an installment loan basis. The interest Ferris will be charged is not subject to the laws governing usury. The creditor takes a risk that Ferris will not pay off the loan. ∎

THE RIGHT TO BE RELIEVED FROM DEBT

Most people in this country do pay their debts, but some people are unable to handle their debts. To help consumers in this situation, Congress, in 1898, passed the Federal Bankruptcy Act. This act, which has been amended several times, helps to relieve a debtor of debt, allowing the debtor to start a new economic life. It also allows unpaid creditors to receive the maximum amount from the debtor's assets.

A person or corporation may be declared bankrupt under the act by committing one or more "acts of bankruptcy." The most common act of bankruptcy is admitting in writing an inability to pay debts as they become due, a condition known as **insolvency**. There are two types of bankrupts: voluntary and involuntary. A **voluntary bankrupt** is a person or corporation that voluntarily files a petition to become a bankrupt. An **involuntary bankrupt** is a person or corporation forced into bankruptcy when a creditor files a petition to have the person or corporation declared bankrupt. Farmers, low-income persons, and nonprofit corporations cannot be forced into involuntary bankruptcy.

The Bankruptcy Act covers four types of bankruptcy proceedings. Chapter 7 of the act covers the most well-known type of bankruptcy proceeding, usually known as ordinary or straight bankruptcy. Chapter 9 covers insolvency of a municipality. Chapter 11 of the act governs reorganization, which permits a debtor to continue in business after working out a payment arrangement with creditors. Chapter 13 permits an individual debtor to work out a payment plan with creditors, thereby avoiding the necessity of going into bankruptcy.

Chapter 7 of the act applies to individuals, partnerships, and corporations. To begin voluntary bankruptcy proceedings, a debtor files a petition in the nearest Federal Bankruptcy Court. (A creditor files the petition for an involuntary bankrupt.) The petition contains information about the bankrupt: a list of creditors, the type and amount of each debt, and a list of the debtor's assets. The debtor must swear to the truth of the information supplied; knowingly giving false information is a crime.

Immediately upon filing a voluntary bankruptcy petition, the debtor is declared a bankrupt. The court notifies all creditors of the filing of the petition and sets a date for a hearing. The court also notifies creditors to file their claims against the bankrupt by a certain date. At the hearing, the court and the creditors may ask the bankrupt about the truth and accuracy of the petition. They will want to know whether any assets have been concealed or given away to try to defraud creditors.

If the bankrupt has no assets, the bankruptcy proceeding is concluded after the hearing and the bankrupt is released from her or his debts. If the bankrupt has assets, they are sold to pay the creditors. Creditors are paid in proportion to the amount they are owed, although some claims, such as taxes owed, have priority.

> Davis owed $200 to the Internal Revenue Service for income taxes, $1,000 to Jones, and $500 to Smith. David filed a petition for bankruptcy. Davis's assets were sold for $800. The Internal Revenue Service would receive the full $200, Jones would receive $400, and Smith would receive $200. ■

To avoid leaving a bankrupt with absolutely nothing, certain assets may not be taken in a bankruptcy proceeding. These assets are exemptions granted under the federal law and under the laws of the state in which the bankruptcy proceeding is held. A bankrupt may choose either federal or state exemptions, except in some states where only the state exemption may be used.

Under federal law, a bankrupt may keep social security benefits, unemployment compensation, and insurance policies. In addition, a bankrupt may keep interest in a home or other real property up to $7,500, equity in a motor vehicle up to $1,200, up to $500 worth of jewelry, up to $4,000 in aggregate value of personal items and household furnishings, and $400 worth of anything else. State exemptions vary, but in most states they include personal property and a portion of the investment in a home.

After all debts, taxes, and administrative expenses have been paid, the bankrupt receives a judgment called a discharge in bankruptcy. A **discharge in bankruptcy** frees the bankrupt from all debts except those for taxes, alimony, child support, and education loans. A discharge will not be granted, however, to a debtor who has fraudulently transferred or concealed property or who has obtained credit by fraudulent means. To avoid abuse of the bankruptcy law by debtors, the law allows a person to file a petition in bankruptcy only once every six years.

A reorganization under Chapter 11 of the Bankruptcy Act enables a debtor to continue in business by making an arrangement with creditors to pay a portion of the outstanding debts over a period of time. Although Chapter 11 is used primarily by corporations, it is available to individuals as well.

A proceeding under Chapter 11 is brought in the same manner as a Chapter 7 proceeding. A petition is filed, listing all debts and creditors.

During the proceedings, the debtor may continue to operate its business but is often supervised by a court-appointed trustee. A committee of unsecured creditors is usually appointed to work with the debtor and trustee to assist in the reorganization.

Ultimately, the debtor proposes a plan of reorganization to the Bankruptcy Court and the creditors. The plan must indicate the different classes of creditors (based on the presence or lack of security, the amount of the claims, and so on), how much will be paid to each class of creditor, and when payment will be made. The plan must also indicate how its goals can be achieved.

If the creditors accept the plan and the Bankruptcy Court finds that the plan is in the best interests of the creditors, the Court confirms it and the debtor continues in business. When the goals of the plan have been achieved, the debtor is discharged.

Chapter 13 of the Bankruptcy Act enables an individual debtor with unsecured debts under $100,000 or secured debts under $350,000 to pay off debts under a court-approved plan. It is similar to a Chapter 11 reorganization (which is also available to individual debtors), except that it is available only to individuals, not partnerships or corporations, and there are debt ceilings, as described above.

A debtor files a petition listing assets and debts. A trustee is appointed to develop with the debtor a reasonable payment plan. The plan provides for payment over a period of time of either all or a portion of the debts. Payment must be made within three years, although an extension of two additional years is available with court approval. Part of the plan must be that the debtor will turn over to the trustee sufficient earnings to ensure the success of the plan.

After the debtor files a plan, the court holds a confirmation hearing. If the plan appears feasible and the secured creditors accept the plan, the court will confirm it, and all debts provided for under the plan will be discharged. As is the case under Chapters 7 and 11 of the act, certain debts, such as alimony, child support, and education loans, are not dischargeable.

After completing the plan, the debtor is fully discharged from the Chapter 13 proceeding. Unlike Chapters 7 and 11 proceedings, a debtor may ask for the Bankruptcy Court's assistance under Chapter 13 any number of times.

Filing for bankruptcy and for assistance under Chapter 13 of the Federal Bankruptcy Act are considered proper solutions for financial distress. However, they are serious matters, and they should not be undertaken unless no other remedies are available. Under federal law, bankruptcy information remains part of a person's credit history for ten years. If a person files for assistance under Chapter 13, the time period is seven years. It becomes virtually impossible for an individual or business to obtain credit during these time periods. The purpose of this is to prevent individuals and businesses from going into bankruptcy solely to avoid paying for their debts.

Other remedies that are available to persons with financial problems are not as drastic as the bankruptcy courts. A person in debt may be able to work out an informal arrangement with creditors to pay debts over a period of time. There are also debt-counseling services, which may be able to work out informal arrangements with creditors. Many of the counseling services are available without charge; others charge for their services.

Summary of Important Legal Concepts

Federal and state governments have enacted many laws to protect consumers who buy on credit and to protect borrowers of money. The areas of protection include the right to obtain credit; the right to be charged only those interest charges permitted by law; the right to receive accurate bills; the right to be free from harassing collection methods; and the right to relief from debt.

The two basic types of credit available to a consumer are unsecured credit, which is based solely on the consumer's promise to repay, and secured credit, which is also based on a pledge of the borrower's property. The three most-used types of credit are charge accounts, installment loans, and bank loans.

The right to obtain credit is controlled by the Equal Credit Opportunity Act. This law prevents creditors from discriminating against certain people and seeks to make sure that credit is based almost solely on the ability to pay. Age, sex, or marital status cannot legally be considered in determining whether to grant credit.

A borrower often does not know what credit is actually going to cost. The Truth in Lending Law helps consumers and borrowers know what they are being charged for the use of credit. This enables them to make intelligent choices when deciding about borrowing money.

Billing errors and disputes can seriously damage a person's credit record. The Fair Credit Reporting Act provides consumers with a way to determine whether their credit records are accurate and with a method for recording any errors in such reports.

When a consumer has purchased goods on credit or borrowed money, it is important that any bills sent be accurate. The Fair Credit Billing Act enables a consumer or borrower to resolve billing errors or disputes in a simplified, inexpensive way.

The Fair Debt Collection Practices Act regulates the collection of all debts except business obligations. The purpose of this law is to control the acts of debt collectors and to prohibit abusive collection tactics.

Debtors are often faced with higher than normal interest charges that they feel powerless to contest. To assist them, most states have enacted usury laws. These laws regulate the interest rate that may be charged and provide penalties for those who charge interest rates higher than those permitted by law. There are some exceptions to usury laws.

Some people are unable to handle their debts and face suits from creditors. The Federal Bankruptcy Act helps debtors to seek relief from debt and get a new start on life. The act covers three types of proceedings. One involves straight bankruptcy, another governs reorganization for individuals and businesses, and the third permits an individual debtor to work out a payment plan with creditors. In addition to the plans permitted under the Bankruptcy Act, many voluntary plans are available, including voluntary arrangements with creditors. The latter may provide less drastic relief than that provided by the Bankruptcy Act, which affects a person's credit history for seven to ten years.

Key Legal Terms to Know

Match the terms with the definitions that follow.

annual percentage rate
charge account
collateral
contract rate
credit
credit card
creditor
debit card
debt collector
debtor
discharge in bankruptcy
exempt property
finance charge

insolvency
installment loan
involuntary bankrupt
legal rate
line of credit
regular charge account
revolving charge account
secured credit
unsecured credit
voluntary bankrupt

1. Inability to pay debts as they become due
2. The right to pay for goods and services after receiving them
3. One who borrows money or buys on credit
4. The cost of borrowing money or buying on credit stated in dollars and cents
5. The maximum interest rate that may be charged when no rate has been agreed to by the parties
6. A judgment relieving a bankrupt from liability for most debts
7. Property that cannot be taken to satisfy a debt
8. The cost of credit stated as a percentage of the amount borrowed
9. The maximum interest rate that may be charged in a credit agreement
10. A person in the business of collecting debts
11. A person who lends money or sells goods on credit
12. An account in which you are expected to pay each bill in full when received
13. An agreement to pay for an item in fixed, regular payments
14. A person or corporation forced into bankruptcy by a creditor
15. An agreement between a consumer and a business allowing the consumer to purchase items now and pay for them later
16. An account in which you may pay a portion of the bill each month
17. A person or corporation that files a petition for bankruptcy
18. The maximum amount that can be owed on a credit card at any one time
19. An asset that may be pledged as security for a loan
20. A card that immediately transfers funds from the user's bank account upon use
21. A card that enables its user to obtain goods and services on credit

22. Credit based solely on a promise to repay
23. Credit based on a promise to repay plus a pledge of the borrower's property, which the lender may sell if the loan is not repaid

Questions and Problems to Discuss

1. What factors may a creditor consider in deciding whether or not to grant credit?
2. What is the difference between a credit card and a debit card?
3. Andrews lost a credit card one evening. The next day, Andrews discovered the loss and notified the card company. In the meantime, Brown found the card and used it to purchase a radio worth $180. The card company billed Andrews for the $180. Should the credit card company collect from Andrews?
4. A credit card company sent a card to Paulson, who hadn't asked for it. A thief stole the card out of Paulson's mailbox, signed Paulson's name to the card, and used the card to buy a boat. Is Paulson liable for the credit card charge?
5. Rodriguez signed a contract to buy a horse trailer from Linden. Rodriguez fell behind in making the payments on the trailer. Linden called her every day at work and also at home to try to collect the debt. May Linden try to collect the amount owed in this manner?
6. Jamison asked the Acme Bank to lend her $15,000 to expand her business. Must Acme disclose the finance charge and annual percentage rate as required by the Truth in Lending Law?
7. Barnes bought a TV set from Janeway on credit. The price tag indicated a price of $400. Barnes signed a contract agreeing to pay for the set in 12 monthly payments of $40 each. The contract contained no other terms. Did the contract violate the Truth in Lending Law?
8. Mason tried to open a charge account at Super Stores. Super Stores checked Mason's credit rating with a credit bureau and learned that Mason was a slow payer. Super Stores refused to open an account for Mason. When Mason insisted on knowing the reason for the refusal, Super Stores refused to answer, claiming the information was confidential. Is Mason entitled to the information?
9. Marshall borrowed $1,000 from a bank, payable at the end of one year at the highest legal interest

rate permitted in that state. The bank gave Marshall only $750, however, keeping the other $250 as part of the "cost" of the loan. Is this loan usurious?

10. Green borrowed money from a bank to finance her education; the loan was guaranteed by the federal government. Green then suffered financial problems and was forced to file a petition in bankruptcy. Is she still obligated to repay the loan?

11. Klaus failed to make three payments on a department store installment loan. A debt collection agency advised Klaus that the store would sue her if the payments were not made up. Is this a violation of the Fair Debt Collection Practices Act?

12. Davis owed $200 to the IRS for income taxes, $300 to Olympia Bank for a student loan, $1,000 to Jones and $500 to Smith. Davis filed a petition for bankruptcy. At the time of filing, Davis's assets were worth $800 and sold for that amount. How much money would each of Davis's creditors receive?

13 Ferris bought a new car and agreed to pay for it on an installment loan basis. A week after Ferris bought the car, he looked over the installment loan contract and discovered that the interest rate being charged was 21 percent, although the laws in his state made it unlawful to charge any rate of interest in excess of 10 percent. Was the interest charged by the automobile dealer a violation of the state usury laws?

14. Because of financial problems, Casey stopped making payments on a VCR he purchased on an installment basis. Each night for two weeks, a debt collector called Casey at his home at 7:30 p.m. and requested payment of the amount due. Were these calls a violation of the Fair Debt Collection Practices Act?

Cases to Decide

1. Martin let someone use his credit card with the understanding that charges would not exceed $500. The user charged much more than that. Is Martin's liability limited to $50? (*Martin* v. *American Express, Inc.*, 361 So 2d 597)

2. Allen took out a loan from Landmark in his own name but used the proceeds to buy a frozen yogurt machine for use in his business. Landmark failed to disclose the information required by the Truth in Lending Law, claiming this was a commercial transaction. Allen claimed the loan was covered by the law because the loan was taken out in his name. Who is correct? (*Allen* v. *Landmark Finance Corporation of Georgia*, USDC, ND of Ga 1979 CCH Consumer Credit Guide, Sec 1007.02)

3. Miller applied for an oil company credit card. He was refused the card because of a poor credit report that was based on incorrect information. Miller sued the credit bureau for violating the Fair Credit Reporting Act by failing to verify the truth of the credit report. The credit bureau claimed that its only duty was to collect information, not to decide whether it was accurate. Will Miller win? (*Miller* v. *Credit Bureau, Inc.*, DC Super, Ct, 1972 CCH Consumer Credit Guide, Sec 680.04, 680.79, 680.61)

4. Mr. and Mrs. Lamb filed a petition in bankruptcy. They claimed that the value of a life insurance policy that they owned was exempt from the demands of creditors because it was exempt under the laws of the state of Louisiana, where they resided. Are they correct? (*Re: Lamb*, 272 F Supp 393)

5. Delta Air Lines offered its customers an opportunity to buy tickets on credit over the telephone. The tickets could either be charged to a credit card or mailed out in advance of payment. If mailing was requested, Delta required payment in advance if the purchaser lived in certain neighborhoods, usually populated by minority groups. May Delta be prohibited from taking this action? (*Delta Air Lines, Inc.*, CAB Order 78-8-101)

6. Branch made false statements in an application for a loan from a bank. When Branch filed a petition in bankruptcy, Mills, a creditor, objected to giving Branch a discharge in bankruptcy. Was Mills correct? (*Branch* v. *Mills and Liption Supply Company*, 348 F2d 901)

7. Carrigan owed a debt to the University of Florida for tuition. Central made many telephone calls to Carrigan requesting payment. Carrigan sent a letter to Central directing Central to cease making any further telephone calls to him, but Central continued to make these calls. Carrigan brought an action against Central for violation of the Fair Debt Collection Practices Act. Will Carrigan succeed? (*Carrigan* v. *Central Adjustment Bureau*, 494 F Supp 824)

8. Mr. and Mrs. McPhee filed a petition in bankruptcy in the U.S. District Court in Connecticut. Two months later, they sought to withdraw the petition in bankruptcy. They were allowed to do so and the matter was dismissed. The McPhees subsequently met their other financial obligations. Two years later, the McPhees applied to a bank for a mortgage and were refused because of a credit report prepared by a consumer reporting agency, which showed that the McPhees had filed for bankruptcy. The information was based on information available at the time the McPhees attempted to get the mortgage. The McPhees brought an action charging violation of the Fair Credit Reporting Act. Are they correct? (*McPhee v. Chilton Corp.*, 468 F Supp 494)

9. Jones and her husband established credit card accounts with Walker Bank. Later, Mr. and Mrs. Jones separated, and Mrs. Jones informed the bank by letter that she would no longer honor any charges made by her husband on their accounts. The bank immediately revoked the accounts and requested the return of the credit cards. Despite numerous requests and notices of revocation, Jones and her husband retained the cards and continued to use them. When Mrs. Jones finally surrendered her cards, the balance showing on their combined accounts was $2,685.70. Walker Bank sued Mrs. Jones but she refused to pay, claiming that the federal Truth In Lending Act limits her liability to a maximum of $50. Is she correct? (*Walker Bank and Trust Company v. Jones*, 672 P2d 73)

Chapter 42

Protecting the Creditor

CHAPTER PREVIEW

Just as consumers and borrowers have certain rights that need protection, so too do those who sell goods on credit and those who lend money. This chapter describes the methods by which creditors can protect themselves to ensure payment. It discusses the different types of debtor-creditor transactions. The chapter also discusses protection for creditors in the form of liens that are provided by statutes. Finally, the chapter describes remedies available to creditors if debtors default in making payments and discusses other devices that may be used to protect creditors.

PROTECTING CREDITORS' RIGHTS

In recent years, the consumer movement has stressed the need to protect the debtor. But creditors also have rights that need protection if creditors are to remain in business. Both statute and case law provide the creditor with methods to ensure payment. These may well be called a "Bill of Rights for the Creditor."

THE RIGHT TO BE PAID

A creditor has an absolute right to be paid unless the debtor has certain defenses against the creditor, such as fraud or misrepresentation. How and in what manner a creditor may enforce this right depends on whether the credit transaction is unsecured or secured.

Unsecured Debts

An **unsecured debt** is one based solely on the debtor's promise to pay. This promise may be made orally or in writing. Much of consumer debt today is of the unsecured type. Examples of unsecured debts are purchases made on a charge account or a personal loan from a friend, family member, or bank.

> You borrowed money from Janus, a friend, and promised to repay the loan in two weeks. The only security Janus has for her loan to you is your promise to repay it. ∎

A creditor holding an unsecured debt is limited in the methods that can be used to collect the debt. If a debtor goes beyond the time for repayment of the debt, a creditor will normally start the collection process by contacting the debtor and asking for payment. If this fails, the creditor may ask a collection agency to collect the debt. If this also fails, the creditor may sue the debtor for payment. If the creditor wins, the creditor will get a judgment against the debtor. A judgment, in this case, is a court order directing the debtor to pay the debt owed to the creditor. Once the creditor has obtained the judgment, the creditor may attempt to collect the amount owed out of the debtor's assets. If the debtor has sufficient assets with which to pay the debt, the creditor will be paid.

If the judgment is not paid, the creditor can obtain an order, or *writ* as it is sometimes called, of execution. The **execution** directs the appropriate enforcement officer, usually a sheriff, to seize the debtor's personal property and sell enough of that property to pay the judgment, plus any costs or expenses. If the execution does not produce enough funds to pay the judgment, the judgment then becomes a lien on any real property owned by the debtor. The debtor's real property may then be sold to satisfy the judgment.

Another method used by a creditor to collect a judgment is garnishment. **Garnishment** is a court-ordered process authorizing an employer to seize (deduct a portion of) the wages of a debtor. A bank account or any amounts owed to the debtor by a third party may also be garnished. The amounts seized are paid to either the court or a sheriff and are then applied against the debt. State laws limit the amount of wages that may be seized so that the debtor is not left penniless. Occasionally, a debtor will voluntarily consent to have a portion of her or his wages turned over to a creditor to repay a debt. This is known as **wage assignment.**

Sometimes a creditor believes that a debtor may dispose of or transfer assets before a judgment can be obtained. If this is the case, the creditor may ask the court to issue an attachment. An **attachment** is an order to seize (attach) and hold property of the debtor before a judgment is obtained. If the creditor later obtains a judgment, the attached property may be sold to satisfy it.

Secured Debts

An unsecured creditor is not only limited in the methods that can be used to collect a debt, but also may face competition from other creditors. Recall from Chapter 41 that some of a debtor's property may even be exempt from execution. To get an extra measure of protection, a creditor may insist on a secured debt. A **secured debt,** created by an agreement between the debtor and the creditor, is one in which the creditor has a claim against specific property of the debtor. The creditor's claim in the property is called a *security interest.* Secured debts occur at all levels of commerce, including the purchase of motor vehicles and the financing of inventory purchases.

A secured debt, or *secured transaction* as it is often called, is created by a **security agreement.** This agreement must be in writing and signed by both the debtor and the creditor. The agreement includes the names and addresses of the debtor and the creditor, the amount of the debt, the terms of payment, and a description of the property in which the creditor gets a security interest. The property pledged by the debtor as security for the debt is the *collateral.*

Collateral may be either tangible or intangible property. Tangible property consists of such things as consumer goods, farm products, equipment, or the inventory of a business. Intangible property refers to the rights (claims) to property, such as money. Stocks and accounts receivable are examples of intangible property.

Gray borrowed $6,000 from Second National Bank to buy a car and gave the bank a security interest in the car. The contract that Gray signed is a security agreement. The car, a consumer good, is the collateral for the loan. ■

Property pledged as collateral may be in the possession of either the debtor or the creditor. In most cases the debtor has possession of the property. For example, if you buy a boat on a secured installment loan, you have possession of the boat, but you must sign a security agreement giving the creditor a security interest in the boat. Occasionally the creditor has possession of the collateral. For example, a pawn shop owner who lends you money on a piece of property (such as a ring or watch) holds the property until you repay the loan.

For certain transactions a **financing statement** must be filed to give public notice that a creditor holds a security interest in specific property of the debtor. A security agreement is valid regardless of whether or not a financing statement is filed. The financing statement is filed only to give notice to third parties. The financing statement identifies the parties to the security agreement (that is, the debtor and the creditor) and describes the property serving as collateral. This public notice warns others who may be interested in buying the collateral or lending money based on its value that a security interest already exists and has first claim on the property. The financing statement is usually filed in a county clerk's office or in the office of a state's motor vehicle bureau. When the debt is paid in full, a notice is filed in the same office indicating that the security interest is no longer claimed. This notice is called a **termination statement.**

Not all security agreements require the filing of a financing statement to protect the creditor. The Uniform Commercial Code distinguishes between a sale of equipment or inventory goods on credit and a sale of consumer goods on credit. A financing statement must be filed for a credit sale of equipment or inventory but is not necessary for most consumer credit sales. The exceptions to this rule involve security interests in automobiles, farm equipment costing over $2,500, and goods such as elevators that are to be attached to buildings or land.

OTHER METHODS OF PROTECTING CREDITORS' RIGHTS

There are many other ways creditors can protect their rights with the consent of the debtor. The two most common means are the use of a suretyship and the use of a guaranty. Both of these involve getting a third party to assume some form of obligation for repayment of the debt.

Suretyship

A **suretyship** is a promise by a third party, the **surety,** to pay a creditor the amount of the debt if the debtor defaults. A surety agrees to be primarily responsible for the amount of the debt if the debtor defaults. That is, the creditor may look to the surety for payment without first having to sue the debtor. If the surety has to pay the creditor, the surety may then sue the debtor for payment. A surety's promise to pay may be oral or written.

> Aldo borrowed money from the Benevolent Finance Company to start a restaurant. Benevolent would not lend the money unless Aldo's brother-in-law agreed to act as surety and be liable for the debt along with Aldo. If Aldo does not repay the loan, Benevolent may go directly to Aldo's brother-in-law and collect the amount due from him. ■

Guaranty

A **guaranty** is similar to a suretyship except that the **guarantor,** the person who gives the guaranty, is not primarily liable for the debt. That is, if the debtor defaults, the creditor must first attempt to collect the debt from the debtor. If that fails, only then may the creditor look to the guarantor for payment. A guaranty must be in writing to be enforceable.

> Drumm agreed to act as guarantor for his sister's loan. If the sister fails to repay the loan, the lender must first sue the sister. If the lender obtains a judgment and still is unable to collect payment from the sister, the lender may proceed to Drumm for payment. ■

Both suretyship and guaranty agreements terminate when the debtor pays the debt in full. They also terminate if the debtor and the creditor make a significant change in the terms of the agreement without the consent of the surety or the guarantor. Such termination protects the surety and guarantor against an increase or change in their liability without their knowledge or agreement.

> Kantell agreed to act as guarantor for a loan of $8,000 made by Ace Loan Company to her brother. Ace later lent her brother an additional $4,000, increasing the loan to $12,000, without notifying Kantell. The additional loan releases Kantell from her obligations under the guaranty. ■

Both a contract of guaranty and a contract of suretyship require consideration to be enforceable. When either contract is made at the same time as the original transaction, the consideration for the original promise is also consideration for the promise of the guarantor or surety. However, when the contract of guaranty or suretyship is entered into after the original transaction, there must be new consideration for the promise of the guarantor or surety.

> Sanders bought a new car and wanted to finance the purchase with a bank loan. Because she was unemployed, the bank would not give Sanders the loan unless her father acted as guarantor. The consideration for his promise as guarantor is the promise made by the bank to grant the loan. ■

Remedies for Debtor's Default

If a debtor cannot or will not make payments, the debtor is said to be "in default." A secured creditor has two options if a debtor defaults. One option is to sell the collateral and use the proceeds to pay the debt. If the creditor has possession of the collateral, such as stocks put up as security for a loan, the creditor may sell the property, keep an amount equal to the unpaid debt and any expenses of the sale, and return any amount left over to the debtor.

If the debtor has possession of the collateral, the creditor may take steps to gain possession of the property. This process is known as **repossession.** In some states the creditor may repossess the collateral without court proceedings if it can be done peacefully. If that is impossible, or if state law requires, the creditor must get a court order authorizing the repossession.

The creditor who has repossessed the collateral does not have to sell it if the debtor agrees. The creditor may lease the collateral or keep it as payment for the debt. The creditor must notify the debtor of this intention. If the debtor objects to the creditor holding the collateral, the creditor must sell the collateral and use the proceeds to pay off the debt. A debtor who has made some payments on the debt may want to force the sale of the collateral to recover any money left over after payment of the debt. Otherwise the debtor would forfeit any amount already paid.

If the creditor does decide to sell the collateral, it may be sold at a public or a private sale and on the creditor's own terms. The sale must be conducted in good faith and the debtor must get advance notice of the sale. After the collateral is sold, the proceeds are used to pay the expenses of repossessing the collateral, the expenses of the sale, and the debt itself. If any money is left, it goes to the debtor. If the proceeds are not enough to pay the debt, the creditor may sue the debtor for the balance of the debt.

> ■ Arthur defaulted on a car installment loan and the bank repossessed the car. The loan balance was $4,000. If the car was sold for $4,500 and the expenses amounted to $800, the bank could sue Arthur for the balance of $300. ■

The second option a creditor has for a debtor's default is to sue the debtor and try to obtain a judgment. If the judgment is granted, the debtor must pay the debt, or assets of the debtor may be taken and sold to pay the debt. After obtaining a judgment, a secured creditor has the same options as an unsecured creditor who obtains a judgment: execution and garnishment.

SECURITY INTERESTS CREATED BY LAW

Some creditors are given a security interest by law to protect them in the event of nonpayment by debtors. This type of security interest, which can be enforced against property, is called a **lien.** The person who has the lien (the creditor) is called the **lienholder.** Liens give a creditor an extra measure of protection over and above the normal rights of an unsecured creditor. There may be many types of liens, including mechanic's liens, tax liens, judgment liens, artisan's liens, and hotelkeeper's liens.

Mechanic's Lien

A **mechanic's lien** is a lien given to those who supply labor, materials, or services in the construction of buildings and other structures. A lien may be placed against the building to ensure that the owner pays for all the materials and services provided in its construction. The lienholder files a notice of the lien in a public office. While the notice is on file, the owner cannot sell or mortgage the property against which the lien has been filed. If a debt is not paid, the lienholder may sue to have the property sold and apply the proceeds to pay the debt.

Tax Lien

A **tax lien** is a lien given to an agency or unit of the government to ensure the payment of property taxes. Most local governments rely on property taxes to supply a large part of their operating funds. They could not continue to operate if they could not collect property taxes. If taxes remain unpaid for a certain period of time, the taxing authority may sell the property and pay the taxes due out of the proceeds. This is a last resort and the property owner has several opportunities to pay the taxes before the property is sold.

Judgment Lien

A **judgment lien** is a lien granted to a creditor who has sued a debtor and obtained a judgment. As discussed earlier in the chapter, the creditor may sell the property of the debtor and pay the judgment out of the proceeds.

Artisan's Lien

An **artisan's lien** is a lien given to someone who has performed labor on or added value to personal property. As long as the property is in the possession of the lienholder and payment is not made, the lienholder may sell the property to satisfy the debt, after giving notice to the owner of the property. Typical lienholders of this type are jewelers, auto repair shops, and dry cleaners.

Hotelkeeper's Lien

A **hotelkeeper's lien** is one placed on a guest's baggage to ensure payment of hotel charges. If the charges are unpaid, the hotelkeeper may satisfy the debt by selling the baggage at a public sale.

Summary of Important Legal Concepts

If creditors are going to continue to sell goods on credit and lend money, their right to be paid must be protected. Statutes and case law both provide creditors with methods to ensure payment.

Debts are either unsecured or secured. The typical debt is unsecured—it is based solely on the debtor's promise to pay. A creditor who is unpaid has only one recourse—to go into court and sue the debtor. Once a creditor obtains a judgment, a number of devices are available to assist in collecting the amount due, including executing on and attacking the debtor's property, garnishment of wages, and a voluntary wage assignment from the debtor to the creditor.

A secured debt is one in which a creditor has a claim against specific property of the debtor. The debtor and creditor enter into a security agreement that establishes the secured transaction. The agreement, or a memorandum of the agreement, is filed in a public office, giving notice to the public of the existence of the security agreement. If the debtor fails to pay the debt, the creditor can seize the property involved, sell it, and satisfy the debt out of the proceeds. A mortgage and an automobile loan are examples of security interests in specific property.

Creditors may also protect their interests by getting a third party to guarantee repayment of a loan. The two methods most often used are suretyship and guaranty. In both cases, a third party guarantees repayment of the debt. The difference between them is that a surety may be held as liable for the debt as the debtor. A guarantor may be held liable only after the debtor is unable or unwilling to pay the debt.

The law gives certain credit extra protection in the form of a security interest known as a lien. A lien is similar to a security interest in specific property. In the event of nonpayment, the creditor may seize the property covered by the security interest, force a sale, and apply the proceeds to pay the debt.

Key Legal Terms to Know

Match the terms with the definitions that follow.

artisan's lien
attachment
execution
financing statement
garnishment
guarantor
guaranty
hotelkeeper's lien
judgment lien
lien
lienholder
mechanic's lien
repossession

secured debt
security agreement
surety
suretyship
tax lien
termination statement
unsecured debt
wage assignment

1. A debt based solely on the debtor's promise to pay
2. A promise by a third party to be secondarily liable for the debt of another person
3. A debt in which the creditor has a claim against specific property of the debtor
4. A promise by a third party to be primarily responsible for another person's debt
5. An agreement giving a creditor a security interest in property belonging to a debtor
6. The seizure of a debtor's property to satisfy a judgment
7. A lien granted to a creditor who has sued a debtor and obtained a judgment against the debtor
8. A public notice of the existence of a security interest in certain property of the debtor
9. A security interest created by law
10. A public notice indicating that a security interest is no longer claimed in certain property
11. A lien given to a government agency to ensure the payment of property taxes
12. Steps taken by a creditor to gain possession of the collateral for a debt
13. A lien given to those who supply labor, materials, or services in construction projects
14. A person holding a lien
15. The seizure of a portion of a debtor's wages to satisfy a judgment
16. The seizure of a debtor's property prior to a judgment
17. A debtor's voluntary transfer of wages to a creditor to repay a debt
18. A third party who agrees to be primarily responsible for another person's debt if the debtor defaults
19. A third party who promises to repay another person's debt if the creditor cannot collect from the debtor
20. The lien a hotel owner has against property of a guest for unpaid bills
21. The lien a service provider has against personal property for unpaid bills

Questions and Problems to Discuss

1. What is the difference between a secured debt and an unsecured debt?
2. Describe the methods available to an unsecured creditor to collect a debt.
3. Why do you think that certain liens, such as tax liens, were created by law?
4. Harper bought a TV set from a department store and charged it on his charge account. When he failed to pay for the set, the store tried to repossess the TV. Can the store legally do this?
5. Hamilton bought an automobile from Muzi Car Sales and financed it as an installment loan. Muzi failed to file the financing statement. Is Muzi protected if Hamilton sells the car to someone else without paying off the installment loan?
6. Exchange Bank agreed to lend $5,000 to Blue if Blue's sister would serve as the guarantor. Blue's sister agreed and the loan was made. The loan agreement provided for weekly payments on Monday of each week. A month after the loan was granted, Blue and the bank agreed to change the day of payment to Wednesday and made the change without notifying Blue's sister. Is Blue's sister released from her guaranty?
7. Friendly agreed to act as surety on a loan given by Ace Finance Company to James. When James could not repay the loan, Ace came directly to Friendly for payment without attempting to get the money from James. Friendly refused to pay, claiming that Ace should first try to collect from James. Is Friendly correct?
8. Ramirez bought a used hay spreader from Hurdle for $3,000, paying $1,000 in cash and the balance in a promissory note secured by a security agreement. Before Hurdle filed the financing statement, Ramirez used the spreader as collateral to obtain a loan from Allen, who did file a financing statement. If Ramirez does not repay the loans, who has a prior right to repossess the spreader, Hurdle or Allen?
9. Liang, an architect, designed a house for Sommers. When Sommers failed to pay Liang for the services rendered, Liang filed a mechanic's lien against the house. Sommers claimed that the lien was invalid because it was not filed for materials used in building the house. Is Sommers correct?
10. Drew sold Maple a car and agreed to take a security interest in the car in return for letting Maple make twelve monthly payments on the balance of the purchase price. When Maple defaulted on the payments, Drew sued Maple. Must Drew repossess the car before bringing a suit against Maple?
11. Young agreed to act as guarantor for a loan made to his sister. The guaranty was made orally over the telephone. Is Young bound by the guaranty?
12. Rey owed Imperial Bank $400. When he couldn't pay, the bank took a judgment against Rey and filed a garnishment against his wages. Rey's employer agreed to turn all of Rey's salary over to the bank until the debt was paid in full. May the employer do this?
13. Jordan bought a boat from Act Marine. Jordan bought the boat on credit and signed a security agreement. Act failed to file the agreement or a financing statement. May Jordan refuse to pay the balance due on the grounds that the security agreement is invalid?
14. Burger borrowed $10,000 on a three-year term from Valley National Bank. Burger's uncle signed as guarantor of the loan. At the end of the three years, Burger requested that the bank extend the loan for an additional three years and the bank agreed. Burger's uncle was never notified of the loan extension. Is Burger's uncle relieved from liability as guarantor of the loan?

Cases to Decide

1. To secure a loan for the purchase of a car, Anderson signed a security agreement giving the bank a security interest in the car. The agreement was never recorded or noted on the automobile title records and no financing statement was filed. When Anderson didn't pay, the bank attempted to repossess the car. Is it entitled to do so? (*Anderson v. First Jacksonville Bank*, Ark 423 SW 2d 273)
2. The Bank of Babylon had a security agreement in connection with a loan to Cherno that authorized the bank, in the event of default, to enter Cherno's home and retake the collateral. Using a key, employees of the bank entered Cherno's home and seized the collateral. Is the bank permitted to do this? (*Cherno v. Bank of Babylon*, NY 54 Misc 2d 277)
3. Dvorak's son wanted to buy a tractor. The bank agreed to lend the son $6,441.90 if Dvorak would

guarantee payment. Dvorak signed an agreement guaranteeing payment of the loan. The tractor's transmission broke and the son borrowed more money from the same bank and signed a new note, which replaced the first note. Dvorak did not sign the second note as guarantor. When the son defaulted on payment and went into bankruptcy, the bank sued Dvorak as a guarantor. Can the bank collect from Dvorak? (*Liberty National Bank & Trust Co.* v. *Dvorak*, 199 NW 2d 414)

4. Muse bought a car from a dealer on an installment contract. The dealer assigned the contract to a credit corporation, which assigned it to Urdang. Muse defaulted in paying the loan, and Urdang repossessed the car. At the time of repossession, the debt was $1,200. Urdang sold the car for $275, even though Muse offered to pay $900 for it. Urdang then sued Muse for the balance of the loan. Can Urdang collect the balance from Muse? (*Urdang* v. *Muse*, NJ 276 A2d 397)

5. Ghosh was the guarantor for a promissory note given to the bank. The original note was renewed by the bank and the maker of the note but Ghosh never consented to the renewal. When the maker defaulted, the bank sued Ghosh. Is Ghosh liable? (*Bank of Waynesboro* v. *Ghosh*, 576 SW 2d 759, Tenn)

6. Penrose borrowed money from Old Colony and, to secure the loan, pledged stock in a corporation that operates a radio station. When Penrose defaulted, Old Colony sold the stock at a private sale instead of at a public sale on the grounds that a radio station was unique and that a private sale might bring in more money than a public sale. Should Old Colony be permitted to do this? (*Old Colony Trust Company* v. *Penrose Industries Corporation*, 280 F Supp 698 aff'd 398 F2d [3d Cir])

7. Butler borrowed money from Ford Motor Credit to purchase a truck. When Butler defaulted on the loan that was secured by the truck, Ford Motor Credit arranged to have the truck repossessed at 2:00 A.M. while the car was parked in an open driveway in front of Butler's house. Butler contends that the repossession was illegal. Is Butler correct? (*Butler* v. *Ford Motor Credit Co.* 829 F2d 568 [5th Cir])

Martinez bought a new piano from Planet Pianos, Inc. for the sum of $10,000. At the time of purchase, Martinez paid $2,000 in cash and gave Planet a note for the $8,000 balance. The balance was payable in sixty monthly installments.

After making the first two payments, Martinez defaulted in making any further payments. Planet then sent a truck to the Martinez home to repossess the piano, but Martinez refused to permit the company to take the piano back. Planet therefore went to court to get an order permitting repossession of the piano.

The Trial

During the trial, Martinez testified that he had signed nothing more than a promissory note and that nothing had been said to him to indicate that the piano could be repossessed if he failed to make the payments. He further testified that he had undergone financial difficulties and that there were a number of creditors who had judgments against him. Planet testified that Martinez had made only two payments and that while it had not had Martinez sign a security agreement in regard to the piano, it was the practice in the industry to repossess musical instruments when there was a default in making payments.

The Arguments at Trial

Martinez's attorney argued that because Martinez had not signed a security agreement covering the piano, Planet's only recourse was to secure a judgment against Martinez and attempt to collect the debt out of all of Martinez's assets. The attorney further argued that to permit Planet to retake the piano would amount to favoring one creditor over another, whereas all creditors should have the right to seek repayment of their debts out of the assets.

Planet's attorney argued that it was understood by both purchasers and sellers of pianos that if payment for such an expensive item was not made in full, the piano company would have the right to repossess the instrument, sell it, and collect any balance due from the purchaser. The attorney further argued that the amount of Martinez's total debts would far exceed the value of the assets and that Planet might recover nothing, or only very little, when all the assets were sold. The attorney argued that this outcome would be unconscionable in view of the fact that Martinez had made only two payments.

Questions to Discuss

1. Who has the stronger argument, Martinez or Planet? Why?
2. If you were the judge or jury hearing this case, for whom would you decide? Why?
3. Do you feel that Planet should be able to repossess the piano even though it does not have a secured interest in the instrument? Why or why not?
4. Do you think that a particular practice in the sale of certain goods should take precedence over the law or over the absence of any written agreement covering this situation?

Appendix A

How to Do
Legal Research

As Chapter 1 of the text indicated, there are many different sources of the law, the most important being **statutes** and **court decisions.** Let's turn first to statutes. You can learn what the law is on a certain subject by researching a particular state's statutes or federal statutes enacted by Congress. Indexes in the statute books will guide you to the laws involving any subject that interests you. Indexes can help you find cases by subject matter, key words (e.g. *whistle blower*), and case titles. Statute books can be found in a public law library, an attorney's office, and often, in a general public library.

Reading and analyzing actual court cases is another way to study law and learn what the law is on a particular subject. Each year, state and federal courts across the country hear and decide thousands of cases. The court decisions are published in legal books called *Reports.* The cases presented in the section, "Cases to Decide," at the end of each chapter of this text are shortened versions of actual court cases.

Reports of state and lower court decisions are printed for each U.S. state. In many states, reports are published both by official state agencies and by private law reporting companies. Regional reports are also published by private companies, and they include decisions from the courts of many states within a geographic region. To make it easier to find court decisions, each reported case decision is assigned a citation, which indicates the volume and the page number where the decision can be found. For example, in *Webster* v. *Blue Ship Tea Room,* 347 Mass 421—a decision of the Massachusetts Supreme Court in which Webster and Blue Ship Tea Room are the parties to the case—the decision can be found in volume 347 of the *Massachusetts Reports,* on page 421. An example of a regional report is *Champaign* vs. *Hanks,* Ill 353 NE 2d 405. Note that NE means Northeast and refers to a case tried in one of certain states located in the northeastern part of the United States.

Decisions of the federal courts are also printed in book form. Decisions of the federal courts are found in the *Federal Supplement,* which is abbreviated as "F Supp." Opinions of the Federal Courts of Appeal are found in the *Federal Reporter,* abbreviated as "F. U.S.". Supreme Court Reports are also published by official reporters and by private law reporting companies.

It is important to know how a court case develops. When judges and juries are called upon to determine the issues in a legal case and to decide who should win the case, they follow several steps.

1. The judge and jury hear testimony that is presented by both parties to the case to support their individual claims.
2. When all testimony has been given, the jury evaluates the testimony and decides the facts that it will believe.
3. The jury members discuss the facts and the issues of the case and reach a decision.
4. Once the jury has reached a decision, that decision is communicated to the court.

In studying the cases in this text, the first task is to "brief" each case. The purpose of the case brief is to organize and summarize the essential elements of a case in order to understand what the case is about. This can best be done using the following method:

1. *Read* the case carefully and determine the relevant facts (circumstances that brought the parties into court). Summarize these facts.
2. *Determine* the legal issue—a one sentence description in the form of a question— that describes the point that the parties are trying to get a decision on in court.
3. *State* your decision in the case, either "yes" or "no."
4. *Give* a reason or reasons for the decision.

Study the following court case and then read the briefed version that follows. It will give you an idea of how to brief a case.

County of *Champaign* vs. *Hanks*, 41 Ill. App. 3d 679. Defendant Hanks, charged with burglary, stated in an affidavit that he was indigent and had no assets. Therefore, the County of Champaign appointed a public defender to represent him at no charge to Hanks. Actually, Hanks was not entitled to free representation by the public defender's office, because he had legal interests in real property. However, he had secretly transferred his interest in the property to some other members of his family in order to avoid legal fees. The County of Champaign now seeks to recover its costs. Hanks claims that the county has no right to collect for the services of the attorneys because he did not agree to pay for these services and couldn't because he was indigent (had no money) during the criminal proceedings. It was determined by the court that Hanks did have to pay based on a legal principle called *quasi contract*, or contract implied in law. The court stated that "a contract implied in law does not depend on the intention of the parties, but exists where there is a duty to perform . . . based on the receipt of a benefit . . . under circumstances where it would be inequitable (not fair, unjust) to retain benefit without compensation." The court went on to say that the facts in this case "reveal that defendant received free legal representation when he clearly was not entitled to such representation and that defendant failed to disclose his assets. Under these circumstances the law will imply a promise by defendant to compensate the county."

County of Champaign vs. Hanks
41 ILL App 3d 679

FACTS:	Defendant Hanks, charged with burglary, swore that he was indigent and had no assets. Consequently, a public defender was appointed to represent him. Actually, Hanks lied about his finances. The County of Champaign is now claiming the right to recover its legal costs.
ISSUE:	Is the County of Champaign entitled to collect its legal costs?
DECISION:	Yes
REASON(S):	Hanks had to pay based on a contract implied in law (quasi contract). A contract implied in law is imposed upon parties when one of these

parties receives a benefit at the expense of the other party. The court in this case therefore implied a contract between Hanks and the county for payment of legal fees because he was able to pay for such services. The court said it would be unfair (unjust) for Hanks to retain a benefit to which he was not entitled without paying the required compensation.

Assume that you now read another case involving similar facts. If the judge in this case follows the decision in the Champaign case above, the decision in the Champaign case is considered a precedent. If, however, the judge does not follow the decision in the Champaign case above, to know what the law is, you would have to determine how the facts differed, and how that difference contributed to a different result. For example, another case might involve a situation in which the defendant possessed assets but the public defender never asked the defendant if he had assets. In such a case, the court might well conclude that, because the defendant did not obtain free legal service through false means, there was no implied contract.

It is only by reading and analyzing many cases that a student of the law can determine what the law actually is on a certain subject.

In addition to books of statute laws and reports of court decisions, many texts summarize and explain what the law is on various matters. These texts usually cover one subject, such as corporations or real estate. All of these sources can help you to understand state and federal statutes and decisions in a particular area of law.

Appendix B

Comparison of Basic Contract Law and the UCC

The two columns below outline the laws relating to important areas of contracts. The LEFT column summarizes basic contract law principles applicable to all transactions other than contracts for the sale of goods. The RIGHT column summarizes the special rules of law, under Article 2 of the UCC, that have changed or modified basic contract laws relating to contracts for the sale of goods. These changes and modifications under the Code conform to the ways that modern business is conducted. Article 2 of the UCC has already been discussed in Part III: PURCHASE AND SALE OF GOODS UNDER THE UCC.

BASIC CONTRACT LAW

Offer

1. The offer must be sufficiently definite in order to be enforceable.

2. Offers generally can be revoked at any time before acceptance, unless the parties have agreed to an "option" contract to keep the offer open.

UCC

1. A sales contract will not fail for indefiniteness even if one or more essential terms (e.g., price, quantity, place and time of delivery, terms of payment) are missing as long as (a) the parties intended to make a contract and (b) there is a reasonably certain basis for the court to make an appropriate award for damages if the contract is breached (§2-204). Rules for filling in the gaps left in the contract are found in sections §2-305 through §2-311 of the Code.

2. If a merchant buyer or seller states in a signed writing that an offer to sell or buy shall remain open for a stated period of time, the offer is "*firm*"—that is, guaranteed (irrevocable) for the time stated, even if the offeree gives no consideration. If no time is stated, the offer remains open for a reasonable time, but no longer than three months. (§2-205)

Acceptance

3. If the offeror does not specify the method of communication to be used, the acceptance is effective when sent if the offeree uses the same method the offeror used. If the offeree uses a different method, acceptance is not effective until received by the offeror (if the offer is still open).

4. When an offer is unilateral, only actual performance of the requested act constitutes acceptance by the offeree. When an offer is bilateral, acceptance occurs when the offeree promises to perform in the manner required by the offer. If the offeree attempts to accept with a response other than that prescribed in the offer, there is no contract. (*Note:* When there is doubt as to whether an offer is unilateral or bilateral, the courts tend to construe the offer as bilateral.)

5. No existing rule.

6. An offeree who is required to accept by doing the act requested (unilateral request) is not required to give notice to the offeror that he or she has started the performance. Such an offeree, however, generally has an implied obligation to give notice to the offeror that he or she (offeree) has completed the performance.

7. An attempted acceptance must match, term by term, the provisions in the offer. Any deviation from these terms, whether by addition, alteration, or omission, makes the communication a counteroffer (mirror-image rule).

3. If the offeror does not specify the method of communication to be used, the UCC permits acceptance by any reasonable means, with this acceptance becoming effective when it is properly sent. (§2-206)

4. An offer to buy goods (buyer initiates the offer) can be treated as though a unilateral contract offer has been made and can be accepted by the seller by shipping either conforming or nonconforming (substitute) goods to the buyer, or the offer may be treated as a bilateral contract offer (exchange of promises) and accepted by the seller by a prompt communication to the offeror promising to ship the goods. (§2-206)

5. A shipment of nonconforming (substitute) goods (where the buyer initiates the offer) is simultaneously regarded as an acceptance of an offer (which results in a contract) and also as a breach of contract for which the buyer may pursue appropriate remedies. However, if the seller states to the buyer that the shipment is nonconforming and is offered only as an accommodation to the buyer, then this shipment would not constitute an acceptance, and the seller would therefore not be in breach of contract. (§2-206) (*Note:* Shipment by the seller is a counteroffer, and the buyer would be free to accept or reject the goods.)

6. Where the beginning of a requested performance (e.g., beginning to manufacture and/or ship the goods) is a reasonable method of acceptance, the offeror must be notified of such beginning within a reasonable time. An offeror who is not reasonably notified of acceptance may treat the offer as having lapsed before acceptance. (§2-206)

7. A definite expression of acceptance of an offer by the offeree amounts to an acceptance, and a contract is formed even if the acceptance adds new terms or proposes terms different from those in the offer, unless acceptance is expressly made conditional on assent to the additional or different terms. Between merchants, additional terms (terms added by the offeree and not found in the original offer) will automatically become part of the contract unless the new terms materially alter

the offer, or the offeror objects to the terms within a reasonable time after receiving the offeree's acceptance, or the original offer expressly limits acceptance to the exact terms of the offer. If one or both parties are nonmerchants, additional terms will not prevent acceptance by the offeree, but these terms will not automatically become part of the contract. They become mere proposals that would have to be agreed to by the offeror. Different terms (terms that change or contradict a term of the offer) which involve minor changes do not become part of the contract, nor do they prevent acceptance. These minor changes will simply be ignored. But different terms that change the offer in any material way do not constitute an acceptance. Instead, they convert the response into a counteroffer and do not become part of the original contract unless specifically accepted by the original offeror. (§2-207)

Consideration

8. A modification of an existing contract must be based on consideration.

8. An agreement modifying a contract for the sale of goods needs no consideration to be binding. The Code treats a modification as a matter of good faith (honesty and fair dealing in the trade) rather than as a matter of consideration. A modification may be made orally. If, however, the original agreement is required to be in writing under the statute of frauds, then the modification must also be in writing. (§2-209)

9. If no price is agreed upon but is to be set in the future, the courts generally will not enforce the contract.

9. The parties can make a contract providing for a determination of the price at a later time. If there is a failure to agree on a definite price, a reasonable price and the time and place of delivery will be allowed. If the parties do not intend to be bound unless a price is agreed upon and an agreed price is never reached, there will be no contract. (§2-305)

10. A written contract in which it is provided that there may be no oral modification can nevertheless be so modified, but only if this modification is supported by consideration.

10. A signed written agreement in which it is provided that there may be no oral modification can be modified only in writing, and only those changes agreed to in the signed writing are enforceable. (*Note:* In a sales contract entered into between a merchant and a nonmerchant (consumer), if the nonmerchant is to be held to such a clause on a form provided by the merchant, the nonmerchant must sign a separate acknowledgement of such a requirement.) (§2-209)

Illegality

11. Unconscionability of contract terms (that is, terms that unreasonably favor the other party) as a defense is available only in courts of equity.

11. Courts of law may now refuse to enforce a contract found to contain terms that are unconscionable. (§2-302)

Statute of Limitations

12. An action for a breach of ordinary contract must be brought within the time fixed by state statute. This time varies from state to state, but the range is from two to fifteen years, depending on whether the contract is oral or written.

12. An action for breach of a sales contract (oral or written) must be brought within four years from the time of the breach. In their original agreement, the parties may reduce the time period to one year (but not less), but they cannot extend it beyond the four-year limitation period. (§2-725)

Statute of Frauds

13. Every state has a statute of frauds that requires certain contracts be in writing to be enforceable. The five types of contracts frequently required to be in writing in the various states are a contract to pay the debt of another person, a contract by an executor or administrator to pay the debts of a deceased person from his or her own pocket, a contract for the sale of real property or an interest in real property, a contract in consideration of marriage, and a contract that cannot be performed within one year.

13. The UCC provision of the statute of frauds requires a writing for a contract involving a sale of goods if the price is $500 or more. (§2-201)

14. The writing must include the subject matter of the contract, the names of the parties, the essential terms of the contract, and (in some states) the consideration.

14. There is only the requirement of "some writing," but this writing must indicate that the parties have entered into a contract for the sale of goods. The one essential term of the sale that must be in the writing is the quantity. Other essential terms in dispute (price, time and place of payment or delivery, the general quality of the goods, and so on) can be proved by oral testimony. (§2-201)

15. The writing must be signed by the party against whom enforcement is sought (normally the buyer). (*Note:* Prior to a dispute, no one can determine which party's signing of the writing may be necessary to prove a case; from the time of contracting, each party should be aware that to him/her, it is signing by the other which is important.)

15. The UCC also requires the writing to be signed by the party against whom enforcement is sought. (§2-201)

16a. No existing rule.

16. The statute of frauds involving the sale of goods may be satisfied with other than a written memorandum under the following circumstances:

a. Contracts for specially manufactured goods for a particular buyer (goods that cannot generally be resold to others in the ordinary course of the seller's business) where the seller, before notice of repudiation is received, has substantially started to manufacture the goods for the buyer or has made commitments for the manufacture of the goods, do not require a writing. (§2-201)

16b. No existing rule.

b. An oral contract is enforceable if the person against whom enforcement is attempted makes a statement in his/her lawsuit admitting that he/she has a sale-of-goods contract with the other party. (Enforceability is limited to the quantity of goods admitted.) (§2-201)

16c. No existing rule.

c. A partial performance rule applies. An oral contract will be enforced if the buyer receives and accepts part of the goods, but only for the portion of the goods that were actually received and accepted by the buyer. Also, an oral contract is binding if the buyer makes a partial payment on the goods. The contract is enforceable, however, only for those goods covered by the party payment. (§2-201) (*Note:* The courts have ruled [*Lockwood* v. *Smigel*, 96 Cal Rptr 289] that an oral contract for the sale of goods consisting of a single item is binding when the buyer makes a down payment.)

16d. No existing rule.

d. If the contract is between merchants, and one of the merchants within a reasonable time sends a written confirmation of the oral agreement to the other merchant, and that merchant fails to object in writing to the confirmation within ten days, the contract is enforceable against the merchant who receives the confirmation even though he or she has not signed anything. (§2-201)

17. The parol evidence rule states that once a contract has been put in writing as the final and complete expression of agreement between the parties, parol evidence—evidence of an oral agreement made prior to or at the time of signing the written agreement—cannot be presented in court to change or add to the terms of the written contract. (In other words, the court presumes that the written contract contained all the terms and provisions intended by the parties.) Parol evidence, however, may be introduced in court to (a) make changes and modifications after the original contract is entered into; (b) give meaning to unclear language; (c) show that the contract was void or voidable; (d) fill in gaps when essential terms are missing; or (e) correct obvious and gross clerical or typographical errors that would change the meaning of what the parties intended.

17. The UCC reaffirms the parol evidence rule and its exceptions as stated under basic contract law, but it goes a step further. The UCC allows oral evidence to explain or supplement the written contract by showing a prior course of dealing, usage of the trade, or course of performance. Evidence from these sources may be introduced even though the court finds the writing to be complete and free from ambiguities. (§2-202)

Rights of Parties

18. An assignment of rights does not impliedly carry with it the delegation of duties; an express assumption of duties is necessary.

18. An assignment of a contract is impliedly a delegation of duties, and an express assumption is not required. (§2-210)

Appendix C

The Constitution of the United States

Preamble

We the People of the United States, in Order to form a more perfect Union, establish Justice, insure domestic Tranquility, provide for the common defence, promote the general Welfare, and secure the Blessings of Liberty to ourselves and our Posterity, do ordain and establish this Constitution for the United States of America.

Article I

Section 1.   All legislative Powers herein granted shall be vested in a Congress of the United States, which shall consist of a Senate and a House of Representatives.

Section 2.   [1] The House of Representatives shall be composed of Members chosen every second Year by the People of the several States, and the Electors in each State shall have the Qualifications requisite for Electors of the most numerous Branch of the State Legislature.

[2] No Person shall be a Representative who shall not have attained to the Age of twenty five Years, and been seven Years a Citizen of the United States, and who shall not, when elected, be an Inhabitant of that State in which he shall be chosen.

[3] Representatives and direct Taxes shall be apportioned among the several States which may be included within this Union, according to their respective Numbers, which shall be determined by adding to the whole Number of free Persons, including those bound to Service for a Term of Years, and excluding Indians not taxed, three-fifths of all other Persons. The actual Enumeration shall be made within three

Years after the first Meeting of the Congress of the United States, and within every subsequent Term of ten Years, in such Manner as they shall by Law direct. The Number of Representatives shall not exceed one for every thirty Thousand, but each State shall have at Least one Representative; and until such enumeration shall be made, the State of New Hampshire shall be entitled to chuse three, Massachusetts eight, Rhode Island and Providence Plantations one, Connecticut five, New York six, New Jersey four, Pennsylvania eight, Delaware one, Maryland six, Virginia ten, North Carolina five, South Carolina five, and Georgia three.

[4] When vacancies happen in the Representation from any State, the Executive Authority thereof shall issue Writs of Election to fill such Vacancies.

[5] The House of Representatives shall chuse their Speaker and other Officers; and shall have the sole Power of Impeachment.

Section 3.   [1] The Senate of the United States shall be composed of two Senators from each State, chosen by the Legislature thereof, for six Years; and each Senator shall have one Vote.

[2] Immediately after they shall be assembled in Consequence of the first Election, they shall be divided as equally as may be into three Classes. The Seats of the Senators of the first Class shall be vacated at the Expiration of the Second Year, of the second Class at the Expiration of the fourth Year, and of the third Class at the Expiration of the sixth Year, so that one third may be chosen every second Year; and if Vacancies happen by Resignation or otherwise, during the Recess of the Legislature of any State, the

Executive thereof may make temporary Appointments until the next Meeting of the Legislature, which shall then fill such Vacancies.

[3] No Person shall be a Senator who shall not have attained to the Age of thirty Years, and been nine Years a Citizen of the United States, and who shall not, when elected, be an Inhabitant of that State for which he shall be chosen.

[4] The Vice President of the United States shall be President of the Senate, but shall have no Vote, unless they be equally divided.

[5] The Senate shall chuse their other Officers, and also a President pro tempore, in the Absence of the Vice President, or when he shall exercise the Office of President of the United States.

[6] The Senate shall have the sole Power to try all Impeachments. When sitting for that Purpose, they shall be on Oath or Affirmation. When the President of the United States is tried, the Chief Justice shall preside: and no Person shall be convicted without the Concurrence of two thirds of the Members present.

[7] Judgment in Cases of Impeachment shall not extend further than to removal from Office, and disqualification to hold and enjoy any Office of Honor, Trust, or Profit under the United States: but the Party convicted shall nevertheless be liable and subject to Indictment, Trial, Judgment, and Punishment, according to law.

Section 4.   [1] The Times, Places and Manner of holding elections for Senators and Representatives, shall be prescribed in each State by the Legislature thereof; but the Congress may at any time by Law make or alter such Regulations, except as to the Places of chusing Senators.

[2] The Congress shall assemble at least once in every Year, and such Meeting shall be on the first Monday in December, unless they shall by Law appoint a different Day.

Section 5.   [1] Each House shall be the Judge of the Elections, Returns, and Qualifications of its own Members, and a Majority of each shall constitute a Quorum to do Business; but a smaller Number may adjourn from day to day, and may be authorized to compel the Attendance of absent Members, in such Manner, and under such Penalties as each House may provide.

[2] Each House may determine the Rules of its Proceedings, punish its Members for disorderly Behavior, and, with the Concurrence of two thirds, expel a Member.

[3] Each House shall keep a Journal of its Proceedings, and from time to time publish the same, excepting such Parts as may in their Judgment require Secrecy; and the Yeas and Nays of the Members of either house on any question shall, at the Desire of one fifth of those Present, be entered on the Journal.

[4] Neither House, during the Session of Congress, shall, without the Consent of the other, adjourn for more than three days, nor to any other Place than that in which the two Houses shall be sitting.

Section 6.   [1] The Senators and Representatives shall receive a Compensation for their Services, to be ascertained by Law, and paid out of the Treasury of the United States. They shall in all Cases, except Treason, Felony and Breach of the Peace, be privileged from Arrest during their Attendance at the Session of their respective Houses, and in going to and returning from the same; and for any Speech or Debate in either House, they shall not be questioned in any other Place.

[2] No Senator or Representative shall, during the Time for which he was elected, be appointed to any civil Office under the Authority of the United States, which shall have been created, or the Emoluments whereof shall have been increased during such time; and no Person holding any Office under the United States shall be a Member of either House during his Continuance in Office.

Section 7.   [1] All Bills for raising Revenue shall originate in the House of Representatives; but the Senate may propose or concur with Amendments as on other Bills.

[2] Every Bill which shall have passed the House of Representatives and the Senate, shall, before it becomes a Law, be presented to the President of the United States; If he approve he shall sign it, but if not he shall return it, with his Objections to the House in which it shall have originated, who shall enter the Objections at large on their Journal, and proceed to reconsider it. If after such Reconsideration two thirds of that House shall agree to pass the Bill, it shall be sent together with the Objections, to the other House, by which it shall likewise be reconsidered, and if approved by two thirds of that House, it shall become a Law. But in all such Cases the Votes of both Houses shall be determined by Yeas and Nays, and the Names of the Persons voting for and against the Bill shall be entered on the Journal of each House respectively. If any Bill shall not be returned by the President within ten Days (Sundays excepted) after it shall have been presented to him, the Same shall

be a Law, in like Manner as if he had signed it, unless the Congress by their Adjournment prevent its Return in which Case it shall not be a Law.

[3] Every Order, Resolution, or Vote, to Which the Concurrence of the Senate and House of Representatives may be necessary (except on a question of Adjournment) shall be presented to the President of the United States; and before the Same shall take Effect, shall be approved by him, or being disapproved by him, shall be repassed by two thirds of the Senate and House of Representatives, according to the Rules and Limitations prescribed in the Case of a Bill.

Section 8. [1] The Congress shall have Power To lay and collect Taxes, Duties, Imposts and Excises, to pay the Debts and provide for the common Defence and general Welfare of the United States; but all Duties, Imposts and Excises shall be uniform throughout the United States;

[2] To borrow money on the credit of the United States;

[3] To regulate Commerce with foreign Nations, and among the several States, and with the Indian Tribes;

[4] To establish an uniform Rule of Naturalization, and uniform Laws on the subject of Bankruptcies throughout the United States;

[5] To coin Money, regulate the Value thereof, and of foreign Coin, and fix the Standard of Weights and Measures;

[6] To provide for the Punishment of counterfeiting the Securities and current Coin of the United States;

[7] To Establish Post Offices and Post Roads;

[8] To promote the Progress of Science and useful Arts, by securing for limited Times to Authors and Inventors the exclusive Right to their respective Writings and Discoveries;

[9] To constitute Tribunals inferior to the supreme Court;

[10] To define and punish Piracies and Felonies committed on the high Seas, and Offenses against the Law of Nations;

[11] To declare War, grant Letters of Marque and Reprisal, and make Rules concerning Captures on Land and Water;

[12] To raise and support Armies, but no Appropriation of Money to that Use shall be for a longer Term than two Years;

[13] To provide and maintain a Navy;

[14] To make Rules for the Government and Regulation of the land and naval Forces;

[15] To provide for calling forth the Militia to execute the Laws of the Union, suppress Insurrections and repel Invasions;

[16] To provide for organizing, arming, and disciplining, the Militia, and for governing such Part of them as may be employed in the Service of the United States, reserving to the States respectively, the Appointment of the Officers, and the Authority of training the Militia according to the discipline prescribed by Congress;

[17] To exercise exclusive Legislation in all Cases whatsoever, over such District (not exceeding ten Miles square) as may, by Cession of particular States, and the Acceptance of Congress, become the Seat of the Government of the United States, and to exercise like Authority over all Places purchased by the Consent of the Legislature of the State, in which the Same shall be, for the Erection of Forts, Magazines, Arsenals, dock-Yards and other needful Buildings;—And

[18] To make all Laws which shall be necessary and proper for carrying into Execution the foregoing Powers, and all other Powers vested by this Constitution in the Government of the United States, or in any Department or Officer thereof.

Section 9. [1] The Migration or Importation of Such Persons as any of the States now existing shall think proper to admit, shall not be prohibited by the Congress prior to the Year one thousand eight hundred and eight, but a Tax or duty may be imposed on such Importation, not exceeding ten dollars for each Person.

[2] The privilege of the Writ of Habeas Corpus shall not be suspended, unless when in Cases of Rebellion or Invasion the public Safety may require it.

[3] No Bill of Attainder or ex post facto Law shall be passed.

[4] No Capitation, or other direct, Tax shall be laid, unless in Proportion to the Census or Enumeration herein before directed to be taken.

[5] No Tax or Duty shall be laid on Articles exported from any State.

[6] No Preference shall be given by any Regulation of Commerce or Revenue to the Ports of one State over those of another: nor shall Vessels bound to, or from, one State be obliged to enter, clear, or pay Duties in another.

[7] No money shall be drawn from the Treasury,

but in Consequence of Appropriations made by Law; and a regular Statement and Account of the Receipts and Expenditures of all public Money shall be published from time to time.

[8] No Title of Nobility shall be granted by the United States: and no Person holding any Office of Profit or Trust under them, shall, without the Consent of the Congress, accept of any present, Emolument, Office, or Title, of any kind whatever, from any King, Prince, or foreign State.

Section 10. [1] No State shall enter into any Treaty, Alliance, or Confederation; grant Letters of Marque and Reprisal; coin Money; emit Bills of Credit; make any Thing but gold and silver Coin a Tender in Payment of Debts; pass any Bill of Attainder, ex post facto Law, or Law impairing the Obligation of Contracts, or grant any Title of Nobility.

[2] No State shall, without the Consent of the Congress, lay any Imposts or Duties on Imports or Exports, except what may be absolutely necessary for executing it's inspection Laws: and the net Produce of all Duties and Imposts, laid by any State on Imports or Exports, shall be for the Use of the Treasury of the United States; and all such Laws shall be subject to the Revision and Control of the Congress.

[3] No State shall, without the Consent of Congress, lay any Duty of Tonnage, keep Troops, or Ships of War in time of Peace, enter into any Agreement or Compact with another State, or with a foreign power, or engage in war, unless actually invaded, or in such imminent Danger as will not admit of delay.

Article II

Section 1. [1] The executive Power shall be vested in a President of the United States of America. He shall hold his Office during the Term of four Years, and, together with the Vice President, chosen for the same Term, be elected, as follows:

[2] Each State shall appoint, in such Manner as the Legislature thereof may direct, a Number of Electors, equal to the whole Number of Senators and Representatives to which the State may be entitled in the Congress; but no Senator or Representative, or Person holding an Office of Trust or Profit under the United States, shall be appointed an Elector.

[3] The Electors shall meet in their respective States, and vote by Ballot for two Persons, of whom one at least shall not be an Inhabitant of the same State with themselves. And they shall make a List of all the Persons voted for, and of the Number of Votes

for each; which List they shall sign and certify, and transmit sealed to the Seat of the Government of the United States, directed to the President of the Senate. The President of the Senate shall, in the Presence of the Senate and House of Representatives, open all the Certificates, and the Votes shall then be counted. The Person having the greatest Number of Votes shall be the President, if such Number be a Majority of the whole Number of Electors appointed; and if there be more than one who have such Majority, and have an equal Number of Votes, then the House of Representatives shall immediately chuse by Ballot one of them for President; and if no Person have a majority, then from the five highest on the List the said House shall in like Manner chuse the President. But in chusing the President, the Votes shall be taken by States the Representation from each State having one Vote; A quorum for this Purpose shall consist of a Member or Members from two thirds of the States, and a Majority of all the States shall be necessary to a Choice. In every Case, after the Choice of the President, the Person having the greatest Number of Votes of the Electors shall be the Vice President. But if there shall remain two or more who have equal Votes, the Senate shall chuse from them by Ballot the Vice President.

[4] The Congress may determine the Time of chusing the Electors, and the Day on which they shall give their Votes; which Day shall be the same throughout the United States.

[5] No person except a natural born Citizen, or a Citizen of the United States, at the time of the Adoption of this Constitution, shall be eligible to the Office of President; neither shall any Person be eligible to that Office who shall not have attained to the Age of thirty-five Years, and been fourteen Years a Resident within the United States.

[6] In case of the removal of the President from Office, or of his Death, Resignation or Inability to discharge the Powers and Duties of the said Office, the Same shall devolve on the Vice President, and the Congress may by Law provide for the Case of Removal, Death, Resignation or Inability, both of the President and Vice President, declaring what Officer shall then act as President, and such Officer shall act accordingly, until the Disability be removed, or a President shall be elected.

[7] The President shall, at stated Times, receive for his Services, a Compensation, which shall neither be increased nor diminished during the Period for

which he shall have been elected, and he shall not receive within that Period any other Emolument from the United States, or any of them.

[8] Before he enter on the Execution of his Office, he shall take the following Oath or Affirmation: "I do solemnly swear (or affirm) that I will faithfully execute the Office of President of the United States, and will to the best of my Ability, preserve, protect and defend the Constitution of the United States."

Section 2. [1] The President shall be Commander in Chief of the Army and Navy of the United States, and of the militia of the several States, when called into the actual Service of the United States; he may require the Opinion, in writing, of the principal Officer in each of the Executive Departments, upon any Subject relating to the Duties of their respective Offices, and he shall have Power to grant Reprieves and Pardons for Offenses against the United States, except in Cases of Impeachment.

[2] He shall have Power, by and with the Advice and Consent of the Senate to make Treaties, provided two thirds of the Senators present concur; and he shall nominate, and by and with the Advice and Consent of the Senate, shall appoint Ambassadors, other public Ministers and Consuls, Judges of the supreme Court, and all other Officers of the United States, whose Appointments are not herein otherwise provided for, and which shall be established by Law; but the Congress may by Law vest the Appointment of such inferior Officers, as they think proper, in the President alone, in the Courts of Law, or in the Heads of Departments.

[3] The President shall have Power to fill up all Vacancies that may happen during the Recess of the Senate, by granting Commissions which shall expire at the End of their next Session.

Section 3. He shall from time to time give to the Congress Information of the State of the Union, and recommend to their Consideration such Measures as he shall judge necessary and expedient; he may, on extraordinary Occasions, convene both Houses, or either of them, and in Case of Disagreement between them, with Respect to the Time of Adjournment, he may adjourn them to such Time as he shall think proper; he shall receive Ambassadors and other public Ministers; he shall take Care that the Laws be faithfully executed, and shall Commission all the Officers of the United States.

Section 4. The President, Vice President and all civil Officers of the United States, shall be removed from Office on Impeachment for, and Conviction of, Treason, Bribery, or other high Crimes and Misdemeanors.

Article III

Section 1. The judicial Power of the United States, shall be vested in one supreme Court, and in such inferior Courts as the Congress may from time to time ordain and establish. The Judges, both of the supreme and inferior Courts, shall hold their Offices during good Behaviour, and shall, at stated Times, receive for their Services a Compensation, which shall not be diminished during their Continuance in Office.

Section 2. [1] The judicial Power shall extend to all Cases, in Law and Equity, arising under this Constitution, the Laws of the United States, and Treaties made, or which shall be made, under their Authority;—to all Cases affecting Ambassadors, other public Ministers and Consuls;—to all Cases of admiralty and maritime Jurisdiction;—to Controversies to which the United States shall be a Party;—to Controversies between two or more States;—between a State and Citizens of another State;—between Citizens of different States;—between Citizens of the same State claiming Lands under the Grants of different States, and between a State, or the Citizens thereof, and foreign States, Citizens or Subjects.

[2] In all Cases affecting Ambassadors, other public Ministers and Consuls, and those in which a State shall be a Party, the supreme Court shall have original Jurisdiction. In all the other Cases before mentioned, the supreme Court shall have appellate Jurisdiction, both as to Law and Fact, with such Exceptions, and under such Regulations as the Congress shall make.

[3] The trial of all Crimes, except in Cases of Impeachment, shall be by Jury; and such Trial shall be held in the State where the said Crimes shall have been committed; but when not committed within any State, the Trial shall be at such Place or Places as the Congress may by Law have directed.

Section 3. [1] Treason against the United States, shall consist only in levying War against them, or, in adhering to their Enemies, giving them Aid and Comfort. No Person shall be convicted of Treason unless on the Testimony of two Witnesses to the same overt Act, or on Confession in open Court.

[2] The Congress shall have Power to declare the Punishment of Treason, but no Attainder of Treason shall work Corruption of Blood, or Forfeiture except during the Life of the Person attainted.

Article IV

Section 1.   Full Faith and Credit shall be given in each State to the public Acts, Records, and judicial Proceedings of every other State. And the Congress may by general Laws prescribe the Manner in which such Acts, Records and Proceedings shall be proved, and the Effect thereof.

Section 2.   [1] The Citizens of each State shall be entitled to all Privileges and Immunities of Citizens in the several States.

[2] A Person charged in any State with Treason, Felony, or other Crime, who shall flee from Justice, and be found in another State, shall on demand of the executive Authority of the State from which he fled, be delivered up, to be removed to the State having Jurisdiction of the Crime.

[3] No Person held to Service or Labour in one State, under the Laws thereof, escaping into another, shall, in Consequence of any Law or Regulation therein, be discharged from such Service or Labour, but shall be delivered up on Claim of the Party to whom such Service or Labour may be due.

Section 3.   [1] New States may be admitted by the Congress into this Union; but no new State shall be formed or erected within the Jurisdiction of any other State; nor any State be formed by the Junction of two or more States, or Parts of States, without the Consent of the Legislatures of the States concerned as well as of the Congress.

[2] The Congress shall have Power to dispose of and make all needful Rules and Regulations respecting the Territory or other Property belonging to the United States; and nothing in this Constitution shall be so construed as to Prejudice any Claims of the United States, or of any particular State.

Section 4.   The United States shall guarantee to every State in this Union a Republican Form of Government, and shall protect each of them against Invasion; and on Application of the Legislature, or of the Executive (when the Legislature cannot be convened) against domestic Violence.

Article V

The Congress, whenever two thirds of both Houses shall deem it necessary, shall propose Amendments to this Constitution, or, on the Application of the Legislatures of two thirds of the several States, shall call a Convention for proposing Amendments, which, in either case, shall be valid to all Intents and Purposes, as part of this Constitution, when ratified by the Legislatures of three fourths of the several States, or by Conventions in three fourths thereof, as the one or the other Mode of Ratification may be proposed by the Congress; Provided that no Amendment which may be made prior to the Year One thousand eight hundred and eight shall in any Manner affect the first and fourth Clauses in the Ninth Section of the first Article; and that no State, without its Consent, shall be deprived of its equal Suffrage in the Senate.

Article VI

[1] All Debts contracted and Engagements entered into, before the Adoption of this Constitution shall be as valid against the United States under this Constitution, as under the Confederation.

[2] This Constitution, and the Laws of the United States which shall be made in Pursuance thereof; and all Treaties made, or which shall be made, under the Authority of the United States, shall be the supreme Law of the Land; and the Judges in every State shall be bound thereby, any Thing in the Constitution or Laws of any State to the Contrary notwithstanding.

[3] The Senators and Representatives before mentioned, and the Members of the several State Legislatures, and all executive and judicial Officers, both of the United States and of the several States, shall be bound by Oath or Affirmation, to support this Constitution; but no religious Test shall ever be required as a Qualification to any Office or public Trust under the United States.

Article VII

The Ratification of the Conventions of nine States shall be sufficient for the Establishment of this Constitution between the States so ratifying the Same.

Amendments

Articles in addition to, and in amendment of, the Constitution of the United States of America, proposed by Congress, and ratified by the Legislatures of the several States pursuant to the Fifth Article of the original Constitution.

Amendment 1 (1791)

Congress shall make no law respecting an establishment of religion, or prohibiting the free exercise thereof; or abridging the freedom of speech, or of the press; or the right of the people peaceably to assemble, and to petition the Government for a redress of grievances.

Amendment 2 (1791)

A well regulated Militia, being necessary to the security of a free State, the right of the people to keep and bear Arms, shall not be infringed.

Amendment 3 (1791)

No Soldier shall, in time of peace be quartered in any house, without the consent of the Owner, nor in time of war, but in a manner to be prescribed by law.

Amendment 4 (1791)

The right of the people to be secure in their persons, houses, papers, and effects, against unreasonable searches and seizures, shall not be violated, and no Warrants shall issue, but upon probable cause, supported by Oath or affirmation, and particularly describing the place to be searched, and the persons or things to be seized.

Amendment 5 (1791)

No person shall be held to answer for a capital, or otherwise infamous crime, unless on a presentment or indictment of a Grand Jury, except in cases arising in the land or naval forces, or in the Militia, when in actual service in time of War or public danger; nor shall any person be subject for the same offence to be twice put in jeopardy of life or limb; nor shall be compelled in any criminal case to be a witness against himself, nor be deprived of life, liberty, or property, without due process of law; nor shall private property be taken for public use without just compensation.

Amendment 6 (1791)

In all criminal prosecutions, the accused shall enjoy the right to a speedy and public trial, by an impartial jury of the State and district wherein the crime shall have been committed, which district shall have been previously ascertained by law, and to be informed of the nature and cause of the accusation; to be confronted with the witnesses against him; to have compulsory process for obtaining witnesses in his favor, and to have the Assistance of Counsel for his defence.

Amendment 7 (1791)

In Suits at common law, where the value in controversy shall exceed twenty dollars, the right of trial by jury shall be preserved, and no fact tried by jury, shall be otherwise re-examined in any Court of the United States, than according to the rules of common law.

Amendment 8 (1791)

Excessive bail shall not be required, nor excessive fines imposed, nor cruel and unusual punishments inflicted.

Amendment 9 (1791)

The enumeration in the Constitution, of certain rights, shall not be construed to deny or disparage others retained by the people.

Amendment 10 (1791)

The powers not delegated to the United States by the Constitution, nor prohibited by it to the States, are reserved to the States respectively, or to the people.

Amendment 11 (1798)

The Judicial power of the United States shall not be construed to extend to any suit in law or equity, commenced or prosecuted against one of the United States by Citizens of another State, or by Citizens or Subjects of any Foreign State.

Amendment 12 (1804)

The Electors shall meet in their respective states and vote by ballot for President and Vice-President, one of whom, at least, shall not be an inhabitant of the same state with themselves; they shall name in their ballots the person voted for as President, and in distinct ballots the person voted for as Vice-President, and they shall make distinct lists of all persons voted for as President, and of all persons voted for as Vice-President, and of the number of votes for each, which lists they shall sign and certify, and transmit sealed to the seat of the government of the United States, directed to the President of the Senate;—The President of the Senate shall, in the presence of the Senate and House of Representatives, open all the certificates and the votes shall then be counted;—The person having the greatest number of votes for President, shall be the President, if such number be a majority of the whole number of Electors appointed; and if no person have such majority, then from the persons having the highest numbers not exceeding three on the list of those voted for as President, the House of Representatives shall choose immediately, by ballot, the President. But in choosing the President, the votes shall be taken by states, the representation from each state having one vote; a quorum for this purpose shall consist of a member or members from two-thirds of the states, and a majority of all states shall be necessary to a choice. And if the House of Representatives shall not choose a President whenever the right of choice shall devolve upon them before the fourth day of March next following, then the Vice-President shall act as President, as in the case of the death or other constitutional disability of the President.—The person having the greatest number of votes as Vice-President, shall be the Vice-President, if such number be a majority of the whole number of Electors appointed, and if no person have a majority, then from the two highest numbers on the list, the Senate shall choose the Vice-President; a quorum for the purpose shall consist of two-thirds of the whole number of Senators, and a majority of the whole number shall be necessary to a choice. But no person constitutionally ineligible to the office of President shall be eligible to that of Vice-President of the United States.

Amendment 13 (1865)

Section 1.   Neither slavery nor involuntary servitude, except as a punishment for crime whereof the party shall have been duly convicted, shall exist within the United States, or any place subject to their jurisdiction.

Section 2.   Congress shall have power to enforce this article by appropriate legislation.

Amendment 14 (1868)

Section 1.   All persons born or naturalized in the United States, and subject to the jurisdiction thereof, are citizens of the United States and of the State wherein they reside. No State shall make or enforce any law which shall abridge the privileges or immunities of citizens of the United States; nor shall any State deprive any person of life, liberty, or property, without due process of law; nor deny to any person within its jurisdiction the equal protection of the laws.

Section 2.   Representatives shall be apportioned among the several States according to their respective numbers, counting the whole number of persons in each State, excluding Indians not taxed. But when the right to vote at any election for the choice of electors for President and Vice President of the United States, Representatives in Congress, the Executive and Judicial officers of a State, or the members of the Legislature thereof, is denied to any of the male inhabitants of such State, being twenty-one years of age, and citizens of the United States, or in any way abridged, except for participation in rebellion, or other crime, the basis of representation therein shall be reduced in the proportion which the number of such male citizens shall bear to the whole number of male citizens twenty-one years of age in such State.

Section 3.   No person shall be a Senator or Representative in Congress, or elector of President and Vice President, or hold any office, civil or military, under the United States, or under any State, who having previously taken an oath, as a member of Congress, or as an officer of the United States, or as a member of any State legislature, or as an executive or judicial officer of any State, to support the Constitution of the United States, shall have engaged in insurrection or rebellion against the same, or given aid or comfort to the enemies thereof. But Congress may by a vote of two-thirds of each House, remove such disability.

Section 4.   The validity of the public debt of the United States, authorized by law, including debts incurred for payment of pensions and bounties for services in suppressing insurrection or rebellion, shall not be questioned. But neither the United States nor any State shall assume or pay any debt or obligation incurred in aid of insurrection or rebellion against the United States, or any claim for the loss of emancipation of any slave; but all such debts, obligations and claims shall be held illegal and void.

Section 5.   The Congress shall have power to enforce, by appropriate legislation, the provisions of this article.

Amendment 15 (1870)

Section 1.   The right of citizens of the United States to vote shall not be denied or abridged by the United States or by any State on account of race, color, or previous condition of servitude.

Section 2.   The Congress shall have power to enforce this article by appropriate legislation.

Amendment 16 (1913)

The Congress shall have power to lay and collect taxes on incomes, from whatever source derived, without apportionment among the several States, and without regard to any census or enumeration.

Amendment 17 (1913)

[1] The Senate of the United States shall be composed of two Senators from each State, elected by the people thereof, for six years; and each Senator shall have one vote. The electors in each State shall have the qualifications requisite for electors of the most numerous branch of the State legislatures.

[2] When vacancies happen in the representation of any State in the Senate, the executive authority of

such State shall issue writs of election to fill such vacancies: *Provided,* That the legislature of any State may empower the executive thereof to make temporary appointments until the people fill the vacancies by election as the legislature may direct.

[3] This amendment shall not be so construed as to affect the election or term of any Senator chosen before it becomes valid as part of the Constitution.

Amendment 18 (1919)

Section 1. After one year from the ratification of this article the manufacture, sale, or transportation of intoxicating liquors within, the importation thereof into, or the exportation thereof from the United States and all territory subject to the jurisdiction thereof for beverage purposes is hereby prohibited.

Section 2. The Congress and the several States shall have concurrent power to enforce this article by appropriate legislation.

Section 3. This article shall be inoperative unless it shall have been ratified as an amendment to the Constitution by the legislatures of the several States, as provided in the Constitution, within seven years from the date of the submission hereof to the States by the Congress.

Amendment 19 (1920)

[1] The right of citizens of the United States to vote shall not be denied or abridged by the United States or by any State on account of sex.

[2] The Congress shall have power to enforce this article by appropriate legislation.

Amendment 20 (1933)

Section 1. The terms of the President and Vice President shall end at noon on the 20th day of January, and the terms of Senators and Representatives at noon on the 3d day of January, of the years in which such terms would have ended if this article had not been ratified; and the terms of their successors shall then begin.

Section 2. The Congress shall assemble at least once in every year, and such meeting shall begin at noon on the 3d day of January, unless they shall by law appoint a different day.

Section 3. If, at the time fixed for the beginning of the term of the President, the President elect shall have died, the Vice President elect shall become President. If the President shall not have been chosen before the time fixed for the beginning of his term, or if the President elect shall have failed to qualify, then the Vice President elect shall act as President

until a President shall have qualified; and the Congress may by law provide for the case wherein neither a President elect nor a Vice President elect shall have qualified, declaring who shall then act as President, or the manner in which one who is to act shall be selected, and such person shall act accordingly until a President or Vice President shall have qualified.

Section 4. The Congress may by law provide for the case of the death of any of the persons from whom the House of Representatives may choose a President whenever the right of choice shall have devolved upon them, and for the case of the death of any of the persons from whom the Senate may choose a Vice President whenever the right of choice shall have devolved upon them.

Section 5. Sections 1 and 2 shall take effect on the 15th day of October following the ratification of this article.

Section 6. This article shall be inoperative unless it shall have been ratified as an amendment to the Constitution by the legislatures of three-fourths of the several States within seven years from the date of its submission.

Amendment 21 (1933)

Section 1. The eighteenth article of amendment to the Constitution of the United States is hereby repealed.

Section 2. The transportation or importation into any State, Territory, or possession of the United States for delivery or use therein of intoxicating liquors, in violation of the laws thereof, is hereby prohibited.

Section 3. This article shall be inoperative unless it shall have been ratified as an amendment to the Constitution by conventions in the several States, as provided in the Constitution, within seven years from the date of the submission hereof to the States by the Congress.

Amendment 22 (1951)

Section 1. No person shall be elected to the office of the President more than twice, and no person who has held the office of President, or acted as President, for more than two years of a term to which some other person was elected President shall be elected to the office of President more than once. But this Article shall not apply to any person holding the office of President when this Article was proposed by the Congress, and shall not prevent any person who may be holding the office of President, or acting as President, during the term within which this Article becomes operative from holding the office of President or acting as President during the remainder of such term.

Section 2. This article shall be inoperative unless it shall have been ratified as an amendment to the Constitution by the legislatures of three-fourths of the several States within seven years from the date of its submission to the States by the Congress.

Amendment 23 (1961)

Section 1. The District constituting the seat of Government of the United States shall appoint in such manner as the Congress may direct:

A number of electors of President and Vice President equal to the whole number of Senators and Representatives in Congress to which the District would be entitled if it were a state, but in no event more than the least populous state; they shall be in addition to those appointed by the states, but they shall be considered, for the purposes of the election of President and Vice President, to be electors appointed by a state; and they shall meet in the District and perform such duties as provided by the twelfth article of amendment.

Section 2. The Congress shall have power to enforce this article by appropriate legislation.

Amendment 24 (1964)

Section 1. The right of citizens of the United States to vote in any primary or other election for President or Vice President, for electors for President or Vice President, or for Senator or Representative in Congress, shall not be denied or abridged by the United States, or any State by reason of failure to pay any poll tax or other tax.

Section 2. The Congress shall have power to enforce this article by appropriate legislation.

Amendment 25 (1967)

Section 1. In case of the removal of the President from office or of his death or resignation, the Vice President shall become President.

Section 2. Whenever there is a vacancy in the office of the Vice President, the President shall nominate a Vice President who shall take office upon confirmation by a majority vote of both Houses of Congress.

Section 3. Whenever the President transmits to the President pro tempore of the Senate and the Speaker of the House of Representatives his written declaration that he is unable to discharge the powers

and duties of his office, and until he transmits to them a written declaration to the contrary, such powers and duties shall be discharged by the Vice President as Acting President.

Section 4. Whenever the Vice President and a majority of either the principal officers of the executive departments or of such other body as Congress may by law provide, transmit to the President pro tempore of the Senate and the Speaker of the House of Representatives their written declaration that the President is unable to discharge the powers and duties of his office, the Vice President shall immediately assume the powers and duties of the office as Acting President.

Thereafter, when the President transmits to the President pro tempore of the Senate and the Speaker of the House of Representatives his written declaration that no inability exists, he shall resume the powers and duties of his office unless the Vice President and a majority of either the principal officers of the executive department or of such other body as Congress may by law provide, transmit within four days to the President pro tempore of the Senate and the Speaker of the House of Representatives their written declaration that the President is unable to discharge the powers and duties of his office. Thereupon Congress shall decide the issue, assembling within forty-eight hours for that purpose if not in session. If the Congress, within twenty-one days after receipt of the latter written declaration, or, if Congress is not in session, within twenty-one days after Congress is required to assemble, determines by two-thirds vote of both Houses that the President is unable to discharge the powers and duties of his office, the Vice President shall continue to discharge the same as Acting President; otherwise, the President shall resume the powers and duties of his office.

Amendment 26 (1971)

Section 1. The right of citizens of the United States, who are eighteen years of age or older, to vote shall not be denied or abridged by the United States or by any State on account of age.

Section 2. The Congress shall have power to enforce this article by appropriate legislation.

Amendment 27 (1992)

No law varying the compensation for the services of the senators and representatives shall take effect until an election of representatives shall have intervened.

Glossary of Legal Terms

A

abandoned property Property purposely parted with by its owner

abandonment Giving up possession of or claim to property

abstract of title Summary of transactions affecting title to real property

acceptance Agreement by offeree to do what offeror requests in offer; agreement by seller of real property to buyer's purchase offer

acceptor Drawee who agrees to pay a draft

accession Acquiring title to property which is added on to original property already owned

accessory One who assists in or conceals the commission of a crime although not directly participating in the crime

accommodation indorsement Indorsement guaranteeing payment of an instrument

accommodation party One who co-makes or indorses a note to help another borrow money

accord Agreement to accept performance different from that in original contract

accounting Financial statement given in a trust relationship

accused One charged with a crime

acknowledgment An oath by one who executed a document that he or she executed it and that it is valid

acquittal Verdict or judgment that a criminal defendant has not been proved guilty beyond a reasonable doubt

action A lawsuit

action at law A civil lawsuit for money damages brought by one party against another party

action in equity A civil lawsuit in which one party is seeking a remedy other than money damages (e.g. an injunction or a decree of specific performance)

act of God Natural occurrence that cannot be foreseen or avoided

actual damages Provable damages

adhesion contract A standardized contract form prepared by one party containing clauses favorable to that party and offered to another party on a "take it or leave it" basis

adjourn To postpone a legal matter

adjudication Judgment in a lawsuit

adjuster One who settles claims for an insurer

administrative agencies Government bodies created to act in the public interest

administrator/administratrix One who manages the estate of an intestate

adversary system System whereby parties to a lawsuit are represented by opposing lawyers

adverse possession Obtaining title to real property by occupying it for a long period without owner's consent

affiant The person who makes an affidavit

affidavit Written statement sworn to under oath

affirmative action Duty of employers to recruit women and minorities for positions usually held by white males

affirmed A decision rendered in a lower court is declared valid by an appellate court

agency by estoppel A situation in which one party creates the appearance that another has the authority to act as an agent

agency coupled with an interest Agency in which agent has a personal interest in subject matter of the agency

agent One who represents another in making business transactions

age of majority Age at which one is legally considered to be an adult

aid and abet To help another commit a crime

alias A fictitious name

alibi Excuse of being somewhere else when a crime was committed

alimony Support given by one spouse to another after a separation or divorce

allegation Statement of fact in a pleading

allonge Attachment to a negotiable instrument on which endorsements are placed

alteration Deliberate material change in a contract by one party without consent

amicus curiae Non-litigant allowed to file briefs with a court in a specific case

amnesty Governmental pardon to one guilty of a crime

annual percentage rate Cost of credit stated as a percentage of amount borrowed

annuity Contract providing an income to holder for a specific time or for life

annul To cancel

annulment Voiding a marriage

answer The formal written statement by a defendant responding to a civil complaint and setting forth the grounds for defense

antedate To date earlier than actual date

anticipatory breach Breach of contract occurring before stated time of performance

antilapse laws Laws providing for distribution of bequests when a beneficiary has predeceased the testator

antitrust laws Laws that prohibit monopolies

apparent authority Authority principal leads third parties to believe agent has because of principal's words or conduct

appeal Request to a higher court made after trial to review a lower court's decision

appellant The party who takes a case from a lower (trial) court to a higher (review) court

appellate court Court that hears appeals of lower-court decisions

appellee The party against whom an appeal to a higher (review) court is directed

appraise To estimate the value of an item

appurtenance Something attached or appended to something else that is more important

arbitration Nonjudicial determination of a dispute rather than by a judge or jury

arraignment Charging a person with a crime and asking for that person's plea

arrears Overdue payments

arrest To take into police custody

arson Intentional, illegal burning of a home or building

articles of incorporation Application for permission to incorporate a business

articles of partnership The agreement entered into by partners that outlines the rights and duties of the partners and governs the operation of the partnership

assault Crime of unlawfully causing physical injury to another; tort of threatening another with bodily harm

asset Property that has value

assign To transfer something to someone else

assigned risk pool Insurance plan for those who cannot get insurance from normal sources

assignee One to whom a contract right is transferred

assignment Transfer of contract rights from one person to another

assignor One who transfers a contract right to another

attachment Lawful seizure of a debtor's property prior to a judgment

attestation Clause in a will stating the witnesses observed the signing of the will

attorney in fact Agent who acts for another person under a power of attorney

attractive nuisance Dangerous condition or property that attracts children who may be injured, making the owner or person in possession liable

authority Power to act for someone else

award Binding decision in an arbitration

B

bad check Check written by a drawer when there is not enough money to cover the check

bail Money or property given to a court to obtain the release of a person from jail

bailee One who accepts possession of another's personal property

bailee's lien Bailee's right to hold bailed property until paid for work or services

bailment Transfer of possession of personal property for a specific time and purpose

bailment by necessity Bailment created when property comes into one's possession by mistake

bailment implied by law Bailment created when one acquires possession of another's personal property without that person's consent

bailment implied in fact Bailment created by actions of bailor and bailee

bailment of lost property Bailment occurring when one obtains possession of lost property

bailor One who gives up possession of personal property to another

bait-and-switch advertising Advertising a product for sale but then trying to sell the consumer another, more expensive product

bankrupt A person declared to be entitled to the protection of the bankruptcy laws

bankruptcy A federal procedure relieving a debtor from his/her debts once the debtor is found to be insolvent (liabilities greater than assets)

bargain and sale deed Deed conveying the interest the seller has and promising that seller has done nothing to disturb the title

battery   Unlawfully striking another person

bearer   A person in possession of an instrument

bench trial   Trial without a jury in which a judge decides the case

bench warrant   A paper issued by the court "from the bench" to secure the arrest of a person who does not appear in court for a legal proceeding when previously ordered to do so

beneficial interest   Right to receive income or property regardless of actual legal ownership

beneficiary   Recipient of the proceeds of a life insurance policy; one who inherits property as specified in a will

bequeath   To give personal property in a will

bid   Offer made at an auction

bilateral contract   Contract in which one party makes a promise in return for a promise made by another party

bill of attainder   A law which inflicts punishment on an individual or group of individuals without a trial (Note: such a law is unconstitutional)

bill of exchange   A draft

bill of lading   Document issued to a consignor by a carrier; receipt for goods shipped, proof of title, and shipping agreement

Bill of Rights   First ten amendments to the U. S. Constitution

bill of sale   Written proof of ownership of goods

binder   Temporary insurance policy

blank indorsement   Indorsement consisting solely of indorser's signature

blue-sky laws   State laws regulating the sale of securities

boardinghouse keeper   One who offers living accommodations to permanent residents

board of directors   Group responsible for setting corporate policy

bodily injury liability insurance   Insurance for one whose car injures or kills another person

bona fide   In good faith

bond   A written promise

boycott   Refusal to do business with someone, usually in combination with others

breach of contract   Failure to perform the obligations required by a contract

brief   Written statement submitted by the attorney for each side in a case that explains to the judge(s) why they should decide the case or the particular part of a case in favor of that lawyer's client

bulk transfer   Sale of all or a major part of a merchant's stock of goods, fixtures, and equipment at one time

burden of proof   The necessity to prove facts in dispute sufficiently enough to prevail during a civil or criminal judicial proceeding

burglary   Unlawfully entering another's home or building with the intent to commit a crime

business guest   One who uses the facilities of a hotel but does not stay there

business law   Law governing business dealings

business trust   Trust set up to run a business

buyer   One who purchases goods

buyer in the ordinary course of business   One who purchases goods in good faith from a seller who normally deals in the goods

bylaws   Rule adopted by a corporation or unincorporated association

C

capitalization   Description of the investment makeup of a corporation

capital stock   Assigned value of all stock issued by a corporation

carrier   One who transports goods or people for pay

case law   Decisions handed down in court cases by judges and juries

cashier's check   Check drawn by a bank on its own funds

cash value   Portion of an insurance premium placed in a savings fund; amount an insured receives if a whole life policy is given up

casual gambler   One who gambles for pleasure

cause of action   Grounds for bringing a lawsuit

caveat emptor   "Let the buyer beware"

caveat venditor   "Let the seller beware"

cease and desist order   Injunction issued by administrative agency ordering a person to stop specific actions

certificate of deposit   Bank's promise to repay an amount left on deposit for a certain time

certified check   Personal check whose payment is guaranteed by a bank

certiorari   Appeal that an appellate court has discretion to hear

challenge for cause   A request to a judge during jury selection (usually by an attorney) that a prospective juror not be permitted to serve on the jury for some reason that questions the impartiality of the juror

chancery   A court of equity

charge to the jury   Judge's instructions to a jury

concerning the law that applies to the facts of the case on trial

charge account Agreement between a consumer and a business allowing consumer to purchase items now and pay for them later

charter Permission by the state to operate a corporation

chattel Personal property

chattel mortgage Mortgage on personal property as security for a debt

chattel real Personal property considered to be real property because of its nature

check Type of draft in which the drawee is always a bank

chose in action Right to sue on a debt or to get damages

circumstantial evidence Facts that indirectly prove a point in question

citation Notice to appear in court; reference to a case or law

citizenship Membership in a community

civil law Law dealing with relationships between individuals

civil rights Freedoms and rights guaranteed by federal and state constitutions

class action suit Suit brought on behalf of a group of consumers

closed corporation Corporation owned by a few people

closing Meeting at which title to real property is transferred from seller to buyer

closing statement Document showing financial details of the transfer of real property

COD Collect on delivery

codicil Addition or amendment to a will

coercion Force or the threat of force

coinsurance Insurance policy clause requiring insured to maintain a certain minimum amount of insurance

collateral Asset that may be pledged as security for a loan

collective bargaining Discussions between union leaders and employer representatives

collective bargaining agreement Contract negotiated between union leaders and company representatives

collision insurance Insurance against damage to insured's car if it collides with something or turns over

commercial paper Written instruments used as substitutes for money

commission merchant Consignee for purposes of a sale

common carrier Carrier that transports people and goods for the general public

common law Unwritten law

common stock Corporation's ordinary stock

community property Right of wife and husband to share equally in property jointly acquired during marriage

comparative negligence Comparing the negligence of the injured party and the one being sued

compensatory damages Actual measurable damages

competent parties Persons legally and mentally capable of entering into contracts

complaint Document listing the details of a lawsuit being filed and the relief sought

composition of creditors Agreement among creditors to accept a percentage of total owed by debtor in full settlement of debt

comprehensive insurance Insurance protecting insured's car against damage from such perils as theft, vandalism, or falling objects

compromise A settlement

computer crime Using a computer for fraudulent purposes

condemnation Right of a government to take private property for public purposes

condition precedent An act that must occur before an obligation is created

condition subsequent Act that creates an obligation if it occurs

conditional sale A contract for the sale of personal property, by which the buyer gets possession but not title until the purchase price has been paid in full

condominium Ownership of a dwelling unit that is one of many

confession Admission of guilt

confession of judgment A written document permitting judgment to be entered against a person for a specific amount

conflict of interest Situation in which one's own interests conflict with those of persons to whom one has a duty

conflict of laws Situation in which laws of more than one state may apply

conforming goods Goods that meet requirements of a contract

consanguinity Relationship by blood

consideration Something of value given by each party to bind an agreement

consignee Bailee in a consignment

consignment Bailment for the purpose of purchase or sale by the bailee

consignor Bailor in a consignment

consolidation The joining of two corporations with one surviving

constitution Principles governing the nature, functions, and limits of a group of people

constructive bailment Bailment implied by law created when one has possession of another's property without that person's knowledge

constructive eviction Action by landlord making it impossible for tenant to occupy leased premises

constructive notice Implied information

consumer One who purchases goods, products, and services for personal use

consumer credit Right to pay for money, property, or services for personal use "on time"

contempt of court Showing disrespect toward the court; disobeying a court order

contingencies Conditions in a contract that may void the contract if not met

contingency fee Fee based on a percentage of an award in a lawsuit

continuance Adjournment of a lawsuit from one day to another

contract Legally binding agreement between two or more competent persons

contract carrier Carrier that transports goods or people under individual contracts for a limited number of customers

contract rate Maximum interest rate that may be charged in a credit agreement

contract to sell Sale in which title to goods passes from seller to buyer at a future time

contributory negligence Defense that injured party's negligence led to injury

conversion Wrongfully exercising control or ownership over another's personal property

conveyance Transfer of title to real property

cooperative Ownership and occupancy of real property through the purchase of stock

copyright Exclusive right to own, produce, sell, and license artistic and intellectual works

corporation Legal entity created by permission of government

corpus delicti Fact that must be proven to determine that a crime has been committed; loosely, the body of a murdered person

co-signer A person who signs a document along with another person and (depending upon state law) who may be equally liable for any debt associated with the document

counterclaim Claim made by a defendant against the plaintiff in a lawsuit

counteroffer Offer made by offeree to offeror changing the terms of original offer

covenant Written promise or obligation; part of a lease listing rights and duties of landlord and tenant; promise made by a grantor in a warranty deed

covenant of quiet enjoyment Tenant's right to have undisturbed possession of leased property

cover Buyer's right to purchase substitute goods if seller does not deliver goods required or sends nonconforming goods

credit Right to pay for goods and services "on time"

credit card Card enabling its user to obtain goods or services on credit

creditor One who loans money or sells goods on credit

crime Wrongful act against society defined by law and made punishable by law

criminal law Law dealing with relationships between individuals and society

criminal mischief Vandalizing property

cross-examination Questioning a witness by the attorney who did not produce the witness

cure Seller's right to correct a defect in nonconforming goods

curtesy A husband's right in the estate of his deceased wife

D

damages Money paid by a defendant to a successful plaintiff in civil cases to compensate the plaintiff for his/her injuries

days of grace Additional days in which to pay something or complete a contract after due date

debenture Unsecured, corporate obligation to pay money

debit card Card that immediately transfers funds from user's bank account upon use

debt collector One who collects debts

debtor One who borrows money or buys on credit

decedent A deceased person

declaratory judgment Court's decision in a case establishing rights of the parties before any action is taken; a court judgment

decree A court judgment

deductible That part of a loss that must be paid for by the insured

deed Formal document transferring title to real property

de facto Existing in fact

defamation Oral or written false statements that injure a person's reputation

defendant Party against whom criminal charges or a lawsuit is brought

defenses Reasons offered by defendant in a lawsuit for being relieved of responsibility

deficiency judgment A judgment requiring payment over and above value of collateral

de jure Existing at law

del credere Agent who sells goods and guarantees payment by buyer

delegation Transfer of performance of one's duty under a contract to another

demurrage Fee charged for unreasonably delaying equipment of a common carrier

demurrer Motion to dismiss a case for insufficiency under the law

deponent One who makes a sworn statement

deposition Testimony of a witness under oath, taken outside the court and put in writing for use as evidence during a court proceeding

depository bank The first bank to which a commercial instrument is transferred for collection even though it may also be the payor bank (UCC 4-105a)

descent Passing of estate through intestacy

devise Gift of real property in a will

dictum Discussion in a legal decision of a point unrelated to matter before the court

directed verdict Judge's instruction to a jury to return a certain verdict

direct examination Questioning a witness by the attorney who called the witness

disability income insurance Insurance providing income to insured who cannot work because of illness or accident

disaffirmance Refusal of incompetent party to carry out the terms of an agreement

disallow To deny

discharge To terminate or end a contract

discharge in bankruptcy Judgment relieving a bankrupt from liability for most debts

disclaimer of warranty Statement in a contract that excludes a warranty

discovery Pretrial steps taken to learn the details of the case

dishonor Refusal of a party to pay or accept an instrument

dismiss an action To issue a court order terminating an action in court

dissent Disagreement with the majority decision in a case

dissolution Termination of a partnership

dividends Portion of corporate profits paid to stockholders

divorce Termination of a marriage by court order

docket Schedule of cases ready for trial

domestic bill of exchange Draft payable within the United States

domicile Legal residence of a person or a corporation

donee Recipient of a gift

donor One making a gift

dormant partner Partner unknown to the public and inactive in management

double indemnity clause Life insurance clause doubling proceeds if insured dies accidentally

double jeopardy Prosecution for a crime for which the person has already been tried

dower Wife's interest in the estate of her deceased husband

draft Instrument in which drawer orders drawee to pay a certain sum to payee

dram shop act Law imposing liability on bars and taverns selling alcoholic beverages to intoxicated persons

drawee Party to a check or draft who is ordered to pay the payee

drawer One who signs a check or draft ordering drawee to pay the payee

due process of law Right to the protections afforded by constitutions, laws, and courts

duress Forcing one to enter into a contract by using violence or threats of violence

duty A legal obligation to another

E

earnest money Deposit made by buyer when purchase offer is submitted or contract of sale of real property is signed

easement Right, granted in writing, to use another's land for a specific purpose

ejectment Action to recover possession and/or title to real property

electronic funds transfer system System allowing depositors to transfer money from their accounts to accounts of creditors and stores

emancipated Self-supporting; no longer under control and authority of parents

embezzlement Unlawfully using or stealing property by one who has been legally entrusted with the property

eminent domain The power of governments to take private property for a public purpose, subject to payment of just compensation

emotional distress Mental suffering caused by another's extreme and outrageous behavior

employee One hired to work

employer One who hires another to work for him or her

encroachment Unlawful use or possession of another's property

encumbrances Interests in property that conflict with owner's title

endowment insurance Life insurance that accumulates a sum of money repaid to insured or beneficiary at later time

entitlement Legal right to another's property

entrapment A defense that excuses the defendant in a criminal action from a crime he or she has been accused of committing because its commission was induced by a law enforcement official

equitable Just or fair

equity Nonmonetary relief granted by courts when money damages are unsuitable

equity of redemption Right of mortgagor to reclaim property after foreclosure

escheat State's right to claim abandoned or unclaimed property

escrow Holding closing documents and funds in trust until title to real property is clear

estate Person's interest in property

estate for life Ownership or possession of property only during one's lifetime

estate in common Estate owned jointly but without the right of survivorship

estate in fee simple Absolute ownership of real property

estate plan Plan to protect and dispose of one's assets

estate tax Tax on transfer of property at one's death

estoppel Being prevented from proving something that already has been proved

eviction Legal action taken by a landlord to force a tenant to leave the premises

evidence Information submitted in testimony that is used to persuade a judge and/or jury to decide the case for one side or the other

exclusion Risk not covered by an insurance policy

exculpatory clause Contract clause excusing a party from liability for negligence

executed contract Contract that has been completely carried out

execution Seizure of a debtor's property to satisfy a judgment

executor/executrix One who administers the estate of a testator/testatrix

executory contract Contract that has not been fully performed by one or all parties

exemplary damages Punitive damages

exempt property Property that cannot be taken to satisfy a debt

exoneration Being cleared of a charge of committing a crime

expert witness Witness at a trial who has special knowledge or experience

ex post facto Law that makes an action a crime after the time when the action was done

express authority Authority specifically given to agent by principal

express contract Contract in which the agreement is specifically stated

express warranty Seller's statement of fact, promise, description, or model that buyer relies upon when purchasing goods

extended coverage rider Additional insurance coverage for loss from windstorms, hail, etc.

extortion Using threats to obtain money or other property

extradition Act of one government giving up to another a person charged with a crime

F

face value Amount of coverage on an insurance policy

false advertising Advertising containing lies or omitting important information

false arrest Unauthorized detainment by an officer of the law

false imprisonment Unlawful restriction of a person's freedom of movement

fee simple Estate with no restrictions on the manner of its disposal

felony Serious crime punishable by death or imprisonment for more than one year

fiduciary One who acts for another in a position of trust

fiduciary relationship Relationship based on trust and confidence

firm offer An offer under the UCC which is irrevocable for a certain period of time

finance charge Cost of borrowing money or buying on credit stated in dollars and cents

financial responsibility laws Laws requiring owners or drivers of cars to prove they can pay for any damage caused by an accident

financing statement Public notice of a security interest in certain property of a debtor

fixture Personal property attached to land or a building and considered real property

floater policy All-risk insurance for loss or damage to personal property from almost any cause

FOB destination Terms indicating that seller has title until goods are actually delivered to buyer's location

FOB shipping point Terms indicating that seller has title until goods are given to the carrier for shipment to buyer

forbearance Refraining from doing something one has a legal right to do

foreclosure Action by a mortgagee to seize mortgaged property in payment of a debt

foreign corporation Corporation doing business in one state but chartered in another

forfeiture Loss of a right or benefit

forged check Check on which drawer's signature is made without authorization

forgery Falsely making or altering a document with intent to deceive

formal contract Written contract prepared with certain formalities, such as a seal

franchise Right or special privilege granted by government

fraud Intentionally misleading a person into making a contract either by making material false statements or concealing material facts

Freedom of Information Act Act permitting persons to obtain data in government files

friendly fire Fire that is not out of control and that stays in its intended place

fringe benefits Non-wage advantages received by an employee from an employer

full performance When both parties do all they agreed to do under a contract

fungible goods Goods easily replaced with others of the same kind, such as grains

future goods Goods not yet in existence and not yet identified

G

gambling agreement Agreement in which one party wins and another loses purely by chance

garnishment Seizure of a portion of a debtor's wages to satisfy a judgment

general agent Agent with authority to perform acts relating to all business matters of principal

general jurisdiction Power of a court to hear almost any case brought before it

general partner Partner fully active and known to the public

gift causa mortis Gift made in anticipation of donor's death

good faith Acting honestly; having a desire to fulfill one's obligations without taking unfair advantage of another party; under the UCC (2-103) good faith means honesty in fact and the observance of reasonable commercial standards of fair dealing in the trade

good will Continued customer patronage

grace period Period of time a policy remains in effect after a premium is missed

grand jury Group of people selected to investigate crimes and to formally charge persons with crimes or dismiss the charges for lack of reasonable evidence

grantee One who receives title to another's property

grantor One who transfers title to real property to another

gratuitous agent Agent who acts for another in business transactions without receiving any compensation

gratuitous bailment Bailment in which only one party benefits

guarantor Third party who promises to repay another's debt if creditor cannot collect from debtor

guaranty Promise by a third party to be secondarily liable for another's debt

guardian Court-appointed adult who has custody and care of an incompetent party

guest laws Laws defining the liability of a motor vehicle owner or operator for injury to passengers

H

habeas corpus Document to obtain immediate freedom for a person believed to be unlawfully detained by legal authorities

health care proxy A power of attorney giving a designated person the authority to make health care decisions

health insurance Insurance for medical expenses and loss of income due to illness

hearsay Statements made by a person based on secondhand knowledge; usually not admissible as evidence in court

heir One who inherits property according to her or his relationship to deceased

holder One in possession of commercial paper

holder in due course One who holds an instrument subject only to real defenses

holding company A corporation which holds the stock of another corporation or corporations

holographic will Will handwritten and signed by the maker

homeowners policy Multi-peril policy insuring homeowners against many risks

homicide Killing of a human being

hospital insurance Insurance covering fees for hospital care

hostile fire Uncontrollable fire that escapes from its usual place

hotelkeeper One who provides accommodations to the public for a limited time

hung jury Trial jury that cannot gather the required votes to reach a verdict

I

identified goods Exact goods being sold that have been decided on by seller and buyer

illicit Unlawful

implied authority Authority agent is understood to have to carry out purpose of the agency

implied contract Contract formed from actions of the parties

implied warranty Obligation imposed upon seller by law

incapacity Physical or mental inability to perform an act

incidental damages Expenses incurred by injured party in connection with a claim for actual damages

incontestable clause Clause preventing insurer from canceling a policy after a set time for any reason except nonpayment of premiums

indemnification Reimbursement for a loss

indemnity A contract by which one party agrees to make good any loss or damage another party may incur

indenture Deed conveying real property by which parties assume certain obligations

independent contractor One hired to perform a task but not under hirer's direction or control

indictment Formal, written accusation by grand jury that one has committed a crime

indorsee One to whom an order instrument is negotiated by indorsement and delivery

indorsement Writing one's name on the back of a negotiable instrument to transfer ownership

indorser One who negotiates an order instrument by indorsement and delivery

infant A minor

informal contract Contract prepared without formalities

information Written statement by a district attorney charging one has committed a minor crime

inheritance Receiving property through the terms of a deceased's will or through laws of descent and distribution upon death of intestate

injunction Court order forbidding a person from doing a certain act

in pari delicto Persons equally at fault or equally guilty

insolvent Unable to pay debts as they fall due

installment loan Agreement to pay for an item in fixed, regular payments

instrument Document that is evidence of an act or an agreement, such as a contract or note

insurable interest Financial interest in the property or life being insured

insurance System of sharing risk of loss among a group of people

insurance agent Insurance company employee who sells insurance only for that company

insurance broker Independent business person who buys insurance for insured from one of many companies

insured One who buys an insurance policy

insurer Company that issues insurance

intangible property Property that has no value in itself but that represents value (e.g. stock certificates and copyrights)

intake Process to determine if a case can be handled in a way other than a formal hearing

interest Fee paid by borrower to lender for the use of money

international bill of exchange Bill of exchange used in international trade

international law Rules that determine rights and duties of nations in their dealings with each other

interstate commerce Business activity conducted in two or more states

inter vivos gift Gift of property by one living person to another, which becomes irrevocable during their lifetimes

intestate One who dies without a will

intrastate commerce Business activity solely within one state

invasion of privacy Violating one's right to be left alone

involuntary bankrupt One forced into bankruptcy by a creditor

ipso facto "By the fact itself"

irrevocable Cannot be withdrawn or called off

issuance Original transfer of commercial paper by maker or drawer to payee

issue Point to be decided in a legal action

J

joint and several contract Contract in which parties are obligated separately and all of them are obligated collectively

joint and several liability Liability of partners as a group or individually

joint estate Property in which two or more persons have the same rights of ownership

joint tenancy Ownership by two or more persons that passes at death to surviving tenant(s)

joint venture Association of two or more companies engaged in a common project

judgment Official decision by a judge in lawsuit tried without a jury

judgment by default Court's decision that plaintiff with proof of a claim may recover damages against a defendant who has not responded to action brought against him or her

judgment lien Lien granted to creditor who has sued a debtor and obtained a judgment

judgment proof A person who lacks the assets to satisfy a judgment for damages

judicial decision Conclusion reached by the court in a case

judicial review Power of a court to review the decisions of a lower court

jurisdiction Power to hear and decide a case

jury Group of people who determine the truth in a civil or criminal case

juvenile delinquent Minor who has committed an unlawful act

L

labor union Organization of employees formed to promote welfare of members in relation to their working conditions

laches Undue delay in seeking a right or claim which would make it unfair to grant the relief requested

landlord One who owns property and rents or leases it to others

larceny Intentionally stealing the money or personal property of another

last clear chance Doctrine that while plaintiff is guilty of contributory negligence, defendant may still be liable if defendant had the last opportunity to avoid the injury by using reasonable care but did not do so

law Enforceable set of rules of conduct

law merchant Laws or customs established by early traders to protect their commercial rights

leading question Question asked by a lawyer in such a way as to suggest the answer

lease Rental agreement between landlord and tenant

legacy Gift of personal property in a will

legal detriment Consideration that is a sacrifice by the offeree

legal rate Maximum interest rate that may be charged when no rate has been agreed to

legal tender Form of money accepted as lawful payment of debts in the United States

lemon laws Laws that protect purchasers of new and used cars

lessee The tenant

lessor The landlord

letter of credit An agreement by a bank to honor drafts or other demands for payment

letters of administration Probate court document authorizing a person to act as administrator/administratrix of deceased's estate

letters testamentary Probate court document authorizing person to act as executor/executrix of deceased's estate

leveraged buyout A method of acquiring control of a corporation by buying stock and financing the purchase with a loan on the assets of the acquired corporation

levy The attachment of property to satisfy a judgment

libel Written false statements that injure a person's reputation

license Temporary right to use another's land

licensing statutes Laws requiring persons to be licensed to practice their occupation

lien A security interest created by law

lienholder One holding a lien

life estate Interest one has in property lasting only for the lifetime of person holding it or of some other person

life insurance   Contract in which insurance company agrees to pay a sum of money to a beneficiary upon insured's death

life insurance trust   Trust set up with proceeds of life insurance policy

limited jurisdiction   Power of a court to hear only certain kinds of cases

limited liability   Liability of stockholder for debts of a corporation

limited partner   Partner whose liability is limited to amount of capital invested

limited payment life insurance   Life insurance paid for after a set number of payments

line of credit   Maximum amount that can be owed on a credit card at any one time

liquid assets   Assets that can be used immediately to pay debts, taxes, and so on

liquidated damages   Damages set in advance by the parties and stated in the contract

liquidated debt   Amount of a debt to be paid that is fixed by agreement or by law

lis pendens   A legal notice that a suit is pending

listing contract   Agreement between owner and broker listing broker's rights and obligations in selling the owner's real property

litigant   Party to a lawsuit

litigation   Lawsuit or legal action

living (inter vivos) trust   Trust set up during trustor's lifetime

living will   A document expressing one's health care preferences

lobbying   Trying to influence lawmakers to vote for or against legislation

loss leader   Item sold at or below cost to attract customers

lost property   Property whose owner has involuntarily parted with

M

Magnuson-Moss Warranty Act   Law preventing deceptive warranties and requiring terms and conditions to be clear and understandable

major medical insurance   Insurance for extraordinary costs of illnesses or accidents

maker   One who makes out and signs a promissory note

mailbox rule   A common law rule used in contracts which states that an acceptance made in response to an offer is binding when placed in the mailbox, properly addressed

malfeasance   Performance of an act that is totally unlawful

malicious prosecution   Wrongfully initiating a lawsuit against one who has done no wrong

malpractice   A professional's improper or immoral conduct in performing duties done intentionally or through carelessness or ignorance

malum in se   An act which is wrong in and of itself without regard of whether it is punishable by law (e.g. murder)

malum prohibitum   An act which is wrong because it is forbidden by law

mandamus   Order to perform a legal duty

manslaughter   The unlawful killing of a person without malice

marine insurance   Insurance covering ships, their crew, and cargo

marital deduction   Estate tax deduction for tax-free transfers of property to a spouse

market price   Price at which goods are currently bought and sold

martial law   Law exercised by military authorities over civilians, usually in time of war, superseding civil law

material   Important or substantial

material breach   A violation of contract that is so substantial that it destroys the value of the contract and therefore excuses further performance by the injured party

maturity   Due date of commercial paper

mechanic's lien   Lien given to those who supply labor, materials, or services in the construction of buildings

mediation   Intervention by a third person to settle a dispute between two parties

medical insurance   Insurance covering emergency room costs and doctor's fees for nonsurgical services

medical payments insurance   Insurance for medical expenses for injuries suffered in a car accident

memorandum   Informal written evidence of an agreement required by the statute of frauds

merchant   One dealing regularly in the sale of goods or having a specialized knowledge of goods

merchantable goods   Goods fit for the purposes for which they would ordinarily be used

merger   The joining of two corporations to form a new one

minor   One under a certain age set by state law

Miranda warnings   Rights read to a suspect upon arrest

mirror image rule A common law contract rule which states that the acceptance must adhere exactly to the offer in order for it to be valid

misdemeanor Less serious crime punishable by a jail sentence of less than one year

mislaid property Property which has been temporarily misplaced by its owner

misrepresentation Stating an untrue fact

mistrial Trial that is invalid

mitigate the damages To try to hold damages down once a breach of contract occurs

modified life insurance Life insurance with gradually increasing premiums

money order Commercial paper that may be purchased from post offices, banks, and private companies

monopoly Limiting competition by act or agreement

moot Undecided; open for discussion

moral law Rules people follow in dealings with others based on their ideas of right and wrong

mortgage Lien against property held by a lender as security for repayment of a loan

mortgage assumption Right of a buyer to take over and be bound by an existing mortgage

mortgage commitment Agreement on the part of lender to grant a mortgage

mortgagee One who borrows money to purchase real property

mortgagor One who lends money used to purchase real property

motion Request to a judge for ruling on point of law

multi-peril policy Insurance combining various types of coverage with emphasis on who is insured rather than perils insured against

mutual benefit bailment Bailment in which both bailor and bailee benefit

mutual mistake Error about certain facts made by both parties to a contract

N

natural law Law derived through human reasoning, often through deductions based on religious and ancient customs

naturalized citizen Alien granted U.S. citizenship under rules passed by Congress

necessaries Things a person needs to live, such as food, clothing, and shelter

negligence Breach of a legal duty to act carefully resulting in injury to another or damage to another's property

negotiable Ability to transfer commercial paper from one person to another

negotiation Transfer of commercial paper in such a way that transferee becomes a holder

net estate Assets left by a person at death, less certain legal deductions

no-bill Conclusion of a grand jury indicating there was insufficient evidence to warrant a "true bill" (formal charge)

no-fault insurance Insurance for bodily injuries regardless of who caused the accident

nolo contendere Statement that defendant in a criminal action will not contest accusation of guilt; implies a plea of guilty

nominal consideration Dollar or other small sum of money used to bind a contract

nominal damages Damages awarded for breach of contract when no real loss or injury occurs

nominal partner One who appears to be but is actually not a partner

nonfeasance Substantial failure, without excuse, to perform a legal duty

nonforfeiture rights Ways of using cash value to prevent an insurance policy from lapsing

nonliquid assets Assets that cannot be used immediately to pay debts, taxes, expenses, etc.

nonmerchant Casual or occasional seller

nonprofit corporation Corporation organized primarily for nonbusiness purposes

nonsuit Termination of an action by a plaintiff who fails to prove the case

nontrading partnership Partnership doing business for professional purposes

no-par stock Stock having no value printed on the stock certificate

notary public Official authorized to certify genuineness of documents and administer oaths

notice of dishonor Notice given to secondary party orally or in writing that primary party has refused to pay instrument

novation Substitution of new party for one of original parties to a contract

nuisance Use of one's property to annoy or disturb others

null and void Having no legal effect

nuncupative will An oral will

O

oath Oral or written promise to perform an act or speak truthfully

obligor One obligated to pay money or complete an act for another under a contract

offer   Promise made by one person to do something if another person either performs an act or promises to do or not to do something

offer and acceptance   Process by which parties to a contract agree to its terms

offeree   One to whom an offer is made

offeror   One making an offer

ombudsperson   Government official who investigates grievances against the government

omnibus clause   Insurance for members of insured's family and those who drive insured's car with permission

open coverage   Amount of insurance proceeds payable for loss or damage based on actual cost of repairs

open shop   Business where employees are not required to join a union

option   Agreement to keep an offer open and irrevocable for a certain time

ordinance   Law passed by a legislature of a locality such as a city, town, or village

ordinary holder   One who does not qualify as holder in due course and is subject to both real and personal defenses

original jurisdiction   Power of a court to try a case first

overdraft   Check written without sufficient funds that will be paid by the bank

overrule   Make a decision in a prior case void

P

panel   Persons required to serve as jurors for a certain period of time or those jurors selected for a particular case

parol   Oral

parol evidence rule   Rule stating that terms of written contract cannot be changed by prior oral or written agreements

parole   Conditional release from prison allowing person to serve the rest of a prison sentence outside prison

par stock   Stock having a value printed on stock certificate

partition   Division of real property between two or more persons, who hold it as co-owners, into separate shares

partners   Co-owners of a business

partnership   Association of two or more persons to carry on, as co-owners, a business for profit

partnership agreement   Written agreement creating a partnership

past consideration   Promise made for an act that has already taken place

patent   Exclusive right to manufacture, sell, or license others to make and sell an invention

pawnbroker   One in the business of taking personal property as security for a loan

payable to bearer   Words directing an instrument to be paid to person holding it

payable to order   Words directing an instrument to be paid to named payee or to whomever payee orders the paper to be paid

payee   One who receives payment on a check, draft, or promissory note

periodic tenancy   Lease that automatically continues for a time equal to original term until canceled by either landlord or tenant

perjury   Making a false statement after taking an oath to be truthful

per se   Something that needs no proof by outside evidence

personal defenses   Defenses arising after an instrument is executed that cannot be used against holder in due course

personal liability insurance   Insurance against claims by persons injured by actions of insured

personal property   Movable property

personal representative   In certain states, the executor/executrix or administrator/administratrix

petit jury (trial jury)   Jury for civil or criminal trial

plaintiff   One who begins a legal action

plea   Answer to a charge, given in court by a person accused of a crime

plea bargaining   Process of negotiating a criminal charge between prosecutor and accused

pledge   Promise to make a gift to a charitable, religious, or educational institution; bailment created when personal property is deposited as security for repayment of a debt

pledgee   One who accepts delivery of personal property that is security for a debt

pledgor   One who transfers possession of personal property as security for a debt

police power   Power of a state to protect the welfare of its citizens

policy   Written contract of insurance between insurer and insured

political rights   Right to participate in process of government

polling the jury   Asking each juror what her or his verdict is before it is recorded

postdated check   Check dated after its actual date of issue

post mortem   After death; examination of a deceased's body to determine cause of death

power of attorney   Formal written document giving agent authority to act

precedent   A court decision in an earlier case with facts and law similar to a dispute currently before the court

pre-emptive right   Right of stockholders to buy new stock before its sale to the public

preferred stock   Stock having a prior right to receive a stated dividend

preliminary negotiations   In contract law, discussions between parties that usually leads one party to make an offer

premium   Cost of insurance coverage

prepayment privilege   Right to pay balance of mortgage before the end of the mortgage term

preponderance of evidence   At least slightly more than half. In order to find for the plaintiff in a civil trial, the jury must believe that the facts are more in favor of the plaintiff than the defendant

prescription   Obtaining an easement by adverse possession or use

presentment   Demand for payment of commercial paper made by holder

present sale   Sale in which title to goods passes from seller to buyer at the time parties make the contract

presumption of fact   Inference that something does or does not exist based on existence of something else already proved

pretrial conference   Hearing before a trial in which parties discuss the facts and which may lead to settlement of the case

price   Consideration for transferring ownership of goods from seller to buyer

price fixing   Agreement among sellers to set price of goods at a certain level

price misrepresentation   Offering an item at discount price higher than regular price

prima facie   Presumed to be true without evidence to the contrary

primary parties   Parties who are first responsible for paying a negotiable instrument

principal   One who authorizes another to act for her or him in business transactions

private carrier   Carrier that transports goods solely for business owning it

privileged communication   Communication between two people in a confidential relationship, such as attorney and client, that need not be revealed in a legal proceeding

privity   Relationship between parties arising from a mutual interest in property or rights

privity of contract   Contractual relationship

probable cause   Reasonable belief that a crime has been committed or certain facts exist

probate   Process of validating a will

probation   Allowing a person convicted of an offense to avoid prison and be free on good behavior, usually under the supervision of a probation officer

product liability   Liability of manufacturers and sellers of products to persons harmed by defects in the products

professional corporation   Corporation organized to operate a professional practice

professional gambler   One who gambles as a profession or business

profit   Right to remove water, natural gas, minerals, or wood from another's land

profit corporation   Corporation organized to earn a profit

promissory note   Instrument by which one promises to pay a sum of money to another

proof   Evidence establishing existence of a fact

proof of claim   Written and verified statement setting forth a claim

property and casualty insurance   Insurance against loss or damage to property

property damage liability insurance   Insurance against claims for damage to another's property

pro-rata liability   Insurance company's liability for loss when there is more than one policy on the same property

prorated premium   Amount of premium returned to insured when insurer cancels the policy

prosecute   To proceed against a person in a criminal trial

protest   Notice given by holder of a bill or note to the drawer or indorser that person required to make payment refused to do so

proximate cause   Direct or natural cause of loss or damage

proxy   Written permission by a stockholder for another to vote her or his shares of stock

public enemy   Military-type force of a foreign country

public liability insurance   Insurance against claims for injuries caused by insured's or guest's negligence

puffing   Salespersons' statements expressing opinions about goods they sell

punitive damages   Damages imposed upon wrongdoer as punishment for intentionally committing a wrongful act

purchase money mortgage New mortgage given for purchase of real property

purchase offer Offer submitted by buyer to seller for purchase of real property

Q

qualified indorsement Indorsement limiting indorser's liability

quantum merit Action based on actual value of one's services regardless of contract price

quasi Similar to; resembling

quasi contract Contract implied in law to prevent one from benefiting at another's expense

quiet enjoyment Lease covenant giving tenant the right of legal, quiet, and peaceful possession during the lease term

quitclaim deed Deed that conveys whatever interest the seller has

quorum Number of members of any body that must be present to transact business coming before that body

R

rain check Coupon allowing one to buy out-of-stock sale item at sale price in the future

ratify To approve something

real defenses Defenses arising when negotiable instruments are created that can be used against all holders

real property Land, rights to land, and anything permanently attached to the land

reasonable care Care taken by average person under ordinary circumstances

reasonable doubt Level of proof required to convict a person of a crime. It doesn't mean that a person is convinced 100%, but the proof must be so conclusive and complete that all reasonable doubts no longer exist in the mind of the ordinary person

reasonable suspicion Information from any source that leads one to believe an unlawful act has been committed

rebate Refund or discount

receiver One appointed by a court to manage property that is the subject of a lawsuit

recourse Right to collect from person secondarily liable on a negotiable instrument

redemption Right to repurchase property after it's been sold, usually after a foreclosure

redress To correct or make right

referee Court-appointed person who takes testimony and decides a matter in dispute

regular charge account Account in which each bill must be paid in full when received

reimburse To pay back

reinstatement clause Insurance clause allowing insured to put policy back into effect after it has lapsed

rejection Refusal of offer by offeree

release Document that is proof of the settlement of a claim

remand When an appellate court sends a case back to a lower court for further proceedings

remedy Course of action injured party may take to get satisfaction for breach of contract

rent Sum of money paid by tenant for use of leased property

replevin Action by buyer to recover through court order goods originally ordered but wrongfully detained by the seller

reply Plaintiff's pleading to answer or counterclaim of a defendant

repossession Steps taken by creditor to gain possession of collateral for a debt

reprieve To temporarily refrain from enforcing a sentence in a criminal matter

repudiate To deny or reject

rescind To cancel a contract by agreement

residuary gift Gift by will of one's entire estate to one or more persons

respondeat superior The doctrine that a principal is liable in certain cases for the wrongful acts of an agent

restitution Paying someone back for lost or stolen property

restraining order Court order requiring a party to cease doing certain acts

restraint of trade Illegal contract or practice that eliminates competition

restrictive covenant Restriction in a deed limiting the use of property

restrictive indorsement Indorsement limiting what transferee may do with instrument

retainer Employment of a lawyer by a client

revocable Right to cancel or rescind an act

revocation Withdrawal of an offer

revolving charge account Account on which portion of bill may be paid each month

rider An addition to a contract, usually an insurance policy

right of action Right to start a lawsuit

right of survivorship Right ensuring ownership interest passes to surviving joint tenant

riparian rights Rights of owner of land adjacent to a body of water

robbery Forcibly taking money or personal property from another

ruling Decision of a judge or court on a question raised during a trial

S

sale Contract that transfers title in goods from seller to buyer for a price

sale on approval Transaction in which goods are delivered to buyer for trial purposes

sale or return Present sale under which buyer may return goods after a set or reasonable time

satisfaction Performance of the terms of a new agreement resulting from an accord

satisfaction piece Document discharging a mortgage

scope of authority Extent of agent's authority to carry out principal's business

scope of the agency Extent of agent's duties to carry out principal's business

secondary parties Parties responsible for payment of a negotiable instrument only if primary party fails to pay

secret partner Partner unknown to the public but active in management

secured debt Debt in which creditor has a claim against specific property of debtor

security agreement Agreement giving creditor security interest in property of a debtor

security deposit Money paid to landlord and applied to any damages caused by tenant

seller One who sells goods

separation of powers Concept of independent branches of government

set off Counterclaim made by defendant to defeat a demand made by plaintiff and having no connection with plaintiff's cause for action

settlement Distribution of estate after all debts, taxes, and expenses have been paid; also when parties to a lawsuit resolve their difference without having a trial

settlement options Ways in which life insurance proceeds may be paid to beneficiaries

several liability When a creditor may sue one of many debtors separately

shoplifting Taking merchandise from a store without paying for it

short rate Amount of premium refunded when insured cancels a policy

silent partner Partner known to the public but inactive in management

sinking fund Reserve fund set aside to repay a loan

slander Oral false statements that injure a person's reputation

small claims court Court that hears minor civil cases involving small amounts of money

sole proprietorship Business owned and operated by one person

sole tenancy Ownership by one person

solvency Ability to pay debts

sovereign The holder of supreme authority

special agent Agent who has authority to perform one type of act or a limited number of acts relating to principal's business

special bailment Bailment in which extraordinary standard of care is imposed on bailee

special damages Damages arising indirectly from an injury

special indorsement Indorsement directing payment to a specified person

specific performance Court order requiring a party to carry out a contract according to its original terms

speculative damages Hypothetical damages that cannot be proven

spendthrift trust A trust in which a beneficiary cannot give away his interest or have it attached by a creditor

standard fire insurance policy Basic insurance policy covering loss from fire and lightning

standby trust Trust that comes into being when a certain event occurs

stare decisis Concept of following decisions in prior cases when a similar case occurs

station in life Person's economic and social status in community

status quo Existing conditions

statute of frauds Law requiring that certain types of contracts be in writing

statute of limitations Law fixing a time limit within which lawsuit for breach of contract must be started

statute law Laws passed by Congress, state legislatures, and local governments

stipulation Agreement between parties to a lawsuit or between their attorneys

stock Ownership interest in a corporation

stock certificate Document indicating ownership interest in a corporation

stockholders   Persons who own a corporation

stoppage in transit   Right of unpaid seller to notify carrier or warehouse operator not to deliver goods to insolvent buyer

stop-payment order   Order to a bank to refuse payment of a check

strict liability   Legal responsibility for harm done to another even when there is no proof of fault on the part of the party that caused the harm

sublease   Transfer of portion of lease term to another tenant

subpoena   Court order requiring testimony in a case

subpoena duces tecum   A command to a witness to produce documents

subrogation   Right of insurance company to recover from person causing a loss

substantial performance   Performance in good faith of all but minor details of a contract

substitute contract   New contract entered into to replace a contract before a breach occurs

subtenant   One to whom a portion of a lease term is transferred

sui juris   A person who has reached the age of majority and is now capable of managing his or her own affairs (e.g. to make a contract)

summons   Written notification to defendant that a lawsuit has been filed

Sunday laws   Laws governing types of transactions that can be performed on Sunday

sunshine laws   Laws requiring public admission to government hearings and proceedings

surety   Third party who agrees to be primarily responsible for another's debt if debtor defaults

suretyship   Promise by third party to be primarily responsible for another's debt

surgical insurance   Insurance for surgical fees for specific operations

surrogate   Probate court judge

survey   Map showing location, boundaries, and size of a piece of real property

syndicate   A joint venture

T

tacking   Adding periods of occupancy by various owners to determine if title has been obtained by adverse possession

tangible property   Real or personal property that has physical existence (i.e., that can be seen and touched)

tax escalator clause   Condition in a lease requiring tenant to pay increases in real estate taxes

tax lien   Lien given to government agency to ensure payment of property taxes

tenancy at sufferance   Tenancy created when a lease ends and tenant is allowed to remain

tenancy at will   Lease for indefinite period of time

tenancy by the entirety   Ownership of land deeded to a husband and wife

tenancy for years   Tenancy for fixed period

tenancy in common   Ownership by two or more persons that passes at death to heirs or beneficiaries

tenant   One who occupies rented property

tender offer   A public offer to stockholders to buy their stock

tender of performance   Offer to perform obligations of a contract

term   Length of time a lease is in effect

termination statement   Public notice that a security interest is no longer claimed

term insurance   Life insurance purchased for a specific period of time

testamentary trust   Trust established according to the terms of a will

testate   Leaving a will upon one's death

testator/testatrix   One who disposes of property by will

testimony   Evidence given under oath by a witness in court

theft of services   Obtaining or attempting to obtain services without paying for them

threshold figure   Amount of medical expenses required before injured person may sue under no-fault laws

title   Interest one has in real property

title insurance   Insurance that compensates owner of real property for damages if title is found to be flawed

title search   Examination of public records to determine if title to real property is clear

Torrens System   System of public registration of titles using title certificates

tort   Wrongful act causing injury to another person or to another's property

tort-feasor   One who commits a tort

trade fixtures   Property considered permanent that remains with leased premises when lease ends

trademark   Exclusive, distinct mark by which a company identifies itself or its products

trading partnership   Partnership doing business for commercial purposes

transcript   Copy of the testimony or records in a court proceeding

transcript on appeal   Record of proceedings filed with an appellate court

transient   One who is not a permanent resident

traveler's check   Check used primarily by travelers in which main feature is security against loss or theft

treasury stock   Issues of its own stock reacquired by a corporation

treble damages   Punitive damages awarded for violation of some government regulations

trespass   Illegally entering or remaining on the property of another

trial   A legal proceeding to determine if a defendant is right or wrong (civil) or is guilty or innocent (criminal)

trial court   Court in which a case is first tried

trust   Plan for transferring and holding property for the benefit of another

trustee   One who manages a trust

trustor   One who establishes a trust

trust receipt   Document in which borrower acknowledges holding property in trust for benefit of lender

U

ultra vires   Acts of a corporation not permitted under its express or implied powers

unconscionable agreements   Contracts so unfair or one-sided that they will not be enforced

unconstitutional   Existing legislation (act, statute, ordinance) or some action that is in conflict with the U.S. Constitution or the constitution of some state

underwriter   Insurer of persons or property

undisclosed principal   Principal whose identity is not known to third parties with whom agent makes contracts

undivided interest   Interest in property of people who hold title jointly

undue influence   Power or dominance used to make persons enter into a contract against their will

unenforceable contract   Contract that is legal but fails to meet some requirement of the law

Uniform Commercial Code   Uniform laws governing commercial transactions

unilateral contract   Contract in which one party makes a promise in return for the performance of an act by the other party

unilateral mistake   Error made by only one party about certain facts in a contract

uninsured motorist insurance   Insurance for injuries caused by a driver who has no insurance or by a hit-and-run driver

union shop   Arrangement whereby new employees must join a union within a certain period of time after being hired

universal defenses   Defenses valid against all holders of negotiable instruments

universal life insurance   Life insurance allowing insured to change premium payments, face value, and period of coverage

unordered goods   Merchandise received even though not requested

unpaid seller's lien   Right of unpaid seller to retain goods sold to insolvent buyer until goods are paid for in cash

unsecured debt   Debt based solely on debtor's promise to pay

usury   Charging a higher rate of interest than allowed by law

V

valid   Legal, lawful

valid contract   Contract containing all the essential elements

valued coverage   Agreed-upon amount of insurance proceeds payable for loss or damage

vandalism   Deliberately damaging another's property

vendee   The buyer of property

vendor   The seller of property

venue   Geographical area in which a case must be tried

verbatim   Word for word

verdict   Decision of a jury

vested   Fixed, legal right

vicarious liability   A person's liability for someone else's acts

void contract   Contract that has no legal effect and cannot be enforced

voidable contract   Contract enforceable against all parties until the party legally entitled to avoid the contract decides to do so

voir dire (meaning "to speak the truth")   Questioning of potential jurors by the judge and opposing attorneys to determine prior knowledge of the facts of the case and a willingness to decide the case only on the evidence presented in court

voluntary bankrupt   One who files a petition for bankruptcy

voucher   A receipt

W

wage assignment Voluntary transfer of wages by debtor to creditor

wager A bet

waiver Voluntary surrender of a given right

waiver of premium clause Insurance policy clause relieving insured from paying premiums if disabled

ward One under a guardian's care by court order

warehouse operator One who stores personal property for another for compensation

warehouse receipt Form issued by a bailee for the storage of personal property

warrant Court order authorizing an arrest or a search of a person's premises

warranty Guarantee by seller that goods are not defective and that they are suitable for intended use

warranty deed Deed that guarantees clear title

warranty of habitability Landlord's implied promise that property is fit for human habitation and free of hazardous conditions

warranty of title Guarantee that title is good

watered stock Issued stock with little or no value

whole life insurance Life insurance on which premiums are paid for as long as insured holds policy

will Document disposing of one's property after death

work permit Document allowing a minor to perform certain types of jobs

workers' compensation State laws providing benefits to employees who are injured or become seriously ill on the job

writ A formal written command issued by the court requiring the performance of a specific act

writ of attachment Legal order authorizing seizure of property

Z

zoning law Ordinance controlling use of land

Index

EFTS, 325, 337–338, 632
Electronic funds transfer system (EFTS), 325, 337–338, 632
Elimination period, *defined*, 574
Emancipated minor, *defined*, 148
Embezzlement, 38
Emergency authority, *defined*, 386
Eminent domain. *See* Condemnation, power of
Employee(s)
    access to personnel records, 347–348
    aliens as, 360
    contract liability of, 387–389
    defined, 345
    hiring of aliens, 360
    invasion of privacy of, 357–358
    rights of, 347–349
    tort liability of, 389–390
Employer(s)
    defined, 345
    rights of, 346–348
    tort liability of, 386–387
Employer-employee relationship
    creation of, 346
    discrimination prohibited in, 345
    vs. principal-agent relationship, 369
    termination of, 349–351
Employment at will, *defined*, 349
Employment discrimination, 352–356
    age discrimination, 353
    sexual harassment, 354–355
Encumbrances, *defined*, 489
Endowment insurance, 565
Enforcement, partially illegal agreements, 167
Entrapment, as defense in crime suit, 44
Environmental protection, 11, 437–438, 458–459
Equal Credit Opportunity Act (1974), 633
Equal Employment Act (1972), 352
Equal Employment Opportunity Commission (EEOC), 352–353
Equal Pay Act (1963), 355
Equity
    defined, 419
    See also Stock(s)
Equity courts, 233
Escheat, *defined*, 451
Escrow, *defined*, 486
Estate
    administration and settlement of, 589
    defined, 581
    distribution of, 583, 590, 591(fig.)
    net, 599
Estate planning
    gifts and, 600
    marital deduction and, 601
    need for, 598–599
    primary goal of, 599–600
    steps in, 603
    taxes and, 599–600
    trusts and, 602–603

Estate tax, *defined*, 599
Estoppel, agency by, 370
Ethics. *See also* Business ethics
    defined, 4
    law, relationship to, 4
Eviction
    constructive, 472
    defined, 469
    notice of, 469(fig.)
Evidence, preponderance of, 94
Exclusions, *defined*, 536
Exculpatory clauses, 162–163
Execution, order (writ) of, 648, 651
Executor/executrix of estate, 175, 191, 587
Executory contracts, 112, 145, 198, 233
Exemplary damages. *See* Punitive damages
Exempt property, *defined*, 638
Express agreement, *defined*, 400
Express authority, *defined*, 385
Express warranty
    defined, 269
    exclusion of, 273
Extended coverage rider, 539
Extortion, 38–39
Extraordinary bailments. *See* Special bailments

F

Face value, of insurance policy, 533, 541
Fair Credit Billing Act (1974), 636–637
Fair Credit Reporting Act (1970), 635–636
    amendment of, 636
Fair Debt Collection Practices Act (1977), 637
Fair Labor Standards Act, 350, 360
False advertising, 610–611
False arrest, 63
False imprisonment, 62–63
Family court, 23
Family income policy, 566
FDA, 617
Federal Bankruptcy Act (1898), 639
Federal Communications Commission, 11
Federal Controlled Substance Act, 40
Federal court(s), participants in legal system, 27–29
Federal court system, 18, 19, 21(fig.)
    establishment of, 23
    intermediate courts of appeal in, 25
    trial courts in, 24–25
    U.S. Supreme Court and, 25, 27
Federal Reserve banks, 335, 336
Federal Reserve Board, 614
Federal Trade Commission Act (1914), 434–435
Federal Trade Commission (FTC), 11
    on advertising, 610–611

    on franchising, 426
    on holder in due course, 319–320
Federal Truth in Lending Law. *See* Truth in Lending Law
Fee shifting, as tort reform, 76–77
Felony
    defined, 35
    examples of, 36, 38, 39
Fiduciary relationship, *defined*, 373
Finance charge, *defined*, 634
Financial responsibility laws, 550
Financing statement, 649
Fire insurance, 538–539, 540–541
Fixture, *defined*, 447–448
Flights
    baggage and, 621
    overbooked or delayed, 620
    rights of air travelers on, 619–621
Floater policy, 539
"Float period," 337
FOB, 243
Food and Drug Administration (FDA), 617
Forbearance, *defined*, 132
Foreclosure, *defined*, 482
Foreseeability, *defined*, 72
Forgery
    of checks and endorsements, 333–334
    defined, 38
    of negotiable instrument, 318
Franchise system, 425–427
Fraud
    as defense against holder of negotiable instrument, 315–316, 318, 320
    as defense in breach of contract suit, 210–212
    defined, 38, 69
    insurance applications and, 534
    remedies for, 216–217
Free-on-board (FOB) sales, 243
Friendly fire, *defined*, 538
FTC. *See* Federal Trade Commission
Full performance, *defined*, 197

G

Gambling statutes, 159–160
Garnishment, 638, 648, 651
General agents, 367
General partner, *defined*, 399
Good faith, *defined*, 248, 254, 314
Goods
    conforming, 254, 255
    defined, 225–226
    delivery of, 254–255
    identified *vs.* future, 241
    inspection of, 255
    merchantable, 271
Government regulation of business
    areas of, 433–438
    authority for, 432–433
    consumer protection and, 610–619

U

UCC. *See* Uniform Commercial Code
ULPA, 407
Ultra vires, *defined*, 421
Unconforming (substitute) goods, 229
Unconscionable agreements, 167, 233–234
Undisclosed principal, 388
Undue influence, 212–213, 216–217
Unemployment insurance, 359
Uniform Commercial Code (UCC), 14
  on auction sales, 245
  on banking rights and duties, 326
  on breach of contract, 230, 256–259
  on bulk transfers, 246
  on commercial paper, 287, 290
  on consideration, 230
  on contracts of sale, 449
  defined, 225
  on endorsement of checks, 304
  on good faith contractual obligations, 254
  on identification of goods, 241
  on instrument for value, 314
  on merchantability, 274
  on negotiability, 290, 294
  on offer and acceptance, 227–230
  on oral sales contracts, 231–233
  parol evidence rule and, 234
  on payment of unsigned checks, 311
  on presentment for payment, 311–312
  on privity requirement, 275
  on risk of loss, 241–244, 242(table)
  sales contracts and, 216, 226–234, 254–262
  on sales on approval and return, 244–245
  on security agreements, 649
  statute of frauds and, 230–231
  statute of limitations and, 230
  on stop-payment orders, 328
  title transfer and, 146
  on unconscionable agreements, 233–234
  on warranties, 269–276
Uniform Limited Partnership Act (ULPA), 407
Uniform Partnership Act, 398–399, 401, 403, 405, 406
Uniform Securities Act, 436
Unilateral contract, 109, 122
Unilateral mistake, 213
Uninsured motorist insurance, 553–554
Unions. *See* Labor unions
Universal life insurance, 565
Unliquidated claim, 135–136
Unordered goods, right to refuse, 613
Unsecured credit, *defined*, 630
Unsecured debt, *defined*, 647
"Unwritten law," 7
U.S. Constitution. *See* Constitution, U.S.
U.S. Immigration and Nationality Act of 1903, 360
U.S. Supreme Court. *See* Supreme Court, U.S.
Usage of trade, 234
Usury statutes, 160–161, 639

V

Valid contract, elements of, 106–108, 109
Valued coverage, *defined*, 536
Variance, *defined*, 458
Verdict, *defined*, 94
Voidable title to goods, 247–248
Voir dire examination, 93

W

Wage and Hour Law, 360
Wage assignment, 188, 648
Wagner Act (1935), 352
Waiver, *defined*, 207
Waiver of premium clause, 569

Warranty, 256–257, 618
  breach of, 256–257, 270, 274–276
  defined, 256, 268–269
  disclaimer of, 273
  exclusion of, 272–274
  express, 269–271, 273
  federal regulation of, 276–277
  full *vs.* limited, 276
  of habitability, 468
  implied, 271–272, 273–274, 276
  oral, 269–270
  of title, 272
Warranty deed, 488(fig.), 489
Warsaw Convention, 525, 621
Whistle-blower laws, 350
Whole life insurance, 564–565
Will(s)
  administering, 588–589
  changing or revoking, 587–588
  handwritten (holographic) wills, 585
  illustrated, 582(fig.)
  intestacy and, 590
  limitations on disposing of property by, 586
  living wills, 590–591, 592(fig.), 594
  nuncupative, 584, 585
  probating, 588–589
  purpose of, 581
  restriction of land use through, 459
  special types of, 585
  steps in making, 586–587
  testamentary capacity of, 583
  valid, requirements of, 583–585
  witnesses to, 584–585
Worker's compensation laws, 358
"Written law," 9
Wrongful death, 68–69

Z

Zoning boards, 11
Zoning laws and regulations, 458–459